Professional Java™, JDK™ 5 Edition

Professional Java™, JDK™ 5 Edition

W. Clay Richardson
Donald Avondolio
Joe Vitale
Scot Schrager
Mark W. Mitchell
Jeff Scanlon

wrox

Programmer to Programmer™

Professional Java™, JDK™ 5 Edition

Published by
Wiley Publishing, Inc.
10475 Crosspoint Boulevard
Indianapolis, IN 46256-5774
www.wiley.com

Published simultaneously in Canada

ISBN: 0-7645-7486-8

Manufactured in the United States of America

10 9 8 7 6 5 4 3 2 1

1MA/RR/QR/QV/IN

For general information on our other products and services please contact our Customer Care Department within the United States at (800) 762-2974, outside the United States at (317) 572-3993, or fax (317) 572-4002.

Wiley also publishes its books in a variety of electronic formats. Some content that appears in print may not be available in electronic books.

Library of Congress Cataloging-in-Publication Data

Professional Java, JDK 5 Edition / W. Clay Richardson . . . [et al.].—
   p. cm.
  Includes bibliographical references and index.
  ISBN 0-7645-7486-8 (paper/web site)
  1. Java (Computer program language) I. Richardson, W. Clay, 1976-
   QA76.73.J38P7623 2004
   005.13'3—dc22

                              2004022626

About the Authors

W. Clay Richardson is a software consultant concentrating on agile Java solutions for highly specialized business processes. He has fielded many Java solutions, serving in roles including senior architect, development lead, and program manager. He is a coauthor of *More Java Pitfalls* and *Professional Portal Development with Open Source Tools* (Wiley). As an adjunct professor of computer science for Virginia Tech, Richardson teaches graduate-level coursework in object-oriented development with Java. He holds degrees from Virginia Tech and the Virginia Military Institute.

Donald Avondolio is a software consultant with over 19 years of experience developing and deploying enterprise applications. He began his career in the aerospace industry developing programs for flight simulators and later became an independent contractor, crafting health-care middleware and low-level device drivers for an assortment of mechanical devices. Most recently, he has built e-commerce applications for numerous high-profile companies, including The Home Depot, Federal Computer Week, the U.S. Postal Service, and General Electric. He is currently a technical architect and developer on several portal deployments. Don serves as an adjunct professor at Virginia Tech, where he teaches progressive object-oriented design and development methodologies, with an emphasis on patterns.

Joe Vitale has been working as a developer for the last ten years. He has worked significantly with the latest Java technologies and also the most-popular open source technologies on the market. Besides being a developer, Vitale is coauthor of *Professional Portal Development with Open Source Tools* (Wiley), which had a strong focus on open source development and the Java Portlet API formally known as JSR 168. Joe currently works for McDonald Bradley as a development manager, where he manages more than 50 developers.

Scot Schrager has consulted extensively in the domains of pharmaceuticals, supply chain management, and the national security market. He has led and participated in various project teams using Java and Object Oriented Analysis & Design techniques. Most recently, Schrager has been focused on distributed application architecture using J2EE technology.

Mark W. Mitchell has extensive experience in enterprise application integration, particularly Web Services integration between Java and the Microsoft platform. He has developed and deployed several mission-critical Web applications. Mitchell holds a degree in computer science from the University of Virginia.

Jeff Scanlon is a senior software engineer at McDonald Bradley in Herndon, Virginia. Scanlon holds both the Sun Certified Java Developer and Microsoft Certified Solutions Developer certifications and has been published in *Software Development* magazine.

Credits

Executive Editor
Robert Elliott

Development Editor
Eileen Bien Calabro

Technical Editor
Dreamtech

Production Editor
William A. Barton

Copy Editor
Luann Rouff

Editorial Manager
Kathryn A. Malm

Vice President and Executive Group Publisher
Richard Swadley

Vice President and Publisher
Joseph B. Wikert

Executive Editor Director
Mary Bednarek

Project Coordinator
Erin Smith

Graphics and Production Specialists
Beth Brooks
Amanda Carter
Sean Decker
Kelly Emkow
Lauren Goddard
Denny Hager
Joyce Haughey
Jennifer Heleine
Barry Offringa

Quality Control Technicians
John Greenough
Susan Moritz

Media Development Specialist
Angie Denny

Text Design and Composition
Wiley Composition Services

Proofreading and Indexing
TECHBOOKS Production Services

This book is dedicated to all those who make the daily sacrifices, especially those who have made the ultimate sacrifice, to ensure our freedom and security.

Acknowledgments

First, I could not have had any chance of actually getting this book done without the support of my wonderful wife, Alicia. She and my daughter Jennifer, who has far less sophisticated expectations from my literary skills, are the joy in my life, and I look forward to spending more time with them. I love both of you more than words can describe. Stephanie, we love you and will never forget you. My fellow authors—Donnie, Mark, Scot, Jeff, and Joe—have been terrific with their hard work on a demanding project. I appreciate each of your contributions to this book. I would like to thank Bob Elliott and Eileen Bien Calabro for all of their hard work and perseverance working with us on this project. I would like to acknowledge my leadership, Joe Duffy, Jim Moorhead, Don Heginbotham, Tom Eger, Mark Cramer, Jon Grasmeder, and Doug Dillingham, for their dedication to the simple concept of doing the right thing for the right people. It is very refreshing to work at a company that exercises the inverse of the cynical "zero sum game." I would like to thank my parents, Bill and Kay, my in-laws, Stephen and Elaine Mellman, my sister Kari, my brother Morgan, and my stepfather Dave for always being there. I would like to acknowledge my grandmothers, Vivian and Sophie, for being what grandmothers should be.

I would also like to acknowledge my team members for the great things they do every day to make the world a better place: Jon Simasek, Rob Brown, Keith Berman, Mauro Marcellino, Terry Trepel, Marshall Sayen, Joe Sayen, Hanchol Do, Greg Scheyer, Scot Schrager, Don Avondolio, and Mark (Mojo) Mitchell. To my duty crew at the Gainesville District VFD: Bob Nowlen, Gary Sprifke, Patrick Vaughn, Seth Bowie, Matt Tyrrell, and Gerry Clemente—we have been through a lot together! To Kevin Smith, I think you were smart to pass on writing to spend more time with Isabella—I think I will do the same with Jennifer. Matt Tyrrell, I thought about giving you a hard time again this time around but decided not to tempt fate too much, so I will just remark the obvious—you are still like a brother to me.—WCR

First, I'd like to thank all of my BV pals: Wendong Wang, Arun Singh, Shawn Sherman, Henry Zhang, Bin Li, Feng Peng, Henry Chang., Sanath Shetty, Prabahkar Ramakrishnan, Yuanlin Shi, Andy Zhang, and John Zhang. Additionally, I'd also like to thank these people for inspiring me in the workplace: Swati Gupta, Chi Louong, Bill Hickey, and Chiming Huang. Thanks to all of the great professors at the Virginia Tech Computer Science/Information Technology Departments: Shawn Bohner, Tarun Sen, Stephen Edwards, and John Viega. I am indebted to all of my students who taught me so much with their dedication, hard work, and insight, which has allowed me to incorporate their development wisdom for instruction in this book. Appreciation goes out to the sponsors and organizers of The Great Cow Harbor Run (Northport, New York) and The Columbia Triathlon (Columbia, Maryland) for organizing world-class events I like to participate in, but more importantly for inspiring me to be a more disciplined and focused person.

Finally, I wish to thank all of the coauthors, who are fun guys to work with and be around: Joe, Jeff, Mark, Scot, and Clay; and my co-workers: Mauro Marcellino, Joe and Marshall Sayen, Jon Simasek, Terry Trepel, Hanchol Do, Keith Berman, and Rob Brown. To all of my family: Mom, Dad, Michael, John, Patricia, Kiel, Jim, Sue, Reenie, Donna, Kelly, Stephen, Emily, Jack, and Gillian, Matt and Danielle, you guys are great. To my wife Van, who I love more than anything for her continual support during the writing of this book.—DJA

Acknowledgments

First, I'd like to thank my wife Jennifer Vitale and my son Andrew. They have been so supportive throughout my book-writing adventures, and without their encouragement I would not have found the time or energy to complete this task. I'd also like to thank my grandfather and grandmother Carlo and Annette Vitale, as well as my father Joseph Vitale, my stepmother Linda Vitale, and my father- and mother-in-law James and Marlaine Moore. Many thanks also go to John Carver, Brandon Vient, and Aron Lee for their great supporting roles as friends. Finally, I'd like to thank all of my co-workers at McDonald Bradley, including Kyle Rice, Danny Proko, Joe Broussard, Rebecca Smith, Joe Cook, Ken Pratt, Adam Dean, Joon Lee, Adam Silver, John Johnson, Keith Bohnenberger, Bill Vitucci, Barry Edmond, Arnold Voketaitis, Steven Brockman, Peter Len, Ken Bartee, Dave Shuping, John Sutton, William Babilon, and many others who have been very supportive. And a special thanks goes to my coauthors for all of their hard work and encouragement. Thank you all!—JV

I would like to dedicate my contribution of this book to the memory of my father. My biggest fan—I know he would have put a copy of this book in the hand of everyone he knew. I appreciate the opportunities I have had as the result of the hard work and sacrifice of both of my parents.

I would like to thank my colleagues for helping me be part of this book. I would especially like to thank Clay and Donnie for their guidance. You make the very difficult seem easy.

This was my first participation in a technical book. I would like to thank my beautiful wife, Heather, for helping me stay the course. I could not have done it without you.

I would also like to thank Don Schaefer. It has been a privilege to work with you. You have taught me several lessons firsthand on leadership, professionalism, and conviction. I learned from you that the quality of a person's ideas should be judged independent of their position in a company.

One of my early mentors was my high school computer science teacher, Mr. John Nadig. I remember specifically having some trouble with an assignment. Instead of just telling me the correct answer, he handed me a thick reference book and said with confidence, "I'm sure you will find the answer in here." Thank you for getting me hooked on solving problems; I have been using that approach ever since.—SRS

I would like to thank my parents: my mother for teaching me how to write and showing me by her example how to work diligently and persistently through any problem and my father for introducing me to computer science and programming very early in my life. I would sit by his side and watch him program and through his patience learned quite a bit—sparking my interest for what would later become my career. I would like to thank the people I work with right now, and whom I have worked with in the past. I have learned a lot simply through watching and listening. There is no greater work atmosphere than the one where you are the least senior—there is something to be learned from everyone, each and every day of the week. I would like to thank my friends for understanding why I was always busy around book deadlines and for continuing to support me even as I became a hermit. Most of all I would like to thank God, as writing this book has been an exercise in faith and trust. Last, but certainly not least, I would like to thank my ever-loving and supporting fiancée, without whose support I certainly would not have been able to complete my chapters. Thank you for planning our wedding and for being patient with me during my many hours of writing. I promise I will spend more time with the wedding planning!—MWM

I would like to thank the people who made this book possible: Dave Nelson for introducing me to the world of software development and for being my long-standing friend; Joe Vitale for his friendship and involving me with this book; and Eileen Bien Calabro for working with us as a developmental editor, helping to ensure that this book succeeds. I would also like to thank those who offer their support and belief in me—my parents, my family, Phil Bickel, Eric Anderton, John Tarcza, Joseph Kapp, Mark Orletsky, Gwynne Sayres, Keith Obenschain, Robert Burtt, Myke Weiskopf, Randy Nguyen, Randy Shine, James Kwon, David Hu, Sung Kwak, Tim Weber, Bobby Suh, Albert Young, Jacob Kim, and a few others I am sure I am forgetting who stand by me.—JS

Contents

Contents

Contents

Contents

Contents

Contents

Contents

Contents

Contents

Introduction

Professional Java, JDK 5 Edition provides a bridge from the "how to" language books that dominate the Java space (*Teach Yourself Hello World in Java in 24 Hours*) and the more detailed, but technologically stovepiped books on topics such as EJB, J2EE, JMX, JMS, and so on. Most development solutions involve using a mix of technologies, and the books for all of these technologies would stand several feet tall. Furthermore, the reader needs but a fraction of the overall content in these books to solve any specific problems. *Professional Java, JDK 5 Edition* provides background information on the technology, practical examples of using the technology, and an explanation of where the reader could find more-detailed information. It strives to be a professional reference for the Java developer.

Who This Book Is For

This book serves three types of readers:

❑   The newly introduced reader who has graduated from *Beginning Java*, by covering more-advanced Java solutions and language features.

❑   The Java developer who needs a good all-purpose reference and a first source when tackling new Java problems that may be outside their technological experience.

❑   The developer who has already had experience with certain solutions, but may not, for example, think it worthwhile to read 500 pages on JMS alone to see if JMS could fit into their solution space. This book can provide reduced barriers to technological entry for these developers.

What This Book Covers

Professional Java, JDK 5 Edition builds upon *Ivor Horton's Beginning Java 2, JDK 5 Edition* by Ivor Horton to provide the reader with an understanding of how professionals use Java to develop software solutions. It starts with a discussion of the tools and techniques of the Java developer, continues with a discussion of the more sophisticated and nuanced parts of the Java SDK, and concludes with several examples of building real Java solutions using Java APIs and open source tools. *Professional Java, JDK 5 Edition* leaves the reader with a well-rounded survey of the professional Java development landscape, without losing focus in exhaustive coverage of individual APIs. This book is the bridge between Java language texts, methodology books, and specialized Java API books. For example, once you have mastered the basics of the Java language, you will invariably encounter a problem, like building a database-driven Web site, which requires you to use a collection of technologies like JSP, and tools like Hibernate; this book provides a concrete solution that integrates both of them. Figure Intro-1 provides a context to this book's coverage in relation to other Java books. As you start with the beginning Java books, you would use this book as a solution primer to introduce you to more in-depth books on a particular subject, such as patterns, Web services, or JDBC.

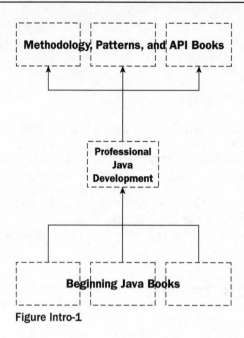

Figure Intro-1

How This Book Is Structured

Working as an effective professional Java developer requires two major skills: thinking like a Java developer and having a broad understanding of Java APIs, tools, and techniques to solve a wide variety of Java problems. Reviewing the structure of the book, you can see how the chapters help you realize the goal of improving these skills.

Thinking Like a Java developer

Experienced Java developers recognize that there is a particular mindset among effective Java developers. The first three chapters provide you with strong coverage of these topics.

Chapter 1: Key Java Language Features and Libraries

Any introductory Java book will cover the features of the Java programming language. This chapter picks up where those books leave off by focusing on a number of the key sophisticated Java language features, such as assertions, regular expression, preferences, and Java logging. Most importantly, this chapter covers a number of key features introduced in the Java 2 Standard Edition 5.0. These include generics, meta data, autoboxing, and more.

Chapter 2: Tools and Techniques for Developing Java Solutions

Making the jump from someone who knows the Java language to a Java developer is an interesting transition. Typically, developers find books that teach the language and books that teach the methodologies. Furthermore, methodology books are often written defensively, as if they are defending a dissertation or prescribing a diet. These books often prescribe ritualistic adherence to their methodology, lest you risk failure. New developers can find this approach quite exhausting, since rarely do you start in a position where you can dictate a team's process. In this book, you will find a developer's focused view on methodology and tools with practical insights into how to allow tools to make your work easier and more productive.

Chapter 3: Exploiting Patterns in Java

Patterns provide an invaluable resource to developers in trying to communicate solutions to common problems. However, as software problems are generally very abstract, understanding common solutions to them—or even the value of the approach—can be a very overwhelming experience.

However, as you might imagine, there are some key problems that recur throughout the Java solution space, and therefore, frameworks and APIs are built upon patterns. As such, having a utilitarian understanding of patterns is invaluable, and arguably unavoidable in becoming an effective Java developer. This chapter will explain the critical importance of patterns, provide a practical understanding of patterns, and demonstrate examples of common patterns found in the Java world.

A Broad Understanding of Java APIs, Tools, and Techniques

The Java platform has extended beyond being a simple applet development language at its inception to three distinct editions targeted at three different platforms. Not only has the platform evolved into a huge undertaking, but the open source movement and the Java community have also added features and tools that provide even more options to the Java developer.

Therefore, you can find yourself easily overwhelmed. This part of the book provides a series of common problems across the Java development space. In each area, you will be introduced to a problem and a focused solution to that problem. These solutions do not attempt to provide comprehensive coverage of all of the involved APIs but rather a primer needed to solve that problem. From there, you could bridge into a book with more-specialized coverage. The primary intent is to not require a three-foot-tall stack of books to address a simple end-to-end solution to a common development problem.

Chapter 4: Developing Effective User Interfaces with JFC

Commonly referred to simply as Swing, the Java Foundation Classes provide the functionality to build user interfaces and desktop applications. As these classes frequently make up most of the logical examples within introductory Java books, it makes logical sense to start with a Swing example. However, this chapter will cover the intricacies of Swing in more detail, including some advanced topics like Layout Managers and Java 2D.

Chapter 5: Persisting Your Application Using Files

One of the more important things for any application to be able to do is persist its state—that is, save. In this chapter, you will discover techniques to implement save and restore functionality, using two different methods, Java object serialization and the Java API for XML Binding (JAXB).

Chapter 6: Persisting Your Application Using Databases

Files are traditionally used to share data in a single-threaded mode—one user at a time. When data must be shared throughout the enterprise, you use a database. In this chapter, you will learn the more advanced features of the Java Database Connectivity API (JDBC) 3.0, including the new Rowset interface. Furthermore, this chapter will address one of the more popular object persistence frameworks (and the foundation for the development of the new EJB 3.0 specification)—Hibernate.

Chapter 7: Developing Web Applications Using the Model 1 Architecture

Those who have been developing Web applications for a long time recognize that the page-centric paradigm, also known as the Model 1 Architecture, has been used across many technology platforms (ASP, Cold Fusion, Perl, and so on) to develop Web applications. Java supports this paradigm through its Java Server Pages 2.0 and Java Standard Tag Library specifications. In this chapter, you will learn about these frameworks as well as other best practices in developing Web applications within the Model 1 Architecture.

Chapter 8: Developing Web Applications Using the Model 2 Architecture

As Web applications have evolved, there has been recognition of some weaknesses in the page-centric approach of the Model 1 Architecture. In this chapter, you will learn about these weaknesses and how they gave rise to the Model 1 Architecture, which is component-centric. You will see how using a component framework like WebWork allows for easy integration of other components like Hibernate.

Chapter 9: Interacting with C/C++ Using Java Native Interface

Frequently, you have application components that are regrettably not written in the Java programming language. This often does not alleviate the need for those components to be accessible by your application. The solution to this problem is the Java Native Interface. This chapter will explain the intricacies of JNI, as well as a number of the potential pitfalls.

Chapter 10: Communicating between Java Components with RMI and EJB

The heart of distributed development is interprocess communication—that is, you have two applications that wish to speak with each other. This is frequently also referred to as Client/Server, instilling the concept of one application process initiating a request upon another application process. This chapter will discuss Java's mechanism for interprocess communication, Remote Method Invocation, or simply, RMI. RMI is the foundation of commonly used technologies like JDBC, though the mechanics are hidden from the developer, by layering a higher-level API (JDBC on top). The chapter builds upon this concept by introducing the enterprise application component framework known as Enterprise JavaBeans (EJB), which is Java's preferred way of building server components.

Chapter 11: Communicating between Java Components and Components of Other Platforms

While RMI has proven to be a good solution for Java to Java communication, there are still a tremendous number of needs to access (or provide access) to components of other platforms. This is particularly true of the Microsoft .NET platform. This chapter will explain the basics of interprocess communication, discuss several techniques for interprocess communication, and culminate in an example using Web services.

Chapter 12: Distributed Processing with JMS and JMX

When performing enterprise application integration of components distributed across many machines and platforms, it is often necessary for you to be able to spread the workload out across many different steps. There are two APIs that are particularly useful in this regard, the Java Message Service (JMS) and the Java Management Extensions (JMX). In this chapter, you will see the core of these two APIs tied together to provide a highly useful architecture.

Chapter 13: Java Security

Information security is tremendously important to Java development. In this chapter, you will see how your application can be secured using the Java Authorization and Authentication Service (JAAS) and how your data can be secured using the Java Cryptography Extensions (JCE).

Chapter 14: Packaging and Deploying Your Java Applications

One of the trickiest and most painful things about developing Java applications, whether they are enterprise or desktop applications, is packaging and deploying your application. There are a multitude of deployment descriptors and packaging rules that exist in many of the Java APIs. There are JARs, WARs, EARs, and more on the way. Often you get cursory understanding of these formats and specifications within each of the stovepipe books. In this chapter, you will learn about a number of the packaging mechanisms that exist in Java, as well as descriptions of the deployment descriptors for each of those mechanisms.

What You Need to Use This Book

This book is based upon Java 2 Standard Edition version 5.0. You might find it helpful to have an Integrated Development Environment (IDE) of your choice—Eclipse is a very good and popular one (http://www.eclipse.org). Furthermore, depending on the chapter, you may need to use an application server like JBoss (http://www.jboss.org) or Tomcat (http://jakarta.apache.org/tomcat). The need to download an application server, as well as any other downloads (of APIs and so on), is addressed in each chapter.

Conventions

To help you get the most from the text and keep track of what's happening, we've used a number of conventions throughout the book.

> **Boxes like this one hold important, not-to-be forgotten information that is directly relevant to the surrounding text.**

Tips, hints, tricks, and asides to the current discussion are offset and placed in italics like this.

As for styles in the text, the following are standard for the book:

❑ Important words are *highlighted* when they are introduced.

❑ Keyboard strokes are shown like this: Ctrl+A.

❑ File names, URLs, and code within the text are like so: persistence.properties.

❑   Code is presented in two different ways:

In code examples, new and important code is highlighted with a gray background.

The gray highlighting is not used for code that's less important in the present context, or has been shown before.

Source Code

As you work through the examples in this book, you may choose either to type in all the code manually or to use the source code files that accompany the book. All of the source code used in this book is available for download at http://www.wrox.com. Once at the site, simply locate the book's title (either by using the Search box or by using one of the title lists) and click the Download Code link on the book's detail page to obtain all the source code for the book.

Because many books have similar titles, you may find it easiest to search by ISBN; for this book the ISBN is 0-7645-7486-8.

Once you download the code, just decompress it with your favorite compression tool. Alternatively, you can go to the main Wrox code download page at http://www.wrox.com/dynamic/books/download.aspx to see the code available for this book and all other Wrox books.

Errata

We make every effort to ensure that there are no errors in the text or in the code. However, no one is perfect, and mistakes do occur. If you find an error in one of our books, like a spelling mistake or faulty piece of code, we would be very grateful for your feedback. By sending in errata you may save another reader hours of frustration, and at the same time you will be helping us provide even higher quality information.

To find the errata page for this book, go to http://www.wrox.com and locate the title using the Search box or one of the title lists. Then, on the book details page, click the Book Errata link. On this page you can view all errata that has been submitted for this book and posted by Wrox editors. A complete book list including links to each book's errata is also available at http://www.wrox.com/misc-pages/booklist.shtml.

If you don't spot the error you are experiencing on the Book Errata page, go to http://www.wrox.com/contact/techsupport.shtml and complete the form there to send us the error you have found. We'll check the information and, if appropriate, post a message to the book's errata page and fix the problem in subsequent editions of the book.

p2p.wrox.com

For author and peer discussion, join the P2P forums at p2p.wrox.com. The forums are a Web-based system for you to post messages relating to Wrox books and related technologies and interact with other readers and technology users. The forums offer a subscription feature to e-mail you topics of interest of your choosing when new posts are made to the forums. Wrox authors, editors, other industry experts, and your fellow readers are present on these forums.

At http://p2p.wrox.com you will find a number of different forums that will help you not only as you read this book, but also as you develop your own applications. To join the forums, just follow these steps:

1. Go to p2p.wrox.com and click the Register link.

2. Read the terms of use and click Agree.

3. Complete the required information to join as well as any optional information you wish to provide and click Submit.

4. You will receive an e-mail with information describing how to verify your account and complete the registration process.

You can read messages in the forums without joining P2P, but to post your own messages, you must join.

Once you join, you can post new messages and respond to messages other users post. You can read messages at any time on the Web. If you would like to have new messages from a particular forum e-mailed to you, click the Subscribe to this Forum icon by the forum name in the forum listing.

For more information about how to use the Wrox P2P, be sure to read the P2P FAQs for answers to questions about how the forum software works as well as many common questions specific to P2P and Wrox books. To read the FAQs, click the FAQ link on any P2P page.

Key Java Language Features and Libraries

Java's initial design opted to leave out many features that programmers knew from C++ and other languages. This made programming and understanding Java a lot simpler since there are fewer syntactic details. The less built into the language, the cleaner the code is. However, since some features are useful and desired by programmers, the new JDK 5 release of Java introduced several important features that were left out of the initial design of the language. Other changes make certain code constructs easier to code, removing the need for repeating common blocks of code. Please note that this book was written while some of these features are in flex, before they enter into their final form. Therefore, certain information may not be accurate by the time this book is published.

The first half of this chapter will explore the new language. The features are new to the language features built into the language, giving you everything you need to know to make full use of these additions. The second half of this chapter details certain key utility packages in the `java.util` branch of the class library.

New Language Features

Sun has added several new features to the Java language itself. All these features are supported by an updated compiler, and all translate to already defined Java bytecode. This means that virtual machines can execute these features with no need for an update.

❑ Generics — A way to make classes type-safe that are written to work on any arbitrary object type, such as narrowing an instance of a collection to hold a specific object type and eliminating the need to cast objects when taking an object out of the collection.

❑ Enhanced `for` loop — A cleaner and less error prone version of the `for` loop for use with iterators.

❑   Variable arguments — Support for passing an arbitrary number of parameters to a method.

❑   Boxing/Unboxing — Direct language support for automatic conversion between primitive types and their reference types (such as `int` and `Integer`).

❑   Type-safe enumerations — Clean syntax for defining and using enumerations, supported at the language level.

❑   Static import — Ability to access static members from a class without need to qualify them with a class name.

❑   Meta data — Coupled with new tools developed by third-party companies, saves developers the effort of writing boilerplate code by automatically generating the code.

These features update the Java language to include many constructs developers are used to in other languages. They make writing Java code easier, cleaner, and faster. Even if you choose not to take advantage of these features, familiarity with them is vital to read and maintain code written by other developers.

Generics

Generics enable compile-time type-safety with classes that work on arbitrary types. Take collections in Java as an example of a good use of the generics mechanism. Collections hold objects of type `Object`, so placing an object into a collection loses that object's type. This means two things. First, any object can be placed into the collection, and second, a cast is required when pulling an object out of the collection. This can be a source of errors since the developer must track what type of object is in each position inside the collection to ensure the correct cast is performed when accessing the collection.

You can design a generic collection such that at the source code level (and verifiable at compile time) the collection will only hold a specific type of object. If a collection is told to only hold objects of type `Integer`, and a `String` is placed into the collection, the compiler will display an error. This eliminates any type ambiguity with the collection and also removes the need to cast the object when retrieving an object from the collection. The class has to be designed to support genericity, and when an object of the collection class is declared, the specific type that that instance of the collection will work on must be specified. There are several syntax changes to the Java language to support generics, but here's a quick taste of what they look like before generics are discussed in detail.

To create an `ArrayList` that holds only `Integer` objects, the syntax for declaring, instantiating, and using the `ArrayList` is the following:

```
ArrayList<Integer> listOfIntegers; // <TYPE_NAME> is new to the syntax
Integer integerObject;

listOfIntegers = new ArrayList<Integer>(); // <TYPE_NAME> is new to the syntax
listOfIntegers.add(new Integer(10)); // Can only pass in Integer objects
integerObject = listOfIntegers.get(0); // no cast required
```

If you have a background in C++, the syntax is quite similar. If you don't, you may have to get used to the syntax, but it shouldn't be too difficult. Let's take a more rigorous look at how generics are supported in the Java language.

Generic Types and Defining Generic Classes

In the terminology of generics, there are parameterized types (the generic classes) and type variables. The generic classes are the classes that are parameterized when the programmer declares and instantiates the class. Type variables are these parameters that are used in the definition of a generic class, and are replaced by specific types when an object of the generic class is created.

Parameterized Types (Classes and Interfaces)

A generic class is also known as a parameterized class. The class is defined with space for one or more parameters, placed between the angle braces, where the type of the parameters is specified during the declaration of a specific instance of the class. For the rest of this section, the term *generic class* will be used to refer to a parameterized class. Also note that a class or an interface in Java can be made generic. For the rest of this section, unless otherwise stated, the word *class* includes classes and interfaces. All instances of a generic class, regardless of what type each instance has been parameterized with, are considered to be the same class.

A type variable is an unqualified identifier that is used in the definition of a generic class as a placeholder. Type variables appear between the angle braces. This identifier will be replaced (automatically) by whatever specific object type the user of the generic class "plugs into" the generic class. In the example at the start of this section, `Integer` is the specific type that takes the place of the type variable for the parameterized `ArrayList`.

The direct super-types of a generic class are the classes in the `extends` clause, if present (or `java.lang.Object` if not present), and any interfaces, if any are present. Therefore, in the following example, the direct super-type is `ArrayList`:

```
class CustomArrayList<ItemType> extends ArrayList {
    // fields/methods here
}
```

The super-types of type variables are those listed in the bounds list for that type variable. If none are specified, `java.lang.Object` is the super-type.

In hierarchies of generic classes, one important restriction exists. To support translation by type erasure (see below for more on type erasure), a class or type variable cannot have two different parameterizations of the same class/interface at the same time. This is an example of an illegal hierarchy:

```
interface BaseInterface<A> {
    A getInfo();
}

class ParentClass implements BaseInterface<Integer> {
    public Integer getInfo()
    {
        return(null);
    }
}

class ChildClass extends ParentClass implements BaseInterface<String> { }
```

The interface BaseInterface is first parameterized with Integer, and later parameterized with String. These are in direct conflict, so the compiler will issue the following error:

```
c:\code\BadParents.java:14: BaseInterface cannot be inherited with different
arguments: <java.lang.String> and <java.lang.Integer>
class ChildClass extends ParentClass implements BaseInterface<String> { }

1 error
```

Raw Types and Type Erasure

A *raw type* is a parameterized type stripped of its parameters. The official term given to the stripping of parameters is *type erasure*. Raw types are necessary to support legacy code that uses nongeneric versions of classes such as collections. Because of type erasure, it is possible to assign a generic class reference to a reference of its nongeneric (legacy) version. Therefore, the following code compiles without error:

```
Vector oldVector;
Vector<Integer> intVector;

oldVector = intVector; // valid
```

However, though not an error, assigning a reference to a nongeneric class to a reference to a generic class will cause an unchecked compiler warning. This happens when an erasure changes the argument types of a method or a field assignment to a raw type if the erasure changes the method/field type. As an example, the following program causes the warnings shown after it. You must pass -Xlint:unchecked on the command line to javac to see the specific warnings:

```
import java.util.*;

public class UncheckedExample {
    public void processIntVector(Vector<Integer> v)
    {
        // perform some processing on the vector
    }

    public static void main(String args[])
    {
        Vector<Integer> intVector = new Vector<Integer>();
        Vector oldVector = new Vector();
        UncheckedExample ue = new UncheckedExample();

        // This is permitted
        oldVector = intVector;
        // This causes an unchecked warning
        intVector = oldVector;
        // This is permitted
        ue.processIntVector(intVector);
        // This causes an unchecked warning
        ue.processIntVector(oldVector);
    }
}
```

Attempting to compile the above code causes the following output:

```
UncheckedExample.java:16: warning: unchecked assignment: java.util.Vector to
java.util.Vector<java.lang.Integer>
        intVector = oldVector; // This causes an unchecked warning

UncheckedExample.java:18: warning: unchecked method invocation:
processIntVector(java.util.Vector<java.lang.Integer>) in UncheckedExample is
applied to (java.util.Vector)
          ue.processIntVector(oldVector); // This causes an unchecked warning

2 warnings
```

Defining Generic Classes

As mentioned earlier, both interfaces and classes can be parameterized. Since type variables have no inherent type, all that matters is the number of type variables that act as parameters in a class. The list of type variables appears between the angle braces (the less-than sign and greater-than sign). An example of changing the existing `ArrayList` class from a nongeneric class to a generic class changes its signature to:

```
public class ArrayList<ItemType> { ... }
```

The type variable here is `ItemType`, and can be used throughout the class as a not-yet-specified type. When an object of the class is defined, a specific type is specified and is "plugged into" the generic class by the compiler. The scope of a type variable extends throughout the class, including the bounds of the type parameter list, but not including static members/methods.

Each type variable can also have bounds that place a restriction on the type variable. The type variable can be forced to extend from a class other than `java.lang.Object` (which it does when no `extends` clause is specified) or implement any number of specific interfaces. For example, if you define an interface `GraphicContext` as part of a graphics library, you might write a specialization of a collection to only hold objects that implement the `GraphicContext` interface. To place only an interface restriction on the type variable, the `extends` clause must be specified, even if it is only `java.lang.Object`, however it is possible to only list interfaces after the `extends` clause. If you only list interfaces, it is implicitly understood that `java.lang.Object` is the base class of the type variable. Note that interfaces are separated by the ampersand ("&"). Any number of interfaces can be specified.

Using Generics

It is straightforward to create objects of a generic type. Any parameters must match the bounds specified. Although one might expect to create an array of a generic type, the early access release of generics forbids it. It is also possible to create a method that works on generic types. This section describes these usage scenarios.

Class Instances

Creating an object of a generic class consists of specifying types for each parameter and supplying any necessary arguments to the constructor. The conditions for any bounds on type variables must be met. Note that only reference types are valid as parameters when creating an instance of a generic class. Trying to use a primitive data type causes the compiler to issue an `unexpected type` error.

This is a simple creation of a `HashMap` that assigns `Floats` to `Strings`:

```
HashMap<String,Float> hm = new HashMap<String,Float>();
```

Here's an example from above, involving bounds:

```
GCArrayList<MemoryDevice> gcal = new GCArrayList<MemoryDevice>();
```

If `MonitorDevice` was specified instead of `MemoryDevice`, the compiler issues the error `type parameter MonitorDevice is not within its bound`.

Arrays

As of the time of this writing, arrays of generic types and arrays of type variables are not allowed. Attempting to create an array of parameterized `Vectors`, for example, causes a compiler error:

```
import java.util.*;

public class GenericArrayExample {
    public static void main(String args[])
    {
        Vector<Integer> vectorList[] = new Vector<Integer>[10];
    }
}
```

If you try to compile that code, the compiler issues the following two errors. This code is the simplest approach to creating an array of a generic type and the compiler tells you explicitly that creating a generic type array is forbidden:

```
GenericArrayExample.java:6: arrays of generic types are not allowed
        Vector<Integer> vectorList[] = new Vector<Integer>[10];
                            ^
GenericArrayExample.java:6: arrays of generic types are not allowed
        Vector<Integer> vectorList[] = new Vector<Integer>[10];
                                           ^ .
2 errors
```

Generic Methods

In addition to the generic mechanism for classes, generic methods are introduced. The angle brackets for the parameters appear after all method modifiers but before the return type of the method. Following is an example of a declaration of a generic method:

```
static <Elem> void swap(Elem[] a, int i, int j)
{
    Elem temp  = a[i];
    a[i] = a[j];
    a[j] = temp;
}
```

The syntax for the parameters in a generic method is the same as that for generic classes. Type variables can have bounds just like they do in class declarations. Two methods cannot have the same name and argument types. If two methods have the same name and argument types, and have the same number of type variables with the same bounds, then these methods are the same and the compiler will generate an error.

Generics and Exceptions

Type variables are not permitted in `catch` clauses, but can be used in `throws` lists of methods. An example of using a type variable in the `throws` clause follows. The `Executor` interface is designed to execute a section of code that may throw an exception specified as a parameter. In this example, the code that fills in the execute method might throw an `IOException`. The specific exception, `IOException`, is specified as a parameter when creating a concrete instance of the `Executor` interface:

```
import java.io.*;

interface Executor<E extends Exception> {
    void execute() throws E;
}

public class GenericExceptionTest {
    public static void main(String args[]) {
        try {
            Executor<IOException> e =
                new Executor<IOException>() {
                public void execute() throws IOException
                {
                    // code here that may throw an
                    // IOException or a subtype of
                    // IOException
                }
            };

            e.execute();
        } catch(IOException ioe) {
            System.out.println("IOException: " + ioe);
            ioe.printStackTrace();
        }
    }
}
```

The specific type of exception is specified when an instance of the `Executor` class is created inside main. The `execute` method throws an arbitrary exception that it is unaware of until a concrete instance of the `Executor` interface is created.

Enhanced for Loop

The `for` loop has been modified to provide a cleaner way to process an iterator. Using a `for` loop with an iterator is error prone because of the slight mangling of the usual form of the `for` loop since the update clause is placed in the body of the loop. Some languages have a `foreach` keyword that cleans up the syntax for processing iterators. Java opted not to introduce a new keyword, instead deciding to keep it simple and introduce a new use of the colon. Traditionally, a developer will write the following code to use an iterator:

```
for(Iterator iter = intArray.iterator(); iter.hasNext(); ) {
    Integer intObject = (Integer)iter.next();
    // ... more statements to use intObject ...
}
```

The problem inherent in this code lies in the missing "update" clause of the `for` loop. The code that advances the iterator is moved into the body of the `for` loop out of necessity, since it also returns the next object. The new and improved syntax that does the same thing as the previous code snippet is:

```
for(Integer intObject : intArray) {
    // ... same statements as above go here ...
}
```

This code is much cleaner and easier to read. It eliminates all the potential from the previous construct to introduce errors into the program. If this is coupled with a generic collection, the type of the object is checked versus the type inside the collection at compile time.

Support for this new `for` loop requires a change only to the compiler. The code generated is no different from the same code written in the traditional way. The compiler might translate the above code into the following, for example:

```
for(Iterator<Integer> $iter = intArray.iterator(); $iter.hasNext(); ) {
    Integer intObject = $iter.next();
    // ... statements ...
}
```

The use of the dollar sign in the identifier in this example merely means the compiler generates a unique identifier for the expansion of the new `for` loop syntax into the more traditional form before compiling.

The same syntax for using an iterator on a collection works for an array. Using the new `for` loop syntax on an array is the same as using it on a collection:

```
for(String strObject : stringArray) {
    // ... statements here using strObject ...
}
```

However, the compiler expands the array version to code slightly longer than the collection version:

```
String[] $strArray = stringArray;

for(int $i = 0; $i < $strArray.length; $i++) {
    String strObject = $strArray[$i];
    // ... statements here ...
}
```

The compiler this time uses two temporary and unique variables during the expansion. The first is an alias to the array, and the second is the loop counter.

Additions to the Java Class Library

To fully support the new `for` loop syntax, the object iterated over must be an array or inherit from a new interface, `java.lang.Iterable`, directly or indirectly. The existing collection classes will be retrofitted for the release of JDK 5. The new `Iterable` interface looks like:

```
public interface Iterable {
    /**
     * Returns an iterator over the elements in this collection.  There are no
     * guarantees concerning the order in which the elements are returned
     * (unless this collection is an instance of some class that provides a
     * guarantee).
     *
     * @return an Iterator over the elements in this collection.
     */
    SimpleIterator iterator();
}
```

Additionally, `java.util.Iterator` will be retrofitted to implement `java.lang.ReadOnlyIterator`, as shown here:

```
public interface ReadOnlyIterator {
    /**
     * Returns true if the iteration has more elements. (In other
     * words, returns true if next would return an element
     * rather than throwing an exception.)
     *
     * @return true if the iterator has more elements.
     */
    boolean hasNext();

    /**
     * Returns the next element in the iteration.
     *
     * @return the next element in the iteration.
     * @exception NoSuchElementException iteration has no more elements.
     */
    Object next();
}
```

The introduction of this interface prevents dependency on the `java.util` interfaces. The change in the `for` loop syntax is at the language level and it makes sense to ensure that any support needed in the class library is located in the `java.lang` branch.

Variable Arguments

C and C++ are the most popular languages that support variable length argument lists for functions. Java decided to introduce this aspect into the language. Only use variable argument parameter lists in cases that make sense. If you abuse them, it's easy to create source code that is confusing. The C language uses the ellipsis (three periods) in the function declaration to stand for "an arbitrary number of parameters, zero or more." Java also uses the ellipsis but combines it with a type and identifier. The type can be anything — any class, any primitive type, even array types. When using it in an array, however, the ellipsis must come last in the type description, after the square brackets. Due to the nature of variable arguments, each method can only have a single type as a variable argument and it must come last in the parameter list.

Following is an example of a method that takes an arbitrary number of primitive integers and returns their sum:

```java
public int sum(int... intList)
{
    int i, sum;

    sum=0;
    for(i=0; i<intList.length; i++) {
        sum += intList[i];
    }

    return(sum);
}
```

All arguments passed in from the position of the argument marked as variable and beyond are combined into an array. This makes it simple to test how many arguments were passed in. All that is needed is to reference the length property on the array, and the array also provides easy access to each argument.

Here's a full sample program that adds up all the values in an arbitrary number of arrays:

```java
public class VarArgsExample {
    int sumArrays(int[]... intArrays)
    {
        int sum, i, j;

        sum=0;
        for(i=0; i<intArrays.length; i++) {
            for(j=0; j<intArrays[i].length; j++) {
                sum += intArrays[i][j];
            }
        }

        return(sum);
    }

    public static void main(String args[])
    {
        VarArgsExample va = new VarArgsExample();
        int sum=0;

        sum = va.sumArrays(new int[]{1,2,3},
                           new int[]{4,5,6},
                           new int[]{10,16});
        System.out.println("The sum of the numbers is: " + sum);
    }
}
```

This code follows the established approach to defining and using a variable argument. The ellipsis comes after the square brackets, that is, after the variable argument's type. Inside the method the argument intArrays is simply an array of arrays.

Boxing/Unboxing Conversions

One tedious aspect of the Java language in the past is the manual operation of converting primitive types (such as `int` and `char`) to their corresponding reference type (for example, `Integer` for `int` and `Character` for `char`). The solution to getting rid of this constant wrapping and unwrapping are boxing and unboxing conversions. A boxing conversion is an implicit operation that takes a primitive type, such as `int`, and automatically places it inside an instance of its corresponding reference type (in this case, `Integer`). Unboxing is the reverse operation, taking a reference type, such as `Integer`, and converting it to its primitive type, `int`. Without boxing, you might add an `int` primitive to a collection (which holds `Object` types) by doing the following:

```
Integer intObject;
int intPrimitive;
ArrayList arrayList = new ArrayList();

intPrimitive = 11;
intObject = new Integer(intPrimitive);
arrayList.put(intObject); // cannot add intPrimitive directly
```

Although this code is straightforward, it is more verbose than necessary. With the introduction of boxing conversions, the above code can be rewritten as follows:

```
int intPrimitive;
ArrayList arrayList = new ArrayList();

intPrimitive = 11;
// here intPrimitive is automatically wrapped in an Integer
arrayList.put(intPrimitive);
```

The need to create an `Integer` object to place an `int` into the collection is no longer needed. The boxing conversion happens such that the resulting reference type's `value()` method (such as `intValue()` for `Integer`) equals the original primitive type's value. Consult the following table for all valid boxing conversions. If there is any other type, the boxing conversion becomes an identity conversion (converting the type to its own type). Note that due to the introduction of boxing conversions, several forbidden conversions referring to primitive types are no longer forbidden since they now can be converted to certain reference types.

Primitive Type	Reference Type
boolean	Boolean
byte	Byte
char	Character
short	Short
int	Integer
long	Long
float	Float
double	Double

Unboxing Conversions

Java also introduces unboxing conversions, which convert a reference type (such as `Integer` or `Float`) to its primitive type (such as `int` or `float`). Consult the following table for a list of all valid unboxing conversions. The conversion happens such that the `value` method of the reference type equals the resulting primitive value.

Reference Type	Primitive Type
Boolean	boolean
Byte	byte
Character	char
Short	short
Integer	int
Long	long
Float	float
Double	double

Valid Contexts for Boxing/Unboxing Conversions

Since the boxing and unboxing operations are conversions, they happen automatically with no specific instruction by the programmer (unlike casting, which is an explicit operation). There are several contexts in which boxing and unboxing conversions can happen.

Assignments

An assignment conversion happens when the value of an expression is assigned to a variable. When the type of the expression does not match the type of the variable, and there is no risk of data loss, the conversion happens automatically. The precedence of conversions that happen is the identity conversion, a widening primitive conversion, a widening reference conversion, and then the new boxing (or unboxing) conversion. If none of these conversions are valid, the compiler issues an error.

Method Invocations

When a method call is made, and the argument types don't match precisely with those passed in, several conversions are possible. Collectively, these conversions are known as method invocation conversions. Each parameter that does not match precisely in type to the corresponding parameter in the method signature might be subject to a conversion. The possible conversions are the identity conversion, a widening primitive conversion, a widening reference conversion, and then the new boxing (or unboxing) conversion.

The most specific method must be chosen anytime more than one method matches a particular method call. The rules to match the most specific method change slightly with the addition of boxing conversions. If all the standard checks for resolving method ambiguity fail, the boxing/unboxing conversion won't be used to resolve ambiguity. Therefore, by the time checks are performed for boxing conversions, the method invocation is deemed ambiguous and fails.

Combining boxing with generics allows you to write the following code:

```
import java.util.*;

public class BoxingGenericsExample {
    public static void main(String args[])
    {
        HashMap<String,Integer> hm = new HashMap<String,Integer>();

        hm.put("speed", 20);
    }
}
```

The primitive integer 20 is automatically converted to an Integer and then placed into the HashMap under the specified key.

Static Imports

Importing static data is introduced into the language to simplify using static attributes and methods. After importing static information, the methods/attributes can then be used without the need to qualify the method or attribute with its class name. For example, by importing the static members of the Math class, you can write abs or sqrt instead of Math.abs and Math.sqrt.

This mechanism also prevents the dangerous coding practice of placing a set of static attributes into an interface, and then in each class that needs to use the attributes, implementing that interface. The following interface should not be implemented in order to use the attributes without qualification:

```
interface ShapeNumbers {
    public static int CIRCLE = 0;
    public static int SQUARE = 1;
    public static int TRIANGLE = 2;
}
```

Implementing this interface creates an unnecessary dependence on the ShapeNumbers interface. Even worse, it becomes awkward to maintain as the class evolves, especially if other classes need access to these constants also and implement this interface. It is easy for compiled classes to get out of synchronization with each other if the interface containing these attributes changes and only some classes are recompiled.

To make this cleaner, the static members are placed into a class (instead of an interface) and then imported via a modified syntax of the import directive. ShapeNumbers is revised to the following:

```
package MyConstants;

class ShapeNumbers {
    public static int CIRCLE = 0;
    public static int SQUARE = 1;
    public static int TRIANGLE = 2;
}
```

A client class then imports the static information from the ShapeNumbers class and can then use the attributes CIRCLE, SQUARE, and TRIANGLE without the need to prefix them with ShapeNumbers and the member operator.

To import the static members in your class, specify the following in the import section of your Java source file (at the top):

```
import static MyConstants.ShapeNumbers.*; // imports all static data
```

This syntax is only slightly modified from the standard format of the import statement. The keyword `static` is added after the `import` keyword, and instead of importing packages, you now always add on the class name since the static information is being imported from a specific class. The chief reason the keyword `static` is added to the import statement is to make it clear to those reading the source code that the import is for the static information.

You can also import constants individually by using the following syntax:

```
import static MyConstants.ShapeNumbers.CIRCLE;
import static MyConstants.ShapeNumbers.SQUARE;
```

This syntax is also what you would expect. The keyword `static` is included since this is a static import, and the pieces of static information to import are each specified explicitly.

You cannot statically import data from a class that is inside the default package. The class must be located inside a named package. Also, static attributes and methods can conflict. For example, below are two classes (located in `Colors.java` and `Fruits.java`) containing static constants:

```
package MyConstants;

public class Colors {
    public static int white = 0;
    public static int black = 1;
    public static int red = 2;
    public static int blue = 3;
    public static int green = 4;
    public static int orange = 5;
    public static int grey = 6;
}
```

```
package MyConstants;

public class Fruits {
    public static int apple = 500;
    public static int pear = 501;
    public static int orange = 502;
    public static int banana = 503;
    public static int strawberry = 504;
}
```

If you write a class that tries to statically import data on both these classes, everything is fine until you try to use a static variable that is defined in both of them:

```
import static MyConstants.Colors.*;
import static MyConstants.Fruits.*;

public class StaticTest {
```

```
        public static void main(String args[])
        {
            System.out.println("orange = " + orange);
            System.out.println("color orange = " + Colors.orange);
            System.out.println("Fruity orange = " + Fruits.orange);
        }
    }
```

The seventh line of the program causes the compiler error listed below. The identifier orange is defined in both Colors and Fruits, so the compiler cannot resolve this ambiguity:

```
StaticTest.java:7: reference to orange is ambiguous, both variable orange in
MyConstants.Colors and variable orange in MyConstants.Fruits match
        System.out.println("orange = " + orange);
```

In this case, you should explicitly qualify the conflicting name with the class where it is defined. Instead of writing orange, write Colors.orange or Fruits.orange.

Enumerations

Java introduces enumeration support at the language level in the JDK 5 release. An enumeration is an ordered list of items wrapped into a single entity. An instance of an enumeration can take on the value of any single item in the enumeration's list of items. The simplest possible enumeration is the Colors enum shown below:

```
public enum Colors { red, green, blue }
```

They present the ability to compare one arbitrary item to another, and to iterate over the list of defined items. An enumeration (abbreviated enum in Java) is a special type of class. All enumerations implicitly subclass a new class in Java, java.lang.Enum. This class cannot be subclassed manually.

There are many benefits to built-in support for enumerations in Java. Enumerations are type-safe and the performance is competitive with constants. The constant names inside the enumeration don't need to be qualified with the enumeration's name. Clients aren't built with knowledge of the constants inside the enumeration, so changing the enumeration is easy without having to change the client. If constants are removed from the enumeration, the clients will fail and you'll receive an error message. The names of the constants in the enumeration can be printed, so you get more information than simply the ordinal number of the item in the list. This also means that the constants can be used as names for collections such as HashMap.

Since an enumeration is a class in Java, it can also have fields and methods, and implement interfaces. Enumerations can be used inside switch statements in a straightforward manner, and are relatively simple for programmers to understand/use.

Here's a basic enum declaration and its usage inside a switch statement. If you want to track what operating system a certain user is using, you can use an enumeration of operating systems, which are defined in the OperatingSystems enum. Note that since an enumeration is effectively a class, it cannot be public if it is in the same file as another class that is public. Also note that in the switch statement, the constant names cannot be qualified with the name of the enumeration they are in. The details are automatically handled by the compiler based on the type of the enum used in the switch clause:

```
import java.util.*;

enum OperatingSystems {
    windows, unix, linux, macintosh
}

public class EnumExample1 {
    public static void main(String args[])
    {
        OperatingSystems os;

        os = OperatingSystems.windows;
        switch(os) {
            case windows:
                System.out.println("You chose Windows!");
                break;
            case unix:
                System.out.println("You chose Unix!");
                break;
            case linux:
                System.out.println("You chose Linux!");
                break;
            case macintosh:
                System.out.println("You chose Macintosh!");
                break;
            default:
                System.out.println("I don't know your OS.");
                break;
        }
    }
}
```

The `java.lang.Enum` class implements the `Comparable` and `Serializable` interfaces. The details of comparing enumerations and serializing them to a data source are already handled inside the class. You cannot mark an `enum` as `abstract` unless every constant has a class body, and these class bodies override the abstract methods in the `enum`. Also note that enumerations cannot be instantiated using `new`. The compiler will let you know that `enum types may not be instantiated`.

Java introduces two new collections, `EnumSet` and `EnumMap`, which are only meant to optimize the performance of sets and maps when using `enum`s. Enumerations can be used with the existing collection classes, or with the new collections when optimization tailored to enumerations is desired.

Methods can be declared inside an `enum`. There are restrictions placed on defining constructors, however. Constructors can't chain to superclass constructors, unless the superclass is another `enum`. Each constant inside the `enum` can have a class body, but since this is effectively an anonymous class, you cannot define a constructor.

You can also add attributes to the enumeration and to the individual `enum` constants. An `enum` constant can also be followed by arguments, which are passed to the constructor defined in the `enum`.

Here's an example enumeration with fields and methods:

```
enum ProgramFlags {
    showErrors(0x01),
    includeFileOutput(0x02),
    useAlternateProcessor(0x04);

    private int bit;

    ProgramFlags(int bitNumber)
    {
        bit = bitNumber;
    }

    public int getBitNumber()
    {
        return(bit);
    }
}

public class EnumBitmapExample {
    public static void main(String args[])
    {
        ProgramFlags flag = ProgramFlags.showErrors;

        System.out.println("Flag selected is: " +
                            flag.ordinal() +
                    " which is " +
                            flag.name());
    }
}
```

The `ordinal()` method returns the position of the constant in the list. The value of `showErrors` is 0 since it comes first in the list, and the ordinal values are 0-based. The `name()` method can be used to get the name of the constant, which provides for getting more information about enumerations.

Meta data

Another feature that Sun has decided to include in the JDK 5 release of Java is a meta data facility. This enables tagging classes with extra information that tools can analyze, and also applying certain blocks of code to classes automatically. The meta data facility is introduced in the `java.lang.annotation` package. An annotation is the association of a `tag` to a construct in Java such as a class, known as a *target* in annotation terminology. The types of constructs that can be annotated are listed in the `java.lang.annotation.ElementType` enumeration, and are listed in the following table. Even annotations can be annotated. `TYPE` covers classes, interfaces, and `enum` declarations.

ElementType Constant
ANNOTATION_TYPE
CONSTRUCTOR
FIELD
LOCAL_VARIABLE
METHOD
PACKAGE
PARAMETER
TYPE

Another concept introduced is the life of an annotation, known as the *retention*. Certain annotations may only be useful at the Java source code level, such as an annotation for the javadoc tool. Others might be needed while the program is executing. The RetentionPolicy enumeration lists three type lifetimes for an annotation. The SOURCE policy indicates the annotations should be discarded by the compiler, that is, should only available at the source code level. The CLASS policy indicates that the annotation should appear in the class file, but is possibly discarded at run time. The RUNTIME policy indicates the annotations should make it through to the executing program, and these can then be viewed using reflection.

There are several types of annotations defined in this package. These are listed in the following table. Each of these annotations inherits from the Annotation interface, which defines an equals method and a toString method.

Annotation Class Name	Description
Target	Specifies to which program elements an annotation type is applicable. Each program element can only appear once.
Documented	Specifies annotations should be documented by javadoc or other documentation tools. This can only be applied to annotations.
Inherited	Inherits annotations from super-classes, but not interfaces. The policy on this annotation is RUNTIME, and it can be applied only to annotations.
Retention	Indicates how long annotations on this program element should be available. See RetentionPolicy discussed earlier. The policy on this annotation is RUNTIME, and it can be applied only to annotations.
Deprecated	Marks a program element as deprecated, telling developers they should no longer use it. Retention policy is SOURCE.
Overrides	Indicates that a method is meant to override the method in a parent class. If the override does not actually exist, the compiler will generate an error message. This can only be applied to methods.

There are two useful source level annotations that come with JDK 5, @deprecated and @overrides. The @deprecated annotation is used to mark a method as deprecated — that is, it shouldn't be used by client programmers. The compiler will issue a warning when encountering this annotation on a class method that a programmer uses. The other annotation, @overrides, is used to mark a method as overriding a method in the parent class. The compiler will ensure that a method marked as @overrides does indeed override a method in the parent class. If the method in the child class doesn't override the one in the parent class, the compiler will issue an error alerting the programmer to the fact that the method signature does not match the method in the parent class.

Developing a custom annotation isn't difficult. Let's create a CodeTag annotation that stores basic author and modification date information, and also stores any bug fixes applied to that piece of code. The annotation will be limited to classes and methods:

```
import java.lang.annotation.*;

@Retention(RetentionPolicy.SOURCE)
@Target({ElementType.TYPE, ElementType.METHOD})
public @interface CodeTag {
    String authorName();
    String lastModificationDate();
    String bugFixes() default "";
}
```

The Retention is set to SOURCE, which means this annotation is not available during compile time and run time. The doclet API is used to access source level annotations. The Target is set to TYPE (classes/interfaces/enums) and METHOD for methods. A compiler error is generated if the CodeTag annotation is applied to any other source code element. The first two annotation elements are authorName and lastModificationDate, both of which are mandatory. The bugFixes element defaults to the empty string if not specified. Following is an example class that utilizes the CodeTag annotation:

```
import java.lang.annotation.*;

@CodeTag(authorName="Dilbert",
         lastModificationDate="Mar 23, 2004")
public class ServerCommandProcessor {
    @CodeTag(authorName="Dilbert",
             lastModificationDate="Mar 24, 2004",
             bugFixes="BUG0170")
    public void setParams(String serverName)
    {
        // ...
    }

    public void executeCommand(String command, Object... params)
    {
        // ...
    }
}
```

Note how annotation is used to mark who modified the source and when. The method was last modified a day after the class because of the bug fix. This custom annotation can be used to track this information as part of keeping up with source code modifications. To view or process these source code annotations, the doclet API must be used.

The doclet API (aka Javadoc API) has been extended to support the processing of annotations in the source code. You use the doclet API by writing a Java class that extends com.sun.javadoc.Doclet. The start method must be implemented as this is the method that Javadoc invokes on a doclet to perform custom processing. A simple doclet to print out all classes and methods in a Java source file follows:

```
import com.sun.javadoc.*;

public class ListClasses extends Doclet {
    public static boolean start(RootDoc root) {
        ClassDoc[] classes = root.classes();
        for (ClassDoc cd : classes) {
            System.out.println("Class [" + cd + "] has the following methods");
            for(MemberDoc md : cd.methods()) {
                System.out.println("  " + md);
            }
        }
        return true;
    }
}
```

The start method takes a RootDoc as a parameter, which is automatically passed in by the javadoc tool. The RootDoc provides the starting point to obtain access to all elements inside the source code, and also information on the command line such as additional packages and classes.

The interfaces added to the doclet API for annotations are AnnotationDesc, AnnotationDesc.ElementValuePair, AnnotationTypeDoc, AnnotationTypeElementDoc, and AnnotationValue.

Any element of Java source that can have annotations has an annotations() method associated with the doclet API's counterpart to the source code element. These are AnnotationTypeDoc, AnnotationTypeElementDoc, ClassDoc, ConstructorDoc, ExecutableMemberDoc, FieldDoc, MethodDoc, and MemberDoc. The annotations() method returns an array of AnnotationDesc.

AnnotationDesc

This class represents an annotation, which is an annotation type (AnnotationTypeDoc), and an array of annotation type elements paired with their values. AnnotationDesc defines the following methods.

Method	Description
`AnnotationTypeDoc annotationType()`	Returns this annotation's type.
`AnnotationDesc.ElementValuePair[] elementValues()`	Returns an array of an annotation's elements and their values. Only elements explicitly listed are returned. The elements that aren't listed explicitly, which assume their default value, are not returned since this method processes just what is listed. If there are no elements, an empty array is returned.

AnnotationDesc.ElementValuePair

This represents an association between an annotation type's element and its value. The following methods are defined.

Method	Description
`AnnotationTypeElementDoc element()`	Returns the annotation type element.
`AnnotationValue value()`	Returns the annotation type element's value.

AnnotationTypeDoc

This interface represents an annotation in the source code, just like `ClassDoc` represents a `Class`. Only one method is defined.

Method	Description
`AnnotationTypeElementDoc[] elements()`	Returns an array of the elements of this annotation type.

AnnotationTypeElementDoc

This interface represents an element of an annotation type.

Method	Description
`AnnotationValue defaultValue()`	Returns the default value associated with this annotation type, or null if there is no default value.

AnnotationValue

This interface represents the value of an annotation type element.

Method	Description
`String toString()`	Returns a string representation of the value.
`Object value()`	Returns the value. The object behind this value could be any of the following.
	* A wrapper class for a primitive type (such as `Integer` or `Float`)
	* A `String`
	* A `Type` (representing a class, a generic class, a type variable, a wildcard type, or a primitive data type)
	* A `FieldDoc` (representing an `enum` constant)
	* An `AnnotationDesc`
	* An array of `AnnotationValue`

Here's an example using the annotation support provided by the doclet API. This doclet echoes all annotations and their values that it finds in a source file:

```
import com.sun.javadoc.*;
import java.lang.annotation.*;

public class AnnotationViewer {
    public static boolean start(RootDoc root)
    {
        ClassDoc[] classes = root.classes();

        for (ClassDoc cls : classes) {
            showAnnotations(cls);
        }

        return(true);
    }

    static void showAnnotations(ClassDoc cls)
    {
        System.out.println("Annotations for class [" + cls + "]");
        process(cls.annotations());

        System.out.println();
        for(MethodDoc m : cls.methods()) {
```

```
            System.out.println("Annotations for method [" + m + "]");
            process(m.annotations());
            System.out.println();
        }
    }

    static void process(AnnotationDesc[] anns)
    {
        for (AnnotationDesc ad : anns) {
            AnnotationDesc.ElementValuePair evp[] = ad.elementValues();

            for(AnnotationDesc.ElementValuePair e : evp) {
                System.out.println("  NAME: " + e.element() +
                                   ", VALUE=" + e.value());
            }

        }
    }
}
```

The `start` method iterates across all classes (and interfaces) found in the source file. Since all annotations on source code elements are associated with the `AnnotationDesc` interface, a single method can be written to process annotations regardless of which source code element the annotation is associated. The `showAnnotations` method prints out annotations associated with the current class and then processes all methods inside that class. The doclet API makes processing these source code elements easy. To execute the doclet, pass the name of the doclet and name of the class to process on the command line as follows:

```
javadoc -source 1.5 -doclet AnnotationViewer ServerCommandProcessor.java
```

The doclet echoes the following to the screen:

```
Loading source file ServerCommandProcessor.java...
Constructing Javadoc information...
Annotations for class [ServerCommandProcessor]
  NAME: CodeTag.authorName(), VALUE="Dilbert"
  NAME: CodeTag.lastModificationDate(), VALUE="Mar 23, 2004"

Annotations for method [ServerCommandProcessor.setParams(java.lang.String)]
  NAME: CodeTag.authorName(), VALUE="Dilbert"
  NAME: CodeTag.lastModificationDate(), VALUE="Mar 24, 2004"

Annotations for method [ServerCommandProcessor.executeCommand(java.lang.String,
java.lang.Object[])]
```

To access annotations at run time, the reflection API must be used. This support is built in through the interface `AnnotatedElement`, which is implemented by the reflection classes `AccessibleObject`, `Class`, `Constructor`, `Field`, `Method`, and `Package`. All these elements may have annotations. The `AnnotatedElement` interface defines the following methods.

Method	Description
`<T extends Annotation>` `T getAnnotation(Class<T> annotationType)`	Returns the annotation associated with the specified type, or null if none exists.
`Annotation[] getAnnotations()`	Returns an array of all annotations on the current element, or a zero-length array if no annotations are present.
`Annotation[] getDeclaredAnnotations()`	Similar to `getAnnotations` but does not return inherited annotations — only annotations explicitly declared on this element are returned. Returns a zero-length array if no annotations are present.
`boolean isAnnotationPresent(Class<?` `extends Annotation> annotationType)`	Returns true if the `annotationType` is present on the current element, false otherwise.

Let's develop an annotation that might be useful in developing a testing framework. The framework invokes test methods specified in the annotation and expects a boolean return value from these testing methods. The reflection API is used to both process the annotation and execute the test methods.

The annotation is listed below:

```
import java.lang.annotation.*;

@Retention(RetentionPolicy.RUNTIME)
@Target({ElementType.TYPE})
public @interface TestParameters {
    String testStage();
    String testMethods();
    String testOutputType(); // "db" or "file"
    String testOutput(); // filename or data source/table name
}
```

An example application of this annotation is to a class of utility methods for strings. You might develop your own utility class and develop testing methods to ensure the utility methods work:

```
@TestParameters(testStage="Unit",
                testMethods="testConcat, testSubstring",
                testOutputType="screen",
                testOutput="")
public class StringUtility {
    public String concat(String s1, String s2)
    {
        return(s1 + s2);
    }

    public String substring(String str, int start, int end)
    {
        return(str.substring(start, end));
    }
```

```
    public boolean testConcat()
    {
        String s1 = "test";
        String s2 = " 123";

        return(concat(s1,s2).equals("test 123"));
    }

    public boolean testSubstring()
    {
        String str = "The cat landed on its feet";

        return(substring(str, 4, 3).equals("cat"));
    }
}
```

Following is an example implementation of the testing framework. It uses reflection to process the annotation and then invoke the testing methods, writing the results to the screen (though other output destinations can be built into the framework). As of the time of this writing, the reflection routines to retrieve annotations on classes and methods were not implemented. In the interest of illustration, the source code is provided here without output:

```
import java.lang.reflect.*;
import java.lang.annotation.*;
import java.util.*;

public class TestFramework {
    static void executeTests(String className) {
        try {
            Object obj = Class.forName(className).newInstance();

            TestParameters tp = obj.getClass().getAnnotation(TestParameters.class);
            if(tp != null) {
                String methodList = tp.testMethods();
                StringTokenizer st = new StringTokenizer(methodList, ",");
                while(st.hasMoreTokens()) {
                    String methodName = st.nextToken();

                    Method m = obj.getClass().getDeclaredMethod(methodName);
                    System.out.println(methodName);
                    System.out.println("----------------");
                    String result = invoke(m, obj);
                    System.out.println("Result: " + result);
                }
            } else {
                System.out.println("No annotation found for " + obj.getClass());
            }
        } catch(Exception ex) {
            ex.printStackTrace();
        }
    }

    static String invoke(Method m, Object o) {
```

```
            String result = "PASSED";

            try {
                m.invoke(o);
            } catch(Exception ex) {
                result = "FAILED";
            }

            return(result);
        }

    public static void main(String [] args) {
        executeTests(args[0]);
        }
    }
```

The `executeTests` method obtains a handle to the `TestParameters` annotation from the class and then invokes each method from the `testMethods()` element of the annotation. This is a simple implementation of the testing framework, and can be extended to support the other elements of the `TestParameters` annotation, such as writing results to a database instead of the screen. This is a practical example of using meta data — adding declarative information to Java source that can then be utilized by external programs and/or doclets for generating documentation.

Important Java Utility Libraries

This section describes several key utility libraries in Java. These libraries are as follows:

- ❑ Java logging — A powerful logging system that is vital for providing meaningful error messages to end users, developers, and people working in the field.

- ❑ Regular Expressions — A powerful "miniature language" used to process strings in a variety of ways, such as searching for substrings that match a particular pattern.

- ❑ Java preferences — A way to store and retrieve both system and user defined configuration options.

Each library is designed for flexibility of usage. Familiarity with these libraries is vital when developing solutions in Java. The more tools on your belt as a developer, the better equipped you are.

Java Logging

Java has a well-designed set of classes to control, format, and publish messages through the logging system. It is important for a program to log error and status messages. There are many people who can benefit from logging messages, including developers, testers, end users, and people working in the field that have to troubleshoot programs without source code. It is vital to include a high number of quality log messages in a program, from status updates to error conditions (such as when certain exceptions are caught). By using the logging system, it is possible to see what the program is doing without consulting the source code, and most importantly, track down error conditions to a specific part of the program. The value of a logging system is obvious, especially in large systems where a casual error with minimal or no log messages might take days or longer to track down.

The logging system in `java.util.logging` is sophisticated, including a way to prioritize log messages such that only messages a particular logger is interested in get logged, and the messages can be output to any source that a `Handler` object can handle. Examples of logging destinations are files, databases, and output streams. Take a close look at Figure 1-1 to see an overview of the entire logging system.

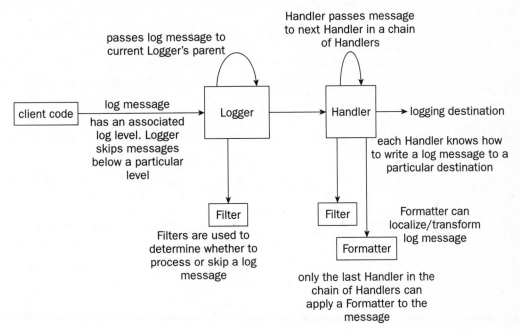

Figure 1-1

The specific `Logger` objects are actually hierarchical, and though not mandatory, can mirror the class hierarchy. When a `Logger` receives a log message, the message is also passed automatically to the `Logger`'s parent. The root logger is named " " (the empty string) and has no parent. Each other `Logger` is usually named something such as `java.util` or `java.util.ArrayList` to mirror the package/class hierarchy. The names of the `Logger` objects, going down the tree, are dot-separated. Therefore, `java.util` is the parent `Logger` of `java.util.ArrayList`. You can name the loggers any arbitrary string, but keeping with the dot-separated convention helps to clarity.

The simplest use of the logging system creates a `Logger` and uses all system defaults (defined in a properties file) for the logging system. The following example outputs the log message using a formatting class called the `SimpleFormatter` that adds time/date/source information to the log message:

```
import java.util.logging.*;

public class BasicLoggingExample {
    public static void main(String args[])
    {
        Logger logger = Logger.getLogger("BasicLoggingExample");

        logger.log(Level.INFO, "Test of logging system");
    }
}
```

The following is output from the `BasicLoggingExample`:

```
Feb 22, 2004 4:07:06 PM BasicLoggingExample main
INFO: Test of logging system
```

The Log Manager

The entire logging system for a particular application is controlled by a single instance of the `LogManager` class. This instance is created during the initialization of the `LogManager`. The `LogManager` contains the hierarchical namespace that has all the named `Logger` objects. The `LogManager` also contains logging control properties that are used by `Handlers` and other objects in the logging system for configuration. These configuration properties are stored in the file `lib/logging.properties` that is located in the JRE installation path.

There are two system properties that can be used to initialize the logging system with different properties. The first way is to override the property `java.util.logging.config.file` and specify the full path to your own version of `logging.properties`. The other property, `java.util.logging.config.class`, is used to point to your own `LogManager`. This custom `LogManager` is responsible for reading in its configuration. If neither of these properties is set, Java will default to the `logging.properties` file in the JRE directory. Consult the following table for properties that can be set on the `LogManager` in this file. You can also specify properties for `Loggers` and `Handlers` in this file. These properties are described later in this section.

Property Key	Property Value
Handlers	Comma separated list of `Handler` classes. Each handler must be located somewhere in the system classpath.
.level	Sets the minimum level for a specific `Logger`.
	The `level` must be prefixed with the full path to a specific `Logger`. A period by itself sets the level for the root logger.

The LogManager Class

The `LogManager` class contains methods to configure the current instance of the logging system through a number of configuration methods, tracks loggers and provides access to these loggers, and handles certain logging events. These methods are listed in the following tables.

Configuration

The methods listed in the following table relate to storage and retrieval of configuration information in the `LogManager`.

Method	Description
`String getProperty(String name)`	Returns the value corresponding to a specified logging property.
`void readConfiguration()`	Reloads the configuration using the same process as startup. If the system properties controlling initialization have not changed, the same file that was read at startup will be read here.
`void readConfiguration(InputStream ins)`	Reads configuration information from an `InputStream` that is in the `java.util.Properties` format.
`void reset()`	Resets the logging system. All `Handlers` are closed and removed and all logger levels except on the root are set to null. The root logger's level is set to `Level.INFO`.

Logger Control

The methods listed in the following table relate to the storage, retrieval, and management of individual `Logger` references. These are the most commonly used methods on the `LogManager` class.

Method	Description
`static LogManager getLogManager()`	Returns the one and only instance of the `LogManager` object.
`boolean addLogger(Logger logger)`	Returns true if the `Logger` passed in is not already registered (its name isn't already in the list). The logger is registered. Returns false if the name of the `Logger` object already exists in the list of registered loggers.
`Logger getLogger(String name)`	Returns a reference to the `Logger` object that is named "name," or null if no logger is found.
`Enumeration getLoggerNames()`	Returns an `Enumeration` containing a list of the names of all currently registered loggers.

Events

The methods listed in the following table provide a way to add and remove references to listeners that should be notified when properties are changed on the `LogManager`.

Method	Description
`void addPropertyChangeListener (PropertyChangeListener l)`	Adds a property change listener to the list of listeners that want notification of when a property has changed. The same listener can be added multiple times.
`void removePropertyChangeListener (PropertyChangeListener l)`	Removes a single occurrence of a property change listener in the list of listeners.

The Logger Class

An instance of the `Logger` class is used by client code to log a message. Both the log message and each logger have an associated level. If the level of the log message is equal to or greater than the level of the logger, the message is then processed. Otherwise, the logger drops the log message. It is an inexpensive operation to test whether to drop the log message or not, and this operation is done at the entry point to the logging system — the `Logger` class. These levels are defined inside the `Level` class. Consult the following table for a full list of levels.

Logger Level	Description
SEVERE	Highest logging level. This has top priority.
WARNING	One level below severe. Intended for warning messages that need attention, but aren't serious.
INFO	Two levels below severe. Intended for informational messages.
CONFIG	Three levels below severe. Intended for configuration-related output.
FINE	Four levels below severe. Intended for program tracing information.
FINER	Five levels below severe. Intended for program tracing information.
FINEST	Lowest logging level. This has lowest priority.
ALL	Special level which makes the system log ALL messages.
OFF	Special level which makes the system log NO messages (turns logging off completely).

Logger Methods

The `Logger` is the main class that is used in code that utilizes the logging system. Methods are provided to obtain a named or anonymous logger, configure and get information about the logger, and log messages.

Obtaining a Logger

The following methods allow you to retrieve a handle to a `Logger`. These are static methods and provide an easy way to obtain a `Logger` without going through a `LogManager`.

Method	Description
`static Logger getAnonymousLogger()static Logger getAnonymousLogger(String resourceBundleName)`	Creates an anonymous logger that is exempt from standard security checks, for use in applets. The anonymous logger is not registered in the `LogManager` name-space, but has the root logger ("") as a parent, inheriting level and handlers from the root logger. A resource bundle can also be specified for localization of log messages.
`static Logger getLogger(String name) static Logger getLogger(String name, String resourceBundleName)`	Returns a named logger from the `LogManager` namespace, or if one is not found, creates and returns a new named logger. A resource bundle can also be specified for localization of log messages.

Configuring a Logger Object

The following methods allow you to configure a `Logger` object. You can add and remove handlers, set the logging level on this `Logger` object, set its parent, and choose whether log messages should be passed up the logger hierarchy or not.

Method	Description
`void addHandler(Handler handler)`	Adds a `Handler` to the logger. Multiple handlers can be added. Also note that the root logger is configured with a set of default `Handlers`.
`void removeHandler(Handler handler)`	Removes a specified handler from the list of handlers on this logger. If the handler is not found, this method returns silently.
`void setLevel(Level newLevel)`	Sets the log level that this logger will use. Message levels lower than the logger's value will be automatically discarded. If null is passed in, the level will be inherited from this logger's parent.
`void setParent(Logger parent)`	Sets the parent for this logger. This should not be called by application code, as it is intended for use only by the logging system.
`void setUseParentHandlers(boolean useParentHandlers)`	Specifies true if log messages should be passed to their parent loggers, or false to prevent the log messages from passing to their parent.

Table continued on following page

Method	Description
Filter getFilter()	Returns the filter for this logger, which might be null if no filter is associated.
Handler[] getHandlers()	Returns an array of all handlers associated with this logger.
Level getLevel()	Returns the log level assigned to this logger. If null is returned, it indicates the logging level of the parent logger that will be used.
String getName()	Returns the name of this logger, or null if this is an anonymous logger.
Logger getParent()	The nearest parent to the current logger is returned, or null if the current logger is the root logger.
ResourceBundle getResourceBundle()	Returns the ResourceBundle associated with this logger. Resource bundles are used for localization of log messages. If null is returned, the resource bundle from the logger's parent will be used.
String getResourceBundleName()	Returns the name of the resource bundle this logger uses for localization, or null if the resource bundle is inherited from the logger's parent.
boolean getUseParentHandlers()	Returns true if log messages are passed to the logger's parent, or false if log messages are not passed up the hierarchy.

Logging Messages

The following methods are all used to actually log a message using a Logger. Convenience methods are provided for logging messages at each logging level, and also for entering and exiting methods and throwing exceptions. Additional methods are provided to localize log messages using a resource bundle.

Method	Description
```void config(String msg) void fine(String msg) void finer(String msg) void finest(String msg) void info(String msg) void severe(String msg) void warning(String msg)```	The `Logger` class contains a number of convenience methods for logging messages. For quickly logging a message of a specified level, one method for each logging level is defined.
```void entering(String sourceClass, String sourceMethod) void entering(String sourceClass, String sourceMethod, Object param1) void entering(String sourceClass, String sourceMethod, Object params[])```	Log a message when a method is first entered. The variant forms take a parameter to the method, or an array of parameters, to provide for more detailed tracking of the method invocation. The message of the log is ENTRY in addition to the other information about the method call. The log level is `Level.FINER`.
```void exiting(String sourceClass, String sourceMethod) void exiting(String sourceClass, String sourceMethod, Object result)```	Log a message when a method is about to return. The log message contains RETURN and the log level is `Level.FINER`. The source class and source method are also logged.
```boolean isLoggable(Level level)```	Checks if a certain level will be logged. Returns true if it will be logged, or false otherwise.
```void log(Level level, String msg) void log(Level level, String msg, Object param1) void log(Level level, String msg, Object[] params) void log(Level level, String msg, Throwable thrown) void log(LogRecord record)```	Standard general logging convenience methods. Variants include the ability to specify a parameter or array of parameters to log, or `Throwable` information. The information is placed into a `LogRecord` object and sent into the logging system. The last variant takes a `LogRecord` object.

Table continued on following page

Method	Description

`void logp(Level level, String sourceClass,`
`String sourceMethod, String msg)`
 	
`void logp(Level level, String sourceClass,`
`String sourceMethod, String msg, Object param1)`
 	
`void logp(Level level, String sourceClass,`
`String sourceMethod, String msg,`
`Object[] params)`
 	
`void logp(Level level, String sourceClass,`
`String sourceMethod, String msg,`
`Throwable thrown)`
	These logging methods take source class and source method names in addition to the other information. All this is put into a `LogRecord` object and sent into the system.

`void logrb(Level level, String sourceClass,`
`String sourceMethod, String bundleName,`
`String msg)`
 	
`void logrb(Level level, String sourceClass,`
`String sourceMethod, String bundleName,`
`String msg, Object param1)`
 	
`void logrb(Level level, String sourceClass,`
`String sourceMethod, String bundleName,`
`String msg, Object[] params)`
 	
`void logrb(Level level, String sourceClass,`
`String sourceMethod, String bundleName,`
`String msg, Throwable thrown)`
	These methods allow you to specify a resource bundle in addition to the other information. The resource bundle will be used to localize the log message.

`void throwing(String sourceClass, String` `sourceMethod, Throwable thrown)`	This logs a throwing message. The log level is `Level.FINER`. The log record's message is set to `THROW` and the contents of `thrown` are put into the log record's `thrown` property instead of inside the log record's message.

The LogRecord Class

The `LogRecord` class encapsulates a log message, carrying the message through the logging system. `Handlers` and `Formatters` use `LogRecords` to have more information about the message (such as the time it was sent and the logging level) for processing. If a client to the logging system has a reference to a `LogRecord` object, the object should no longer be used after it is passed into the logging system.

LogRecord Methods

The LogRecord contains a number of methods to examine and manipulate properties on a log record, such as message origination, the log record's level, when it was sent into the system, and any related resource bundles.

Method	Description
Level getLevel()	Returns the log record's level.
String getMessage()	Returns the unformatted version of the log message, before formatting/localization.
long getMillis()	Returns the time the log record was created in milliseconds.
Object[] getParameters()	Returns an array of parameters of the log record, or null if no parameters are set.
long getSequenceNumber()	Returns the sequence number of the log record. The sequence number is assigned in the log record's constructor to create a unique number for each log record.
Throwable getThrown()	Returns the Throwable associated with this log record, such as the Exception if an exception is being logged. Returns null if no Throwable is set.
String getLoggerName()	Returns the name of the logger, which might be null if it is the anonymous logger.
String getSourceClassName()	Gets the name of the class that might have logged the message. This information may be specified explicitly, or inferred from the stack trace and therefore might be inaccurate.
String getSourceMethodName()	Gets the name of the method that might have logged the message. This information may be specified explicitly, or inferred from the stack trace and therefore might be inaccurate.
int getThreadID	Returns the identifier for the thread that originated the log message. This is an ID inside the Java VM.

Setting Information about Message Origination

The following methods allow you to set origination information on the log message such as an associated exception, class and method that logged the message, and the ID of the originating thread.

Method	Description
void setSourceClassName (String sourceClassName)	Sets the name of the class where the log message is originating.
void setSourceMethodName (String sourceMethodName)	Sets the name of the method where the log message is originating.
void setThreadID (int threadID)	Sets the identifier of the thread where the log message is originating.
void setThrown (Throwable thrown)	Sets a Throwable to associate with the log message. Can be null.

Resource Bundle Methods

The following methods allow you to retrieve and configure a resource bundle for use with the log message. Resource bundles are used for localizing log messages.

Method	Description
ResourceBundle getResourceBundle()	Returns the ResourceBundle associated with the logger that is used to localize log messages. Might be null if there is no associated ResourceBundle.
String getResourceBundleName()	Returns the name of the resource bundle used to localize log messages. Returns null if log messages are not localizable (no resource bundle defined).
void setResourceBundle (ResourceBundle bundle)	Sets a resource bundle to use to localize log messages.
void setResourceBundleName (String name)	Sets the name of a resource bundle to use to localize log messages.

Setting Information about the Message

The following methods configure the log message itself. Some of the information you can configure related to the log message are its level, the contents of the message, and the time the message was sent.

Method	Description
void setLevel(Level level)	Sets the level of the logging message.
void setLoggerName(String name)	Sets the name of the logger issuing this message. Can be null.
void setMessage(String message)	Sets the contents of the message before formatting/localization.

Method	Description
`void setMillis(long millis)`	Sets the time of the log message, in milliseconds since 1970.
`void setParameters(Object[] parameters)`	Sets parameters for the log message.
`void setSequenceNumber(long seq)`	Sets the sequence number of the log message. This method shouldn't usually be called, since the constructor assigns a unique number to each log message.

The Level Class

The `Level` class defines the entire set of logging levels, and also objects of this class represent a specific logging level that is then used by loggers, handlers, and so on. If you desire, you can subclass this class and define your own custom levels, as long as they do not conflict with the existing logging levels.

Logging Levels

The following logging levels are defined in the `Level` class.

Log Level	Description
OFF	Special value that is initialized to `Integer.MAX_VALUE`. This turns logging off.
SEVERE	Meant for serious failures. Initialized to 1,000.
WARNING	Meant to indicate potential problems. Initialized to 900.
INFO	General information. Initialized to 800.
CONFIG	Meant for messages useful for debugging. Initialized to 700.
FINE	Meant for least verbose tracing information. Initialized to 500.
FINER	More detailed tracing information. Initialized to 400.
FINEST	Most detailed level of tracing information. Initialized to 300.
ALL	Special value. Logs ALL messages. Initialized to `Integer.MIN_VALUE`.

Level Methods

The `Level` class defines methods to set and retrieve a specific logging level. Both numeric and textual versions of levels can be used.

Method	Description
`static Level parse(String name)`	Returns a `Level` object representing the name of the level that is passed in. The string `name` can be one of the logging levels, such as `SEVERE` or `CON-FIG`. An arbitrary number, between `Integer.MIN_VALUE` and `Integer.MAX_VALUE` can also be passed in (as a string). If the number represents one of the existing level values, that level is returned. Otherwise, a new `Level` is returned corresponding to the passed in value. Any invalid name or number causes an `IllegalArgumentException` to get thrown. If the name is null, a `NullPointerException` is thrown.
`boolean equals(Object ox)`	Returns true if the object passed in has the same level as the current class.
`String getLocalizedName()`	Returns the localized version of the current level's name, or the nonlocalized version if no localization is available.
`String getName()`	Returns the nonlocalized version of the current level's name.
`String getResourceBundleName()`	Returns the name of the level's localization resource bundle, or null if no localization resource bundle is defined.
`int hashCode()`	Returns a hash code based on the level value.
`int intValue()`	Returns the integer value for the current level.
`String toString()`	Returns the nonlocalized name of the current level.

The Handler Class

The `Handler` class is used to receive log messages and then publish them to an external destination. This might be memory, a file, a database, a TCP/IP stream, or any number of places that can store log messages. Just like loggers, a handler has an associated level. Log messages that are less than the level on the handler are discarded. Each specific instance of a `Handler` has its own properties and is usually configured in the `logging.properties` file. The next section discusses the various handlers that are found in the `java.util.logging` package. Creating a custom handler is straightforward, since implementations of only `close()`, `flush()`, and `publish(LogRecord record)` are needed.

Handler Methods

The `Handler` class defines three abstract methods that need specific behavior in inheriting classes. The other methods available on the `Handler` class are for dealing with message encoding, filters, formatters, and error handlers.

Key Abstract Methods

When developing a custom handler, there are three abstract methods that must be overridden. These are listed in the following table.

Method	Description
`abstract void close()`	This method should perform a `flush()` and then free any resources used by the handler. After `close()` is called, the Handler should no longer be used.
`abstract void flush()`	Flushes any buffered output to ensure it is saved to the associated resource.
`abstract void publish(LogRecord record)`	Takes a log message forwarded by a logger and then writes it to the associated resource. The message should be formatted (using the `Formatter`) and localized.

Set and Retrieve Information about the Handler

The methods listed in the following table allow you to retrieve information about the handler, such as its encoding, associated error manager, filter, formatter, and level, and also set this configuration information.

Method	Description
`String getEncoding()`	Returns the name of the character encoding. If the name is null, then the default encoding should be used.
`ErrorManager getErrorManager()`	Returns the `ErrorManager` associated with this Handler.
`Filter getFilter()`	Returns the `Filter` associated with this `Handler`, which might be null.
`Formatter getFormatter()`	Returns the `Formatter` associated with this `Handler`, which might be null.
`Level getLevel()`	Returns the level of this handler. Log messages lower than this level are discarded.
`boolean isLoggable(LogRecord record)`	Returns true if the `LogRecord` passed in will be logged by this handler. The checks include comparing the record's level to the handler's, testing against the filter (if one is defined), and any other checks defined in the handler.
`void setEncoding(String encoding)`	Sets the encoding to a specified character encoding. If null is passed in, the default platform encoding is used.

Table continued on following page

Method	Description
void setErrorManager (ErrorManager em)	Sets an ErrorManager for the handler. If any errors occur while processing, the Error Manager's error method is invoked.
void setFilter (Filter newFilter)	Sets a custom filter that decides whether to discard or keep a log message when the publish method is invoked.
void setFormatter (Formatter newFormatter)	Sets a Formatter that performs custom formatting on log messages passed to the handler before the log message is written to the destination.
void setLevel(Level newLevel)	This method sets the level threshold for the handler. Log messages below this level are automatically discarded.

Stock Handlers

The java.util.logging package includes a number of predefined handlers to write log messages to common destinations. These classes include the ConsoleHandler, FileHandler, MemoryHandler, SocketHandler, and StreamHandler. These classes provide a specific implementation of the abstract methods in the Handler class. All the property key names in the tables are prefixed with java.util. logging in the actual properties file.

The StreamHandler serves chiefly as a base class for all handlers that write log messages to some OutputStream. The subclasses of StreamHandler are ConsoleHandler, FileHandler, and SocketHandler. A lot of the stream handling code is built into this class. See the following table for a list of properties for the StreamHandler.

Property Name	Description	Default Value
StreamHandler.level	Log level for the handler	Level.INFO
StreamHandler.filter	Filter to use	Undefined
StreamHandler.formatter	Formatter to use	java.util.logging. SimpleFormatter
StreamHandler.encoding	Character set encoding to use	Default platform encoding

The following methods are defined/implemented on the `StreamHandler` class.

Method	Description
`void close()`	The `head` string from the `Formatter` will be written if it hasn't been already, and the `tail` string is written before the stream is closed.
`void flush()`	Writes any buffered output to the stream (flushes the stream).
`boolean isLoggable(LogRecord record)`	Performs standard checks against `level` and `filter`, but also returns false if no output stream is open or the record passed in is null.
`void publish(LogRecord record)`	If the record passed in is loggable, the `Formatter` is then invoked to format the log message and then the message is written to the output stream.
`void setEncoding(String encoding)`	Sets the character encoding to use for log messages. Pass in null to use the current platform's default character encoding.
`protected void setOutputStream (OutputStream out)`	Sets an `OutputStream` to use. If an `OutputStream` is already open, it is flushed and then closed. The new `OutputStream` is then opened.

The `ConsoleHandler` writes log messages to `System.err`. It subclasses `StreamHandler` but overrides `close()` to only perform a flush, so the `System.err` stream does not get closed. The default formatter used is `SimpleFormatter`. See below for specific information about formatters. See the following table for properties that can be defined in the `logging.properties` file for the `ConsoleHandler`.

Property Name	Description	Default Value
`ConsoleHandler.level`	Log level for the handler	`Level.INFO`
`ConsoleHandler.filter`	Filter to use	Undefined
`ConsoleHandler.formatter`	Formatter to use	`java.util.logging.SimpleFormatter`
`ConsoleHandler.encoding`	Character set encoding to use	Default platform encoding

The `SocketHandler` writes log messages to the network over a specified TCP port. The properties listed in the following table are used by the `SocketHandler`. The default constructor uses the properties defined, and a second constructor allows the specification of the host and port `SocketHandler(String host, int port)`. The `close()` method flushes and closes the output stream, and the `publish()` method flushes the stream after each record is written.

Property Name	Description	Default Value
SocketHandler.level	Log level for the handler	Level.INFO
SocketHandler.filter	Filter to use	undefined
SocketHandler.formatter	Formatter to use	java.util.logging. XMLFormatter
SocketHandler.encoding	Character set encoding to use	Default platform encoding
SocketHandler.host	Target host name to connect to	undefined
SocketHandler.port	Target TCP port to use	undefined

The FileHandler is able to write to a single file, or write to a rotating set of files as each file reaches a specified maximum size. The next number in a sequence is added to the end of the name of each rotating file, unless a *generation* (sequence) pattern is specified elsewhere. See below for a discussion of patterns to form filenames. The properties for the FileHandler are listed in the following table.

Property Name	Description	Default Value
FileHandler.level	Log level for the handler	Level.INFO
FileHandler.filter	Filter to use	undefined
FileHandler.formatter	Formatter to use	java.util.logging. XMLFormatter
FileHandler.encoding	Character set encoding to use	Default platform encoding
FileHandler.limit	Specifies approximate maximum number of bytes to write to a file. 0 means no limit.	0
FileHandler.count	Specifies how many output iles to cycle through.	1
FileHandler.pattern	Pattern used to generate output filenames. See below for more information.	%h/java%u.log
FileHandler.append	Boolean value specifying whether to append to an existing file or overwrite it.	false

The FileHandler class supports filename patterns, allowing the substitution of paths such as the user's home directory or the system's temporary directory. The forward slash (/) is used as a directory separator, and this works for both Unix and Windows machines. Also supported is the ability to specify where the generation number goes in the filename when log files are rotated. These patterns are each prefixed with a percent sign (%).To include the percent sign in the filename, specify two percent signs (%%). The following table contains all the valid percent-sign substitutions.

Pattern	Description
%t	Full path of the system temporary directory
%h	Value of the user.home system property
%g	Generation number used to distinguish rotated logs
%u	Unique number used to resolve process conflicts

For example, if you're executing this on Windows 95 and specify the filename pattern %t/app_log.txt, the FileHandler class expands this to C:\TEMP\app_log.txt. Note that the %t and %h commands do not include the trailing forward slash.

The %u is used to account for when multiple threads/processes will access the same log file. Only one process can have the file open for writing, so to prevent the loss of logging information, the %u can be used to output to a log file that has a similar name to the others. For example, the filename pattern %t/logfile%u.txt can be specified, and if two processes open this same log file for output, the first will open C:\TEMP\logfile0.txt and the second will open C:\TEMP\logfile1.txt.

The MemoryHandler is a circular buffer in memory. It is intended for use as a quick way to store messages, so the messages have to be sent to another handler to write them to an external source. Since the buffer is circular, older log records eventually are overwritten by newer records. Formatting can be delayed to another Handler, which makes logging to a MemoryHandler quick. There are conditions that will cause the MemoryHandler to send data (push data) to another Handler. These conditions are as follows:

❑ A log record passed in has a level greater than a specified pushLevel.

❑ Another class calls the push method on the MemoryHandler.

❑ A subclass implements specialized behavior to push data depending on custom criteria.

The properties on the MemoryHandler are listed in the following table.

Property Name	Description	Default Value
MemoryHandler.level	Log level for the handler	Level.INFO
MemoryHandler.filter	Filter to use	undefined
MemoryHandler.size	Size of the circular buffer (in bytes)	1,000
MemoryHandler.push	Defines the push level — the minimum level that will cause messages to be sent to the target handler	Level.SEVERE
MemoryHandler.target	Specifies the name of the target Handler class	Undefined

The constructors create a `MemoryHandler` with a default or specific configuration.

Constructor	Description
`MemoryHandler()`	Creates a `MemoryHandler` based on the configuration properties.
`MemoryHandler(Handler target, int size, Level pushLevel)`	Creates a `MemoryHandler` with a specified target handler, size of the buffer, and push level.

The methods provided by the `MemoryHandler` create and configure the behavior of the memory handler.

Method	Description
`void publish(LogRecord record)`	Stores the record in the internal buffer, if it is loggable (see `isLoggable`). If the level of the log record is greater than or equal to the `pushLevel`, all buffered records, including the current one, are written to the target `Handler`.
`void close()`	Closes the handler and frees the associated resources. Also invokes `close` on the target handler.
`void flush()`	Causes a `flush`, which is different from a `push`. To actually write the log records to a destination other than memory, a `push` must be performed.
`Level getPushLevel()`	Returns the current push level.
`boolean isLoggable(LogRecord record)`	Compares the log level's versus the handler's log level, and then runs the record through the filter if one is defined. Whether the record will cause a push or not is ignored by this method.
`void push()`	Sends all records in the current buffer to the target handler, and clears the buffer.
`void setPushLevel(Level newLevel)`	Sets a new `push` level.

The Formatter Class

The `Formatter` class is used to perform some custom processing on a log record. This formatting might be localization, adding additional program information (such as adding the time and date to log records), or any other processing needed. The `Formatter` returns a string that is the processed log record. The `Formatter` class also has support for `head` and `tail` strings that come before and after all log records. An example that will be implemented later in this section is a custom `Formatter` that writes log records to an HTML table. For this formatter, the head string would be the `<table>` tag, and the tail string is the `</table>` tag. The methods defined in the `Formatter` class are listed in the following table.

Method	Description
`abstract String format(LogRecord record)`	Performs specific formatting of the log record and returns the formatted string.
`String formatMessage(LogRecord record)`	The message string in the `LogRecord` is localized using the record's `Resource-Bundle`, and formatted according to `java.text` style formatting (replacing strings such as `{0}`).
`String getHead(Handler h)`	Returns the header string for a specified handler, which can be null.
`String getTail(Handler h)`	Returns the tail string for a specified handler, which can be null.

Stock Formatters

The logging package comes already equipped with a couple of useful formatters. The `SimpleFormatter` provides a basic implementation of a formatter. The `XMLFormatter` outputs log records in a predefined XML format. These two stock formatters will cover a variety of basic logging scenarios, but if you need behavior not supplied by either of these formatters, you can write your own.

SimpleFormatter

The `SimpleFormatter` does a minimal level of work to format log messages. The format method of the `SimpleFormatter` returns a one- or two-line summary of the log record that is passed in. Logging a simple log message, such as `test 1`, using the `SimpleFormatter` will issue the following output:

```
Apr 18, 2004 12:18:25 PM LoggingTest main
INFO: test 1
```

The `SimpleFormatter` formats the message with the date, time, originating class name, originating method name, and on the second line, the level of the log message and the log message itself.

XMLFormatter

The `XMLFormatter` formats the log records according to an XML DTD. You can use the `XMLFormatter` with any character encoding, but it is suggested that it is only used with `"UTF-8"`. The `getHead()` and `getTail()` methods are used to output the start and end of the XML file, the parts that aren't repeated for each log record but are necessary to create a valid XML file.

Example output from the `XMLFormatter` follows:

```
<?xml version="1.0" encoding="windows-1252" standalone="no"?>
<!DOCTYPE log SYSTEM "logger.dtd">
<log>
<record>
  <date>2004-04-18T12:22:36</date>
  <millis>1082305356235</millis>
  <sequence>0</sequence>
  <logger>LoggingTest</logger>
```

```
    <level>INFO</level>
    <class>LoggingTest</class>
    <method>main</method>
    <thread>10</thread>
    <message>test 1</message>
</record>
<record>
    <date>2004-04-18T12:22:36</date>
    <millis>1082305356265</millis>
    <sequence>1</sequence>
    <logger>LoggingTest</logger>
    <level>INFO</level>
    <class>LoggingTest</class>
    <method>main</method>
    <thread>10</thread>
    <message>test 2</message>
</record>
</log>
```

The XML DTD that the logging system uses is shown here:

```
<!-- DTD used by the java.util.logging.XMLFormatter -->
<!-- This provides an XML formatted log message. -->

<!-- The document type is "log" which consists of a sequence
of record elements -->
<!ELEMENT log (record*)>

<!-- Each logging call is described by a record element. -->
<!ELEMENT record (date, millis, sequence, logger?, level,
class?, method?, thread?, message, key?, catalog?, param*, exception?)>

<!-- Date and time when LogRecord was created in ISO 8601 format -->
<!ELEMENT date (#PCDATA)>

<!-- Time when LogRecord was created in milliseconds since
midnight January 1st, 1970, UTC. -->
<!ELEMENT millis (#PCDATA)>

<!-- Unique sequence number within source VM. -->
<!ELEMENT sequence (#PCDATA)>

<!-- Name of source Logger object. -->
<!ELEMENT logger (#PCDATA)>

<!-- Logging level, may be either one of the constant
names from java.util.logging.Constants (such as "SEVERE"
or "WARNING") or an integer value such as "20". -->
<!ELEMENT level (#PCDATA)>

<!-- Fully qualified name of class that issued
logging call, e.g. "javax.marsupial.Wombat". -->
<!ELEMENT class (#PCDATA)>

<!-- Name of method that issued logging call.
```

```
It may be either an unqualified method name such as
"fred" or it may include argument type information
in parenthesis, for example "fred(int,String)". -->
<!ELEMENT method (#PCDATA)>

<!-- Integer thread ID. -->
<!ELEMENT thread (#PCDATA)>

<!-- The message element contains the text string of a log message. -->
<!ELEMENT message (#PCDATA)>

<!-- If the message string was localized, the key element provides
the original localization message key. -->
<!ELEMENT key (#PCDATA)>

<!-- If the message string was localized, the catalog element provides
the logger's localization resource bundle name. -->
<!ELEMENT catalog (#PCDATA)>

<!-- If the message string was localized, each of the param elements
provides the String value (obtained using Object.toString())
of the corresponding LogRecord parameter. -->
<!ELEMENT param (#PCDATA)>

<!-- An exception consists of an optional message string followed
by a series of StackFrames. Exception elements are used
for Java exceptions and other java Throwables. -->
<!ELEMENT exception (message?, frame+)>

<!-- A frame describes one line in a Throwable backtrace. -->
<!ELEMENT frame (class, method, line?)>

<!-- an integer line number within a class's source file. -->
<!ELEMENT line (#PCDATA)>
```

Creating Your Own Formatter

It isn't too difficult to develop a custom `Formatter`. As an example, here's an implementation of the `HTMLTableFormatter` that was mentioned earlier. The HTML code that is output looks like this:

```
<table border>
    <tr><th>Time</th><th>Log Message</th></tr>
    <tr><td>...</td><td>...</td></tr>
    <tr><td>...</td><td>...</td></tr>
</table>
```

Each log record starts with `<tr>` and ends with `</tr>` since there is only one log record per table row. The `<table>` tag and the first row of the table make up the `head` string. The `</table>` tag makes up the tail of the collection of log records. The custom formatter only needs an implementation of the `getHead()`, `getTail()`, and `format(LogRecord record)` methods:

```
import java.util.logging.*;

class HTMLTableFormatter extends java.util.logging.Formatter {
    public String format(LogRecord record)
    {
        return("  <tr><td>" +
                record.getMillis() +
                "</td><td>" +
                record.getMessage() +
                "</td></tr>\n");
    }

    public String getHead(Handler h)
    {
        return("<table border>\n  " +
                "<tr><th>Time</th><th>Log Message</th></tr>\n");
    }

    public String getTail(Handler h)
    {
        return("</table>\n");
    }
}
```

The Filter Interface

A filter is used to provide additional criteria to decide whether to discard or keep a log record. Each logger and each handler can have a filter defined. The `Filter` interface defines a single method:

```
boolean isLoggable(LogRecord record)
```

The `isLoggable` method returns true if the log message should be published, and false if it should be discarded.

Creating Your Own Filter

An example of a custom filter is a filter that discards any log message that does not start with `"client"`. This is useful if log messages are coming from a number of sources, and each log message from a particular client (or clients) is prefixed with the string `"client"`:

```
import java.util.logging.*;

public class ClientFilter implements java.util.logging.Filter {
    public boolean isLoggable(LogRecord record)
    {
        if(record.getMessage().startsWith("client"))
            return(true);
        else
            return(false);
    }
}
```

The ErrorManager

The `ErrorManager` is associated with a handler and is used to handle any errors that occur, such as exceptions that are thrown. The client of the logger most likely does not care or cannot handle errors, so using an `ErrorManager` is a flexible and straightforward way for a `Handler` to report error conditions. The error manager defines a single method:

```
void error(String msg, Exception ex, int code)
```

This method takes the error message (a string), the `Exception` thrown, and a code representing what error occurred. The codes are defined as static integers in the `ErrorManager` class and are listed in the following table.

Error Code	Description
CLOSE_FAILURE	Used when `close()` fails.
FLUSH_FAILURE	Used when `flush()` fails.
FORMAT_FAILURE	Used when formatting fails for any reason.
GENERIC_FAILURE	Used for any other error that other error codes don't match.
OPEN_FAILURE	Used when open of an output source fails.
WRITE_FAILURE	Used when writing to the output source fails.

Logging Examples

By default, log messages are passed up the hierarchy to each parent. Following is a small program that uses a named logger to log a message using the `XMLFormatter`:

```java
import java.util.logging.*;

public class LoggingExample1 {
    public static void main(String args[])
    {
        try{
            LogManager lm = LogManager.getLogManager();
            Logger logger;
            FileHandler fh = new FileHandler("log_test.txt");

            logger = Logger.getLogger("LoggingExample1");

            lm.addLogger(logger);
            logger.setLevel(Level.INFO);
            fh.setFormatter(new XMLFormatter());

            logger.addHandler(fh);
            // root logger defaults to SimpleFormatter.
            // We don't want messages logged twice.
            //logger.setUseParentHandlers(false);
            logger.log(Level.INFO, "test 1");
            logger.log(Level.INFO, "test 2");
            logger.log(Level.INFO, "test 3");
```

```
                fh.close();
            } catch(Exception e) {
                System.out.println("Exception thrown: " + e);
                e.printStackTrace();
            }
        }
    }
```

What happens here is the XML output is sent to `log_test.txt`. This file is listed below:

```xml
<?xml version="1.0" encoding="windows-1252" standalone="no"?>
<!DOCTYPE log SYSTEM "logger.dtd">
<log>
<record>
  <date>2004-04-20T2:09:55</date>
  <millis>1082472395876</millis>
  <sequence>0</sequence>
  <logger>LoggingExample1</logger>
  <level>INFO</level>
  <class>LoggingExample1</class>
  <method>main</method>
  <thread>10</thread>
  <message>test 1</message>
</record>
<record>
  <date>2004-04-20T2:09:56</date>
  <millis>1082472396096</millis>
  <sequence>1</sequence>
  <logger>LoggingExample1</logger>
  <level>INFO</level>
  <class>LoggingExample1</class>
  <method>main</method>
  <thread>10</thread>
  <message>test 2</message>
</record>
</log>
```

Because the log messages are then sent to the parent logger, the messages are also output to `System.err` using the `SimpleFormatter`. The following is output:

```
Feb 11, 2004 2:09:55 PM LoggingExample1 main
INFO: test 1
Feb 11, 2004 2:09:56 PM LoggingExample1 main
INFO: test 2
```

Here's a more detailed example that uses the already developed `HTMLTableFormatter`. Two loggers are defined in a parent-child relationship, `ParentLogger` and `ChildLogger`. The parent logger will use the `XMLFormatter` to output to a text file, and the child logger will output using the `HTMLTableFormatter` to a different file. By default, the root logger will execute and the log messages will go to the console using the `SimpleFormatter`. The `HTMLTableFormatter` is extended to an `HTMLFormatter` to generate a full HTML file (instead of just the table tags):

```
import java.util.logging.*;
import java.util.*;

class HTMLFormatter extends java.util.logging.Formatter {
    public String format(LogRecord record)
    {
        return("      <tr><td>" +
                (new Date(record.getMillis())).toString() +
                "</td>" +
                "<td>" +
                record.getMessage() +
                "</td></tr>\n");
    }

    public String getHead(Handler h)
    {
        return("<html>\n  <body>\n" +
                "    <table border>\n      " +
                "<tr><th>Time</th><th>Log Message</th></tr>\n");
    }

    public String getTail(Handler h)
    {
        return("    </table>\n  </body>\n</html>");
    }
}

public class LoggingExample2 {
    public static void main(String args[])
    {
        try {
            LogManager lm = LogManager.getLogManager();
            Logger parentLogger, childLogger;
            FileHandler xml_handler = new FileHandler("log_output.xml");
            FileHandler html_handler = new FileHandler("log_output.html");
            parentLogger = Logger.getLogger("ParentLogger");
            childLogger = Logger.getLogger("ParentLogger.ChildLogger");

            lm.addLogger(parentLogger);
            lm.addLogger(childLogger);

            // log all messages, WARNING and above
            parentLogger.setLevel(Level.WARNING);
            // log ALL messages
            childLogger.setLevel(Level.ALL);
            xml_handler.setFormatter(new XMLFormatter());
            html_handler.setFormatter(new HTMLFormatter());

            parentLogger.addHandler(xml_handler);
            childLogger.addHandler(html_handler);

            childLogger.log(Level.FINE, "This is a fine log message");
            childLogger.log(Level.SEVERE, "This is a severe log message");
            xml_handler.close();
            html_handler.close();
```

```
        } catch(Exception e) {
            System.out.println("Exception thrown: " + e);
            e.printStackTrace();
        }
    }
}
```

Here's what gets output to the screen:

```
Apr 20, 2004 12:43:09 PM LoggingExample2 main
SEVERE: This is a severe log message
```

Here's what gets output to the `log_output.xml` file:

```xml
<?xml version="1.0" encoding="windows-1252" standalone="no"?>
<!DOCTYPE log SYSTEM "logger.dtd">
<log>
<record>
  <date>2004-04-20T12:43:09</date>
  <millis>1082479389122</millis>
  <sequence>0</sequence>
  <logger>ParentLogger.ChildLogger</logger>
  <level>FINE</level>
  <class>LoggingExample2</class>
  <method>main</method>
  <thread>10</thread>
  <message>This is a fine log message</message>
</record>
<record>
  <date>2004-04-20T12:43:09</date>
  <millis>1082479389242</millis>
  <sequence>1</sequence>
  <logger>ParentLogger.ChildLogger</logger>
  <level>SEVERE</level>
  <class>LoggingExample2</class>
  <method>main</method>
  <thread>10</thread>
  <message>This is a severe log message</message>
</record>
</log>
```

The contents of the `log_output.html` file are as follows:

```html
<html>
  <body>
    <table border>
      <tr><th>Time</th><th>Log Message</th></tr>
      <tr><td>Tue Apr 20 12:43:09 EDT 2004</td><td>This is a fine log
message</td></tr>
      <tr><td>Tue Apr 20 12:43:09 EDT 2004</td><td>This is a severe log
message</td></tr>
    </table>
  </body>
</html>
```

Note that the root logger, by default, logs messages at level INFO and above. However, because the ParentLogger is only interested in levels at WARNING and above, log messages with lower levels are immediately discarded. The HTML file contains all log messages since the ChildLogger is set to process all log messages. The XML file only contains the one SEVERE log message, since log messages below the WARNING level are discarded.

Regular Expressions

Regular expressions are a powerful facility available to solve problems relating to the searching, isolating, and/or replacing of chunks of text inside strings. The subject of regular expressions (sometimes abbreviated regexp or regexps) is large enough that it deserves its own book — and indeed, books have been devoted to regular expressions. This section will provide an overview of regular expressions and discuss the support Sun has built in to the java.util.regex package.

Regular expressions alleviate a lot of the tedium of working with a simple parser, providing complex pattern matching capabilities. Regular expressions can be used to process text of any sort. For more sophisticated examples of regular expressions, consult another book that is dedicated to regular expressions.

If you've never seen regular expressions before in a language, you've most likely seen a small subset of regular expressions with file masks on Unix/DOS/Windows. For example, you might see the following files in a directory:

```
Test.java
Test.class
StringProcessor.java
StringProcessor.class
Token.java
Token.class
```

You can type dir *.* at the command line (on DOS/Windows) and every file will be matched and listed. The asterisks are replaced with any string, and the period is taken literally. If the file mask T*.class is used, only two files will be matched — Test.class and Token.class. The asterisks are considered meta-characters, and the period and letters are considered normal characters. The meta-characters are part of the regular expression "language," and Java has a rich set of these that go well beyond the simple support in file masks. The normal characters match literally against the string being tested. There is also a facility to interpret meta-characters literally in the regular expression language.

Several examples of using regular expressions are examined throughout this section. As an initial example, assume you want to generate a list of all classes inside Java files that have no modifier before the keyword class. Assuming you only need to examine a single line of source code, all you have to do is ignore any white space before the string class, and you can generate the list.

A traditional approach would need to find the first occurrence of class in a string and then ensure there's nothing but white space before it. Using regular expressions, this task becomes much easier. The entire Java regular expression language is examined shortly, but the regular expression needed for this case is \s*class. The backslash is used to specify a meta-character, and in this case, \s matches any white space. The asterisk is another meta-character, standing for "0 or more occurrences of the previous term." The word class is then taken literally, so the pattern stands for matching white space (if any exists) and then matching class. The Java code to use this pattern is shown next:

```
Pattern pattern = Pattern.compile("\\s*class");
// Need two backslashes to preserve the backslash

Matcher matcher = pattern.matcher("\t\t    class");
if(matcher.matches()) {
    System.out.println("The pattern matches the string");
} else {
    System.out.println("The pattern does not match the string");
}
```

This example takes a regular expression (stored in a `Pattern` object) and uses a matcher to see if the regular expression matches a specific string. This is the simplest use of the regular expression routines in Java. Consult Figure 1-2 for an overview of how the regular expression classes work with each other.

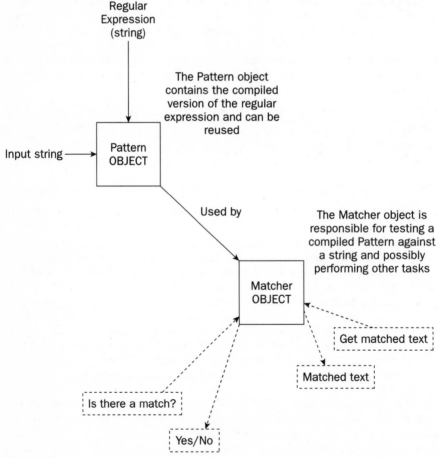

Figure 1-2

The designers of the regular expression library decided to use a *Pattern-Matcher* model, which separates the regular expression from the matcher itself. The regular expression is compiled into a more optimized form by the `Pattern` class. This compiled pattern can then be used with multiple matchers, or reused by the same matcher matching on different strings.

In a regular expression, any single character matches literally, except for just a few exceptions. One such exception is the period (.), which matches any single character in the string that is being analyzed. There are sets of meta-characters predefined to match specific characters. These are listed in the following table.

Meta-Character	Matches
\\	A single backslash
\0n	An octal value describing a character, where n is a number such that $0 <= n <= 7$
\0nn	
\0mnn	An octal value describing a character, where m is $0 <= m <= 3$ and n is $0 <= n <= 7$
\0xhh	The character with hexadecimal value hh (where $0 <= h <= F$)
\uhhhh	The character with hexadecimal value hhhh (where $0 <= h <= F$)
\t	A tab (character '\u0009')
\n	A newline (linefeed) ('\u000A')
\r	A carriage-return ('\u000D')
\f	A form-feed ('\u000C')
\a	A bell/beep character ('\u0007')
\e	An escape character ('\u001B')
\cx	The control character corresponding to x, such as \cc is control-c
.	Any single character

The regular expression language also has meta-characters to match against certain string boundaries. Some of these boundaries are the beginning and end of a line, and the beginning and end of words. The full list of boundary meta-characters can be seen in the following table.

Meta-Character	Matches
^	Beginning of the line
$	End of the line
\b	A word boundary
\B	A nonword boundary
\A	The beginning of the input

Table continued on following page

Meta-Character	Matches
\G	The end of the previous match
\Z	The end of the input before any line terminators (such as carriage-return or linefeed)
\z	The end of the input

Regular expression languages also have characters classes, which are a way of specifying a list of possible characters that can match any single character in the string you want to match. If you want to specify a character class explicitly, the characters go between square brackets. Therefore, the character class [0123456789] matches any single digit. It is also possible to specify "any character except one of these" by using the caret after the first square bracket. Using the expression [^012], any single digit *except* for 0, 1, and 2 is matched. You can specify character ranges using the dash. The character class [a-z] matches any single lowercase letter, and [^a-z] matches any character except a lowercase letter. Any character range can be used, such as [0-9] to match a single digit, or [0-3] to match a 0, 1, 2, or 3. Multiple ranges can be specified, such as [a-zA-Z] to match any single letter. The regular expression package contains a set of predefined character classes, and these are listed in the following tables.

Character Class Meta-Character	Matches
.	Any single character
\d	A digit [0-9]
\D	A nondigit [^0-9]
\s	A whitespace character [\t\n\x0B\f\r]
\S	A nonwhitespace character [^\s]
\w	A word character [a-zA-Z_0-9]
\W	A nonword character [^\w]

Additionally, there are POSIX character classes and Java character classes. These are listed in the following tables, respectively.

Character Class Meta-Character	Matches
\p{Lower}	Lowercase letter [a-z]
\p{Upper}	Uppercase letter [A-Z]
\p{ASCII}	All ASCII [\x00-\x7F]
\p{Alpha}	Any lowercase or uppercase letter

Character Class Meta-Character	Matches
`\p{Digit}`	A digit `[0-9]`
`\p{Alnum}`	Any letter or digit
`\p{Punct}`	Punctuation `[!"#$%&'()*+,-./:;<=>?@[\]^_`{|}~]`
`\p{Graph}`	A visible character: any letter, digit, or punctuation
`\p{Print}`	A printable character; same as `\p{Graph}`
`\p{Blank}`	A space or tab `[ \t]`
`\p{Cntrl}`	A control character `[\x00-\x1F\x7F]`
`\p{XDigit}`	Hexadecimal digit `[0-9a-fA-F]`
`\p{Space}`	A whitespace character `[ \t\n\x0B\f\r]`

Character Class	Matches
`\p{javaLowerCase}`	Everything that `Character.isLowerCase()` matches
`\p{javaUpperCase}`	Everything that `Character.isUpperCase()` matches
`\p{javaWhitespace}`	Everything that `Character.isWhitespace()` matches
`\p{javaMirrored}`	Everything that `Character.isMirrored()` matches

Another feature of the regular expression language is the ability to match a particular character a specified number of times. In the previous example, the asterisk was used to match zero or more characters of whitespace. There are two general ways the repetition operators work. One class of operators is greedy, that is, they match as much as they can, until the end. The other class is reluctant (or lazy), and matches only to the first chance they can terminate. For example, the regular expression `.*;` matches any number of characters up to the *last* semicolon it finds. To only match up to the first semicolon, the reluctant version `.*?;` must be used. All greedy operators and the reluctant versions are listed in the following two tables, respectively.

Greedy Operator	Description
`X?`	Matches X zero or one time
`X*`	Matches X zero or more times
`X+`	Matches X one or more times
`X{n}`	Matches X exactly n times, where n is any number
`X{n,}`	Matches X at least n times
`X{n,m}`	Matches X at least n, but no more than m times

Reluctant (Lazy) Operator	Description
`X??`	Matches X zero or one time
`X*?`	Matches X zero or more times
`X+?`	Matches X one or more times
`X{n}?`	Matches X exactly n times, where n is any number
`X{n,}?`	Matches X at least n times
`X{n,m}?`	Matches X at least n, but no more than m times

The language also supports capturing groups of matching characters by using parentheses inside the regular expression. A back reference can be used to reference one of these matching subgroups. A back-reference is denoted by a backslash followed by a number corresponding to the number of a subgroup. In the string `(A(B))`, the zero group is the entire expression, then subgroups start numbering after each left parenthesis. Therefore, `A(B)` is the first subgroup, and `B` is the second subgroup. The backreferences then allow a string to be matched. For example, if you want to match the same word appearing twice in a row, you might use `[([a-zA-Z])\b\1]`. Remember that the `\b` stands for a word boundary. Because the character class for letters is inside parentheses, the text that matched can then be referenced using the backreference meta-character `\1`.

The Pattern Class

The `Pattern` class is responsible for compiling and storing a specified regular expression. There are flags that control how the regular expression is treated. The `regex` is compiled to provide for efficiency. The textual representation of a regular expression is meant for ease of use/understanding by programmers.

Method	Description

`static Pattern compile(String regex)`
 	
 `static Pattern compile(String regex, int flags)`
	The compile method accepts a regular expression in a string and compiles it for internal use. The variant form allows you to specify flags that modify how the regular expression is treated.

`static boolean matches(String regex, CharSequence input)`	Compiles a specified regular expression and matches it against the `input`. Returns true if the regular expression describes the input data, and false otherwise. Use this only for quick matches. To match a regular expression repeatedly against different input, the regular expression should only be compiled once.
`static String quote(String s)`	Returns a literal regular expression that will match the string passed in. The returned string starts with `\Q` followed by the string passed in, and ends with `\E`. These are used to quote a string, so what would be meta-characters in the regular expression language are treated literally.

Method	Description
`int flags()`	Returns an integer containing the flags set when the regular expression was compiled.
`Matcher matcher (CharSequence input)`	Returns a `Matcher` to use for matching the pattern against the specified input.
`String pattern()`	Returns the regular expression that was used to create the pattern.

`String[] split(CharSequence input)`
 	
`String[] split(CharSequence input, int limit)`
	Returns an array of strings after splitting the input into chunks using the regular expression as a separator. The `limit` can be used to limit how many times the regular expression is matched. The matching text does not get placed into the array. If `limit` is positive, the pattern will be applied at least "limit minus 1" times. If `limit` is 0, the pattern will be applied as many times as it can, and trailing empty strings are removed. If `limit` is negative, the pattern will be applied as many times as it can, and trailing empty strings will be left in the array.

The Matcher Class

The `Matcher` class is used to use a pattern to compare to an input string, and perform a wide variety of useful tasks. The `Matcher` class provides the ability to get a variety of information such as where in the string a pattern matched, replace a matching subset of the string with another string, and other useful operations.

Method	Description
`static String quoteReplacement(String s)`	Returns a string that is quoted with \Q and \E and can be used to match literally with other input.
`Matcher appendReplacement (StringBuffer sb, String replacement)`	First appends all characters up to a match to the string buffer, then replaces the matching text with `replacement`, then sets the index to one position after the text matched to prepare for the next call to this method. Use `appendTail` to append the rest of the input after the last match.
`StringBuffer appendTail (StringBuffer sb)`	Appends the rest of the input sequence to the string buffer that is passed in.
`MatchResult asResult()`	Returns a reference to a `MatchResult` describing the matcher's state.
`int end()`	Returns the index that is one past the ending position of the last match.

Table continued on following page

Method	Description
`int end(int group)`	Returns the index that is one past the ending position of a specified capturing group.
`boolean find()`	Returns true if a match is found starting at one index immediately after the previous match, or at the beginning of the line if the matcher has been reset.
`boolean find(int start)`	Resets the matcher and attempts to match the pattern against the input text starting at position `start`. Returns true if a match is found.
`boolean hitEnd()`	Returns true if the end of input was reached by the last match.
`boolean requireEnd()`	Returns true if more input could turn a positive match into a negative match.
`boolean lookingAt()`	Returns true if the pattern matches, but does not require that the pattern has to match the input text completely.
`boolean matches()`	Returns true if the pattern matches the string. The pattern must describe the entire string for this method to return true. For partial matching, use `find()` or `lookingAt()`.
`Pattern pattern()`	Returns a reference to the pattern currently being used on the matcher.
`Matcher reset()`	Resets the matcher's state completely.
`Matcher reset(CharSequence input)`	Resets the matcher's state completely and sets new input to `input`.
`int start()`	Returns the starting position of the previous match.
`int start(int group)`	Returns the starting position of a specified capturing group.
`Matcher usePattern(Pattern newPattern)`	Sets a new pattern to use for matching. The current position in the input is not changed.
`String group()`	Returns a string containing the contents of the previous match.
`String group(int group)`	Returns a string containing the contents of a specific matched group. The 0-th group is always the entire expression.
`int groupCount()`	Returns the number of capturing groups in the matcher's pattern.

Method	Description
`Matcher region(int start, int end)`	Returns a `Matcher` that is confined to a substring of the string to search. The caret and dollar sign meta-characters will match at the beginning and end of the defined region.
`int regionEnd()`	Returns the end index (one past the last position actually checked) of the currently defined region.
`int regionStart()`	Returns the start index of the currently defined region.
`String replaceAll(String replacement)`	Replaces all occurrences of the string that match the pattern with the string `replacement`. The `Matcher` should be reset if it will still be used after this method is called.
`String replaceFirst(String replacement)`	Replaces only the first string that matches the pattern with the string `replacement`. The `Matcher` should be reset if it will still be used after this method is called.

The MatchResult Interface

The `MatchResult` interface contains the group methods, and `start` and `end` methods, to provide a complete set of methods allowing for describing the current state of the `Matcher`. The `Matcher` class implements this interface and defines all these methods. The `toMatchResult` method returns a handle to a `MatchResult`, which provides for saving and handling the current state of the `Matcher` class.

Regular Expression Example

Let's use the `Pattern`/`Matcher` classes to process a Java source code file. All classes that aren't public will be listed (all classes that have no modifiers, actually), and also all doubled words (such as two identifiers in a row) are listed utilizing backreferences.

The input source code file (which does not compile) is shown as follows:

```
import java.util.*;

class EmptyClass {
}

class MyArrayList extends extends ArrayList {
}

public class RETestSource {
    public static void main(String args[]) {
        System.out.println("Sample RE test test source code code");
    }
}
```

The program utilizing regular expressions to process this source code follows:

```java
import java.util.*;
import java.util.regex.*;
import java.io.*;

public class RegExpExample {

    public static void main(String args[])
    {
        String fileName = "RETestSource.java";

        String unadornedClassRE = "^\\s*class (\\w+)";
        String doubleIdentifierRE = "\\b(\\w+)\\s+\\1\\b";

        Pattern classPattern = Pattern.compile(unadornedClassRE);
        Pattern doublePattern = Pattern.compile(doubleIdentifierRE);
        Matcher classMatcher, doubleMatcher;

        int lineNumber=0;

        try {
            BufferedReader br = new BufferedReader(new FileReader(fileName));
            String line;

            while( (line=br.readLine()) != null) {
                lineNumber++;

                classMatcher = classPattern.matcher(line);
                doubleMatcher = doublePattern.matcher(line);

                if(classMatcher.find()) {
                    System.out.println("The class [" +
                                        classMatcher.group(1) +
                                "] is not public");
                }

                while(doubleMatcher.find()) {
                    System.out.println("The word \"" + doubleMatcher.group(1) +
                                "\" occurs twice at position " +
                                doubleMatcher.start() + " on line " +
                                lineNumber);
                }
            }
        } catch(IOException ioe) {
            System.out.println("IOException: " + ioe);
            ioe.printStackTrace();
        }
    }
}
```

The first regular expression, ^\\s*class (\\w+), searches for unadorned class keywords starting at the beginning of the line, followed by zero or more whitespace characters, then the literal class. The group operator is used with one or more word characters (A–Z, a–z, 0–9, and the underscore), so the class name gets matched.

The second regular expression, \\b(\\w+)\\s+\\1\\b, uses the word boundary meta-character (\b) to ensure that words are isolated. Without this, the string public class would match on the letter c. A back reference is used to match a string already matched, in this case, one or more word characters. One or more characters of whitespace must appear between the words. Executing the above program on the test Java source file listed above gives you the following output:

```
The class [EmptyClass] is not public
The class [MyArrayList] is not public
The word "extends" occurs twice at position 18 on line 6
The word "test" occurs twice at position 32 on line 11
The word "code" occurs twice at position 49 on line 11
```

Java Preferences

Programs commonly must store configuration information in some manner that is easy to change and external to the program itself. Java offers utility classes for storing and retrieving system-defined and user-defined configuration information. There are separate hierarchies for the user and system information. All users share the preference information defined in the system tree; each user has his or her own tree for configuration data isolated from other users. This allows for custom configuration, including overriding system values.

The core of the preferences class library is the abstract class java.util.prefs.Preferences. This class defines a set of methods that provides for all the features of the preferences library.

Each node in a preference hierarchy has a name, which does not have to be unique. The root node of a preference tree has the empty string ("") as its name. The forward slash is used as a separator for the names of preference nodes, much like it is used as a separator for directory names on Unix. The only two strings that are not valid node names are the empty string (since it is reserved for the root node) and a forward slash by itself (since it is a node separator). The root node's path is the forward slash by itself. Much like with directories, absolute and relative paths are possible. An absolute path always starts with a forward slash, since the absolute path always starts at the root node and follows the tree down to a specific node. A relative path never starts with a forward slash. A path is valid as long as there aren't two consecutive forward slashes in the pathname, and no path except the path to root ends in the forward slash.

Since preferences are implemented by a third-party implementer, changes to the preferences aren't always immediately written to the backing store.

The maximum length of a single node's name and any of its keys is 80 characters. The maximum length of a string value in a node is 8,192 characters.

The Preference Class

The Preference class is the main class used for dealing with preferences. It represents a node in the preference's tree and contains a large number of methods to manipulate this tree and also nodes in the tree. It is basically a one-stop shop for using preferences. The Preference class has the following methods.

Operations on the Preferences Tree

The Preferences class defines a number of methods that allow for the creation/deletion of nodes, and the retrieval of certain nodes in the tree.

Method	Description
`Preferences node(String pathName)`	Returns a specified node. If the node does not exist, it is created (and any ancestors that do not exist are created) and returned.
`boolean nodeExists(String pathName)`	Returns true if the path to a node exists in the current tree. The path can be an absolute or relative path.
`void removeNode()`	Removes this preference node and all of its children. The only methods that can be invoked after a node has been removed are `name()`, `absolutePath()`, `isUserNode()`, `flush()`, and `nodeExists("")`, and those inherited from `Object`. All other methods will throw an `IllegalStateException`. The removal may not be permanent until `flush()` is called to persist the changes to the tree.
`static Preferences systemNodeForPackage(Class c)`	This method returns a preference node for the package that the specified class is in. All periods in the package name are replaced with forward slashes. For a class that has no package, the name of the node that is returned is literally <unnamed>. This node should not be used long term, as it is shared by all programs that use it. If the node does not already exist, the node and all ancestors that do not exist will automatically be created.
`static Preferences systemRoot()`	This method returns the root node for the system preference tree.
`static Preferences userNodeForPackage(Class c)`	This method returns a preference node for the package that the specified class is in. All periods in the package name are replaced with forward slashes. For a class that has no package, the name of the node that is returned is literally <unnamed>. This node should not be used long term, as it is shared by all programs that use it, so configuration settings are not isolated.

Method	Description
	If the node does not already exist, the node and all ancestors that do not exist will automatically get created.
static Preferences userRoot()	This method returns the root node for the user preference tree.

Retrieving Information about the Node

Each node has information associated with it, such as its path, parent and children nodes, and the node's name. The methods to manipulate this information are shown here.

Method	Description
String absolutePath()	This method returns the absolute path to the current node. The absolute path starts at the root node, /, and continues to the current node.
String[] childrenNames()	Returns an array of the names of all child nodes of the current node.
boolean isUserNode()	Returns true if this node is part of the user configuration tree, or false if this node is part of the system configuration tree.
String name()	Returns the name of the current node.
Preferences parent()	Returns a Preferences reference to the parent of the current node, or null if trying to get the parent of the root node.

Retrieving Preference Values from the Node

The following methods act much like those from the Hashtable class. The key difference is that there are versions of the get for most primitive types. Each type is associated with a specific key, a string standing for the name of the configuration parameter.

Method	Description
String[] keys()	Returns an array of strings that contains the names of all keys in the current preferences node.
String get(String key, String def)	Returns the string associated with a specified key. If the key does not exist, it is created with the default value def and this default value is then returned.

Table continued on following page

Method	Description
boolean getBoolean(String key, boolean def)	Returns the boolean associated with a specified key. If the key does not exist, it is created with the default value def and this default value is then returned.
byte[] getByteArray(String key, byte[] def)	Returns the byte array associated with a specified key. If the key does not exist, it is created with the default value def and this default value is then returned.
double getDouble(String key, double def)	Returns the double associated with a specified key. If the key does not exist, it is created with the default value def and this default value is then returned.
float getFloat(String key, float def)	Returns the float associated with a specified key. If the key does not exist, it is created with the default value def and this default value is then returned.
int getInt(String key, int def)	Returns the integer associated with a specified key. If the key does not exist, it is created with the default value def and this default value is then returned.
long getLong(String key, long def)	Returns the long associated with a specified key. If the key does not exist, it is created with the default value def and this default value is then returned.

Setting Preference Values on the Node

Along with each get method is a put version intended for setting the information associated with a given configuration parameter's key name.

Method	Description
void put(String key, String value)	These methods set a configuration parameter (the name of which is passed in as key) to a specific type. If key or value is null, an exception is thrown. The key can be at most 80 characters long (defined in MAX_KEY_LENGTH) and the value can be at most 8,192 characters (defined in MAX_VALUE_LENGTH).
void putBoolean(String key, boolean value)	
void putByteArray(String key, byte[] value)	
void putDouble(String key, double value)	
void putFloat(String key, float value)	
void putInt(String key, int value)	
void putLong(String key, long value)	

Events

Two events are defined for the `Preference` class—one fires when a node is changed in the preference tree, and the second fires when a preference is changed. The methods for these events are listed in the next table.

Method	Description
`void addNodeChangeListener (NodeChangeListener ncl)`	Adds a listener for notification of when a child node is added or removed from the current preference node.
`void addPreferenceChangeListener` `(PreferenceChangeListener pcl)`	Adds a listener for preference change events—anytime a preference is added to, removed from, or the value is changed, listeners will be notified.
`void removeNodeChangeListener (NodeChangeListener ncl)`	Removes a specified node change listener.
`void removePreferenceChangeListener (PreferenceChangeListener pcl)`	Removes a specified preference change listener.

Other Operations

The following table lists the other methods in the `Preference` class, such as writing any pending changes to the backing store, resetting the preference hierarchy to empty, saving the hierarchy to disk, and other operations.

Method	Description
`void clear()`	Removes all preferences on this node.
`void exportNode(OutputStream os)`	Writes the entire contents of the node (and only the current node) to the output stream as an XML file (following the `preferences.dtd` listed below).
`void exportSubtree(OutputStream os)`	Writes the entire contents of this node and all nodes located below this node in the preferences tree to the output stream as an XML file (following the `preferences.dtd` listed below).
`void flush()`	Writes any changes to the preference node to the backing store, including data on all children nodes.
`void remove(String key)`	Removes the value associated with the specified key.

Table continued on following page

Method	Description
`void sync()`	Ensures that the current version of the preference node in memory matches that of the stored version. If data in the preference node needs to be written to the backing store, it will be.
`String toString()`	Returns a string containing User or System, depending on which hierarchy the node is in, and the absolute path to the current node.

Exporting to XML

The Preferences system defines a standard operation to export the entire tree of keys/values to an XML file. This XML file's DTD is available at http://java.sun.com/dtd/preferences.dtd. This DTD is also included here:

```
<?xml version="1.0" encoding="UTF-8"?>

    <!-- DTD for a Preferences tree. -->

    <!-- The preferences element is at the root of an XML document
        representing a Preferences tree. -->
    <!ELEMENT preferences (root)>

    <!-- The preferences element contains an optional version
        attribute, which specifies version of DTD. -->
    <!ATTLIST preferences EXTERNAL_XML_VERSION CDATA "0.0" >

    <!-- The root element has a map representing the root's preferences
        (if any), and one node for each child of the root (if any). -->
    <!ELEMENT root (map, node*) >

    <!-- Additionally, the root contains a type attribute, which
        specifies whether it's the system or user root. -->
    <!ATTLIST root
            type (system|user) #REQUIRED >

    <!-- Each node has a map representing its preferences (if any),
        and one node for each child (if any). -->
    <!ELEMENT node (map, node*) >

    <!-- Additionally, each node has a name attribute -->
    <!ATTLIST node
            name CDATA #REQUIRED >

    <!-- A map represents the preferences stored at a node (if any). -->
    <!ELEMENT map (entry*) >

    <!-- An entry represents a single preference, which is simply
        a key-value pair. -->
    <!ELEMENT entry EMPTY >
```

```
<!ATTLIST entry
         key   CDATA #REQUIRED
         value CDATA #REQUIRED >
```

Using Preferences

The following example sets a few properties in a node in the user tree, prints out information about the node, and then exports the information to an XML file:

```java
import java.util.*;
import java.util.prefs.*;
import java.io.*;

public class PreferenceExample {
    public void printInformation(Preferences p)
        throws BackingStoreException
    {
        System.out.println("Node's absolute path: " + p.absolutePath());

        System.out.print("Node's children: ");
        for(String s : p.childrenNames()) {
            System.out.print(s + " ");
        }
        System.out.println("");

        System.out.print("Node's keys: ");
        for(String s : p.keys()) {
            System.out.print(s + " ");
        }
        System.out.println("");

        System.out.println("Node's name: " + p.name());
        System.out.println("Node's parent: " + p.parent());
        System.out.println("NODE: " + p);
        System.out.println("userNodeForPackage: " +
                Preferences.userNodeForPackage(PreferenceExample.class));
        System.out.println("All information in node");
        for(String s : p.keys()) {
            System.out.println("  " + s + " = " + p.get(s, ""));
        }
    }

    public void setSomeProperties(Preferences p)
        throws BackingStoreException
    {
        p.put("fruit", "apple");
        p.put("cost", "1.01");
        p.put("store", "safeway");
    }

    public void exportToFile(Preferences p, String fileName)
        throws BackingStoreException
    {
        try {
```

```
            FileOutputStream fos = new FileOutputStream(fileName);

            p.exportSubtree(fos);
            fos.close();
        } catch(IOException ioe) {
            System.out.println("IOException in exportToFile\n" + ioe);
            ioe.printStackTrace();
        }
    }

    public static void main(String args[])
    {
        PreferenceExample pe = new PreferenceExample();
        Preferences prefsRoot = Preferences.userRoot();
        Preferences myPrefs = prefsRoot.node("PreferenceExample");

        try {
            pe.setSomeProperties(myPrefs);
            pe.printInformation(myPrefs);
            pe.exportToFile(myPrefs, "prefs.xml");
        } catch(BackingStoreException bse) {
            System.out.println("Problem with accessing the backing store\n" + bse);
            bse.printStackTrace();
        }
    }
}
```

The output to the screen is shown here:

```
Node's absolute path: /PreferenceExample
Node's children:
Node's keys: fruit cost store
Node's name: PreferenceExample
Node's parent: User Preference Node: /
NODE: User Preference Node: /PreferenceExample
userNodeForPackage: User Preference Node: /<unnamed>
All information in node
  fruit = apple
  cost = 1.01
  store = safeway
```

The exported information in the XML file is listed here:

```
<?xml version="1.0" encoding="UTF-8"?>
<!DOCTYPE preferences SYSTEM "http://java.sun.com/dtd/preferences.dtd">
<preferences EXTERNAL_XML_VERSION="1.0">
  <root type="user">
    <map/>
    <node name="PreferenceExample">
      <map>
        <entry key="fruit" value="apple"/>
        <entry key="cost" value="1.01"/>
        <entry key="store" value="safeway"/>
```

```
        </map>
      </node>
    </root>
  </preferences>
```

Summary

This chapter introduced the new language features that Sun built into the JDK 5 release of the Java programming language. You should have all you need to know to understand and utilize these new features. You may find that a number of programming tasks you've accomplished in the past are now made simpler and clearer, and perhaps even some problems that never had a good solution now do.

Also covered in this chapter are several of the most important utility libraries in Java. The preferences library allows you to store and retrieve configuration information for your application. The logging library provides a sophisticated package of routines to track what your program is doing and offer output to a variety of people that need it. The regular expression library provides routines for advanced processing of textual data.

You should now be well-equipped to solve a variety of real-world problems and get the most out of the JDK 5 release of Java.

Now that you have learned about the advanced language features in Java, the next two chapters will take you inside a modern Java development shop. In Chapter 2, the habits, tools, and methodologies that make an effective Java developer will be discussed.

2

Tools and Techniques for Developing Java Solutions

Many beginning Java developers master the concepts of the Java programming language fairly well and still have a difficult time reaching the next level as a professional Java developer.

This is because most Java books simply focus on teaching just the Java language, a Java tool (like Ant or JUnit), or a language-neutral software methodology. This leaves you to learn techniques and practices from other software developers or at the proverbial "school of hard knocks."

In Chapter 1, I discussed the advanced features of the Java language — a continuation on the theme of most beginning Java books. But now, you are starting the transition to a new kind of Java book, one more experience-centric, starting with this chapter. In this chapter, you will get a feel for the tools and techniques of modern Java development. It will introduce you to "thinking like a professional Java developer," which continues in the next chapter — a discussion of Java design patterns.

By the end of this chapter, you should have acquired the following skills:

❑ Familiarity with the principles of quality software development

❑ Familiarity with the habits of an effective software developer

❑ Awareness of a number of the prominent software development methodologies

❑ Acquaintance with many of the tools commonly found in Java development environments

Principles of Quality Software Development

So, you have figured out how to build your Java applications, and they work just like the ones from which you learned. You are getting paid to write these applications, so you are now a professional Java developer. But how do you know if you are doing a good job?

There are literally thousands upon thousands of articles debating the measures of quality software with each of them offering you their own solution for how you should answer this question. Realizing that this discussion is well beyond the scope of this book (thankfully), this body of work can be boiled down to a few questions:

❑   **Does the software do what it is supposed to do?**

Of course, this is a loaded question. It is entirely possible to say that a piece of software does what it is supposed to do (as defined by a requirements specification), but this is absolutely worthless. In essence, you are talking about a failure of your requirements gathering process, which leads you to build the wrong thing. Your software is being built to serve a particular need, and if it does not satisfy that need (for whatever reason), the software is a failure.

❑   **Does the software do things it shouldn't do?**

Developers like to refer to this phenomenon as undocumented features, but your users will refer to them as bugs. Everyone prefers to build bug-free software, but in the real world, this just doesn't happen. All men may be created equal, but all bugs are not. Bugs that do not impact the functioning of the system — or the business process that they support — are obviously far less important than those that do.

❑   **Did you deliver the software in a timely manner?**

Timing is everything, and this is true nowhere more than in software in which the pace of change is incredible. If your software takes so long to deliver that it is no longer appropriate to the business process it supports, then it is worthless. The great untold secret behind the high percentage of software projects that end in failure is that many of them simply could not keep up with the pace of technological innovation — and died trying.

❑   **Could you do it again if you had to?**

Of course, you will have to! This is *the job* — writing and delivering software that complies with the above questions. The key here is that you should not have to learn all of your hard knocks lessons every time you build software. You will invariably be asked to deliver your software again with fixes and enhancements, and you hopefully do not have to fix the same bugs over and over again nor have the same integration challenges repeatedly. "At least we don't have to deal with this next time" should be a truth that comforts you in your integration and bug fixing and not a punch line to a development team joke.

These questions may seem like common sense — because they are! But there is an old saying that "common sense is neither," so it is important to not assume that everyone is on the same sheet of music. Furthermore, the US Army Rangers have a saying, "Never violate any principles, and do not get wrapped up in technique." You will find this a helpful maxim in dealing with the maze of processes, products, and techniques involved in software development. These are the core principles of software development, and how you get there is technique. Do not lose sight of the distinction between these two things.

Habits of Effective Software Development

Motivational sayings and common sense questions do not make a strategy for making you into an effective Java developer. You need to consider *the how* in delivering on quality software. Along those lines, there are a set of habits that are shared among effective software developers. They are as follows:

Communicate

The picture of the egg-headed recluse software engineer sitting in the dark part of some basement while banging away on a keyboard like an eccentric secretary is an outmoded stereotype (well mostly, the dark is good). As you learned before, software is built to satisfy a need in some particular business process. In order to be successful, you need to tap in and really appreciate that need. This is very difficult to do by reading a specification. You want to talk to the users, and, if you cannot talk to the users, you want to talk to someone who was a user or speaks with users. You want to learn what it is they do, how they are successful, and how your software will help them be more successful. If the use of your software is simply by management fiat, then your software purpose is already on critical life support.

You also want to communicate with your fellow developers—explaining to them what you learned, learning from their mistakes, and coordinating how your software will work together. Make it a point to try to establish some social interaction amongst your teammates, even if it is an occasional lunch or brief chat. Software can be a hard and stressful job; it helps if you have a basic familiarity with your teammates.

Model

Before you go running out to buy the latest in fashion apparel, check the cover of this book. It is pretty clear that this book will not have you doing any posing! Modeling builds upon communication by allowing a more tangible way to visualize a given concept or idea.

Don't assume that everyone on your team needs to attend UML training or buy thousands of dollars of UML modeling software. UML is a great package for expressing a lot of things in a common format that should be understandable by a wide variety of people—from users to developers. Of course, you know this is not the case. The key to any notation is that it must be well understood by those who read it. If your team is UML-savvy or will commit to being that way, then it is a fantastic notation—planned out by a large committee of very smart people.

Of course, the old joke is, "A camel is a horse designed by a committee." This means that you should recognize that UML contains a toolset that extends well beyond what you may need for your project's modeling needs. The key is to find a notation that everyone (including users) understands and sticks with it.

Also, if your tools provide more of a hindrance than an aid in your modeling, then don't use them. Ambler suggests in his book *Agile Modeling* that you can draw your models on a whiteboard, take a digital camera snapshot of the whiteboard, and have exactly what you need—without the burden or cost of a tool. [AMBLER]

Be Agile

Change is an inevitable part of software development. Not only is technology consistently changing, but so is your customer's business process, if for no other reason than the fact that you have actually provided some automation support.

Teaching a course in Object Oriented Software Development, I often point out to my students that, despite being a sophisticated software engineering professional who has developed many software solutions to improve the way people do business, I could not easily come up with a set of requirements for a system that would improve my business process. The fact is — like most people in the working world — I don't spend a lot of time thinking about how I do what I do. If asked to do so, I would probably relate my ideal system as an approximation of what I already experience. This would immediately change when you, the software team, introduced a new system to me because my entire frame of reference is now relative to what you have placed before me. Things that I once thought were important would no longer be so — improvements that I assumed would be better turn out not to be, and so on. Ultimately, it is a very natural and appropriate thing for my requirements to change!

You frequently hear software engineers bemoan the fact that the requirements keep changing. This is quite puzzling because software engineers presumably chose their profession based on the desire to develop software, and changing requirements facilitate that goal. The requirements changing is not really the problem. The problem is that the software team is not in the habit of accommodating change; that is, they are not very agile.

Lou Holtz once said, "Life is 10 percent what happens to you and 90 percent how you respond to it." This saying goes a long way towards distilling the attitude that a software engineer should possess to be effective in modern Java development.

Be Disciplined

Before you go running out and hacking and slashing your way to programming heaven, ensure that you maintain your discipline. Discipline is about maintaining your focus in the presence of a tremendous amount of distraction. This is not about holding your hand over a hot candle or walking across burning coals. You do what you should do, not what you can do.

Recall the principles of quality software development and ensure that you are not violating any of them. Often, rushing to do something will actually cause you to take longer. Be mindful of things slipping, like little bugs that should have been caught before or lapses in judgment for the sake of expediency.

However, in the same regard, do not slow things down simply for the sake of caution. Simply slowing down to avoid making a mistake will not definitely allow you to avoid the mistake, but it will certainly reduce the amount of time you have to correct it.

This is a very typical concern when trying to fix a bug or develop an innovative way to handle something that was unanticipated. By desiring to do something new and cool, you can lose sight of how important it really is in accomplishing the goal of the system.

Trace Your Actions to Need

Discipline goes hand in hand with tracing your actions to the need that your software is meant to address. It is very important that you are able to understand why each of you built each of the components of your system.

Traceability refers to the ability for you to follow your need all the way through the system. For example, you may have a need to provide a printed report. You would then see that traced into a set of use cases, or software requirements, which would then be realized in certain design elements, which would then be implemented in certain pieces of code, which would then be compiled into certain executables/libraries, which would then be deployed to a certain machine, and so forth.

So, you are thinking, "Well, that is really neat, but what does all of that really buy me?" The answer is simple. Say you received a request to change the code to support another type of printer. By being able to trace your code through, you would understand where your potential adaptations could be made.

Traceability is not meant to be some huge undertaking requiring mountains of paperwork and a large database, spreadsheet, or document, nor does it require some dumbed-down version of the code in order to explain it to those who are not able to read or write code. Traceability only requires that someone who can do something about it should be able to find his or her way through the code.

Don't Be Afraid to Write Code

It seems self-evident, but you would be surprised how often coding is relegated to such a minor part of software development — particularly on complex systems, where it is most needed. Often, there is a desire to figure it out on paper first, find the right design pattern, or model it just right.

However, certain logical constructs are simply unable to be elegantly expressed anywhere but in the code. Also, a compiler verifies a number of assumptions in your design, and your runtime environment will do the same.

It is also easier to estimate how long it will take to do something if you actually do something very similar. A scaled-back prototype that covers the bounds of your system can go a long way to understanding exactly how complex or time-consuming a particular task may actually be.

Furthermore, in Java development, you simply do not have the luxury of assuming that you understand everything about your system. With the high degree of reuse that exists in Java development, your system is invariably dependent on code developed outside of your design space. So, it is foolish to assume that a given API works like you assume it does. There are too many variables involved in the equation.

Part of the fearlessness towards writing code involves changing code. Refactoring — changing the design of existing code — is an important part of software development. [FOWLER]

Think of Code as a Design, not a Product

Refactoring demonstrates a key habit in effective software development. Code should not be considered the product that you deliver. After all, you rarely actually deliver the source code to the user. Instead, you deliver them a compiled byte code that operates in accordance with your source code.

This is because your source code is part of the design. As mentioned previously, there are some logical constructs that cannot be expressed anywhere but inside code. Furthermore, source code provides a human-understandable expression of logic that is then compiled into byte codes (and further gets converted into machine instructions).

You may be saying, "Well, of course, source code is not the product, who said it was?" You may never run into a problem with an organization that fails to realize this premise, but it is unlikely. Simply pay careful attention to the disproportionate focus paid to the design phase and the relative number of designers who cannot write code. This will demonstrate that the focus of the project is misplaced.

Read a LOT!

This may seem like a shameless plug by a self-serving author, but the simple fact is that software is always changing and improving. There are new technologies, implementations, APIs, standards, and so forth. Software development is a knowledge occupation, and part of the job (as well as developing any system) is learning. Learning new technologies, learning better approaches, and even learning more about the tools and APIs currently used in your solutions are critical to success.

A large part of this has to do with the rise of the Internet and open source software. Java has extended beyond just being a programming language and more towards a software development community.

If you have a software problem, you should first check online to see if someone has already solved that problem. Furthermore, you could check to see how others in your situation have overcome problems you have yet to encounter.

Build Your Process from the Ground Up

Your process is the way you, as a team, do business. No matter what your management tries to do in terms of instituting a process, your team will have to buy into how you will do business. The key to building an effective process is to start from the ground up. Management will set expectations for the outcomes they want and how they will measure your performance. If they place a high value on documentation and paperwork, then you need to ensure those expectations are met.

The key part is that your team will need to work together and that will decide how you meet the expectations of management. If you do not agree as a team to a process, then process can become a political football. You do not want to get into a situation where process is used to try to differentiate between co-workers. Once that starts happening, you will find that the techniques become more important than good software principles, and you start to lose the ability to trace your actions to your software's need.

An important consideration in building your process from the ground up is recognizing where your process really begins and ends. Development team wars have been waged simply on the basis of the question of integrated development environment (IDE) standardization, like Eclipse. You should really ask yourselves whether you really want to standardize on an IDE. Even though you certainly need something to be able to interoperate among team members with effective configuration management (discussed subsequently), you still don't want to make someone have to fight their development tools. Software is hard enough without having to fight against your tools.

This is the key consideration in building your process. Decide on what your team can agree on to make everyone the most effective. If you cannot agree, then management may have to get involved, but this should be avoided.

Manage Your Configuration

Configuration management is important because stuff happens. A hard drive goes bad, your latest improvement goes very badly, and so forth. These are all examples of things that happen in the normal course of software development.

You should recognize that there is a distinct difference between configuration management and source code control. Configuration management is a process in which you control how your system is put together. The key goal in configuration management is that you can replicate your configuration in another place. You do not just maintain configuration control of your source code but also your runtime environment (including dependent libraries, application server configuration, Java Runtime Environment, or database schema), that is, anything you would need in order to recreate your system.

Source code control using a tool like the Concurrent Versioning System (CVS) is used to allow multiple developers to work on files and integrate their changes while saving the history of previous revisions. CVS is the dominant tool in the open source environment and is cleanly integrated into most of the major IDEs. Of course, source control is useless if you do not *commit your changes*!

Unit Test Your Code

When you design and write code, you are writing test cases. You are writing test cases to handle the intended case, that is, how the system should behave as you go through the system. As you do that, you are making certain assumptions about how your system will react given a certain set of circumstances. For example, if I check to see that an object is not null here, then I am assuming that it will not be null up to a certain point.

As you write code, you tend to develop your complex logic to support the intended case, checking for needed preconditions required for your code to work. However, there is often a set of scenarios for which your code was designed to work. Unit testing allows you to test those scenarios.

I will discuss how to use an open source tool called JUnit to perform unit testing, but unit testing becomes an important part of the habit known as continuous integration.

Continuously Integrate

Having a strong set of unit tests that ensure the functionality of the individual components of your system, you could now combine these together into one cohesive product and run all of the unit tests on all the components to see how well the system as a whole functions, as illustrated in Figure 2-1.

You should note that, even if you are not very good about unit testing, continuous integration can still apply and provide great value to your development team. As you combine the efforts of your entire development team, you will see how things actually play together and ensure valid assumptions towards each other's code.

The more you integrate your system together, the more confident you will become in the success of the product as a whole. This helps mitigate risk by discovering problems early when they can be fixed. Continuous integration ties directly into maintaining short development iterations.

Maintaining Short Iterations

As previously noted, the sooner you discover problems, the less likely they are to affect your overall development success. The trick to doing this is to maintain short development iterations. This means that you should be able to go through the development life cycle (requirements, code, design, and test) in a short period of time.

You should try to involve your customer in each iteration if possible because, as mentioned previously, your software will change their context. This means they will start describing what they want within the context of what you built, not in some abstract concept.

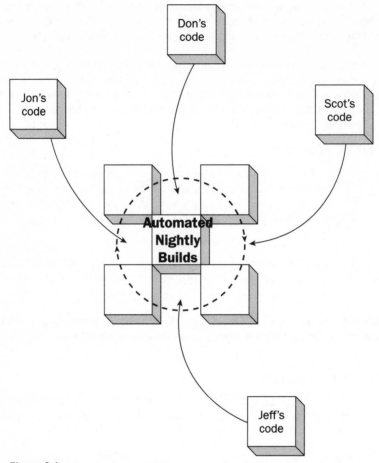

Figure 2-1

How short depends on your team, but, for the purposes of this discussion, you should measure it in weeks, not months. You want to put enough in an iteration to be meaningful in the shortest period of time. Two weeks to a month is a good rough estimate for your first iteration. After that, you can use your own success or failure to determine your next iteration.

Measure What You Accomplished — Indirectly

There is an old joke in software estimation, "What is the difference between a fairy tale and a software estimate? One doesn't start with once upon a time." This joke takes to task the idea that software estimation is really hard, and most techniques are frequently described as black magic.

However, successful software estimates are based on experience. Experience is based on trying to quantify what you have done before (and how long it took) as a predictor of how long the next thing will take. Because the typical workplace doesn't punish overestimation as much as underestimation — early is good, late is bad — you start to have these highly defensive estimates of software effort. These estimates start to build on one another and, because you cannot come in too low or your next estimate will not be as believable, you start to have down time. You start to gold plate (that is, add unnecessary and untraceable features) your system and gain a sense of inactivity.

The opposite phenomenon also occurs. Because software developers cannot be trusted to make estimates (because they are gold plating and sitting around), management steps in and promises software based on its guesses on how long something should take. Usually, they are setting aggressive schedules simply for some marketing purpose and frame it as a technical challenge to the developers. Developers are optimists and fighters, so they accept the ridiculous schedules until they get burned out and leave for a new job.

So, how do you avoid these dysfunctional circumstances? You measure what you have done by using an indirect measure to keep you honest. eXtreme Programming (XP) has a concept known as velocity. XP will be discussed subsequently, but the concept can be paraphrased as follows:

1. You have a set of tasks that, each of which, you assign a certain number of points related to how much effort it will take to accomplish it.

2. You then estimate how many points each of the developers on your team will be able to accomplish for a given iteration — taking into account leave and so forth. Your iteration is timeboxed to a specific amount of time (for example, two weeks is common).

3. You perform the work and keep track of how many points you were actually able to accomplish.

4. You start the process over for new tasks, adjusting them based on the actual results. As you get better or your system becomes better understood, your velocity will increase.

Of course, nothing scares developers more than metrics. As Mark Twain once said, "There are three types of lies: lies, damned lies, and statistics." Developers understand that metrics can be oversimplified or distorted beyond their actual meaning. This is why teamwork and communication is so important. You should only allow these metrics to be visible to those who actually are involved in using these metrics. You can make it a secret handshake; that is, if you don't have a velocity, you don't get to know the velocity.

Of course, on the subject of sensitive but necessary measures of your development performance, you should also look into tracking your issues.

Track Your Issues

Another volatile subject on a development team is bug reporting and tracking. As previously mentioned, it is hard for you to understand what your customers want, and it is hard for them to understand what they want. Furthermore, your users will use your software in ways that you did not anticipate and they will discover undocumented features of your system.

However, if you get past the concept of blame and simply focus on the inevitability of bugs and changes, you can make your issue tracking system a good way of keeping track of things that need to be done.

Whether you use a sophisticated online system or a simple spreadsheet, it is important that you keep track of the loose ends. You will find that it is a great practice to allow your users to directly input feedback on your product. How you choose to triage your responses is up to you, but it is very helpful to always have an open ear to listen to the user. Of course, if you let them constantly enter things in the system, you will need to make it appear that you are actually listening on the other end.

Development Methodology

Now that you have reviewed the principles of quality software development and many of the habits that help to facilitate achieving those principles, it is time to learn some actual full up methodologies used in many Java development shops.

There is a joke, "What is the difference between a methodologist and a terrorist? You can negotiate with a terrorist!" This joke pokes fun at a very real problem. Often, methodologies are evaluated as if they must account for every possible circumstance in the development life cycle and must be ritualistically adhered to — or the methodology magic will not work. Of course, all methodologies have to be tailored to your own development scenario, but you need to know the particulars of a methodology before you can tailor it.

A full examination and comparison of development methodologies is beyond the scope of this book, but you will learn some of the most popular ones in use today.

Waterfall Methodology

The grandfather of all software methodologies is the Waterfall methodology. It is known as the Waterfall methodology because the sequences flow through each other sequentially, as demonstrated in Figure 2-2.

The Waterfall methodology consists of a series of activities separated by control gates. These control gates determine whether a given activity has been completed and would move across to the next activity. The requirements phase handles determining all of the software requirements. The design phase, as the name implies, determines the design of the entire system. Next, the code is written in the code phase. The code is then tested. Finally, the product is delivered.

The primary criticism of the Waterfall methodology is that it takes too long to gain feedback on how things are going. As you read previously, some parts of your software are well understood and others are not. Therefore, trying to do all of the requirements first (which is to say, quantify the need into tangible specifications) is very hard when your user may not have a good understanding of the problem at hand. Furthermore, if you make a mistake in the requirements, then it will propagate to the design, the code, and so on. Also, there is no real capability to go back in the process. So, if you get into testing and discover that a part of the design simply doesn't work, you end up making changes to fix that issue, but you lose all context of your design activity — you are literally band-aiding the system on purpose!

Recognizing this problem, the Waterfall methodology has been adapted in several other forms, like the spiral methodology, which entails simply having multiple waterfalls. The idea is to shorten the time of the life cycle down; that is, create an iterative solution to the problem.

Ultimately, you cannot escape the waterfall because it really is the common-sense approach. First, you decide what it is you are going to build. Then, you decide how it is that you are going to build it. Next, you actually build it. Finally, you ensure that you actually built what you wanted (and it works). The major distinction with the next two methodologies that you will read about has to do with how much of the overall effort you try to build at a time.

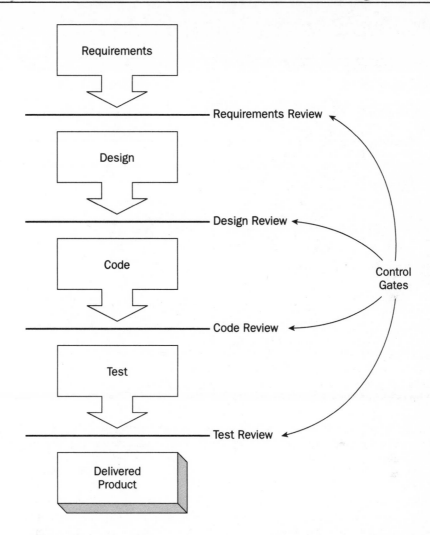

Figure 2-2

Unified Process

In Craig Larman's *Applying UML and Patterns*, he discusses an agile version of the Unified Process (UP), a process originally developed from the merger of several object-oriented development methodologies. The Unified Process entails short iterations of development based on tackling the most important aspects of your system first, which is illustrated in Figure 2-3. [LARMAN]

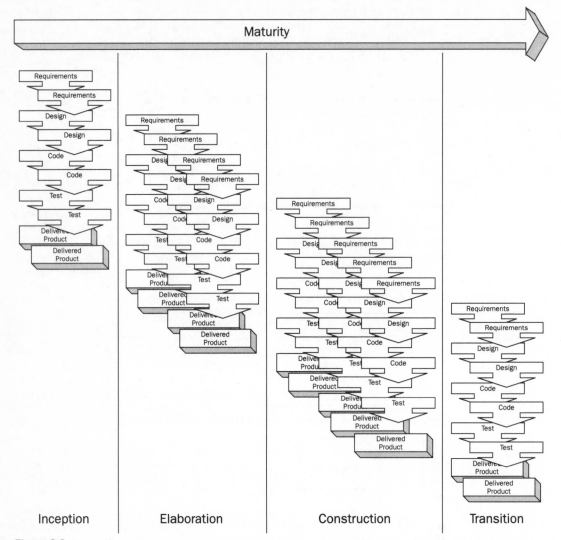

Figure 2-3

You develop a survey of use cases (that is, brief descriptions of user interactions with the system) and start working them off in the order of which they pose a risk to the overall success of the system. You can add or remove use cases from your survey, as appropriate, through your development. The phases illustrated in Figure 2-3 define and measure the relative maturity of the system.

The phases of the Unified Process are as follows:

- ❑ **Inception:** The system is still being felt out to determine the scope of the system — what will the system do and what are its boundaries. This phase can be very short if the system is well understood.

- ❑ **Elaboration:** You are mitigating the architectural risks to the system. This is a fancy way of saying, "Have you solved all of your hard problems?" or "Do you know how to do all the things you are going to need to do?"

- ❑ **Construction:** You are finishing all of the relevant use cases to make the system production ready, that is, to go into beta.

- ❑ **Transition:** You move the system through its final release stages and beta releases. It could include the operations and maintenance of the software.

This is an agile process that focuses on maintaining momentum, but it still sticks to a lot of the traditional practices of use case development, modeling, and so forth. The next methodology is also an agile process, but it has a different focus in terms of how to accomplish it.

eXtreme Programming

Kent Beck's *eXtreme Programming Explained* introduced a radically new methodology into the software development community. Based on his experiences on a project at Chrysler, he proposed making coding the central part of your development effort. [BECK]

You have your user come up with stories describing how the system should work, and order them based on their relative importance. You then take on a set of stories for your team to accomplish in a given iteration, about two weeks in length — working 40-hour work weeks. You split your team into pairs to work on each of the stories, allowing a certain amount of built-in peer review of the code as it is being written. You and your partner start by writing unit tests to go along with your source code. After you are done with your particular piece of code, you take it over to the integration machine where you add to the code baseline and run all of the unit tests accumulated from everyone's code. After each iteration, you should have a working system that your user can review to ensure that you are meeting their needs. This whole process is shown in Figure 2-4.

Note that XP doesn't place a high emphasis on designing the software; instead, it holds that most upfront design is not very helpful to the overall effort and ends up being changed with actual development.

XP is rather good at continuously having a working system. It can be tough when you lack an involved user or have a project of a large size (50 or more developers), when coordination and design activities actually could provide more value.

XP's system of velocity, described previously, provides a good sense of understanding the capability of your team so that you can effectively plan, which thus avoids burning out your engineers or sandbagging your customer.

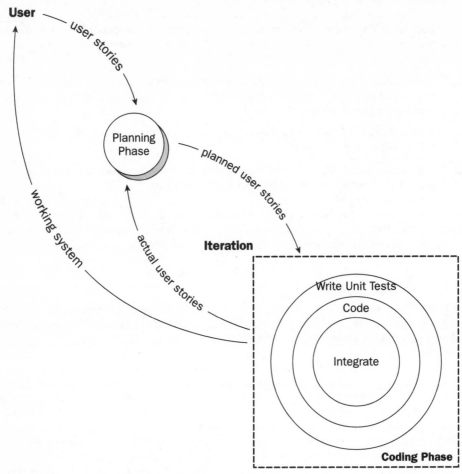

Figure 2-4

Observations on Methodology

There are several critical points that you can take away from reviewing these three divergent methodologies:

❑   Ultimately, you are doing the same task in each methodology. It is about how much scope you attempt to address in each activity that defines the real difference.

❑   The agile methodologies, like UP and XP, seek to be reactive rather than proscriptive. That is, they attempt to assess the success and adjust direction of the effort continuously rather than relying on the pass/fail nature of waterfall control gates.

❑   The methodologies vary in how much importance they grant to the design phase and the accoutrements that surround them (UML modeling tools and so forth). The Waterfall process finds this phase incredibly important, and UP recognizes that for the part of the system you are addressing in your iteration. XP believes that coding is design, and all of the additional work is built around considering scenarios that are not actually addressed in the functionality of the system. After all, you are coding the actual user stories.

❑   All of the methodologies recognize the importance of use cases; though, they address them in different forms. The Waterfall methodology sees use cases as a tool for generating the explicit requirements of the system, providing background information. UP finds them important as an inventory of scope. The survey report contains a simplified explanation of each use case and then relies upon them to build its design models in each of its iterations. XP is based directly on developing to satisfy what it calls user stories, which are more informal in format but still essentially the same thing.

There is no one-size-fits-all methodology. As mentioned in *Habits of Effective Software Development*, it is important that you and your team determine the process by which you will accomplish addressing the need for which your software is being built. This section was meant to provide you with a background on some of the most common methodologies in software today, and the next section will discuss some of the common tools used in software development in the context of practical development scenarios.

Practical Development Scenarios

Distributing J2EE applications across tiers is a challenging task to tackle because of all of the underlying implications of mixing and matching components with connectors across a system. The J2EE architecture consists of four tiers: the client, Web, business, and Enterprise Information System (EIS). The client tier is comprised of applets, HTML, and Java components. The Web tier is made up of servlets and Java Server Pages that operate in a Web container. The business tier manages all of the data transactions and persistence mechanisms of a system as well as resource allocations. The EIS tier is accountable for all of the back-end database systems that application components must integrate with.

With all of these components and connectors, consideration must be given to the construction of processes that manage and test these entities to ensure that consistencies are attained during development and deployment. Many open source tools have been developed to facilitate technological timing issues so that business challenges can be met. The remaining sections of this chapter will discuss some of these tools so that you can apply them in your operations to realize those consistencies, which should facilitate your development activities and help you become more successful with your integrations and deployments.

This chapter will investigate some scenarios on how to apply scripting tools like Ant, Maven, and XDoclet to manage your component builds and packaging, along with JUnit and JMeter to test your applications in an automated fashion to ensure that your development operations can behave in a harmonious manner.

Ant

All software projects need consistent builds from a common repository to ensure applications are deployed properly. For many software projects (both commercial and open source), Ant has been used to compile, test, and package components for distribution (see Figure 2-5).

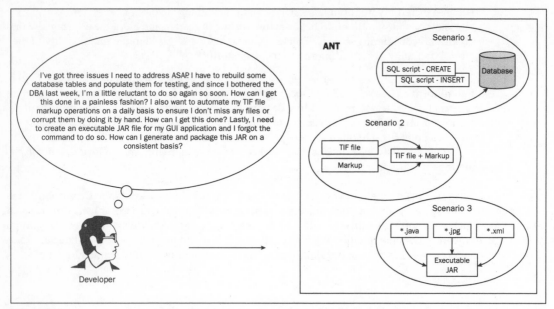

Figure 2-5

With Ant, a series of targets are implemented to construct processes to build your system components. This section will take you through three different scenarios that you might encounter in your development activities that can be tackled with Ant.

Scenario 1

In general, most Ant scripts start with property settings that are used to establish proper directory structures for file creation and transfer during your build activities. Similarly, parameters that are needed for processing can be defined like they are for database operations used in all three target entries in the following Ant script. Users can also send these parameters to the Ant script from the command line using the -D operation:

```
<project name="Database creation" default="createTables_MySQL" basedir=".">
<!-- could use a property file, we opted for property settings in script
<property file="${basedir}/build.properties"/> -->

<property name="sql.driver" value="org.gjt.mm.mysql.Driver"/>
<property name="sql.url" value="jdbc:mysql://localhost/sample_project"/>

<property name="sql.user" value=""/>
<property name="sql.pass" value=""/>
```

The `createTables_MySQL` target executes three SQL scripts for `employees`, `project`, and `timetable` table creation. The idea here is to be able to generate your tables on the fly just in case you need to deploy your database tables on a new platform for testing and/or deployment:

```
    <target name="createTables_MySQL">
        <sql driver="${sql.driver}" url="${sql.url}" userid="${sql.user}"
password="${sql.pass}" >
            <classpath>
            <pathelement location="mysql-connector-java-3.0.9-stable-bin.jar"/>
</classpath>
            use sample_project;
            <transaction src="employees.sql"/>
            <transaction src="project.sql"/>
            <transaction src="timetable.sql"/>
        </sql>
    </target>
```

The `createDB_MySQL` script works in conjunction with the `sample_project.sql` file to create a database in MySQL so that tables can be added to it. The following code snippet outlines how this is done, first by dropping any preexisting tables for `employees`, `project`, and `timetable`. After that has been performed, then the database will be created for table aggregations:

```
BEGIN;
DROP TABLE IF EXISTS employees;
DROP TABLE IF EXISTS project;
DROP TABLE IF EXISTS timetable;
DROP DATABASE IF EXISTS sample_project;
COMMIT;

CREATE DATABASE sample_project;
    <target name="createDB_MySQL">
        <sql driver="${sql.driver}"
            url="${sql.url}"
            userid="${sql.user}"
            password="${sql.pass}"
            classpath="mysql-connector-java-3.0.9-stable-bin.jar"
            src="sample_project.sql"/>
    </target>
```

The last target, `dropDB_MySQL`, is used to drop the database, `sample_project`, just in case something has gone wrong and a user wants to start over from scratch. Prior to performing this operation, a user should probably provide a query asking the user if this operation is really desired, as shown below:

```
    <target name="dropDB_MySQL">
        <input message="Do you really want to delete this table (y/n)?"
validargs="y,n" addproperty="do.delete" />
        <condition property="do.abort">
            <equals arg1="n" arg2="${do.delete}"/>
        </condition>
        <fail if="do.abort">Build aborted by user.</fail>
        <sql driver="${sql.driver}" url="${sql.url}" userid="${sql.user}"
password="${sql.pass}" >
            <classpath>
            <pathelement location="mysql-connector-java-3.0.9-stable-bin.jar"/>
</classpath>
            drop database sample_project;
```

```
        </sql>
    </target>
</project>
```

Sequence	Target	Action
2	createTables_MySQL	Creates tables for operations/testing
1	createDB_MySQL	Creates database for table adds
3	dropDB_MySQL	Drops database

Scenario 2

Scenario 2 addresses the image file markup that could be part of your workflow processes in your development operations. The following Ant script invokes the application necessary to aggregate your TIF files, depending on the date passed into your process. After all of the files have been collected, they will be sequentially run through a markup process that will tag the documents with the text provided:

```
<target name="run" description="Run the application.">
    <java classname="book.WorkFlow" fork="true" failonerror="true">
        <classpath>
            <pathelement location="${run.dir}"/>
        </classpath>
    </java>
</target>
```

The WorkFlow application employs the Ant library DirectoryScanner to determine which files will be marked, and all files collected will be marked up using Sun's Java Image I/O APIs:

```
package book;

import java.awt.Color;
import java.awt.Font;
import java.awt.Graphics;
import java.awt.image.BufferedImage;
import java.io.File;
import java.io.FileInputStream;
import java.io.IOException;
import java.text.SimpleDateFormat;
import java.util.ArrayList;
import java.util.Date;
import java.util.Iterator;
import java.util.List;

import javax.imageio.ImageIO;
import javax.imageio.stream.ImageOutputStream;

import org.apache.commons.logging.Log;
import org.apache.commons.logging.LogFactory;
import org.apache.tools.ant.DirectoryScanner;
import org.apache.tools.ant.types.Parameter;
import org.apache.tools.ant.types.selectors.BaseSelector;
```

```
import org.apache.tools.ant.types.selectors.DateSelector;
import com.sun.media.imageio.plugins.tiff.TIFFImageWriteParam;

public class WorkFlow {

  private static Log log = LogFactory.getLog(WorkFlow.class);
  private String workfilePath = "c://java_1.5_book/ant";

  public synchronized void processDocument(String s) {

    // perform timing tests
    long start = System.currentTimeMillis();

    log.info("[WorkFlow:processDocument()] ");

    if (s.length() <= 0) {
      String date = new Date().toString();
      log.info("date = " + date);
      SimpleDateFormat sdfLog = new SimpleDateFormat("MM/dd/yyyy HH:mm aa");

log.info("formatted date = " + sdfLog.format(new Date()));
      s = sdfLog.format(new Date());
    }
    log.info("passing date: " + s);
```

The string variable that is passed into the `processDocument` method represents the date that will be used to collect the image documents. If an empty value is passed, then the current date will be used. Now pass that date along to the `createWorkFiles` method, which returns a `String` array of all of the files to be processed.

The `String` array returned from `createWorkFiles` is propagated to the `documentsToProcess` method that might perform checks on the individual files to ensure that bad files are not passed along for marking:

```
    List list = documentsToProcess(createWorkFiles(s));
    Iterator it = list.iterator();

    if (!list.isEmpty()) {
      while (it.hasNext()) {
        log.info("[WorkFlow:processDocument] processing item:" + it.next());
    }
    } else {
        log.info("[WorkFlow:processDocument] list is NULL.");
    }

    // finalize timing tests
    long elapsedTimeMillis = System.currentTimeMillis()-start;
    log.info("Time (ms)  :" + elapsedTimeMillis + " ms");
    log.info("Time (secs):" + (elapsedTimeMillis/1000F) + " secs");

  }
```

The `markImage` method receives three parameters, which represent an input and output file as well as a `String` markup that will be pasted on the top and bottom of the document being processed:

```
    public void markImage(String inFile, String outFile, String marking) {

      try {

        BufferedImage  image = ImageIO.read(new File(inFile));

        Graphics graphics = image.getGraphics();
        graphics.setColor(Color.black);
        graphics.setFont(new Font("Arial", Font.BOLD | Font.ITALIC, 60));

        graphics.drawString(marking, (image.getWidth()*4/10) , (image.getHeight() -
  (image.getHeight()/20)));
        graphics.drawString(marking, (image.getWidth()*4/10) , image.getHeight()/20);
  // save modified image
        String format = "tiff";

        // Create Image
        IIOImage iioImage = new javax.imageio.IIOImage(image, null, null);

        // Get TIFF Writer
        Iterator writers = ImageIO.getImageWritersByFormatName("tiff");
        ImageWriter writer = (ImageWriter)writers.next();

        // Set WriteParam's
        TIFFImageWriteParam writeParam =
  (TIFFImageWriteParam)writer.getDefaultWriteParam();
        writeParam.setCompressionMode(ImageWriteParam.MODE_EXPLICIT);
        writeParam.setCompressionType("CCITT T.6");

        // Create File to save the image
        File f = new File(outFile);
        if (!f.exists()) f.createNewFile();
        ImageOutputStream ios = createImageOutputStream(f);
        writer.setOutput(ios);

        // Save the image
        writer.write(null, iioImage, writeParam);
        ios.close();

      } catch (IOException e) {
        log.error("FILE FAILED:" + inFile);
      }
    }
```

The `createWorkFiles` method receives a `date` value in string form to be used by the `DateSelector` object to collect files with `*.TIF` extensions that were created after the date specified for markup processing. Once the `workfilePath` directory has been scanned for those files adhering to the data constraints established and stored in a `String` array, that object will be passed back to the calling method in `processDocument`:

```java
public String[] createWorkFiles(String date) {
  log.info("[WorkFlow:createWorkFiles()] ");
  DateSelector selector = new DateSelector();

  Parameter param = new Parameter();
  param.setName(DateSelector.WHEN_KEY);
  param.setValue("after");

  // test date = "01/01/2004 23:15 PM";
  selector.setParameters(new Parameter[]{param});
  selector.setDatetime(date);

  DirectoryScanner ds = new DirectoryScanner();
  ds.setBasedir(workfilePath);
  ds.setIncludes(new String[]{"*.TIF"});
  ds.setSelectors(new BaseSelector[]{selector});
  ds.scan();
  return ds.getIncludedFiles();

}
```

The documentsToProcess method can be omitted if the checks are not going to be performed on the artifacts collected. The method itself just parses through the String array of filenames collected using the Ant library DateSelector:

```java
public List documentsToProcess(String[] s) {
  List docList = new ArrayList();

  for (int i=0; i < s.length; i++) {
    log.info("s[" + i + "]= " + s[i]);
    // not shown, but could perform checks to ensure
    // that improper files are not propagated forward
    docList.add(s[i]);
  }
  return docList;
}

// test
public static void main(String[] args) {

  WorkFlow testWorkFlow = new WorkFlow();
  String date = "";
  String[] s = testWorkFlow.createWorkFiles(date);
  if (s.length > 0) {
    log.info("s.length = " + s.length);
  } else {
    log.info("Files NOT found.");
  }

  testWorkFlow.processDocument(date);

  String workfilePath = "c://java_1.5_book/ant";
  testWorkFlow.markImage(workfilePath + File.separatorChar + "test.TIF",
workfilePath + File.separatorChar + "tests.TIF",
```

```
                                    "Test");
    }

}
```

Scenario 3

Scenario 3 addresses the creation of executable JAR files for a sample GUI application called `BookAuthorSearch`. Notice the following `<manifest>` tag that specifies the application's main class name. This is provided so that the `create` JAR file can be clicked and the application will be run automatically:

```xml
<project name="test" default="all" >

    <target name="init" description="initialize the properties.">
      <tstamp/>
      <property name="build" value="./build" />
    </target>

    <target name="clean" depends="init" description="clean up the output
directories.">
      <delete dir="${build}" />
    </target>

    <target name="prepare" depends="init" description="prepare the output
directory.">
      <mkdir dir="${build}" />
    </target>

    <target name="compile" depends="prepare" description="compile the Java
source.">
        <javac srcdir="./src/book" destdir="${build}">
        </javac>
    </target>

    <target name="package" depends="compile" description="package the Java classes
into a jar.">
      <jar destfile="${build}/BookAuthorSearch.jar" basedir="${build}">
        <manifest>
          <attribute name="Main-Class" value="book.BookAuthorSearch" />
        </manifest>
      </jar>
    </target>
```

The last target, `run`, is used to invoke the `BookAuthorSearch` JAR file for execution. The JAR file is an important feature that allows Java applications to be easily packaged for deployment:

```xml
    <target name="run" description="Run the application.">
        <classpath>
            <pathelement location=" BookAuthorSearch.jar "/>
        </classpath>
    </java>
    </target>
```

```
    <target name="all" depends="clean,package" description="Compile and package."/>

</project>
```

With tightened schedules, smaller development teams, and remote development operations, it is paramount for projects to employ Ant so that important processes can be captured and implemented in an easy manner by anyone. Consistent process operations ensure that builds are not corrupted and development and deployment activities can go forward in a less painful way than those programs that operate in an ad hoc fashion.

Maven

Maven is a build tool that allows users to build a project using its Project Object Model (POM) and Ant build files to perform uniform build activities. Maven is integrated with Gump to help projects maintain backward compatibility, and it utilizes a project descriptor, `project.xml`, to dictate how your project will be built.

Some of the elements of a project descriptor can include the following.

Element	Description
Extend	Specifies the location of the parent project if it exists
PomVersion	The current version of the project descriptor
Id	The short name of the project
Name	The full name of the project
GroupId	The short name of the project group
CurrentVersion	The current version of the project
Organization	The organization that owns the project
InceptionYear	The year of the project's start (specified with four digits)
Package	The Java package name of the project
Logo	The URL to the project's logo image
GumpRepositoryId	(Optional) The Id of the Gump repository
Description	(Optional) A detailed description of the project
ShortDescription	A brief description of a project
url	The homepage's URL
IssueTrackingUrl	(Optional) URL of issue tracking system
SiteAddress	(Optional) Web server directory where project resides
SiteDirectory	(Optional) The public site directory
DistributionSite	(Optional) The site where public distributions reside

Table continued on following page

Element	Description
Repository	Source configuration management repository information
Versions	(Optional) Contains information on previous version releases
Branches	(Optional) Contains information on previous project branches
mailingLists	Contains mailing lists for project
Developers	Describes the committers to a project
Contributors	Describes contributors to a project
Licenses	Describes licenses for a project
Dependencies	Describes the dependencies of a project
Build	Describes the environment of a project
Reports	Describes the reports that should be included with distribution
Properties	Project properties that will be used

For the sake of brevity, this example will not include many of the project elements described above. As shown in the Ant example previously, consistency across your builds is a important goal for development operations. Maven will allow you to satisfy your build and deployment goals, like Ant, but with a different technique. This scenario will give you a small taste on how to implement Maven to automate your build activities (see Figure 2-6).

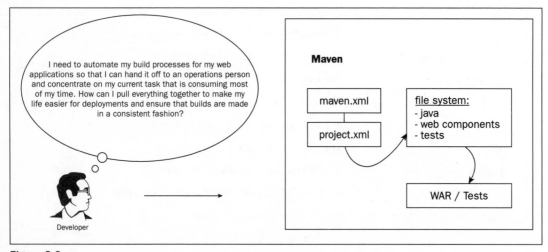

Figure 2-6

When you run this example, the target sequence will be war:init, war:web-app, followed by war:war when a user types in **maven** at the command line:

```
<!-- maven.xml ‡
<project default="war"
  xmlns:j="jelly:core"
  xmlns:m="maven"
  xmlns:deploy="deploy">
</project>
```

The project descriptor, `project.xml`, dictates all of the relevant elements that will be utilized for the Web application build:

```
<!-- project.xml ‡
<?xml version="1.0"?>
<project>
  <pomVersion>1</pomVersion>
  <id>maven-war-example</id>
  <name>Maven Example</name>
  <currentVersion>1.0</currentVersion>
  <package>org.apache.maven.examples.war</package>
```

The `<dependencies>` tag indicates what libraries are needed for the application build to be successful. The following example specifies dependencies with the log4j and servlet 2.3 libraries:

```
<dependencies>
  <dependency>
    <id>log4j</id>
    <version>1.2.8</version>
    <properties><war.bundle>true</war.bundle></properties>
  </dependency>
  <dependency>
    <id>servletapi</id>
    <version>2.3</version>
  </dependency>
</dependencies>
```

The `<build>` tag indicates where the source and test code directories are on the file system for compilation and testing by JUnit test scripts:

```
<build>
  <sourceDirectory>src/java</sourceDirectory>
  <unitTestSourceDirectory>src/test/java</unitTestSourceDirectory>
  <unitTest>
    <resources><resource>
      <directory>src/test/java</directory>
      <includes><include>**/*</include></includes>
      <excludes><exclude>**/*.java</exclude></excludes>
    </resource></resources>
    <includes>
      <include>**/*Test.java</include>
    </includes>
  </unitTest>
</build>
</project>
```

You can generate a build script with countless operations to manipulate and package your applications for deployment. The table below specifies a few for consideration in your build coverage.

Target	Action
Maven clean	Clean up directories
Maven	Compile source code and build WAR file
Maven test	Compile code and run tests on it

JUnit

Countless books have been written about JUnit and its numerous library extensions. Their usefulness in testing applications does not need to be recounted, but it is important to remember, when developing these tests with JUnit tools, to consider the objectives behind your testing coverage.

Ideally, your tests will exercise the constraints of your deployment system. This generally means that valid/invalid inputs of application components (`Textfield`, `RadioButton`, and so forth) will be tested as well as data points on your system. This testing needs to have a complementary problem-tracking tool to support your iterative development practices and to ensure that problems have been recorded and addressed in a timely fashion.

JUnit incorporates the XP philosophy of testing continuously so that problems do not manifest themselves in the latter stages of your development activities, which will bog down deployment schedules.

The scenario described here is an all too often occurrence that can be handled with the use of JUnit test scripts that allow developers to better understand the current state of their code and where it needs to be (see Figure 2-7).

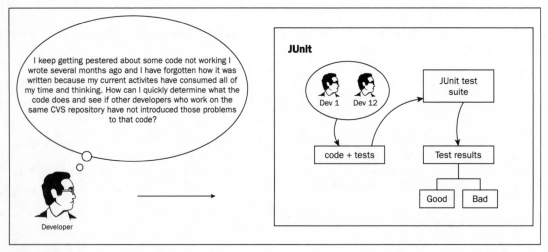

Figure 2-7

The `build.xml` file runs two test scenarios, `test1` and test2, after compiling the test code to ensure that your source code has not been corrupted by modifications to that code. Ideally, you would want to create a target in your build file to check out both the test and source code files from a common repository to ensure that your tests are being performed on working code that is being implemented in your development and deployments:

```xml
<?xml version="1.0"?>

<project name="junitTest" default="test">

<target name="init">
  <property name="test.dir" value="." />
</target>

<target name="compile" depends="init">
  <javac srcdir="." destdir="." classpath="junit.jar" />
</target>

<target name="test1" depends="compile">
  <echo message="Running JUnit tests (1)." />
  <junit printsummary="true">
  <!-- <formatter type="plain" usefile="false" /> -->
  <formatter type="xml" />
  <test name="TestScenarios1" />
<classpath>
      <pathelement location="." />
    </classpath>
  </junit>
  <junitreport todir=".">
    <fileset dir=".">
      <include name="TEST-*.xml" />
    </fileset>
    <report format="frames" todir="." />
  </junitreport>
</target>

<target name="test2" depends="compile">
  <echo message="Running JUnit tests (2)." />
  <junit printsummary="true">
  <!-- <formatter type="plain" usefile="false" /> -->
  <formatter type="xml" />
  <test name="TestScenarios2" />
    <classpath>
      <pathelement location="${testdir}" />
    </classpath>
  </junit>
  <junitreport todir=".">
    <fileset dir=".">
      <include name="TEST-*.xml" />
    </fileset>
    <report format="frames" todir="." />
  </junitreport>
</target>

</project>
```

The `TestScenarios1` test script reads the meta data affiliated with the employees table in the `sample_project` database and checks the attribute names of that table to ensure that someone has not corrupted the table itself. Alternatively, tests can be performed on database connections and the data that is stored in that table to ensure that bugs have not been introduced into the table:

```java
import java.sql.*;
import java.util.*;
import junit.framework.TestCase;

public class TestScenarios1 extends TestCase {

  private static final String DRIVER="org.gjt.mm.mysql.Driver";
  private static final String URL="jdbc:mysql://localhost/project-sample";
  private static final String USER="";
  private static final String PASSW="";
  private static final String QUERY="Select * from employees";

  public DbTestCase(String name) {super(name);}
  public void noTestCase() {}
  public void testCase() {}
  public void testCase(int arg) {}

void testCase1() {

try {

  Class.forName(DRIVER);
  // connect to the MySQL db
  Connection conn = DriverManager.getConnection(URL, USER, PASS);
  Statement stmt = conn.createStatement();
  ResultSet rslt = stmt.executeQuery(QUERY);

  // Get the resultset meta-data
  ResultSetMetaData rmeta = rslt.getMetaData();

  // Use meta-data to determine column #'s in each row
  int numColumns = rmeta.getColumnCount();
  String[] s = new String[numColumns];

  for (int i=1; i < numColumns; i++) {
    s[i] = rmeta.getColumnName(i);
  }

  // check to see if db columns are correct
  assertTrue(s[1].equals("employee-id"));
  assertTrue(s[2].equals("employee-name"));
  assertTrue(s[3].equals("employee-salary"));
  assertTrue(s[4].equals("position-desc"));
  assertTrue(s[5].equals("start-date"));
  assertTrue(s[6].equals("end-date"));
  assertTrue(s[7].equals("conditions-of-discharge"));
```

```
    assertTrue(s[8].equals("salary"));

    // close connection
    conn.close();
}
catch(Exception e) {}
}

}
```

When automated JUnit tests discover that code does not do what requirements prescribe, or indicate that an error has been introduced into your build, developers can use these tests as a point of reference to discover what is wrong with code and rectify it in a procedural manner. The alternative is to code and fix on the fly without any process to ensure things have been rectified properly and hope that things work out in the end, which is not a promising practice.

XDoclet

XDoclet is a wonderful tool that can be downloaded from the SourceForge Web site at `http://xdoclet.sourceforge.net/` to ensure that consistencies are realized with your development operations. XDoclet can be especially helpful on projects that involve disparate sets of developers who are working from a common source code repository. Consider all the times you have halted your development activities because someone forgot to add entries in the deployment descriptor and included the code that refers to that entry or when the entry itself was delivered but the code was not checked in. That can be particularly frustrating during final deployment migrations. XDoclet can alleviate those occurrences because developers can embed their mapping in their code and build files can parse through that code to generate the appropriate mappings needed for deployment. Additionally, extraneous mappings can be appended to the deployment descriptor (`web.xml`) by making entries in `servlets.xml` and `servlet-mappings.xml`. This scenario appends JavaServer Page mappings to the deployment descriptor through the `servlets.xml` file for browser visualization (see Figure 2-8).

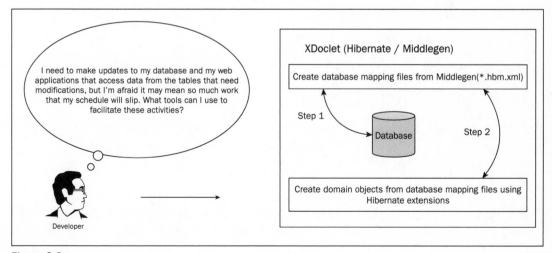

Figure 2-8

You can implement the following script to properly map your servlet and JSP entries in your deployment descriptor using the XDoclet libraries. Naturally, the first part of your script outlines the properties needed for file transfer, manipulation, and packaging:

```xml
<?xml version="1.0" encoding="UTF-8"?>

<project name="XDoclet servlet/jsp" default="build-war" basedir=".">

<description>XDoclet script generation for Servlets/JSPs</description>

  <property name="app.name" value="resubmit"/>

  <property name="src.dir" location="src"/>
  <property name="build.dir" location="build"/>
  <property name="dist.dir" location="dist"/>
  <property name="lib.dir" location="lib"/>
  <property name="merge.dir" location="mergeDir"/>
  <property name="generated.dir" location="generated"/>
  <property name="web.deployment.dir" location="${generated.dir}/webdeployment"/>
<property name="xdoclet.lib.dir" location="xdocletlib"/>

  <path id="compile.path">
    <fileset dir="${lib.dir}" includes="*.jar"/>
  </path>

  <path id="xdoclet.lib.path">
<fileset dir="${lib.dir}" includes="*.jar"/>
    <fileset dir="${xdoclet.lib.dir}" includes="*.jar"/>
  </path>
```

The clean target is typically used to clean up operations prior to operations so that a clean slate can be worked on without having to worry about residual files corrupting processing activities. The target block also creates new directories for file transfer and deployment once the previous directories have been purged from the file system:

```xml
<target name="clean">
  <delete dir="${gen.src.dir}/org"/>
  <delete dir="${web.deployment.dir}"/>
  <delete dir="${build.dir}"/>
  <delete dir="${dist.dir}"/>
  <delete dir="${generated.dir}"/>
  <mkdir dir="${build.dir}" />
  <mkdir dir="${build.dir}/WEB-INF" />
  <mkdir dir="${build.dir}/WEB-INF/classes" />
  <mkdir dir="${build.dir}/WEB-INF/lib" />
</target>
```

The generate-web target implements the WebDocletTask libraries to parse the servlet source file to strip the servlet's mapping attributes. Once that has been performed, the Ant script copies the deployment descriptor to the /WEB-INF directory of the Web application and the JavaServer Pages to the Web directory:

```
    <target name="generate-web">
      <taskdef name="webdoclet" classname="xdoclet.modules.web.WebDocletTask"
classpathref="xdoclet.lib.path"/>
      <webdoclet destdir="${build.dir}/WEB-INF/classes" mergeDir="${merge.dir}">
<fileset dir="${src.dir}">
          <include name="**/*.java" />
        </fileset>
        <deploymentdescriptor destdir="${web.deployment.dir}" distributable="false"
/>
      </webdoclet>
      // copy files to appropriate directories
      <copy todir="${build.dir}/WEB-INF">
        <fileset dir="${web.deployment.dir}">
          <include name="**/*.xml" />
        </fileset>
      </copy>
      <copy todir="${build.dir}">
        <fileset dir="${basedir}/web/jsp">
          <include name="**/*.jsp" />
        </fileset>
      </copy>
    </target>
```

The `compile` target is invoked from the `build-clean` target. This compiles the source code so that it can be properly packaged for deployment:

```
    <target name="compile" depends="generate-web">
      <javac destdir="${build.dir}/WEB-INF/classes" classpathref="xdoclet.lib.path">
      <src path="${src.dir}"/>
      </javac>
    </target>
```

The `package` target creates a Web ARchive file (WAR) for distribution. Ideally, you could build a target to deploy the WAR file to your application server's Web container for execution:

```
    <target name="package" depends="generate-web">
      <jar destfile="${build.dir}/${app.name}.war" basedir="${build.dir}"/>
    </target>

    <target name="build-clean" depends="clean,compile"/>
    <target name="build-war" depends="build-clean,package"/>

  </project>
```

The next scenario is common for many distributed system applications that use Hibernate as their Object/Relational (O/R) tool to gain access to back-end data with domain objects (see Figure 2-9).

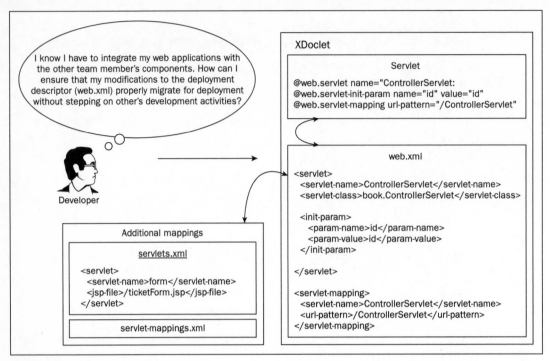

Figure 2-9

The DOCTYPE script uses XML entity references to include the test.xml fragment where the script includes an &database reference. As in all of these scripts, property settings precede the targets' entries to ensure proper paths are specified prior to file manipulation and migration:

```
<?xml version="1.0"?>
<!DOCTYPE project [
    <!ENTITY database SYSTEM "file:./config/database/test.xml">
]>
<project name="Middlegen Hibernate" default="all" basedir=".">

    <property file="${basedir}/test.properties"/>

<property name="name" value="test"/>
    <property environment="env"/>
    <property name="build.dir"                  value="${basedir}/build"/>

    <property name="lib.dir"                    value="${basedir}/lib"/>
    <property name="src.dir"                    value="${basedir}/src"/>
    <property name="build.java.dir"             value="${build.dir}/java"/>
    <property name="build.gen-src.dir"          value="${build.dir}/gen-src"/>
    <property name="build.classes.dir"          value="${build.dir}/classes"/>
```

```
    &database;

    <property name="datasource.jndi.name"                value="${name}/datasource"/>
```

The `path id` element is created so that similar path-like structures can be used for one or more tasks. The `<path>` element is placed at the same level as targets in your script, and they are referenced via their id attribute:

```
    <path id="lib.class.path">
        <pathelement path="${database.driver.classpath}"/>
        <fileset dir="${lib.dir}">
            <include name="*.jar"/>
        </fileset>
        <fileset dir="${basedir}/middlegen-lib">
            <include name="*.jar"/>
        </fileset>
        <fileset dir="${build.gen-src.dir}">
            <include name="**/*.hbm.xml"/>
        </fileset>
    </path>
```

The `middlegen` target runs the Middlegen application that opens up a user-specified database and creates mappings of its tables. Table mappings contain `*.hbm.xml` extensions. Once these are created, then the `hbm2java` target can run to generate `*.java` domain object files to access your database:

```
    <target name="middlegen" description="Run Middlegen">

        <mkdir dir="${build.gen-src.dir}"/>
        <taskdef
            name="middlegen"
            classname="middlegen.MiddlegenTask"
            classpathref="lib.class.path"
        />

        <middlegen
            appname="${name}"
            prefsdir="${src.dir}"
            gui="${gui}"
            databaseurl="${database.url}"
            initialContextFactory="${java.naming.factory.initial}"
            providerURL="${java.naming.provider.url}"
            datasourceJNDIName="${datasource.jndi.name}"
            driver="${database.driver}"
            username="${database.userid}"
            password="${database.password}"
    schema="${database.schema}"
            catalog="${database.catalog}"
        >

        <hibernate
            destination="${build.gen-src.dir}"
```

```
            package="${name}.hibernate"
            genXDocletTags="false"
            genIntergratedCompositeKeys="false"
            javaTypeMapper="middlegen.plugins.hibernate.HibernateJavaTypeMapper"
    />

    </middlegen>

    <mkdir dir="${build.classes.dir}"/>
</target>
```

The `hbm2java` target determines where the database table mappings reside using the `path id` element and then creates the hibernate mappings to be used to access the items in the tables of the targeted database:

```
<path id="project.class.path">
    <pathelement path="${build.gen-src.dir}"/>
    <pathelement path="${build.gen-src.dir}/test/hibernate"/>
    <fileset dir="${build.gen-src.dir}/test/hibernate">
        <include name="**/*.hbm.xml"/>
    </fileset>
    <fileset dir="lib">
        <include name="**/*.jar"/>
    </fileset>
 </path>

<!-- Hibernate mapping files -->
<fileset id="hibernate.mapping.files" dir="${build.gen-src.dir}/test/hibernate">
    <include name="**/*.hbm.xml" />
</fileset>

<target name="hbm2java" description="Generate .java from .hbm files.">

    <pathconvert refid="hibernate.mapping.files" property="hibernate.mappings"
pathsep=" "/>
    <java classname="net.sf.hibernate.tool.hbm2java.CodeGenerator" fork="true">
        <classpath refid="project.class.path" />
        <arg line="--config=test.xml"/>
        <arg line="${hibernate.mappings}"/>
    </java>
</target>
```

The `test.xml` file passed as a parameter to the `CodeGenerator` application specifies the renderer operations that will be performed during code generation. This code snippet tells you what is needed for a basic rendering procedure:

```
<codegen>
    <generate renderer="net.sf.hibernate.tool.hbm2java.BasicRenderer"/>
    <generate suffix="Finder"
renderer="net.sf.hibernate.tool.hbm2java.FinderRenderer"/>
</codegen>
```

The next target, `compile-hibernate`, performs Java compilation of the domain model objects that were created by the mapping and conversion procedures:

```
    <target name="compile-hibernate" depends="middlegen" description="Compile
hibernate Business Domain Model">
      <javac
          srcdir="${build.gen-src.dir}"
          destdir="${build.classes.dir}"
          classpathref="lib.class.path"
      >
          <include name="**/hibernate/**/*"/>
      </javac>
    </target>

    <target name="all" description="Build everything" depends="compile-hibernate"/>

    <target name="clean" description="Clean all generated stuff">
      <delete dir="${build.dir}"/>
    </target>

</project>
```

JMeter

Software development typically is performed as a solitary endeavor until it is time to integrate with new and existing components on your deployment system. Understanding how your applications will perform under real-life conditions is a legitimate concern for all software developers.

With the JMeter application available at `http://jakarta.apache.org/jmeter/`, you can generate and manage user simulations for your applications using a robust GUI application console to collect performance measurements. This is performed by adding ThreadGroups to your test plans to simulate users and configuration elements that simulate and stimulate your applications (see Figure 2-10).

With enterprise development efforts, performance discovery cannot be performed early enough in your development activities to determine what kind of loads your applications can handle alone and when packaged with other applications targeted for deployment.

Rather than delving into a broad range of scenarios to demonstrate the load testing abilities of JMeter and the wide range of testing protocols that can be applied, it would probably be more beneficial to describe from a high-level view all of the different capabilities that the tool possesses that can facilitate your development operations.

JMeter is comprised of six different components (Listeners, Config Elements, Assertions, Pre- and Post-Processors, and Timers) to measure your application's performance in your development space.

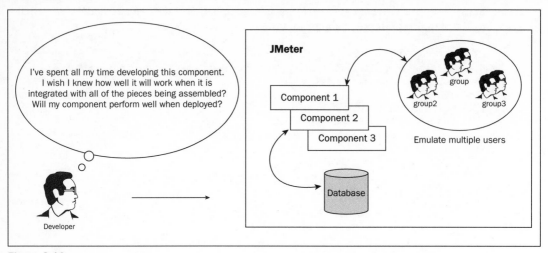

Figure 2-10

Listeners are conduits to data that is collected by the JMeter application during testing operations. Data collections can either be saved off to files or shown in graphical representations like graphs and tables.

Config Elements are used by the JMeter application to perform disparate protocol requests to back-end components like Web, database, and Lightweight Directory Access Protocol (LDAP) servers. TCP and FTP requests can also be performed to test your system's components.

Assertions can be implemented to discover problems with HTML tags and error strings that can be introduced by testing activities.

Pre- and Post-Processor tests act a lot like servlet filters that can manipulate code prior to being run as well as after. These components allow Web requests to be modified prior to being passed along for interpretation. An example of this would be to translate an XML response to HTML during Web application transactions.

By establishing test plans using ThreadGroups, users can manually craft simulations through the GUI controls as well as generate capture and replay tests automatically by recording navigation flows using JMeter's Recording Controller.

The latest JMeter 2.0 release has introduced many new features, as shown in Figure 2-11, to load test the functional behavior of your system and gather performance metrics so that your applications can be deployed with some assurance that they can handle difficult user loads.

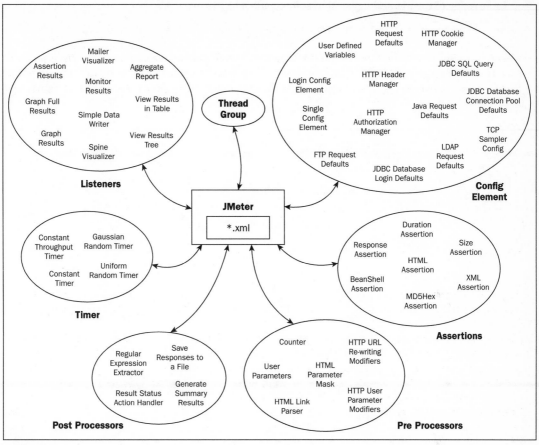

Figure 2-11

Summary

This chapter carried you from the abstract concepts of what it means to write quality software to the concrete details of how software tools are used in Java development environments. Along the way, you were provided information to give you a feel for what it is like to be a Java developer, including the following points:

❑ The principles of software quality by which developers live

❑ The habits that an effective software developer exhibits

❑   A few of the methodologies that software developers use

❑   How and why to use many of the tools found in Java development environments

Chapter 3 continues the brief aside into thinking like a professional Java developer by discussing design patterns, which provide an intellectual repository from which you can learn to avoid common problems that face many Java developers, as well as how the developers of the Java programming language solved many of their issues.

3

Exploiting Patterns in Java

In Chapter 2, you learned about half of "thinking like a Java developer" when I discussed software development methodologies. This chapter handles the other half—the use of patterns to make you an effective Java developer.

This is not a patterns book. This chapter is included because patterns are critical to understanding and communicating the designs of application programming interfaces, tools, and other applications. This is because the vast majority of these technologies are built on top of design patterns.

If I had to pick one aspect of software engineering that I absolutely love, hands down, it would be software design. Designing software well is challenging and it requires a combination of creativity and problem-solving skills. The experience of creating a solution in software can be very rewarding. If you are just becoming familiar with the Java programming language, software design can be a little overwhelming. It's like a blank canvas with a lot of colors from which to choose. Design decisions are difficult to make because—without experience—it is difficult to understand how the choices you make will affect the application later.

Learning design patterns is the single best way to increase your abilities as a software engineer. Technology changes very quickly. To give things a little perspective, learning a new technology is like reading a good book; learning patterns is like learning to read.

The focus of this chapter is to communicate why design patterns are important and highlight commonly occurring patterns. Hopefully, if you haven't been turned on to patterns already, this chapter will give you some reasons to pursue them.

> *There are plenty of patterns books. I feel these three represent some of the best work written on the subject: Refactoring: Improving the design of Existing Code by Martin Fowler; Design Patterns: Elements of Reusable Objected-Oriented Software by Erich Gamma, Richard Helm, Ralph Johnson, and John Vlissides; and Applying UML and Patterns: An Introduction to Objected-Oriented Analysis and Design and the Unified Process by Craig Larman.*

This chapter will provide you with a strong definition of a pattern, an understanding of why patterns are important, tricks to understanding a pattern, and an explanation of important Java patterns. This chapter is divided into three main sections. The first section will discuss the rationale behind learning patterns and some examples of where they are used in software design. The second section, building patterns from design principles, will walk you through a series of exercises that show how to form patterns from basic design principles. Finally, the important patterns section will walk you through code examples of a subset of well-known design patterns.

Why Patterns Are Important

One of my father's favorite quotes was, "Experience is a good teacher, but a fool will learn from no other." In software, experience is a good teacher, but lessons learned from experienced designers can help accelerate your design skills. A pattern is a documented lesson learned.

A pattern is a proven solution to a software problem enabling reuse of software at the design level. The purpose of a pattern is to conceptually pair a problem with its design solution and then apply the solution to similar problems. Code level reuse of software is desirable, but design level reuse is far more flexible.

With each application you work on, none of them will be the same. There will be similarities. Being able to recognize these similarities, combined with your knowledge of design patterns, will help bring confidence to the design decisions you make.

Patterns are one of the greatest resources you will have in the design of object-oriented software. They will definitely help you to master the Java programming language, be more productive, and develop effective Java solutions.

Keys to Understanding the Java Programming Language

Patterns help you understand the Java programming language. Compared to other programming languages, Java has a steep learning curve. It's not that Java is harder to learn than other languages. Just the opposite, it has a very clean syntax and its structure is similar to other OO languages.

The language becomes difficult once you confront the vast number of APIs available to the Java programmer. The number of APIs available is a very good thing. Each API should be viewed as a tool in the toolbox for solving problems.

Leveraging existing software is a core practice in thinking like a professional Java developer. This allows you to save time and be more productive. The collection of APIs provided in the 1.5 JDK, as well as countless open source projects, represent what you don't have to build from scratch.

This book examines several APIs such as Collections, Java2D, JMX, XML, EJB, JMS, JDBC, RMI, and Web Service. The list is pretty long, but it only scratches the surface on the number of APIs available. The truth is you cannot sit down and learn them all. Thankfully, there is no reason to learn them all. This is why design patterns are so important to learning Java.

Design patterns allow you to learn a new API quickly. If you understand the patterns used in an API, then you will be able to quickly understand, evaluate, and potentially integrate that code into your solution. It is much easier to learn and build on top of existing API's than it is to reinvent the wheel and start from nothing.

This is especially true when working with the J2EE framework. If you are working on a project and hear that a decision has been made to ignore the distributed transaction processing capabilities of a J2EE application server in favor of a homegrown solution, run and don't look back. As a Java developer, you learn as much as you can and only build what you need.

J2EE is a standards-based solution. One misconception about the J2EE framework is that it is considered a product. J2EE is not a product. It is a specification that Sun published as a set of documents describing how a Web and EJB containers must behave. Then software vendors implement the specs and sell their products as part of a standards-based solution. This is important because the folks at Sun are pattern savvy. The APIs are all based on patterns. This is very good news for you and an excellent reason to gain a strong understanding of design patterns. If you do, you will be able to understand and leverage anything Sun throws your way.

Keys to Understanding Tools Used in Java Development

In addition to the wealth of APIs available to Java developers, there is also a large number of development tools for improving the software development process. A few tools are ANT, JUnit, and XDoclet. These tools offer extension points for integration as well as good working examples of the power of design patterns.

ANT

ANT is an XML-based build tool with several uses. One of the uses is to automate the building of a software project. It can also do the work of most scripting languages without being OS dependent. It's built using a combination of several design patterns.

JUnit

JUnit is a unit-testing framework. Establishing automated unit tests is an excellent way to prove code changes so as to prevent introducing new bugs into your software. To use JUnit, you must extend the framework. By understanding the patterns JUnit is built on, you will be able to take advantage of automated unit testing.

XDoclet

XDoclet is a code-generating framework. It allows you to imbed meta data in the comments of your code. The meta data is used to generate supporting code as well as XML descriptor files. XDoclet makes it easy to sync derived software artifacts common when developing EJBs, Servlets, and persistent data objects such as `hibernate` and `JDO`.

There are numerous other tools available to the Java developer. Understanding the patterns these tools are built on takes some of the magic out of how they work. By understanding design patterns you will be able to use and extend these tools to build better software.

Keys to Developing Effective Java Solutions

Patterns help you build effective solutions using Java. Patterns help you communicate design concepts as well as gain an appreciative knowledge of underlying design principles.

Develop Common Design Vocabulary

There is a lot of value in the pattern name. The name provides a common vocabulary for software engineers to use to communicate. The patterns in this book are taken from the widely accepted GoF.

For example, say you need two to parts of a system to communicate even though they expect different interfaces. Use the Adapter pattern. If you have a situation where several algorithms will solve the same problem, use the Strategy pattern. This chapter goes into those two patterns, as well as several others, in detail. The point of mentioning them now is to show the value in understanding patterns.

Understand the Fundamentals of Design

This reason for learning patterns is near and dear to me. Initially, after being introduced to the concepts of object-oriented programming, I failed to see the relevance of the object-oriented concepts. It seems like more work with limited benefits. It wasn't until I was exposed to design patterns that I started to gain a real appreciation for the power of the OO concepts.

Patterns will help you fully understand fundamental design principles. Understanding the fundamentals of software design is critical to becoming a confident software designer. Patterns provide a concrete example of how to apply various design principles. Essentially, design is about making decisions. Knowing which decisions lead to good software design, and which lead to problems in the future, makes all the difference in building effective solutions.

Design decisions center on identifying the pieces of your software system and how they will work together to accomplish your objective. Good design is the result of the lessons learned often from living through a bad design nightmare.

Abstraction, *polymorphism*, and *inheritance* are the three principal concepts of object-oriented design, Abstraction is the practice of modeling the relevant aspects of real-world concepts. Polymorphism is type substitution allowing one class to take the place of another. Inheritance is the practice of creating specialization and generalization relationships between classes.

Some design criteria to consider when building a Java solution include:

❏ **Protected Variations.** This means that you need to isolate volatility in your application. If you feel an application component could change, then take steps to segregate that component using interfaces. Interfaces will allow you to change the implementing class without affecting existing application dependencies.

❏ **Low Coupling.** The purpose of this design concept is to ensure that changes made in one section of code don't adversely affect another unrelated section. For example, does a user interface change require a change to the database? If so, the application could be brittle where any small change propagates throughout the software system.

❏ **High Cohesion.** The practice of tying closely related things together tightly.

This is important to understanding design patterns because each pattern is the application of one or more design principles. Once you understand abstraction, polymorphism, and inheritance, it is easier to understand how patterns can reduce the complexity of software design.

Software design goals are important, but there is a large gap between goals and real implementations. Patterns bridge this gap and realize these goals; nothing teaches like a good example. The next section discusses some foundation on how to get started with patterns.

Building Patterns with Design Principles

At the core of any pattern is a collection of design principles. This section looks at a simple and unconventional approach to building patterns from the ground up. The approach is to start with a simple design and gradually make changes so that the design is more flexible. Each design change becomes a step in building more complex design patterns. By following the exercises in this section, it will be clear how applying design principles makes software more flexible. This allows the reader to understand the mechanics behind patterns a small piece at a time.

This section starts off with the design of a single class. From this single class design an association is added, followed by an interface. These two steps add flexibility to the single class design. Understanding this flexibility has important ramifications for understanding design patterns. The final section shows an example of merging the concepts of association and inheritance, which is common in a number of design patterns.

Designing a Single Class

A single class doesn't constitute a design pattern, but it is a design. And there is nothing wrong with simplicity. Part of the design process is assigning responsibility to an object, as in Figure 3-1.

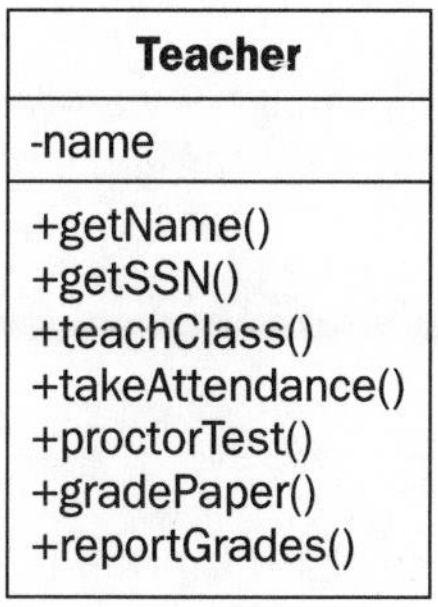

Teacher
-name
+getName() +getSSN() +teachClass() +takeAttendance() +proctorTest() +gradePaper() +reportGrades()

Figure 3-1

It is very common for a class to become bloated with several methods not related to the abstraction the class represents. This can cause dependency problems down the line and does not fit with the high cohesion design principle. In this example, the `Teacher` class contains several methods related to teacher responsibilities. The solution is to *push to the right* or delegate the methods that do not belong with the abstraction. The phrase "do not belong" is subjective. Any design decision could be wrong. As long as you justify it with sound OO principles, don't worry — you can always change it later when the problem is clearer.

Creating an Association between Classes

All the teacher responsibilities have been delegated to a class called `TeacherResponsibilities`. Again visualize the methods being pushed to the right. Figure 3-2 shows how responsibility has been delegated through an association.

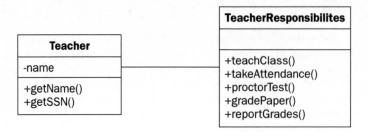

Figure 3-2

For the `TeacherResponsibilities` class to do work on behalf of the `Teacher` class, an association has to be created. The `Teacher` object holds a reference to the `TeacherResponsibilities`.

There are basically three ways this can happens:

1. The `TeacherResponsibilities` object is passed to the `Teacher` object as a parameter.

```
Teacher teacher = new Teacher("Heather");
TeacherResponsibilities responsibilities= new TeacherResponsibilities ();
teacher.setResponsibilities ( responsibilities);
```

2. The `Teacher` object creates the `TeacherResponsibilities` object.

```
public class Teacher {

private TeacherResponsibilities responsibilities = new TeacherResponsibilites();

}
```

3. The `TeacherResponsibilites` object is passed back from a method call.

```
public class Teacher {
      public Teacher() {
Administration admin = new Administration();
         responsibilities = admin.getResponsibilites();
    }
  }
```

These three methods determine the visibility an object shares with another in making up an association. The design might be done, but there is another design principle to address: *loose-coupling*. In specifying an association, a tight dependency between the `Teacher` and the `TeacherResponsibilites` classes has been created. The relationship is restricted to the `Teacher` and the `TeacherResponsibilites` types. That would be fine, except that it may be felt that the responsibilities will change over time. *How do you loosen the relationship and address this volatility?* The answer is to *push up* an interface.

Creating an Interface

An interface is a software contract between classes. By using the interface, the current class is allowed to provide the implementation. If in the future the implementation changes, you can replace the current class with a new class. Since the `Teacher` class only depends on the `Responsibilities` interface, the `Teacher` class will not need to be modified. The UML for this design is shown in Figure 3-3.

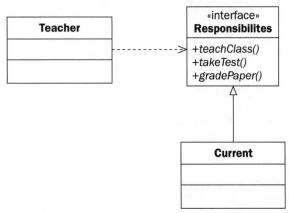

Figure 3-3

> Just a word of warning, each artifact you add to the design is one more thing to manage. Interfaces are great when establishing dependencies across components to isolate volatility, but they are not needed everywhere.

In the next section, we will combine delegation and inheritance, the concepts of the previous two sections, to create powerful object structures. An inheritance loop combines the pluggable functionality of inheritance with the separation of concerns gained with an association.

Creating an Inheritance Loop

By relating two classes with both an association and an inheritance, it is possible to create trees and graphs. Think of this as *reaching up* the class hierarchy. The inheritance relationship causes the nodes in the object structure to be polymorphic. In the example shown in Figure 3-4, a `WorkFriends` group can be manipulated using the same interface declared by the `Person` class. Another common example would be how files and folders on a file system have similar behavior. They both use common functionality such as copy, delete, and more.

Figure 3-4 shows the resulting class and object view of an *inheritance loop*. This is a common structure used in many design patterns including composition.

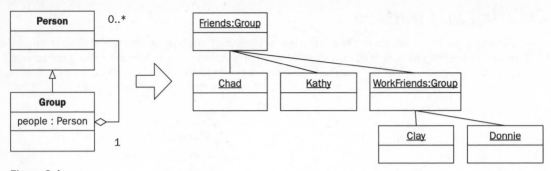

Figure 3-4

I refer to an inheritance loop as reaching up the hierarchy, as depicted in Figure 3-4. By reaching up the hierarchy, you create a relationship known as *reverse containment*. By holding a collection of a superclass from one of its subclasses it is possible to manipulate different subtypes as well as collections with the same interface.

Figure 3-5 shows one subtle change to the example in Figure 3-4. By changing the cardinality of the association between the super- and subtypes to many-to-many, it is possible to represent graphs as well as trees.

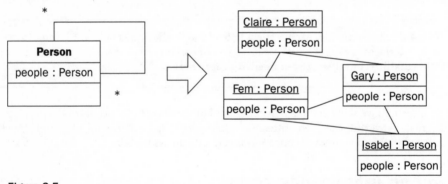

Figure 3-5

Finally, Figure 3-6 adds subtype relationships to the inheritance loop, allowing the representation of a complex data structure with methods that can be invoked with a polymorphic interface.

We have also created a common interface for each responsibility allowing us to add new responsibilities with limited impact to the application.

The purpose of this section was to learn tricks to understanding patterns. By creating associations and using inheritance, you have been able to build some complex designs from these principles. You learned to apply these principles by remembering simple actions: push to the right, push up, and reach up. Learning these tricks will help you understand the well-known patterns in the next section.

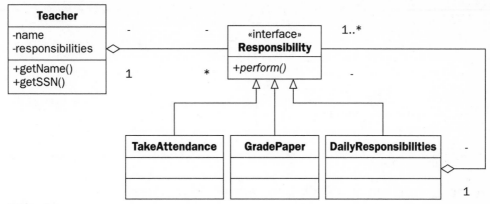

Figure 3-6

Important Java Patterns

The next section will show examples of very important and well-known patterns. By learning each of these patterns, you will develop your pattern vocabulary and add to your software design toolbox. Each pattern discussed below includes a description of the problem the pattern solves, the underlying principles of design at work in the pattern, and the classes that make up the pattern and how they work together.

This section will highlight a few well-known patterns. The focus of this section is not to describe patterns in a traditional sense, but instead to provide code and concrete examples to demonstrate the types of problems that each pattern can solve. All the patterns discussed in this section are well known and oft-adapted GoF patterns.

The patterns in this section include Adapter, Model-View-Controller, Command, Strategy, and Composite.

What is important to take away from the discussion of each pattern is how the classes that make up the pattern work together to solve a specific problem. Each pattern will be discussed with a text description and a diagram showing the pattern as well as the example classes fulfilling their corresponding pattern role.

Adapter

An Adapter allows components with incompatible interfaces to communicate. The Adapter pattern is a great example of how to use object-oriented design concepts. For one reason, it's very straightforward. At the same time, it's an excellent example of three important design principles: delegation, inheritance, and abstraction. Figure 3-7 shows the class structure of the Adapter pattern as well as the example classes used in this example.

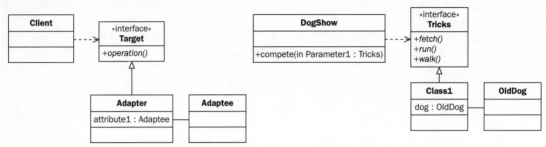

Figure 3-7

The Adapter Pattern Is a Collaboration of Four Classes

The four classes that make up the Adapter pattern are the *Target, Client, Adaptee, and Adapter*. Again, the problem the Adapter pattern is good at solving is incompatible interfaces. In this example, the adaptee class does not implement the target interface. The solution will be to implement an intermediary class, an Adapter, that will implement the target interface on behalf of the Adaptee. Using polymorphism, the client can use either the Target interface or the Adapter class with little concern over which is which.

Target

Start off with the Target interface. The Target interface describes the behavior that your object needs to exhibit. It is possible in some cases to just implement the Target interface on the object. In some cases it is not. For example, the interface could have several methods, but you need custom behavior for only one. The java.awt package provides a Window adapter for just this purpose. Another example might be that the object you want to adapt, called the Adaptee, is vendor or legacy code that you cannot modify:

```
package wrox.pattern.adapter;

public interface Tricks {

    public void walk();
    public void run();
    public void fetch();
}
```

Client

Next, look at the Client code using this interface. This is a simple exercise of the methods in the interface. The compete() method is dependent on the Tricks interface. You could modify it to support the Adaptee interface, but that would increase the complexity of the Client code. You would rather leave the Client code unmodified and make the Adaptee class work with the Tricks interface:

```
public class DogShow {

    public void compete( Tricks target){
        target.run( );
        target.walk( );
        target.fetch( );
    }
}
```

Adaptee

Now the Adaptee is the code that you need to use, but it must exhibit the `Tricks` interface without implementing it directly:

```
package wrox.pattern.adapter;

public class OldDog {
  String name;

  public OldDog(String name) {
    this.name= name;
  }
  public void walk() {
    System.out.println("walking..");
  }
  public void sleep() {
    System.out.println("sleeping..");
  }
}
```

Adapter

As you can see from the `OldDog` class, it does not implement any of the methods in the `Tricks` interface. The next code passes the `OldDog` class to the Adapter, which does implement the `Tricks` interface:

```
package wrox.pattern.adapter;

public class OldDogTricksAdapter implements Tricks {
  private OldDog adaptee;

  public OldDogTricksAdapter(OldDog adaptee) {
    this.adaptee= adaptee;
  }
  public void walk() {
    System.out.println("this dog can walk.");
    adaptee.walk();
  }
  public void run() {
    System.out.println("this dog doesn't run.");
    adaptee.sleep();
  }
  public void fetch() {
    System.out.println("this dog doesn't fetch.");
    adaptee.sleep();
  }
}
```

The Adapter can be used anywhere that the `Tricks` interface can be used. By passing the `OldDogTricksAdapter` to the `DogShow` class, you are able to take advantage of all the code written for the `Tricks` interface as well as use the `OldDog` class unmodified.

The next section looks at how to establish the associations and run the example:

```java
package wrox.pattern.adapter;

public class DogShow {
  //methods omitted.

  public static void main(String[] args) {

    OldDog adaptee = new OldDog("cogswell");
    OldDogTricksAdapter adapter = new OldDogTricksAdapter( adaptee );
    DogShow client = new DogShow( );
    client.compete( adapter );

  }
}
```

Model-View-Controller

The purpose of the Model-View-Controller pattern is to separate your User Interface Logic from your business logic. By doing this it is possible to reuse the business logic and prevent changes in the interface from affecting the business logic. MVC, also known as Model-2, is used extensively in Web development. For that reason, Chapter 8, "Developing Web Applications Using the Model 2 Architecture," is focused completely on this subject. You can also learn more about developing Swing clients in Chapter 4, "Effective User Interfaces with JFC." Figure 3-8 shows the class structure of the Model-View-Controller pattern along with the classes implementing the pattern in this example.

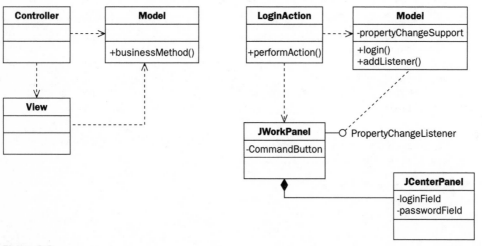

Figure 3-8

This pattern example will be a simple swing application. The application functionality will implement the basic login functionality. More important than the functionality is the separation of design principles that allow the model (data), controller (action), and the view (swing form) to be loosely coupled together.

Model-View-Controller is actually more than a simple pattern. It is a separation of responsibilities common in application design. An application that supports the Model-View-Controller design principle needs to be able to answer three questions. How does the application change the model? How are changes to the model reflected in the view? How are the associations between the model, view, and controller classes established? The next sections show how these scenarios are implemented in this example using a swing application.

Scenario 1: Changing to the Model

Changes to the model are pushed from the outside in. The example uses Java swing to represent the interface. The user presses a button. The button fires an event, which is received by the controlling action. The action then changes the model (see Figure 3-9).

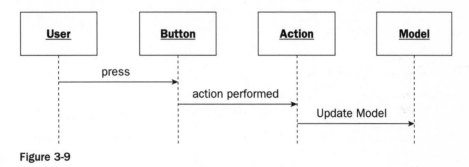

Figure 3-9

Scenario 2: Refreshing When the Model Changes

The second scenario assumes that the model has been updated by an action. The views might need to know this information, but having the model call the view direction would break the MVC separation principle requiring the model to have knowledge of the view. To overcome this, Java provides the Observer Design pattern, allowing changes from the model to "bubble out" to the view components. All views that depend on the model must register as a ChangeListener. Once registered, the views are notified of changes to the model. The notification tells the view to pull the information it needs directly from the model (see Figure 3-10).

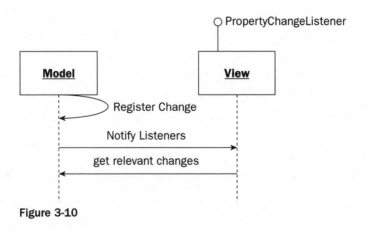

Figure 3-10

123

Scenario 3: Initializing the Application

The third scenario shows how to initialize the action, model, and view objects and then establish dependencies between the components (see Figure 3-11).

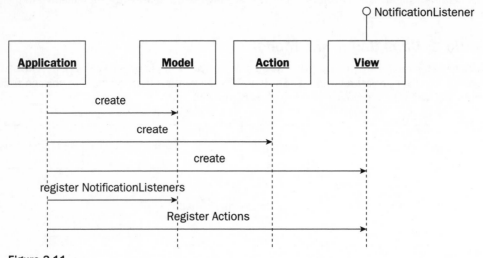

Figure 3-11

The views are registered with the model and the actions are registered with the views. The application class coordinates this.

Having discussed the collaboration scenarios between the model, view, and controller components, the next sections will delve into the internals of each component, starting with the model.

Model

The Model can be any Java object or objects that represent the underlying data of the application, often referred to as the domain model. For this example, we will use a single Java object called `Model`.

The functionality of the Model in this example is to support a login function. In a real application, the Model would encapsulate data resources such as a relational database or directory service:

```
package wrox.pattern.mvc;
import java.beans.PropertyChangeListener;
import java.beans.PropertyChangeSupport;

public class Model {
```

The first thing of interest in the Model is the `PropertyChangeSupport` member variable. This is part of the Event Delegation Model (EDM) available since JDK 1.1. The EDM is an event publisher-subscriber mechanism. It allows views to register with the Model and receive notification of changes to the Model's state:

```
private PropertyChangeSupport changeSupport= new PropertyChangeSupport(this);
private boolean loginStatus;
private String login;
private String password;
public Model() {
  loginStatus= false;
}
public void setLogin(String login) {
  this.login= login;
}
public void getPassword(String password) {
  this.password= password;
}
public boolean getLoginStatus() {
  return loginStatus;
}
```

Notice that the setLoginStatus() method fires a property change:

```
public void setLoginStatus(boolean status) {
  boolean old= this.loginStatus;
  this.loginStatus= status;
  changeSupport.firePropertyChange("model.loginStatus", old, status);
}

public void login(String login, String password) {
  if ( getLoginStatus() ) {
    setLoginStatus(false);
  } else {
    setLoginStatus(true);
  }
}
```

This addPropertyChangeListener() is the method that allows each of the views interested in the model to register and receive events:

```
public void addPropertyChangeListener(PropertyChangeListener listener) {
  changeSupport.addPropertyChangeListener(listener);
}
}
```

Notice that there are no references to any user interface components from within the Model. This ensures that the views can be changed without affecting the operations of the model. It's also possible to build a second interface. For example, you could create an API using Web services to allow automated remote login capability.

View

The view component of the application will consist of a swing interface. Figure 3-12 shows what the user will see when the application is run.

There are two JPanel components that make up the user interface. The first is the CenterPanel class that contains the login and password text boxes. The second is the WorkPanel that contains the login and exit command buttons as well as the CenterPanel.

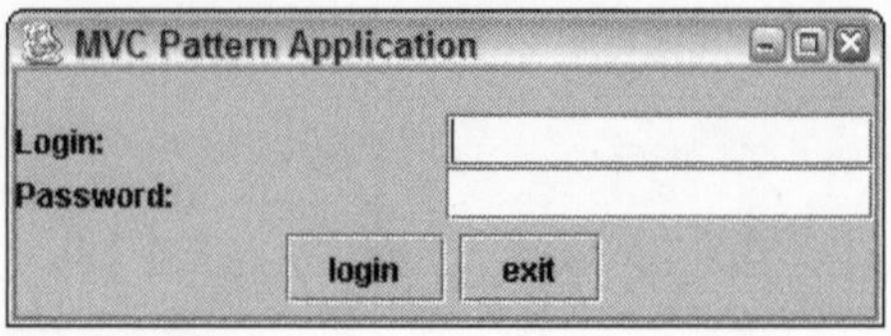

Figure 3-12

The CenterPanel is a typical user data entry form. It's important to notice that there is no code to process the login in this class. Its responsibility is strictly user interface:

```java
package wrox.pattern.mvc;
import java.awt.GridLayout;
import javax.swing.JLabel;
import javax.swing.JPanel;
import javax.swing.JTextField;

public class CenterPanel extends JPanel {

  private JTextField login= new JTextField(15);
  private JTextField password= new JTextField(15);

  public CenterPanel() {
    setLayout(new GridLayout(2, 2));
    add(new JLabel("Login:"));
    add(login);
    add(new JLabel("Password:"));
    add(password);
  }
  public String getLogin() {
    return login.getText();
  }
  public String getPassword() {
    return password.getText();
  }
}
```

The next user interface component, WorkPanel, contains CenterPanel. Notice that there are no references to the WorkPanel from the CenterPanel. This is an example of composition, allowing the CenterPanel to be switched out for another form, or viewed in a different frame:

```java
package wrox.pattern.mvc;
import java.awt.BorderLayout;
import java.beans.PropertyChangeEvent;
import java.beans.PropertyChangeListener;
import javax.swing.Action;
import javax.swing.JButton;
import javax.swing.JLabel;
import javax.swing.JPanel;
```

As you can see from the class declaration, the `WorkPanel` is a swing component. In addition, it also implements the `PropertyChangeListener` interface. This allows the `WorkPanel` to register with the application Model and have change Notifications published to it when the `Model` changes. The `WorkPanel` is registered with the Model as a `PropertyChangeListener`. This provides low coupling between the interface and domain logic, allowing the view to be changed with changes to the `Model`:

```java
public class WorkPanel extends JPanel implements PropertyChangeListener {
  private Model model;

  private JPanel center;
  private JPanel buttonPanel= new JPanel();
  private JLabel loginStatusLabel= new JLabel("  ");

  public WorkPanel(JPanel center, Model model) {
    this.center= center;
    this.model= model;
    init();
  }
  private void init() {
    setLayout(new BorderLayout());
    add(center, BorderLayout.CENTER);
    add(buttonPanel, BorderLayout.SOUTH);
    add(loginStatusLabel, BorderLayout.NORTH);
  }
```

When the `Model` changes. The `propertyChange()` method is called for all classes that registered with the Model:

```java
public void propertyChange(PropertyChangeEvent evt) {
  if (evt.getPropertyName().equals("model.loginStatus")) {
    Boolean status= (Boolean)evt.getNewValue();
    if (status.booleanValue()) {
      loginStatusLabel.setText("Login was successful");
    } else {
      loginStatusLabel.setText("Login Failed");
    }
  }
}
```

The `addButton()` method allows you to do two things. First, you can configure any number of buttons. Second, it provides the action classes. They specify the work each performs when the button is pressed. The action represents the final part of the MVC pattern: the controller. The controller will be discussed in the next section.

```java
public void addButton(String name, Action action) {
  JButton button= new JButton(name);
  button.addActionListener(action);
  buttonPanel.add(button);
}

}
```

Controller

The purpose of the controller is to serve as the gateway for making changes to the model. In this example, the controller consists of two `java.swing.Action` classes. These Action classes are registered with one or more graphical components via the components' `addActionListener()` method. There are two `Action` classes in this application. The first attempts to login with the Model. The second exits the application:

```
package wrox.pattern.mvc;

import java.awt.event.ActionEvent;
import javax.swing.AbstractAction;
```

The `LoginAction` extends the `AbstractionAction` and overrides the `actionPerformed()` method. The `actionPerformed()` method is called by the component, in this case the command button, when it is pressed. The action is not limited to registration with a single user interface component. The benefit of separating out the controller logic to a separate class is so that the action can be registered with menus, hotkeys, and toolbars. This prevents the action logic from being duplicated for each UI component:

```
public class LoginAction extends AbstractAction {

  private Model model;
  private CenterPanel panel;
```

It is common for the controller to have visibility of both the Model and the relevant views; however, the model cannot invoke the actions directly. Ensuring the separation of business and interface logic remains intact:

```
  public LoginAction(Model model, CenterPanel panel ) {
    this.model= model;
    this.panel = panel;
  }
   public void actionPerformed(ActionEvent e) {
    System.out.println("Login Action: "+ panel.getLogin() +" "+ panel.getPassword()
);
    model.login( panel.getLogin(), panel.getPassword()  );
  }
}
```

The `ExitAction` strictly controls the behavior of the user interface. It displays a message when the Exit button is pressed confirming that the application should close:

```
package wrox.pattern.mvc;
import java.awt.event.ActionEvent;
import javax.swing.AbstractAction;
import javax.swing.JFrame;
import javax.swing.JOptionPane;
public class ExitAction extends AbstractAction {

  public void actionPerformed(ActionEvent e) {

    JFrame frame= new JFrame();
    int response= JOptionPane.showConfirmDialog(frame,
                                         "Exit Application?",
```

```
                                                    "Exit",JOptionPane.OK_CANCEL_OPTION);
      if (JOptionPane.YES_OPTION == response) {
        System.exit(0);
      }
    }
  }
```

Finally, you can view the `Application` class. The `Application` class is responsible for initialization, and it creates the associations that establish the MVC separation of logic design principles:

```
package wrox.pattern.mvc;
import java.awt.event.WindowAdapter;
import java.awt.event.WindowEvent;
import javax.swing.JFrame;

public class Application extends JFrame {
  private Model model;
```

The Swing Application creates an association to the Model class, shown in the following code in the application constructor:

```
public Application(Model model) {
  this.model= model;
```

Then, create the Views to display the swing interface:

```
CenterPanel center= new CenterPanel();
WorkPanel work= new WorkPanel(center, model);
```

Create the Action classes that represent the controller and register them with the command buttons:

```
work.addButton("login", new LoginAction(model, center));
work.addButton("exit", new ExitAction() );
model.addPropertyChangeListener(work);
setTitle("MVC Pattern Application");
```

Use Swing housekeeping to display the application:

```
getContentPane().add(work);
pack();
show();
addWindowListener(new WindowAdapter() {
  public void windowClosing(WindowEvent e) {
    System.exit(0);
  }
});
}
public static void main(String[] args) {
  Model model= new Model();
  Application application= new Application(model);
}
}
```

The Model-View-Controller pattern is a combination of best practices in software design. It prompts a separation of concern between the user interface and business layers of an application. This example covered a number of design patterns: composition, action, and event publish-subscribe. The next pattern is the Command pattern. The Command pattern provides a consistent means of handling user requests.

Command

The Command pattern provides a standard interface for handling user requests. Each request is encapsulated in an object called a Command. Figure 3-13 shows the classes involved in the Command pattern.

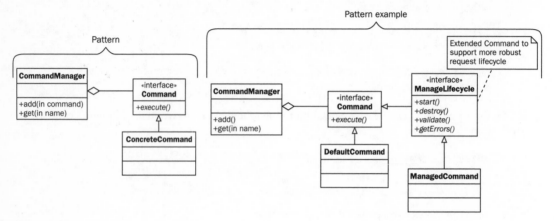

Figure 3-13

The three classes of the command pattern are the Command, CommandManager, and Invoker. The Command class represents an encapsulation of a single behavior. Each behavior in an application, such as save or delete, would be modeled as a command. In that way the behavior of an application is a collection of command objects. To add behavior to an application, all a developer needs to do is implement additional command objects. The next component in the Command pattern is the CommandManager. This class is responsible for providing access to the commands available to the application. The final component is the Invoker. The Invoker is responsible for executing the command classes in a consistent manner. The next section will look at the anatomy of the Command class.

Command

The first part of the Command pattern is the Command interface identified by a single method:

```
package wrox.pattern.command;

public interface Command {

    public void execute();
}
```

The life cycle is different from calling a typical method. For example, if you need to pass in an object parameter like the following method:

```
public void getTotal(Sale) {
//calculate the sale.
}
```

As a command you would write the following:

```
public CalculateSale implements Command {
private Sale sale;

public void setSale( Sale sale ) {
this.sale = sale;
}
public void execute( ) {
 // calculate the sale.
}
```

For the purpose of the example, we will use an empty command to demonstrate the interaction between the classes in this pattern:

```
package wrox.pattern.command;

public class DefaultCommand implements Command {

    public void execute() {
        System.out.println("executing the default command");
    }
}
```

The next section will look at the class that manages the command for an application.

CommandManager

The CommandManager class will process all requests. Using a HashMap, all of the commands will be initialized before requests are processed, then retrieved by name. They are stored using the add() method, and retrieved through the getCommand() method:

```
package wrox.pattern.command;
import java.util.HashMap;
import java.util.Map;
public class CommandManager {
    private Map commands= new HashMap();

    public void add(String name, Command command) {
        commands.put(name, command);
    }
    public Command getCommand(String name) {
        return (Command)commands.get(name);
    }
}
```

Invoker

A standalone client will demonstrate the execution of the Command pattern. When the Client constructor is called it adds the DefaultCommand to the manager:

```
package wrox.pattern.command;
import java.util.Collection;
import java.util.HashMap;
import java.util.Map;
```

```
public class Client {
  private CommandManager manager= new CommandManager();

  public Client() {
    manager.add("default", new DefaultCommand());
  }
```

Here, the command mapping has been hard coded. A more robust implementation would initialize the command map from a resource file:

```
<commands>
  <command name="default" class="wrox.Pattern.command.DefaultCommand" />
</commands>
```

Then, as requests are received by the `invoke(String name)` method, the command name is looked up in the `CommandManager` and the `Command` object is returned:

```
  public void invoke(String name) {
    Command command= manager.getCommand(name);
      command.execute();
  }

  public static void main(String[] args) {
    Client client= new Client();
    client.invoke("default");
  }
}
```

This is an important part of most Web frameworks like Struts or WebWork. In WebWork there is a specific Command pattern component called xWork. It is described in detail in Chapter 8, "Developing Web Applications Using the Model 2 Architecture."

By handling each request as a `Command` object, it is possible to apply common services to each command. Some common services could be things such as security, validation, and auditing. The next section will extend the current `Command` pattern and implement a `ManagedLifecycle` interface. This interface will define a set of methods that are called during each request:

```
package wrox.Pattern.command;

import java.util.Collection;
import java.util.Map;

public interface ManagedLifecycle extends Command {

  public void initialize();
  public void setApplicationContext(Map context);
  public boolean isValidate();
  public Collection getErrors( );
  public void destroy();

}
```

The `ManagedLifecycle` interface is a contract between the `Command` object and the client code.

The following is an example command that implements the `ManagedLifecycle` interface:

```java
package wrox.pattern.command;
import java.util.Collection;
import java.util.Map;
import java.util.HashMap;

public class ManagedCommand implements ManagedLifecycle {
  private Map context;
  private Map errors= new HashMap( );
  public void initialize() {
    System.out.println("initializing..");
  }
  public void destroy() {
    System.out.println("destroying");
  }
  public void execute() {
    System.out.println("executing managed command");
  }
  public boolean isValidate() {
    System.out.println("validating");
    return true;
  }
  public void setApplicationContext(Map context) {
    System.out.println("setting context");
    this.context= context;
  }
  public Collection getErrors() {
    return errors.getValues();
  }
}
```

The following code shows initialization and invocation of two types of commands, the standard and managed:

```java
package wrox.pattern.command;
import java.util.Collection;
import java.util.HashMap;
import java.util.Map;

public class Client {
  private Map context= new HashMap();
  private CommandManager manager= new CommandManager();

  public Client() {
    manager.add("default", new DefaultCommand());
```

A new `ManagedCommand` has been added to the `CommandManager`:

```java
    manager.add("managed", new ManagedCommand());
  }
  public void invoke(String name) {
    Command command= manager.getCommand(name);
```

Next, a check is put in place to determine whether the command being executed implements the
`ManagedLifecycle` interface:

```
if (command instanceof ManagedLifecycle) {
   ManagedLifecycle managed= (ManagedLifecycle)command;
   managed.setApplicationContext(context);
   managed.initialize();
   if (managed.isValidate()) {
      managed.execute();
   } else {
      Collection errors = managed.getErrors();
   }
   managed.destroy();
} else {
   command.execute();
}
}
```

The calling sequence of the `ManagedLifecycle` is richer with functionality compared with its single
method version. First it passes required application data, calls the initialize method, performs validation,
and then calls the execute method.

> **Allowing the client invoker to pass resources to the command is a very powerful
> concept referred to as IOC inversion of control. This eliminates the need for the
> Command class to look up services and resources that are available to the invoker.**

Strategy

The Strategy pattern allows you to replace algorithms on the fly. To implement the solution, you represent each algorithm as a strategy class. The application then delegates to the current strategy class to execute the strategy specific algorithm. Figure 3-14 shows the UML for the strategy pattern alongside the
example for this section.

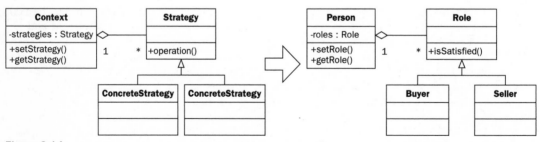

Figure 3-14

A common mistake in domain modeling is the overuse of *subtyping*. A subtype should be created only when a specific "is-a" type relationship can be described between a subtype and its super-type. For example, when modeling a person within a domain model, it is tempting to create a subtype for each role for which a person is a participating. There is no wrong way of modeling a problem, but in this case each person can take on several roles. This doesn't pass the "is-a" relationship test for subtyping. It is fitting that a person's behavior varies by his role; this concept can be expressed using the Strategy pattern.

The example application in this section looks at the roles of buyers and sellers, showing how their differing behavior can be abstracted out into a strategy.

This is a mistake locking each person into one role or the other. The need to be able to switch between the behaviors of classes in a class hierarchy is the motivation for using the Strategy pattern. Figure 3-15 shows the wrong way to model the "play's a role" relationship.

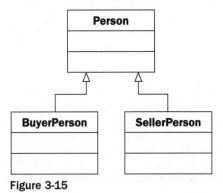

Figure 3-15

The Strategy pattern is made up of an interface that defines the pluggable behavior, implementing subclasses to define the behavior, and then an object to make use of the strategy.

Strategy

The solution is to model each role as a class and delegate role-specific behavior from the `Person` class to the `Role` current State. First, look at the behavior that will differ by the current state object. The example uses the interface `Role` to declare the strategy behavior, and the two concrete classes, `Buyer` and `Seller`, to implement the differing behavior.

To provide a little context to the example, the `Buyer` and `Seller` are trying to agree on a product price. The `isSatisified()` method is passed a `Product` and a `Price` and both parties must determine if the deal is acceptable:

```java
package wrox.pattern.strategy;

public interface Role {

    public boolean isSatisfied( Product product, double price );
}
```

Of course, the `Seller` and `Buyer` have differing objectives. The `Seller` is looking to make a profit, setting a 20 percent profit margin on any products sold. The following code makes that assumption:

```java
package wrox.pattern.strategy;
public class Seller implements Role {

  /*
   * Seller will be happy if they make 20% profit on whatever they sell.
   * (non-Javadoc)
   * @see wrox.Pattern.strategy.Role#isSatisfied(wrox.Pattern.strategy.Product,
double)
   */
  public boolean isSatisfied(Product product, double price) {
    if (price - product.getCost() > product.getCost() * .2) {
      return true;
    } else {
      return false;
    }
  }
}
```

The `Seller`, on the other hand, is looking for a product that is within a spending limit. It is important to note that the `Buyer` class is not limited to the methods described by the `Role` interface, making it possible to establish the `limit` member variable in the `Buyer` class that is not present in the `Seller` class.

The algorithm for what is acceptable is an arbitrary part of this example, but it is set so that the `Buyer` cannot spend above the chosen limit and will not pay more that 200 percent of the initial product cost. The role of `Buyer` is expressed in the `isSatisfied()` method:

```java
package wrox.Pattern.strategy;
public class Buyer implements Role {

  private double limit;

  public Buyer(double limit) {
    this.limit= limit;
  }
  /*
   * The buyer is happy if he can afford the product,
   *  and the price is less then 200% over cost.
   * @see wrox.Pattern.strategy.Role#isSatisfied(wrox.Pattern.strategy.Product,
double)
   */
  public boolean isSatisfied(Product product, double price) {
    if ( price < limit && price < product.getCost() * 2 ) {
      return true;
    } else {
      return false;
    }

  }
}
```

The code example that follows uses a class for the abstraction of a product. It's a data object that is part of the scenario. The code is as follows:

```
package wrox.pattern.strategy;
public class Product {
  private String name;
  private String description;
  private double cost;

  public Product(String name, String description, double cost) {
      this.name = name;
      this.description = description;
      this.cost = cost;
  }
  // Setters and Getter Omitted.
```

The next section looks at the class that uses the pluggable strategy.

Context

Next, let's look at the `Person` class that manages the `Role` objects. First, the `Person` class has an association with the `Role` interface. In addition, it is important to note that there is a setter and getter for the `Role`. This allows the person's roles to change as the program executes. It's also much cleaner code. This example uses two roles: `Buyer` and `Seller`. In the future, other `Role` implementing objects such as `Wholesaler`, `Broker`, and others can be added because there is no dependency to the specific subclasses:

```
package wrox.pattern.strategy;

public class Person {
  private String name;
  private Role role;
  public Person(String name) {
    this.name= name;
  }
  public Role getRole() {
    return role;
  }
  public void setRole(Role role) {
    this.role= role;
  }
```

Another key point is that the satisfied method of the `Person` class delegates the `Role` specific behavior to its `Role` interface. *Polymorphism* allows the correct underlying object to be chosen:

```
public boolean satisfied(Product product, double offer) {
    return role.isSatisfied(product, offer);
  }
}
```

Now, the code of the pattern has been implemented. Next, lets view what behavior an application can exhibit by implementing this pattern. To start, you can establish `Products`, `People`, and `Roles`:

```
package wrox.pattern.strategy;

public class Person {
// previous methods omitted.

  public static void main(String[] args) {
      Product house= new Product("house", "4 Bedroom North Arlington", 200000);
      Product condo= new Product("condo", "2 Bedroom McLean", 100000);
      Person tim= new Person("Tim");
      Person allison= new Person("Allison");
```

You are buying and selling houses. The next step is to establish initial roles and assign the roles to the people. The people will then exhibit the behavior of the role they have been assigned:

```
      tim.setRole(new Buyer(500000));
      allison.setRole(new Seller());

      if (!allison.satisfied(house, 200000)) {
        System.out.println("offer of 200,000 is no good for the seller");
      }
      if (!tim.satisfied(house, 600000)) {
        System.out.println("offer of 600,000 is no good for the buyer");
      }
      if (tim.satisfied(house, 390000) && allison.satisfied(house, 390000)) {
        System.out.println("They Both agree with 390,000 ");
```

To further demonstrate the capabilities of the Strategy pattern, switch the initial Seller to the Buyer by calling setRole() on the Person object. It is possible to switch to a Buyer without modifying the Person object:

```
      allison.setRole(new Buyer(190000));
      if (allison.satisfied(condo, 110000)) {
        System.out.println("As a buyer she can afford the condo ");
      }
    }
  }
}
```

By implementing the Strategy pattern, it is possible to change an object's behavior on the fly with no affect on its implementation. This is a very powerful tool in software design. In the next section, the composite patterns will build on the same principle of abstracting behavior to treat a class hierarchy with a single common interface.

Composite

The Composite design pattern allows you to treat a collection of objects as if they were one thing. In this way you can reduce the complexity of the code required if you were going to handle collections as special cases. Figure 3-16 shows the structure of the composite pattern in conjunction with the classes implementing the pattern in this example.

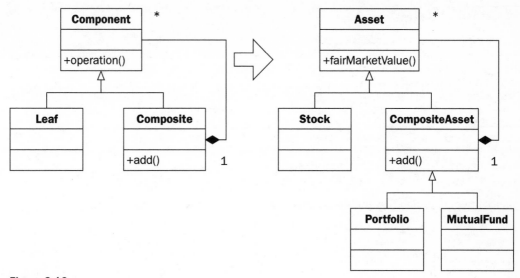

Figure 3-16

The example used here to demonstrate this behavior is a portfolio management system that consists of stocks and mutual funds. A mutual fund is a collection of stocks, but you would like to apply a common interface to both stocks and mutual funds to simplify the handling of both. This allows you to perform operations such as calculate Fair Market Value, buy, sell, and assess percent contribution with a common interface. The Composition pattern would clearly reduce the complexity of building these operations. The pattern consists of the classes, a leaf, and composite. Figure 3-16 should look similar to the example built in the earlier section of this chapter.

Component

First is the component interface; it declares the common interface that both the single and composite nodes will implement. The example is using `fairMarketValue`, an operation that can be calculated over stocks, mutual funds, and portfolios:

```
package wrox.pattern.composite;

public interface Asset {

    public double fairMarketValue();
}
```

Leaf

The leaf class represents the singular atomic data type implementing the component interface. In this example, a `Stock` class will represent the leaf node of the pattern. The `Stock` class is a leaf node in that it does not hold a reference to any other `Asset` objects:

```
package wrox.pattern.composite;

public class Stock implements Asset {

  private String name;
  private double price;
  private double quantity;

  public Stock(String name, double price, double quantity) {
    this.name= name;
    this.price= price;
    this.quantity= quantity;
  }
```

Stock price is calculated by multiplying share price times quantity:

```
  public double fairMarketValue() {

    return price * quantity;
  }
}
```

Composite

The following section declares the Composite object called CompositeAsset. Notice that CompositeAsset is declared abstract. A valid composite asset, such as a mutual fund or portfolio, extends this abstract class:

```
package wrox.pattern.composite;
import java.util.ArrayList;
import java.util.Iterator;
import java.util.List;

public abstract class CompositeAsset implements Asset {
  private List assets= new ArrayList();

  public void add(Asset asset) {
    assets.add(asset);
  }
```

Iterate through the child investments. If one of the child investments happens to also be a composite asset, it will be handled recursively without requiring a special case. So, for example, it would be possible to have a mutual fund comprising mutual funds:

```
  public double fairMarketValue() {
    double total = 0;
    for (Iterator i= assets.iterator(); i.hasNext();  ) {
      Asset asset= (Asset)i.next();
      total = total + asset.fairMarketValue();
    }
    return total;
  }
}
```

Once that is complete, what follows is to build the concrete composite objects: `MutualFund` and `Portfolio`. Nothing significant is required for the `Mutual Fund` class; its behavior is inherited from the `CompositeAsset`:

```java
package wrox.pattern.composite;

public class MutualFund extends CompositeAsset{

  private String name;

  public MutualFund(String name) {
    this.name = name;
  }

}
```

The `Portfolio` class extends `CompositeAsset` as well; the difference is that it calls the super class directly and modifies the resulting calculation for fair market. It subtracts a 2 percent management fee:

```java
package wrox.pattern.composite;

public class Portfolio extends CompositeAsset {
  private String name;
  public Portfolio(String name) {
    this.name= name;
  }
  /* Market value - Management Fee
   * @see wrox.Pattern.composite.CompositeAsset#fairMarketValue()
   */
  public double fairMarketValue() {
    return super.fairMarketValue() - super.fairMarketValue() * .02;
  }

}
```

The only thing left to do is exercise the code. The next class is of an `Investor`. The `Investor` is the client code taking advantage of the Composite design pattern:

```java
package wrox.pattern.composite;

public class Investor {
  private String name;
  private Portfolio porfolio;
  public Investor(String name, Portfolio portfolio) {
    this.name= name;
    this.porfolio= portfolio;
  }
```

By calling the fair market value on the investor's portfolio, the Composite pattern will be able to traverse the collection of stocks and mutual funds to determine the value of the whole thing without worrying about the object structure:

```
public double calcNetworth( ){

   return porfolio.fairMarketValue();
}

public static void main(String[] args) {
    Portfolio portfolio= new Portfolio("Frequently Used Money");
    Investor investor= new Investor("IAS", portfolio);

    portfolio.add(new Stock("wrox", 450, 100));

    MutualFund fund= new MutualFund("Don Scheafer's Intellectual Capital");
    fund.add(new Stock("ME", 35, 100) );
    fund.add(new Stock("CV", 22, 100) );
    fund.add(new Stock("BA", 10, 100) );
    portfolio.add(fund);

    double total =investor.calcNetworth();

    System.out.println("total =" + total);
}
}
```

With the composite pattern, it is very easy to simplify operations over complex data structures.

Summary

This chapter gave you a strong appreciation of the value of patterns in developing Java solutions. They are critical in learning from the experience of others, but also in understanding APIs used by the Java platform.

In this chapter, you learned about patterns, why they're important, tricks to understanding them, and several important patterns in Java programming.

Now that you have learned how to think like a Java developer, the rest of the book will focus on practical examples of developing Java solutions. These chapters will not be comprehensive examinations of the technologies in each chapter, but rather a real-life example of a development problem, which is solved using various technologies.

The first chapter in this new phase of the book is Chapter 4, "Developing Effective User Interfaces with JFC." In this chapter, you will learn how to use Swing to build Java desktop applications.

4

Developing Effective User Interfaces with JFC

Java Foundation Classes (JFC) is a package of libraries for developing robust graphical user displays for client-side applications that can be implemented on enterprise systems. The JFC API libraries comprise five different components:

- ❑ **AWT.** The Abstract Windowing Toolkit (AWT) classes are comprised of legacy graphics code from Java 1.x that were developed to create simple user interfaces for applications and applets.

- ❑ **Accessibility.** The Accessibility classes accommodate assistive technologies that provide access to information in user interface components.

- ❑ **Java 2D.** The Java 2D classes contain a broad set of advanced graphics APIs that allow users to create and manipulate image, shape, and text components.

- ❑ **Drag and Drop.** The Drag and Drop classes allow users to initiate drag operations so that components can be dropped on designated target areas. This is accomplished by setting up a drop target listener to handle drop events and a management object to handle drag and drop operations.

- ❑ **Swing.** The Swing classes are built atop of the AWT classes to provide high-quality GUI components for enterprise applications.

Large tomes have been written about JFC, specifically Swing libraries and their advanced presentation features, with numerous pages of APIs affiliated with those libraries that could easily be acquired by your Integrated Development Environment (IDE) or the Internet during your development activities. Along with those library presentations were some simple applications that provided little instructional value other than to demonstrate how things work in a basic fashion. Rather than getting bogged down with a recital of those voluminous API's, this chapter will concentrate the discussion on many of the Swing features that you will need to incorporate into your professional development activities to be successful. You'll learn advanced GUI applications that combine multiple layout managers to achieve relevant presentation applications that manage data and navigation flow in an efficient manner. All of the sample applications incorporate listeners and their interfaces to manage events generated by users in their navigation activities along with Gang of Four (GoF) design patterns to promote best practices in your modeling and implementation operations.

This chapter starts by demonstrating some foundation knowledge about layout managers so that you can conceptualize Swing layout designs from a high-level perspective and then implement them using JFC libraries in an efficient manner. With a solid handle on what these libraries can do for you, you will be able to approach your development tasks with greater confidence, which will result in more germane product development. The next two sections of this chapter will cover some practical applications, the first being an Annotation Editor that links meta data to passages in a text file followed by an illustration of how an Installation Wizard can easily be crafted with JFC libraries and GoF design patterns to manage navigation flows and data persistence.

Layout Managers

Layout managers are used in Java Swing applications to arrange objects when they are added to a `Container` object. The `setLayout()` method is used to override default layout managers appropriated to `JPanel` (`FlowLayout`) and `JFrame` (`BorderLayout`) containers.

This section of the chapter will discuss seven important layout managers:

- ❑   BorderLayout
- ❑   BoxLayout
- ❑   CardLayout
- ❑   FlowLayout
- ❑   GridbagLayout
- ❑   GridLayout
- ❑   SpringLayout

All of these layout managers will be covered at length within interesting Swing applications that implement listeners to react to user selections on various visualization components. Most importantly, these applications will demonstrate how the different layout managers can be amalgamated to craft relevant GUI presentations.

BorderLayout

The `BorderLayout` manager is the default layout for a frame. A `BorderLayout` uses five regions in its display space. Those regions are generally referred to as: NORTH, SOUTH, WEST, EAST, and CENTER. Those regions generally refer to the same attributes that a map would use. The NORTH and SOUTH regions extend to the top and bottom areas of the Container, while the EAST and WEST regions extend from the bottom of the NORTH and top of the SOUTH regions and to the left and right sides of the Container, respectively. The CENTER region occupies all of the residual space the remains in the center of the Container.

The `BorderLayout` manager is typically generated by instantiating a new `BorderLayout` class with a constructor that has no parameters, or with a constructor that specifies two integer values that specify the horizontal and vertical pixels between components in this fashion: new `BorderLayout(int hGap, int vGap)`.

The constructor methods for the `BorderLayout` manager are shown in the method summary table that follows.

Method	Description
`public BorderLayout()`	No parameters
`public BorderLayout(int hGap, int vGap)`	The `hGap` and `vGap` integer parameters specify the horizontal and vertical pixels between components

The following `BorderLayout` example emulates a test application that quizzes the user with five fairly simple arithmetic queries. As a user sequentially steps through the test questions, a progress bar will track where the test taker is with respect to the end of the test and what the running score is. Figure 4-1 provides a model of the application and shows how the different GUI components will occupy the `BorderLayout` panel.

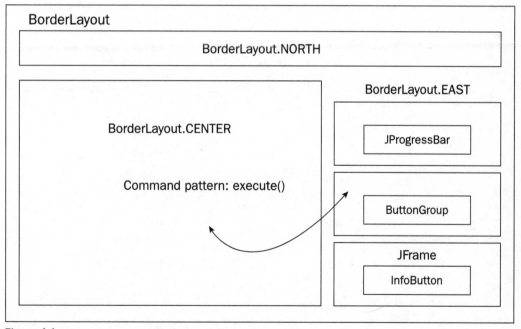

Figure 4-1

The `BorderLayoutPanel` application will incorporate the Command pattern to handle button requests for quiz questions and the answers to those questions by the user. Some of the benefits and drawbacks of the Command pattern are outlined in the table that follows.

Pattern	Benefits	Consequences
Command	Acts as a delivery mechanism that carries behavior rather than data in an application Delivers encapsulated actions to a method or object for easier program control.	Creation of a lot of little classes to accommodate component actions

The following code segment outlines the `BorderLayoutPanel` application how the model in Figure 4-1 is realized:

```
[BorderLayoutPanel.java]
// package name and import statements omitted

public class BorderLayoutPanel extends JPanel implements ActionListener {
```

The following section performs object declaration and initialization activities necessary for the Arithmetic Test application. Many of these actions are omitted from this example, as well as many of the layout manager programs, to provide better reading clarity. Note that the `ButtonText` variable uses HTML scripting text to allow for the spanning of text in the `JButton` Swing component to which it will be applied. The Command pattern interface is implemented so that the application can polymorphically derive proper event actions during run time based on the user's navigation operations:

```
private static Logger logger = Logger.getLogger("FlowLayout");

// some declarations omitted for the sake of brevity [Please check download code]
private final static String[] ButtonText =
    { "<html><center><font size='+2'>Basic Arithmetic</font><br><br>( click for
question )</center></html>" };
private static String[] questions =
                { "1, 2, What is 1 + 1 ?, 0, 1, 2, 3",
                  "2, 0, What is 1 - 1 ?, 0, 1, 2, 3",
                  "3, 2, What is 5 - 3 ?, 0, 1, 2, 3",
                  "4, 3, What is 4 - 1 ?, 0, 1, 2, 3" };

private Hashtable hashtableQuestions = new Hashtable();

public interface Command {
    public void execute();
}

public BorderLayoutPanel(String FrameTitle) {
    initComponents();
}
```

The `initComponents()` method is created to separate relevant initialization tasks so that it can be invoked by the constructor during inception and when the user has finished the test and wants to reset the application. Here, all of the panels are derived that will be deployed by the `BorderLayout` manager:

```
public void initComponents() {
    try {
        removeAll();

        northPanel = new JPanel();
        answerPanel = new JPanel();
        centerPanel = new JPanel();
        eastPanel = new JPanel();
        msgText = new JLabel("Click button to start!");
        InfoScreenButton = new RulesButton("Rules");
        optGroup = new ButtonGroup();
        progressBar = new JProgressBar();

        questionCount = 1;
        correctAnswerCount = 0;
        numberQuestionsAnswered = 0;

        String[] strLine;
        for (int x = 0; x < questions.length; x++) {
            strLine = questions[x].split(",");
            hashtableQuestions.put(strLine[0], strLine);
        }

        buttons = new JQuestionButton[numberButtons];
        for (int i = 0; i < numberButtons; i++) {
            buttons[i] = new JQuestionButton("Question");
            buttons[i].setText(ButtonText[i]);
            centerPanel.add(buttons[i]);
            buttons[i].addActionListener(this);
        }

        InfoScreenButton.addActionListener(this);
```

At this point in the application, the layout of the Swing components are established and the answers for the quiz are saved to the ButtonGroup component for visual rendering. It is important to note how layout managers are intermingled to get the desired visual effect. The answerPanel uses the GridLayout class to enforce 0 rows and 1 column so that the answers available to the user are lined up in a single column prior to being added to the eastPanel component below the progress bar and above the rules button:

```
        centerPanel.setLayout(new GridLayout(0, 1));

        answerPanel.setLayout(new GridLayout(0, 1));

        Answer = new JRadioButtonAnswer[numberAnswers];
        for (int i = 0; i < numberAnswers; i++) {
            Answer[i] = new JRadioButtonAnswer(A[i]);
            answerPanel.add(Answer[i]);
            Answer[i].addActionListener(this);
            optGroup.add(Answer[i]);
        }

        BlankRadioButton = new JRadioButton();
        optGroup.add(BlankRadioButton);
```

```
            northPanel.setBackground(new Color(255, 255, 220));
            northPanel.add(msgText);

            eastPanel.setLayout(new GridLayout(0, 1));
            eastPanel.add(progressBar);
            eastPanel.add(answerPanel);
            eastPanel.add(InfoScreenButton);

            setLayout(new BorderLayout());
            add(eastPanel, "East");
            add(northPanel, "North");
            add(centerPanel, "Center");

            setSize(600, 600);
            questionAnswered = true;
            answerPanel.setVisible(false);

            progressBar.setMaximum(numberQuestions);
            progressBar.setValue(0);
            progressBar.setIndeterminate(false);

            resetButton = new JResetButton("Reset Game");
            resetButton.addActionListener(this);

        } catch (Exception e) {
            logger.info("Exception: " + e.toString());
        }
    }
```

The JQuestionButton class implements the Command interface so that user invocations on that button will dynamically determine — through the ActionListener implementation — that the execute() method associated with this button should be invoked. Once invoked, the application will use a key based on the question count to search the hashtableQuestions collection class for the proper question to render on the display:

```
private class JQuestionButton extends JButton implements Command {

    public JQuestionButton(String caption) { super(caption); }
    public void execute() {
        try {
            if (numberQuestionsAnswered < numberQuestions) {
                answerPanel.setVisible(true);
                northPanel.setBackground(new Color(255, 255, 220));
                if (questionAnswered) {
                    optGroup.setSelected(BlankRadioButton.getModel(), true);
                    questionAnswered = false;
                    try {
                        String key = Integer.toString(questionCount);
                        if (hashtableQuestions.containsKey(key)) {
                            Question = (String[]) hashtableQuestions.get(key);
                            questionCount++;
                        } else {
                            logger.info("key NOT found" + key);
```

```
                              }
                      } catch (Exception e) { throw e; }

                      msgText.setText(Question[2]);
                      for (int i = 0, x = 3; i < numberAnswers; i++) {
                          Answer[i].setText(Question[x + i]);
                      }
                  }
              }
          }
      } catch (Exception e) {
          logger.info("Exception: " + e.toString());
      }
  }
}
```

The JRadioButtonAnswer class also implements the Command interface to polymorphically determine
behavior needed when a user clicks on the radio button answer to the question posed by the test application. If the user response is correct, the background color of the northPanel will be turned green,
indicating a positive response to the question, and if another question is available, the JButton
setText() method will be used to display the user's score and the progressBar component will
exhibit the percentage of the test that the user has covered:

```
private class JRadioButtonAnswer extends JRadioButton implements Command {
    public JRadioButtonAnswer(String caption) {}
    public void execute() {
        try {
            if (!questionAnswered) {
                if (Question[1].trim().equals(getText().trim())) {
                    msgText.setText("Correct!!!");
                    northPanel.setBackground(Color.green);
                    correctAnswerCount++;
                } else {
                    msgText.setText(
                        "Wrong!!! The correct answer is: " + Question[1]);
                    northPanel.setBackground(Color.red);
                }

                questionAnswered = true;
                numberQuestionsAnswered++;

                buttons[0].setText(
                    ("<html><center><font size='+2'>( click for question )</font>"
                    + "<br><br>"
                    + " Score= "
                    + correctAnswerCount
                    + "/"
                    + numberQuestionsAnswered).toString()
                    + "</center></html>");

                progressBar.setValue(numberQuestionsAnswered);
                progressBar.setStringPainted(true);
                progressBar.setString(
                Double.toString(Math.round(progressBar.getPercentComplete() * 100))+
"%");

                if (numberQuestionsAnswered >= numberQuestions) {
```

149

```
                        buttons[0].setBackground(new Color(255, 255, 220));
                        buttons[0].setText("Finished. Score= " + String.valueOf(
(float) correctAnswerCount / (float) numberQuestionsAnswered * 100) + "%");
                        // setup reset button
                        answerPanel.removeAll();
                        answerPanel.add(resetButton);
                    }
                } else {
                    msgText.setText(
                    "You have answered this question, please select a new Question");
                }

            } catch (Exception e) {
                logger.info("Exception occured: " + e.toString());
            }
        }
    }
```

The `actionPerformed` method is an implementation of the `ActionListener` interface, which is invoked when an event is created by user operations. The `Command` pattern implementation determines which button was selected by the user and the proper `execute()` method to invoke based on that event:

```
public void actionPerformed(ActionEvent e) {
    Command obj = (Command) e.getSource();
    obj.execute();
}
```

The `RulesButton` class also implements the `Command` interface so that a new frame will be kicked off when a user selects the Rules button in the test application. The `JResetButton` button is used to supplant the answers in the `answerPanel` when all five questions have been answered by the test taker. This allows the user to retake the test by resetting the answers in the test. Ideally, you would want to randomize those answers to make the test more difficult, but this application was developed to demonstrate, in a simple fashion, how the `BorderLayout` class can be used with other layout managers to develop relevant GUI applications:

```
class RulesButton extends JButton implements Command {

    public RulesButton(String Title) { super(Title); }
    public void execute() {
        JLabel InfoLabel = new JLabel(
            "<html> How To Play:<br> Click on button to generate questions "
            + "on the right side of the user display. A progress bar will "
            + "indicate where the tester is with respect to the entire test.");
        JFrame InfoFrame = new JFrame("How To Play");
        InfoFrame.getContentPane().add(InfoLabel);
        InfoFrame.setSize(400, 150);
        InfoFrame.show();
    }
}

private class JResetButton extends JButton implements Command {

    public JResetButton(String caption) {
```

```
            super(caption);
        }
        public void execute() {
            initComponents();
        }
    }
    // main method omitted for the sake of brevity


}
```

Figure 4-2 represents the finished product of the BorderLayoutPanel application. Test questions are rendered in the NORTH section of the BorderLayout, while test progress statistics, answers, and a Rules component reside on the EAST. Users navigate through the test by clicking on the questionPanel in the BoderLayout.CENTER, which will retrieve and display the questions for the user to answer.

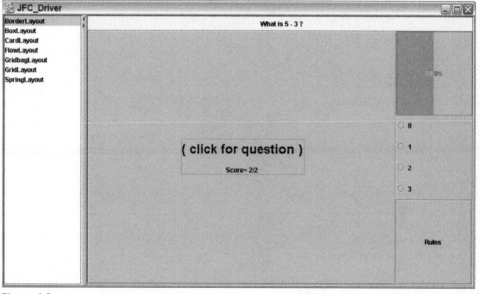

Figure 4-2

BoxLayout

The BoxLayout manager arranges components horizontally from left to right, or vertically from top to bottom, without the wraparound capability in the FlowLayout manager. The implementation of the BoxLayout manager warrants the instantiation of the BoxLayout class with two parameters, the first being the Container panel that will be displayed, followed by an integer axis value that indicates the placement of the components on the panel. An axis value of Boxlayout.X_AXIS indicates left to right layout management, while a value of BoxLayout.Y_AXIS signifies a top to bottom layout.

The constructor methods for the BoxLayout manager are shown in the following method summary table.

Method	Description
public BoxLayout(Container panel, int axis)	The panel parameter signifies the container that will be mapped out, while the axis parameter indicates where the components will be placed. An axis value of BoxLayout.Y_AXIS indicates left to right placement and an axis value of BoxLayout.Y_AXIS indicates a top to bottom placement.

The following BoxLayout example will apply the Decorator pattern in its implementation so that users can add behavior dynamically through drag and drop operations. Figure 4-3 provides a model of the application and how the different image components occupy the BoxLayout panel real estate.

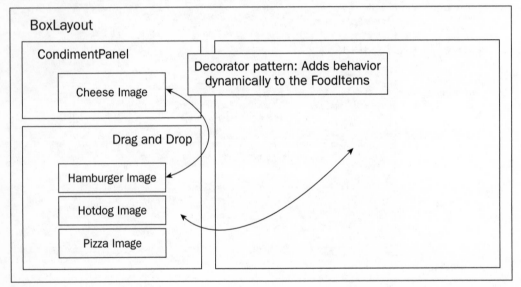

Figure 4-3

Dynamic behavior transfer occurs when a user drags the Cheese condiment image onto one of the three food item images on the left panel. Some of the benefits of the `Decorator` pattern are defined in the table below.

Pattern	Benefits	Consequences
Decorator	Can add or remove responsibilities of individual objects dynamically without affecting other objects during run time A class can be wrapped in another object to provide added functionalities	Generates a lot of similar objects

The `FoodCourt` interface allows the `BoxLayout` application to dynamically add behaviors to the three different food items (Hamburger, Hotdog, and Pizza) during run time when the Cheese object is dragged and dropped on the food items. Additionally, get methods are modeled so that relevant data can be retrieved from objects. The `FoodCourt` interface class allows behaviors to be defined across the class hierarchy of the `BorderLayout` sample application with private implementations to address individual needs:

```
[FoodCourt.java]
// package name omitted
public interface FoodCourt {
    public String getName();
    public float getCost();
    public FoodGraphic getGraphic();
    public void addBehavior(String b);
    public String getDescription();
    public void setGraphicHandler(FoodCourt h);

    public void handleClick();
}
```

The `FoodGraphic` class controls the user events associated with the three different food images. The `FoodImage` class is implemented to handle image files affiliated with the different food items in the `BoxLayout` demonstration. The `paintComponent(Graphics g)` method ensures that image files are drawn properly throughout the lifetime of the `JPanel` component `FoodImage`:

```
[FoodGraphic.java]
// package name and import statements omitted

public class FoodGraphic extends JPanel implements DropTargetListener,
MouseListener {

  // declarations omitted for the sake of brevity [Please check download code]
    private class FoodImage extends JPanel {
        private Image image = null;
        public FoodImage(String imageFile) {
            super();
            URL url = FoodImage.class.getResource(imageFile);
            image = Toolkit.getDefaultToolkit().getImage(url);
        }
```

```
      public void paintComponent(Graphics g) {
         super.paintComponent(g);
         g.drawImage(image, 0, 0, this);
      }
   }

   public FoodGraphic(FoodCourt hand, String imageFile, int w, int h, boolean
tipsFlag) {
       this(hand, imageFile, w, h);
       updateTips = tipsFlag;
   }
```

The `FoodGraphic` method receives a handler object from the `Food` class, which is instantiated in the `FoodItems` class when the three different food items are created. A new `dropTarget` object reference is created with the `DropTarget` class to tell the application that the Food object is willing to accept drops during drag and drop operations.

The `DropTargetListener` interface performs callback notifications on registered subjects to signal event changes on the target being dropped on:

```
   public FoodGraphic(FoodCourt hand, String imageFile, int w, int h) {
       super();
       handler = hand;
       imageFileName = imageFile;

       imagew = w;
       imageh = h;

       dropTarget = new DropTarget(this, DnDConstants.ACTION_COPY_OR_MOVE, this);
       setBackground(Color.white);
       name = handler.getName();

       image = new FoodImage(imageFile);
       image.setPreferredSize(new Dimension(imagew,imageh));
       image.setMaximumSize(new Dimension(imagew,imageh));
       image.setMinimumSize(new Dimension(imagew,imageh));
       image.setAlignmentX(CENTER_ALIGNMENT);

       label = new JLabel(name,SwingConstants.CENTER);
       label.setPreferredSize(new Dimension(imagew,25));
       label.setMaximumSize(new Dimension(imagew,25));
       label.setMinimumSize(new Dimension(imagew,25));
       label.setAlignmentX(CENTER_ALIGNMENT);

       setLayout(new BoxLayout(this, BoxLayout.Y_AXIS));
       setBorder(BorderFactory.createLineBorder(Color.blue, 2));

       add(image);
       add(label);

       setToolTipText(name);

       addMouseListener(this);
   }
```

A method summary of the `DropTargetListener` interface class and its methods is illustrated in the following table.

Method	Description
void dragEnter(DropTargetDragEvent d)	Method called when the mouse pointer enters the operable part of the drop site for the target registered with a listener
void dragExit(DropTargetEvent d)	Method called when the mouse pointer has exited the operable part of the drop site for the target registered with a listener
void dragOver(DropTargetDragEvent d)	Method called when the mouse pointer is still over the operable part of the drop site for the target registered with a listener
void drop(DropTargetDropEvent d)	Method called when the drag operation has terminated with a drop on the operable part of the drop site for the target registered with a listener
void dropActionChanged(DropTargetDragEvent d)	Method called if the user has modified the current drop gesture

The `drop(DropTargetDropEvent e)` method in the following code implements the `DataFlavor` class, which represents a format style that can be conveyed across an application. If the flavor being dragged and dropped across the GUI display is supported and verified by the `isDataFlavorSupported` method, then the drag and drop operation of the cheese condiment onto one of the three food items will be allowed to occur and the behavior affiliated with that operation will be added to the object handler so that a description of that action can be obtained through the `getDescription()` method.

The `dragEnter` and `dragExit` methods are used to visually color the borders of the items being dragged and dropped in the GUI presentation:

```
public void drop(DropTargetDropEvent e) {
    try {
        DataFlavor stringFlavor = DataFlavor.stringFlavor;
        Transferable tr = e.getTransferable();
        if (e.isDataFlavorSupported(stringFlavor)) {
            String behavior = (String)tr.getTransferData(stringFlavor);
            e.acceptDrop(DnDConstants.ACTION_COPY_OR_MOVE);
            e.dropComplete(true);

            handler.addBehavior(behavior);

            if (handler != null && updateTips) {
                setToolTipText(handler.getDescription());
            }
        } else {
```

```
                e.rejectDrop();
            }
        } catch (Exception ex) {}
            setBorder(BorderFactory.createLineBorder(Color.blue, 2));
    }

    public void dragEnter(DropTargetDragEvent e) {
        setBorder(BorderFactory.createLineBorder(Color.red, 3));
    }
    public void dragExit(DropTargetEvent e) {
        setBorder(BorderFactory.createLineBorder(Color.blue, 2));
    }
    public void dragOver(DropTargetDragEvent e){}
    public void dropActionChanged(DropTargetDragEvent e) { }

    public void setHandler(FoodCourt h) {
        handler = h;
    }

    public void setBorderColor(Color col) {
        setBorder(BorderFactory.createLineBorder(col, 2));
    }
```

Click-handling routines are implemented through the FoodCourt interface with the assistance of the mouse event listeners. The Food class handleClick() method is invoked when a user clicks on the hamburger, hotdog, and pizza food items:

```
    public void addClickHandler(FoodCourt h) {
        clickHandler = h;
    }

    public void mouseClicked(MouseEvent e) {
        if (clickHandler != null) {
            clickHandler.handleClick();
        }
    }

    public void mouseEntered(MouseEvent e) {}
    public void mouseExited(MouseEvent e) {}
    public void mousePressed(MouseEvent e) {}
    public void mouseReleased(MouseEvent e) {}
}
```

The CondimentPanel class generates a decorator object for the cheese item and associates a coin value with that object so that it can be passed along to the food item it is decorated with. A hamburger costs $1.35 alone, but will add to, or decorate, that cost by 35 cents if cheese is appended to it. The panel layout consists of a combination GridLayout manager called pictures, with the cheese image and label, added to a BoxLayout manager that combines this panel with a label component for presentation in the GUI display above the three different food items:

```
[CondimentPanel.java]
// package name and import statements omitted
```

```
public class CondimentPanel extends JPanel {

  private static Logger logger = Logger.getLogger("CondimentPanel");

  JPanel pictures = null;
  GridLayout pictureLayout = null;
  Hashtable condimentPrices = new Hashtable();

  public CondimentPanel(String title) {
    super();
    setBackground(Color.white);

    pictures = new JPanel();
    pictureLayout = new GridLayout(1, 1);
    pictures.setLayout(pictureLayout);
    pictures.setAlignmentX(CENTER_ALIGNMENT);
    pictures.setBorder(BorderFactory.createLineBorder(Color.red));

    pictures.add(new FoodDecoratorGraphic("Cheese", "resources/Cheese.gif",
0.35f));
    condimentPrices.put("Cheese", new Float(0.35f));

    JLabel label = new JLabel(title, SwingConstants.CENTER);
    label.setPreferredSize(new Dimension(200, 25));
    label.setMinimumSize(new Dimension(200, 25));
    label.setMaximumSize(new Dimension(200, 25));
    label.setAlignmentX(CENTER_ALIGNMENT);

    setLayout(new BoxLayout(this, BoxLayout.Y_AXIS));

    add(label);
    add(pictures);
  }
}
```

The Food class implements the FoodCourt interface so that the application can polymorphically discover the methods needed for processing during run time. The FoodItems class invokes this method three times for the three different food items displayed in the application (hamburger, hotdog, pizza):

```
[Food.java]
// package name and import statements omitted
public class Food implements FoodCourt {

  private static Logger logger = Logger.getLogger("Food");
  private FoodItems item = null;
  private FoodGraphic graphic = null;
  private String name = null;
  private float cost = 0.0f;

  public Food(FoodItems fooditem, String name, String imageFile, float cost) {
    super();

    item = fooditem;
    name = name;
    cost = cost;
```

```
            graphic = new FoodGraphic(this, imageFile, 100, 35);
            graphic.addClickHandler(this);
    }

    public String getName() { return name; }

    public FoodGraphic getGraphic() { return graphic; }

    public float getCost() { return cost; }
```

The addBehavior(String b) method takes the food item object reference and invokes the
addMemberBehavior(String name, String b) method to aggregate the behavior of your only
condiment item, cheese, with the food item it is being added to. If the food item alone is clicked by the
user, the handle event method named handleClick() will add the food item description to the test area
display using the static class DisplayPanel:

```
    public void addBehavior(String b) { item.addMemberBehavior(name, b); }

    public String getDescription() { return name; }

    public void setGraphicHandler(FoodCourt h) { graphic.setHandler(h); }


    public void handleClick() {


        DisplayPanel.write(getDescription() + " ");
        DisplayPanel.write("selected. That'll cost you " + getCost());
        DisplayPanel.writeLine("");
    }
}
```

The final class that will be discussed for the BoxLayoutPanel application is the FoodItems class.
FoodItems implements its layout in a similar fashion to the CondimentPanel class. A GridLayout
manager is crafted to accommodate the food item images, which is then added to a BoxLayout manager
for the final presentation. The static helper component named Box.createVerticalGlue lets the application adjust when the parent container is resized by the user so that the box layout maintains its
spacing:

```
[FoodItems.java]
// package name and import statements omitted
public class FoodItems extends JPanel {

    private static Logger logger = Logger.getLogger("FoodItems");

    // declarations omitted for the sake of brevity [Please check download code]
    public FoodItems(BoxLayoutPanel p, Hashtable condimentPrices) {
        super();

        this.name = "Condiments";
        this.panel = p;
        this.condimentPrices = condimentPrices;
```

```
         members = new HashMap();

         setBackground(new Color(204,204,102));

         pictures = new JPanel();
         pictureLayout = new GridLayout(3, 2);
         pictureLayout.setHgap(5);
         pictureLayout.setVgap(5);
         pictures.setLayout(pictureLayout);
         pictures.setAlignmentX(CENTER_ALIGNMENT);

         imagePanel = new JPanel();
         imagePanel.setBackground(Color.white);
         imagePanel.setLayout(new BoxLayout(imagePanel, BoxLayout.X_AXIS));

         JLabel label = new JLabel("", SwingConstants.CENTER);
         label.setAlignmentX(CENTER_ALIGNMENT);
         label.setPreferredSize(new Dimension(200,20));
         label.setMinimumSize(new Dimension(200,20));
         label.setMaximumSize(new Dimension(200,20));

         setLayout(new BoxLayout(this, BoxLayout.Y_AXIS));

         Component padding = Box.createRigidArea(new Dimension(100, 1));
```

This code segment illustrates how the `Food` objects are instantiated and manipulated by the `addMember(FoodCourt fc)` method that adds a new food item to the members collection class structure for future reference and to the pictures panel for visual rendering:

```
         food = new Food(this, "Hamburger", "resources/Hamburger1.gif", 1.35f);
         addMember(food);
         food = new Food(this, "Hotdog", "resources/Hotdog1.gif", 1.15f);
         addMember(food);
         food = new Food(this, "Pizza", "resources/Pizza1.gif", 1.05f);
         addMember(food);

         add(label);
         add(padding);
         add(pictures);
         add(Box.createVerticalGlue());
     }

     public void addMember(FoodCourt fc) {
         if (!members.containsKey(fc.getName())) {
             members.put(fc.getName(), fc);
             pictures.add(fc.getGraphic());
         }
     }
```

The `addMemberBehavior(String n, String b)` method outputs the food item description and cost to the static `DisplayPanel` text area component. The `condimentPrices` collection class is used to derive the cost of the cheese condiment, the only condiment in the `BoxLayoutPanel` application, so that its cost can be added to the cost of the food item:

```
   public void addMemberBehavior(String n, String b) {

      Float condimentCost = (Float)condimentPrices.get(b.trim());

      FoodCourt m = (FoodCourt) members.get(n);
      DisplayPanel.writeLine("Adding " +
                         b +
                         " (" +
                         condimentCost +
                         ") to " +
                         m.getDescription() +
                         " which costs $" +
                         m.getCost() +
                         " for a total cost of $" +
                         (m.getCost() + condimentCost.floatValue())));
   }

   // getName(), getGraphic() and getDescription() methods omitted for better
clarity

   public String getDescription(String n) {
      FoodCourt m = (FoodCourt) members.get(n);
      if (m != null) {
         return m.getDescription();
      } else {
         return "";
      }
   }

   public void setGraphicHandler(FoodCourt h) {
      graphic.setHandler(h);
   }

}
```

The BoxLayoutPanel display is demonstrated in Figure 4-4. Users can drag and drop the cheese condiment on the three different food items to determine the total cost of the two products combined. Additionally, users can click on the individual food items to determine the cost of that single item. All events that are generated by mouse clicks or drag and drop operations are tracked by listener classes and logged to the text area display to track the users' navigation activities. The Decorator pattern implementation in the BoxLayoutPanel application allows behaviors to be dynamically aggregated during run time.

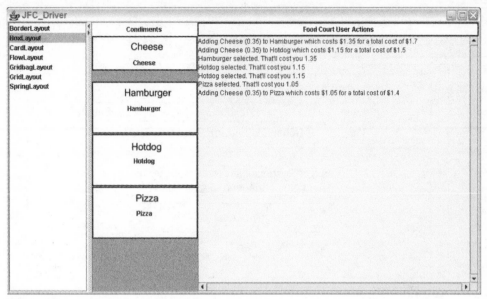

Figure 4-4

FlowLayout

The FlowLayout manager arranges components from left to right in the Container space; if the space on a line is exhausted, then the components that are part of this manager will flow to the next line. By default, all components of the FlowLayout manager are centered in a horizontal fashion on each line. Three different constructors can be invoked to instantiate a FlowLayout manager object. The first constructor requires no parameters while the second constructor requires an integer alignment value that indicates how components will be justified during construction. The last constructor method uses an integer alignment value like the aforementioned method, but also requires two integer values that specify horizontal and vertical gap values for pixel spacing.

The constructor methods for the FlowLayout manager are shown in the method summary table that follows.

Method	Description
public FlowLayout()	No parameters
public FlowLayout(int align)	Align parameter may be one of three class constants: LEFT, RIGHT, or CENTER to indicate how components will be justified
public FlowLayout (int align, int hGap, int vGap)	Where align indicates how the components will be justified and the hGap and vGap parameters specify the horizontal and vertical pixels between components

The following `FlowLayout` example accepts a dollar value from the user and calculates the coin distribution using the Chain of Responsibility pattern. Figure 4-5 provides a high-level view of the `FlowLayoutPanel` application and how the Swing components are positioned on the `FlowLayout` panel.

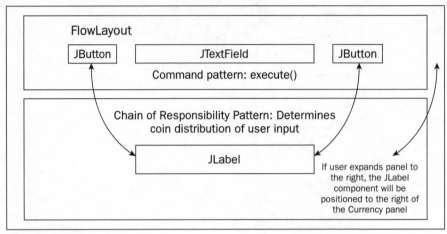

Figure 4-5

Request processing in the `FlowLayputPanel` application is handled with the Chain of Responsibility pattern that accepts the dollar amount from the user and cascades downward from the four different coin handlers (`QuarterHandler`, `DimeHandler`, `NickelHandler`, `PennyHandler`) until all the coins have been accounted for in the dollar amount specified by the user.

Pattern	Benefits	Consequences
Chain of Responsibility	Reduces coupling by allowing several objects the opportunity to handle a request Distributes responsibilities among objects	Requests can go unhandled with improper chain configuration

The `FlowLayoutPanel` class below illustrates how the `FlowLayout` manager can be implemented. This sample application implements the `JFormattedTextField` class to dictate how the data must be input by the user and the `NumberFormat` class to establish what that format will be. Two buttons are created as extensions to the `JButton` class, one for kicking off the Chain of Responsibility pattern named `"Determine Coins"` and the other for clearing the text in the coin display panel:

```
[FlowLayoutPanel.java]
// package name and import statements omitted

public class FlowLayoutPanel extends JPanel implements ActionListener,
PropertyChangeListener {
```

```
        private JFormattedTextField amountField;
        private NumberFormat amountDisplayFormat;
        private NumberFormat amountEditFormat;
        // some GUI component initializations/declarations omitted for the sake of brevity
        private JButtonCoins coinButton = new JButtonCoins("Determine Coins");
        private JButtonClear clearButton = new JButtonClear("Clear");

        private QuarterHandler quarterHandler;
        private DimeHandler dimeHandler;
        private NickelHandler nickelHandler;
        private PennyHandler pennyHandler;

        public FlowLayoutPanel() {
            setSize(700, 150);

            // Coin Button
            coinButton.setActionCommand("Coins");
            coinButton.addActionListener(this);

            // Clear button
            clearButton.setActionCommand("clear");
                clearButton.addActionListener(this);
```

The `FlowLayoutPanel` constructor establishes the currency display format using the `NumberFormat` class, which is the abstract base class for all number formats. The `setMinimumFractionDigits(int newValue)` method sets the minimum number of digits permitted in the fraction portion of a number. Once the format styles have been created, they can then be applied to the `JFormattedTextField` class used for rendering the dollar amount specified by the user. The `PropertyChangeListener` interface forces the application to deploy the `propertyChange` method `(PropertyChangeEvent evt)` to handle events when the dollar amount has been modified. The `BorderLayout` manager is applied to the `topPanel` component that organizes the `coinButton`, `amountField`, and `clearButton` components, which is added to the `FlowLayout` manager of the overall application by default:

```
        amountDisplayFormat = NumberFormat.getCurrencyInstance();
        amountDisplayFormat.setMinimumFractionDigits(0);
        amountEditFormat = NumberFormat.getNumberInstance();

        amountField = new JFormattedTextField(new DefaultFormatterFactory
                    (new NumberFormatter(amountDisplayFormat),
                     new NumberFormatter(amountDisplayFormat),
                     new NumberFormatter(amountEditFormat)));
        amountField.setValue(new Double(amount));
        amountField.setColumns(10);
        amountField.addPropertyChangeListener("value", this);

        topPanel.add(coinButton);
        topPanel.add(amountField);
        topPanel.add(clearButton);

        messageText = new JLabel("Coin Amounts");
        results.add(messageText);
        results.setPreferredSize(new Dimension(400, 100));
```

```
        results.setBorder(BorderFactory.createLineBorder (Color.blue, 2));
        results.setBackground(DIGIT_COLOR);

        JPanel borderPanel = new JPanel(new BorderLayout());
        borderPanel.setBorder(new TitledBorder("Formatted Currency"));
        borderPanel.add(topPanel, BorderLayout.CENTER);
        borderPanel.setSize(200,200);

        add(borderPanel);
        add(results);
```

The following code section implements the coin handlers that implement the Chain of Responsibility pattern to process all of the coins that are derived from the amount specified by the user in the GUI panel. The `setSuccessor(TestHandler successor)` method is used to specify the successor object along the chain of objects:

```
        // setup chain of responsibility pattern implementation
        try {
            quarterHandler = new QuarterHandler();
            dimeHandler = new DimeHandler();
            nickelHandler = new NickelHandler();
            pennyHandler = new PennyHandler();

            quarterHandler.setSuccessor( dimeHandler );
            dimeHandler.setSuccessor( nickelHandler );
            nickelHandler.setSuccessor( pennyHandler );
        } catch( Exception e ) {
            e.printStackTrace();
        }
    }

    public void propertyChange(PropertyChangeEvent e) {
        Object source = e.getSource();
        amount = ((Number)amountField.getValue()).doubleValue();

    }

    public void actionPerformed(ActionEvent e) {
        Command obj = (Command)e.getSource();
        obj.execute();
    }
```

The `JButtonCoins` method implements the `Command` interface to invoke the `execute()` method of the class when the user clicks on the Determine Coins button. The dollar amount is read from the `amountField` component and passes that value to the `quarterHandler` object for coin processing. When all of the coins have been accounted for, the coin distribution will be displayed in the `messageText` component:

```
    class JButtonCoins extends JButton implements Command {

        public JButtonCoins(String caption) { super(caption); }
        public void execute() {

            amountField.setValue(new Double(amount));
```

```
        int coinAmount = (int)(amount * .100);
        quarterHandler.handleRequest(coinAmount);
        messageText.setText(" QUARTERS= " + quarterHandler.getCount() +
                        " DIMES= " + dimeHandler.getCount() +
                        " NICKELS= " + nickelHandler.getCount() +
                        " PENNIES= " + pennyHandler.getCount());
    }
}

class JButtonClear extends JButton implements Command {

    public JButtonClear(String caption) { super(caption); }

    public void execute() {

        amountField.setValue(new Double(0));
        messageText.setText("User cleared text: ");
    }
}

public interface Command {
    public void execute();
}

// main method omitted for the sake of brevity


}
```

The `TestHandler` class is inherited by the individual coin handlers so that get/set successor methods can be used to determine the successor objects that are implemented along the chain of coin handlers:

```
[TestHandler.java]
// package name and import statements omitted
public class TestHandler {

    private TestHandler successor;

    public void setSuccessor( TestHandler successor ) { this.successor = successor; }
    public TestHandler getSuccessor() { return successor; }

    public void handleRequest(int coinAmount) { successor.handleRequest(coinAmount);
}
}
```

The `QuarterHandler` class inherits the successor classes from its superclass `TestHandler` and takes the coin amount to determine how many quarters can be found in the dollar total. The modulus % operator divides the coin amount by 25 to determine the number of quarters in the sum, and takes the remainder and passes it along the chain of coin handlers for dimes, nickels, and pennies. For all of the handlers, if a remainder of zero is discovered, then the chain processing is halted:

```
[QuarterHandler.java]
// package name and import statements omitted
public class QuarterHandler extends TestHandler {
  private static Logger logger = Logger.getLogger("QuarterHandler");
  private int count;
  public void handleRequest(int coinAmount) {

    int numberQuarters = coinAmount / 25;
    coinAmount %= 25;
    this.count = numberQuarters;
    if (coinAmount > 0) getSuccessor().handleRequest(coinAmount);
  }
  public int getCount() {
    return this.count;
  }
}
```

Figure 4-6 represents the finished product of the `FlowLayoutPanel` application. When users add a dollar amount in the text field of the GUI application and click the Determine Coins button, the coin distribution will be displayed in the panel below the Currency panel. With the Chain of Responsibility pattern implementation, the coins are handled sequentially from quarters to dimes to nickels to pennies until all coins have been accounted for. An important point to take away from the Chain of Responsibility pattern is that rather than calling a single method to satisfy a request, multiple methods in a chain have a chance to fulfill that request.

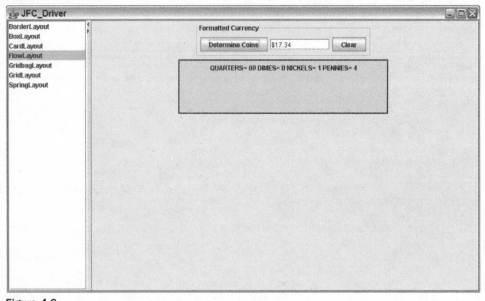

Figure 4-6

GridLayout

The GridLayout manager arranges its components in a rectangular, gridlike fashion. When components are added to the GridLayout manager, rows are populated first.

The constructor methods for the GridLayout manager are shown in the method summary table that follows.

Method	Description
public GridLayout()	No parameters — creates a grid layout with a default of one column per component, in a single row
public GridLayout(int rows, int columns)	Row and column parameters specify the size of the grid
Public GridLayout(int rows, int columns, int hGap, int vGap)	Row and column parameters specify the size of the grid and the hGap and vGap parameters specify the horizontal and vertical pixels between components

The following GridLayout example processes mouse events on buttons generated with Java 2D classes. Figure 4-7 shows how the buttons are organized on the GridLayoutPanel display.

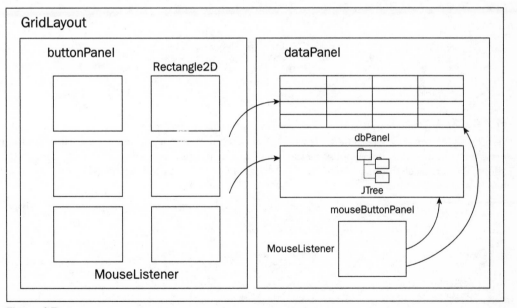

Figure 4-7

The following `GridLayoutPanel` code segment aggregates the different Java 2D components along with the Swing `JTree` and `JTable` components on the grid display. The `Java2DPanel` and `Java2DPanelMouseover` classes generate Java 2D button images that set the Cola row value of the `JTable` component, and store the proper Cola data value to the `JTree` component when the user clicks on them:

```
[GridLayoutPanel.java]
// package name and import statements omitted

public class GridLayoutPanel extends JPanel {

    // declarations omitted for the sake of brevity [Please check download code]
    public GridLayoutPanel() {

        JPanel panelAll = new JPanel(new GridLayout(0,2,5,5));

        DBPanel dbPanel = new DBPanel();
        Java2DPanel buttonPanel = new Java2DPanel(dbPanel);
        Java2DPanelMouseover mouseButtonPanel = new Java2DPanelMouseover(dbPanel);
        JPanel dataPanel = new JPanel(new GridLayout(0,1,5,5));
        dbPanel.add(mouseButtonPanel);
        panelAll.add(dbPanel);

        panelAll.add(buttonPanel);
        panelAll.add(dataPanel);

        add(panelAll);
        setVisible(true);

    }

    // main method omitted for the sake of brevity

}
```

The `Java2DPanel` class implements the `Rectangle2D` class to create buttons to obtain information concerning six different Cola selections. These buttons are attached to a `mouseListener` handler to determine if a user has clicked the mouse inside one of those buttons. The `setPreferredSize` method allows the constructor class for `Java2DPanel` to set the panel display to a desired dimension using height and width values:

```
[Java2DPanel.java]
// package name and import statements omitted

public class Java2DPanel extends JPanel implements MouseListener {

    Rectangle2D rect1, rect2, rect3, rect4, rect5, rect6;
    DBPanel dbRef;

    public Java2DPanel(DBPanel db) {

        dbRef = db;
```

```
        rect1 = new Rectangle2D.Double(25, 25, 100, 100);
        rect2 = new Rectangle2D.Double(150, 25, 100, 100);
        rect3 = new Rectangle2D.Double(25, 150, 100, 100);
        rect4 = new Rectangle2D.Double(150, 150, 100, 100);
        rect5 = new Rectangle2D.Double(25, 275, 100, 100);
        rect6 = new Rectangle2D.Double(150, 275, 100, 100);

        this.addMouseListener(this);

        setBackground(Color.white);
        setPreferredSize(new Dimension(300, 200));
    }
```

The `paintComponent(Graphics g)` method is called when a window becomes visible or is resized, and when a mouse listener detects a new user-generated event to draw the background graphics components on the panel display. Six rectangle class components are constructed by instantiating `Rectangle` class objects and filling them by implementing the `Graphics2D fill(Shape s)` method:

```
    public void paintComponent(Graphics g) {
        clear(g);

        Graphics2D g2 = (Graphics2D) g;
        g2.setRenderingHint(RenderingHints.KEY_ANTIALIASING,
RenderingHints.VALUE_ANTIALIAS_ON);

        Rectangle rectangle1 = new Rectangle(35, 40, 100, 100);
        Rectangle rectangle2 = new Rectangle(160, 40, 100, 100);
        Rectangle rectangle3 = new Rectangle(35, 165, 100, 100);
        Rectangle rectangle4 = new Rectangle(160, 165, 100, 100);
        Rectangle rectangle5 = new Rectangle(35, 290, 100, 100);
        Rectangle rectangle6 = new Rectangle(160, 290, 100, 100);

        g2.setPaint(new Color(204, 255, 153));
        g2.fill(rectangle1);
        g2.fill(rectangle2);
        g2.fill(rectangle3);
        g2.fill(rectangle4);
        g2.fill(rectangle5);
        g2.fill(rectangle6);
        g2.setColor(new Color(123,123,45));
        g2.fill(rect1);
        g2.fill(rect2);
```

Now that the six different background buttons have been created and filled, the foreground buttons are created by using the `Graphics2D drawstring(String str, int x, int y)` method to place string text on the button display and the `fill(Shape s)` method to draw the button shape:

```
        g2.setColor(Color.black);
        g2.setFont(new Font("Serif", Font.BOLD, 18));
        g2.drawString("Cola 1", (float)(rect1.getX())+25,
(float)(rect1.getY()+rect1.getHeight()/2));
        g2.drawString("Cola 2", (float)(rect2.getX())+25,
(float)(rect2.getY()+rect2.getHeight()/2));
```

```
        g2.setColor(new Color(123,123,45));
        g2.fill(rect3);
        g2.fill(rect4);

        g2.setColor(Color.black);
        g2.setFont(new Font("Serif", Font.BOLD, 18));
        g2.drawString("Cola 3", (float)(rect3.getX())+25,
(float)(rect3.getY()+rect3.getHeight()/2));
        g2.drawString("Cola 4", (float)(rect4.getX())+25,
(float)(rect4.getY()+rect4.getHeight()/2));

        g2.setColor(new Color(123,123,45));
        g2.fill(rect5);
        g2.fill(rect6);

        g2.setColor(Color.black);
        g2.setFont(new Font("Serif", Font.BOLD, 18));
        g2.drawString("Cola 5", (float)(rect5.getX())+25,
(float)(rect5.getY()+rect5.getHeight()/2));
        g2.drawString("Cola 6", (float)(rect6.getX())+25,
(float)(rect6.getY()+rect6.getHeight()/2));
    }
```

The `mousePressed(MouseEvent e)` method checks the user's mouse event to see if it was clicked inside one of the Rectangle2D button shapes. If the application detects a click inside the button display area, then the data values associated with that button will be set in the `JTree` and `JTable` components:

```
    public void mousePressed(MouseEvent e) {
        if ( insideRectangle(e.getX(), e.getY(), rect1.getX(), rect1.getY(),
rect1.getWidth(), rect1.getHeight()) ) {
            dbRef.setRow(0);
            dbRef.addTreeData(0);
        }
        if ( insideRectangle(e.getX(), e.getY(), rect2.getX(), rect2.getY(),
rect2.getWidth(), rect2.getHeight()) ) {
            dbRef.setRow(1);
            dbRef.addTreeData(1);
        }
        if ( insideRectangle(e.getX(), e.getY(), rect3.getX(), rect3.getY(),
rect3.getWidth(), rect3.getHeight()) ) {
            dbRef.setRow(2);
            dbRef.addTreeData(2);
        }
        if ( insideRectangle(e.getX(), e.getY(), rect4.getX(), rect4.getY(),
rect4.getWidth(), rect4.getHeight()) ) {
            dbRef.setRow(3);
            dbRef.addTreeData(3);
        }
        if ( insideRectangle(e.getX(), e.getY(), rect5.getX(), rect5.getY(),
rect5.getWidth(), rect5.getHeight()) ) {
            dbRef.setRow(4);
            dbRef.addTreeData(4);
        }
```

```
      if ( insideRectangle(e.getX(), e.getY(), rect6.getX(), rect6.getY(),
rect6.getWidth(), rect6.getHeight()) ) {
          dbRef.setRow(5);
          dbRef.addTreeData(5);
      }
   }
```

The insideRectangle method returns a boolean true or false value depending on whether or not the user has clicked the mouse inside the button shape on the panel display based on the coordinates passed to the routine:

```
   public boolean insideRectangle(int xMouse, int yMouse, double x, double y, double
width, double height) {
       if ( (xMouse >= x && xMouse <= x+width) && (yMouse >= y && yMouse <= y+height)
) {
           return true;
       }
       return false;
   }

   protected void clear(Graphics g) {
      super.paintComponent(g);
   }


   public void mouseDragged(MouseEvent e) {}
   public void mouseReleased(MouseEvent e) {}
   public void mouseMoved (MouseEvent e) {}
   public void mouseEntered (MouseEvent e) {}
   public void mouseExited (MouseEvent e) {}
   public void mouseClicked (MouseEvent e) {}

   // main method omitted for the sake of brevity


}
```

The Java2DPanelMouseover class only generates a single Java 2D button that acts differently than the Java2DPanel buttons in that when a user passes the mouse over the button, the Cola value will automatically be set in the JTree and JTable data stores. The Java2DPanel application requires that a user click inside the button display area to emulate the same behavior:

```
[Java2DPanelMouseover.java]
// package name and import statements omitted

public class Java2DPanelMouseover extends JPanel {

   // declarations omitted for the sake of brevity [Please check download code]
   public Java2DPanelMouseover(DBPanel dbRef) {

      this.dbRef = dbRef;

      setPreferredSize(new Dimension(100, 100));
      setSize(100,100);
```

```
        this.mouseOverColor = new Color(123,123,45);
        this.normalColor = new Color(204, 255, 153);
        this.paintColor = normalColor;
```

The addMouseListener method is used to track the individual mouse movements of the user across the panel component. When the user crosses enters the button space with the Cola 1 label, the mouseOverColor will displace the normalColor value and the JTable and JTree components will point to the data associated with the Cola1 item using the displayTableRow1() method:

```
        this.addMouseListener(new MouseListener() {
            public void mouseEntered(MouseEvent e) {
                displayTableRow1();
                paintColor = mouseOverColor;
                repaint();
            }
            public void mouseExited(MouseEvent e) {
                paintColor = normalColor;
                repaint();
            }
            public void mouseDragged(MouseEvent e) {}
            public void mouseClicked(MouseEvent e) {}
            public void mousePressed(MouseEvent e) {}
            public void mouseReleased(MouseEvent e) {}
        });
    }

    public void displayTableRow1() {
        dbRef.setRow(0);
        dbRef.addTreeData(0);
    }
```

The paintComponent(Graphics g) method applies the proper paint color inside the Java 2D button using the value stored in the paintColor variable. The MouseEntered method sets the paintColor to the mouseOverColor value and when the user exits the button space, it is reset to the normalColor value:

```
    public void paintComponent(Graphics g) {

        Graphics2D g2d = (Graphics2D) g;

        g2d.setRenderingHint(RenderingHints.KEY_ANTIALIASING,
RenderingHints.VALUE_ANTIALIAS_ON);
        Dimension d = this.getSize();

        g2d.clearRect(0, 0, d.width, d.height);

        int centerX = d.width / 2;
        int centerY = d.height / 2;

        int xOffset = d.width / 2 - 3;
        int yOffset = d.height / 2 - 3;

        g2d.setColor(this.paintColor);
```

```
            g2d.fillRect(0, 0, 100, 100);

            g2d.setColor(Color.black);
            g2d.setFont(new Font("Serif", Font.BOLD, 18));
            g2d.drawString("Cola 1", 25, 50);

    }
}
```

The DBPanel class below stores the six different Cola values in the JTable component and dynamically sets the row value inside the populated table associated with the button value as the user clicks on the different Java 2D button components. The DBPanel constructor method is called when the class is first invoked, where an object reference of the MyTableModel class, named mtm, invokes the populateTable(String[] s) method to initialize the table values to empty strings prior to establishing the layout managers needed to place the visual components on. Three different GridLayout managers are instantiated, and two of those—panelData and panelTree—are placed upon the panelAll layout panel:

```
[DBPanel.java]
// package name and import statements omitted

  public class DBPanel extends JPanel implements PropertyChangeListener,
TableModelListener {
      // declarations omitted for the sake of brevity [Please check download code]
      public DBPanel() {
          JPanel panelAll = new JPanel(new GridLayout(0,1,5,5));
          JPanel panelData = new JPanel(new GridLayout(0,1,5,5));
          panelData.add(panelTable());

          setPreferredSize(new Dimension(300, 450));
          String[] s = { "", "", "", "" };
          mtm.populateTable(s);
          addTableData();

          panelAll.add(panelData);

          JPanel panelTree = new JPanel(new GridLayout(0,1,5,5));
          panelTree.add(treePanel());

          panelAll.add(panelTree);
          addTreeData(0);

          add(panelAll);
          setBackground(Color.white);
      }
```

The addTableData() method populates the array of string values called s with the four different Cola attributes (Brand, Cost, Calories, and Size) and passes that array to the populateTable method for display. The addTree(int row) method allows users to add the Cola data to the row value passed into the method:

```
    public void addTableData() {
        String[] s = { "", "", "", "" };
        for (int i=0; i < tableData.length; i++) {
            s[0]=tableData[i][0]; s[1]=tableData[i][1]; s[2]=tableData[i][2];
s[3]=tableData[i][3];
            mtm.populateTable(s);
        }
    }

    public void addTreeData(int row) {
        root = new DefaultMutableTreeNode("Cola Attributes");
        tree = new JTree(root);
        DefaultMutableTreeNode items;

        items = new DefaultMutableTreeNode("Cola " + (row+1));
        root.add(items);
        items.add(new DefaultMutableTreeNode("Brand= " + tableData[row][0]));
        items.add(new DefaultMutableTreeNode("Cost= " + tableData[row][1]));
        items.add(new DefaultMutableTreeNode("Calories= " + tableData[row][2]));
        items.add(new DefaultMutableTreeNode("Size= " + tableData[row][3]));
        scrollPane.getViewport().add( tree );
        tree.expandRow(0);
    }
```

The `panelTable()` method creates a new `MyTableModel` object reference and adds it to a `JTable` object called `tree`, which in turn is placed inside a scroll pane component so that users can navigate up and down in the table when cola data attributes are added to the table component. The `ListSelectionModel` interface is implemented to maintain the tables' row selection state. The `addListSelectionListener` method monitors the list so that changes to that list are reflected in the GUI representation:

```
    public JPanel panelTable() {

        JPanel tablePanel = new JPanel(new GridLayout(0,1,5,5));

        mtm = new MyTableModel();
        table = new JTable(mtm);
        table.setPreferredScrollableViewportSize(new Dimension(250, 70));
        JScrollPane scrollPane = new JScrollPane(table);

        tablePanel.add(scrollPane);

        table.setSelectionMode(ListSelectionModel.SINGLE_SELECTION);
        ListSelectionModel rowSM = table.getSelectionModel();
        rowSM.addListSelectionListener(new ListSelectionListener() {
            public void valueChanged(ListSelectionEvent e) {
                //Ignore extra messages.
                if (e.getValueIsAdjusting()) return;

                lsm = (ListSelectionModel)e.getSource();
                if (lsm.isSelectionEmpty()) {
                    //no rows are selected
                } else {
                    selectedRow = lsm.getMinSelectionIndex();
```

```
            }
          }
      });
      // titledBorder logic omitted for the sake of brevity


      return tablePanel;
   }
```

The `treePanel()` method establishes a new `GridLayout` manager so that a `JTree` structure can be embedded within a scroll pane, which will allow the user to vertically scroll up and down the tree structure. The `BorderFactory` class is implemented so that a compound border titled Tree Information frames the tree component:

```
      public JPanel treePanel() {
         JPanel tablePanel = new JPanel(new GridLayout(0,1,5,5));

         scrollPane = new JScrollPane();
         scrollPane.setVerticalScrollBarPolicy(
            JScrollPane.VERTICAL_SCROLLBAR_ALWAYS);
            scrollPane.setPreferredSize(new Dimension(250, 150));
            scrollPane.setBorder(
            BorderFactory.createCompoundBorder(BorderFactory.createCompoundBorder(
            BorderFactory.createTitledBorder("Tree Information"),
            BorderFactory.createEmptyBorder(5,5,5,5)),
            scrollPane.getBorder()));

         root = new DefaultMutableTreeNode("Annotations");
         tree = new JTree(root);
         scrollPane.getViewport().add( tree );

         tablePanel.add(scrollPane);
         return tablePanel;
      }

      public void propertyChange( PropertyChangeEvent e ) {}
      public void tableChanged(TableModelEvent e) {}
```

The `MyTableModel` class handles all of the table data for the six different Cola types through its method implementations. The `setValueAt` method stores an individual object value at a designated row and column value. The `populateTable` method reads in a string array and populates the table with those values. The `fireTableDataChanged()` method tells the application's listeners that changes have been made to the table and need to be shown in the GUI representation:

```
      class MyTableModel extends AbstractTableModel {
         String[] columnNames= { "Brand", "Cost", "Calories", "Size" };
         private Object[][] data;
         public int getColumnCount() { return columnNames.length; }
         public int getRowCount() { return (data == null) ? 0 : data.length; }
         public String getColumnName(int col) { return columnNames[col]; }
         public Object getValueAt(int row, int col) { return data[row][col]; }
            // addRow() and deleteRow(int row) methods were omitted for sake of brevity
```

```
        public void setValueAt(Object value, int row, int col) {
            data[row][col] = value;
        }
```

The `populateTable` method receives a string array of table data that relates to the Cola button selection so that it can be added to the `JTable` component for observation. Once the table has been populated, then the `fireTableDataChanged()` method is invoked so that these table changes are updated in the GUI view:

```
        public void populateTable(String[] s) {
            // if data exists in table, rewrite table for new entry
            int rowCount = getRowCount();
            if (rowCount != 0) {
                // add another row
                Object[][] temp = data;
                data = new Object[rowCount+1][getColumnCount()];
                // copy old items into new structure
                for (int i=0; i < temp.length; i++) {
                    data[i][0] = temp[i][0];
                    data[i][1] = temp[i][1];
                    data[i][2] = temp[i][2];
                    data[i][3] = temp[i][3];
                }
                for (int i=0; i < getColumnCount(); i++)
                    setValueAt(s[i], rowCount-1, i);
            } else {
                data = cData;
                for (int i=0; i < getColumnCount(); i++)
                    setValueAt(s[i], 0, i);
            }
            fireTableDataChanged();
        }
    }

    public void setRow(int row) {
        table.setRowSelectionInterval(row, row);
    }

    // main method omitted for the sake of brevity

}
```

Figure 4-8 represents the `GridLayoutPanel` application defined in the source code above. When users click on the Java 2D button images, proper Cola values will be highlighted in the Swing components on the right side of the GUI display.

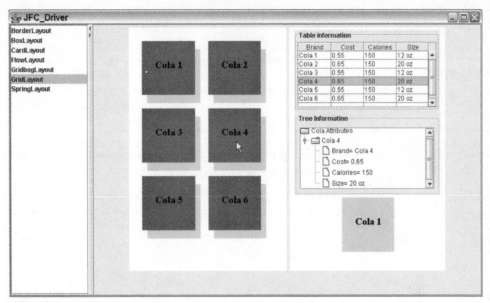

Figure 4-8

GridBagLayout

The `GridBagLayout` manager manages its components both vertically and horizontally by maintaining a rectangular grid of cells in its display area. Components are manipulated through constraint parameters using the `GridBagConstraints` class. These constraints specify where a component's display area should be positioned on the grid and its size using minimum and preferred size attributes. The constructor methods for the `GridBagLayout` manager are shown in the method summary table that follows.

Method	Description
`public GridBagLayout()`	No parameters

The table below outlines the different instance variables that can be implemented with the `GridBagLayout` manager. These variables can be implemented interchangeably to satisfy an application's visual requirements.

Instance Variables	Description
`gridx, gridy`	The `gridx` and `gridy` instance variables specify the cells containing the leading corner of the component's display area, where the cell at the origin of the grid has address x = 0 degrees and y = 0 degrees. For applications that have horizontal left-to-right layouts, the leading corner is on the upper left. For applications that have horizontal right-to-left layouts, the leading corner is on the upper right.

Table continued on following page

Instance Variables	Description
weightx, weighty	The weightx and weighty instance variables are used to determine how to distribute space for resizing. All components are placed together in the middle of a container unless a weightx or weighty value is specified. The GridBagLayout manager appends additional space between its cells and the container edges when the default weight is initialized to zero.
insets	The insets instance variable specifies the component's padding, which amounts to the minimum space available between the component and the display area edges.
fill	The fill instance variable is implemented when the component's display area is larger than the component's requested size to determine whether (and how) to resize the component. GridBagConstraints.NONE (the default) GridBagConstraints.HORIZONTAL — enables the component to fill its display area horizontally, not vertically GridBagConstraints.VERTICAL — allows the component to fill its display area vertically, not horizontally GridBagConstraints.BOTH — allows the component to fill its display area both vertically and horizontally

The following GridBagLayout example applies both the Command and Visitor patterns to handle user events and message generation from Swing component activities. Figure 4-9 provides a model of the application and the component distribution on the GridBagLayout and their listeners.

The GridBagLayoutPanel application will incorporate the Command and Visitor patterns to handle button requests for answers to the questions selected by the user in the different question components. Some of the benefits and shortcomings of these patterns are shown in the following table.

Pattern	Benefits	Consequences
Visitor	Separates operations from the objects that perform operations on it. Objects of the primary type *accept* the visitor and then call the visitor's dynamically bound method in a process referred to as *double dispatch*. Adding new operations is facilitated, no need for recompilation.	Difficult to maintain Forces you to provide public operations that access internal state data, which may break encapsulation

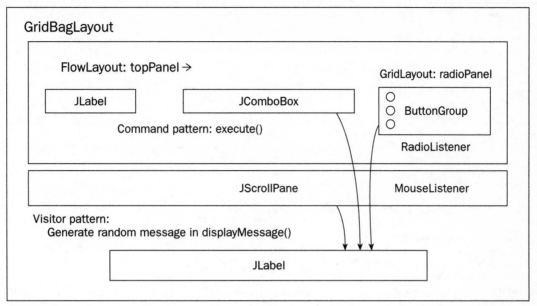

Figure 4-9

The `GridBagLayoutPanel` class incorporates the `GridBagLayout` manager, which allows for the place-ment of GUI components in a grid formation of rows and columns. The width and height of the rows and columns do not necessarily have to be the same size throughout a panel display, but this sample application maintains consistency across rows and columns for its GUI components:

```
[GridBagLayoutPanel.java]
// package name and import statements omitted

public class GridBagLayoutPanel extends JPanel implements ActionListener {
  // declarations omitted for the sake of brevity [Please check download code]
```

The `GridBagLayoutPanel` constructor method declares and initializes the Swing components used for the fortune teller application. First a `JcomboBox` component is created with a list of questions that can be selected from the drop-down box. Next, a group of radio buttons is created, grouped together, and regis-tered to the application using the `RadioListener` class. Those radio buttons are grouped vertically and appended to the `radioPanel`. Both the drop-down list and the radio buttons are appended to the `topPanel` display. Lastly, a list of questions is generated and added to a `JScrollPane` component and registered with a `MouseListener` to generate fortunes when a user double-clicks a question in the list:

```
public GridBagLayoutPanel() {

    setSize(200, 150);
    cbQuestion = new JComboQuestion();
    cbQuestion.addActionListener(this);

    label = new JLabel("Question: ");
    label.setFont(messageFont);

    RadioListener radioListener = new RadioListener();
```

```
        question1Button.setMnemonic('1');
        question2Button.setMnemonic('2');
        question3Button.setMnemonic('3');
        question1Button.addActionListener(radioListener);
        question2Button.addActionListener(radioListener);
        question3Button.addActionListener(radioListener);
        ButtonGroup group = new ButtonGroup();
        group.add(question1Button);
        group.add(question2Button);
        group.add(question3Button);

        JPanel radioPanel = new JPanel();
        radioPanel.setLayout(new GridLayout(0, 1));
        radioPanel.add(question1Button);
        radioPanel.add(question2Button);
        radioPanel.add(question3Button);

        String[] data = {"Will the Yankees win the pennant?",
                         "Will the Giants win the Super Bowl?",
                         "Will the Rangers win the Stanley Cup?"};
```

In the code snippet below, a `JList` component is instantiated and attached to a mouse listener so that user clicks are detected upon that list. If a user double-clicks a list item, then the `displayMessage()` method will be invoked with a randomly generated fortune related to the question selected by the user in the list:

```
        final JList list = new JList(data);
        MouseListener mouseListener = new MouseAdapter() {
            public void mouseClicked(MouseEvent e) {
                if (e.getClickCount() == 2) {
                    logger.info("Double clicked: " + list.locationToIndex(e.getPoint()));
                    displayMessage();
                }
            }
        };
        list.setFont(listFont);
        list.addMouseListener(mouseListener);
        JScrollPane listScroller = new JScrollPane(list);
        listScroller.setPreferredSize(new Dimension(100, 125));
        listScroller.setBorder(new TitledBorder("Double-click query for fortune"));
        topPanel.add(label);
        topPanel.add(cbQuestion);
        topPanel.add(radioPanel);
        topPanel.setBorder(new TitledBorder("Question components"));

        messageText = new JLabel("Please pick a question...");
        messageText.setFont(messageFont);
        results.add(messageText);
        results.setPreferredSize(new Dimension(400, 50));
        results.setBorder(BorderFactory.createLineBorder (Color.blue, 2));
        results.setBackground(Color.yellow);
```

The following code segment demonstrates how the components are rendered using the `GridBagLayout` manager. The `GridBagConstraints` class is instantiated so that constraints can be specified for the GUI components in the application using the `GridBagLayout` manager:

```
        setLayout(new GridBagLayout());

        GridBagConstraints c = new GridBagConstraints();
        c.gridx = 0;
        c.gridy = 0;
        c.weightx = 0.5;
        c.insets = new Insets( 2, 2, 2, 2 );
        c.fill = GridBagConstraints.BOTH;
        add(topPanel, c);

        c.gridy = 1;
        c.weightx = 0.5;
        c.gridwidth = 1;
        c.fill = GridBagConstraints.HORIZONTAL;
        add(listScroller, c);

        c.gridx = 0;
        c.gridy = 2;
        c.weightx = 0.0;
        c.insets = new Insets( 50, 50, 0, 0 );
        c.fill = GridBagConstraints.NONE;
        add(results, c);
    }

    public void actionPerformed(ActionEvent e) {
        JComboQuestion cb = (JComboQuestion)e.getSource();
        Command obj = (Command)e.getSource();
        String question = (String)cb.getSelectedItem();

        if (!question.equals("Pick a question?")) {
            obj.execute();
        }
    }
}
```

The JComboQuestion class implements the Command pattern interface so that the GridBagLayoutPanel class can invoke its execute() method when a user clicks the combo box affiliated with a question list reference qbQuestion. The Command pattern increases reuse by decoupling the interface from the implementation, which means that all GUI components in the GridBagLayoutPanel class can use the public execute() method interface to serve as a gateway to private implementations associated with them:

```
class JComboQuestion extends JComboBox implements Command {

    public JComboQuestion() {
        this.addItem("Pick a question?");
        this.addItem("Will I pass my class?");
        this.addItem("Will my candidate win the election?");
        this.addItem("Will I grow up to be a doctor?");
        setFont(messageFont);
    }
    public void execute() {
        displayMessage();
    }
}
```

The `displayMessage()` method selects a random number between 1 and 3 and uses that number to generate a fortune using the `Visitor` pattern. The `Visitor` pattern implementation polymorphically determines the proper accept method to call during operations:

```java
public void displayMessage() {
    MessageText mt = new MessageText();
    int number = (int) (Math.random () * 3 + 1);
    switch(number) {
        case 1: ((FortuneTeller)new Message1()).accept(mt); break;
        case 2: ((FortuneTeller)new Message2()).accept(mt); break;
        case 3: ((FortuneTeller)new Message3()).accept(mt); break;
    }
    messageText.setFont(messageFont);
    messageText.setText(mt.toString());
    results.add(messageText);
}

public interface Command {
    public void execute();
}

class RadioListener implements ActionListener {
    public void actionPerformed(ActionEvent e) {
        displayMessage();
    }
}

static public void main(String argv[]) {
    JFrame frame = new JFrame("GridBagLayout");
    frame.addWindowListener(new WindowAdapter() {
        public void windowClosing(WindowEvent e) {System.exit(0);}
    });
    frame.getContentPane().add(new GridBagLayoutPanel(), BorderLayout.CENTER);
    frame.pack();
    frame.setVisible(true);
}
}
```

Figure 4-10 shows the visual representation of the `GridLayoutPanel` application. Random fortunes will be generated by the `Visitor` pattern implementation when the user selects a question from the different Swing components.

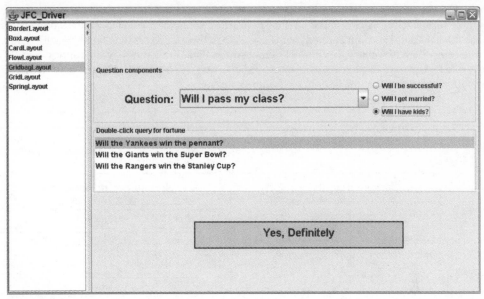

Figure 4-10

SpringLayout

The SpringLayout manager lays out its Container components according to user-specified constraint parameters. Each constraint, represented by a Spring object, controls the vertical or horizontal distance between two component edges. The edges can belong to any child of the container, or to the container itself.

The SpringLayout manager does not set the location of its components automatically like some of the other layout managers. Component locations need to be initialized through constraint parameters so that minimum, maximum, and preferred lengths can be contained and bound. The constructor methods for the SpringLayout manager are shown in the method summary table below.

Method	Description
SpringLayout()	Constructor (no parameters)

The following are some of the fields used to describe the constraints for component placement.

Field	Description
static String EAST	Right edge of component
static String NORTH	Top edge of component
static String SOUTH	Bottom edge of component
static String WEST	Left edge of component

The following SpringLayout example allows users to generate log entries for their triathlon events using a simple form display. Simple checks will be performed on the data prior to submission to ensure that all of the relevant data has been entered by the user. When the user saves that event, it will be stored in a JTable component for review. Figure 4-11 demonstrates what the SpringLayout application will look like. Only one tabbed panel will be on display at a time, which will be dictated by the user navigations from the button components at the bottom of the application.

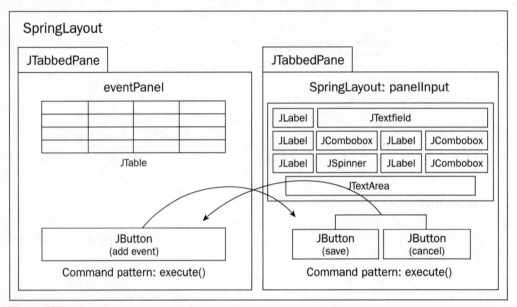

Figure 4-11

The following code segment outlines in code how the model in Figure 4-11 will be realized:

```
[SpringLayoutPanel.java]
// package name and import statements omitted

public class SpringLayoutPanel extends JPanel implements ActionListener {

  // declarations omitted for the sake of brevity [Please check download code]
  public SpringLayoutPanel(String name) {
    initComponents();
  }

  private void initComponents() {
    tabPanel = new JTabbedPane();

    eventPanel = new JPanel();
    eventPanel.setLayout(new BorderLayout());
    eventPanel.setPreferredSize(new Dimension(350, 400));
    eventPanel.setToolTipText("Event");
```

```
                eventPanel.add("Center", EventPanel());

                tabPanel.addTab("Triathlon Record Log", eventPanel);
                add(tabPanel, BorderLayout.CENTER);
        }
```

The EventPanel() method initializes many of the Swing components in the SwingLayoutPanel application and combines BorderLayout and GridLayout manager panels to obtain its visualization needs:

```
public JPanel EventPanel() {
    JPanel ePanel = new JPanel(new GridLayout(0, 1, 5, 5));
    ePanel.setMaximumSize(new Dimension(350, 400));
    ePanel.setMinimumSize(new Dimension(350, 400));
    ePanel.setPreferredSize(new Dimension(350, 400));

    eventPanel = new JPanel();
    eventButtonPanel = new JPanel();
    addEventButton = new JAddEventButton();

    eventPanel.setLayout(new BorderLayout());
    eventPanel.setMinimumSize(new Dimension(350, 400));
    eventPanel.setPreferredSize(new Dimension(350, 400));

    gridPanel = new JPanel(new GridLayout(0, 1, 5, 5));
    gridPanel.add(panelTable());

    eventButtonPanel.setLayout(new GridLayout(1, 2));

    addEventButton.setText("Add New Event");
    addEventButton.setToolTipText("Add New Event");
    addEventButton.addActionListener(this);
    eventButtonPanel.add(addEventButton);
    eventButtonPanel.setPreferredSize(new Dimension(350, 30));
    eventPanel.add(eventButtonPanel, BorderLayout.SOUTH);
    eventPanel.add(gridPanel, BorderLayout.NORTH);

    String[] s = { "", "", "", "" };
    mtm.populateTable(s);

    ePanel.add(eventPanel);

    return ePanel;
}
```

The panelTable method implements a GridLayout manager to accommodate the inclusion of a JTable component that will store the different triathlon log entries. A ListSelectionListener is instantiated to handle user events that affect the table:

```
public JPanel panelTable() {

    JPanel tablePanel = new JPanel(new GridLayout(0, 1, 5, 5));

    mtm = new MyTableModel();
```

```
        table = new JTable(mtm);
        table.setPreferredScrollableViewportSize(new Dimension(250, 70));
        JScrollPane scrollPane = new JScrollPane(table);
        tablePanel.add(scrollPane);

        table.setSelectionMode(ListSelectionModel.SINGLE_SELECTION);
        ListSelectionModel rowSM = table.getSelectionModel();
        rowSM.addListSelectionListener(new ListSelectionListener() {
            public void valueChanged(ListSelectionEvent e) {
                if (e.getValueIsAdjusting()) return;

                lsm = (ListSelectionModel) e.getSource();
                if (lsm.isSelectionEmpty()) {
                    //no rows are selected
                } else {
                    selectedRow = lsm.getMinSelectionIndex();
                    logger.info("selectedRow= " + selectedRow);
                }
            }
        });
        return tablePanel;
    }
```

The `formPanel()` method implements a SpringLayout manager where all of the log entry components are placed so that user training activities can be tracked. Two Swing library layout managers, BorderLayout and GridLayout, are combined so that a SpringLayout manager that holds the triathlon training attributes can be placed above the Save and Cancel buttons:

```
    public JPanel formPanel() {

        springLayout = new SpringLayout();
        panelInput = new JPanel(springLayout);
        panelInput.setMinimumSize(new Dimension(350, 370));
        panelInput.setPreferredSize(new Dimension(350, 370));

        eventPanel = new JPanel();
        eventPanel.setLayout(new BorderLayout());
        eventPanel.setPreferredSize(new Dimension(350, 400));

        panelButton = new JPanel();
        panelButton.setLayout(new GridLayout(1, 4));

        panelButton.setMinimumSize(new Dimension(350, 30));
        panelButton.setPreferredSize(new Dimension(350, 30));

        textareaDescription = new JTextArea();

        buttonSave = new JButtonSave();
        buttonCancel = new JButtonCancel();

        comboboxTime = new JComboBox();

        trainingLength = new String[] { "15 min", "30 min", "45 min", "1 hr", "2 hrs"
};
        comboboxLength = new JComboBox(trainingLength);
```

```
textfieldTitle = new JTextField();
category = new String[] { "Swim", "Bike", "Run", "Other" };
comboboxCategory = new JComboBox(category);

model = new SpinnerDateModel();
model.setCalendarField(Calendar.WEEK_OF_MONTH);
spinner = new JSpinner(model);
JSpinner.DateEditor editor =
    new JSpinner.DateEditor(spinner, "MMMMM dd, yyyy");
spinner.setEditor(editor);
ChangeListener listener = new ChangeListener() {
    public void stateChanged(ChangeEvent e) {
        SpinnerModel source = (SpinnerModel) e.getSource();
        System.out.println("The value is: " + source.getValue());
    }
};
model.addChangeListener(listener);

// label declarations and initializations for Title, Date, Category, Time,
Duration, and Description omitted for better clarity
```

The code segment below establishes two button components and a text area display for the triathlon entry form. The text area named textareaDescription is enabled and has an etched border frame to surround it. Minimum and maximum size constraints are defined as well as column values and line wrapping so that text entered by a user remains in sight of that user. Buttons for both the save and cancel operations have text labels attached to them with new font declarations and tool tip text for mouse over pop-ups that indicate what purpose those buttons serve:

```
textareaDescription.setEnabled(true);
textareaDescription.setBorder(BorderFactory.createEtchedBorder());
textareaDescription.setMinimumSize(new Dimension(85, 51));
textareaDescription.setPreferredSize(new Dimension(85, 51));
textareaDescription.setText("");
textareaDescription.setColumns(25);
textareaDescription.setLineWrap(true);

buttonSave.setText("Save event");
buttonSave.setFont(new java.awt.Font("Dialog", 1, 12));
buttonSave.addActionListener(this);
buttonSave.setToolTipText("Save event.");
buttonSave.setPreferredSize(new Dimension(58, 25));

buttonCancel.setText("Return to event list.");
buttonCancel.setFont(new java.awt.Font("Dialog", 1, 12));
buttonCancel.addActionListener(this);
buttonCancel.setToolTipText("Return to event list.");
buttonCancel.setPreferredSize(new Dimension(58, 25));
```

The following code segment dictates how to implement SpringLayout constraints to achieve the look and feel of the disparate Swing components for tracking. The Constraints object of the SpringLayout manager positions the edges of the children in the container object through vertical and horizontal values:

```
      //Add the components to the panel using SpringLayout.
      panelInput.add(labelTitle,new
SpringLayout.Constraints(Spring.constant(15),Spring.constant(21)));
      panelInput.add(textfieldTitle,new
SpringLayout.Constraints(Spring.constant(45),Spring.constant(17)));
      panelInput.add(labelTime,new
SpringLayout.Constraints(Spring.constant(13),Spring.constant(69)));
      panelInput.add(comboboxTime,new
SpringLayout.Constraints(Spring.constant(45),Spring.constant(63)));
      panelInput.add(labelLength,new
SpringLayout.Constraints(Spring.constant(190),Spring.constant(69)));
      panelInput.add(comboboxLength,new
SpringLayout.Constraints(Spring.constant(250),Spring.constant(63)));
      panelInput.add(labelCategory,new
SpringLayout.Constraints(Spring.constant(190),Spring.constant(115)));
      panelInput.add(comboboxCategory,new
SpringLayout.Constraints(Spring.constant(250),Spring.constant(109)));
      panelInput.add(labelDate,new
SpringLayout.Constraints(Spring.constant(15),Spring.constant(115)));
      panelInput.add(spinner,new
SpringLayout.Constraints(Spring.constant(45),Spring.constant(111)));
      panelInput.add(textareaDescription,new
SpringLayout.Constraints(Spring.constant(10),Spring.constant(217)));
      panelInput.add(labelDescription,new
SpringLayout.Constraints(Spring.constant(11),Spring.constant(201)));

      for (int i = 0; i < 24; i++) {
          timeString = Integer.toString(i);
          if (timeString.length() == 1)
             timeString = "0" + timeString;
          if (i != 0) {
             comboboxTime.addItem(timeString + "00");
             comboboxTime.addItem(timeString + "15");
             comboboxTime.addItem(timeString + "30");
             comboboxTime.addItem(timeString + "45");
          } else {
             comboboxTime.addItem(timeString + "00");
             comboboxTime.addItem(timeString + "15");
             comboboxTime.addItem(timeString + "30");
             comboboxTime.addItem(timeString + "45");
          }
      }
      comboboxTime.addItem("2400");
      comboboxTime.setSelectedItem("0930");

      eventPanel.add(BorderLayout.CENTER, panelInput);
      eventPanel.add(BorderLayout.SOUTH, panelButton);

      JPanel ePanel = new JPanel(new BorderLayout());
      ePanel.add(eventPanel, BorderLayout.CENTER);

      panelButton.add(buttonSave);
      panelButton.add(buttonCancel);
```

```
            return ePanel;
    }
```

The JAddEventButton class handles mouse events on the first tabbed pane display that occur when the user clicks the Add Event button on the bottom of the display. The application polymorphically invokes the execute() method, which removes all of the current panel components with the removeAll() method, and then creates a new layout so that the SpringLayout manager can be applied from the formPanel() method:

```java
class JAddEventButton extends JButton implements Command {
    public JAddEventButton() {
        super();
    }
    public void execute() {
        logger.info("[JAddEventButton:execute]");
        eventPanel.removeAll();
        eventPanel.setLayout(new BorderLayout());
        eventPanel.add(formPanel());
        eventPanel.requestFocusInWindow();
        eventPanel.validate();
    }
}
```

The JButtonSave component handles user events that occur when the user clicks the Save Event button. A cursory data check is performed on the title field to ensure that a proper title has been entered by the user prior to moving back to the initial tabbed panel screen with the user entry displayed in a JTable component:

```java
class JButtonSave extends JButton implements Command {
    public JButtonSave() {
        super();
    }
    public void execute() {
        if (textfieldTitle.getText().length() == 0 || textfieldTitle.getText() ==
null) {
            Toolkit.getDefaultToolkit().beep();
            JOptionPane.showMessageDialog(null, "Please Enter Event Title",
                                 "Error", JOptionPane.ERROR_MESSAGE);
            textfieldTitle.requestFocusInWindow();
            textfieldTitle.selectAll();
            return;
        }

        JOptionPane.showMessageDialog(null, "Event saved.",
                        "Operation Completed",
JOptionPane.INFORMATION_MESSAGE);

        restoreLogPanel();
        String[] s = { "", "", "", "" };
        s[0] = (String) comboboxCategory.getSelectedItem();
        s[1] = textareaDescription.getText();
        s[2] = (String) comboboxTime.getSelectedItem();
```

```
            mtm.populateTable(s);
      }
   }

   class JButtonCancel extends JButton implements Command {
      public JButtonCancel() {
         super();
      }
      public void execute() {
         logger.info("[JButtonCancel:execute] date = " + getDate());
         restoreLogPanel();
      }
   }
```

The getDate() method returns a string value from the JSpinner component that represents the date affiliated with the triathlon event. The restoreLogPanel() method invokes the removeAll() method to clear the panel display, establishes a new BorderLayout presentation panel, and initializes that new panel with the triathlon event components for logging operations. The requestFocusInWindow() method is called to request that the panel component gets the input focus. Lastly, the validate() method is implemented to cause the container to lay out its subcomponents again:

```
   public String getDate() {
      return ((JSpinner.DateEditor) spinner.getEditor()).getTextField().getText();
   }

   public void restoreLogPanel() {
      removeAll();
      setLayout(new BorderLayout());
      initComponents();
      requestFocusInWindow();
      validate();
   }

   public void actionPerformed(ActionEvent e) {
      Command obj = (Command) e.getSource();
      obj.execute();
   }

   // main method omitted for better clarity

}
```

Figure 4-12 represents the SpringLayoutPanel tabbed panel application that appears on the user display when a user invokes the Add Event button. The form display performs a cursory check on the data to ensure proper data is entered by the user when the Save Event button is clicked. The SpringLayout manager distributes JTextfield, JComboBox, JSpinner, and JTextArea components using constraint values positioning.

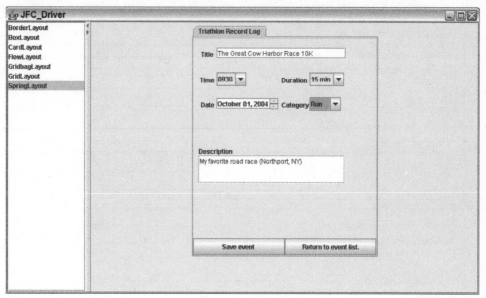

Figure 4-12

CardLayout

The CardLayout manager organizes its components as a stack of cards, where components are displayed one at a time. This allows components to be easily swapped in and out like a slide show presentation. The constructor methods for the CardLayout manager are shown in the method summary table below.

Method	Description
`public CardLayout()`	No parameters
`public CardLayout(int hGap, int vGap)`	Constructor where the `hGap` and `vGap` parameters specify the horizontal and vertical pixels between components

The following CardLayout example employs the Command and Strategy patterns to encapsulate behavior that will be applied to the user text. Figure 4-13 shows the CardLayout model and the different Swing components applied to that layout manager panel.

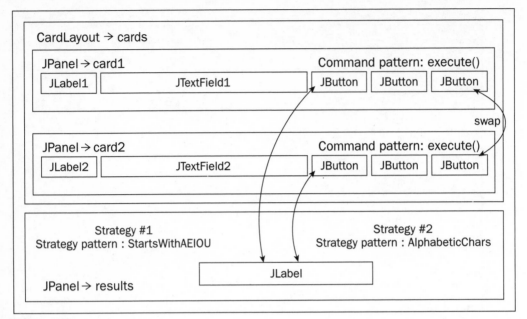

Figure 4-13

The CardLayoutPanel application utilizes the Strategy pattern to apply different algorithms to user specified text. The Command pattern is used to polymorphically determine what strategy to apply during run time. Some of the benefits and drawbacks of these two patterns are shown in the following table.

Pattern	Benefits	Consequences
Strategy	Decouples algorithms so that programs can be more flexible in their execution of logic and behavior Reduces multiple conditional statements	Increases number of objects

The CardLayoutPanel source code follows to demonstrate how the model in Figure 4-13 can be developed:

```
[CardLayoutPanel.java]
// package name and import statements omitted

public class CardLayoutPanel extends JPanel implements ActionListener, ItemListener
{

   // declarations omitted for the sake of brevity [Please check download code]
```

The CardLayoutPanel constructor lays out the manager for the two card panels, card1 and card2. The card1 panel contains two independent buttons that implement the Strategy pattern on user specified text. The card2 panel reveals the text that results from the State pattern algorithm application. The JButtonStrategy1 class applies the Pig-Latin algorithm to the use text when solicited by the user. The JButtonStrategy2 button converts the user text to uppercase text by applying the AlphabeticChars algorithm in its operations:

```java
public CardLayoutPanel() {

    setSize(700, 150);
    cards = new JPanel(new CardLayout());
    card1 = new JPanel();
    card2 = new JPanel();
    card3 = new JPanel();

    // swap buttons
    swapButton1.addActionListener(this);
    swapButton1.setActionCommand("Swap to Strategy 2");
    swapButton2.addActionListener(this);
    swapButton2.setActionCommand("Swap to Strategy 1");

    // Strategy Buttons
    strategyButton1.setActionCommand("Strategy #1");
    strategyButton1.addActionListener(this);
    strategyButton2.setActionCommand("Strategy #2");
    strategyButton2.addActionListener(this);

    // Clear button
    clearButton1.setActionCommand("clear");
    clearButton1.addActionListener(this);
    clearButton2.setActionCommand("clear");
    clearButton2.addActionListener(this);

    topPanel1.add(labelText1);
    topPanel1.add(textfield1);
    topPanel1.add(strategyButton1);
    topPanel1.add(clearButton1);
    topPanel1.add(swapButton1);

    topPanel2.add(labelText2);
    topPanel2.add(textfield2);
    topPanel2.add(strategyButton2);
    topPanel2.add(clearButton2);
    topPanel2.add(swapButton2);

    messageText = new JLabel("Enter messages");
    results.add(messageText);
    results.setPreferredSize(new Dimension(700, 100));
    results.setBorder(BorderFactory.createLineBorder (Color.blue, 2));
    results.setBackground(DIGIT_COLOR);

    card1.add(topPanel1);
    card2.add(topPanel2);

    cards.add(cardText[0], card1);
```

```
        cards.add(cardText[1], card2);

        card3.add(results, "Results Panel");

        add(cards);
        add(card3);
    }
```

The CardLayoutPanel class implements the ActionListener interface so that component objects created with that class can be registered using the addActionListener(ActionListener l) method shown in the previous code segment. The actionPerformed(ActionEvent e) method then processes those requests that are registered through the action listener. All of the JButton components in CardLayoutPanel implement the Command pattern interface method named execute() so that the appropriate button control method logic is executed when the user clicks that component. This is feasible because the application uses the object reference to that execute() method for execution. If one of the swap buttons is selected, then the sample application will alternate between strategy operations. The CardLayout next method is implemented to swap operations, but alternative code that performs that same operation using the swapNumber token and the CardLayout show method also demonstrate how to swap layouts:

```
public void actionPerformed(ActionEvent e) {
    if (e.getActionCommand.startsWith("Swap")) {
        CardLayout cardLayout = (CardLayout)(cards.getLayout());
        // ++swapNumber;
        // cardlayout.show(cards, cardText[swapNumber%2]);
        cardLayout.next(cards);
    } else {
        Command obj = (Command)e.getSource();
        obj.execute();
    }
}
```

The testStrategy(TestStrategy strategy, String m) method allows the application to send in the appropriate Strategy algorithm class along with a String variable that will be applied to that algorithm. The object reference, called strategy, invokes the test() method in the TestStrategy interface:

```
public boolean testStrategy(TestStrategy strategyApproach, String s) {
    return strategyApproach.test(s);
}
```

The JButtonStrategy1 class invokes the execute() method when the user clicks the Strategy #1 button on the GUI panel. The text specified in the text field is stripped into individual tokens that are passed into the StartsWithAEIOU strategy class to return a boolean value, true or false, if the token starts with either an a, e, i, o, or u. Strings that satisfy this test are converted to Pig-Latin by appending the word *way* to the end of the string. Tokens that don't match that test have their initial consonant value stripped from the start of the word and appended to the end along with the letters *ay*:

```
class JButtonStrategy1 extends JButton implements Command {

    public JButtonStrategy1(String caption) { super(caption); }
    public void execute() {
        String s = textfield1.getText();
        String[] sArray = s.split("[ ,]+");
        StringBuffer sb = new StringBuffer();
```

```
            sb.append("PIG-LATIN: ");

            for (int i=0; i < sArray.length; i++) {
               if (testStrategy(new StartsWithAEIOU(), sArray[i])) {
                  sb.append(sArray[i] + "way ");
               } else {
                  sb.append(sArray[i].replaceAll("^([^aeiouAEIOU])(.+)", "$2$1ay "));
               }
            }
            messageText.setText(sb.toString());
         }
   }
```

The JButtonStrategy2 class invokes the execute() method when the user clicks the Strategy #2 button on the GUI panel. The text specified in the text field is stripped into individual tokens that are passed into the AlphabeticChars strategy class to determine if they can be properly converted to uppercase lettering:

```
class JButtonStrategy2 extends JButton implements Command {

   public JButtonStrategy2(String caption) { super(caption); }
   public void execute() {
      String s = textfield2.getText();
      String[] sArray = s.split("[ ,]+");
      StringBuffer sb = new StringBuffer();
      sb.append("UPPERCASE: ");

      for (int i=0; i < sArray.length; i++) {
         if (testStrategy(new convertUppercase(), sArray[i])) {
            sb.append(sArray[i].toUpperCase());
            sb.append(" ");
         }
      }
      messageText.setText(sb.toString());
   }
}

class JButtonClear extends JButton implements Command {

   public JButtonClear(String caption) { super(caption); }
   public void execute() {
      textfield1.setText("");
      textfield2.setText("");
      messageText.setText("User cleared text: ");
   }
}

public void itemStateChanged(ItemEvent evt) {
   CardLayout cl = (CardLayout)(cards.getLayout());
   cl.show(cards, (String)evt.getItem());
}

public interface Command {
   public void execute();
}
```

The TestStrategy interface is implemented by the StartsWithAEIOU and AlphabeticChars classes so that the CardLayoutPanel application can apply different string algorithms to the user-specified text. Regular expression constructs are used to determine the patterns of the strings passed into the test method:

```
public interface TestStrategy {
    public boolean test(String s);
}

public class StartsWithAEIOU implements TestStrategy {
    public boolean test(String s) {
        if( s == null || s.length() == 0) return false;
            return (s.toUpperCase().charAt(0) == 'A' ||
                    s.toUpperCase().charAt(0) == 'E' ||
                    s.toUpperCase().charAt(0) == 'I' ||
                    s.toUpperCase().charAt(0) == 'O' ||
                    s.toUpperCase().charAt(0) == 'U'
                );
    }
}

public class convertUppercase implements TestStrategy {
    public boolean test(String s) {
        if( s == null || s.length() == 0 ) return false;
        Pattern pattern = Pattern.compile("[a-zA-Z]");
        Matcher match = pattern.matcher(s);
        if (!match.find()) {
            return false;
        } else {
            return (true);
        }
    }
}

// main routine omitted for brevity

}
```

Figure 4-14 represents the CardLayoutPanel application modeled in the source code above. Users can enter text in the card layout show in the top panel and hit either strategy pattern button to apply the appropriate Strategy algorithm to that text. Results of those actions will be rendered in the card layout below. All of the button components employ the Command pattern to allow the application to determine at run time the proper execute() method to invoke based on the user's navigations.

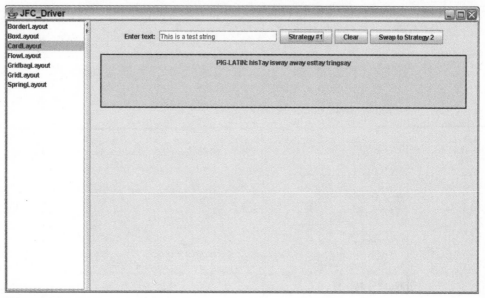

Figure 4-14

JFrame and JDialog Components

The JFrame class is used in Java applications to construct a top-level window for GUI components with a border and title, as well as buttons for minimization, maximization, and closure. The JDialog class is used to build pop-up windows for user decision making and aggregating unified data entries. Both classes are important features of the Swing libraries to build cohesive GUI components.

This portion of the chapter will disclose how the JFrame and JDialog classes can be used in tandem to build an effective Annotation Editor application. The sample application will allow users to mark up text files so that meta data, in the form of comments and associated attributes, can be linked to a document passage from a user-specified file. Annotations typically mean comments, notes, or explanations that can be attached to the text without actually needing to touch the document. When a user opens a document in the editor, all meta data text that is persisted in a MySQL database will be attached to the text marked up by users who have commented on passages in that file (see Figure 4-15).

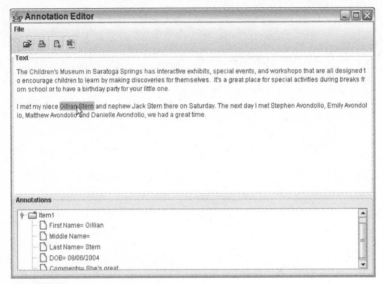

Figure 4-15

The code here demonstrates how the Annotation Editor was developed. A MySQL database is used to persist meta data associated with marked text in the document. Additionally, logic was added to save the annotation to Microsoft Excel spreadsheet artifacts using Jakarta POI libraries, as well as XML documents using dom4j libraries:

```
// package name and import statements omitted

public class AnnotationEditor extends JFrame {

    // declaration omitted for sake of brevity [please check out source download]

    public AnnotationEditor() {
        super("Annotation Editor");

        initPopupMenu();
        popupListener = new PopupListener();
        componentListener = new ComponentListener();

        textComp = createTextComponent();
        textComp.addMouseListener(popupListener);
        textComp.addCaretListener(componentListener);
        textComp.setBorder(BorderFactory.createCompoundBorder(
                        BorderFactory.createCompoundBorder(
                        BorderFactory.createTitledBorder("Text"),
                        BorderFactory.createEmptyBorder(5,5,5,5)),
                        textComp.getBorder()));
                        textComp.setEditable(false);

        scrollPane = new JScrollPane();
        scrollPane.setVerticalScrollBarPolicy(JScrollPane.VERTICAL_SCROLLBAR_ALWAYS);
        scrollPane.setPreferredSize(new Dimension(350, 150));
```

```
            scrollPane.setBorder(BorderFactory.createCompoundBorder(
                          BorderFactory.createCompoundBorder(
                          BorderFactory.createTitledBorder("Annotations"),
                          BorderFactory.createEmptyBorder(5,5,5,5)),
                          scrollPane.getBorder())));

        root = new DefaultMutableTreeNode("Annotations");
        tree = new JTree(root);
        scrollPane.getViewport().add( tree );

        content = getContentPane();
        content.add(textComp, BorderLayout.CENTER);
        content.add(createToolBar(), BorderLayout.NORTH);
        content.add(scrollPane, BorderLayout.SOUTH);
        setJMenuBar(createMenuBar());
        setSize(700, 500);
    }
```

The `AnnotationEditor(String filename)` constructor method invokes the `createTextComponent()` method to instantiate a JTextArea component used to display the file used for annotating text. The FileReader class is used to read the file for annotation and posit in the text area display textComp. The center and north quadrants of a BorderLayout manager are used to display the annotation file and tool-bar components:

```
    public AnnotationEditor(String filename) {
        super("Annotation Editor");

        textComp = createTextComponent();
        File file = new File(filename);
        if (file == null) return;

        FileReader reader = null;
        try {
            reader = new FileReader(file);
            textComp.read(reader, null);
        } catch (IOException ex) {
            JOptionPane.showMessageDialog(AnnotationEditor.this,
            "File Not Found", "ERROR", JOptionPane.ERROR_MESSAGE);
        }
        finally {
            if (reader != null) {
                try {
                    reader.close();
                } catch (IOException x) {}
            }
        }

        Container content = getContentPane();
        content.add(textComp, BorderLayout.CENTER);
        content.add(createToolBar(), BorderLayout.NORTH);
        setJMenuBar(createMenuBar());
        setSize(320, 240);
    }

    protected JTextComponent createTextComponent() {
```

```
        JTextArea ta = new JTextArea();
        ta.setLineWrap(true);
        return ta;
    }
```

The initPopupMenu() method kicks off a dialog panel that allows users to input meta data associated with the person highlighted in the editor display. The actionPeformed(ActionEvent evt) method is implemented to handle mouse events when the user right-clicks text within the GUI display. If the user selects the Person link inside the pop-up panel, then the application will pop up the AnnotationPeopleDialog component so that users can attach meta data to the text highlighted by the user:

```
    protected void initPopupMenu() {
        popup = new JPopupMenu();
        ActionListener menuListener = new ActionListener() {
            public void actionPerformed(ActionEvent event) {
                if ("Person".equals(event.getActionCommand())) {
                    String[] markedText = textComp.getSelectedText().trim().split("[
]+");

                    for (int i=0; i < markedText.length; i++)
                      AnnotationPeopleDialog dlg =
                          new AnnotationPeopleDialog(textComp.getSelectedText().trim(),
                                                    filename.toString(),
                                                    getAnnotationStart(),
                                                    getAnnotationEnd());
                    dlg.show();
                    highlight(textComp, textComp.getSelectedText().trim());
                } else if ("Annotations".equals(event.getActionCommand())) {
                    AnnotationSearchResultsDialog d = new AnnotationSearchResultsDialog();
                    d.show();
                }
            }
        };
```

Users can kick off the dialog panel for annotation entry by right-clicking their mouse inside the GUI presentation, which will pop up a panel with two user selections, Person or Export Excel. If the user selects Person, then the dialog will present the data input form. Alternatively, if the user clicks Export Excel, then all of the annotations that reside in the database will be exported to an Excel spreadsheet. Figure 4-16 illustrates how the AnnotationPeopleDialog display is rendered so that users can attach meta data to the highlighted Gillian Stern text.

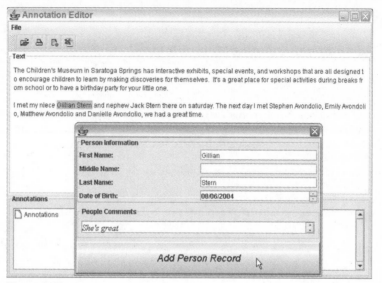

Figure 4-16

```
      // add images and listeners
      itemPerson = new JMenuItem("Person", createImageIcon("images/people.gif"));
      itemPerson.setActionCommand("Person");
      itemPerson.addActionListener(menuListener);
      popup.add(itemPerson);
      itemExportExcel = new JMenuItem("Export Excel",
createImageIcon("images/excel.gif"));
      itemExportExcel.setActionCommand("Export Excel");
      itemExportExcel.addActionListener(menuListener);
      popup.add(itemExportExcel);

      // The code here is commented out, but is a new feature of J2SDK1.5 that
      // allows users to easily implement context-sensitive menus that appear when
      // a user right-clicks over a specified area in a GUI display. Rather than
      // checking the trigger within the MouseEvent class, control is passed to
      // to the JpopupMenu class itself. If the code below is commented out, then
      // the PopupListener class below should be omitted, as well as the
      // instantiation of that class above and its ties to the JTextArea mouse
      // listener in the textComp.addMouseListener(popupListener) operation
      //
      // JButton button = new JButton("Test");
      // button.setComponentPopupMenu(popup);
      // getContentPane().add(button, BorderLayout.CENTER);

   }

   class PopupListener extends MouseAdapter {
      public void mousePressed(MouseEvent e) { showPopup(e); }
      public void mouseClicked(MouseEvent e) { showPopup(e); }
      public void mouseReleased(MouseEvent e) { showPopup(e); }
```

```
        private void showPopup(MouseEvent e) {
            if (e.isPopupTrigger()) {
                popup.show(e.getComponent(), e.getX(), e.getY());
            }
        }
    }
```

The ComponentListener class implements the CaretListener interface to process the user marking activities inside the editor application. The Select operation in the PreparedStatement below takes the start and end positions of the annotation text to determine what annotations have been affiliated with that text:

```
public class ComponentListener implements CaretListener {

    public void caretUpdate(CaretEvent e) {
        displaySelectionInfo(e.getDot(), e.getMark());
    }

    protected void displaySelectionInfo(final int dot, final int mark) {
        SwingUtilities.invokeLater(new Runnable() {
            public void run() {

                setAnnotationInfo(mark, dot);
                // retrieve annotation text
                try {
                    Class.forName("org.gjt.mm.mysql.Driver");
                    Connection conn =
DriverManager.getConnection("jdbc:mysql://localhost/annotationtest", "", "");
                    PreparedStatement preparedStmt =
                        conn.prepareStatement("SELECT F_FILENAME, ANNOTATION_TYPE,
ANNOTATION_TEXT FROM ANNOTATION_TABLE WHERE ? >= ANNOTATION_START AND ? <=
ANNOTATION_END");
                    preparedStmt.setInt( 1, mark );
                    preparedStmt.setInt( 2, dot );
                    ResultSet result = preparedStmt.executeQuery();
                    if (result != null) {
                        String annotationFilename="";
                        String annotationType="";
                        while (result.next()) {
                            annotationFilename = result.getString(1);
                            annotationType = result.getString(2);
                        }
```

If the annotation filename is not empty, then all of the attributes of the annotation file are retrieved (so that they can be added to the JTree component for visualization) and the database connection is closed:

```
                        if (!annotationFilename.equals("")) {
                            preparedStmt =
                                conn.prepareStatement("SELECT * FROM " + annotationType +
" WHERE FILENAME = ?" +
                                    " AND ? >= ANNOTATION_START AND ? <= ANNOTATION_END");
                            preparedStmt.setString( 1, annotationFilename );
                            preparedStmt.setInt( 2, mark );
                            preparedStmt.setInt( 3, dot );
```

```
                        result = preparedStmt.executeQuery();

                        int itemsCount = 0;
                        root = new DefaultMutableTreeNode("Annotations");
                        tree = new JTree(root);
                        DefaultMutableTreeNode items;

                        if (annotationType.equals("PERSON")) {
                            while (result.next()) {
                                items = new DefaultMutableTreeNode("Item" +
(++itemsCount));
                                root.add(items);
                                items.add(new DefaultMutableTreeNode("First Name= " +
result.getString(2)));
                                items.add(new DefaultMutableTreeNode("Middle Name= " +
result.getString(3)));
                                items.add(new DefaultMutableTreeNode("Last Name= " +
result.getString(4)));
                                items.add(new DefaultMutableTreeNode("DOB= " +
result.getString(5)));
                                items.add(new DefaultMutableTreeNode("Comments= " +
result.getString(6)));
                            }
                        }
                        scrollPane.getViewport().add( tree );
                        tree.expandRow(0);
                    }
                }
                conn.close();
            } catch (Exception e) {
                logger.info("Exception: " + e.toString());
            }
        }
    });
    }

  }
    // setAnnotationInfo(), getAnnotationStart() and getAnnotationEnd() omitted for
the sake of brevity
```

The createToolBar() method instantiates a new toolbar component to add the actions that a user can perform in the editor application. Those actions include the opening and printing of files and the exporting of annotations to XML and Excel spreadsheet artifacts:

```
    protected JToolBar createToolBar() {
      JToolBar bar = new JToolBar();
      bar.add(getOpenAction()).setText("");
      bar.add(getPrintAction()).setText("");
      bar.add(getXmlAction()).setText("");
      bar.add(getExcelAction()).setText("");
      return bar;
    }
```

The highlight and removeHighlights methods are invoked by the user when text inside the editor is marked and unmarked by mouse activities by the user. The text marked inside the text area component textComp is collected by the invocation of the getHighlighter() method, and the text is highlighted in the view by the addHighlight method. Alternatively, text highlights are removed by invoking the removeHighlights method:

```java
public void highlight(JTextComponent textComp, String pattern) {

    try {
        hilite = textComp.getHighlighter();
        doc = textComp.getDocument();
        String text = doc.getText(0, doc.getLength());
        int pos = 0;

        // save annotation position and length for future reference
        int x = text.indexOf(pattern, pos);
        if (x > 0) {
            hilite.addHighlight(x, x+pattern.length(), myHighlightPainter);
        }
    } catch (BadLocationException e) {
        logger.severe("BadLocationException e" + e.toString());
    }
}

public void removeHighlights(JTextComponent textComp) {
    Highlighter hilite = textComp.getHighlighter();
    Highlighter.Highlight[] hilites = hilite.getHighlights();

    for (int i=0; i<hilites.length; i++) {
        if (hilites[i].getPainter() instanceof MyHighlightPainter) {
            hilite.removeHighlight(hilites[i]);
        }
    }
}
```

The HighlightPainter class is instantiated with color attributes sent to the Color constructor so that all highlights in the text document persist the same color throughout the text. The `createMenuBar()` method returns a JMenuBar object with actions for opening and printing files, as well as for persisting the annotations in XML and Microsoft Excel files and finally for exiting the application altogether:

```java
Highlighter.HighlightPainter myHighlightPainter = new MyHighlightPainter(new
Color(255,204,51));

class MyHighlightPainter extends DefaultHighlighter.DefaultHighlightPainter {
    public MyHighlightPainter(Color color) {
        super(color);
    }
}

protected JMenuBar createMenuBar() {
    JMenuBar menubar = new JMenuBar();
    JMenu file = new JMenu("File");
    menubar.add(file);

    file.add(getOpenAction());
```

```
        file.add(getPrintAction());
        file.add(getXmlAction());
        file.add(getExcelAction());
        file.add(new ExitAction());
        return menubar;
    }
```

The Action interface provides an extension to the ActionListener interface whereby an application needs to implement an actionPerformed() method to obtain desirable system behavior. That behavior could be for a fly-over text display or to modify component event generation. The AnnotationEditor establishes four user actions for File Open, Print, XML, and Excel spreadsheet generation operations.

The peopleAction method kicks off a dialog that allows users to add people information that has been marked in the editor display. When invoked, the application creates a new instance of the AnnotationPeopleDialog class, the class reference invoked the show() method to display the panel to the user for data input:

```
    protected Action getOpenAction() { return openAction; }
    protected Action getPrintAction() { return printAction; }
    protected Action getXmlAction() { return xmlAction; }
    protected Action getExcelAction() { return excelAction; }

    protected JTextComponent getTextComponent() { return textComp; }


    protected Action getPeopleAction() { return peopleAction; }

    public class peopleAction extends AbstractAction {
        public peopleAction() {
            super("People", new ImageIcon("images/people.gif"));
        }
        public void actionPerformed(ActionEvent ev) {
            AnnotationPeopleDialog dlg = new AnnotationPeopleDialog();
            dlg.show();
        }
    }

    public class ExitAction extends AbstractAction {
        public ExitAction() { super("Exit"); }
        public void actionPerformed(ActionEvent ev) { System.exit(0); }
    }
```

The PrintAction class collects all information from the Person database table and kicks off a print GUI to allow users to dictate where the aggregated people information will be printed. All of the annotation text that will be submitted for printout will be aggregated through the Select construct placed in the PreparedStatement that follows. Each individual row of the Person table will be stuffed into an instance of a AnnotationPersonRecord object and added to a list collection before it is passed to the printArrays method of the AnnotationPrint class:

```
    public class PrintAction extends AbstractAction {
        public PrintAction() {
            super("Print", new ImageIcon("icons/print.gif"));
        }
        public void actionPerformed(ActionEvent ev) {
```

```
        try {
            Class.forName("org.gjt.mm.mysql.Driver");
            Connection conn =
                DriverManager.getConnection("jdbc:mysql://localhost/annotationtest",
"", "");

            PreparedStatement preparedStmt =
                conn.prepareStatement("SELECT * FROM PERSON WHERE FILENAME = ?");
            preparedStmt.setString( 1, filename.toString());

            ResultSet result = preparedStmt.executeQuery();
            ArrayList list = new ArrayList();
            while (result.next()) {
                AnnotationPersonRecord person = new AnnotationPersonRecord();
                person.setFirstName(result.getString(2));
                person.setMiddleName(result.getString(3));
                person.setLastName(result.getString(4));
                person.setDob(result.getString(5));
                person.setComments(result.getString(6));
                person.setFilename(result.getString(7));
                person.setAnnotationStart(result.getString(8));
                person.setAnnotationEnd(result.getString(9));
                list.add(person);
            }
            if (list != null) {
                for (int i=0; i < list.size(); i++) {
                    AnnotationPersonRecord element =
(AnnotationPersonRecord)list.get(i);
                }
                AnnotationPrint.printArrayS( list );
            }
        } catch (Exception e) {
            logger.info("Exception: " + e.toString());
        }
    }
}
```

The createDocument(ResultSet rs) method works in conjunction with the XMLAction class to export annotation data to an XML file upon user request. Libraries are used from the dom4j package to craft an XML file artifact with the annotation text. The addElement method adds a new Element node to the topic branches of the document data structure:

```
static public org.dom4j.Document createDocument(ResultSet rs) {

    org.dom4j.Document document = org.dom4j.DocumentHelper.createDocument();
    org.dom4j.Element root = document.addElement( "Annotation" )
                                    .addAttribute("text", "Default annotation")
                                    .addAttribute("value", "default");

    try {
        org.dom4j.Element topic = null;
        int item=0;
        while (rs.next()) {
            ++item;
            topic = root.addElement( "person" ).addAttribute( "value", "item"
).addAttribute( "text", String.valueOf(item));
```

```
            topic.addElement( "attribute" ).addAttribute( "value", "First Name"
).addAttribute( "text", rs.getString(2) );
            topic.addElement( "attribute" ).addAttribute( "value", "Middle Name"
).addAttribute( "text", rs.getString(3) );
            topic.addElement( "attribute" ).addAttribute( "value", "Last Name"
).addAttribute( "text", rs.getString(4) );
            topic.addElement( "attribute" ).addAttribute( "value", "DOB"
).addAttribute( "text", rs.getString(5) );
            topic.addElement( "attribute" ).addAttribute( "value", "Comments"
).addAttribute( "text", rs.getString(6) );
            topic.addElement( "attribute" ).addAttribute( "value", "Filename"
).addAttribute( "text", rs.getString(7) );
        }
    } catch (Exception sqle) {
        logger.info("SQLException: " + sqle.toString());
    }
    return document;
}
```

The XMLAction class establishes a database connection to the annotationtest database and performs a select operation so that the attributes of the annotation table will be output to an XML file. The data collected from the SQL operation is passed to the createDocument method described earlier:

```
public class XmlAction extends AbstractAction {
    public XmlAction() {
        super("XML", new ImageIcon("icons/xml.gif"));
    }
    public void actionPerformed(ActionEvent ev) {
        logger.info("Generating XML.");
        try {
            Class.forName("org.gjt.mm.mysql.Driver");
            Connection conn =
                DriverManager.getConnection("jdbc:mysql://localhost/annotationtest",
"", "");
            PreparedStatement preparedStmt =
                conn.prepareStatement("SELECT * FROM PERSON WHERE FILENAME = ?");
            preparedStmt.setString( 1, filename.toString());

            ResultSet result = preparedStmt.executeQuery();
            XMLWriter writer = new XMLWriter(new FileWriter( "Annotation.xml" ),
OutputFormat.createPrettyPrint());
            writer.write( createDocument( result ) );
            writer.close();
        } catch(Exception e) {
            logger.info("Exception: " + e.toString());
        }
    }
}
```

The ExcelAction class implements the Open-source Jakarta POI libraries to convert the Person table data to an Excel spreadsheet document. New workbook and sheet objects are created with the POI libraries and the annotation attributes that make up the annotation table are saved to those objects. For demonstration purposes, only the first, middle, and last name values are placed in the worksheet template:

```
    public class ExcelAction extends AbstractAction {
        public ExcelAction() {
            super("Excel", new ImageIcon("icons/excel.gif"));
        }
        public void actionPerformed(ActionEvent ev) {
            logger.info("Generating Excel Spreadsheet.");
            int rownum;

            try {

                FileOutputStream out = new FileOutputStream("annotations.xls");
                HSSFWorkbook wb = new HSSFWorkbook();

                HSSFSheet s = wb.createSheet();

                HSSFRow r = null;

                HSSFCell c = null;
                HSSFCellStyle cs = wb.createCellStyle();
                HSSFDataFormat df = wb.createDataFormat();
                HSSFFont f = wb.createFont();

                f.setFontHeightInPoints((short) 12);

                cs.setFont(f);

                cs.setDataFormat(HSSFDataFormat.getBuiltinFormat("text"));

                wb.setSheetName(0, "Test", HSSFWorkbook.ENCODING_COMPRESSED_UNICODE );
                // set title row
                String[] titles = {"First Name", "Middle Name", "Last Name" };
                r = s.createRow(0);
                for (int i=0; i < titles.length; i++ ) {
                    s.setColumnWidth((short) (i + 1), (short) ((50 * 8) / ((double) 1 /
20))));
                    c = r.createCell((short) (i + 1));
                    c.setCellStyle(cs);
                    c.setEncoding( HSSFCell.ENCODING_COMPRESSED_UNICODE );
                    c.setCellValue( titles[i] );
                }
```

The following code segment demonstrates how the SQL construct is built and executed so that the data collected can be saved to the Excel template file:

```
            try {
            Class.forName("org.gjt.mm.mysql.Driver");
            Connection conn =
                DriverManager.getConnection("jdbc:mysql://localhost/annotationtest",
"", "");
            PreparedStatement preparedStmt =
                conn.prepareStatement("SELECT * FROM PERSON");
            ResultSet result = preparedStmt.executeQuery();
            int row = 1;
            while (result.next()) {
```

```
                r = s.createRow(row);
                c = r.createCell((short) (1));
                c.setCellStyle(cs);
                c.setEncoding( HSSFCell.ENCODING_COMPRESSED_UNICODE );
                c.setCellValue( result.getString(2) );
                c = r.createCell((short) (2));
                c.setCellStyle(cs);
                c.setEncoding( HSSFCell.ENCODING_COMPRESSED_UNICODE );
                c.setCellValue( result.getString(3) );
                c = r.createCell((short) (3));
                c.setCellStyle(cs);
                c.setEncoding( HSSFCell.ENCODING_COMPRESSED_UNICODE );
                c.setCellValue( result.getString(4) );
                row++;
            }

        } catch (Exception e) {
            logger.info("Exception: " + e.toString());
        }
        wb.write(out);
        out.close();
    } catch(IOException ioe) { logger.info("IOException= " + ioe.toString()); }
    }
}
```

The OpenAction class uses the JFileChooser class to enable users to dynamically determine the files that will read into the AnnotationEditor for annotation operations. When a user selects the Open link in the menu bar, the showOpenDialog method will pop up a dialog box that allows users to drill across the system's file structures for retrieval and manipulation:

```
// An action that opens an existing file
class OpenAction extends AbstractAction {
  public OpenAction() {
    super("Open", new ImageIcon("icons/open.gif"));
  }

  // Query user for a filename and attempt to open and read the file into the
  // text component.
  public void actionPerformed(ActionEvent ev) {
    JFileChooser chooser = new JFileChooser();
    if (chooser.showOpenDialog(AnnotationEditor.this) !=
JFileChooser.APPROVE_OPTION)
      return;
    filename = chooser.getSelectedFile();
    if (filename == null)
      return;

    FileReader reader = null;
    try {
      reader = new FileReader(filename);
      textComp.read(reader, null);
      // read annotations and markup text here
      try {
        Class.forName("org.gjt.mm.mysql.Driver");
```

The code snippet below establishes a database connection with the annotationtest database to retrieve the annotations associated with the document opened in the code above. Once all of the annotations have been retrieved, then the text associated with those annotations is highlighted in the AnnotationEditor application:

```
            Connection conn =
                DriverManager.getConnection("jdbc:mysql://localhost/annotationtest",
"", "");
            PreparedStatement preparedStmt =
                conn.prepareStatement("SELECT ANNOTATION_START, ANNOTATION_END,
ANNOTATION_TEXT FROM ANNOTATION_TABLE");
            ResultSet result = preparedStmt.executeQuery();
            while (result.next()) {
                highlight(textComp, result.getString(3));
            }

        } catch (Exception e) {
            logger.info("Exception: " + e.toString());
        }

    } catch (IOException ex) {
    JOptionPane.showMessageDialog(AnnotationEditor.this,
    "File Not Found", "ERROR", JOptionPane.ERROR_MESSAGE);
    } finally {
    if (reader != null) {
      try {
        reader.close();
      } catch (IOException x) {}
    }
    }
  }
 }
    // main method omitted for the sake of brevity
}
```

The importance of dialog components cannot be understated because they allow applications to organize and prioritize data for your user interface so that information can be properly propagated to your data persistence mechanism, which might be a database or collection class implementation. When an application invokes a dialog box, it forces the user to aggregate information in a controlled fashion from a user so that information can be added or modified for your application's operations.

Some dialog applications are modal, which means that they block all user input to windows in a program when they are visible, but the AnnotationDialog application is nonmodal because it uses the JDialog class directly.

The AnnotationDialog application below enables users to dynamically add information about people that a user has marked for insertion by the user in the editor application (see Figure 4-17).

Figure 4-17

```
// [AnnotationPeopleDialog.java]
// package name and import statements omitted
public class AnnotationPeopleDialog extends JDialog implements ActionListener {
   // declarations omitted for the sake of brevity [please look at source downloads]
   public interface Command {
      public void execute();
   }

   public AnnotationPeopleDialog(String annotation, String filename,
                                 int annotationStart, int annotationEnd) {
      // parameter save omitted for the sake of brevity
      createGUIDisplay();
   }

   public AnnotationPeopleDialog() {
      createGUIDisplay();
   }

   public void createGUIDisplay() {
      JPanel panelAll = new JPanel(new GridLayout(0,1,5,5));
      JPanel panelTest1 = new JPanel(new GridLayout(0,1,5,5));
      panelTest1.add(panelGUI());

      JPanel panelTest2 = new JPanel(new GridLayout(0,1,5,5));
      panelTest2.add(panelComments());

      panelAll.add(panelTest1);
      panelAll.add(panelTest2);

      String[] name = annotation.trim().split("[ ]+");
      if (name.length == 3) {
         firstName.setText(name[0]);
         middleName.setText(name[1]);
         lastName.setText(name[2]);
      } else {
         firstName.setText(name[0]);
         lastName.setText(name[1]);
      }
      getContentPane().add(panelAll);
      getContentPane().setVisible(true);

      pack();
   }
```

The panelGUI() method establishes a GridLayout display so that users can enter user data that will be affiliated with highlighted text inside the AnnotationEditor. Figure 4-16 represents the GUI presentation that will be rendered when the panelGUI() method is invoked:

```
public JPanel panelGUI() {
   JPanel peoplePanel = new JPanel(new GridLayout(0,2,5,5));

   firstName = new JTextField(20);
   middleName = new JTextField(20);
   lastName = new JTextField(20);
```

```
        model1 = new SpinnerDateModel();
        model1.setCalendarField(Calendar.WEEK_OF_MONTH);
        spinner1 = new JSpinner(model1);
        JSpinner.DateEditor editor1 = new JSpinner.DateEditor(spinner1, "MM/dd/yyyy");
        spinner1.setEditor(editor1);

        // add items to panel
        peoplePanel.add(new JLabel("First Name:"));
        peoplePanel.add(firstName);
        peoplePanel.add(new JLabel("Middle Name:"));
        peoplePanel.add(middleName);
        peoplePanel.add(new JLabel("Last Name:"));
        peoplePanel.add(lastName);
        peoplePanel.add(new JLabel("Date of Birth:"));
        peoplePanel.add(spinner1);
        titledBorder = BorderFactory.createTitledBorder(new EtchedBorder
 (EtchedBorder.LOWERED), "Person Information");
        titledBorder.setTitleJustification(TitledBorder.LEFT);
        peoplePanel.setBorder(titledBorder);

        return peoplePanel;
    }
```

The panelComments() method generates the text area component that collects user comments that will be associated with the name and date of birth text in the AnnotationPeopleDialog class:

```
    public JPanel panelComments() {

        JPanel peoplePanel = new JPanel(new GridLayout(0,1,5,5));

        peopleComments = new JTextArea("");
        peopleComments.setFont(new Font("Serif", Font.ITALIC, 16));
        peopleComments.setLineWrap(true);
        peopleComments.setWrapStyleWord(true);
        areaScrollPane1 = new JScrollPane(peopleComments);
        areaScrollPane1.setVerticalScrollBarPolicy(
            JScrollPane.VERTICAL_SCROLLBAR_ALWAYS);
        areaScrollPane1.setPreferredSize(new Dimension(50, 50));
        areaScrollPane1.setBorder(BorderFactory.createCompoundBorder(
                            BorderFactory.createCompoundBorder(
        BorderFactory.createTitledBorder(" People Comments"),
        BorderFactory.createEmptyBorder(5,5,5,5)),
        areaScrollPane1.getBorder()));

        addPersonRecord = new JAddPersonButton(" Add Person Record ");
        addPersonRecord.addActionListener(this);
        addPersonRecord.setFont(navigationFont);
        addPersonRecord.setBorder(raisedBevelBorder);

        peoplePanel.add(areaScrollPane1);
        peoplePanel.add(addPersonRecord);

        return peoplePanel;
    }
```

The ComboListener class listens for user actions on the combobox component on the GUI display. The actionPerformed(ActionEvent e) method implements the Command pattern so that user activities are handled appropriately by the AnnotationEditor application:

```
class ComboListener implements ActionListener {
    public void actionPerformed(ActionEvent e) {
        JComboBox cb = (JComboBox)e.getSource();
        logger.info("Combo selection= " + (String)cb.getSelectedItem());
    }
}

public void actionPerformed(ActionEvent e) {
    Command obj = (Command)e.getSource();
    try {
        obj.execute();
    } catch (Exception ex) {
        logger.info("Exception: " + ex);
    }
}
```

The JAddPersonButton method polymorphically invokes the `execute()` method, which uses the JOptionPane class to pop up a standard dialog box to collect relevant annotation data that relates to the person highlighted in the Annotation Editor. The showConfirmDialog method asks the user whether or not the information entered should be persisted by the application or neglected when the dialog box exits. If the user selects Yes when queried, "Are You Sure?", then an SQL prepared statement is constructed to aggregate the user information for insertion to the person and annotation_table tables, respectively:

```
class JAddPersonButton extends JButton implements Command {

    public JAddPersonButton(String caption) { super(caption); }
    public void execute() {
        int selection = JOptionPane.showConfirmDialog(null, "Are you sure?",
                          "People database insert.",
JOptionPane.YES_NO_CANCEL_OPTION);
        if (selection == 0) {

            try {
                Class.forName("org.gjt.mm.mysql.Driver");
                Connection conn =
DriverManager.getConnection("jdbc:mysql://localhost/annotationtest", "", "");
                PreparedStatement preparedStmt =
                    conn.prepareStatement("INSERT INTO PERSON (FIRST_NAME, MIDDLE_NAME,
LAST_NAME, DOB, COMMENTS, FILENAME, ANNOTATION_START, ANNOTATION_END) VALUES
(?,?,?,?,?,?,?,?)");

                preparedStmt.setString( 1, firstName.getText().toString() );
                preparedStmt.setString( 2, middleName.getText().toString() );
                preparedStmt.setString( 3, lastName.getText().toString() );
                preparedStmt.setString( 4,
((JSpinner.DateEditor)spinner1.getEditor()).getTextField().getText() );
                preparedStmt.setString( 5, peopleComments.getText().toString() );
                preparedStmt.setString( 6, filename );
```

```
                    preparedStmt.setInt( 7, annotationStart );
                    preparedStmt.setInt( 8, annotationEnd );
                    preparedStmt.executeUpdate();

                    preparedStmt =
                        conn.prepareStatement("INSERT INTO ANNOTATION_TABLE (F_FILENAME,
ANNOTATION_TYPE, ANNOTATION_START, ANNOTATION_END, ANNOTATION_TEXT) VALUES
(?,?,?,?,?)");
                    preparedStmt.setString( 1, filename );
                    preparedStmt.setString( 2, "PERSON" );
                    preparedStmt.setInt( 3, annotationStart);
                    preparedStmt.setInt( 4, annotationEnd);
                    preparedStmt.setString( 5, annotation );
                    preparedStmt.executeUpdate();

                    conn.close();

                } catch(Exception e) { logger.info("Exception = " + e.toString());}
            } else {
                logger.info("User selected: NO");
            }
            hidePanel();

        }
    }

    public void hidePanel() {
        setVisible(false);
    }

    // main method omitted for brevity

}
```

Managing Navigation Flows in Swing Applications

Installation wizards are common Swing applications to consign software applications and their libraries to their file systems during their development or deployment tasks. Wizards typically perform initialization activities, gather user directory designations, and perform post-installation tasks for clean-up actions by leading users through a series of requests to ensure that applications and their libraries are configured properly for operations. This last segment of the chapter will demonstrate how an InstallationWizard application can be developed using the State Pattern, a GoF behavioral pattern, to delegate behaviors across objects during user navigations at run time. Each state, or step, of the wizard is encapsulated as an object, which is affiliated to a subclass of an abstract class for proper state management This same application could have easily been developed with the CardLayout manager using its first(), last(), previous(), and next() methods, but the intent was to show how you could manage those flows in a different fashion. Additionally, the Singleton pattern is implemented in the sample application to demonstrate how a single object can be created and referenced from a program without incurring the overhead of creating superfluous objects.

The following table outlines some of benefits and drawbacks of implementing both patterns in your applications.

Pattern	Benefits	Consequences
Singleton	Direct control over how many instances can be created Ensures that a class has only one instance and enforces controlled access to the sole instance	Inability to subclass an application that implements it, which prevents extendibility
State	Allows an object to modify its behavior when its state changes internally Localizes all behavior of a particular state in a single object Polymorphically defines behaviors and states of an object	Preponderance of classes to support the different states of an application

The individual panel display components represent state-specific behaviors that are derived from the abstract State class. The application maintains a pointer to the current state position in the installation process and reacts to changes by the user as navigation is performed in a forward and backward direction using the Previous and Next buttons on the GUI display (see Figure 4-18).

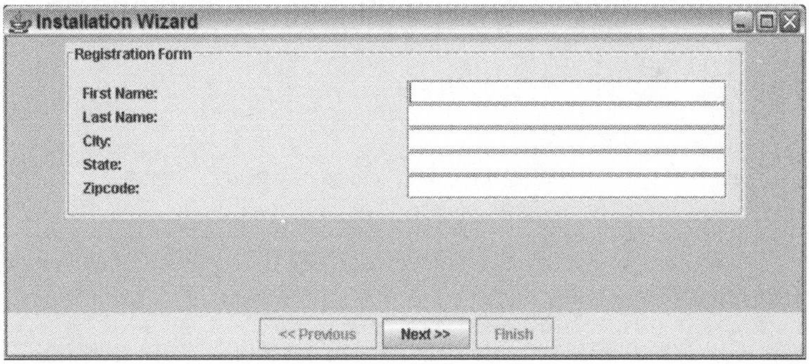

Figure 4-18

The InstallationWizard application implements two JPanel components, componentPanel and buttonPanel, to display the individual Swing visualizations for user input and the buttons used for previous/next operations, respectively:

```
// [InstallationWizard.java]
// package name and import statements omitted

public class InstallationWizard extends JFrame implements ActionListener {

    private static Logger logger = Logger.getLogger("InstallationWizard");
```

```
private JPreviousButton previousButton = new JPreviousButton("<< Previous");
private JNextButton nextButton = new JNextButton("Next >>");
private JFinishButton finishButton = new JFinishButton("Finish");
private JPanel componentPanel;
private JPanel buttonPanel;
private Context context = new Context();

InstallationWizard() {
    super("State Pattern");
    setDefaultCloseOperation(EXIT_ON_CLOSE);
```

The application establishes a context reference that the application uses to determine proper panel visualization flows. The FlowLayout manager is used with the buttonPanel to position the buttons used for directing the wizard flow. The context reference invokes the `getColor()` method to set the background color of the panel component (the default color is Yellow) with the `setBackground(Color bg)` method. Additionally, the previousButton and finishButton components are disabled by the `setEnabled(Boolean b)` method:

```
    context = new Context();

    componentPanel = new JPanel();

    previousButton.addActionListener(this);
    nextButton.addActionListener(this);
    finishButton.addActionListener(this);

    buttonPanel = new JPanel();
    buttonPanel.setLayout(new FlowLayout());
    buttonPanel.add(previousButton);
    buttonPanel.add(nextButton);
    buttonPanel.add(finishButton);

    getContentPane().add(componentPanel, BorderLayout.CENTER);
    getContentPane().add(buttonPanel, BorderLayout.SOUTH);

    // default is yellow
    componentPanel.setBackground(context.getColor());
    previousButton.setEnabled(false);
    finishButton.setEnabled(false);
    componentPanel.add(context.getPanel(), BorderLayout.CENTER);
    componentPanel.setBackground(context.getColor());
    componentPanel.validate();

    setSize(700,300);
}

public void actionPerformed(ActionEvent e) {
    Command obj = (Command)e.getSource();
    obj.execute();
}

public interface Command {
    public void execute();
}
```

The JPreviousButton component manages all user requests when the Previous button is clicked by the user. The execute() method uses the application's context reference to invoke the previous() and getState() methods to set the application to its previous state. The removeAll() method of the Container class is then used to remove all of the components from the container so that the appropriate panel display will be positioned in the user visualization:

```
class JPreviousButton extends JButton implements Command {

    public JPreviousButton(String caption) { super(caption); }
    public void execute() {
        context.previous();
        context.getState();

        componentPanel.removeAll();
        componentPanel.add(context.getPanel(), BorderLayout.CENTER);
        componentPanel.setBackground(context.getColor());
        componentPanel.validate();

        nextButton.setEnabled(true);
        finishButton.setEnabled(false);
        if (context.getColor() == Color.yellow) {
            previousButton.setEnabled(false);
        } else {
            previousButton.setEnabled(true);
        }
    }
}
```

The JNextButton component implements the same methods as the JPreviousButton component to render the appropriate user display when the installation invokes the Next button on the GUI presentation. When the Next button is invoked by the user, all of the components on the panel display will be removed using the removeAll() method. Once the remove operation has been executed, the next color panel will be discovered by using the reference state of the application using the context reference:

```
class JNextButton extends JButton implements Command {

    public JNextButton(String caption) { super(caption); }
    public void execute() {
        context.next();
        context.getState();

        componentPanel.removeAll();
        componentPanel.add(context.getPanel(), BorderLayout.CENTER);
        componentPanel.setBackground(context.getColor());
        componentPanel.validate();

        previousButton.setEnabled(true);
        if (context.getColor() == Color.blue) {
            nextButton.setEnabled(false);
            finishButton.setEnabled(true);
        } else {
            nextButton.setEnabled(true);
            finishButton.setEnabled(false);
```

```
            }
        }
    }
```

The FinishButton class is enabled when the user has reached the final panel display in the series of four panel components:

```
class JFinishButton extends JButton implements Command {

    public JFinishButton(String caption) { super(caption); }
    public void execute() {
        System.exit(1);
    }
}

public static void main(String s[]) {
    InstallationWizard st = new InstallationWizard();
    st.setVisible(true);
}

}
```

The abstract State class is a generalized class used by the Context class to establish a blueprint needed to describe the methods needed to handle the state flows in the wizard across the different panel displays. Two get methods, getColor() and getPanel(), are used to retrieve color and panel values of the individual JPanel components implemented for display:

```
[State.java]
public abstract class State {
    public abstract void handlePrevious(Context c);
    public abstract void handleNext(Context c);
    public abstract Color getColor();
    public abstract JPanel getPanel();
}
```

The Context class below sets the initial state to yellow, so the YellowState application will start the installation program and create objects for the four color applications: Blue, Green, Orange, and Yellow:

```
// [Context.java]
// package name and import statements omitted

public class Context {

    private State state = null;
    public BlueState blueState;
    public GreenState greenState;
    public OrangeState orangeState;
    public YellowState yellowState;

    public Context(State state) { this.state = state; }
    public Context() {
        // get instances for all panels
        blueState = new BlueState();
        greenState = new GreenState();
```

```
            orangeState = new OrangeState();
            yellowState = new YellowState();

            state = getYellowInstance();
    }
    public State getState() { return state; }
    public void setState(State state) { this.state = state; }
    public void previous() { state.handlePrevious(this); }
    public void next() { state.handleNext(this); }
    public Color getColor() {
        return state.getColor();
    }
    public JPanel getPanel() {
        return state.getPanel();
    }
```

The following methods are used to return references to the object instances of the four different panel displays:

```
    public BlueState getBlueInstance() {
        return blueState.getInstance();
    }

    public GreenState getGreenInstance() {
        return greenState.getInstance();
    }

    public OrangeState getOrangeInstance() {
        return orangeState.getInstance();
    }

    public YellowState getYellowInstance() {
        return yellowState.getInstance();
    }

}
```

The YellowState class is the first panel display invoked by the Installation Wizard to start the install process. The YellowState constructor method initializes all of the different textfield components that are used for data collection. The getInstance() method creates a new YellowState instance for reference by other objects if the reference has not been created. If a reference value has already been established, then the reference will be returned to the object that references it:

```
// [YellowState.java]
// package name and import statements omitted

public class YellowState extends State {

    // component declarations and initialization omitted for better clarity

    static private YellowState _instance = null;

    public YellowState() {
        firstName = "";
```

```
        lastName = "";
        city = "";
        state = "";
        zipcode = "";
        generatePanel();
    }

    static public YellowState getInstance() {
        if(null == instance) {
            instance = new YellowState();
        }
        return instance;
    }
```

The handlePrevious(Context c) and handleNext(Context c) methods invoke the setValues() method to persist the values entered into the form display by the user. Once the data has been saved off the local instance variables, the context reference is implemented to obtain the reference to the next panel display. The get<color>Instance() method acquires the Singleton instance generated in the individual panel components:

```
    public void handlePrevious(Context c) {
        setValues();
        c.setState(c.getBlueInstance());
    }

    public void handleNext(Context c) {
        setValues();
        c.setState(c.getOrangeInstance());
    }

    public Color getColor() { return (Color.yellow); }

    public JPanel getPanel() {
        return panelYellow;
    }

    public void generatePanel() {
        log.info("[YellowState:generatePanel]");
        panelYellow = new JPanel(new GridLayout(0,1));
        panelYellow.setSize(200,200);

        formPanel.add(fnameLabel);
        formPanel.add(fnameTextfield);
        formPanel.add(lnameLabel);
        formPanel.add(lnameTextfield);
        formPanel.add(cityLabel);
        formPanel.add(cityTextfield);
        formPanel.add(stateLabel);
        formPanel.add(stateTextfield);
        formPanel.add(zipcodeLabel);
        formPanel.add(zipcodeTextfield);

        Border etchedBdr = BorderFactory.createEtchedBorder();
        Border titledBdr = BorderFactory.createTitledBorder(etchedBdr, "Registration
Form");
```

```
        Border emptyBdr   = BorderFactory.createEmptyBorder(15,15,15,15);
        Border compoundBdr=BorderFactory.createCompoundBorder(titledBdr, emptyBdr);
        formPanel.setBorder(compoundBdr);

        getValues();

        panelYellow.add(formPanel);
    }
```

The `getValues()` method sets the text in the various textfield components using the `setText` methods that are part of the JTextField class. The `setValues()` method retrieves the text from the textfield components and saves them to the various instance variables associated with the panel display:

```
    public void getValues() {
        fnameTextfield.setText(firstName);
        lnameTextfield.setText(lastName);
        cityTextfield.setText(city);
        stateTextfield.setText(state);
        zipcodeTextfield.setText(zipcode);
    }

    public void setValues() {
        firstName = fnameTextfield.getText();
        lastName = lnameTextfield.getText();
        city = cityTextfield.getText();
        state = stateTextfield.getText();
        zipcode = zipcodeTextfield.getText();
    }

}
```

An important object-oriented (OO) concept to remember is that the InstallationWizard uses object composition to alter the behavior of the objects during run time. The wizard application delegates behavior to a known interface and varies the implementation details for the different installation panels.

Summary

This chapter covered a tremendous amount of ground regarding all of the JFC components. All of the Swing top-level containers were discussed (JFrame, JDialog, and JPanel), as well as many of the other Swing visualization components (JButton, JLabel, JSpinner, JTextField, JTextArea, and others). Lastly, Swing listener and layout managers were implemented along with GoF design patterns to craft effective user interface displays. All of the sample applications should help developers address complex GUI development activities and influence designers with their modeling conceptualizations.

The difficulty in explaining the Java Foundation Class (JFC) libraries is that they're broad and varied. The complexities of their implementation can be overcome, as with many things in software development, by actually doing it. With a better understanding of what is possible with JFC packages, a developer can approach a task with confidence that it will get done.

5

Persisting Your Application Using Files

Saving an application's state is one of the most important qualities necessary to reuse an application. Imagine what life would be like if word processors could not save documents, or image manipulation programs could not save images! If a user had to retype a document every time he or she wanted to print it, many tasks now common to computers would probably still be done by hand. An end user calls the ability of a word processing application to save its state *saving a document*. To the software developer, saving a document means saving the internal memory state of the word processing application in such a way as to be able to recreate it exactly as it was left at a future point in time. In this chapter, there will be more references to persisting an application's state than to saving a document, but in reality, they are similar phrases — the former is simply more precise (since an application's state can be saved in other ways than to a file).

Different applications need to save different pieces of information to disk to properly recreate their state. Some applications only need to save their configuration settings to disk, as they may save their other data to a database (see the subsequent chapter to see how to persist your application's data to a database). A typical single-user application such as a word processor or image manipulation program will need to save its state to files (for example, Word documents or JPEG images). Java provides a couple built-in mechanisms for saving or serializing data to files. The two major APIs in the JDK for persisting application data to disk are: the Java Serialization API for generic serialization and the XMLEncoder/Decoder API for serializing Java Bean components. These two APIs will be discussed in depth in this chapter along with the Java API for XML Binding (JAXB). JAXB provides the ability to read and write data to user-defined XML formats. Each of these three APIs has a different approach to serialization and as such should be used in different circumstances. In this chapter, you will first look at how application data is structured in memory, and then apply the Java Serialization API, the XMLEncoder/Decoder API, and the JAXB API to actually serialize the data to disk. These three APIs are a great foundation for persisting your application's data to disk.

The *Imager Application* — Since saving an application's state can be a rather abstract topic, the various persistence strategies that are appropriate to use with the three different APIs with concrete examples will be discussed. A hypothetical image manipulation program will be created and the focus will be on using the Java Serialization API, the XMLEncoder/Decoder API, and JAXB to persist its state to disk. The image manipulation program will be referred to as The *Imager Application* throughout the chapter, and is hypothetical because it will not actually implement image manipulation, since the focus of this chapter is persistence, not GUI development (see the previous chapter for more information on building graphical user interfaces with Swing and the Java Foundation Classes).

Application Data

Every application has some sort of in-memory data structure from which to retrieve its data. Besides data structures like maps, lists, sets, and trees, custom data structures are often built. For an application to save its state, the data in these structures must be saved to disk, and then at a later time, loaded back into the same data structure. Web browsers, for example, create what's called a Document Object Model (DOM) in memory for every Web page that is loaded. It is their internal data structure for displaying HTML pages. Word processors also keep some sort of document object model as well — some way to represent the fact that certain pieces of text are aligned to the right, or possibly that other paragraphs of text are highlighted in a particular color. These custom data structures are necessary for the application to display the data properly to the user.

Viewer applications like Web browsers essentially read files and display them to the user. Web browsers first read HTML files over a network or from a disk, and then parse the data into its internal in-memory data structure, the DOM. Once the data is in the Web browser's data structure, its rendering functions can now properly display the page to the user. Image viewing programs are similar, in that they read an image into their internal data structure representing images, and then display that image to the user. Other types of applications, though, also allow the user to manipulate the data. Word processors, in addition to reading files into their internal data structures and displaying them, also must allow the user to manipulate the data, and therefore the internal data structure, and then write the data back to disk.

Many of these other applications that allow the user to manipulate data follow the Model-View-Controller (MVC) design pattern (see Chapter 3 more for information on design patterns). In this pattern, the internal data structures of the application are called its *data model*. This data model is contained in structures that are separate from UI components and UI-related data structures. In Java-based applications, the data model usually consists of Java Bean components, along with other data storage and collection classes. These data classes are manipulated and modified by UI controller classes (such as events generated by buttons, menus, et cetera), and viewed and presented by other UI components. A simple MVC diagram is shown in Figure 5-1, illustrating how only the *data model* of an MVC-based application needs to be saved to restore the state of the application. Swing or other UI toolkit/utility classes would be in both the view and controller areas while the internal data model specific to the domain of the application would be contained in the *data model*. This step of separating domain data from UI components allows for a much easier process of saving and loading the data from disk since the data is all in one place: the model.

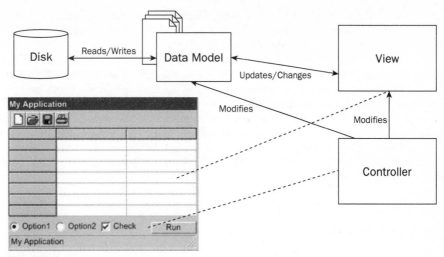

Figure 5-1

Once all the domain data is contained in its own model, separate from the UI components, the parts of the data model that need to be persisted can be identified. Some pieces of an internal data structure need not necessarily be saved. Some parts of the data structure in an application will not change from time to time or they can be recreated given that certain other aspects of the data structure exist. Developers wishing to save the state of their application must look carefully at the data they hold in memory in their model, identify the pieces of it that must be saved, and then write routines for saving and loading the data from the data structure to and from disk.

Saving Application Data

Now that application data structures have been discussed in a general sense, it is time to move to something a little more tangible and realistic. How exactly do Java applications store their data model in memory? Since Java is an object-oriented language, most applications have a set of data classes (which is the application's *data model*). Instances of these data classes reside in memory. The viewer and controller components (the UI) of the application interact with them to produce the functionality of the application.

Any Java class that has attributes (or properties in Java Bean terms) can be thought of as a data structure. A simplistic data structure could be simply a `Person` class with two `String` attributes, representing a first name and last name. More complex classes, which in addition to storing primitive data types contain references to other classes, effectively form an *object graph*. An object graph is a graph in which objects are the nodes in the graph and the connections are references from one instance of an object to another. The notion of object graphs is important because when you want to serialize the information contained in a class, you must also consider what data the class relies on that is stored in other classes, the dependencies these other classes have, and so on. In the next section, a tangible data model for *The Imager* will be outlined and its object graph will be viewed.

A Configuration Data Model for the Imager Application

Throughout this chapter, you will be developing a sample application to demonstrate different strategies for persisting application data using the three APIs discussed (Java Serialization, the XMLEncoder/Decoder APIs, and JAXB). The application is called *The Imager*, and is some sort of image editing and drawing program. You will not be implementing any actual image manipulation functionality in the application, but merely persistence and serialization code to show how to save the application's data model to disk — how to persist the state of the application.

Since your application is merely a placeholder for learning serialization, you will delve into designing a data model for the Imager's configuration settings. Many applications have various preferences, settings, and options available for users to change and modify. Web browser's can store a user's HTTP proxy settings; mail client programs store the server names and passwords for a user's e-mail account. These preferences are generally stored on disk, sometimes in the user's home directory, sometimes in the application's root directory. The first step to building any sort of data model that can eventually be persisted to disk is identifying attributes you want to save. Your Imager program probably should have settings for, at the least, the following properties:

❏   Location of the user's home directory or default directory to load and save files

❏   A list of recent files loaded or saved by the user

❏   Whether or not the application should use a tabbed windowed interface or a multiple document interface (MDI) with child windows

❏   Foreground and background colors last used (for drawing or painting operations)

❏   The last positions of the tool and palette windows within the application when the application was last closed

In a full-fledged paint or photo editing application, there would probably be many more configuration options that users could potentially persist to a file. However, the process is the same, and can also be applied to saving application data such as a custom image format, or reading and writing other image formats into your application's structure. Persisting information in Java objects to the file system is the same whether it is application configuration data or simply application domain data itself. Figure 5-2 shows the actual model of the data in UML and Figure 5-3 shows an example object graph of an actual instance of the data model.

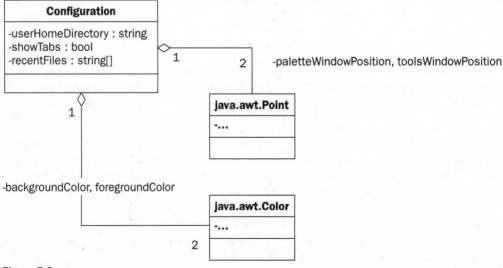

Figure 5-2

`Configuration` is the root object. It uses classes from `java.awt` to represent colors and points. In the object graph below, you can see that an instance of configuration also contains references to instances of `java.awt.Color` and `java.awt.Point`. When you persist the information in a `Configuration` instance to disk, you must also save the information contained in the `Color` and `Point` instances (and any other class instances *they* may also reference), if you want to be able to recreate your `Configuration` object at a later point in time.

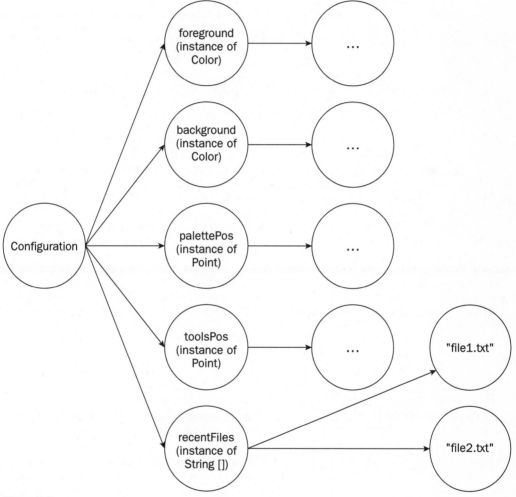

Figure 5-3

You will design `Configuration` using the Java Beans architecture (`getXXX` and `setXXX` for all properties in your class). Your application itself will read the configuration settings from this class and appropriately apply them throughout the application. It is typical to use Java Beans conventions to store data in Java-based data models. The standard mechanism by which to set and get data properties allows the designer to use many tools that are based on those standards (XMLEncoder/Decoder as you will later see for one). Object-relational-mapping tools allow the developer to map Java objects to a database. Almost all of these tools require the data to be accessible by using Java Beans conventions. It is just good practice and design.

Java Serialization: Persisting Object Graphs

One approach to saving a data model to disk is to write all of the object instances in the data model's object graph to disk, and then simply reload them at a later time. This is the approach taken by the Java Serialization API. It saves actual object in-memory instances to disk. *Serializing* an object is the process of writing its data members to disk. *Deserializing* an object is the process of reconstructing the object instance from the data members written to disk. Suppose you have a simple class MyPoint:

```
package book;

public class MyPoint {
  public int x;
  public int y;

  public void doSomething() { ... }
}
```

To save an instance of MyPoint to disk, its two data members must be written to disk. Saving x and y allow you to create a new instance of MyPoint at a later point in time and set its x and y values to the ones saved to disk—effectively recreating the original instance. The method doSomething() is already specified in the compiled class file, and there is no need to store any method information in the serialization process. All a class instance is in memory is the values for all of its attributes. To serialize an instance to disk, all of its data members must be saved. What if a data member is a reference to another object instance? The reference itself is just a memory address and would obviously be meaningless to save. The object instance the reference points to also would need to be saved as well. Suppose you add a color attribute to MyPoint:

```
package book;

import java.awt.Color;

public class MyPoint {
  public int x;
  public int y;

  private Color pointColor;

  public void doSomething() { ... }
}
```

The data members of the instance of java.awt.Color must now also be saved. As you can see, the entire object graph of an object instance must be saved when it is serialized to disk. If only x and y were saved from MyPoint and then subsequently recreated in MyPoint later, its color information would be lost. So how is an external API able to access all of the fields of a particular class? Java's reflection mechanism allows the dynamic ability to find out the fields and field values of any class, whether those fields are marked public or private. Thankfully, the Java Serialization API takes care of all these details for us, and it is easy to serialize object instances to disk.

> *Note: It is important to note that the file format used by the Java Serialization API is a special binary file format developed specifically for Java Serialization and therefore not human-readable. It is an efficient format, but also specific to Java.*

Key Classes

The Java Serialization API hides most of the complexity required to save off object graphs to disk (such as circular references and multiple references to the same object). There are really only two interfaces and two classes that need to be learned in order to use the API. `ObjectInputStream` and `ObjectOutputStream` are two stream classes that can be wrapped around any type of `java.io.InputStream` or `java.io.OutputStream`, respectively, making it possible to send serialized objects over a network or simply save them to disk. The two interfaces, `Serializable` and `Externalizable`, allow for implementing classes to be serialized. If a class does not implement one of these two interfaces, it cannot be serialized using the API. This means that if a class that *does* implement either `Serializable` or `Externalizable` contains a reference to a class that does *not* implement that interface somewhere in its object graph, it cannot be serialized successfully without some modification (discussed later on in this chapter).

Class or Interface (From java.io)	Function
Serializable	Interface for marking the fact that a class supports serialization
ObjectInputStream	Input stream used to read object instances that were written by an ObjectOutputStream
ObjectOutputStream	Output stream used to write object instance data that can later be read by an ObjectInputStream
Externalizable	Interface that extends Serializable to give a class complete control over how it is read and written to streams

Serializing Your Objects

Performing the actual serialization of objects is straightforward. There are four main steps.

1. Make sure the class to be serialized has a default constructor (one that takes no arguments).

2. Implement the `Serializable` or `Externalizable` interface to mark the class as supporting serialization.

3. Use `ObjectOutputStream` to serialize a class instance.

4. Use `ObjectInputStream` to read a serialized instance back into memory.

Classes you wish to serialize must have default constructors. This is because the serialization API needs to create blank instances of the class when it recreates object instances saved to disk — it does so by calling the default constructor. After it creates the new class, it simply populates the data members of the class via reflection (so accessor and mutator methods are not required for private data members). The class must also be marked as serializable by implementing the `Serializable` interface. The `Serializable` interface contains no method definitions; it is simply a marker to the serialization API to indicate that the class is indeed serializable. Not all classes store their data — the classic example is `java.sql.ResultSet`, which is used in the Java DataBase Connectivity API (JDBC) to access data from a database. The `ResultSet` object is querying the database for data when its methods are called and hence it does not store the information it returns. Since it is a mediator between the client and the database, it has no information to serialize! The `Serializable` interface exists to give developers the ability to mark certain classes as potentially serializable — essentially meaning the author of a particular class planned for the fact that the class may be saved to disk. The `Externalizable` interface gives developers more control over the actual serialization process, and it will be discussed in more detail later on in this chapter.

Configuration Example: Saving Your App's Configuration to Disk

Earlier, you developed the high-level data model for a sample configuration for your generic image manipulation application. Suppose that now you want to develop that data model and the UI components to save and load it from disk. The first step is translating your data model into code. You will have one class, `Configuration`, represent the application's configuration. You will model it using the Java Bean conventions, implicitly provide it a default constructor (by having no constructors), and implement the `Serializable` interface. The two classes referenced in `Configuration`, `java.awt.Point`, and `java.awt.Color` also both implement `Serializable`, so the entire graph is guaranteed to serialize. The code for `Configuration` is as follows:

```java
package book;

import java.awt.Color;
import java.awt.Point;
import java.io.Serializable;

public class Configuration implements Serializable {

  private String userHomeDirectory;

  private Color backgroundColor;
  private Color foregroundColor;

  private boolean showTabs;

  private Point paletteWindowPosition;
  private Point toolsWindowPosition;

  private String[] recentFiles;


  public Color getBackgroundColor() {
    return backgroundColor;
  }

  public void setBackgroundColor(Color backgroundColor) {
    this.backgroundColor = backgroundColor;
  }

  public Color getForegroundColor() {
    return foregroundColor;
  }

  public void setForegroundColor(Color foregroundColor) {
    this.foregroundColor = foregroundColor;
  }
```

```
    public Point getPaletteWindowPosition() {
      return paletteWindowPosition;
    }

    public void setPaletteWindowPosition(Point paletteWindowPosition) {
      this.paletteWindowPosition = paletteWindowPosition;
    }

    public String[] getRecentFiles() {
      return recentFiles;
    }

    public void setRecentFiles(String[] recentFiles) {
      this.recentFiles = recentFiles;
    }

    public boolean isShowTabs() {
      return showTabs;
    }

    public void setShowTabs(boolean showTabs) {
      this.showTabs = showTabs;
    }

    public Point getToolsWindowPosition() {
      return toolsWindowPosition;
    }

    public void setToolsWindowPosition(Point toolsWindowPosition) {
      this.toolsWindowPosition = toolsWindowPosition;
    }

    public String getUserHomeDirectory() {
      return userHomeDirectory;
    }

    public void setUserHomeDirectory(String userHomeDirectory) {
      this.userHomeDirectory = userHomeDirectory;
    }
  }
```

Writing the Configuration to Disk

With your configuration data model in hand, you can write the code to serialize and deserialize instances of Configuration. Saving an instance of Configuration is almost too easy. First, you create an ObjectOutputStream object, and since you want to save your instance of Configuration to a file, you wrap it around a FileOutputStream:

```
ObjectOutputStream out = new ObjectOutputStream(
                              new FileOutputStream("appconfig.config"));
```

Now you can create an instance of `Configuration` and save it to the file `appconfig.config`:

```
Configuration conf = new Configuration();
// ... set its properties

out.writeObject(conf);
```

Now all you have to do is close the stream:

```
out.close();
```

> *Note: Multiple object instances (of potentially differing types) can be written to the same **ObjectOutputStream**. Simply call **writeObject()** more than once, and the next object is appended to the stream. Also note that the file extension config, appended to the file, was arbitrarily chosen.*

Reading the Configuration from Disk

Deserializing objects back into memory is as easy as serializing them. To read your configuration data model from disk, you create an `ObjectInputStream` wrapped around a `FileInputStream` (since in this case you saved your `Configuration` instance to a file):

```
ObjectInputStream in = new ObjectInputStream(
                            new FileInputStream("appconfig.config"));
```

The counterpart to `ObjectOutputStream`'s `writeObject()` is `readObject()` in `ObjectInputStream`. If more than one object was explicitly written with multiple calls to `writeObject()`, `readObject()` can be called more than once. The method `readObject()` returns an `Object` that needs to be cast the proper type—so the developer must know some of the details about the order in which object instances were saved to the stream. In addition to potentially throwing a `java.io.IOException` if the stream was corrupted or other I/O error, `readObject()` can throw a `java.lang.ClassNotFoundException`. The `ClassNotFoundException` occurs if the VM cannot find the class for the type of the object instance being deserialized on the classpath. The following line of code reads your `Configuration` object back into memory:

```
Configuration conf = (Configuration) in.readObject();
```

After reading the object back in, you can use it like you use any normal Java object. After you are done with your `ObjectInputStream`, you close it as you do any other subclass of `InputStream`:

```
in.close();
```

As you can see, reading and writing objects using `ObjectInputStream` and `ObjectOutputStream` is a simple process with powerful functionality. Later on in this Java Serialization section there will be talk about customizing and extending the serialization process, as well as some of the pitfalls that can occur along the way.

Wrapping Serialization and Deserialization Code into Swing Actions

Now that you have seen how to create and store data models, it is time to see your configuration data model serialization and deserialization code in the context of a real application. Since your application is a JFC-based Swing application, you will integrate your code to serialize and deserialize Configuration into the UI framework via Swing's javax.swing.Action interface. Actions are a useful way to generalize UI commands — such as a *save* or *open* command. These commands usually appear in multiple places in a UI. In the case of *save* and *open*, usually in the File menu and on the application's toolbar. Swing components such as menus and toolbars allow actions to be added and they create the necessary events and properties to control them. Actions abstract away some of the UI code, and allow the developer to concentrate on the logic of an action, like saving a file to disk. Your actions will need a reference to your application, to get and set its configuration before it serializes or deserializes the Configuration instance. Your actions will inherit from the class javax.swing.AbstractAction as that class takes care of all of the methods in the Action interface except for the event method actionPerformed(). The class diagram that follows in Figure 5-4 illustrates where your actions, LoadConfigurationAction and SaveConfigurationAction, fit with respect to Action and AbstractAction.

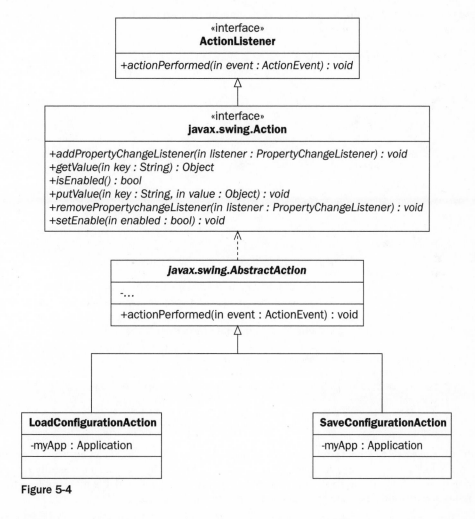

Figure 5-4

All of the code for both of these actions will reside in the event-driven method, actionPerformed(). When the user of the application clicks the save configuration menu item or button, this code will be invoked. The same goes for the action to load the application's configuration.

The main area of interest in any `Action` implementation is the `actionPerformed()` method. This method is called when a user clicks the menu item or button containing the `Action`. For your save action, you want the user first to be prompted to choose a file location, and then save the application's `Configuration` object instance to that file location. The implementation is fairly straightforward. First, a file chooser is displayed, and if the user selects a file, the application's `Configuration` instance is retrieved:

```
public void actionPerformed(ActionEvent evt) {
  JFileChooser fc = new JFileChooser();
  if (JFileChooser.APPROVE_OPTION == fc.showSaveDialog(myApp)) {
    try {
      Configuration conf = this.myApp.getConfiguration();
```

Now that you know the file location to save to, you simply serialize the `Configuration` object to disk to eventually be loaded at a later point in time:

```
      ObjectOutputStream out = new ObjectOutputStream(
                                  new FileOutputStream(fc.getSelectedFile()));

      out.writeObject(conf);

      out.close();

    } catch (IOException ioe) {
      JOptionPane.showMessageDialog(this.myApp, ioe.getMessage(), "Error",
                                    JOptionPane.ERROR_MESSAGE);

      ioe.printStackTrace();

    }
  }
}
```

The load action is similar to the save action. Again, the user is first prompted for a file. If the user selects a file, you will try to open it. To read your `Configuration` object instance back into memory so it can then be loaded into the application, you must create an `ObjectInputStream`. The `ObjectInputStream` is creating a `FileInputStream`, which reads the data from the file the user selected:

```
public void actionPerformed(ActionEvent evt) {
  JFileChooser fc = new JFileChooser();
  if (JFileChooser.APPROVE_OPTION == fc.showOpenDialog(myApp)) {
    try {
      ObjectInputStream in = new ObjectInputStream(
                                  new FileInputStream(fc.getSelectedFile()));
```

If the user selects a file that is not a serialized instance of `Configuration`, an `IOException` will be thrown when `readObject()` is called. If the instance of `Configuration` is successfully read, load it into the application via the application's `setConfiguration()` method. It's that simple — the application has now loaded a previously saved instance of `Configuration`:

```
        Configuration conf = (Configuration) in.readObject();

        in.close();

        myApp.setConfiguration(conf);
    } catch (IOException ioe) {
    JOptionPane.showMessageDialog(this.myApp,
                        "File is not a configuration file!", "Error",
                            JOptionPane.ERROR_MESSAGE);

        ioe.printStackTrace();

    } catch (ClassNotFoundException clEx) {
    JOptionPane.showMessageDialog(this.myApp,
                        "Classpath incorrectly set for application!",
                        "Error", JOptionPane.ERROR_MESSAGE);

        clEx.printStackTrace();
    }
  }
}
```

Giving Your Application a Time-based License Using Serialization

Serialization can be used in a variety of helpful ways. It is easy to save Java Beans and the data models for various kinds of application data as seen in the last example. Serialization, though, is not limited to simply saving objects to disk. Since `ObjectInputStream` and `ObjectOutputStream` are subclasses of `InputStream` and `OutputStream`, respectively, they can be used in any situation that a normal stream could be. Objects can be serialized over the network or read from a JAR file. Serialization is a fundamental aspect of Java's Remote Method Invocation (RMI) — it is the technology behind passing objects by value in RMI method calls.

To continue with the Imager Application example, suppose you want to give it a time-based license. For the demo version of the application, it should only be fully active for 30 days. After 30 days, users will be required to purchase a full license to use the product. There are many ways to do this, but using the serialization API could be an effective way to produce a time-based license file. The biggest challenge to creating time-based licenses is making it difficult for the user to overcome the license, which they usually can do by setting their computer's clock to an incorrect time, or by modifying whatever license file gets distributed (or registry key for some Windows' based applications, et cetera). Since Java's serialization produces a binary format that is unfamiliar to anyone except Java developers, it will make a good format for the application's license file. The application will also need some mechanism to guard against users setting the incorrect date on their computer clock to give them a longer license. To do so, the application will authenticate the license file against a timeserver on your network. The high-level design is shown in Figure 5-5.

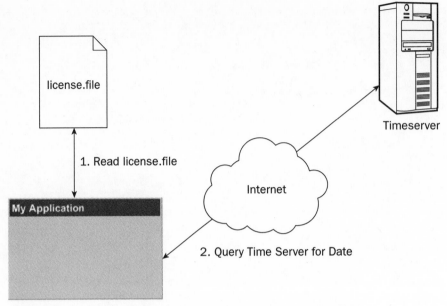

1. Read license.file

Internet

Timeserver

My Application

2. Query Time Server for Date

3. If server date is after the date in license.file, start the application

Figure 5-5

The next step in the design is to model the license file. Since you are using Java Serialization, all that needs to be done is to produce a class that implements `Serializable` and contains the necessary fields to do license validation against the timeserver. The `License` class will look like Figure 5-6.

License
-expirationDate : Calendar -timeServerHost : URL
+isValid() : boolean

Figure 5-6

Implementing the License

The license file for the application will consist of a serialized instance of the `License` class. The two data attributes it contains are: `expirationDate`, which is the date when the license expires (stored in a `java.util.Calendar` instance), and `timeServerHost`, which is the `java.net.URL` representing the Internet address of your timeserver. This address, as well as the expiration date, has been saved to prevent tampering with the URL. The `isValid()` method gets the current date from the timeserver and checks to see if the expiration date is before the date returned from the timeserver. If it is, the license is valid. Actually implementing the `License` yields the following code listing:

```
package book;

import java.io.IOException;
import java.io.ObjectInputStream;
import java.io.Serializable;
```

```java
import java.net.URL;
import java.util.Calendar;

public class License implements Serializable {
  private Calendar expirationDate;

  private URL timeServerHost;

  public boolean isValid() throws IOException, ClassNotFoundException {
    ObjectInputStream in = new ObjectInputStream(timeServerHost.openStream());

    Calendar serverDate = (Calendar) in.readObject();

    in.close();

    return serverDate.before(expirationDate);
  }

  public Calendar getExpirationDate() {
    return expirationDate;
  }

  public void setExpirationDate(Calendar expirationDate) {
    this.expirationDate = expirationDate;
  }

  public URL getTimeserverHost() {
    return timeServerHost;
  }

  public void setTimeServerHost(URL timeServerHost) {
    this.timeServerHost = timeServerHost;
  }
}
```

Look into the implementation for isValid(). One detail of the design that has not yet been discussed is the protocol you need to define between the timeserver and the License. How does the isValid() method get the current date from the timeserver? A normal HTTP GET request is sent to the URL in timeServerHost, which resides on the timeserver, and instead of it returning an HTML page, it will return an instance of java.util.Calendar. Using this timeServerHost URL object, the connection to the timeserver via an HTTP request over the network is established and an ObjectInputStream is constructed to read a serialized Calendar instance:

```java
ObjectInputStream in = new ObjectInputStream(timeServerHost.openStream());
```

Now a Calendar object is read just like any other object in Java serialization. After the object is read in, the expirationDate can be compared with the date returned from the timeserver to see whether the license is valid:

```java
Calendar serverDate = (Calendar) in.readObject();

in.close();

return serverDate.before(expirationDate);
```

Serialization can make complex tasks very straightforward. Java programmers can serialize and deserialize information without ever really leaving the Java environment in the sense that *actual class instances* can be serialized. Rather than creating your own date format on the server, an instance of Calendar was returned. All the low-level details of marshalling information over the network and finding a format you can use for date information were all taken care of by Java Serialization and the URL class.

Implementing the Timeserver

So now that you know what the timeserver is supposed to do, you must actually implement it. The timeserver will run as a Java Web Application (see Chapters 7 and 8 for much more detailed information on Web applications). A simple servlet is all that is necessary to implement the timeserver. The servlet will take care of the HTTP request and response, and allow you to write a Calendar object out to the client. Here is the servlet code that runs on the timeserver:

```
package book;

import java.io.IOException;
import java.io.ObjectOutputStream;
import java.util.Calendar;
import java.util.GregorianCalendar;
import java.util.logging.Logger;

import javax.servlet.ServletConfig;
import javax.servlet.ServletException;
import javax.servlet.http.HttpServlet;
import javax.servlet.http.HttpServletRequest;
import javax.servlet.http.HttpServletResponse;

public class ServerDate extends HttpServlet {

  private Logger logger;

  public void init(ServletConfig config) throws ServletException {
    logger = Logger.getLogger(ServerDate.class.getName());
  }

  public void doGet(HttpServletRequest req, HttpServletResponse resp)
                    throws IOException, ServletException {

    logger.info("Received date request");

    ObjectOutputStream out = new ObjectOutputStream(resp.getOutputStream());
    Calendar calendar = new GregorianCalendar();

    out.writeObject(calendar);

    out.close();

    logger.info("Wrote the date: " + calendar.getTime());
  }
}
```

By implementing the `doGet()` method, your servlet handles HTTP GET requests (which is expected from your `License` clients). The method is straightforward. All you do is wrap an `ObjectOutputStream` around the normal `ServletOutputStream`:

```
ObjectOutputStream out = new ObjectOutputStream(resp.getOutputStream());
```

Now that the output stream back to the client has been wrapped in an `ObjectOutputStream`, a new `Calendar` instance (which corresponds to the current date and time *on the server*) can be written back to the client:

```
Calendar calendar = new GregorianCalendar();

out.writeObject(calendar);

out.close();
```

The `License` class and `ServerDate` servlet take care of the actual license file and the means to validate the date it stores, respectively. In the next section, you will see how to integrate the components in this example, with your configuration data model and Swing actions, into the actual Swing implementation of the Imager Application.

Tying Your Serialization Components into the Application

You have developed Swing actions that load and save your configuration data model. You wrote a licensing system that uses serialization to specify both the license file format, as well as specifying the date and time format of your simple timeserver. Actually tying these pieces into the Imager Application is not very difficult, but helps to paint the larger picture of how serialization can fit into a real application design.

The first task your application does at startup is to load the license file and verify that the date contained therein is before the date returned on the timeserver. The `license.file` is read in from the application's Java Archive file (JAR) and then the validity of the license is verified against the timeserver found at the URL in the serialized license:

```
try {
    ObjectInputStream in = new ObjectInputStream(
                    Application.class.getResourceAsStream("license.file"));

    License license = (License) in.readObject();

    in.close();

    if (!license.isValid()) {
      JOptionPane.showMessageDialog(this, "Your license has expired",
                                    "License", JOptionPane.ERROR_MESSAGE);
      System.exit(1);
    }

} catch (Exception ex) {
    JOptionPane.showMessageDialog(this, ex.getMessage(), "License",
                                    JOptionPane.ERROR_MESSAGE);
    System.exit(1);
}
```

Notice how the license file, `license.file`, is loaded as a resource. Your application assumes that the license was packaged into the same JAR file as the application. This means that there must be some sort of license managing utility to create and put a valid `license.file` into the same JAR file as the application — it will not be discussed though, as it is irrelevant to this example. Getting the `license.file` from the JAR file reduces the risk of a user attempting to tamper with its contents to gain a longer license. The Java Serialization API is a binary format that is not human-readable, but could potentially be recognized by another Java developer. If you really cared an awful lot about anyone tampering with your `license.file`, it could always be encrypted using the Java Cryptography Extension (JCE) (included in the JDK). JCE allows one to encrypt any `OutputStream` and hence you could encrypt (and later decrypt) an `ObjectOutputStream`.

Adding your Swing actions to the File menu looks like the following:

```
fileMenu.add(new JMenuItem(new LoadConfigurationAction(this)));
fileMenu.add(new JMenuItem(new SaveConfigurationAction(this)));
```

Now you have tied in all of your components based on serialization. Below is a stripped-down code listing for the basic application, showing your serialization code in the context of the application. Look at the `setConfiguration()`, `loadConfiguration()`, and `getConfiguration()` methods as these are what your Swing actions manipulate:

```
package book;

import java.awt.Color;
import java.awt.GridLayout;
import java.awt.event.ActionEvent;
import java.awt.event.ActionListener;
import java.io.IOException;
import java.io.ObjectInputStream;

import javax.swing.*;

public class Application extends JFrame {

    private Configuration configuration = new Configuration();

    private JButton hdButton;

    private JButton bcButton;
    private JButton fgButton;
    private Color defaultColor;

    private JCheckBox showTabsCheckBox;

...

    public Application() {
        this.setDefaultCloseOperation(JFrame.EXIT_ON_CLOSE);
        this.setTitle("The Imager");

        try {
            ObjectInputStream in = new ObjectInputStream(
                            Application.class.getResourceAsStream("license.file"));
```

```
          License license = (License) in.readObject();

          in.close();

          if (!license.isValid()) {
            JOptionPane.showMessageDialog(this, "Your license has expired",
                                          "License", JOptionPane.ERROR_MESSAGE);
            System.exit(1);
          }

        } catch (Exception ex) {
          JOptionPane.showMessageDialog(this, ex.getMessage(), "License",
                                             JOptionPane.ERROR_MESSAGE);
          System.exit(1);
        }

...

        JMenuBar menu = new JMenuBar();
        JMenu fileMenu = new JMenu("File");
        fileMenu.add(new JMenuItem(new LoadConfigurationAction(this)));
        fileMenu.add(new JMenuItem(new SaveConfigurationAction(this)));
        fileMenu.addSeparator();
...
        this.pack();
        this.setVisible(true);
      }

      private JPanel createConfigDisplayPanel() {
...
        return panel;
      }

      private void loadConfiguration() {
        hdButton.setText(this.configuration.getUserHomeDirectory());

        Color bcColor = this.configuration.getBackgroundColor();
        if (bcColor != null) {
          bcButton.setBackground(bcColor);
          bcButton.setText(null);
        } else {
          bcButton.setText("<No color set>");
          bcButton.setBackground(this.defaultColor);
        }

        Color fgColor = this.configuration.getForegroundColor();
        if (fgColor != null) {
          fgButton.setBackground(fgColor);
          fgButton.setText(null);
        } else {
          fgButton.setText("<No color set>");
          fgButton.setBackground(this.defaultColor);
        }

        showTabsCheckBox.setSelected(this.configuration.isShowTabs());
      }
```

```java
public Configuration getConfiguration() {
    return configuration;
}

public void setConfiguration(Configuration configuration) {
    this.configuration = configuration;

    this.loadConfiguration();
}

public static void main(String[] args) {
    Application app = new Application();
}
}
```

In Figure 5-7 that follows, your application is editing part of your configuration data model. To get to this screen means that the application was able to verify the license (since the license is verified before the main application window is even fully loaded). Notice in the `loadConfiguration()` method in the preceding code listing how the color buttons are set, the checkbox is checked, and the user's home directory is placed on the first button when a configuration is loaded. The user can then change these options, which modifies the application's `Configuration` object.

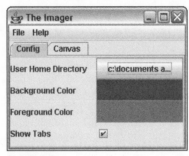

Figure 5-7

Once the data in the `Configuration` object is changed, it can be saved back to disk. Since the whole configuration data model is rooted in the `Configuration` object, all you need to do is export it to disk using your action, as shown in the screen shot in Figure 5-8.

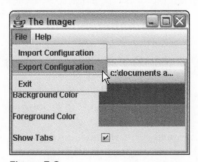

Figure 5-8

Extending and Customizing Serialization

Though most of the time, the Java Serialization API provides plenty enough functionality out of the box, there are some times when a greater level of control is necessary for the developer. Sometimes a developer will not want every field of a class serialized to disk. Other times, the developer may want to append additional information not included in class fields into the stream — or maybe modify the class's data structure before serialization occurs. When a class definition is modified (in other words, the code is changed and the class recompiled — that is, fields are renamed, or other fields are added and still others removed), classes serialized previously to these changes will have errors upon deserialization. In this section, some of the commonly used mechanisms for customizing and extending Java Serialization will be discussed.

The Transient Keyword

The `transient` keyword in the Java language is used for Java Serialization. Any field marked `transient` will not be saved to disk. This is useful when a class contains a reference to another object that does not implement `Serializable`, but you still would like to persist a class instance to disk. Sometimes certain fields are runtime-dependent and should not be persisted. Suppose in your `Configuration` object you wanted to additionally store a reference to your Application (for callbacks perhaps). When you saved your application to disk, you would certainly not want to persist the `Application` and every object associated with it on its object graph (even if all its objects implemented `Serializable` anyhow). To mark a field `transient`, simply put the keyword before the definition of the object or primitive:

```
private transient Application application;
```

The `transient` keyword is an easy way to quickly mark which fields of your class you would like the Serialization API to skip over and not save.

Note, though, that when a class is reconstructed after being serialized, these fields marked transient will be null (or if they are primitives, their default value), unless they are given a default value or set in the default constructor of the class.

Customizing the Serialization Format

Sometimes there is a need to perform additional operations either right before an object is serialized or right after it is deserialized. This need could arise if a class must retrieve data that is externally stored, such as on a server or in a cache, right before it is serialized. Objects may wish to verify some of their fields right after deserialization and fill in or create some of the fields marked `transient`. There are two methods you can add to a class to add additional behavior to the serialization and deserialization process. These methods are not part of any interface, and for them to be called, they must have the exact signature as shown. These are `writeObject()` and `readObject()`, as defined by the following:

```java
private void writeObject(ObjectOutputStream out) throws IOException {
  // can do things like validate values, get data from an external source, etc

  out.defaultWriteObject(); // invokes normal serialization process on this object
}

private void readObject(ObjectInputStream in) throws IOException,
ClassNotFoundException {
```

```
        in.defaultReadObject(); // invokes normal deserialization process on this object

    // can do things like validate values, produce new values based on data, etc
  }
```

The method `writeObject()` is called right before a class is serialized. The user can control when the class is actually serialized by calling `defaultWriteObject()` on the `ObjectOutputStream` as shown above. Doing so invokes the normal Java Serialization process on the current object. Before or after the object is written to the stream though, values to current data members could be changed or updated. Additional information can also be written to the `ObjectOutputStream` at this time. The `ObjectOutputStream` also implements the `java.io.DataOutput` interface, which includes methods for writing primitives (and `Strings`).

The `readObject()` method is called right before an object is deserialized. It is the natural counterpart to `writeObject()`. Similarly, the user can control when the object is deserialized by calling `defaultReadObject()` on the `ObjectInputStream`. After an object is deserialized, fields that did not have values could be assigned default values, or the values that were assigned could be checked. If any extra data was written to the `ObjectOutputStream` in `writeObject()` it *must* be read back in the `readObject()` method. For example, if the user wrote the `java.util.Date` object to the stream before writing the current object (to signify when the object was serialized), the `Date` object would have to be read in *before* `defaultReadObject()` was called.

Verification and Validation for Configuration

One example of how implementing `writeObject()` and `readObject()` could be useful to your `Configuration` object is data verification and validation. Your `Configuration` object stores the user's home directory and a list of recently accessed files. Between the time when a `Configuration` instance is serialized and later deserialized, the files and directory may not exist (they could have been moved or deleted). When your `Configuration` instance is deserialized, you want to remove the references to the directory or files that no longer exist to where they originally were. To do this, the `readObject()` method is implemented as shown below. After `defaultReadObject()` is called to populate the current instance of your object, the `userHomeDirectory` field and the `recentFiles` field can be verified to check if the files (and directory) exist. Any file or directory that does not exist will simply be set to `null`:

```
    private void writeObject(ObjectOutputStream out) throws IOException {
      out.defaultWriteObject();
    }

    private void readObject(ObjectInputStream in) throws IOException,
  ClassNotFoundException {
      in.defaultReadObject();

      if (this.userHomeDirectory != null) {
        File f = new File(this.userHomeDirectory);
        if (!f.exists())
          this.userHomeDirectory = null;
      }

      if (this.recentFiles != null) {
        List list = new LinkedList();
        Collections.addAll(list, this.recentFiles);
```

```
        ListIterator it = list.listIterator();
        while (it.hasNext()) {
          String curr = (String) it.next();
          File f = new File(curr);
          if (!f.exists()) {
            it.remove();
          }
        }

        this.recentFiles = new String[list.size()];
        list.toArray(this.recentFiles);
    }
}
```

The Externalizable Interface

Besides implementing `readObject()` and `writeObject()`, there is also an interface that extends `Serializable` that allows for greater customization of serialization and deserialization. This interface, `java.io.Externalizable`, allows more control of the serialization *format* than `readObject()` and `writeObject()`. It exists to allow developers to write their own custom formats for a class. With `Externalizable`, only the class identity is written to the stream by the Java Serialization API, the rest is left for the developer. The `Externalizable` interface looks like the following:

```
public interface java.io.Externalizable extends java.io.Serializable {
   public void readExternal(java.io.ObjectInput in) throws java.io.IOException,
       java.lang.ClassNotFoundException { }

   public void writeExternal(java.io.ObjectOutput out) throws java.io.IOException
       { }
}
```

The methods `writeExternal()` and `readExternal()` are public, instead of private like `readObject()` and `writeObject()`. Other classes can call these methods to read and write a class to disk without specifically invoking Java Serialization. `Externalizable` is not generally used very often, because when you normally want to save a class to disk, there is no need to completely customize the format. However, there may be times when `Externalizable` could come in handy. If you wanted to serialize a class that represented an image, and the in-memory representation was huge because it represented every pixel (like a bitmap), the `Externalizable` interface could be used to write the image in a different and compressed format (such as JPEG). The same could be done with `readObject()` and `writeObject()`, but these methods are not public, and in the case of your image-saving class, you may also want to save your image to disk outside of a serialization stream.

Versioning

The biggest stumbling block most developers run into with serialization is *versioning*. Many times classes will be serialized to disk, and then the definition of the class will change as source code is modified and the class recompiled. Maybe a field is added, or one is taken away. Design decisions could force the change of some internal data structures, say, from lists to maps or trees. Any change to a class, by default, results in the inability to restore any previously serialized instance — a version error results. Serialization versioning works by default by hashing a class based on its fields and class definition. Even if one of the field *names* is changed (but not its data type), previously serialized instances will not deserialize — the hash for the class has changed, and when the definition of a class is changed, there is no way to retain backward compatibility with previously saved instances. For smaller changes, especially things like name changes or the addition or removal of one field, you will probably want to retain backward compatibility with previously saved instances.

The Java Serialization API provides a way to manually set the hash of a class. The following field must be specified exactly as shown to provide the hash of the class:

```
private static final long serialVersionUID = 1L;  // version 1 of our class
```

If the `serialVersionUID` is specified (and is `static` and `final`), the value given will be used as the hash for the class. This means that if you define a `serialVersionUID` for your class and keep it the same value between different class versions, then you will not get versioning errors when deserializing instances of previous class definitions. The Serialization API provides a best-effort matching algorithm to try to best deserialize classes saved with an older class definition against a newer definition. If a field was added since a class was serialized, upon deserialization, that field will be `null`. Fields in which names have changed or types have changed will be `null`. Fields removed will not be set. The developer will still need to account for these older versions, but by setting the `serialversionUID`, the developer is given the chance to do so, rather than just have an exception thrown right when the deserialization process is attempted. It is recommended to always set a `serialVersionUID` for a class that implements `Serializable`, and change it only when you want previously serialized instances to be incompatible.

So, say you have previously serialized class instances and want to change a field or add another. You did not originally set a `serialVersionUID`, so *any* change you make will render it impossible to deserialize the old instances. The JDK provides a tool to identify a class's hash that has not been manually set. The `serialver` tool identifies the JVM's current hash of a compiled class file. Before you modify your class, you can find the hash previously being used. For your `Configuration` object, for example, you did not previously define a `serialVersionUID` field. If you add a field, you will not be able to deserialize old instances. *Before* modifying the class, you need to find the hash. By running the `serialver` tool, you find the hash by the following:

```
serialver book.Configuration
```

`Configuration` must be on the classpath for the `serialver` tool to work. The output of the tool is shown in Figure 5-9.

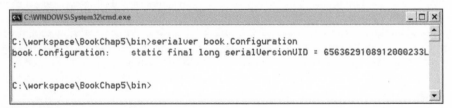

Figure 5-9

Note: Serialver is located in the \bin directory of your JDK.

Now this `serialVersionUID` value can be added to your `Configuration` class:

```
private static final long serialVersionUID = 6563629108912000233L;
```

New fields can now be added without breaking backward compatibility with your older instances. Versioning is such an issue with serialization that it is recommended to *always* set a `serialVersionUID` for any class that implements `Serializable` right off the bat. This is especially important since different JVMs can utilize different hashing algorithms — manually setting the `serialVersionUID` from the get-go mitigates this issue.

When to Use Java Serialization

Java Serialization is a simple but very powerful API. It is easy to use and can serialize most any type of data your application could have. Its main strengths follow:

- ❑ Simplicity
- ❑ Efficient binary file format

The file format defined by the Serialization API is usually what determines its suitability for an application. It is a fairly efficient file format, since it is binary as opposed to XML or other textual file formats. However, the file format also produces the following weaknesses (though possibly not weaknesses depending on your requirements or design decisions):

- ❑ Not human-readable
- ❑ Only Java-based applications can access the serialized data

Since the data is in a binary format, it cannot be edited with simple text editors. Your application's configuration from the example could only be modified from the application. The data was not in an XML format (or other textual format) where you could edit it in both the application or in an external editor. Sometimes this is important, but certainly not always. The key downside to Java Serialization is that only Java-based applications can access the serialized data. Since the serialization format is storing actual Java class instances in a file specification particular to Java, no parsers have been written in other languages for parsing data serialized with the Java serialization API.

The Java Serialization API is most useful when developing data models for Java applications and persisting them to disk. If your application needs a common file format with other applications not written in Java, serialization is the wrong design choice. If the files do not need to be human-readable, and the only applications written for reading them will be in Java, serialization is a great design choice.

Serialization can usually be a good temporary solution. Every Java application will have some sort of in-memory data model. Certain classes will store data in memory for the application to use. These classes could be persisted to disk, or populated from reading some other file format. Serialization could be initially used to save and restore these class instances, especially because of the little effort it takes to write serialization and deserialization code. Later on though, as the need for a common file format between non-Java based applications arises, routines could be written to take the data in those classes and persist it to another format. In other words, the same classes would still be used for the application's internal memory model, but the load and save routines would have to change. You will see in the next sections how you can serialize the application's configuration data in other formats and still retain the use of `Configuration` as your in-memory way of representing that data. Only the load and save code will need to change — *not the actual data model*.

Java Beans Long-Term Serialization: XMLEncoder/Decoder

The XMLEncoder/Decoder API is the new recommended persistence mechanism for Java Beans components starting from the 1.4 version of the JDK. It is the natural progression from serialization in many respects, though it is not meant to replace it. Like Java Serialization, it too serializes object graphs. XMLEncoder/Decoder came around in response to the need for long-term persistence for Swing toolkit components. The Java Serialization API was only good for persisting Swing components in the short term because it was only guaranteed to work for the same platform and virtual machine version. The reason for this is that some of the core UI classes that Swing depends on must be written in a platform/VM dependent manner, and thus their private data members may not always match up — leading to incompatibility problems in using the normal Serialization API. The Swing API has also had a lot of fluctuation in its implementation. Classes like JTable used to take up 30 megabytes of memory alone in memory. As the implementations have improved, especially in the new 5.0 release of the JDK, the internal implementations of many of these Swing classes have drastically changed. A new serialization API was developed in response to the challenge of true portability between different implementations and versions of the JDK for Swing/JFC classes. XMLEncoder/Decoder thus has a different set of design criteria than the original Java Serialization API. It was designed for a different usage pattern. Both APIs are necessary, with XMLEncoder/Decoder filling in some of the gaps of the Java Serialization API. XMLEncoder is a more robust and resilient API for long-term serialization of object instances, but is limited to serializing only Java Beans components, and not any Java class instances.

Design Differences

Since the XMLEncoder/Decoder API was designed to serialize only Java Beans components, the designers had the freedom to make XMLEncoder/Decoder more robust. Some of the key issues many developers had with the original Java Serialization API were version and portability problems. The XMLEncoder/Decoder API was written in response to these issues. Unlike the Java Serialization API, the XMLEncoder/Decoder API serializes object instances without *any* knowledge of their private data members. It serializes based upon the object's methods, its Java Bean properties, exposed through the Java Beans convention of getters and setters (getXXX and setXXX). By storing an object based upon its interface rather than its underlying implementation, the underlying implementation is free to change without affecting previously serialized instances (as long as the interface remains the same). This allows for long-term persistence. The class's internal structure could be completely rewritten, or differ across platforms, and the serialized instance would still be valid (and truly portable). A simple example of a Java Bean follows:

```java
public class MyBean {
  private String myName;

  public String getMyName() { return this.myName; }

  public void setMyName(String myName) { this.myName = myName; }
}
```

Internal data members could be added, the field myName could be changed to a character array or StringBuffer, or some other mechanism of storing a string. As long as the methods getMyName() and setMyName() did not change, the serialized instance could be reconstructed at a later time regardless of other changes. You will notice that `MyBean` does not implement `Serializable`. XMLEncoder/Decoder does not require classes it serializes to implement `Serializable` (or any other interface for that matter). Only two requirements are levied upon classes for XMLEncoder/Decoder to serialize:

❑ The class must follow Java Bean conventions.

❑ The class must have a default constructor (a constructor with no arguments).

In the upcoming "Possible Customization" section, you will see how both of these requirements can possibly be sidestepped, but at the expense of writing and maintaining additional code to help the XMLEncoder/Decoder API.

XML: The Serialization Format

The XMLEncoder/Decoder API naturally lives true to its name and has its serialization format based in XML text (in contrast to the binary format used by Java Serialization). The format is essentially a series of processing instructions telling the API how to recreate a given object. The processing instructions instantiate classes, and set Java Bean properties. This idea of serializing *how* to recreate an object, rather than every private data member of an object, leads to a robust file format capable of withstanding any internal class change (obviously not changes to the interface of the properties stored, though). You will not get into the nitty-gritty details of the file format. It is helpful, though, to see the result of serializing a Java Bean using the XMLEncoder/Decoder API. Below is the output of an instance of the `Configuration` object, serialized using the XMLEncoder/Decoder API. Since `Configuration` already follows Java Bean conventions (as most all Java data models should), no special code additions were necessary to serialize an instance using XMLEncoder/Decoder. Notice how the whole object graph is again saved like the Java Serialization API, and since `java.awt.Color` and `java.awt.Point` follow Java Bean conventions, they are persisted as part of the graph. XMLEncoder/Decoder also optimizes what information is saved — if the value of a bean property is its default value, it does not save the information:

```xml
<?xml version="1.0" encoding="UTF-8"?>
<java version="1.5.0-beta3" class="java.beans.XMLDecoder">
 <object class="book.Configuration">
  <void property="recentFiles">
   <array class="java.lang.String" length="3">
    <void index="0">
     <string>c:\mark\file1.proj</string>
    </void>
    <void index="1">
     <string>c:\mark\testproj.proj</string>
    </void>
    <void index="2">
     <string>c:\mark\final.proj</string>
    </void>
   </array>
  </void>
  <void property="userHomeDirectory">
   <string>C:\Documents and Settings\Mark\My Documents</string>
  </void>
  <void property="showTabs">
   <boolean>true</boolean>
  </void>
  <void property="foregroundColor">
   <object class="java.awt.Color">
    <int>255</int>
```

```
      <int>255</int>
      <int>51</int>
      <int>255</int>
     </object>
    </void>
    <void property="backgroundColor">
     <object class="java.awt.Color">
      <int>51</int>
      <int>51</int>
      <int>255</int>
      <int>255</int>
     </object>
    </void>
   </object>
  </java>
```

One key point about the XML file format used by XMLEncoder/Decoder is that even though an XML parser in any language could read the file, the file format is still specific to Java. The file format encodes processing instructions used to recreate serialized Java Bean class instances, and is therefore not directly useful to applications written in other languages. It would be possible of course to implement a reader in another language that read some data from this file format, but it would be a large and fairly difficult task (at least to write a generalized one). The other language would also need to have some sort of notion of Java Bean. In other words, think of this as a Java-only file format and do not rely on it for transmitting data outside of the Java environment. The Java API for XML Binding (JAXB) will be discussed, which is far more suited to exporting data to non-Java consumers.

Since XML is text and therefore human-readable, it is possible to save class instances to disk and then edit the information with a text file. However, editing the preceding XML document would not be for the casual user; it would be more useful to a developer, since some knowledge of how the XMLEncoder/Decoder API stores information is necessary to understand *where* to modify the file. If you wanted users to be able to save your Configuration object to disk and then edit it outside of your application, you probably would not choose the XMLEncoder/Decoder XML file format. In the file above, for example, java.awt.Color was persisted using four integer values, described only by int for each one. What casual user would know that they correspond to the red, blue, green, and alpha channels of a color, and that they can range from 0 to 255? A descriptive configuration file format in XML would probably be a task for JAXB, as discussed in the next section. The file format used by XMLEncoder/Decoder is Java-specific and is also not well suited for general hand editing like many XML formats are. XML was simply the storage mechanism chosen — why define a new file format when you can use XML?

Key Classes

Using the XMLEncoder/Decoder API is very similar to using the Java Serialization API. It was developed to have the same core methods, and as such, java.beans.XMLEncoder and java.beans .XMLDeocoder could literally be substituted for ObjectOutputStream and ObjectInputStream, respectively. XMLEncoder and XMLDecoder are the only classes needed to serialize Java Beans. In the "Possible Customization" section, some other classes that are needed to serialize Java Beans that do not completely follow Java Bean conventions will be briefly discussed. Below is a table of the classes needed to use XMLEncoder/Decoder.

Class (From java.beans)	Function
XMLEncoder	Class that takes an instance of a Java Bean and writes the corresponding XML representation of it to the java.io.OutputStream it wraps
XMLDecoder	Class that reads a java.io.InputStream and decodes XML formatted by XMLEncoder back into instances of Java Beans

Serializing Your Java Beans

The process of serializing Java Beans using XMLEncoder/Decoder is almost exactly like the process of serializing a Java class using normal Java Serialization. There are also four steps to serialization:

1. Make sure the class to be serialized follows Java Bean conventions.

2. Make sure the class to be serialized has a default (no argument) constructor.

3. Serialize your Java Bean with XMLEncoder.

4. Deserialize your Java Bean with XMLDecoder.

To save an instance of your Configuration object to disk, you simply begin by creating an XMLEncoder with a FileOutputStream object:

```
XMLEncoder encoder = new XMLEncoder(
                          new FileOutputStream("c:\\mark\\config.bean.xml"));
```

Then you simply write your instance of Configuration, conf, to disk and close the stream:

```
encoder.writeObject(conf);

encoder.close();
```

Reading the serialized instance of Configuration back into memory is just as simple. First the XMLDecoder object is created with a FileInputStream:

```
XMLDecoder decoder = new XMLDecoder(
                          new FileInputStream("c:\\mark\\config.bean.xml"));
```

Next you read in your object, much like you did with ObjectInputStream, and then close your stream:

```
Configuration config = (Configuration) decoder.readObject();

decoder.close();
```

On the surface, XMLEncoder/Decoder works much like Java Serialization. The underlying implementation though, is much different, and allows for the internal structure of classes you serialize to change drastically, yet still work and be compatible with previously saved instances. XMLEncoder/Decoder offers many ways to customize how it maps Java Beans to its XML format; some of these will be discussed in the "Possible Customization" section.

Note: Just like the Java Serialization API, multiple objects can be written to the same stream.
***XMLEncoder**'s* **writeObject()** *method can be called in succession to serialize more than one object instance. When instances are deserialized though, they must be deserialized in the same order in which they were written.*

Robustness Demonstrated: Changing Configuration's Internal Data

Suppose you want to change the way your `Configuration` object stores the references to the user's recently accessed files of your application. They were stored previously using a string array. There were two methods that gave access to the bean property, `recentFiles`: `getRecentFiles()` and `setRecentFiles()`. Your `Configuration` object looked like:

```
package book;

import java.awt.Color;
import java.awt.Point;
import java.beans.XMLDecoder;
import java.io.File;
import java.io.FileInputStream;
import java.util.ArrayList;
import java.util.List;

public class Configuration {

...

  private String[] recentFiles;

  public String[] getRecentFiles() {
    return recentFiles;
  }

  public void setRecentFiles(String[] recentFiles) {
    this.recentFiles = recentFiles;
  }

...

}
```

Now you would like to store the `recentFiles` property internally as a `java.util.List` full of `java.io.File` objects. If you do not change the signature of the `getRecentFiles()` and `setRecentFiles()`, you can do whatever you like with the underlying data structure. The modified `Configuration` class below illustrates how the storage of recent files could be changed to a `List` *without* changing your method signatures for the `recentFiles` bean property:

```
package book;

import java.awt.Color;
import java.awt.Point;
import java.beans.XMLDecoder;
import java.io.File;
import java.io.FileInputStream;
import java.util.ArrayList;
```

```
import java.util.List;

public class Configuration {

...

  private List recentFiles;

  public String[] getRecentFiles() {
    if (this.recentFiles == null || this.recentFiles.isEmpty())
      return null;

    String[] files = new String[this.recentFiles.size()];

    for (int i = 0; i < this.recentFiles.size(); i++)
      files[i] = ((File) this.recentFiles.get(i)).getPath();

    return files;
  }

  public void setRecentFiles(String[] files) {
    if (this.recentFiles == null)
      this.recentFiles = new ArrayList();

    for (int i = 0; i < files.length; i++) {
      this.recentFiles.add(new File(files[i]));
    }
  }

...

}
```

Notice how in the setRecentFiles() method, an array of String objects is converted to a List of File objects. In the getRecentFiles() method, the intenal List of File objects is converted back into an array of String objects. This conversion is the key to the information hiding principle that XMLEncoder/Decoder uses to serialize and deserialize object instances. Since XMLEncoder/Decoder only works with the operations and interface to a class, the private data members can be changed. By keeping the interface the same, your Configuration class can undergo all kinds of incremental changes and improvements under the hood without affecting previously saved instances. This is the key benefit of XMLEncoder/Decoder that provides its ability to serialize instances not just in the short-term, but also in the long-term, by weathering many types of changes to a class definition.

The main() method below demonstrates XMLDecoder deserializing an instance of Configuration previously saved with your older version of Configuration that stored the recentFiles property as a String array. The file this method is loading is the one shown previously in this section as sample output for XMLEncoder/Decoder (see the previous section "XML: The Serialization Format"):

```
public static void main(String[] args) throws Exception {
    XMLDecoder decoder = new XMLDecoder(
                  new FileInputStream("c:\\mark\\config.bean.xml"));

    Configuration conf = (Configuration) decoder.readObject();
```

```
    decoder.close();

    String[] recentFiles = conf.getRecentFiles();
    for (int i = 0; i < recentFiles.length; i++)
      System.out.println(recentFiles[i]);
  }
```

As you can see, the output from your `main()` method confirms that not only was your old `Configuration` instance successfully read by the XMLEncoder/Decoder API, but your new `List` of `File` objects is working properly and is populated with the correct objects:

```
c:\mark\file1.proj
c:\mark\testproj.proj
c:\mark\final.proj
```

Possible Customization

XMLEncoder/Decoder supports serialization of Java Beans out of the box, but it can also be customized to serialize any class — regardless of whether or not it uses Java Beans conventions. In fact, throughout the Swing/JFC class library you will find classes that do not fully conform to Java Bean conventions. Many types of collection classes do not; some Swing classes have other ways of storing data besides getters and setters. The following XML file is a serialized instance of a `java.util.HashMap`, and a `javax.swing.JPanel`. Both of these classes have their data added to them by methods that do not follow the Java Beans convention:

```
<?xml version="1.0" encoding="UTF-8"?>
<java version="1.5.0-beta3" class="java.beans.XMLDecoder">
 <object class="java.util.HashMap">
  <void method="put">
   <string>Another</string>
   <string>AnotherTest</string>
  </void>
  <void method="put">
   <string>Mark</string>
   <string>Test</string>
  </void>
 </object>
 <object class="javax.swing.JPanel">
  <void method="add">
   <object class="javax.swing.JLabel">
    <void property="text">
     <string>Mark Label</string>
    </void>
   </object>
  </void>
 </object>
</java>
```

Note how data is added to a `HashMap` by the `put()` method, and components are added to `JPanel`s by the `add()` method. How does the XMLEncoder/Decoder API know how to look for this — or even find the data that should be inserted via those methods? Since its file format is a series of processing instructions, XMLEncoder/Decoder can serialize the information necessary to make method calls to disk. This generic ability lets XMLEncoder/Decoder do any kind of custom initialization or setting of data that a class may require — and all through its methods, its interface. Just because the file format supports this type of generic processing instruction, though, does not mean that the XMLEncoder automatically knows how to use them. The solution is the API's `java.beans.PersistenceDelegate` class.

Persistence Delegates

Every class serialized and deserialized has an instance of `java.beans.PersistenceDelegate` associated with it. It may be the default one, included for classes following the Java Beans conventions, or it could be a custom subclass of `PersistenceDelegate` that writes the processing instructions needed to recreate a given instance of a class. Persistence delegates are responsible only for writing an object to disk — not reading them. This is because all objects are written in terms of known processing instructions. These instructions can be used to recreate the object without the need of any custom information contained in the persistence delegate. How to write a custom persistence delegate is a fairly complex topic that is out of the scope of this section. It is what allows classes like `HashMap` and `JPanel` to be successfully serialized. The XMLEncoder/Decoder includes a number of `PersistenceDelegates` used for classes found in the JDK that do not fully conform to Java Beans conventions.

For detailed information on how to use and create custom persistence delegates, see the following article, written by Philip Mine, the designer and author of XMLEncoder/Decoder API:

```
http://java.sun.com/products/jfc/tsc/articles/persistence4/
```

When to Use XMLEncoder/Decoder

Use of the XMLEncoder/Decoder API over the Java Serialization API is generally preferred when you are serializing object graphs consisting of Java Beans and Swing components. It was designed precisely for that purpose and fixes the more generic Java Serialization API's shortcomings with respect to both Java Beans, but especially Swing components. Prior to the XMLEncoder/Decoder API, there was no built-in mechanism for the long-term serialization of Swing components. XMLEncoder/Decoder has only been around since JDK 1.4; if you must support any JDK released before 1.4, you cannot use XMLEncoder/Decoder.

Thinking in more general terms, and assuming your application has a data model you wish to persist to disk, XMLEncoder/Decoder has the following advantages:

- ❑ It's simple to implement.

- ❑ You can add properties and remove properties from your Java Beans class definitions without breaking previously serialized instances.

- ❑ The internal private data structure of your beans can change without breaking previously serialized instances.

- ❑ Instances are saved in XML, making the resulting files human-readable.

Some of the potential downsides to choosing the XMLEncoder/Decoder for serializing your object graph of Java Beans follow:

❑ Even though the file format is human-readable, it is editable in the real world only by developers or power users.

❑ Even though the file format is XML, it is still Java-specific — it would take great effort to allow a non-Java-based application to read the data.

❑ Every piece of data you want persisted in the class must be a Java Bean property (or customized with a special persistence delegate).

The XMLEncoder/Decoder API is perfect for what it is designed for — the long-term serialization of Java Beans components for use later on by Java-based applications. Because it is so customizable, it can often be used for a variety of other purposes, and serialize a lot of data beyond ordinary Java Beans. Generally, though, its main advantage over normal Java Serialization is its robustness, even through class definition changes. Apart from that, however, it still has the same limitations of the Java Serialization API. When you have an internal data model based with Java Beans, XMLEncoder/Decoder makes sense. If you would like your application's file formats to be read by other non-Java applications, eventually you will have to specify some other custom file format or write to an existing standard.

XML Schema-Based Serialization: Java API for XML Binding (JAXB)

The last method to be discussed in this chapter for persisting an application's data is the Java API for XML Binding (JAXB). This method is fundamentally different from the other two serialization methods that have already been discussed (the Java Serialization API and the XMLEncoder/Decoder API). Both of these models involve taking a data model consisting of classes already defined and persisting instances of these classes. Later on, the information on disk could then be used to reconstruct the object graph back into the in-memory model used by an application. Both of these models map Java classes to a file format. JAXB takes the opposite approach. It maps a file format to Java classes. The diagram shown in Figure 5-10 illustrates this difference.

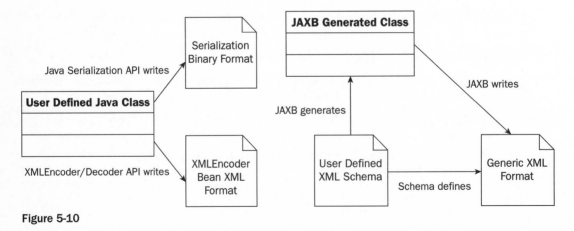

Figure 5-10

Instead of defining Java classes, which in turn are written to predefined file formats, the developer defines the file format in the XML schema language. Once the file format is defined, JAXB generates a set of Java classes that read and write the XML instance documents that correspond to the defined XML schema.

> The XML schema language is the World Wide Web Consortium's standard for defining XML instance documents of a particular type. It is a widely accepted standard and already defines many different types of XML documents. XML schemas also let XML parsers validate an XML instance document to verify that they conform to the schema's requirements. This can greatly reduce the time it takes to write code that must read XML, as it does a lot of the validation for you. View the XML schema specification at the following URL: `http://www.w3.org/TR/xmlschema-0/`.

JAXB generally requires more work on the part of the developer. The benefit is that other applications can easily read and write the data model defined by the XML schema. Because XML schema is a well-accepted standard, other languages and development languages also have tools to generate data storage classes based on an XML schema. This makes JAXB ideal for applications that must share a common data format. When other applications specify their file formats in XML schema, JAXB makes life simple for the developer, since the developer already has a file format specification defined and simply has to generate the Java classes that bind to XML documents that follow the schema.

Since JAXB *generates* Java classes based on a particular XML schema, the developer does not have as much room to customize the data structure. In most cases, developers will find themselves going back to the XML schema, modifying it, and regenerating the classes's additional information or changes to current information that must be stored. Generated code provides a set of different issues for the developer. Names for data members, while following the schema, can be tedious to work with, and code using generated classes can easily become difficult to read. Many times developers will be forced with the additional burden of mapping data in JAXB-generated classes to classes in the JDK — like mapping color information to a `java.awt.Color` instance, or constructing a `java.net.URL` or file path from a String. This additional overhead is one of the downsides of JAXB — it is usually worth the effort though, if interoperability and a readable file format are requirements of your application. The quick and easy days of the Java Serialization API and the XMLEncoder/Decoder API give way to the slightly more tedious JAXB methodology of programming. Anytime you need to interface with non-Java applications, the complexity increases.

Sample XML Document for Your Configuration Object

Suppose you want to take your `Configuration` data model and define an XML schema to represent it. You will not be able to write an XML schema that maps directly to your already-existing `Configuration` class, but you can write an XML schema that saves all the necessary data attributes to recreate your Configuration instance. This is where the extra effort comes in on the part of the developer. After the in-memory data model is defined, in your case the `Configuration` object, an XML schema must additionally be defined to represent all the necessary data attributes to recreate it. If you did not already have a class for your `Configuration` data model, you would still have to write some sort of conversion between types like `java.awt.Color` and the JAXB class that you generate with that same information — after all, other Swing classes were developed to interact with `java.awt.Color`, not whatever custom class JAXB decides to generate for you! To refresh your memory on what data attributes are stored in `Configuration`, Figure 5-11 is the original data model diagram displayed earlier in the chapter.

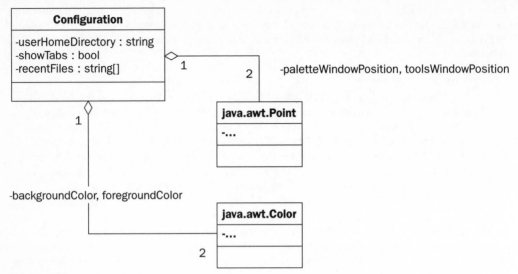

Figure 5-11

Essentially, data representing a color, a point, directory and file locations, and a boolean variable needs to be stored. XML schema is more than equipped to handle this — you just have to actually define it. Below is an XML instance document that contains all of the information you would need to recreate your Configuration object. Notice how it is not only human-readable in the sense that it is text, but it is also conceivably modifiable by a user. Colors are obviously defined, and the user's home directory is easily modified. The XML below is far more readable than the output from the XMLEncoder/Decoder API:

```xml
<?xml version="1.0" encoding="UTF-8" standalone="yes"?>
<configuration xmlns="http://book.org/Configuration">
    <user-settings>
        <user-home-directory>C:\Documents and Settings\Mark\My Documents</user-home-
directory>

        <recent-files>
            <recent-file>c:\mark\file1.proj</recent-file>

            <recent-file>c:\mark\testproj.proj</recent-file>

            <recent-file>c:\mark\final.proj</recent-file>
        </recent-files>
    </user-settings>

    <ui-settings>
        <palette-window-position>
            <x-coord>5</x-coord>

            <y-coord>5</y-coord>
        </palette-window-position>

        <tools-window-position>
```

```
            <x-coord>10</x-coord>

            <y-coord>10</y-coord>
        </tools-window-position>

        <background-color>
            <red>51</red>

            <green>51</green>

            <blue>255</blue>

            <alpha>255</alpha>
        </background-color>

        <foreground-color>
            <red>255</red>

            <green>255</green>

            <blue>51</blue>

            <alpha>255</alpha>
        </foreground-color>

        <show-tabs>true</show-tabs>
    </ui-settings>
</configuration>
```

Note though, that this XML file is *not* the XML schema; it is a document that conforms to the XML schema defined in the next section of this chapter. JAXB will generate Java classes that read and write files like the preceding XML conforming to your schema. It will give you Java Bean–like access to all of the data contained in the document.

Defining Your XML Format with an XML Schema

Now that you have looked at a sample XML instance document containing a sample set of `Configuration` data for your data model, you can look under the hood and see how to specify the file format. In this section, the various data types for your configuration will be analyzed and then defined in a schema. To reiterate the following data is necessary to store in your configuration data model:

❑ The user's home directory, a string value

❑ A flag whether or not to use a tabbed interface, a boolean value

❑ A list of recently accessed files by the user, an array of string values

❑ Two colors, foreground and background, for drawing operations, color values

❑ Two points, for the last position of the tool and palette windows, point values

While this section will not be a thorough guide in any sense to XML schema, you will go through how to define the data bullets listed earlier. First, though, XML schema must be briefly discussed. XML schema is a simple but powerful language for defining and specifying what types various XML elements can be, and where they can appear in a document. Essentially, there are two types of XML elements you can define with XML schema: simple elements and complex elements. Simple elements have no attributes and contain only text data — they also have no child elements. An example of a simple element follows:

```
<hello>world</hello>
```

Complex elements can have attributes, child elements, and potentially mix their child elements with text. The following is an example of a complex element:

```
<complex c="12">
    <hello>world</hello>
</complex>
```

XML schema is fairly intuitive, but a full and thorough coverage of it is beyond the scope of this book. A great online tutorial can be found at the following URL:

```
http://www.w3schools.com/schema/default.asp
```

Defining Your Data: Configuration.xsd

To define your data, you will be using both simple and complex elements. Looking back at the bullet list of data points necessary, both the user's home directory and your tabbed interface flag (the first two bullets) can probably be modeled with simple elements. Here is how you will model them in XML schema:

```
<xs:element name="user-home-directory" type="xs:string" />
<xs:element name="show-tabs" type="xs:boolean" />
```

You are defining elements and requiring that the text within those elements be of the type specified. An instance example of both of these elements follows:

```
<user-home-directory>c:\mark</user-home-directory>
<show-tabs>true</show-tabs>
```

The string array of recent files is slightly more complex to model. It will be modeled as a complex element, with a child element for each individual recent file. First, you define your complex type:

```
<xs:complexType name="recentFilesType">
    <xs:sequence>
        <xs:element name="recent-file" type="xs:string" maxOccurs="unbounded" />
    </xs:sequence>
</xs:complexType>
```

After defining your complex type, which is a sequence of `recent-file` elements, you can define your element that uses your custom XML type. Note how the `type` attribute in the element definition that follows corresponds to the `name` attribute in your preceding complex type definition:

```
<xs:element name="recent-files" type="recentFilesType" minOccurs="0" />
```

An example instance of your `recent-files` element looks like the following:

```
<recent-files>
    <recent-file>c:\mark\file1.proj</recent-file>

    <recent-file>c:\mark\testproj.proj</recent-file>

    <recent-file>c:\mark\final.proj</recent-file>
</recent-files>
```

Defining colors presents an interesting challenge. You must make sure you have enough information specified in the XML file to construct a `java.awt.Color` object. If you specify in the XML file the red, green, blue, and alpha components of a color, you will have enough information to construct a `java.awt.Color` instance. The color type can then be modeled as follows:

```
<xs:complexType name="colorType">
    <xs:sequence>
        <xs:element name="red" type="xs:int" />

        <xs:element name="green" type="xs:int" />

        <xs:element name="blue" type="xs:int" />

        <xs:element name="alpha" type="xs:int" default="255" />
    </xs:sequence>
</xs:complexType>
```

As you can see, your complex type (`colorType`) contains child elements for the RGBA components. These components are integer values and if the alpha component is not specified, it defaults to 255 (a totally opaque color). After defining two elements that take your newly defined type (`colorType`), the foreground and background colors for your application's configuration data model can be declared:

```
<xs:element name="background-color" type="colorType" minOccurs="0" />
<xs:element name="foreground-color" type="colorType" minOccurs="0" />
```

An example instance of a `foreground-color` element is shown as follows:

```
<foreground-color>
    <red>255</red>

    <green>255</green>

    <blue>51</blue>

    <alpha>255</alpha>
</foreground-color>
```

The last major custom type you must define is your type for point objects. This type must have enough information encoded in the XML to construct a `java.awt.Point` instance. All you essentially need are integer values representing the x and y coordinates of a point. The last two element definitions that use your new XML type for points, `pointType`, are also listed below. These elements represent the positions of the palette window and the tool window of your application:

```
    <xs:complexType name="pointType">
        <xs:sequence>
            <xs:element name="x-coord" type="xs:int" />

            <xs:element name="y-coord" type="xs:int" />
        </xs:sequence>
    </xs:complexType>

<xs:element name="palette-window-position" type="pointType" minOccurs="0" />
<xs:element name="tools-window-position" type="pointType" minOccurs="0" />
```

Now that you have defined all of your basic types in your schema, they can be organized around other elements for better readability of your XML instance documents. The actual schema listed at the end of this section will have more element and complex type definitions to account for document readability. The next step will be to generate JAXB classes from your schema in order to start reading and writing XML documents that conform to your schema.

The full XML Schema Definition (XSD) file for your configuration data model, configuration.xsd, is listed as follows:

```
<?xml version="1.0" encoding="utf-8" ?>
<xs:schema targetNamespace="http://book.org/Configuration"
elementFormDefault="qualified" xmlns="http://book.org/Configuration"
xmlns:xs="http://www.w3.org/2001/XMLSchema">
    <xs:complexType name="configurationType">
        <xs:sequence>
            <xs:element name="user-settings" type="user-settingsType" />

            <xs:element name="ui-settings" type="ui-settingsType" />
        </xs:sequence>
    </xs:complexType>

    <xs:complexType name="recentFilesType">
        <xs:sequence>
            <xs:element name="recent-file" type="xs:string" maxOccurs="unbounded" />
        </xs:sequence>
    </xs:complexType>

    <xs:complexType name="pointType">
        <xs:sequence>
            <xs:element name="x-coord" type="xs:int" />

            <xs:element name="y-coord" type="xs:int" />
        </xs:sequence>
    </xs:complexType>

    <xs:complexType name="colorType">
        <xs:sequence>
            <xs:element name="red" type="xs:int" />

            <xs:element name="green" type="xs:int" />

            <xs:element name="blue" type="xs:int" />
```

```
            <xs:element name="alpha" type="xs:int" default="255" />
        </xs:sequence>
    </xs:complexType>

    <xs:complexType name="ui-settingsType">
        <xs:sequence>
            <xs:element name="palette-window-position" type="pointType" minOccurs="0"
            />

            <xs:element name="tools-window-position" type="pointType" minOccurs="0" />

            <xs:element name="background-color" type="colorType" minOccurs="0" />

            <xs:element name="foreground-color" type="colorType" minOccurs="0" />

            <xs:element name="show-tabs" type="xs:boolean" />
        </xs:sequence>
    </xs:complexType>

    <xs:complexType name="user-settingsType">
        <xs:sequence>
            <xs:element name="user-home-directory" type="xs:string" />

            <xs:element name="recent-files" type="recentFilesType" minOccurs="0" />
        </xs:sequence>
    </xs:complexType>

    <xs:element name="configuration" type="configurationType" />

</xs:schema>
```

Generating JAXB Java Classes from Your Schema

Generating JAXB classes from an XML schema requires the Java Web Services Development Pack from Sun. The latest version of JWSDP from Sun is version 1.4 and version 1.0 of the JAXB specification (implemented by version 1.03 of Sun's reference implementation). Sun's reference distribution of JAXB includes an XML schema compiler. This compiler outputs Java classes that read and write the particular XML schema from which they were generated. The JWSDP installer can be downloaded from Sun's Web site from the following URL:

```
http://java.sun.com/webservices/jwsdp/index.jsp
```

Installing it is straightforward, as it installs much like any Windows application. JWSDP includes many tools besides JAXB, but JAXB is all that will be discussed in this chapter. To use the XML schema compiler, you must make sure your PATH environment variable includes the /jaxb/bin directory under the folder where you installed JWSDP. Sun's compiler is called by the xjc batch file located in the /jaxb/bin directory. Once it is on your PATH, running it is straightforward. You saved your schema to the file configuration.xsd. To compile your schema, you simply type the following at the command prompt:

```
xjc -d gen configuration.xsd
```

The -d option simply tells the compiler in which directory to put the generated Java source files. In your case, you have a directory under your main project specifically for generated source files, gen, so that if you modify your schema, you can easily regenerate the files to this same location. Figure 5-12 shows the output of the xjc compiler.

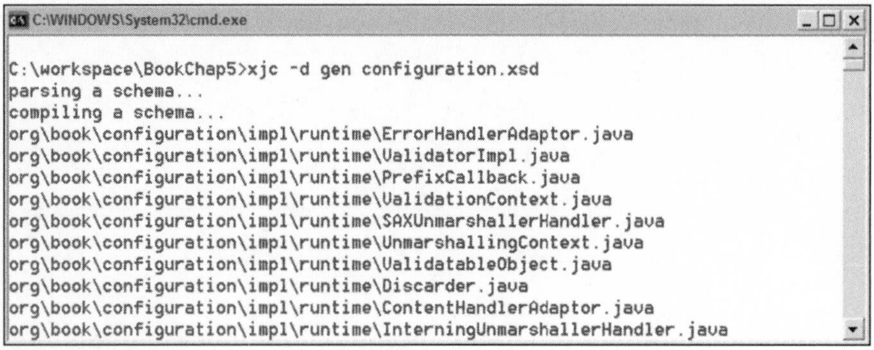

```
C:\WINDOWS\System32\cmd.exe                                              _ □ ×

C:\workspace\BookChap5>xjc -d gen configuration.xsd
parsing a schema...
compiling a schema...
org\book\configuration\impl\runtime\ErrorHandlerAdaptor.java
org\book\configuration\impl\runtime\ValidatorImpl.java
org\book\configuration\impl\runtime\PrefixCallback.java
org\book\configuration\impl\runtime\ValidationContext.java
org\book\configuration\impl\runtime\SAXUnmarshallerHandler.java
org\book\configuration\impl\runtime\UnmarshallingContext.java
org\book\configuration\impl\runtime\ValidatableObject.java
org\book\configuration\impl\runtime\Discarder.java
org\book\configuration\impl\runtime\ContentHandlerAdaptor.java
org\book\configuration\impl\runtime\InterningUnmarshallerHandler.java
```

Figure 5-12

After the xjc compiler is run to compile your schema, the following Java source files and resources are generated:

```
org\book\configuration\bgm.ser
org\book\configuration\ColorType.java
org\book\configuration\Configuration.java
org\book\configuration\ConfigurationType.java
org\book\configuration\jaxb.properties
org\book\configuration\ObjectFactory.java
org\book\configuration\PointType.java
org\book\configuration\RecentFilesType.java
org\book\configuration\UiSettingsType.java
org\book\configuration\UserSettingsType.java
org\book\configuration\impl\ColorTypeImpl.java
org\book\configuration\impl\ConfigurationImpl.java
org\book\configuration\impl\ConfigurationTypeImpl.java
org\book\configuration\impl\JAXBVersion.java
org\book\configuration\impl\PointTypeImpl.java
org\book\configuration\impl\UiSettingsTypeImpl.java
org\book\configuration\impl\UserSettingsTypeImpl.java
```

Note: *There are also many Java sources generated in the org\book\configuration\impl\runtime folder. These sources are required in addition to the JAXB library JAR files at run time. You will not be analyzing them or their content, however; just be aware that they are necessary at run time. There is a command-line option to disable the runtime package generation — if you generate classes for more than one schema, you only need to reference one runtime package. In those scenarios, the runtime classes are not needed (though you will need to pass along where a current runtime package exists for the xjc compiler to disable the generation of the runtime package).*

Generated JAXB Object Graphs

JAXB generates its classes to follow certain conventions that correspond to how an XML schema is written. Package names for generated classes follow whatever XML namespace the elements have in the schema (though the package names can be changed with a certain command-line argument to the `xjc` compiler). Every top-level XML element or complex type defined in a schema gets its own `interface` in the root package generated by JAXB. A top-level element or complex type in an XML schema is one that is not nested in other elements — its definition is a direct child element to the root element of the schema definition. For example, in your schema, the complex type `pointType` is a top-level definition because its location in the schema is right under the parent schema definition element. The only interface that represents an element definition in your list of generated files is the `org.book.configuration.Configuration` interface. This interface corresponds to the following element definition from the schema:

```
<xs:element name="configuration" type="configurationType" />
```

*Note: The type **org.book.configuration.Configuration** is different from the type **book.Configuration** that has been referred to in the earlier sections of this book (though it represents the same logical data points). The type **org.book.configuration.Configuration** is the JAXB-generated class that represents the data defined in your XML schema.*

As you can see, the name of the interface comes from the name of the element. Every top-level element in a schema definition gets its own interface that extends the interface `javax.xml.bind.Element`. This is JAXB's way of marking that a particular interface is a top-level element in an XML schema. It is similar in concept to `java.io.Serializable`, in the sense that it contains no methods. It is also similar because in JAXB, you cannot serialize or deserialize any structure that is not a `javax.xml.bind.Element` (much like you cannot use the Java Serialization API to serialize any class not marked `Serializable`). This is important to know, because when you define your schema, you must have at least one top-level element definition. These top-level element definitions are potential root elements in an XML instance document.

You may have guessed by now that the rest of the root package `org.book.configuration` consists mainly of all interfaces. That is the case, and the `org.book.configuration.impl` package contains the implementations of these interfaces. The rest of the interfaces in your package all correspond to top-level complex type definitions in your schema. A couple of them will be looked at in detail, namely `ColorType` and `PointType`. Any interface that represents a complex type definition will have the `Type` suffix appended to the complex type name, hence your interfaces `PointType` and `ColorType` represent the complex schema types `pointType` and `colorType`, respectively (the generator is smart enough not to make the name `PointTypeType`, since you already appended type to the name of your complex type definitions in the schema; see Figure 5-13).

As you can see from the diagram in Figure 5-13, JAXB maps XML elements and attributes of complex types to Java Bean properties. The complex type `colorType` in the schema had four subelements: `red`, `blue`, `green`, and `alpha`. These were all mapped to Java Bean `int` properties. They were mapped to `int` because that was the type specified in their element definitions. Their type could also potentially be another complex type, which would map to another generated JAXB interface, rather than a Java primitive type like `int`.

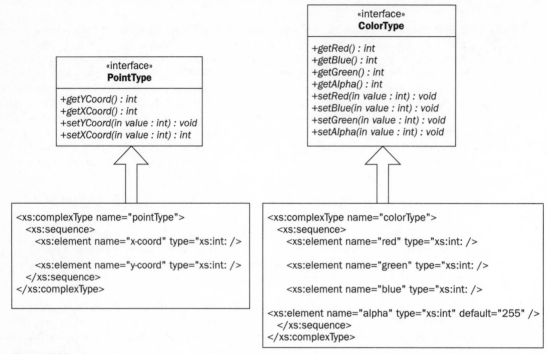

Figure 5-13

Since XML documents are hierarchical in nature, the structure the generated JAXB classes naturally take on is hierarchical. JAXB serializes and deserializes root elements in an XML document. It is the beginning of an object graph. The XML complex type pointType, for instance, has subelements x-coord and y-coord; they are therefore properties of pointType. In the generated JAXB class, these coordinates become properties of the PointType interface. Figure 5-14 shows the generated JAXB object graph from the root element of your configuration data model, configuration. The Configuration interface not only extends javax.xml.bind.Element because it is a root element, but since it is an instance of XML complex type configurationType, it also extends the org.book.configuration.ConfigurationType interface. This interface has the properties as shown in the diagram. The object graph then extends out from there.

The complete class diagram of all of the JAXB generated interfaces from your XML schema are pictured in Figure 5-15. Notice how only the Configuration interface extends javax.xml.bind.Element. This means that it is the only element that can be serialized or deserialized by JAXB. The rest are all subtypes and elements branching off from Configuration. By looking at the object graph above and the class diagram below, you can match up the XML element and its place in the object graph with the JAXB interface that implements it.

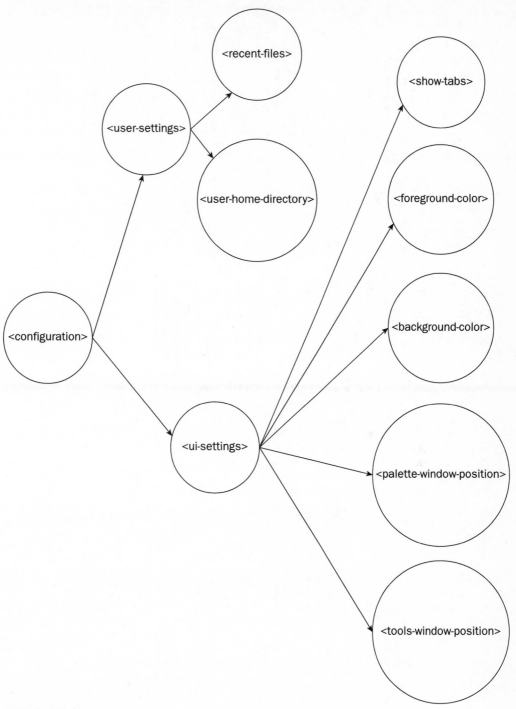

Figure 5-14

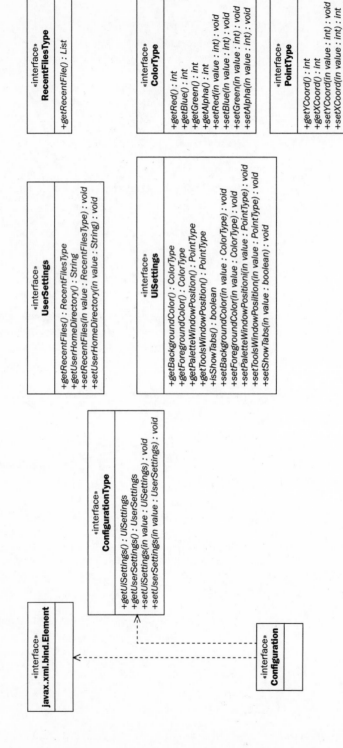

Figure 5-15

JAXB API Key Classes

The classes that the `xjc` compiler generates are not the classes that are used by the developer to serialize or unserialize any data, or in JAXB terms, marshall or unmarshall any data. The classes and resources generated by JAXB from an XML schema merely provide the rules and data structure necessary for the JAXB runtime libraries to marshall and unmarshall XML data conforming to that schema. Because the JAXB run time must be made aware of the particular constraints and rules for each individual schema, a `JAXBContext` object must first be created with the particular context of the particular schema and data structure classes to be used. From there, `Marhsallers` and `Unmarshallers` can be created to actually serialize and deserialize XML data.

Class or Interface (From javax.xml.bind)	Function
JAXBContext	The JAXBContext is the initial class; one creates Marshaller and Unmarshaller classes for various JAXB-generated types
Marshaller	Interface that allows for the marshalling of JAXB-generated objects to XML in various formats (stream, DOM nodes, SAX events, and so on)
Unmarshaller	Interface that allows for the unmarshalling of various XML representations (from a stream, a DOM tree, or SAX events) to populate instances of JAXB-generated classes
Validator	Interface through which JAXB-generated class instances can be verified that the data they contain conforms to the XML schema they were generated against

Marshalling and Unmarshalling XML Data

The process of marshalling and unmarshalling data into and from JAXB classes occurs through three classes: `JAXBContext`, `Marshaller`, and `Unmarshaller`. Both `Marshaller` and `Unmarshaller` are created from an instance of `JAXBContext`, and they do the actual work of marshalling and unmarshalling the data, respectively. A different `JAXBContext` is required for every different XML namespace from XML schemas, or more specifically, the Java package that contains the generated JAXB classes. This allows the `JAXBContext` to set up the `Marshaller` and `Unmarshaller` objects with that particular schema's rules and constraints. There are three steps to unmarshalling XML instance data conforming to a schema into a JAXB-generated object graph:

1. Retrieve an instance of `JAXBContext` specific to the root package of the generated JAXB classes.

2. Create an `Unmarshaller` object from the `JAXBContext` instance.

3. Use the `Unmarshaller` to unmarshall XML data into instances of the generated JAXB classes.

You will now unmarshall XML data conforming to your `configuration.xsd` schema into your generated JAXB classes. First, the `JAXBContext` is retrieved:

```
JAXBContext ctx = JAXBContext.newInstance("org.book.configuration");
```

Then `Unmarshaller` can then be created from the context:

```
Unmarshaller u = ctx.createUnmarshaller();
```

Now that you have an `Unmarshaller`, various representations of XML data can be passed to it to transform the XML into instances of the JAXB-generated object graph. In this example, you will pass it a `FileInputStream` corresponding to an XML file saved on disk that conforms to your schema:

```
org.book.configuration.Configuration conf = (org.book.configuration.Configuration)
                        u.unmarshal (new
FileInputStream("c:\\mark\\configuration.xml"));
```

The Unmarshaller returns a populated instance of `Configuration`, which represents the root node of the XML file, and is the root of your object graph. The XML data can now be used as necessary in your application. Marshalling data back into XML is just as straightforward as unmarshalling. The three steps to marshall data mirror the three steps to unmarshall it:

1.   Retrieve an instance of `JAXBContext` specific to the root package of the generated JAXB classes.

2.   Create a `Marshaller` object from the `JAXBContext` instance.

3.   Use the `Marshaller` to marshall XML data into instances of the generated JAXB classes.

Now instances of `org.book.configuration.Configuration` can be marshalled back to disk (or to DOM or SAX representations). Just like before, the `JAXBContext` particular for your package of JAXB-generated classes must be obtained:

```
JAXBContext ctx = JAXBContext.newInstance("org.book.configuration");
```

The `Marshaller` can then be created from the context:

```
Marshaller m = ctx.createMarshaller();
```

The `Marshaller` instance can now be used to serialize the information in your `conf` instance of `org.book.configuration.Configuration` to a `FileOutputStream` (and hence a file on the file system):

```
m.marshal (conf, new FileOutputStream("c:\\mark\\configuration.xml");
```

That's all there is to marshalling and unmarshalling data. As you can see, the difficult part of using JAXB is writing the schema.

> *Note: If the* ***org.book.configuration.Configuration*** *type is not populated with all the data the schema requires, the instance will not be able to be marshalled into XML. By the same token, XML documents containing errors — in other words not exactly conforming to the schema — will not be able to be unmarshalled. Exceptions will be thrown and the instance document will have to be fixed.*

Creating New XML Content with JAXB-Generated Classes

You have looked at how to load XML data into a JAXB object graph. You have looked into saving an existing JAXB object graph back into XML. How would you create a new JAXB graph and populate it programmatically (to later save to XML)? Unfortunately, this is one area where JAXB becomes a little unwieldy. In JAXB, every set of generated classes comes with an `ObjectFactory` class at the root package of the generated classes. You may have noticed the class `org.book.configuration` `.ObjectFactory` back when you generated your set of classes for your `configuration.xsd` schema. This is the class necessary to create blank new instances of every JAXB object. Since every JAXB representation of either an element or complex type definition corresponds to a Java interface, the `ObjectFactory` finds the right implementation class (from the generated package's subpackage, `impl`) and creates it. In any given JAXB object graph, there are potentially many element and complex type definitions turned into interfaces, and each of these must be created with the `ObjectFactory`. Once these types are created, though, it is easy to populate them with data, since they all follow Java Bean conventions. The example below shows the creation and population of an `org.book.configuration` `.Configuration` instance:

```
ObjectFactory factory = new ObjectFactory();

ConfigurationType configType = factory.createConfiguration();
UiSettingsType uiSettingsType = factory.createUiSettingsType();
UserSettingsType userSettingsType = factory.createUserSettingsType();

configType.setUiSettings(uiSettingsType);
configType.setUserSettings(userSettingsType);
ColorType fgColorType = factory.createColorType();
fgColorType.setRed(255);
fgColorType.setBlue(255);
fgColorType.setGreen(0);

uiSettingsType.setForegroundColor(fgColorType);

uiSettingsType.setShowTabs(true);

userSettingsType.setUserHomeDirectory("c:\\mark");

... // continue on as such, populating the entire object graph
```

One thing to take into consideration when manually populating JAXB object graphs is completeness and conformance to the schema. While it is easy to populate your JAXB objects and use the data in a Java application, if you want to save the data you are populating out to disk (or somewhere else) as XML, every schema-required piece of data must exist in your newly created object graph. In the example above, if you did not create a `UserSettingsType` instance and set it on your `Configuration` instance, JAXB exceptions would be thrown when the instance was later marshalled to disk.

Using JAXB-Generated Classes in Your Application

One of the potential issues that arise whenever information is saved and loaded from a file is that the information must be turned into objects used by the application. The nice thing about the Java Serialization API and XMLEncoder/Decoder is that they save the actual Java class instances used by an application, so there is no need to transform the data loaded into a format used internally by the application — it is already in the format used by the application. The classes that JAXB generates can be used as the in-memory data model for your application, but generally, there is a need to perform at least some transformations. The Java classes in the JDK are rich and full of functionality — and it would be wasteful to ignore them. Why store URLs as `String`s? Why store `File` objects as `String`s? Why not represent a color with a `java.awt.Color` object? Because it makes sense to use the classes in the JDK, a lot of the time you will find yourself taking data from the Java Beans generated by JAXB, and putting them into your own data structures. You will find yourself adding JAXB classes to your own lists, maps, trees, and other data structures, especially since `java.util.List` is the only collection class ever used by JAXB-generated classes. This is the added burden of using JAXB over using Java Serialization or XMLEncoder/Decoder. Not only do you have to create schema, but also it is often a necessity to transform some of the data from the JAXB classes into classes more usable by your application. In the example configuration data model used throughout this chapter for the Imager Application, you use an instance of `book.Configuration` to represent the model. It contains Java representations of points and colors that could be used by the AWT and Swing UI frameworks. To use your JAXB-generated configuration data model in your application, you will as such have to transform it to and from your `book` `.Configuration` data model. It is not a difficult task, but must be done for things like your color and point representations to have any meaning to your application. The diagram in Figure 5-16 that follows shows where your transformations fit into the bigger picture of your application.

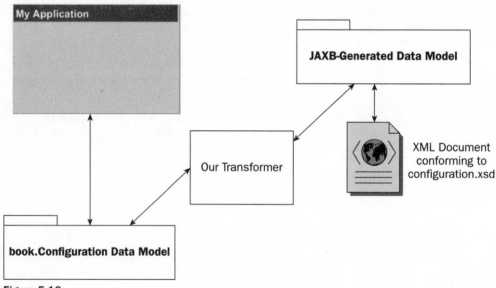

Figure 5-16

In your original `Configuration` data model example, you wrapped your serialization code into Swing actions to use in the UI for the Imager Application. This let you easily add your code to save and load configuration data to your menus and buttons in your application. You will do the same for your code to save and load your configuration data, this time with your XML format based on your `configuration` `.xsd` schema file. The key difference, though, will be that you need to integrate transformation functionality into these actions, since a conversion needs to be done between your JAXB-generated data model and your original `Configuration` data model (as shown in Figure 5-16). Other than this transformation, your new XML save and load Swing actions will be very similar in structure and nature to your older actions.

Implementing Your Save Action

As shown in the code that follows, your save action's `actionPerformed()` method will start out the same way as your original save action — by prompting the user for a file in which to save the configuration information:

```
package book;

...

import org.book.configuration.ColorType;
import org.book.configuration.ConfigurationType;
import org.book.configuration.ObjectFactory;
import org.book.configuration.PointType;
import org.book.configuration.RecentFilesType;
import org.book.configuration.UiSettingsType;
import org.book.configuration.UserSettingsType;

public class SaveXMLConfigurationAction extends AbstractAction {

  private Application myApp;

  public SaveXMLConfigurationAction(Application app) {
    super("Export XML Configuration");

    this.myApp = app;
  }

  public void actionPerformed(ActionEvent arg0) {
    JFileChooser fc = new JFileChooser();
    if (JFileChooser.APPROVE_OPTION == fc.showSaveDialog(myApp)) {
      try {
```

If the user chooses a file to save the configuration to, the application's `book.Configuration` object is retrieved, and the process of mapping its data to a new JAXB `org.book.configuration` `.Configuration` object is begun. The first step to completing this mapping is to create the `ObjectFactory`. After the factory is created, all of the types necessary, starting with `ConfigurationType`, can be created. Notice in the code that follows how values are then retrieved from the application's `book.Configuration` data model, and then mapped into their appropriate place in the JAXB-generated `ConfigurationType` data model:

```
Configuration conf = this.myApp.getConfiguration();

JAXBContext ctx = JAXBContext.newInstance("org.book.configuration");

Marshaller m = ctx.createMarshaller();
ObjectFactory factory = new ObjectFactory();

ConfigurationType configType = factory.createConfiguration();
UiSettingsType uiSettingsType = factory.createUiSettingsType();
UserSettingsType userSettingsType = factory.createUserSettingsType();

configType.setUiSettings(uiSettingsType);
configType.setUserSettings(userSettingsType);
```

```
Color fgColor = conf.getForegroundColor();
if (fgColor != null) {
  ColorType fgColorType = factory.createColorType();
  fgColorType.setRed(fgColor.getRed());
  fgColorType.setBlue(fgColor.getBlue());
  fgColorType.setGreen(fgColor.getGreen());
  fgColorType.setAlpha(fgColor.getAlpha());

  uiSettingsType.setForegroundColor(fgColorType);
}

Color bgColor = conf.getBackgroundColor();
if (bgColor != null) {
  ColorType bgColorType = factory.createColorType();
  bgColorType.setRed(bgColor.getRed());
  bgColorType.setBlue(bgColor.getBlue());
  bgColorType.setGreen(bgColor.getGreen());
  bgColorType.setAlpha(bgColor.getAlpha());

  uiSettingsType.setBackgroundColor(bgColorType);
}

Point ppPoint = conf.getPaletteWindowPosition();
if (ppPoint != null) {
  PointType ppPointType = factory.createPointType();
  ppPointType.setXCoord(ppPoint.x);
  ppPointType.setYCoord(ppPoint.y);

  uiSettingsType.setPaletteWindowPosition(ppPointType);
}

Point tpPoint = conf.getToolsWindowPosition();
if (ppPoint != null) {
  PointType tpPointType = factory.createPointType();
  tpPointType.setXCoord(tpPoint.x);
  tpPointType.setYCoord(tpPoint.y);

  uiSettingsType.setToolsWindowPosition(tpPointType);
}

uiSettingsType.setShowTabs(conf.isShowTabs());

userSettingsType.setUserHomeDirectory(conf.getUserHomeDirectory());
String[] recentFiles = conf.getRecentFiles();
if (recentFiles != null) {
  RecentFilesType rFilesType = factory.createRecentFilesType();

  Collections.addAll(rFilesType.getRecentFile(), recentFiles);

  userSettingsType.setRecentFiles(rFilesType);
}
```

Finally, after you finish mapping the data, the JAXB data model is marshalled to XML in the file specified by the user:

```
        m.marshal (configType, new FileOutputStream(fc.getSelectedFile()));

    } catch (IOException ioe) {
    JOptionPane.showMessageDialog(this.myApp, ioe.getMessage(), "Error",
                                JOptionPane.ERROR_MESSAGE);

    ioe.printStackTrace();

    } catch (JAXBException jaxbEx) {
    JOptionPane.showMessageDialog(this.myApp, jaxbEx.getMessage(), "Error",
                                JOptionPane.ERROR_MESSAGE);

    jaxbEx.printStackTrace();
    }
  }
 }
}
```

Note how you must catch `JAXBException` in the above code. Most JAXB operations can throw a `JAXBException`—when saving it can mean that you did not populate all the information that was required in your generated object structure as specified in the originating XML schema.

Implementing Your Load Action

The load action is of course similar to your original load action—and probably most actions that load files, actually. As shown in the code that follows, the user is prompted for a file from which to load the configuration at the beginning of the `actionPerformed()` method:

```
package book;

...

import javax.xml.bind.JAXBContext;
import javax.xml.bind.JAXBException;
import javax.xml.bind.Unmarshaller;

import org.book.configuration.ColorType;
import org.book.configuration.ConfigurationType;
import org.book.configuration.PointType;
import org.book.configuration.RecentFilesType;

public class LoadXMLConfigurationAction extends AbstractAction {

  private Application myApp;

  public LoadXMLConfigurationAction(Application app) {
    super("Import XML Configuration");
    this.myApp = app;
```

```
        }

        public void actionPerformed(ActionEvent evt) {
          JFileChooser fc = new JFileChooser();
          if (JFileChooser.APPROVE_OPTION == fc.showOpenDialog(myApp)) {
            try {
```

Once the user has picked the file, you begin the process of unmarshalling the XML data contained in the file to your JAXB-generated data model. The code below shows the XML file the user specified being unmarshalled into a new instance of org.book.configuration.Configuration, the JAXB object representing the root node of the XML document specified in your configuration.xsd schema file:

```
        JAXBContext ctx = JAXBContext.newInstance(ConfigurationType.class
                                               .getPackage().getName());

        Unmarshaller u = ctx.createUnmarshaller();
        org.book.configuration.Configuration configType =
                            (org.book.configuration.Configuration)
                                u.unmarshal (fc.getSelectedFile());
```

Now that the data has been unmarshalled, the data from the JAXB model must be mapped back from the JAXB model to your original book.Configuration model. This is essentially the reverse-process of what occurred in your save action. You are converting things like your JAXB ColorType back into a form that can be displayed in your Swing user interface, the java.awt.Color object. After the data has been mapped into your book.Configuration class, it can then be loaded into the application via the myApp.setConfiguration() method:

```
        Configuration conf = new Configuration();

        ColorType bgColorType = configType.getUiSettings().getBackgroundColor();
        if (bgColorType != null) {
          Color bgColor = new Color(bgColorType.getRed(),
                          bgColorType.getGreen(), bgColorType.getBlue(),
                          bgColorType.getAlpha());

          conf.setBackgroundColor(bgColor);
        }

        ColorType fgColorType = configType.getUiSettings().getForegroundColor();
        if (fgColorType != null) {
          Color fgColor = new Color(fgColorType.getRed(),
                          fgColorType.getGreen(), fgColorType.getBlue(),
                          fgColorType.getAlpha());

          conf.setForegroundColor(fgColor);
        }

        PointType ppPointType = configType.getUiSettings()
                                .getPaletteWindowPosition();

        if (ppPointType != null) {
```

```
            Point ppPoint = new Point(ppPointType.getXCoord(),
                                      ppPointType.getYCoord());

            conf.setPaletteWindowPosition(ppPoint);
          }

          PointType tpPointType = configType.getUiSettings()
                                 .getToolsWindowPosition();

          if (tpPointType != null) {
            Point tpPoint = new Point(tpPointType.getXCoord(),
                                      tpPointType.getYCoord());

            conf.setToolsWindowPosition(tpPoint);
          }

          conf.setShowTabs(configType.getUiSettings().isShowTabs());

          conf.setUserHomeDirectory(
                     configType.getUserSettings().getUserHomeDirectory());

          RecentFilesType rFilesType =
                          configType.getUserSettings().getRecentFiles();

          if (rFilesType != null) {
            List recentFileList = rFilesType.getRecentFile();
            if (recentFileList != null) {
              String[] recentFiles = new String[recentFileList.size()];

              recentFileList.toArray(recentFiles);

              conf.setRecentFiles(recentFiles);
            }
          }


          myApp.setConfiguration(conf);
        } catch (JAXBException jaxb) {
          JOptionPane.showMessageDialog(this.myApp, jaxb.getMessage(), "Error",
                                        JOptionPane.ERROR_MESSAGE);

          jaxb.printStackTrace();

        }
      }
    }
  }
```

Similar to your save action, you must also catch JAXBException. If an error occurs while loading the file, that is, if it does not conform to your configuration.xsd schema or the file could not be found, etc., the exception will be thrown.

The Swing actions you just developed get integrated into your application the same way the previous ones did. Your application now has two mechanisms for persisting its configuration data model. One is user-friendly to edit, the other one cannot be edited outside of the application. JAXB takes more effort on the part of the developer, but can provide added value over normal Java Serialization. Figure 5-17 shows a screen shot of your updated application.

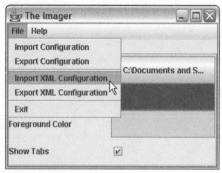

Figure 5-17

When to Use JAXB

JAXB is fundamentally different from either the Java Serialization API or the XMLEncoder/Decoder API. It takes a completely different approach. Instead of first specifying a data structure using Java classes, one first specifies the serialization format itself. The two are drastically different design approaches. In the Java Serialization and XMLEncoder/Decoder API, you design Java classes and do not worry about the serialization file format — that is taken care of by the APIs. However, it has the unfortunate disadvantage of limiting the use of the serialized objects to only Java-based applications. JAXB generates your Java data classes for you (at the expense of a very loose integration of your data with the JDK libraries) from the specification of a file format in a W3C standard XML Schema Definition. JAXB adds more complexity to an application and requires more development effort. Its advantages are as follows:

❑ Reads and writes standard file formats that applications written in any language can read, and in many languages generates classes to use the data similarly to how JAXB generates classes based on the file

❑ Resulting serialized documents are human-readable and as friendly to edit as they are defined

❑ Fast way to read XML data based on an XML schema — uses far less memory to represent an XML document in memory than a DOM tree

Its disadvantages are namely the following:

❑ Requires more development effort — sometimes it is necessary to manage *two* data models: one your application can more efficiently use and the JAXB-generated data model

❑ Working with JAXB objects can be unwieldy since they are generated — things like naming and object creation are more tedious to develop with than custom Java classes

JAXB should be used when you want a human-readable file format that can be edited by users. It should be used when you are developing a file format you want non-Java-based applications to be able to read. It can be used in conjunction with other XML technologies, and to read third-party XML documents based on third-party XML schemas. It is a valuable tool that requires more development effort and more design, but its benefits far outweigh its costs — if you need a universal file format or just simply human-readable XML.

Future Direction of JAXB 2.0

JAXB 2.0 will fix the one main problem with JAXB 1.0. It will allow developers to map *existing* Java classes to an XML schema. Essentially this solves the problem you had to deal with when you had to transform your JAXB-generated configuration data model to the Swing/UI-friendly one you custom developed. If JAXB had given you the ability to map your original `book.Configuration` data model to XML directly, there would have been no need to generate an additional data model and convert between the two. JAXB 2.0 will build on some of the new JDK 5.0 language features, such as annotations. Developers will have the ability to annotate their classes to define how they will be serialized to XML. This really is the best of both Java Serialization or XMLEncoder/Decoder and JAXB. Developers can design their data model in a way friendly to the Java environment, building their in-memory representations of the data, and then simply map it straight to human-readable and XML schema conforming XML. Once JAXB 2.0 is released, it will become probably the best way to serialize your classes out of the three technologies discussed in this chapter for most all design cases (though certainly not all). You can view the JAXB 2.0 specification online at the following URL:

```
http://www.jcp.org/aboutJava/communityprocess/edr/jsr222/
```

Summary

Saving the state of an application to a file is saving all of the pieces of its in-memory data model necessary to reconstruct it exactly as it was at a later point of time. Most object-oriented applications store their data model as a set of data storage classes. In Java, it is standard practice to have the data model represented as a series of classes following the Java Beans conventions and utilizing collection classes where necessary (such as lists, maps, trees, sets, etc.). In applications that have graphical user interfaces, it is best to separate the in-memory data structure from the GUI toolkit classes as much as possible. The standard Java GUI toolkit, Swing, follows the Model-View-Controller design pattern to accomplish this separation. This way, to persist the state of an application, *only* the data model needs to be written to disk — the GUI is simply a transient aspect of the state of the application. Normally, when you say you want to be able to save an application's state, you are referring to saving some sort of file that an application produces, whether an image file, a word processing document, or a spreadsheet. These types of files are simply a data model persisted to disk. By keeping your data model separate from your GUI classes, it is easier to save it off to a file. The Java Serialization API and the XMLEncoder/Decoder API have been looked at in this chapter. These APIs literally take a set of Java classes, and persist enough information to disk to reconstruct the actual object instances as they used to look in memory. This methodology makes adding serialization capabilities to an application very easy, but at the cost of limiting the use of the serialized information to Java-based applications.

The JAXB API takes a fundamentally different approach, and first defines a common file format that can be read from any application using the W3C standard XML schema technology. From this schema, JAXB generates the in-memory data model for an application. It is essentially the reverse design process of the Java Serialization API and the XMLEncoder/Decoder API. Both the JAXB API and the XMLEncoder/Decoder API persist their information in XML — but the XML produced by the XMLEncoder/Decoder API can only be used by Java-based applications. The Java Serialization API serializes its information in a Java-specific binary format that is much more efficient than XML, but again, is only useful by Java applications and is not human readable. Persisting your applications using files can require as little design and development time as you give it. If you use JAXB, it takes a little more time. Your application's in-memory data model is probably the most important aspect of your data design. Once that exists, the various serialization and persistence strategies found in this chapter can all be applied. The next chapter talks about how to serialize your application's data model using a database, which is usually necessary for multi-user systems.

Persisting Your Application Using Databases

In the last chapter, you learned about how to persist the state of your application using file-based mechanisms. This is a useful way to handle things in a single-user model, but when multiple users need to share the same data, databases are the solution. Now, you will learn about how to persist your application to a database.

Persisting your data to a database has always required true effort, regardless of your development language. Java has been making substantial leaps in this area and has come a long way in making the task much easier with their addition of the JDBC 3.0 API. Java also has an ever-growing open source community that is releasing new and improved technologies every year.

This chapter will discuss how to persist your application's data to a database using features of the JDBC 3.0 API, such as RowSets and Distributed Transactions. It will also allow you to take an in-depth look at *Hibernate*, a powerful object/relational mapping tool that is used to store and retrieve Java objects to and from relational databases.

Java and its open source community are becoming extremely aware of the importance of data persistence, especially for a developer in a J2EE architecture. Therefore they continue to enhance the JDBC API to support the ever-growing needs of its developers.

JDBC API Overview

The JDBC API provides a simple way for Java applications to access data from one or more relational data sources. A Java developer can use the JDBC API to do the following things:

- ❑ Connect to a data source
- ❑ Execute complex SQL statements

Chapter 6

❑ Persist changes to a data source

❑ Retrieve information from a data source

❑ Interact with legacy filesystems

The JDBC API is based on the specification X/Open SQL Call Level Interface (CLI), which provides an application with an alternative method for accessing databases with embedded SQL calls. This specification has been accepted by the International Organization for Standards (ISO) as an international standard. ODBC is also based on this standard, and the JDBC API can interface with ODBC through JDBC-ODBC bridge drivers.

The JDBC API makes it relatively simple to send SQL statements to databases, and it doesn't matter what platform, what database vendor, or what combination of platform and vendor you choose to use. It's all done through one common API layer for all platforms. This is what makes Java the front-runner of programming languages in today's market. Although there are different vendors who are creating their own drivers, they all must follow the JDBC 3.0 specification. With that said, all drivers fit into four categories.

Driver Type	Description
JDBC-ODBC Bridge Driver	This is a JDBC driver that is used to bridge the gap between JDBC and ODBC. It allows them to communicate and is mostly used in three-tier architectures. This is not a pure Java solution.
Native API/Part Java Driver	This type of driver is specific to a DBMS (Database Management System) and converts JDBC calls to specific client calls for the DBMS being used. This type of driver is usually operating-system specific and is also not a pure Java solution.
JDBC-Net Pure Java Driver	This type of driver uses net server middleware for connecting Java clients to DBMS. It converts the JDBC calls into an independent protocol that can then be used to interface with the DBMS. This is a pure Java solution with the main drawback being security.
Native-Protocol Pure Java Driver	This type of driver is provided by the database vendor, and its main purpose is to convert JDBC calls into the network protocol understood by the DBMS. This is the best solution to use and is pure Java.

The first two driver-type options are usually temporary solutions to solve the problem, where the JDBC driver for the particular DBMS (Database Management System) in use does not exist. The third and fourth driver-type options represent the normal, preferred usage of JDBC because they keep the platform-independent fundamentals in place. If you would like to find out if your DBMS vendor supports a particular version of the JDBC API, please check out the following Web site for details: `http://servlet.java.sun.com/products/jdbc/drivers`.

The JDBC API is contained in two Java packages — java.sql and javax.sql. The first package, java.sql, contains the original core APIs for JDBC. The second package, javax.sql, contains optional, more advanced features such as row sets, connection pooling, and distributed transaction management. It is important to determine your application's data access needs and architecture ahead of time to properly assess which packages you need to import.

Setting Up Your Environment

To use the JDBC API and its advanced features, it is recommended that you install the latest Java 2 SDK Standard Edition. The JDBC API is currently shipping with both Java 2 SDK SE and Java 2 SDK Enterprise Edition (the latter is a must if you are doing server-side development).

You will also need to install a JDBC driver that implements the JDBC 3.0 features. Your driver vendor may not support all the features that are in the javax.sql package, so you should check with them first.

Finally you will need access to a Database Management System that is supported by your driver. Further information on JDBC support can be found at `http://java.sun.com/products/jdbc/`.

JDBC API Usage in the Real World

The JDBC API is most commonly used by applications to access data in two main models: the two-tier model and three-tier model, both of which will be covered in the following paragraphs.

Understanding the Two-Tier Model

The two-tier model is the simplest of the models. It comprises a *client layer* and a *server layer*. The client layer interacts directly with the server layer, and no middleware is used. The business logic, application/presentation layer, transaction management, and connection management are all handled by the client layer. The server layer contains only the data source and doesn't manage anything that the client is doing, except for user access and rights. Figure 6-1 illustrates the two-tier model.

This is a good design for small applications but would present a scalability dilemma for larger applications requiring more robust connection and transaction management.

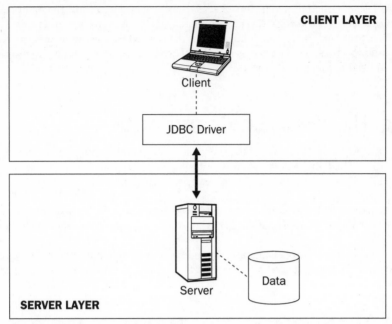

Figure 6-1

Understanding the Three-Tier Model

The three-tier model is the most complex and the most scalable of the models. It removes the business logic and adds a layer of abstraction to the data sources. This model is shown in Figure 6-2.

The *client layer* in this model is a thin client layer that contains only very lightweight presentation layers that will run on Web browsers, Java Programs, PDAs, Tablet PCs, and so forth. It does not handle business logic, methods of accessing the data sources, the drivers used to provide access, or the methods in which data is saved.

The *middle layer* is where the core of the functionality exists in the three-tier model. The thin clients interact with applications that support the business logic and interactions with data sources. Connection pools, transaction management, and JDBC drivers can all be found here. This is the layer that adds increased performance and scalability compared to the two-tier model.

The *data layer* is where the data sources such as database management systems and files exist. The only interaction that occurs here is from the middle layer to the data layer through a JDBC driver.

The main benefit of the three-tier model is the fact that it adds layers of abstraction that can be scaled, removed, added, and improved upon. It also adds extra performance benefits when simultaneously accessing multiple data sources. The main drawback is that it can be expensive, depending on the choices made for the application server software and the hardware to run the system.

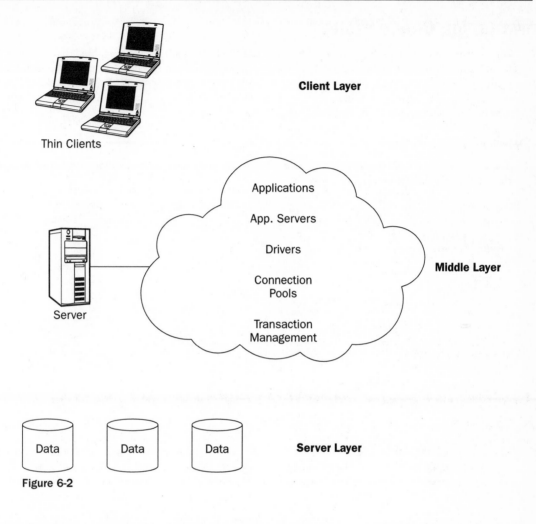

Client Layer

Thin Clients

Applications

App. Servers

Drivers

Middle Layer

Connection
Pools

Server

Transaction
Management

Data   Data   Data   **Server Layer**

Figure 6-2

Grasping JDBC API Concepts

For this part of the chapter, you will explore the main usage of the JDBC API before moving on to more advanced topics, such as managing database meta data, utilizing RowSets, connection pooling, and managing transactions to insure that you have a solid foundation with which to start your JDBC API journey. This section will also act as a good review for those of you who need it, and it will cover the following topics:

❑ Managing JDBC API connections using the DriverManager class and the new DataSource interface

❑ Creating, defining, and understanding statements

❑ Utilizing result sets to retrieve and manage database information

Managing Connections

A Java application can establish a connection to a data source via a JDBC API–enabled driver. Connections are maintained in code by the Connection object. A Java application can have multiple connections to multiple data sources at the same time using multiple Connection objects. A Connection object can be obtained by a Java application in two ways: through a DriverManager class or through an implementation of the DataSource interface.

DriverManager Class

The traditional method to establish a connection is to use the DriverManager class, load the driver, and then make the connection:

```
String sDriver   = "com.sybase.jdbc2.jdbc.SybDataSource";
String sURL      = "jdbc:sybase:Tds:127.0.0.1:3000?ServiceName=sybase";
String sUsername = "Andrew";
String sPassword = "Vitale";

try {
   // Load the driver
   Class.forName(sDriver);

   // Obtain a connection
   Connection cConn = DriverManager.getConnection(sURL, sUsername, sPassword);
} catch (...) {
} finally {
   if (cConn != null) {
       cConn.close(); // Close the connection
   }
}
```

The driver is loaded into memory for use by the `Class.forName(driver)` call, and then a Connection object is obtained by a static DriverManager API call, `getConnection(JDBCURL, Username, Password)`. A connection is now established. The driver itself views the Connection object as the user's session.

DataSource Interface

The preferred method to establishing a connection is to use the DataSource interface. The DataSource interface is preferred because it makes the code more portable, it allows for easier program maintenance, and it permits the Connection object to participate in distributed transaction management as well as transparent connection pooling. Connection pooling is a great idea when performance is the primary goal for your application. The ability to reuse Connection objects eliminates the need to constantly create a new physical connection every time a connection request is made. Distributed transactions allow you to create applications that work well in robust enterprise architectures where an enormous amount of concurrent database tasks are likely to occur.

The DataSource interface utilizes the Java Naming and Directory Interface (JNDI) to store a logical name for the data source instead of using the fully qualified driver name to connect to the data source. This type of usage aids in code portability and reusability. One of the very neat features of a DataSource object is that it basically represents a physical data source; if the data source changes, the changes will be automatically reflected in the DataSource object without invoking any code.

Using JNDI, a Java application can find a remote database service by its logical name. For the application to use the logical name, it must first be registered with the JNDI naming service. The following code shows an example of how to register a data source with the JNDI naming service:

```
VendorDataSource vdsDataSource = new VendorDataSource();
vdsDataSource.setServerName("Our_Database_Server_Name");
vdsDataSource.setDatabaseName("Our_Database_Name");
vdsDataSource.setDescription("Our database description");

// Get the initial context
Context ctx = new InitialContext();

// Create the logical name for the data source
ctx.bind("jdbc/OurDB", vdsDataSource);
```

If JNDI is new to you, it can best be thought of as a directory structure like that of your file system that provides network-wide naming and directory services. However, it is independent of any naming or directory service. For more information on JNDI, please visit http://java.sun.com/products/jndi/.

Once you have registered the data source with the JNDI naming service, establishing a connection to the data source is very straightforward:

```
Context ctx = InitialContext();

// Look up the registered data source from JNDI
DataSource dsDataSource = (DataSource) ctx.lookup("jdbc/OurDB");

// Obtain a Connection object from the data source
Connection cConn = dsDataSource.getConnection("username", "password");

// Close the connection
cConn.close();
```

Now that you have established a connection, there are a couple of things that can occur that are transparent to the developer. The first thing is that the data source's properties that you are connected to can change dynamically. These changes will be automatically reflected in the DataSource object. The second thing that could occur, which is very nice, is that the middle tier managing the connections could seamlessly switch the data source to which you are connected, without your knowledge. This is definitely a benefit for fail-over, clustered, and load-balanced enterprise architectures.

Understanding Statements

Statements are essential for communicating with a data source using embedded SQL. There are three main types of statements. The first one is the Statement interface. When objects are created from Statement interface implementations, they are generally used for executing generic SQL statements that do not take any parameters. The second type of statement is the PreparedStatement, which inherits from the Statement interface. PreparedStatement objects are useful when you need to create and compile SQL statements ahead of time. PreparedStatement objects also accept IN parameters, which will be discussed further in this section under the title "Setting IN Parameters." The final type of statement is the CallableStatement. The CallableStatement inherits from the PreparedStatement and accepts both IN and OUT parameters. Its main purpose is to execute stored database procedures.

Investigating the Statement Interface

The basic Statement object can be used to execute general SQL calls once a connection has been established and a Connection object exists:

```
Connection cConn = dsDataSource.getConnection("username", "password");

Statement sStatement = cConn.createStatement();

// Execute the following SQL query
ResultSet rsResults = sStatement.executeQuery("SELECT * FROM PLAYERS WHERE" +
                                              "AGE=25");

while (rsResults.next()) {
      // Perform operations
}
```

You can see from the previous code that once you establish a connection, creating a Statement object is trivial. The main area of importance is the Statement execution method, called executeQuery, which executes the given SQL command with the data source. The following list describes the different execution methods that can be used with a Statement object.

Method	Description
boolean execute(String sql)	Use this method to execute a generic SQL request. It may return multiple results. Use getResultSet to retrieve the ResultSet.
boolean execute(String sql, int autoGenKeys)	This method executes the SQL request and also notifies the driver that auto-generated keys should be made accessible.
boolean execute(String sql, int [] columnIndexes)	This method allows you to specify, via the array, which auto-generated keys should be made accessible.
boolean execute(String sql, String [] columnNames)	This method also allows you to specify, via the array, which auto-generated keys should be made accessible.
int [] executeBatch()	This method executes a batch of database commands and returns an array of update counts.
ResultSet executeQuery(String sql)	This method executes the SQL string and returns a single ResultSet object.
int executeUpdate(String sql)	This method executes an SQL string, which must be an INSERT, UPDATE, DELETE, or a statement that doesn't return anything.

Method	Description
int executeUpdate(String sql, int autoGeneratedKeys)	This method executes an SQL string, which must be an INSERT, UPDATE, DELETE, or a statement that doesn't return anything. It will also allow you to notify the driver that auto-generated keys should be made accessible.
int executeUpdate(String sql, int[] columnIndexes)	This method executes an SQL string, which must be an INSERT, UPDATE, DELETE, or a statement that doesn't return anything. It will also allow you to specify, via the array, which auto-generated keys should be made accessible.
int executeUpdate(String sql, String[] columnNames)	This method executes an SQL string, which must be an INSERT, UPDATE, DELETE, or a statement that doesn't return anything. It will also allow you to specify, via the array, which auto-generated keys should be made accessible.

Exploring the PreparedStatement Interface

If you need to execute an SQL statement many times, the PreparedStatement is the perfect choice for the task because it increases program efficiency and performance. The PreparedStatement is the logical name choice for the interface because it contains an SQL statement that has been previously compiled and sent to the DBMS of choice, hence the term *prepared*. The PreparedStatement is a subclass of the Statement interface; therefore, it inherits all of the functionality listed in the previous "Investigating the Statement Interface" section, with a few exceptions. When using the execute methods with a PreparedStatement object, you should never attempt to pass parameters to the methods execute(), executeQuery(), or executeUpdate(). These methods have been modified to be parameterless for the PreparedStatement interface and should be called without parameters.

Setting IN Parameters

The PreparedStatement also gives the developer the ability to embed IN parameters in the SQL statement contained in the PreparedStatement object. These IN parameters are denoted in the SQL statement by the question mark symbol. Anywhere in the SQL statement where an IN parameter occurs, you must have your application fill in a value for the IN parameter using the appropriate setter method before executing the PreparedStatement. The most common setter methods are listed in the following table.

> *Note: There are many more setter methods from which to choose than those listed in this table. These are just the ones that are most commonly used.*

Method	Description
void setBoolean(int paramIndex, boolean x)	Sets the IN parameter to a boolean value
void setDate(int paramIndex, Date x)	Sets the IN parameter to a java.sql.Date value
void setDouble(int paramIndex, double x)	Sets the IN parameter to a double value
void setFloat(int paramIndex, float x)	Sets the IN parameter to a float value
void setInt(int paramIndex, int x)	Sets the IN parameter to an int value
void setLong(int paramIndex, long x)	Sets the IN parameter to a long value
void setString(int paramIndex, String x)	Sets the IN parameter to a String value
void clearParameters()	Clears the parameter values set by the setter methods

The following is a code example of how to effectively use a PreparedStatement with IN parameters:

```
// Remember, the "?" symbol denotes an IN parameter
PreparedStatement psStatement = cConn.prepareStatement("SELECT * FROM PLAYERS" +
                                " WHERE AGE=? AND TEAM=?");

// Set the first IN parameter to 25
psStatement.setInt(1, 25);

// Set the second IN parameter to Titans
psStatement.setString(2, "Titans");

// Execute the statement
ResultSet rsResults = psStatement.executeQuery();

// Clear parameters
psStatement.clearParameters();
```

You'll notice at the end of the code example, you call psStatement.clearParameters. This call clears any parameters that are currently set for the PreparedStatement object. Therefore, if you wanted to execute the PreparedStatement again, you would have to reset all the IN parameters with the appropriate values you would want to send to the DBMS.

IN Parameter Pitfalls

There are certain pitfalls that can occur when setting parameters with the setter methods that may not be obvious to you. Anytime you set a parameter and then execute the PreparedStatement object, the JDBC driver will convert the Java type into a JDBC type that the DBMS understands. For instance, if you were to set a parameter to a Java float type and pass it to a DBMS that is expecting an INTEGER JDBC type, you could run into serious problems: potential data loss or exceptions, depending on how the DBMS handles the situation. Trying to write code that is portable to different vendors is possible, but it definitely requires knowledge of the mappings that occur between Java types and JDBC types. The following table lists the most commonly used Java types and their mappings to JDBC types.

Java Object/Type	JDBC Type
Int	INTEGER
Short	SMALLINT
Byte	TINYINT
Long	BIGINT
Float	REAL
Double	DOUBLE
java.math.BigDecimal	NUMERIC
Boolean	BOOLEAN or BIT
String	CHAR, VARCHAR, or LONGVARCHAR
Clob	CLOB
Blob	BLOB
Struct	STRUCT
Ref	REF
java.sql.Date	DATE
java.sql.Time	TIME
java.sql.Timestamp	TIMESTAMP
java.net.URL	DATALINK
Array	ARRAY
byte[]	BINARY, VARBINARY, or LONGVARBINARY
Java class	JAVA_OBJECT

Specifying JDBC Types with setObject

A way around the potential mapping pitfalls of using IN parameters is by using the `PreparedStatement.setObject()` method for setting IN parameters:

```
void setObject(int paramIndex, Object x, int targetSqlType)
```

The `setObject` method allows you to pass a Java object and specify the targeted JDBC type. This method will ensure that the conversion from the Java type to the JDBC type occurs as you intend. Here is an example using `setObject` to specify a JDBC type:

```
PreparedStatement psStatement = cConn.prepareStatement("SELECT * FROM PLAYERS WHERE
TEAM=?");

// Set the IN parameter to Titans using setObject
```

```
psStatement.setObject(1, "Titans", java.sql.Types.VARCHAR);

// Execute the statement
ResultSet rsResults = psStatement.executeQuery();

// Clear parameters
psStatement.clearParameters();
```

User Defined Types (UDT), which are classes that implement the SQLData interface, can also be used as a parameter for the setObject method. All of the conversion details are kept from the programmer, so it is important to use the following form of the setObject method rather than the previous form, which explicitly maps the Java types to JDBC Types:

```
void setObject(int paramIndex, Object x)
```

The difference between the two setObject methods is that this form intentionally omits the parameter for specifying the target JDBC type. Another valuable method that requires mentioning is the setNull method, which allows you to send a NULL for a specific JDBC type to the DBMS:

```
void setNull(int paramIndex, int sqlType)
```

Even though you are sending a NULL value to the DBMS, you still must specify the JDBC type (java.sql.Types) for which the NULL will be used.

Retrieving Meta data about Parameters

Using the getParameterMetaData method of a PreparedStatement object, an application can retrieve information about the properties and types of parameters contained in a PreparedStatement object. The results are returned in a ParameterMetaData object, which can then be manipulated to find the specific information in question. For example, if you wanted to know the name type, the mode, whether it is nullable, or the JDBC type of a specific parameter, you could issue the following method calls:

```
ParameterMetadata pmdMetaData = psStatement.getParameterMetaData();

String sTypeName  = pmdMetaData.getParameterTypeName(1);
int nMode         = pmdMetaData.getParameterMode(1);
int nJDBCType     = pmdMetaData.getParameterType(1);

int nNullable     = pmdMetaData.isNullable(1);

// Print out values...
```

You can also retrieve the parameter count, the fully-qualified Java class name, the decimal digits, the scale of the decimal digits, and information about whether a parameter can be a signed number all from the ParameterMetadata object.

Exploring the CallableStatement Interface

Occasionally you may run into to a situation where you will need to execute stored procedures on a Remote Database Management System (RDBMS). The CallableStatement provides a standard way to call stored procedures using the JDBC API stored procedure SQL escape syntax. The SQL escape syntax supports two forms of stored procedures. The first form includes a result parameter known as the OUT parameter, and the second form doesn't use OUT parameters. Each form may have IN parameters. The IN parameters are discussed in depth earlier in the "Exploring the PreparedStatement Interface" section of this chapter. The syntax of the two forms is listed as follows:

```
This form does not return a result.
{call <procedure name>[(?,?, ...)]}
This form does return a result.
{? = call <procedure name>[(?,?, ...)]}
```

The CallableStatement interface extends PreparedStatement and therefore can use all of the methods contained in the PreparedStatement interface. As a result, IN parameters are handled the same way as in the PreparedStatement; however, OUT parameters must be handled differently. They must be registered before the CallableStatement object can be executed. Registration of the OUT parameters is done through a method contained in the CallableStatement object called registerOutParameter. The intent is to register the OUT parameters with the appropriate JDBC type (java.sql.Types), not the Java type. Here is the registerOutParameter method in its simplest form:

```
void registerOutParameter (int paramIndex, int sqlType) throws SQLException
```

There is one more type of parameter that hasn't yet been discussed, and it is called the INOUT parameter. This simply means that an IN parameter that you are passing in will also have a new value associated with it on the way out. These must also be registered as OUT parameters with the registerOutParameter method. Listed below are code examples that show how to prepare a callable statement, and they also illustrate all three parameter types (IN, OUT, and INOUT).

❑   CallableStatement using an IN parameter:

```
CallableStatement cStatement = cConn.prepareCall(
                        "{CALL setPlayerName(?)}";

cStatement.setString("John Doe");

cStatement.execute();
```

❑   CallableStatement using an OUT parameter:

```
CallableStatement cStatement = cConn.prepareCall(
                "{CALL getPlayerName(?)}";

cStatement.registerOutParameter(1, java.sql.Types.STRING);

cStatement.execute();

// Retrieve Player's name
String sName = cStatement.getString(1);
```

❑   CallableStatement using an INOUT parameter:

```
CallableStatement cStatement = cConn.prepareCall(
                    "{CALL getandsetPlayersName(?)}";

cStatement.setString("John Doe");
cStatement.registerOutParameter(1, java.sql.Types.STRING);
```

293

```
cStatement.execute();

// Retrieve Player's name
String sName = cStatement.getString(1);
```

There is another escape syntax that has not been discussed because it may be supported differently by different vendors. It is the escape syntax for *scalar functions* and its form is as follows:

```
{ fn <function name> (?, ...)}
```

To figure out which scalar functions your DBMS uses, the JDBC API provides several methods in the DatabaseMetaData class for retrieving a comma-separated list of the available functions. These methods are shown in the following table.

Method	Description
String getNumericFunctions()	Returns a comma-separated list of math functions available for the given database. Example: POWER(number, power)
String getStringFunctions()	Returns a comma-separated list of string functions available for the given database. Example: REPLACE(string)
String getSystemFunctions()	Returns a comma-separated list of system functions available for the given database. Example: IFNULL(expression, value)
String getTimeDateFunctions()	Returns a comma-separated list of time and date functions available for the given database. Example: CURTIME()

The DatabaseMetaData class contains an enormous amount of useful functions for retrieving meta data about a database. This will be discussed more in the "Managing Database Meta Data" section of this chapter. However, there are two other methods of the DatabaseMetaData class that are worth mentioning here because they relate to stored procedures. They are the supportsStoredProcedures method and the getProcedures method. The supportsStoredProcedures method returns *true* if the DBMS supports stored procedures. The getProcedures method returns a description of the stored procedures available in a given DBMS.

Utilizing Batch Updates

To improve performance, the JDBC API provides a batch update facility that allows multiple updates to be submitted for processing at one time. Statement, PreparedStatement, and CallableStatement all support batch updates. Imagine a case where you have to input 100 new changes to a database using single calls to it. Wouldn't it be easier if you could just send the request at one time instead of making 100 calls to the database? Well, that is exactly the type of functionality that batch updates provide. This portion of the chapter will explain how to create batch updates for the Statement, PreparedStatement, and CallableStatement objects.

Creating Batch Updates Using a Statement Object

The Statement object can submit a set of updates to a DBMS in one single execution; however, statement objects are initially created with empty batch command lists. Therefore you must invoke the Statement. addBatch method to add SQL commands to the Statement object. The SQL commands must return an update count and are not allowed to return anything else, like *Resultsets*. If a return value other than that of an update count is returned, a BatchUpdateException is thrown and must be processed. An application can determine why the exception occurred by calling the BatchUpdateException.getUpdateCounts method to retrieve an integer array of update counts, which allows you to determine the cause of the failure.

To properly process batch commands, you should always set auto-commit to *false* so that the DBMS's driver will not commit the changes until you tell it to do so. This will give you a chance to catch exceptions and clear the batch list, if necessary. To clear a batch list that has not been processed, use the Statement. clearBatch method. This will clear the Statement object's batch list of all commands. If a batch is successfully processed, it is automatically cleared.

When a Statement.executeBatch is successful, it will return an array of update counts that are in the same order as the commands were when added to the batch of the Statement. Each entry in the array will contain one of the following:

❏ A value that is 0 or greater, which means the command was processed successfully. If the value is greater than 0, the number signifies the number of rows that were affected when the command was executed.

❏ A Statement.SUCCESS_NO_INFO, which signifies that the particular command was processed successfully; however, it did not contain any information about the number of rows that were affected by the command.

In the event of a failure during the execution of the batch command, a BatchUpdateException will be thrown. Certain drivers may continue with the execution of the batch commands, and others will stop execution all together. If the batch command fails and the driver stops processing after the first failure, it will return the number of update counts via the BatchUpdateException.getUpdateCounts. If the batch command fails and the driver continues to process other commands in the batch list, it will return in its update counts array a value of Statement.EXECUTE_FAILED for the command or commands that failed during the batch execution. You can determine which type of driver you have by checking to see whether an error occurs and whether the size of the returned array from BatchUpdateException.getUpdateCounts is equal to the same number of commands submitted.

JDBC drivers do not have to support batch updates. Typically you will know if your driver supports batch updates via its documentation. If you don't know, you can always detect it in code using the DatabaseMetaData.supportsBatchUpdates method.

The following is an example of creating a batch update to enter five new team members into a TEAMS table and checking to make sure that the database driver supports batch updates:

```
try {
  // Make sure that autocommit is off
  cConn.setAutoCommit(false);

  // Retrieve metadata info about the data source
```

```
        DatabaseMetaData dbmData = cConn.getMetaData();

    // Make sure our driver supports batch updates
    if (dbmData.supportsBatchUpdates()) {

        Statement sStatement = cConn.createStatement();

        // Add batch commands
        sStatement.addBatch("INSERT INTO TEAMS VALUES ("'Joon Lee')");
        sStatement.addBatch("INSERT INTO TEAMS VALUES ('Jennie Vitale')");
        sStatement.addBatch("INSERT INTO TEAMS VALUES ('Kyle Rice')");
        sStatement.addBatch("INSERT INTO TEAMS VALUES ('Steve Brockman')");
        sStatement.addBatch("INSERT INTO TEAMS VALUES ('Arnie Voketaitis')");

        int []uCounts = sStatement.executeBatch();

        // Commit the changes
        cConn.commit();
    } else {
        System.err.print("Your driver does not support batch updates!");
    }
} catch(BatchUpdateException batchEx) {
    int []uCounts = batchEx.getUpdateCounts();
    for (int  i = 0; i < uCounts.length; i ++) {
        System.err.print("Count #" + i + "=" + uCounts[i] + "\n");
    }
    // Handle errors further here if necessary
}
```

Creating Batch Updates Using a PreparedStatement Object

The PreparedStatement object batch updates follow mostly the same method of operations as the Statement object batch updates, with the exception that you now have to deal with parameterized SQL statements and setting each parameter before adding a batch command. So for each command you will need to set the necessary IN parameter before issuing a PreparedStatement.addBatch call. The following code example shows how to correctly add batch commands to a PreparedStatement object:

```
try {
    // Make sure that autocommit is off
    cConn.setAutoCommit(false);

    // Retrieve metadata info about the data source
    DatabaseMetaData dbmData = cConn.getMetaData();

    // Make sure our driver supports batch updates
    if (dbmData.supportsBatchUpdates()) {
        PreparedStatement psStatement = cConn.prepareStatement(
                "INSERT INTO TEAMS VALUES (?)");

        // Set the IN parameter
        psStatement.setString(1, "Jennie Vitale");

        // Add batch command
        psStatement.addBatch();
```

```
        // Set the IN parameter for the next command
        psStatement.setString(1, "Andrew Vitale");

        // Add batch command
        psStatement.addBatch();

        int []uCounts = psStatement.executeBatch();

        // Commit the changes
        cConn.commit();
    } else {
      System.err.print("Your driver does not support batch updates!");
    }
} catch(BatchUpdateException batchEx) {
}
```

The key point to note from the code above is where the PreparedStatement.addBatch methods occur. They occur after the IN parameters are set, so you simply change the IN parameters for each batch command you wish to execute.

Creating Batch Updates Using a CallableStatement Object

The CallableStatement object handles batch commands in the exact same way as the PreparedStatement object. Now I know what you are thinking, "What about all the stored procedures that require OUT or INOUT parameters?" Well the answer is that OUT and INOUT parameters are *not allowed* to be used to call stored procedures in a batched fashion. If you did call a stored procedure that required either an OUT or an INOUT parameter, a BatchUpdateException would be thrown because SQL commands must return an update count and are not allowed to return anything else, such as result sets. So the code syntax looks remarkably the same as the PreparedStatement object, with the exception that you are calling stored procedures. The following code illustrates using a CallableStatement object to perform batch updates:

```
// Make sure that autocommit is off
cConn.setAutoCommit(false);
CallableStatement csStatement = cConn.prepareCall(
            "{call updatePlayers(?)}");

// Set the IN parameter
csStatement.setString(1, "Jennie Vitale");

// Add batch command
csStatement.addBatch();

// Set the IN parameter for the next command
csStatement.setString(1, "Andrew Vitale");

// Add batch command
csStatement.addBatch();
int []uCounts = csStatement.executeBatch();

// Commit the changes
cConn.commit();
```

Utilizing Result Sets

In simple terms, a ResultSet object is a Java object that is created to contain the results of an SQL query that has been executed. The results are in table row fashion, meaning they contain column headers, types, and values. All this information can be obtained through either the ResultSet object or the ResultSetMetaData object.

ResultSet objects are very common, and you will interface with them on a continuous basis when doing JDBC programming, so it is important to understand the different types of ResultSet objects that are available for you to exploit. Understanding how ResultSet objects are created and manipulated is crucial when you are designing different algorithms, especially with regard to performance. So find the best possible option for executing a query, and manipulate its results for your particular situation.

Investigating Types of Result Sets

There are two main areas of interest when dealing with result sets of which you must be aware. The first area of interest is the concentration on how the cursor in a result set can be exploited. Cursors can be limited to only moving forward, or they can be allowed to move in both forward and backward directions. The second area of interest is how changes in the data source affect the result set. You can instruct a result set to be aware of changes that occur in an underlying data source and have a ResultSet object reflect those changes.

There are three types of result sets that warrant explanation. Each of these types will be scrollable or non-scrollable, sensitive or insensitive. Scrollable means that the cursor in the result set can move both forward and backward. Non-scrollable signifies that the cursor can only move in one direction: forward. If the result set is sensitive to change, it will reflect changes that occur while the result set is open. If the result set is insensitive to change, it will usually remain fixed with no change to its structure, even if the underlying data source changes. The following is a list of constants that are in the ResultSet interface that you can use to specify a result set type:

❑ TYPE_FORWARD_ONLY — The result set cursor can only be moved forward from the beginning to the end. It cannot move backwards. Also, the result set is not sensitive to change from the data source.

❑ TYPE_SCROLL_INSENSITIVE — The result set cursor can move forward and backward and jump to rows specified by the application. Also, the result set is not sensitive to change from the data source.

❑ TYPE_SCROLL_SENSITIVE — The result set cursor can move forward and backward and jump to rows specified by the application. This time the result is sensitive to changes to the data source while the result set is open. This provides a dynamic view to the data.

Setting Concurrency of Result Sets

Result sets have only two levels of concurrency: *read-only* and *updatable*. To find out if your driver supports a specific concurrency type, use the DatabaseMetaData.supportResultSetConcurrency method to find out. The following is a list of constants that are in the ResultSet interface that you can use to specify a result set concurrency type:

❑ CONCUR_READ_ONLY — Specify this constant when you want your result set to be read-only, meaning it cannot be updated programmatically.

❑ CONCUR_UPDATABLE — Specify this constant when you want your result set to be updatable, meaning it can be updated programmatically.

Setting Holdability of Result Sets

Result sets are generally closed when a transaction has been completed. This means that a Connection. commit has been called, which in turn closes any related result sets. In special cases, this may not be the desired behavior that you were hoping for. It is possible to hold a result set open and keep its cursor position in the result set after a Connection.commit has been called by creating your statements with the following ResultSet interface constants present:

❑ HOLD_CURSORS_OVER_COMMIT — Specifies that a ResultSet object will not be closed when a Connection.commit is called. Instead, it will remain open until the program calls the method ResultSet.close. If you are interested in better performance, this is usually *not* the best option.

❑ CLOSE_CURSORS_AT_COMMIT — Specifies that a ResultSet object will be closed when a Connection.commit occurs. This is the best performance option.

Another interesting point to note is that the default holdability is determined by the DBMS that you are interfacing with. In order to determine the default holdability, use the DatabaseMetaData.getResultSetHoldability method to retrieve the default holdability for the DBMS.

Using Result Sets

Now that you know the different types of result sets that exist and the concurrency and holdability levels, it is time to see what a result set looks like in action. The following code shows how to create a statement that is scrollable, updatable, insensitive to data source changes, and closes the cursor when a commit occurs:

```
// Look up the registered data source from JNDI
DataSource dsDataSource = (DataSource) ctx.lookup("jdbc/OurDB");

// Obtain a Connection object from the data source
Connection cConn = dsDataSource.getConnection("username", "password");

Statement sStatement = cConn.createStatement(
            ResultSet.CONCUR_UPDATABLE,
            ResultSet.TYPE_SCROLL_INSENSITIVE,
            ResultSet.CLOSE_CURSORS_AT_COMMIT
);

ResultSet rsResults = sStatement.executeQuery("SELECT NAME, TEAM FROM PLAYERS");

// Though we have not done anything to warrant a commit we put this here to show
// where the ResultSet would be closed
cConn.commit();

// Close the connection
cConn.close();
```

Navigating Result Sets

The ResultSet interface of the JDBC API provides a rich set of methods for navigating through ResultSet objects. If your ResultSet object is scrollable, you can easily jump to different rows in the ResultSet object with little effort. Here is a list of the main methods provided in the ResultSet interface for navigation with a ResultSet object.

Method	Description
First	This method moves the cursor to the first row in the ResultSet object. Returns true if successful. Returns false if there are no rows in the ResultSet object.
Last	This method moves the cursor to the last row in the ResultSet object. Returns true on success. Returns false if there are no rows in the ResultSet object.
Next	This method moves the cursor one row forward in the Result object. It will return true if successful and false if the cursor has been moved past the last row.
Previous	This method moves the cursor one row backwards in the Result object. It will return true if successful and false if the cursor has been moved past the first row.
absolute(int)	This method will move the cursor to the row specified by the int parameter. The first row is represented by the number 1. If you send a 0 as a parameter, the cursor is moved just before the first row. If the integer specified is a negative number, it will move the number of rows specified backwards from the end of the ResultSet object.
BeforeFirst	This method will move the cursor to the beginning of the ResultObject just before the first row.
AfterLast	This method will move the cursor to the end of the ResultObject just after the last row.
relative(int)	Depending on whether the integer specified is negative or positive, this method will move the cursor the number of rows specified from its current position. A positive value signifies a forward movement. A negative value signifies a backward movement. A zero signifies that the cursor remains in the same position.

Manipulating Result Sets

The ResultSet interface has an enormous number of methods that can be used for updating a ResultSet object. The majority of the methods are prefixed with the word *update*. In order to be able to update a ResultSet object, it must have a concurrency of type CONCUR_UPDATABLE. If a ResultSet object is updatable, its columns can be altered, its rows can be deleted, new rows can be added, and its data can be changed. The following code example shows several ways to manipulate a ResultSet object:

```
Statement sStatement = cConn.createStatement(
         ResultSet.CONCUR_UPDATABLE,
         ResultSet.TYPE_SCROLL_INSENSITIVE,
         ResultSet.CLOSE_CURSORS_AT_COMMIT
);

ResultSet rsResults = sStatement.executeQuery("SELECT NAME, TEAM, AGE, " +
```

```
                                       "RANK FROM PLAYERS");

// Move to the last row
rsResults.last();

// Update specific data in the row
rsResults.updateString(2, "Hornets");
rsResults.updateInt(3, 27);
rsResults.updateLong(4, 5021);

// Commit the changes to the row
rsResults.updateRow();
cConn.commit();

// Close the connection
cConn.close();
```

The following example will show you how to insert and delete rows. Inserting rows is not a difficult process but it does require a bit of know-how since it is not initially intuitive. In order to insert a row into a ResultSet object, you must first make a call to ResultSet.moveToInsertRow. This may seem confusing, but the JDBC API defines a concept of an insert row in the ResultSet object. When you call ResultSet. moveToInsertRow, this essentially allows you to remember your current cursor position, move to a temporary area in memory, perform the creation of your new row, and call the ResultSet.insertRow to insert the newly created row into the ResultSet object at the cursor position you were at before calling ResultSet. moveToInsertRow.

Deleting a row is much more trivial than inserting a row. To delete a row, you simply move to the row you want to delete and call ResultSet.deleteRow. The following code will demonstrate how to delete and insert a row using the methods that were just described:

```
Statement sStatement = cConn.createStatement(ResultSet.CONCUR_UPDATABLE);

ResultSet rsResults = sStatement.executeQuery("SELECT NAME, TEAM, AGE," +
                                              "RANK FROM PLAYERS");

// Move to the fourth row
rsResults.absolute(4);

// Delete the fourth row
rsResults.deleteRow();

// Now let's insert a new row
rsResults.moveToInsertRow();

// Build data for new row
rsResults.updateString(1, "Ken Pratt");
rsResults.updateString(2, "Tigers");
rsResults.updateInt(3, 32);
rsResults.updateLong(4, 7521);

// Add the new row to the ResultsSet
```

```
    rsResults.insertRow();

    // Move the cursor back the original position
    rsResults.moveToCurrentRow();

    // Commit changes
    cConn.commit();

    // Close the connection
    cConn.close();
```

Closing Result Sets

If the Statement object that created the ResultSet object is not yet closed, you can use the ResultSet.close method to close a ResultSet object and free its resources. If you specified the HOLD_CURSORS_OVER_COMMIT flag when you created the Statement object, then you will also need to call the ResultSet.close method when you are done with the ResultSet object. Otherwise it would remain open even if a Connect.commit is called. However, if the Statement object that created the ResultSet object is closed, the ResultSet object would be closed as well even if the HOLD_CURSORS_OVER_COMMIT was specified during creation.

Examining JDBC Advanced Concepts

This portion of the chapter will discuss concepts that are generally used in advanced Java applications that definitely fall in the three-tier model that was described in the section "JDBC API Usage in the Real World," earlier in this chapter. This section will cover the following:

❑ Meta data—Explore retrieving meta data about your data source and understanding how to use it.

❑ RowSets—Explain RowSets in depth.

❑ Connection Pooling—Discuss all the ins and outs of connection pooling.

❑ Transactions—Both standard and distributed transactions.

Managing Database Meta Data

Sometimes the JDBC-supported applications that you write may need to acquire more information about a data source. Specifically, information that is not readily available through Statement objects with embedded SQL calls or through the results that they return. Suppose you want to obtain information about whether or not your DBMS supports transactions, batch updates, or save points. The only way to determine this type of information is through the DBMS's meta data. The JDBC API has an interface called *DatabaseMetaData* that allows an application to retrieve meta data about a DBMS through an enormous array of methods. These methods can be used to retrieve meta data information that is classified into the following categories:

❑ Discovering limitations of the data source

❑ Determining what capabilities and features a data source supports

❑ Retrieving general information about a data source such as a database version or what SQL keywords it supports

With the DatabaseMetaData interface, you can even retrieve the tables, columns, user-defined types, and the schema of a particular data source. This can be a very useful tool when you know very little about the data source with which you are interfacing.

Discovering Limitations of a Data Source

Discovering the limitations of a data source is easily done using a DatabaseMetaData object. Most of the limitations methods are prefixed with the words *getMax*. For example, DatabaseMetaData.getMaxConnections retrieves the maximum number of connections that can occur at the same time within a data source. Listed below are some of the more common limitation methods that are used for a given data source. To see a list of all the limitation methods, please see the DatabaseMetaData Java doc.

Method	Description
int getMaxColumnsInTable()	Returns the maximum number of columns that a table is allowed to have.
int getMaxRowSize()	Returns the maximum size a row can be in bytes.
int getMaxStatements()	Returns the maximum number of statements a data source can have open at the same time.
int getMaxStatementLength()	Returns the maximum length an SQL statement can be.
int getMaxUserNameLength()	Returns the allowed maximum length a user name can be.

Determining Which Features a Data Source Supports

The DatabaseMetaData object provides numerous methods for determining whether or not your DBMS driver supports a feature that you are interested in using. Most of the methods begin with the prefix *supports*. The most commonly used features are listed in the following table:

Method	Description
boolean supportsBatchUpdates()	Returns true if the data source supports batch updates or false if it does not.
boolean supportsSavepoints()	Returns true if the data source supports savepoints or false if it does not.
boolean supportsStoredProcedures()	Returns true if the data source supports stored procedures or false if it does not.
boolean supportsTransactions()	Returns true if the data source supports transactions or false if it does not.
boolean supportsGroupBy()	Returns true if the data source supports the GROUP BY clause or false if it does not.

Retrieving General Information about a Data Source

There is an enormous amount of general information that can be retrieved about a data source using the DatabaseMetaData methods. There are over 100 methods, so I decided to focus on a few of the core methods that you are most likely to use, such as: retrieving the database schema; obtaining the names of the tables in the database; and retrieving the columns for a specific table. The rest of the methods can be found in the DatabaseMetaData Java docs that come with the Java SDK 1.5 documentation.

I decided to show you a practical example of how to use these methods, rather than bore you with the details of how each method operates. This example will show you how to create a *keyword search* that can explore an entire database without knowing anything about it except how to connect to it and retrieve specific rows that contain the keywords for which you are searching. The keyword search example has three main classes that make up its architecture: *DBDatabase*, *DBTable*, and *DBColumn*. DBDatabase handles the connection to the data source, reading meta data information such as tables and columns, and searching for specific keywords.

The DBTable class stores information about a table's makeup as well as its individual columns that are associated with the table. The column objects are stored in an ArrayList and can be accessed via the DBTable.getColumns method:

```java
public class DBTable {
  private String     m_sTblName;
  private ArrayList  m_alColumns;

  public DBTable(String sName) {
      m_sTblName = sName;
      m_alColumns = new ArrayList();
  }
   public String getTableName() {
      return m_sTblName;
  }
  public void addColumn(DBColumn Column) {
      m_alColumns.add((DBColumn) Column);
  }

  public ArrayList getColumns() {
      return m_alColumns;
  }
}
```

The DBColumn class contains information about a specific column that belongs to a table. This information consists of the table name it belongs to, the column's name, the SQL data type of the column, the size of the data contained in the column, and whether or not the column is nullable:

```java
public class DBColumn {
  private String m_sTblName;
  private String m_columnName;

  private String m_datatype;
  private int m_datasize;
  private int m_digits;
```

```
    private boolean m_nullable;

    public DBColumn(String sTableName, String sCol, String sDType, int idsize,
                int idigits, boolean bnullable) {
        // Initialize variables here
    }

    // getter methods
    public String getTableName()   { return m_sTblName; }
    public String getColumnName()  { return m_columnName;           }
    public String getDataType()    { return m_datatype; }
    public int getDataSize()       { return m_datasize; }
    public int getDecimalDigits()  { return m_digits; }
    public boolean isNullable()    { return m_nullable; }

}
```

The final class in this example is the DBDatabase class, which is too large to display in its entirety so I will only illustrate its basic structure. Its main purpose is to create a connection with a database and start the process to load the DBTable and DBColumn objects with data through the load, readTables, and readTableColumns methods. The searchAllByKeyword method allows the application to search an entire database for a specific keyword:

```
public class DBDatabase {
 private Connection m_cConnection;

 private ArrayList m_alTables;
 private ArrayList m_alResults;

 public DBDatabase(String sDriver, String sURL, String sUser, String sPass)
 { }

 public boolean load()
 { }

  public void readTables(Connection currentConnection) throws Exception
  { }

  public void readTableColumns(DatabaseMetaData meta, DBTable table) throws
Exception
  { }

 public ArrayList searchAllByKeyword(String saKeyword)
  { }
```

I demonstrate the classes that are contained in this example and show the steps in action to execute a keyword search of the database. Here are the steps:

1. The first thing you need to do is call the DBDatabase.load method to create a connection to the data source and read the meta data from the data source that contains the tables and columns. The DBDatabase.readTables creates a DBTable object for each table in the database and also calls the DBDatabase.readTableColumns method to associate DBColumn objects with the appropriate DBTable objects.

Once a connection is established through the DBDatabase.load method, it will call the DBDatabase.readTable method to get the table and column meta data:

```
// Setup and retrieve the metadata info
DatabaseMetaData metadata = null;
metadata = currentConnection.getMetaData();

String[] names = {"TABLE"};
ResultSet tableNames = metadata.getTables(null,"%", "%", names);

while (tableNames.next()) {
  String sTName = tableNames.getString("TABLE_NAME");
  if (sTName != null) {
      DBTable dTable = new DBTable(sTName);
      readTableColumns(metadata, dTable);
      m_alTables.add((DBTable) dTable);
  }
}
```

Each DBTable object that is created will call the DBDatabase.readTableColumns automatically to create DBColumns objects for the given DBTable:

```
ResultSet columns = meta.getColumns(null, "%", table.getTableName(), "%");

while (columns.next()) {
      String columnName = columns.getString("COLUMN_NAME");
      String datatype = columns.getString("TYPE_NAME");

      int datasize = columns.getInt("COLUMN_SIZE");
      int digits = columns.getInt("DECIMAL_DIGITS");
      int nullable = columns.getInt("NULLABLE");
      boolean bNull = (nullable == 1);

      DBColumn dCol = new DBColumn((String)table.getTableName(),
                        columnName, datatype, datasize, digits, bNull);

      table.addColumn((DBColumn)dCol);
}
```

2. Once you have created a connection and obtained the table and column meta data you need, then execute the DBDatabase.searchAllByKeyword method to search the entire data source for the given keyword in all tables and all columns:

```
public ArrayList searchAllByKeyword(String saKeyword)
{
 try {

    // Clear result list
    m_alResults.clear();

    // Get size of Tables ArrayList
    int nSize = m_alTables.size();

    // Create our basic SQL statement
```

```
String sStartSQL = "Select * from ";

DBTable dbTable;

for (int i = 0; i < nSize; i++) {
   String sSQL = sStartSQL;

    // Get table
   dbTable = (DBTable) m_alTables.get(i);
   if (dbTable == null) {
        break;
   }

   // Add the table name
   sSQL = sSQL + "[" + dbTable.getTableName() + "] WHERE ";

    // Get column objects
   ArrayList alCols = dbTable.getColumns();

   if (alCols == null) {
      continue;
   }

   int nColSize = alCols.size();
   if (nColSize <= 0) {
      continue;
   }

   String sSQLColumns = "";

   // Get individual columns for table and add to SQL
   for (int k = 0; k < nColSize; k++) {
      DBColumn dbCol = (DBColumn) alCols.get(k);

      if (dbCol != null) {
         if (k == 0) {
            sSQLColumns = dbCol.getColumnName();
         } else {
            sSQLColumns = sSQLColumns + " & " + dbCol.getColumnName();
         }
      }
   }

   // Add keyword to SQL string
   sSQL = sSQL + sSQLColumns + " LIKE '%" + saKeyword + "%'";

   // Search Table and Save result set
   Statement statement = m_cConnection.createStatement();

   // Execute SQL statement
   ResultSet resultSet = statement.executeQuery(sSQL);

   // Add to resultset array list
   m_alResults.add(resultSet);
}
```

```
        } catch(Exception e) {
            System.out.println(e);
            e.printStackTrace(System.out);
    }
    return m_alResults;
}
```

This code is an excellent example of how you can utilize the DatabaseMetaData object to create code that does not fit under normal database operations. Using the DatabaseMetaData object, you were able to design code that has the ability to grab all the meta data information, create a list of all tables and all columns, and search the entire database for a specific keyword.

Utilizing RowSets

A RowSet represents a set of rows obtained from a tabular form of data such as a result set. RowSet interfaces are a JavaBeans component; therefore they support event notifications and property manipulations. RowSets can be used in Integrated Development Environments (IDE) that support visual JavaBeans development. This allows you to create a RowSet at design time and then execute its methods at run time.

RowSets are usually implemented as either *connected* or *disconnected* implementations. Connected RowSet implementations establish a connection with a data source and keep the connection until the RowSet is discarded. Disconnected RowSet implementations are very interesting because they don't require a JDBC driver or the full use of the JDBC API until they need to establish a connection to retrieve or update data. Once the operations are finished, the RowSet disconnects. The disconnected RowSet implementation stores all the data and meta data about a data source in memory; so most manipulations of the data can occur offline until there is a need to commit the data. RowSets provide the perfect mechanism for sending formatted data over a low bandwidth network to clients that do not possess an extreme amount of capabilities for data processing.

Understanding RowSet Events

RowSets support JavaBeans events that notify other JavaBeans components that implement the RowSetListener interface and are registered with the appropriate RowSet object. In order to register with a RowSet object, the method `RowSet.addRowSetListener()` is provided for applications to use. There are three types of events that can occur which will cause an event to fire:

❑   cursorMoved—Notifies listeners that the cursor has moved within the RowSet object.

❑   rowChanged—Notifies listeners that the RowSet object has changed one of its rows.

❑   rowSetChanged—Notifies listeners that the entire content of the RowSet object has changed.

RowSet Standard Implementations

Up until this point in time there have not been any finalized standard implementations on RowSets. Now there are five available for use in the J2SE 1.5 platform that are maintained by the Java Community Process (JCP) under the alias JSR 114.

Implementation	Description
CachedRowSetImpl	Used for RowSets that want to cache rows in memory. It is a disconnected RowSet.
FilteredRowSetImpl	Provides filtering capabilities on RowSets without using a heavyweight query language.
JdbcRowSetImpl	This is basically a wrapper for ResultSet objects. This essentially turns a ResultSet into a JavaBeans component. This RowSet implementation is classified as a connected RowSet.
JoinRowSetImpl	This implementation allows disconnected RowSet objects to perform SQL JOIN operations between RowSet objects without having to reconnect to the data source.
WebRowSetImpl	This implementation is provided to allow a standard way of describing a JDBC RowSet in XML.

Using the New JdbcRowSetImpl

The *JdbcRowSetImpl* is a new implementation of the JdbcRowSet interface that is provided with J2SE 1.5. This implementation essentially encapsulates a ResultSet and in turn makes the ResultSet and its driver usable as a JavaBeans component. The JdbcRowSetImpl supports all the *ResultSet* methods and it even has the added benefit of making nonscrollable ResultSets scrollable. So you could take a nonscrollable ResultSet, plug it into a JdbcRowSetImpl and make it scrollable as well as updatable:

```
JdbcRowSetImpl jrsRowSet = new JdbcRowSetImpl();

jrsRowSet.setURL(jdbc:sybase:Tds:127.0.0.1:3000?ServiceName=Sybase");
jrsRowSet.setUsername("jconnelly");
jrsRowSet.setPassword("secret");

jrsRowSet.setCommand("SELECT * FROM EMPLOYEES WHERE TITLE = ? AND AGE = ?");
jrsRowSet.setString(1, "SOFTWARE ENGINEER");
jrsRowSet.setInt(2, 27);

// This establishes the connection, creates the prepared statement, and creates the
// ResultSet if successful
jrsRowSet.execute();
```

The code in the sample above creates a JdbcRowSetImpl called *jrsRowSet* and then sets its properties, which include a JDBC URL to the data source, a username and password for the data source, and an SQL command to be executed. Once all the properties are set, the JdbcRowSetImpl.execute method is called, which internally establishes a connection to the data source, creates any necessary prepared statements, and executes the statements, which in turn generate a ResultSet. The jrsRowSet can now be traversed just like any other scrollable, updatable ResultSet object.

The beauty of it all is that now the jrsRowSet that contains a ResultSet object can be a component in a Swing application, if so desired.

Connection Pooling

The trouble with the normal way of connecting to a data source is that, if your application requires numerous connections to occur with a data source, every time you close the Connection object, the physical connection is closed. Therefore, every time you open a connection, the connection has to be reestablished with the data source, initialized, and eventually closed again before repeating the same process over and over again. This is a performance and scalability nightmare.

Connection pooling is the answer to this problem. It provides a way to maintain a certain amount of physical database connections that can be reused by applications as necessary. Connection pooling is typically used in a three-tier environment, but it can be used in a two-tier environment as well if the JDBC driver provides an implementation of the ConnectionPoolDataSource interface.

From an applications standpoint, connection pooling is virtually transparent. There are only two things you need to know in order to utilize connection pooling correctly, and they are listed here:

❑   Never use the DriverManager class to get a Connection object; always use the DataSource object to create a Connection object.

❑   Always use finally statements to close a Connection object.

Administrators of application servers are responsible for managing the connection pools, so talk to your application server administrator to find out specifics for your particular server.

Managing Transactions

Transaction management is extremely important when dealing with data sources. Transaction management ensures data integrity and data consistency; without it, it would be very easy for applications to corrupt data sources or cause problems with the synchronization of the data. Therefore, all JDBC drivers are required to provide transaction support.

What Is a Transaction?

To explain transactions best, take using an ATM machine as an example. The steps to retrieve money are as follows:

1.   Swipe your ATM card.
2.   Enter your PIN number.
3.   Select the withdrawal option.
4.   Enter the amount of money to withdraw.
5.   Agree to pay the extremely high fee.
6.   Collect your money.

If anything was to go wrong along the way and you didn't receive your money, you would definitely not want that to reflect on your balance. So a transaction encompasses all the steps above and has only two possible outcomes: *commit* or *rollback*. When a transaction commits, all the steps had to be successful. When a transaction fails, there should not be any damage done to the underlying data source. In this case, the data that stores your account balance!

Standard Transactions

JDBC transactions are extremely simple to manage. Transaction support is implemented by the DBMS, which eliminates your having to write anything — code-wise — that would be cumbersome. All the methods you need are contained in the Connection object. There are two main methods you need to be concerned about: *Connection.commit* and *Connection.rollback*. There isn't a begin transaction method because the beginning of a transaction is implied when the first SQL statement is executed.

In JDBC 3.0, there is a new concept called a *savepoint*. Savepoints allow you to save moments in time inside a transaction. For example, you could have an application that sends an SQL statement, then invokes a savepoint, tries to send another SQL statement, but a problem arises and you have to rollback. Now instead of rolling back completely, you can choose to rollback to a given savepoint. The following code example demonstrates JDBC transactions and the new savepoint method, *Connection.setSavepoint*:

```
Statement stmt = cConn.createStatement();

int nRows = stmt.executeUpdate("INSERT INTO PLAYERS (NAME) " +
                                        VALUES ('Roger Thomas')");

// Create our save point
Savepoint spOne = cConn.setSavepoint("SAVE_POINT_ONE");

nRows = stmt.executeUpdate("INSERT INTO PLAYERS (NAME) " +
                                    VALUES ('Jennifer White')");

// Rollback to the original save point
cConn.rollback(spOne);

// Commit the transaction.
cConn.commit();
```

From this example, the second SQL statement never gets committed because it was rolled back to SAVE_POINT_ONE before the transaction was committed.

Distributed Transactions

Participation in distributed transaction management is the same as participating in connection pooling. You must create connections from the DataSource interface. Transactions are no longer maintained by applications; rather, they are now maintained by transaction managers outside your control. Therefore, your program must not call any of the following methods:

- ❑ commit
- ❑ rollback
- ❑ setSavePoint
- ❑ setAutoCommit(true) — false is acceptable

If your application calls any of these methods while participating in a distributed transaction architecture, an SQLException will be thrown. The following are the two things you do need to do to participate fully in a distributed transaction management architecture:

❑   Never use the DriverManager class to get a connection; *always* use the DataSource interface to create a new Connection object.

❑   Always use finally statements to close Connection objects.

Object to Relational Mapping with Hibernate

Object to Relational Mapping (ORM) technologies are becoming very popular in today's fast-paced, develop-it-yesterday environment. ORM is an approach to developing applications that persist objects to relational databases. Another term that is frequently used when discussing ORM technologies is *transparent persistence*. Simply stated, it is the ability to store objects in a database using an object-oriented programming language while hiding the details from the application. Hibernate does exactly that.

Hibernate (`http://www.hibernate.org`) is one of the most popular and versatile ORM tools on the market. It acts as a persistent service for your applications to store and retrieve Java objects to and from relational databases. Hibernate is designed to be as transparent to the developer as possible and one of the main architectural features it possesses to accomplish this is the use of runtime reflection instead of build-time code generation. This type of architecture allows you to write and compile your code without Hibernate intruding on the build process. Hibernate doesn't enter the picture until the application is actually executed.

Hibernate, like most ORM tools, has its own query language called *Hibernate Query Language* (HQL). HQL is an object-oriented query language that looks very similar to SQL. It supports the use of subqueries; *group by*, *having*, and *order by*; retrieval of arbitrary data objects using its select new construct; table joins; native SQL Queries; SQL functions and operators; aggregate functions; and query by criteria.

Hibernate handles the object to relational bridge through plain-text XML files that map classes and variables of those classes to tables and columns in a relational database. It also has mapping support for one-to-one, many-to-one, one-to-many, and many-to-many relationships. If your particular application will require complex mapping of an already existing database, I recommend a third-party tool called *MiddleGen* (`http://middlegen.codehaus.org/`) to perform all of your mapping needs. MiddleGen provides a Hibernate plug-in that supports the creation of Hibernate's mapping configuration files and eliminates the need for you to generate the mappings by hand. For more information on how MiddleGen interacts with Hibernate, please visit `http://www.hibernate.org/98.html`.

Exploring Hibernate's Architecture

Hibernate's architecture is very flexible, and trying to narrow it down to one specific, overall architecture is rather difficult. The reason is that Hibernate can basically plug in to any J2EE architecture without hampering it. So the majority of its use will be based upon your architectural needs. This is not a drawback but a major winning point for Hibernate. You can base your needs on your requirements and not worry about how they will affect the tool. Figure 6-3 shows a very basic architecture that shows where Hibernate could reside.

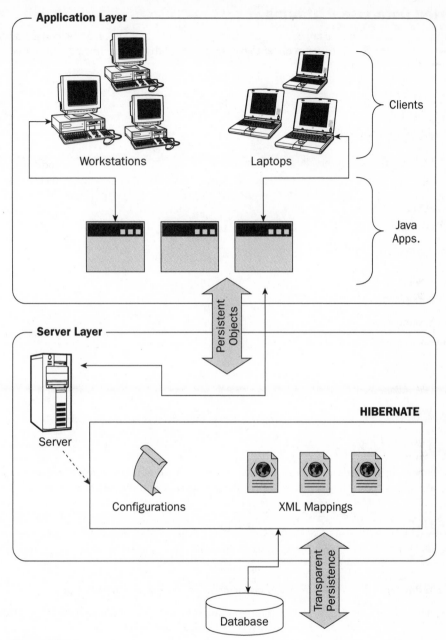

Figure 6-3

Supported Database Platforms

Hibernate supports a large array of database platforms to which objects may be persisted. Each database will require its own JDBC driver in order to communicate with it. The currently supported database platforms are as follows:

- ❑ MySQL
- ❑ Oracle
- ❑ Sybase
- ❑ Microsoft SQL Server
- ❑ Informix
- ❑ DB2
- ❑ PostgreSQL
- ❑ SAP DB
- ❑ HypersonicSQL
- ❑ Interbase
- ❑ Pointbase
- ❑ Mckoi SQL
- ❑ Progress
- ❑ FrontBase

You can always add more database platforms when their drivers become available.

Plugging Hibernate In

To use Hibernate in your application, you need to understand what is required in order to set up Hibernate successfully. The JARs that Hibernate uses are listed in the following table.

JAR File	Description
hibernate2.jar	This is the main jar that contains the portable hibernate functionality
cglib-2.0-rc2.jar	Code generation library used at run time
commons-collections-2.1.jar	Random utilities provided by the Apache Jakarta Commons project that Hibernate uses
commons-logging-1.0.3.jar	Used in conjunction with log4j-1.2.8.jar for log support
dom4j-1.4.jar	Used for XML parsing and mappings
Ehcache-0.6.jar	Support for caching needs

JAR File	Description
log4j-1.2.8.jar	The commons-logging-1.0.3.jar uses this file for specific logging needs — Hibernate uses the commons-logging-1.0.3.jar for its logging needs
odmg-3.0.jar	ODMG compliant persistence manager interface

Depending on your particular needs, some of these JARs can be optionally included.

Developing with Hibernate

This section will explore how to develop applications using Hibernate. The section will end with a complete working example of a forum that allows users to collaborate via a Web browser on various topics. This example will also show how to use Hibernate with Tomcat.

Understanding Mappings

The XML mapping files are a great place to start when learning Hibernate. This is the area where you will build your object mappings to the relational database of choice. No code has to be written at this point because Hibernate can actually generate the stub classes for you using the CodeGenerator that ships with the Hibernate Extensions package. If you have downloaded and installed the Hibernate Extension package, you can issue the following command on your mapping files to generate the source stubs:

```
java -cp classpath net.sf.hibernate.tool.hbm2java.CodeGenerator options
mapping_files
```

Mapping documents are usually created in the same directory as your generated class files where your source files are. If you had a class named Employee, then the mapping file for that class should be called *Employee.hbm.xml*. Below is a sample mapping file showing the basics of how to map a generic class, in this case *Employee*, to a relational data source:

```
<hibernate-mapping package="org.hibernate">
  <class name="Employee" table="tblEmployees">

    <id name="id" column="employee_id" type="long" unsaved-value="null">
      <generator class="native"/>
    </id>

    <property name="name" column="employee_name" type="string"
        length="25" not-null="true"/>

    <set name="Payroll" cascade="all" inverse="true" lazy="true">
      <key column="employee_id"/>
      <one-to-many class="Employee"/>
    </set>

  </class>
</hibernate-mapping>
```

The mapping file is fairly straightforward once you understand the basic principles in mapping a class to a table in a relational data source. The first element is the beginning `<hibernate-mapping/>` element. It contains one attribute called *package* that simply states the package name that the class elements belong to. This is an optional attribute. The `<class/>` element in the above example maps the class named Employee to a table in a relational database named tblEmployees.

Mapping classes are also required to define an `<id/>` element, which defines the mapping of a class property to a primary key column in the data source. Primary keys must be available in all the tables you plan to use from a data source. A required child element of the `<id/>` element, `<generator>` is used to generate unique identifiers for the instance of the persistent class. The following are the ten built-in generator shortcut names that can ultimately be used.

Generator	Description
Assigned	Allows the application to specifically assign an identifier to the object prior to calling the `save()` method.
Foreign	Primarily used in `<one-to-one>` key associations, this uses an identifier of another object.
Hilo	Uses a hi/lo algorithm to generate identifiers of type int, long, or short. Please be aware that this generator uses a table and a column, which can be supplied to generate the identifiers. See the Hibernate documentation for more details.
Identity	This generator returns an identifier of type int, long, or short and is designed for use with identity columns in DB2, HypersonicSQL, MS SQL Server, and MySQL.
Increment	Not to be used with clusters, this generates identifiers of type int, long, and short that are only unique when a table is currently not being used by a process to insert data.
Native	This generator decides which generator to use based on the data source. It will pick one of the following to use: hilo, identity, or sequence.
Seqhilo	Generates identifiers of type int, long, or short based upon a hi/lo algorithm and the given named database sequence.
Sequence	This generator returns an identifier of type int, long, or short based on a sequence in either DB2, PostgreSQL, Oracle, SAP DB, McKoi, or a generator in Interbase.
uuid.hex	Returns a UUID encoded string of hexadecimal digits of length 32.
uuid.string	Returns a UUID encoded string of 16 ASCII characters. Not recommended for PostgreSQL.

The `<property/>` element is used to map a Java attribute to a column in a table. You can specify the SQL type, column length, and whether to allow NULL values or not.

The `<set name="Payroll">` element is an example of how to use Hibernate's one-to-many mapping features. The `<key/>` element depicts a foreign key and the `<one-to-many>` element specifies the relationship between the Employee class and the Payroll class. The `<set name="Payroll">` element also has an attribute `<lazy>` and it is set to true. This means that the collection of objects will not automatically be populated when first acquired from the data source. It will be populated when the application decides to use it.

Setting Hibernate Properties

Hibernate uses a *hibernate.properties* file for its main configurations. This file should be stored in your class path and will be used to set configurations such as the following:

- ❏ Query language constants
- ❏ Database platform and connection properties
- ❏ Connection pool settings
- ❏ Query cache properties
- ❏ JNDI settings
- ❏ Transaction API properties
- ❏ Miscellaneous settings such as showing SQL statements

The ability to store all these settings in a properties file eliminates the need to hard code them into your source code. This is a huge plus when you need to quickly configure your application for a particular architecture.

Using Hibernate's APIs for Persistence

The basic Hibernate APIs needed to persist objects to a data source are described in this section. In order to persist an object using Hibernate, one of the first requirements is to create a *SessionFactory* object. A SessionFactory can be created once the *net.sf.hibernate.cfg.Configuration* object has loaded all the necessary mappings into memory. The following code shows an example of the appropriate way to load the mappings into a Configuration object and how to create a SessionFactory object once the new Configuration object has been populated:

```
SessionFactory factory;

// Load configurations
Configuration cfg = new Configuration()
        .addClass(Category.class)
        .addClass(Post.class)
        .addClass(Topic.class);

// Create a new SessionFactory
factory = cfg.buildSessionFactory();
```

The Configuration object, cfg, is populated with mappings for the three classes listed in the example: Category.class, Post.class, and Topic.class. Hibernate knows to search for the XML files containing the mappings for the classes in the directory in which they are stored. The XML files should be named with the prefix of the class name and the suffix *hbm.xml*. So, for the Category.class file, the name of its XML mapping file should be *Category.hbm.xml*.

The next steps on your way to persisting your objects are the following:

1. Open a session with the data source.

2. Start a transaction.

3. Create the objects that you want to persist and populate them with data.

4. Save the objects to the session.

5. Commit the changes to the data source and close your connection.

The following code illustrates these steps in detail:

```
// Step 1, open a session with the data source
Session snSession = factory.openSession();

// Step 2, start a transaction
Transaction tTransaction = snSession.beginTransaction();

// Step 3, create the objects we want to persist.
Category cat = new Category();

cat.setCategoryMsg("Astronomy");
cat.setDescription("Discuss all your Astronomy topics here!");

// step 4, save the objects to the session
snSession.save(cat);

// Step 5, commit the changes and close our session
tTransaction.commit();
snSession.close();
```

Your object Category is now persisted to the data source with little effort. You did not have to know anything about the columns, tables, JDBC types, and so on to accomplish your goal because all the work had been done up front with the XML mapping files. The underlying mapping files and data sources could change without affecting your code.

You can also search for specific data in a data source using Hibernate's Criteria query API. This API allows you to avoid embedding long SQL strings in queries and provides you with an object-oriented approach to queries. The following is an example of how to query specific information by criteria:

```
Session snSession = factory.openSession();
Transaction tTransaction = null;

try {
   tTransaction = snSession.beginTransaction();

    // Retrieve a list of Category objects that have an "id"
    // greater than 0.
```

```
    List list = snSession.createCriteria(Category.class)
            .add( Expression.gt("id", new Long(0L)) )
            .list();

  if (list.size() == 0) return;

  Iterator it = list.iterator();
  while (it.hasNext()) {
    Category cat = (Category) it.next();
    System.out.println("Category Description = " + cat.getDescription());
  }

  tTransaction.commit();

} catch (Exception e) {
  // Handle Exceptions
}finally {
  snSession.close();
}
```

The code is designed to return all the Category objects that have an id that is greater than 0 into a net.sf. hibernate.collection.List object. Once the List object is populated, you then iterate through the list pulling out the Category objects and printing information from each one to the console. Session.createCriteria is a very versatile API and it should contain enough functionality to satisfy your most complicated searching needs.

The *Session* operations that can be performed are extensive. The following table describes some of the core functionality. For an extensive list, please see Hibernate's Java docs.

Method	Description
Transaction beginTransaction()	Creates a Transaction object and returns it for use.
Connection close()	This method completely ends the session and disconnects it from the JDBC connections.
Criteria createCriteria(Class persistentClass)	This method allows you to create a Criteria instance and allows you to query the persistentClass using the specific Criteria instance for information.
void delete(Object object)	Deletes the specific object from the data source.
List find(String query)	This method allows you to find specific information using an HQL string.
void saveOrUpdate(Object object)	Depending on the value of its identifier property, this method will either save or update the given instance. Its default behavior is to issue a save() call.
void update(Object object)	This method updates the given instance.

Putting It All Together: The Forum Example

The forum example will demonstrate the creation of a fully functional forum where users can create categories, create topics for a specific category, and generate posts that reside inside topics. You will use Hibernate to perform all of the necessary database transactions utilizing its object to relational mapping capabilities. To develop this type of example in JDBC would have been very time-consuming, but by using Hibernate it can be developed relatively quickly.

Understanding the Forum Architecture

The forum is housed in a Web application that resides on an Apache Tomcat server and is accessed via a Web browser by the user. The Web application uses Java Server Pages (JSPs) for the presentation layer, which will process user requests. Figure 6-4 illustrates the architecture of the forum example and where each component resides.

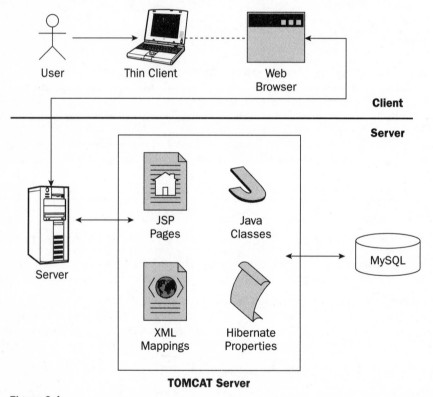

Figure 6-4

The Java classes, Hibernate libraries and settings, and JSP pages are all encapsulated in a Web application called *forum*. The database used is a MySQL database that stands alone as a self-contained DBMS.

The Forum's Database

The forum's database comprises three tables, which are used to store user posts, user topics, and user categories. The table schemas are illustrated in Figure 6-5.

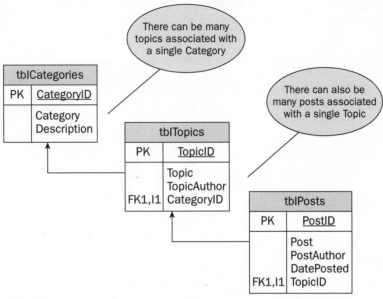

Figure 6-5

The tblCategories table is used to store category information. An example of a category would be music. Each category could then have subcategories called topics. The tblTopics table stores information on a specific topic such as what category it belongs to, who created the topic, and the description of the topic itself. An example of a topic that could fall under the category astronomy could be telescopes. Users would post information to the different topic areas such as questions or technical information. The tblPosts table stores topic posts that users have submitted. This table stores information on posts such as who posted the information, what topic the post belongs to, the date the post occurred, and of course the post itself.

The Forum's File Structure

The forum example utilizes the Apache Tomcat server to host your Web application. Because of this, Hibernate must be configured in such a way that it will play nicely with Tomcat. You must put your JDBC driver that you wish to use in the TOMCAT/COMMON/LIB directory; all the other files will be contained in your forum Web application directory. The required libraries, properties, classes, and JSP files that make the forum example are illustrated in Figure 6-6. Please take note that all the properties files (including the hibernate.properties file) should be contained in the WEB-INF/classes directory.

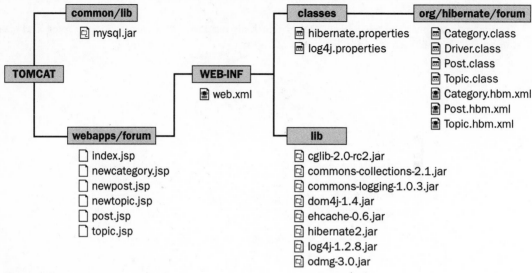

Figure 6-6

The Forum's User Interface

The forum's user interface comprises six JSP pages. Three are used for displaying categories, topics, and posts; the other three are used for submitting categories, topics, and posts. The first user interface shown in Figure 6-7 is the interface for viewing categories. Its filename is index.jsp and it is the first page that the user will see upon accessing the forum webapp. This page retrieves the categories using Hibernate, which are in turn contained in the table tblCategories of the forum database.

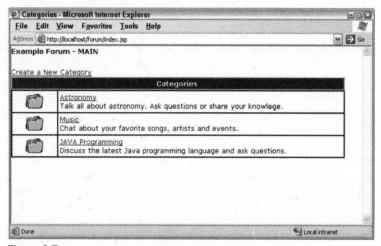

Figure 6-7

The second user interface (UI) shown in Figure 6-8 is the interface used for displaying topics that are stored in the table tblTopics of the forum database. The user would first need to select a category from the category user interface, which would then trigger the topic UI to display the topics related to that specific category. The topic UI knows which category it belongs to because a parameter (cid) is passed to the underlying JSP (topic.jsp) that represents the category ID.

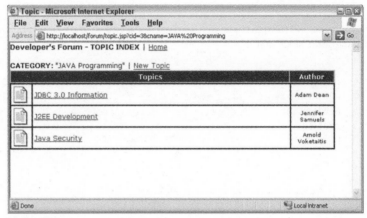

Figure 6-8

The third user interface shown in Figure 6-9 is the interface used to display posts that are associated with a particular topic. These posts are stored in the table tblPosts of the forum database. The user would first need to select a topic from the topic user interface which would display the post UI and display the appropriate posts. The post UI obtains the topic ID through a parameter (TID) that is passed to its JSP (post.jsp).

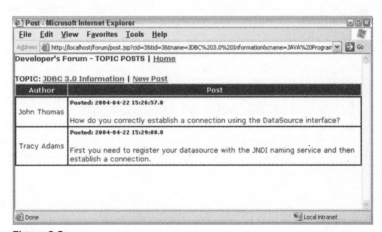

Figure 6-9

The other three interfaces are used for submitting new posts (newpost.jsp), topics (newtopic.jsp), and categories (newcategory.jsp). These interfaces and all the source code can be found at http://www.wrox.com.

The Forum's Code

The forum is made up of Java Server Pages (JSPs), which interact with the Hibernate API. The mapping files that Hibernate uses are mapped to Java classes, which you created by hand. As stated earlier, it is possible to have Hibernate generate the classes for you if you downloaded the Hibernate Extensions package. Simply use the utility net.sf.hibernate.tool.hbm2java.CodeGenerator to generate the code after you have created the mapping files.

The first code example I will show you is the Category class and its mapping file, *Category.hbl.xml*. Here is the Category mapping file:

```xml
<?xml version="1.0"?>
<!DOCTYPE hibernate-mapping PUBLIC
 "-//Hibernate/Hibernate Mapping DTD 2.0//EN"
 "http://hibernate.sourceforge.net/hibernate-mapping-2.0.dtd">

<hibernate-mapping package="org.hibernate.forum">

 <class name="Category" table="tblcategories">
        <id name="id" column="CategoryID">
                <generator class="native"/>
        </id>

        <property name="CategoryMsg" column="`Category`"/>
        <property name="Description" column="`Description`"/>
 </class>

</hibernate-mapping>
```

The element `<hibernate-mapping>` contains a package attribute that specifies the package name in which the Category class is contained. In this case, it is org.hibernate.forum. The `<class>` element has an attribute called name, which is the name of the Java class to use, and a table element called tblcategories that specifies the name of the table to which the class maps. The `<id>` element has a attribute called name, which has a value of id. This id value is the name of an attribute in the Category Java class. The column attribute of `<id>` has a value of CategoryID, which is the column name of the primary key in the table tblcategories. Simply stated, the Java attribute id contained in the class Category now maps to the primary key CategoryID in the table tblcategories of the forum database. The `<id>` element is required and any tables that you intend to map with must have a primary key. There is a child element called `<generator>` that is used to automatically generate a unique ID.

The `<property>` element is used to map Java class attributes to columns in the specified table. Here we are mapping CategoryMsg to column Category and Description to column Description. The code example that follows shows the code for the Category class:

```java
package org.hibernate.forum;
import java.util.*;


public class Category
{
 private Long     id;
 private String   CategoryMsg;
```

```
    private String    Description;

    public Long getId() {
        return id;
    }
    public String getCategoryMsg() {
        return CategoryMsg;
    }
    public String getDescription() {
        return Description;
    }

    public void setId(Long nID) {
        id = nID;
    }
    public void setCategoryMsg(String string) {
        CategoryMsg = string;
    }
    public void setDescription(String string) {
        Description = string;
    }
}
}
```

The preceding code shows all the Java class attributes that were referred to in the mapping example. The Java class is also required to provide `getter` and `setter` methods for each attribute that is mapped. Hibernate will use these methods to communicate with the class.

> Note: The **getter** and **setter** method names must be prefixed with **get** or **set** and be completed with exact spelling of the attribute name.

The other two classes that are mapped are the Topic and Post classes. They are mapped in the exact same fashion as the preceding examples; therefore, they will not be displayed here. If you are interested in looking at them, the code for the example is available at `http://www.wrox.com`.

At this point, you haven't had to use any Hibernate APIs in your code, mainly because Hibernate uses runtime reflection instead of compile-time code. Where you will need to utilize the Hibernate APIs is in the code for the JSPs that access the information from the data source. There are six JSPs in this example: three for viewing data, three for submitting data. I will now demonstrate and explain the post.jsp and the newpost.jsp. All the other JSPs use similar coding techniques and are less complicated than these two particular JSPs.

The newpost.jsp purpose is to insert a new posting to the database for a specific topic. The code that follows shows the core code that does all the work:

```
public void createPost(Long lTopicID, String sAuthor, String sPost) throws
Exception {

  SessionFactory factory;

  // Load configurations
  Configuration cfg = new Configuration()
        .addClass(Category.class)
```

```
            .addClass(Post.class)
            .addClass(Topic.class);

    // Create a new SessionFactory
    factory = cfg.buildSessionFactory();

    // Open Session
    Session sn = factory.openSession();
    Transaction transaction = null;

    try {
      tx = sn.beginTransaction();

      // Create a new Post object with a specified Topic ID
      Post post = new Post(lTopicID);

      // Populate the post object before saving it
      post.setPostDate(new java.sql.Date(System.currentTimeMillis()));
      post.setPostMsg(sPost);
      post.setPostAuthor(sAuthor);

      // Save the Post object
      sn.save(post);

      // Commit the transaction and close the session
      transaction.commit();
      sn.close();
    } catch (Exception e) {
      if (transaction!= null) {
          transaction.rollback();
          throw e;
      }finally {
          sn.close();
      }
}
```

The post.jsp allows the user to view posts for a specific topic. It utilizes the following code, which queries the data source for posts that have the same topic id associated with them as the topic id that is being passed to the viewPosts method:

```
public void viewPosts(JspWriter out, Long catID, Long topID) throws Exception {

    // final Driver test = new Driver();
    SessionFactory factory;

    Configuration cfg = new Configuration()
            .addClass(Category.class)
            .addClass(Post.class)
            .addClass(Topic.class);

    factory = cfg.buildSessionFactory();

    Session s = factory.openSession();
```

```
        Transaction tx=null;

    try {
        tx = s.beginTransaction();
        List list = s.createCriteria(Post.class)
                        .add( Expression.eq("TopicID", topID) )
                        .list();

        if (list.size()==0) return;
            Iterator it = list.iterator();

            while (it.hasNext()) {
                Post post = (Post) it.next();

                out.write("<tr>");
                    // Insert information from Post object here to display
                    // to the user.
                out.write("</tr>");

                tx.commit();
    } catch (Exception e) {
                if (tx!=null) tx.rollback();
                    throw e;
            } finally {
                s.close();
            }
    }
```

The forum example that was just demonstrated is a lightweight use of Hibernate's capabilities. Its main intent was to help you get your feet wet with Hibernate and provide you with an end-to-end example that doesn't cover the query language or mapping collections in great depth. These particular topics will be covered in greater detail later on in the book.

Summary

Developing applications that are required to persist data to relational database management systems is a need that continues to grow throughout the IT industry. This chapter provided you with a strong sense of how Java technologies and open source products are being used to solve data persistence issues. Java 2 SDK 1.5 edition provides extensive data persistence support through its new and improved JDBC API. The different features that the JDBC API provides were discussed in-depth and intuitive examples were created that should help you choose the best features to fit your particular application's architecture.

Through the use of Hibernate, this chapter was able to show you just how easy it is to utilize an object with the relational mapping technology in your application. It also explored why Hibernate is one of the most popular tools on the market based on its ability to provide scalability and performance benefits with little effect on your existing applications code.

Simple Web applications were also used to demonstrate Hibernate's persistence. In the next couple chapters, your focus will turn more toward Web applications themselves. Chapter 7 starts with building Web applications using the Model 1 Architecture.

7

Developing Web Applications Using the Model 1 Architecture

Software development activities generally involve domain-driven speculations that attempt to tackle complexity by aggregating knowledge of a subject matter so that it can be handled for your own purposes. This reflection generally involves experimentation by software and domain experts to organize knowledge for use by development teams. Ultimately, these modeling tasks involve the abstraction and filtering of nonessential data and the attainment of purposeful knowledge so that developer needs are served and proper deployments are made to customers.

This chapter will demonstrate how you can overcome speculation over how to construct a Web application using the Model 1 Architecture by constructing a hands-on Contact Management Tool. Two different types of Java syntax, JSTL 1.1 and JSP 2.0, will be utilized to craft the sample GUI component that will allow users to manage contact information through upload and query activities. The sample application's use of Model 1 was chosen to suit design and implementation needs for a quick prototype that can be implemented by novice Java Web developers in an easy fashion, and to demonstrate some of the new Java language enhancements that were delivered with the JSTL 1.1 and JSP 2.0 specifications.

What Is Model 1? Why Use It?

The Model 1 Architecture is a *page-centric* approach where page flows are handled by individual Web components. This means that request and response processing are hard-coded into pages to accommodate user navigations in a Web application. With Model 2 Architecture, navigation flows are generally handled by a servlet controller that works in conjunction with configuration files to dictate page renderings during application operations.

Naturally, this presents maintenance problems when logic modifications are needed to accommodate changes in requirements and end-user needs. Those changes would oblige developers to comb through code to ensure that all logic flows are properly handled as users navigate through a Web application. Along with the responsibilities of maintaining navigation flow in Model 1 deployments is the need to manage concerns regarding security and application state.

Model 1 Architecture concerns are certainly difficult design decisions to tackle at the inception of a project, but limitations in your team's development expertise, the scope of your application, and time to delivery might persuade you to adopt this development philosophy to get your project going. Adoption of the Model 1 philosophy is not necessarily a bad decision depending on your predicament and your estimation of what and how your team will deliver in an allotted delivery schedule. Model 2 implementations would most likely help you overcome maintenance issues in the long run, so it is paramount that your team overcomes its deficiencies by practicing with Model 2 frameworks and their configurations to better understand their intricacies so that your earlier Model 1 applications can be migrated fairly easily.

Figure 7-1 provides a high-level overview of a Model 1 template used for the sample Contact Management application that will be built to demonstrate Web application assembly combining JSP and JSTL technologies. Notice the individual JSP components (`header`, `leftNav`, `content`, and `footer`) that are all aggregated in the `home` page. As a user navigates the taxonomy in the application, indexes are established and passed along all of the individual pages so that operations can be performed inside those pages based on those indexes.

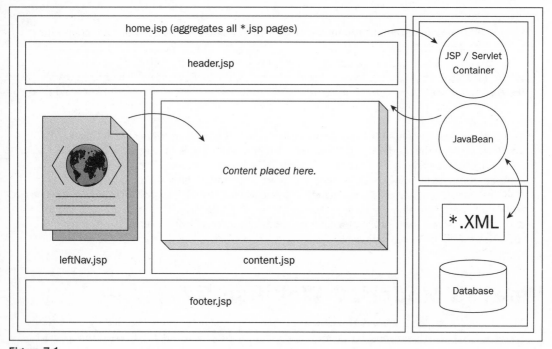

Figure 7-1

On many Web application components, content is typically retrieved from Java Bean components that persist data on the back-end tier of an enterprise system for visualization on the client tier. The sample application modeled in Figure 7-1 aggregates content from a MySQL database by using indexes from the left panel drill-down to determine proper page inclusion demonstrated in the *content.jsp* code shown below. When a user clicks on the initial Tasks link in the left panel, three navigation links will be presented (Add Profile, Add Contact, and View Contacts) so that contact names can be saved and queried:

```
<!--content.jsp -‡
<%@ taglib prefix="c" uri="http://java.sun.com/jstl/core" %>

<link href="CMS.css" rel="stylesheet" type="text/css">

<c:if test="${param.taxonomyIndex == '101'}">
    <jsp:include page="addProfile.jsp"/>
</c:if>

<c:if test="${param.taxonomyIndex == '102'}">
    <jsp:include page="addContact.jsp"/>
</c:if>

<c:if test="${param.taxonomyIndex == '103'}">
    <jsp:include page="viewContacts.jsp"/>
</c:if>
```

The Expression Language (EL) construct `<c:if>` is used in `content.jsp` to evaluate the three different test conditions so that the appropriate JSP script will be included, which will in turn collect the proper content for visualization.

Java Server Page (JSP) 2.0 and Java Standard Template Library (JSTL) 1.1 are both important Web application components for constructing dynamic content on J2EE platforms. JSP 2.0 scripts can easily construct HTML content and access JavaBean properties through Expression Language libraries. JSTL components encapsulate functionalities that allow developers to iterate through data, perform XSLT transform operations, and access both database and object data. Both technologies can be combined to craft presentation-tier components to display and interact with back-end data models.

This section will discuss JSP 2.0 and JSTL 1.1 technologies by presenting overviews of their capabilities followed by some individual components of their libraries and demonstrate their usage in figures and source code listings.

JSP 2.0 Overview

The viability of the Model 1 Architecture depends heavily on a number of the new features in the JSP 2.0 specification. In this section you will learn about the following:

❑ Servlet 2.4 specification support

❑ Expression Language (EL) support

❑ Code reuse with *.tag and *.tagx files

❑ JSP page extensions (*.jspx)

❑ Simple Invocation Protocol

331

The introduction of these new script language constructs with the JSP 2.0 and JSTL 1.1 specifications was meant to eliminate the need to include Java expressions in script code, which would result in scriptless page development. These enhancements will certainly provide more controlled interactions and flexibility with other components as well as reusability among common actions.

Servlet 2.4 Support

The JSP 2.0 specification uses the Servlet 2.4 specification for its syntax, which allows applications to handle Expression Language (EL) expressions as native syntax.

The following table describes some of the ServletRequest methods that were introduced with the Servlet 2.4 specification to determine client connection attributes.

Method	Description
getRemotePort()	Method that returns the IP address of the port that sent a request
getLocalName()	Method that returns the hostname of the IP address from which the request was received
getLocalAddr()	Method that returns the IP Address from which the request was received
getLocalPort()	Method that returns the IP port number from which the request was received

This code segment illustrates how these methods can be implemented to realize these client connection values:

```
<html>
<head>
<title>Servlet 2.4 Features</title>
</head>
<body>
<h2>Servlet 2.4 Features</h2>
<%
out.println("Remote Port : " + request.getRemotePort() + "<br>");
out.println("Local Name : " + request.getLocalName() + "<br>");
out.println("Local Address : " + request.getLocalAddr() + "<br>");
out.println("Local Port : " + request.getLocalPort() + "<br>");
%>
</body>
</html>
```

Additionally, Servlet 2.4 support includes the introduction of new features for the RequestDispatcher and ServletRequest listener classes, as well as login capabilities related to the HttpSession class.

Expression Language Support

The Expression Language implementation in JSP 2.0 allows easy access to data from JSP scripts. This enhancement has allowed developers to avoid writing scriptlets inside their pages, which should result in cleaner and more readable JSP pages.

Expression Language syntax is purported to be more user-friendly than Java and was introduced to encourage its use for accessing data over Java language implementations. The power of Expression Language constructs is that they allow users to embed Java code in a Java Server Page through scripting elements. Three types of scripting elements are shown in the following table.

Scripting Element	Example
expressions	<jsp:expression> objectRef.loadValues() </:jsp:expression>
scriptlets	<% for (int increment = 0; increment < 25; increment++) { }
declarations	<%! boolean firstPass = true; %>

The following code examples use Expression Language features to perform pig Latin word translations and string replacement operations. The tag library prefix `test` is used to access the `pigLatin` and `dwReplacement` methods to perform string operations on user specified text that is saved in the `sampleText` parameter:

```
<%-- index.jsp --%>
<%@ taglib prefix="test" uri="/WEB-INF/el-taglib.tld"%>

<html>
  <head>
    <title>Expression Language Examples</title>
  </head>
  <body>
  <h1>Expression Language Examples</h1>

    <form action="functions.jsp" method="GET">
    sampleText = <input type="text" name="sampleText"
value="${param['sampleText']}">
         <input type="submit">
    </form>

    <table border="0">
    <tr>
      <td bgcolor="#ffff99">Pig-Latin = </td>
      <td bgcolor="#ffff99">${test:pigLatin(param["sampleText"])} </td>
    </tr>
    <tr>
      <td bgcolor="#ffff99">Dirty Word Replacement = </td>
      <td bgcolor="#ffff99">${test:dwReplacement(param["sampleText"])} </td>
    </tr>
    </table>

  </body>
</html>
```

The Java method below performs regular expression string manipulation operations on the text expressions specified by the user in the text field components of `index.jsp`. For the `pigLatin` method, a check is performed on the first character of the string passed in to see if that character is a vowel; if so, then the string will be returned with the word "way" appended to the end of it. Strings that start with consonants will have their first character moved to the end of the string and then have "ay" added to the end of string:

```java
// [StringMethods.java]
package examples.el;

import java.util.*;
import java.util.regex.*;

public class StringMethods {

    public static String pigLatin( String text) {
        // works for one word ONLY
        Pattern pattern = Pattern.compile("^([aeiouAEIOU])");
        Matcher matcher = pattern.matcher(text);
        if (matcher.find())
            return text+"way";
        else
            return text.replaceAll("^([^aeiouAEIOU])(.+)", "$2$1ay");
    }

    public static String dwReplacement( String text ) {
        Pattern pattern = Pattern.compile("(darn|damn|stupid|dummy)");
        Matcher matcher = pattern.matcher(text);
        text = matcher.replaceAll("#%&@");
        return text;
    }
}
```

The tag library definition file below defines the two different text functions, pigLatin and dwReplacement, that are invoked in the index.jsp file and defined in StringMethods.java:

```xml
<!-- el-taglib.tld -->
<?xml version="1.0" encoding="UTF-8" ?>

<taglib xmlns="http://java.sun.com/xml/ns/j2ee"
    xmlns:xsi="http://www.w3.org/2001/XMLSchema-instance"
    xsi:schemaLocation="http://java.sun.com/xml/ns/j2ee web-jsptaglibrary_2_0.xsd"
    version="2.0">

    <description>Function Examples</description>
    <tlib-version>1.0</tlib-version>
    <short-name>Function Examples</short-name>
    <uri>/el</uri>

    <function>
    <description>PIG-Latin</description>
        <name>pigLatin</name>
    <function-class>examples.el.StringMethods</function-class>
    <function-signature>
        java.lang.String pigLatin( java.lang.String )
    </function-signature>
```

```
          </function>
          <function>
          <description>Dirty Word Replacement</description>
                <name>dwReplacement</name>
          <function-class>examples.el.StringMethods</function-class>
          <function-signature>
              java.lang.String dwReplacement( java.lang.String )
          </function-signature>
          </function>

     </taglib>
```

As this example demonstrates, Expression Language library extensions are powerful features that strengthen developer's capabilities for Web development. The function methods described here are mapped to public static methods in Java classes that can be accessed through Expression Language constructs throughout your Web application.

Code Reuse with *.tag and *.tagx Files

The implementation of *.tag and *.tagx files allows for better code reuse among developers. With these tags, developers can encapsulate common behavior that will support reuse activities.

The following code snippet demonstrates how tag files can be implemented for reuse by other Web applications. In this example, a portlet-like visualization component is crafted using a tagged file named portlet.tag. Two parameters, title and color, are passed into the portlet tag file to dynamically alter those properties in the component display:

```
<%@ taglib prefix="tags" tagdir="/WEB-INF/tags" %>
<html>
<head><title>tagx test</title>
</head>
<body>
<table width="100%"><tr><td>
   <tags:portlet title="Portlet" color="#0000ff"> Test 1
   </tags:portlet>
</td></tr></table>
</body>
</html>
```

The portlet.tag file encapsulates the portlet component and renders the title and color features passed into the file by the preceding script:

```
<!--portlet.tag -->
<%@ attribute name="title" required="true" %>
<%@ attribute name="color" required="true" %>

<table width="250" border="1" cellpadding="2" cellspacing="0">
  <tr bgcolor="${color}" color="#ffffff">
    <td nowrap>
      ${title}
    </td>
  </tr>
```

```
    <tr>
      <td valign="top">
          &#149;  <a href="">Test1</a><br>
          &#149;  <a href="">Test2</a><br>
      </td>
    </tr>
  </table>
```

These tag files can be important components for header and footer implementations that contain common information that can be easily propagated to the Web pages in your project.

JSP Page Extensions (*.jspx)

Java Server Pages that have *.jspx extensions are meant to advocate the use of XML syntax to generate XML documents in JSP 2.0 compliant Web containers.

The code specified below describes how jspx files can be implemented when you develop Web applications to generate user displays:

```
<!--forms.jspx ‡
<?xml version="1.0"?>
<tags:test xmlns:tags="urn:jsptagdir:/WEB-INF/tags"
           xmlns:jsp="http://java.sun.com/JSP/Page"
           xmlns:c="http://java.sun.com/jsp/jstl/core"
           xmlns="http://www.w3.org/1999/xhtml">
<jsp:directive.page contentType='text/html'/>
<head><title>Form Test</title></head>
<body>
  <c:choose>
  <c:when test='${param.name == null} and ${param.address == null}'>
      <form action="form.jspx">
          Please enter your name and address:<br/>
          <input name="name" size="40"/><br/>
          <input name="address" size="40"/><br/>
          <input type="submit"/>
      </form>
  </c:when>
  <c:otherwise>
User entered name=${param.name}, address=${param.address}<br/>
  </c:otherwise>
  </c:choose>
</body>
</tags:test>
```

The test.tag file below is used to invoke the JSP fragments using the `<jsp:doBody>` standard action:

```
<!DOCTYPE html PUBLIC "-//W3C//DTD XHTML Basic 1.0//EN"
"http://www.w3.org/TR/xhtml-basic/xhtml-basic10.dtd">
<html xmlns="http://www.w3.org/1999/xhtml">
<jsp:doBody/>
</html>
```

As the JSP 2.0 specification indicates, Web applications that contain files with an extension of .jspx will have those files interpreted as JSP documents by default.

Simple Invocation Protocol

This API enhancement was developed to exploit the use of scriptless pages among Web developers using JSP libraries in their development activities for implementing tag files.

In the code example below, the `<lottery:picks/>` tag file invocation demonstrates how simple it is to incorporate logic into a Web page using tag libraries:

```
<%@ taglib uri="/WEB-INF/tlds/lottery.tld" prefix="lottery" %>
<html>
<head>
<title>Lottery Picks</title>
</head>
<body>
<h2>Lottery Picks</h2>
Lottery number generated is...<lottery:picks/>
</body>
</html>
```

The lottery tag library descriptor file, lottery.tld, outlines the lottery tag file application invoked from the preceding Web application:

```
<!--lottery.tld ‡
<?xml version="1.0" encoding="UTF-8" ?>
<taglib xmlns="http://java.sun.com/xml/ns/j2ee"
    xmlns:xsi="http://www.w3.org/2001/XMLSchema-instance"
    xsi:schemaLocation="http://java.sun.com/xml/ns/j2ee/web-jsptaglibrary_2_0.xsd"
    version="2.0">

    <description>
     Lottery picks
    </description>
    <jsp-version>2.0</jsp-version>
    <tlib-version>1.0</tlib-version>
    <short-name>picks</short-name>
    <uri></uri>

    <tag>
        <name>picks</name>
        <tag-class>lottery.LotteryPickTag</tag-class>
        <body-content>empty</body-content>
        <description>Generate random lottery numbers</description>
    </tag>
</taglib>
```

The `LotteryPickTag` application below illustrates how the SimpleTagSupport class can be extended to allow developers to craft tag handlers. The `doTag()` method is invoked when the end element of the tag is realized. In the sample Lottery application, the `getSixUniqueNumbers()` method is called from the doTag method which in turn displays the string output of six unique lottery numbers generated in random fashion:

```
package lottery;

import java.io.*;
import java.util.*;
import javax.servlet.jsp.*;
import javax.servlet.jsp.tagext.SimpleTagSupport;

public class LotteryPickTag extends SimpleTagSupport {

    public LotteryPickTag(){}

    public void doTag() throws JspException, IOException {
        getJspContext().getOut().write("Random #'s =" + getSixUniqueNumbers());
    }

    public String getSixUniqueNumbers() {
        StringBuffer sb = new StringBuffer();
        int count = 0, number = 0;
        int numbers[] = {0,0,0,0,0,0,0};
        boolean found;

        while (count < 6) {
            number = (int)(Math.random()*59) + 1;
            found = false;
            for (int i=0; i < numbers.length; i++)
                if (numbers[i] == number) found = true;
            if (!found) {
                if (count != 0) sb.append(" - ");
                sb.append(number);
                numbers[count++] = number;
            }
        }
        return sb.toString();
    }
}
```

JSP tag files are converted into Java code by the JSP container in the same fashion that JSP scripts are translated into servlets. It should be fairly evident from this example how easily tag files can be constructed for deployment in Web components for enterprise systems because they hide the complexity of building custom JSP tag libraries, which makes them easier to maintain in the long run.

Figure 7-2 outlines visually some of the enhancements of the JSP 2.0 specification along with some of the backwards compatibility issues that are addressed in the JSP 2.0 specification.

Certainly, the JSP 2.0 upgrade, with its ready-made Expression Language implementations, along with improvements in Java Server Pages Standard Tag Libraries, will enhance developer's abilities to build cohesive and robust Web components.

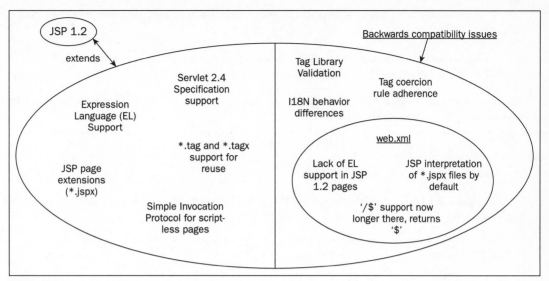

Figure 7-2

Integrated Expression Language (EL)

The following section concentrates on the Expression Language (EL) and its implementation in JSP applications. Certainly, there is ample content in the JSP 2.0 specification to discuss and demonstrate, especially some of the Servlet 2.4 features that were discussed briefly above, but this section will concentrate on EL implementations because they are exploited prominently in the Contact Management Tool. Some of the other aspects of that specification are fairly involved and extend beyond the scope of this chapter.

Expression Language (EL) expressions can be used with three different attribute values. First, they can be applied when an attribute value has a single expression; second, they can be used when the attribute value contains one or more expressions surrounded or separated by text; and lastly, they can be used when the attribute value contains only text. The table below shows how these operations can be implemented.

EL Expressions	Implementation
Single expression	\<xyz.tag value="${expression}"/>
One or more expressions	\<xyz.tag value="abc${expression}text${expression}"/>
Text only	\<xyz.tag value="abc text"/>

JSP 2.0 scripts allow EL expressions to perform conditional operations on your Web page variables. An example of this follows:

```
<c:if test="${param.Comments > 250}">
</c:if>
```

The parameter `param.Comments` is checked to see if it is greater than 250; if so, then the logic that lies between the `if` statement is executed.

The JSTL core tag libraries can also be used for variable output. Here is an example of this:

```
<c:out value="${testELexpression}"/>
```

JSP 2.0 pages implement several different implicit objects through EL expressions; the table below lists some examples.

Implicit Object	Description
pageContext	Accesses the PageContext object, which provides access to all the namespaces associated with a JSP page
pageScope	A Map that contains page-scoped attribute names and values
requestScope	A Map that contains request-scoped attribute names and values
sessionScope	A Map that contains session-scoped attribute names and values
applicationScope	A Map that contains application-scoped attribute names and values
Param	A Map that correlates parameter names to single String parameter values
paramValues	A Map that correlates parameter names to a String[] of all values of that parameter
header	A Map that contains header names in a String
headerValues	A Map that contains header names in a String array component
Cookie	A Map that contains Web cookie objects
initParam	A Map that holds context initialization parameter names and their values

Implicit objects, for example, objects that don't need to be declared and are declared automatically, allow developers to access Web container services and resources.

JSTL 1.1 Overview

Capabilities of the Java Standard Template Library (JSTL 1.1) specification are too numerous to elaborate on in great depth, so this chapter will concentrate on two tag library capabilities that are helpful in the sample Contact Management Tool (CMT). The CMT application persists data in a MySQL database during storage and retrieval operations so that the SQL Actions libraries are implemented and the Function Tag Library operations are used for string manipulation. So the latter will be discussed too.

Function Tag Library

The Function Tag Library capabilities were introduced with the JSP 2.0 specification to allow developers to extend Expression Language (EL) functionalities with string manipulation libraries. The JSTL 1.1 specification outlines these functions as follows. The following table demonstrates some of the new method functions available as part of the expression language support in JSP 2.0.

Function [fn:]	Description of Function
fn:contains(string, substring)	If the substring exists in a specified string value, *true* will be returned to the user, otherwise *false*. Example, fn:contains("independence", "depend") returns *true*
fn:containsIgnoreCase(string, substring)	Ignoring case differences, if a substring exists in a specified string value, *true* will be returned to the user, otherwise *false*. Example, fn:containsIgnoreCase("independence", "DEPEND") returns *true*
fn:endsWith(string, suffix)	Tests the end of a string with the suffix specified to determine if there is a match. Example, fn:endsWith("whirlyjig", "jag") returns *false*
fn:escapeXml(string)	Escape characters that might be XML Example, fn.escapeXml("<test>yea</test>") returns converted string
fn:indexOf(string, substring)	Returns integer value of the first occurrence of the specified substring in a string. Example, fn:indexOf("democratic", "rat") returns 6
fn:join(array, separator)	Joins elements from an array into a string with a specified separator Example, array[0]="X", array[1]="Y" fn:join(array,";") returns String = "X;Y"
fn:length(item)	Returns a collection count or the number of characters in a string as an integer value Example, fn.length("architecture") returns 12
fn:replace(string, before, after)	Returns a new string after replacing all occurrences of the *before* string with the *after* string. Example, fn:replace("downtown", "down", "up") returns *uptown*
fn:split(string, separator)	Returns an array where all the items of a string are added based on a specified delimiter Example, fn:split("how now brown cow"," ") returns array[0]="how", array[1]="now", array[2]="brown", array[3]="cow"

Table continued on following page

Function [fn:]	Description of Function
fn:startsWith(string, prefix)	Returns a boolean value (true/false) depending on whether or not a string contains a specified prefix value Example, fn:startsWith("predicament", "pre") returns *true*
fn:substring(string, begin, end)	Returns a substring of a string based upon specified index values Example, fn:substring("practical", 2,5) returns *act*
fn:substringAfter(string, substring)	Returns a string value that follows a specified substring Example, fn:substringAfter("peppermint","pepper") returns *mint*
fn:substringBefore(string, substring)	Returns a string value that precedes a specified substring value Example, fn:substringBefore("peppermint", "mint") returns *pepper*
fn:toLowerCase(string)	Converts all the characters of a specified string to lowercase Example, fn:toLowerCase("Design Patterns") returns *design patterns*
fn.toUpperCase(string)	Converts all the characters of a specified string to uppercase Ex., fn:toUpperCase("Patterns") returns *PATTERNS*
fn:trim(string)	Eliminates leading and trailing white space from a specified string Example, fn:trim(" almost done　") returns *"almost done"*

Since text manipulation is so prevalent in Web applications, these function libraries are invaluable components for your development and deployment operations. Many of these functions mirror the same APIs that the Java String class possesses, so they should be learned fairly easily.

SQL Actions

A general rule of thumb for SQL transactions on enterprise systems is to handle database operations within business logic operations; we'll demonstrate that with the Add Contact component below. But, sometimes you might want to perform those activities with the SQL tag libraries that are part of the JSTL 1.1 libraries.

JSTL SQL Actions allow developers to interact with databases on the presentation layer. An overview of its capabilities include the ability to perform queries through *select* statements, database updates with *insert*, *update*, and *delete* operations, and transactional activities that allow the aggregation of database operations.

The following table illustrates the SQL Action tags for establishing a data source.

Tag	Description

<sql:setDataSource>	This tag exports a data source.
	<sql:setDataSource
	        {datasource="dataSource" |
	        url = "jdbcUrl"
	        [driver = "driverClassName"]
	        [user = "userName"]
	        [password = "password"] }
	        [var="varName"]
	        [scope="{page | request | session | application}"]/>

The following table illustrates the SQL Action tags for query operations.

Tag	Description

<sql:query>	This tag queries the database.
	Without body content
	<sql:query sql="queryString"
	        var="varName"
	        [scope="{page | request | session | application}"]
	        [maxRows="maxRows"]
	        [startRow="startRow"] />
	With a body for query parameters
	<sql:query sql="queryString"
	        var="varName"
	        [scope="{page | request | session | application}"]
	        [maxRows="maxRows"]
	        [startRow="startRow"]
	    <sql:param> actions
	  </sql:query>
	With a body for query parameters and options
	<sql:query sql="queryString"
	        var="varName"
	        [scope="{page | request | session | application}"]
	        [maxRows="maxRows"]
	        [startRow="startRow"]
	    query optional
	    <sql:param> actions
	  </sql:query>

The following table illustrates the SQL Action tags for update operations.

Tag	Description

<sql:update>	This tag executes an INSERT, UPDATE, or DELETE statement.
	Without body content
	<sql:update sql="updateString"
	        [datasource="datasource"]
	        [var="varName"]
	        [scope="{page | request | session | application}"]/>
	With a body for query parameters
	<sql:update sql="updateString"
	        [datasource="datasource"]
	        [var="varName"]
	        [scope="{page | request | session | application}"]
	    <sql:param> actions
	  </sql:update>
	With a body for query parameters and options
	<sql:update sql="updateString"
	        [datasource="datasource"]
	        [var="varName"]
	        [scope="{page | request | session | application}"]
	    update statement optional
	    <sql:param> actions
	  </sql:update>

The SQL Action tags elaborated on above certainly are powerful mechanisms to perform SQL transactions inside your JSP Web components without having to worry about back-end JavaBean applications to perform the same duties. Ultimately, developers must decide during their coding operations if they opt to perform script or JavaBean queries in their deployments. Fortunately, the Contact Management Tool illustrates both to facilitate your design decisions.

Developing Your Web Application Visualizations with JSTL

Our code example below demonstrates the use of SQL actions mentioned previously. The first course of action in our code is to establish a data source object that will allow the application to connect to the *picture* database so that queries can collect data for visualization on your JSP page:

```
<%@ page language="java"
    contentType="text/html"
    import="java.util.*,java.lang.*,java.io.*" %>

<%@ taglib prefix="c" uri="http://java.sun.com/jstl/core_rt" %>
<%@ taglib prefix="sql" uri="http://java.sun.com/jstl/sql" %>

<HTML><HEAD><TITLE>Contact Management Tool</TITLE>
<link href="CMT.css" rel="stylesheet" type="text/css">

<sql:setDataSource
```

```
        var="pictures"
        driver="org.gjt.mm.mysql.Driver"
        url="jdbc:mysql://localhost/picture"
        user=""
        password=""
        scope="page"/>
```

After the data source has been established, a query is performed using the database reference *${pictures}* where the result set is stored in the *results* variable:

```
<sql:query var="results" dataSource="${pictures}">
    select * from picture
</sql:query>


<br>
<br>
```

The result set variable is then used to iterate through the individual database entries so that they can be shown on the user display:

```
<table cellSpacing=0 cellPadding=4 align=center><tr><td bgColor=#7b849c>
    <table border="0"><tr><td>
        <c:forEach var="row" items="${results.rows}" varStatus="counter">
            <tr class="row1">
            <td>
            <table cellSpacing="0" cellPadding="0" border="0">
                <td valign="top"><b>${counter.count}.</b></td>
                <td>
                <table width="500" border="0">
                  <tr>
                      <td class="smallblue" noWrap align="middle">
                          <a href="">${row.marking}</a>
                      </td>
                      <td>
                          <u>Attributes:</u>
                      </td>
                  </tr>
                  <tr>
                      <td align="middle">
                       <a href="">
                          <img src="./images/${row.name}" width=50 border=0>
                       </a>
                      </td>
                      <td>
                      <table>
                      <tr>
                        <td>Phone Number:</td>
                        <td>${row.telephone_num}</td>
                      </tr>
                      <tr>
                        <td>Comments:</td>
                        <td>${row.comments}</td>
```

```
                    </tr>
                  </table>
                </td>
              </tr>
          </table>
          </td>
      </table>
      </td>
      </tr>
    </c:forEach>
  </td></tr></table>
</td></tr></table>
<br>
<br>
```

The resulting display is demonstrated in the Contact Management Tool screenshot (see Figure 7-3 following). The JSP script culls the *picture* database for the image and meta data associated with that image for rendering. The person that is marked in the file text is hyperlinked so that users can click it and obtain more information about the selected contact.

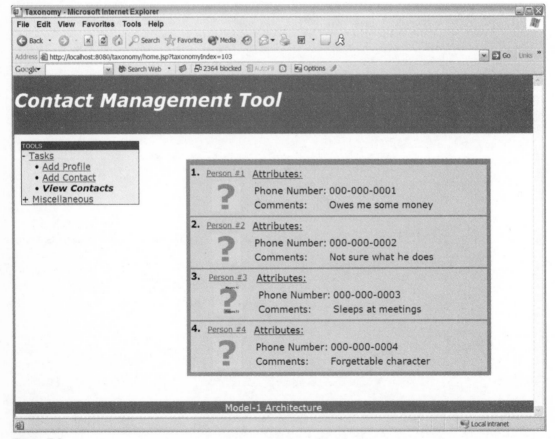

Figure 7-3

The next application, *addProfile.jsp*, uses both the core tag libraries for logic operations and the SQL actions to perform form processing actions on the Add Profile page. Once the form has been properly filled out, checks will be done to ensure that required fields have been entered. Once those checks have been performed, and the application has determined that the form entries can be pushed to the back-end database, the application will send the data to the *registration* database for storage and subsequent retrievals:

```
<%@ taglib prefix="c" uri="http://java.sun.com/jstl/core" %>
<%@ taglib prefix="fmt" uri="http://java.sun.com/jstl/fmt" %>
<%@ taglib uri="http://java.sun.com/jstl/sql_rt" prefix="sql" %>

<script language="JavaScript">
function textCounter(field, countfield, maxlimit) {
if (field.value.length > maxlimit) {
field.value = field.value.substring(0, maxlimit);
} else {
countfield.value = maxlimit - field.value.length;
}
}
</script>
```

The JSTL 1.1 core library tags are used below to perform logic operations on the form entries specified by the user. If either firstName, lastName, or email is empty, the application will not allow the form to pass the data to the back-end *registration* database:

```
<c:if test="${param.submitted}">

  <c:if test="${empty param.firstName}" var="noFirstName" />
  <c:if test="${empty param.lastName}" var="noLastName" />
  <c:if test="${empty param.email}" var="noEmail" />

  <c:if test="${not (noFirstName or noLastName or noEmail)}">
    <c:set value="${param.firstName}" var="firstName" scope="request"/>
    <c:set value="${param.lastName}" var="lastName" scope="request"/>
    <c:set value="${param.email}" var="email" scope="request"/>
```

Once the proper form entries have been entered by the user, the data source will be established with the SQL action tags by passing familiar JDBC driver, URL, username, and password parameters to the library to create a connection. After the connection has been created, then the SQL update tag can be used to perform an insert operation on the *registration* database using a prepared statement construct:

```
    <sql:setDataSource
        var="datasource"
        driver="org.gjt.mm.mysql.Driver"
        url="jdbc:mysql://localhost/registration"
        user=""
        password=""
        scope="page"/>

    <sql:update dataSource="${datasource}">
        INSERT INTO registration (registration_id, first_name, last_name, email)
VALUES(?, ?, ?, ?)
```

```
      <sql:param value="${param.firstName}" />
      <sql:param value="${param.lastName}" />
      <sql:param value="${param.email}" />
    </sql:update>

  </c:if>
</c:if>
```

The following code represents the registration form and its components that will be used to register contacts in the Contact Management Tool. Expression Language constructs, like `${param.lastName}`, are used to represent and persist data items entered by the form user:

```
<form method="post">

<table border="0" cellpadding="0" cellspacing="0"><tbody>

<tr valign="bottom">
<td nowrap="nowrap">

<table cellspacing="2" cellpadding="2" bgcolor="#336699">
<tbody>

  <tr>
    <td nowrap="nowrap" colspan="2">Registration</td>
  </tr>

  <tr>
    <td nowrap="nowrap" class="mandatory">First Name: (required)</td>
    <td class="value">
    <input name="firstName" value="${param.firstName}" size="25" maxlength="50">
    <c:if test="${noFirstName}">
        <small><font color="red">
        Please enter a First Name
        </font></small>
    </c:if>
    </td>
  </tr>

  <tr>
    <td nowrap="nowrap" class="mandatory">Last Name: (required)</td>
    <td class="value">
    <input name="lastName" value="${param.lastName}" size="25" maxlength="50">
    <c:if test="${noLastName}">
        <small><font color="red">
        Please enter a Last Name
        </font></small>
    </c:if>
    </td>
```

```
      </tr>

      <!--- Email, Gender, Marital Status, Date of Birth, Country, Zip Code, Age,
Place of Birth, Occupation and Interests components were omitted for the sake of
brevity -- >

      <tr>
        <td align="left" nowrap="nowrap" class="field" colspan="2">
        Characters remaining: 
        <input readonly="readonly" type="text" name="inputcount" size="5"
maxlength="4" value="" class="text">
        <br>
        <script language="JavaScript">
        document.form1.inputcount.value = (200 -
document.form1.interests.value.length);
        </script>
        </td>
      </tr>

      <tr>
        <td nowrap="nowrap" class="field" align="middle" colspan="2">
        <input type="hidden" name="submitted" value="true" />
        <input type="submit" value="Register" />
        </td>
      </tr>

    </tbody>
    </table>

  </form>
```

The form visualization (see Figure 7-4 following) is the result of the code fragments in the *addProfile.jsp* script described above. Some JavaScript code was used for the comments section to provide client-side validation, which ensures that the user does not enter more than 200 characters.

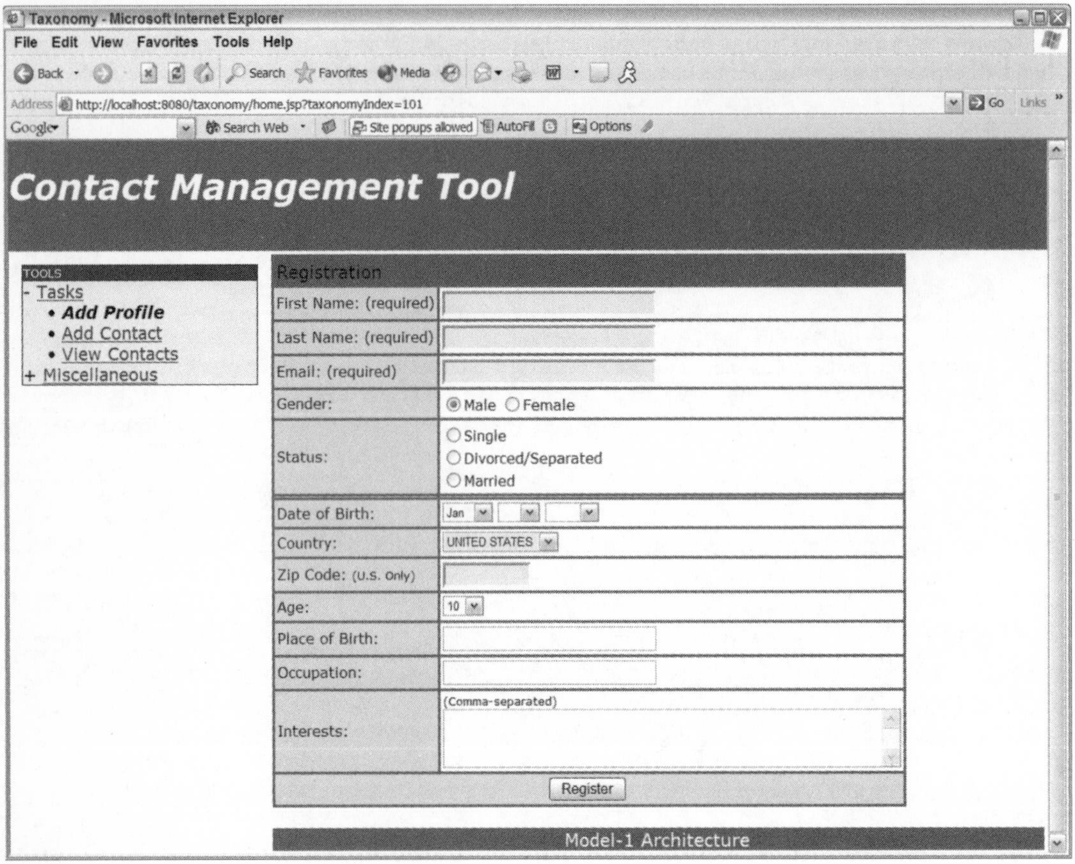

Figure 7-4

Developing Your Web Application Visualizations with JSP 2.0

Java Server Pages (JSPs) are generally implemented in distributed systems to aggregate content with back-end components for user visualizations. When application servers first receive a request from a JSP component, the JSP engine compiles that page into a servlet. Additionally, when changes to a JSP occur, that same component will be recompiled into a servlet again where it will be processed by a class loader so that it can restart its life cycle in the Web container.

A general best practice for developing Web components is to use JSPs for display generation and servlets for processing requests. The idea is to encapsulate complicated business logic in JavaBean components written in Java that are entirely devoid of scriptlet syntax so that display scripts are not obfuscated with complicated logic that might make your code hard to decipher for maintenance purposes. Naturally, your JavaBean code artifacts will transfer across platforms because they are written in Java, which accommodates reuse in your overall development operations.

The benefits of JSP technology include the following points:

❑ **Code reuse across disparate platforms.** Components and tag libraries can be shared in development operations and among different tools.

❑ **Separation of roles.** Web designers can work presentation scripts and developers can work back-end data transaction activities.

❑ **Separation of content.** Both static and dynamic content can be "template-tized", which inevitably facilitates coding operations.

A JSP page has two distinct phases during operations: translation and execution. During translation, the Web container validates the syntax of a JSP script. The Web container manages the class instances of a JSP during the execution phase as user requests are made for it.

Figure 7-5 conceptualizes how a Web page can be constructed using the Model 1 Architecture.

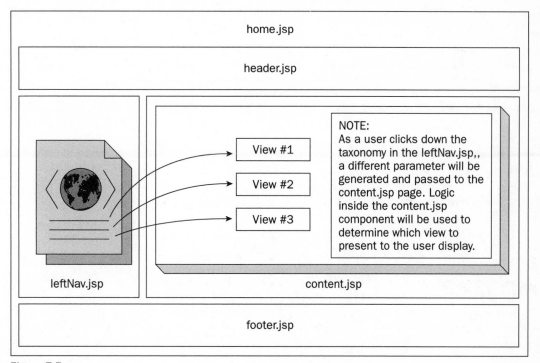

Figure 7-5

The following code is used by the leftNav.jsp page to read an XML file so that a drill-down navigation component can be used by a user to select different views for presentation. This application uses an open source product called dom4j to extract and navigate links from a hierarchical tree in an XML file. The dom4j library is a great tool for parsing and manipulating content because it offers full support for JAXP, SAX, DOM, and XSLT. It also has Xpath support for navigating XML artifacts, and is based on Java interfaces for flexible support:

```
package taxonomy;

/**
 * @author MMitchell
 *
 * To change this generated comment edit the template variable "typecomment":
 * Window>Preferences>Java>Templates.
 * To enable and disable the creation of type comments go to
 * Window>Preferences>Java>Code Generation.
 */

import java.net.*;
import java.util.*;
import javax.naming.*;
import java.util.logging.*;
import org.dom4j.*;
import org.dom4j.io.*;

public class TopicGenerator {

    protected static String EXPANDED_SYMBOL = "- ";
    protected static String COLLAPSED_SYMBOL = "+ ";
    protected static String LEAF = "&#149; ";
    protected static String SPACER = " ";
    protected static String TOPIC_CSS_CLASS = "SelectedTopic";

    private Document document;
    private static Logger log = Logger.getLogger("TopicGenerator");
```

The following code represents the constructor methods for the TopicGenerator application that reads the *Topic.xml* file into memory so that it can be navigated by users in the Contact Management Tool, which in turn will render a different view in the content.jsp page:

```
    public TopicGenerator() throws NamingException {
        Context initCtx = new InitialContext();
        Context ctx =  (Context) initCtx.lookup("java:comp/env");
        String topicsDirectory = (String) ctx.lookup("topicsDirectory");
        setFilename(topicsDirectory + java.io.File.separator + "Topic.xml");
        log.info("topicsDirectory= " + topicsDirectory);
    }

    public TopicGenerator(String fileName) throws Exception {
        parseDocument(fileName);
        if (this.document == null)
            throw new Exception("Problem initializing TopicGenerator");
    }

    public void setFilename(String fileName) {
        parseDocument(fileName);
    }
```

The `parseDocument` method initiates the application by reading the filename *Topic.xml* into memory for manipulation:

```
private void parseDocument(String fileName) {
    try {
        SAXReader reader = new SAXReader();
        document = reader.read(fileName);
    } catch (DocumentException de) {
        log.info("Problem initializing TopicGenerator.");
        de.printStackTrace();
    } catch (MalformedURLException me) {
        log.info("Malformed URL.");
        me.printStackTrace();
    }
}
```

The `addElement` method adds hyperlinked elements to the navigation tree for visualization. The implementation of the *StringBuffer* class is preferred over *String* class concatenation because of significant performance differences:

```
private void addElement(StringBuffer sb, Set set, Element element, String topicId,
                        String topicParamName, String href, String extraParams,
                        int level) {

    if (level != -1) {
        // write current node
        for (int i = 0; i < level*4; i++)
            sb.append(TopicGenerator.SPACER);

        if (element.elements().isEmpty())
            sb.append(TopicGenerator.LEAF);
        else if (set.contains(element))
            sb.append(TopicGenerator.EXPANDED_SYMBOL);
        else sb.append(TopicGenerator.COLLAPSED_SYMBOL);

        String thisTopicId = element.attributeValue("value");

        if (topicId.equals(thisTopicId))
            sb.append("<a class=\"" + TopicGenerator.TOPIC_CSS_CLASS + "\" ");
        else
            sb.append("<a ");

        sb.append("href=\"");
        sb.append(href);
        sb.append('?');
        sb.append(topicParamName);
        sb.append('=');
        sb.append(thisTopicId);
        sb.append(extraParams);
        sb.append("\">" + element.attributeValue("text") + "</a><br>");
```

```
        }

    if (set.contains(element) || level == -1) {
        Iterator it = element.elementIterator();
        while (it.hasNext()) {
            Element currElement = (Element) it.next();
            addElement(sb, set, currElement, topicId, topicParamName, href,
extraParams,
                          level + 1);
        }
    }
}
```

The `generateParams` method receives a HashMap object from the `getTopics` method so that it can generate the parameters needed for traversal. Please note that it is always a good practice to check the input parameters that are passed into a method prior to performing operations on them as has been done in the following example code:

```
private String generateParams(HashMap params) {
    if (params == null || params.isEmpty())
        return "";

    StringBuffer toReturn = new StringBuffer();

    Iterator keys = params.keySet().iterator();
    while (keys.hasNext()) {
        String currParam = (String) keys.next();
        String currParamValue = (String) params.get(currParam);

        if (currParamValue != null) {
            toReturn.append('&');
            toReturn.append(currParam);
            toReturn.append('=');
            toReturn.append(currParamValue);
        }
    }

    return toReturn.toString();
}
```

The `getTopics` method establishes a tree structure based on the taxonomies residing in the Topic.xml file, which is discovered by a context lookup at the onset of the application. The overloaded `getTopics` methods return the topic values that are read from the taxonomy for user navigation:

```
    public String getTopics(String topicId, String topicParamName, String href,
                        HashMap params) {
      if (topicId == null)
         topicId = "";

      Element taxonomy = (Element)
document.selectSingleNode("/navigation/taxonomy");

      List list = taxonomy.selectNodes("//topic[@value='" + topicId + "']/
ancestor-or-self::*");

      Set expandedNodeSet = new HashSet(list);
      StringBuffer toReturn = new StringBuffer();

      addElement(toReturn, expandedNodeSet, taxonomy, topicId, topicParamName,
href,
                  generateParams(params), -1);

      return toReturn.toString();
    }

    public String getTopics(String topicId, String topicParamName, String href) {
      HashMap params = new HashMap();
      return getTopics(topicId, topicParamName, href, params);
    }

    public static void main(String[] args) throws Exception {
      String s = "c:\\tomcat5019\\webapps\\mojo\\WEB-INF\\classes\\Topic.xml");"
      TopicGenerator tg = new TopicGenerator(s);
    }
}
```

In our GUI presentation shown in Figure 7-6, when a user attempts to add a new contact to the Contact Management Tool, a form will be presented to the user for a picture and meta data that will be associated with that picture. The Web application uses JSP 2.0 Expression Language (EL) features to present data, and JavaBean components to persist and manipulate contact data for retrieval and storage.

```
<%@ page language="java"
    contentType="text/html"
    import="java.util.*,java.nio.channels.*,java.lang.*,java.io.*,com.model1.*"  %>

<jsp:useBean id="fd" class="com.model1.FileDir" scope="request">
    <jsp:setProperty name="fd" property="*"/>
</jsp:useBean>

<title>Insert Contact</title>
```

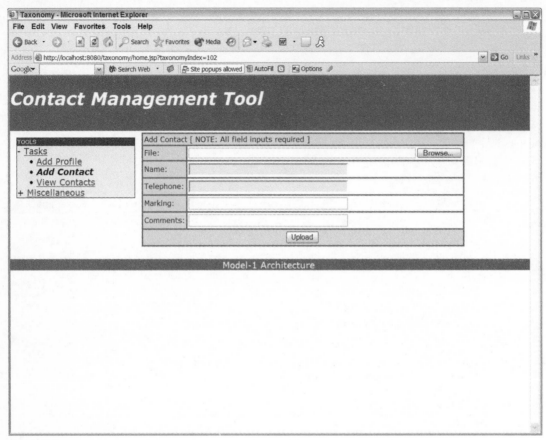

Figure 7-6

The code below performs Expression Language checks to ensure that the user-specified filename is not null and its length is greater than zero. The code also performs checks with the JavaBean `FileDir` to determine if all of the input fields (Name, Telephone, Marking, Comments) have been properly entered. If that action has been performed properly, then the application will use that bean to upload the image file designated for upload and insert the meta data associated with that image into the *picture* database for future retrieval. The string validation checks are redundant for the filename attribute, but were shown to demonstrate how user form inputs might be implemented to ensure that proper data is propagated to back-end components:

```
<c:if test="${param.filename != null && fn:length(param.filename) > 0}">
<%
if (fd.isValid()) {
    if (fd.fileUpload(fd.getFilename())) {
        fd.addMetadata(fd.getName(), fd.getTelephone(), fd.getMarking(),
fd.getComments());
    }
} else {
    System.out.println("INVALID...");
```

```
}
%></c:if>

<form method="post" action="home.jsp?taxonomyIndex=102">

<table border="0" cellpadding="0" cellspacing="0" bgcolor="#336699"><tbody>
<tr valign="bottom"><td nowrap="nowrap">
```

The following code represents the form values for input. Notice the JSP 2.0 syntax without scriptlets, like `${fd.filename}`. The Servlet 2.4 container, along with the JSP 2.0 container, now can handle EL expressions as native JSP syntax:

```
<table cellspacing="2" cellpadding="2">
<tbody>

    <tr>
        <td nowrap="nowrap" class="mandatory" colspan="2">
        Add Contact [ NOTE: All field inputs required ]
        </td>
    </tr>
    <tr>
        <td nowrap="nowrap" class="mandatory">File:</td>
        <td class="value">
        <input type="file" size="60" name="filename" value="${fd.filename}">
        </td>
    </tr>
    <tr>
        <td nowrap="nowrap" class="mandatory">Name:</td>
        <td class="value">
        <input name="name" value="${fd.name}" size="40" maxlength="50">
        </td>
    </tr>
    <tr>
        <td nowrap="nowrap" class="mandatory">Telephone:</td>
        <td class="value">
        <input name="telephone" value="${fd.telephone}" size="40" maxlength="50">
        </td>
    </tr>
    <tr>
        <td nowrap="nowrap" class="mandatory">Marking:</td>
        <td class="value">
        <input name="marking" value="${fd.marking}" size="40" maxlength="50">
        </td>
    </tr>
    <tr>
        <td nowrap="nowrap" class="mandatory">Comments:</td>
        <td class="value">
        <input name="comments" value="${fd.comments}" size="40" maxlength="50">
        </td>
    </tr>
    <tr>
      <td align="middle" class="mandatory" colspan="2">
```

```
        <input type="submit" name="UploadFile" value="Upload">
        </td>
    </tr>

</tbody>
</table>

</td></tr>
</tbody>
</table>

</form>
```

The Java Bean `FileDir` below accepts the inputs from the `addContact.jsp` file and performs checks to ensure that all of the proper fields have been entered prior to uploading the user-specified image and its related meta data:

```java
// FileDir.java

package com.model1;

import java.io.*;
import java.net.*;
import java.sql.*;
import java.util.*;
import java.util.logging.*;
import java.nio.channels.*;

// needed for marking
import java.awt.*;
import java.awt.image.BufferedImage;
import javax.imageio.*;
import javax.imageio.stream.*;
import javax.imageio.ImageIO.*;
import com.sun.media.imageio.plugins.tiff.TIFFImageWriteParam;
import javax.imageio.plugins.jpeg.JPEGImageWriteParam;

public class FileDir {

    private static Logger log = Logger.getLogger("FileDir");

    private String txtPath = "C:\\tmp"; // image repository directory
    private Connection connection;
    private Statement statement;
    private String driverName = "";
    private String className = "";
    private String user = "";
    private String pass = "";

    // form entries
    private String filename;
    private String name;
    private String telephone;
    private String marking;
    private String comments;
```

The `FileDir` constructor uses a class loader object to discover the *file.properties* file that outlines the JDBC parameters needed to connect to the *picture* database. If all goes well, a connection object will be instantiated to perform operations on that database:

```java
public FileDir() throws ClassNotFoundException, SQLException {

    Properties resource = new Properties();
    try {
       URL url =
this.getClass().getClassLoader().getResource("file.properties");
       resource.load( new FileInputStream(url.getFile()) );
       // Get properties
       driverName = resource.getProperty("driverName");
       className = resource.getProperty("className");
       user = resource.getProperty("user");
       pass = resource.getProperty("pass");
       log.info("Using parameters from the file.properties file for Contact
Information.");
    } catch (Exception e) {
       log.info("[FileDir()] EXCEPTION. " + e.toString());
    }

    Class.forName(className);
    connection = DriverManager.getConnection(driverName,user, pass);
    statement = connection.createStatement();
}
```

The `fileUpload` method is passed the filename specified by the user in the Add Contact form above so that it can be uploaded to the filesystem for rendering when queried by the View Contact page. The method uses the NIO (New IO) libraries to stream the data from the local filesystem. A local file copy routine was introduced here for demonstration purposes only; normally, an enterprise Web upload application would handle remote file upload, too:

```java
public boolean fileUpload(String srcFilename) {

    String dstFilename = "";
    log.info("srcFilename= " + srcFilename);

    if ((srcFilename != null) && (!srcFilename.equals(""))) {

        int x = srcFilename.lastIndexOf(File.separatorChar)+1;
        if (x > 0) {
            dstFilename = txtPath + File.separatorChar + srcFilename.substring(x);
            log.info("dstFilename= " + dstFilename);

            try {
                File f = new File(dstFilename).getParentFile();
                if (f.mkdirs() || f.isDirectory()) {
                    FileChannel srcChannel = new
FileInputStream(srcFilename).getChannel();
                    FileChannel dstChannel =
                        new FileOutputStream(dstFilename).getChannel();
                    dstChannel.transferFrom(srcChannel, 0, srcChannel.size());
```

```
                        srcChannel.close();
                        dstChannel.close();
                        log.info("uploaded to " + txtPath + " file -> " + dstFilename);
                    } else {
                        log.info("FAILURE with file [f]");
                        return false;
                    }
                } catch (IOException e) {
                    log.info("IOException= " + e.toString());
                    return false;
                }

            } else {
                log.info("could not parse: " + srcFilename);
                return false;
            }
        }
    }
    return true;
}
```

The `markImage` method allows users to pass an image file with a marking value so that the marking can be overlayed on to that image file. The Java Image IO libraries are used to perform these actions. The sample application is set up so that *.jpeg images can be uploaded for tag marking. Logic has also been added to accommodate *.tif files, which would need to be uncommented in order to work:

```
public void markImage(String inFile, String outFile, String marking) {

    try {

        BufferedImage  image = ImageIO.read(new File(inFile));

        Graphics graphics = image.getGraphics();
        graphics.setColor(Color.black);
        graphics.setFont(new Font("Arial", Font.BOLD | Font.ITALIC, 20));

        graphics.drawString(marking, (image.getWidth()*4/10),
                                (image.getHeight() - (image.getHeight()/10)));
        graphics.drawString(marking, (image.getWidth()*4/10) ,
image.getHeight()/10);


        // Create Image
        IIOImage iioImage = new javax.imageio.IIOImage(image, null, null);

        //  If TIFF document used, uncomment this and comment JPEG
        // Iterator writers = ImageIO.getImageWritersByFormatName("tiff");
        Iterator writers = ImageIO.getImageWritersByFormatName("jpeg");
        ImageWriter writer = (ImageWriter)writers.next();

        // Set WriteParam's
        // TIFFImageWriteParam writeParam =
(TIFFImageWriteParam)writer.getDefaultWriteParam();
```

```
            // writeParam.setCompressionMode(ImageWriteParam.MODE_EXPLICIT);
            JPEGImageWriteParam writeParam =
(JPEGImageWriteParam)writer.getDefaultWriteParam();
            // writeParam.setCompressionType("CCITT T.6"); // for TIF compression
            writeParam.setCompressionType("JPEG");

            // Create File to save the image
            File f = new File(outFile);
            if (!f.exists()) f.createNewFile();
            ImageOutputStream ios = createImageOutputStream(f);
            writer.setOutput(ios);

            // Save the image
            writer.write(null, iioImage, writeParam);
            ios.close();

        } catch (IOException e) {
            log.info("FILE FAILED:" + inFile);
        }
    }
```

The addMetadata method adds the meta data associated with the image file uploaded to the *picture* database. Additional checks on the meta data passed for database insertion could also be added to this routine to ensure that properly formatted data is passed to the database, but such checks were omitted for the sake of brevity. The string value passed in for marking text is passed along to the markImage method, which inserts that marking into the image file using the Java IO image libraries:

```
    public void addMetadata(String name, String telephone, String marking,
                            String comments) {
        StringBuffer sqlString = new StringBuffer();

        sqlString.append("INSERT INTO picture (name, telephone_num, marking,
comments) VALUES (");
        sqlString.append("'" + name + "',");
        sqlString.append("'" + telephone + "',");
        sqlString.append("'" + marking + "',");
        sqlString.append("'" + comments + "');");

        try {
            statement.executeUpdate(sqlString.toString());
            // mark images.
            markImage(dstFilename, dstFilename, marking);
        } catch (SQLException sqle) {
            log.info("SQLException: " + sqle.toString());
        }
    }
```

The getFiles method can be used to check the file system for files loaded to the c:\\tmp directory, which is the designated repository for image file uploads. Checks are performed on the filesystem to ensure that only *.gif and *.jpg files are loaded to the Map object that is returned to the routine that invoked it:

```java
public Map getFiles() {

    Map map = new HashMap();
    map = new TreeMap();

    File dir = new File("C:\\tmp");

    String[] children = dir.list();

    if (children == null) {
        log.info("Directory does not exist, or perhaps is NOT a directory.");
    } else {

        for (int i=0; i < children.length; i++) {
            // Get filename of file or directory
            String filename = children[i];
            if ((filename.endsWith(".gif")) || (filename.endsWith(".jpg")))
                map.put(filename, filename);
            }
            // Iterate over the keys in the map
            Iterator it = map.keySet().iterator();
            while (it.hasNext()) {
                Object key = it.next();
                log.info("[FileDir] key= " + key);
            }
        }
        return map;
}
```

The next section of the FileDir code represents the setter methods that are used by the Add Contact form to persist the form parameters that have been entered by the form user:

```java
// setters
public void setFilename(String filename) {
    this.filename = filename;
}

public void setName(String name) {
    this.name = name;
}

public void setTelephone(String telephone) {
    this.telephone = telephone;
}

public void setMarking(String marking) {
    this.marking = marking;
}

public void setComments(String comments) {
    this.comments = comments;
}
```

The getter methods below retrieve the form values so that the user form can ensure that all the fields have been properly entered by the user, prior to having the `FileDir` JavaBean application upload and save the meta data:

```
// getters
public String getFilename() {
   return filename;
}

public String getName() {
   return name;
}

public String getTelephone() {
   return telephone;
}

public String getMarking() {
   return marking;
}

public String getComments() {
   return comments;
}

public boolean isValid() {
   return ( (filename != null) && (!filename.equals("")) &&
            (name != null) && (!name.equals("")) &&
            (telephone != null) && (!telephone.equals("")) &&
            (marking != null) && (!marking.equals("")) &&
            (comments != null) && (!comments.equals("")) );
}

public static void main(String[] args) {

   try {
      FileDir fd = new FileDir();
      log.info("getting files...");
      fd.getFiles();
      String s = "c:\\tmp\\test\\screenshot1.gif";
      fd.fileUpload(s);
   } catch(Exception e) {
      log.info("EXCEPTION: " + e.toString());
   }


}
}
```

The FileDir Bean application demonstrates how Java components can be constructed with robust libraries to facilitate form processing and data persistence activities. The key to good bean development is to migrate common methods with one another for easy maintenance and to provide simple interfaces to data so that users will be more likely to incorporate them into their presentation code.

Summary

This chapter has demonstrated two different implementations of database transactions using both tag libraries and JavaBean components within the Contact Management Tool incorporating the Model 1 Architecture approach. The page flows were hard-coded to accommodate user navigations from a taxonomy drill-down component, with the assistance of core tag library logic operators and JavaBean validation methods. Naturally, not all of the features of the JSP 2.0 and JSTL 1.1 specifications and API libraries could be discussed in this chapter alone, but the sample Web application that was constructed should provide ample knowledge on how to craft J2EE Web components for the needs of the presentation tier.

Hopefully, you will find that this chapter eliminates some of your problems with your development operations and enhances your ability to make knowledgeable design decisions concerning Model 1 Architecture deployments.

Developing Web Applications Using the Model 2 Architecture

In the last chapter, you learned about building Web applications using the Model 1 Architecture, which is heavily dependent on a page-centric development focus. In this chapter, you will review and apply a prominent pattern in software development known as Model-View-Controller (MVC) to build Web applications in a more modular and componentized manner. You will learn a little about the Model 2 Architecture, particularly a framework known as WebWork, and its use of a concept known as Inversion of Control. You will see an example of how componentized development with WebWork provides a tremendous advantage to you as a Web developer, as it saves you time in having to rebuild the same components over and over in your application.

The Problem

Imagine your office needed a centralized contact manager for referencing people that could be used for given projects. You know that such functionality would be useful, but are worried about trying to do something too ad hoc and inflexible, leading to it being quickly thrown away.

You need something quick, but flexible. You need something where you can reuse a lot of components to build your solution. You need to look at a Model 2 Architecture framework.

What Is Model 2?

In order to understand Model 2, you should review the Model-View-Controller paradigm, which you examined in depth in Chapter 3, "Exploiting Patterns in Java." As you saw in Chapter 3, MVC is often described in the context of Swing, so you may be wondering, "But these are Web applications, how could they have much to do with each other?" So, you should remember that the Model-View-Controller Architecture simply refers to breaking your system into distinct components to satisfy three concepts:

- ❑ The *Model* refers to the real-world representation of your domain. For example, if I have a golf scoring system, I would have objects to represent things like a golf hole, a score, and so on.

- ❑ The *View* refers to the ways that you view the data you are managing. For example, you may have a view of every player on a given hole, or you may have a scorecard for a given player over the whole course.

- ❑ The *Controller* refers to the actual discrete actions that the system can perform. For example, "enter a score," "generate a leaderboard," and so on.

Of course, there are wide debates about where the divisions really exist — is your model just data objects and does your controller handle the business logic? For purposes of this book, just simplify it down to three basic concepts: The model is "what it is"; the view is "what it looks like"; and the controller is "what it does."

So, how does the Model 2 Architecture actually work? Figure 8-1 demonstrates the Model 2 Architecture in action.

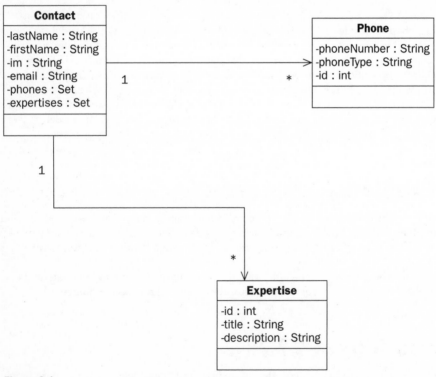

Figure 8-1

The Model 2 Architecture works like this:

1. The Request comes into the Controller.

2. The Controller performs a given action with the provided parameters.

3. The Controller forwards control to the View in order to give the response.

4. The View refers to the domain model to build the presentation.

5. The View is passed back in the Response to the user.

A critical thing that is usually missed by a lot of people who look at this diagram is the concept of "scope." Think of it like this. There are objects that are along for the ride, whether they are along for the duration of the request, the session, or the application.

Those are the key principles of Model 2 Architectures; now you will learn why the Model 2 Architecture is good for use in Web applications.

Why Use Model 2?

Now that you have a good sense of what the Model 2 Architecture is, you may be asking, "Why do I need this?" or "Isn't that a lot of effort for a Web page?" Well, there are a number of significant advantages to the Model 2 architectures, particularly in large-scale applications. Here are several of the advantages of the Model 2 Architecture.

Advantage	Description
Flexibility	Model 2 is flexible because it separates your application into components by their relevant piece of what they do. This allows you to plug in new views or actions as needed without having to rewrite everything. You can even reuse your components in other application platforms like Swing.
Reuse	Since Model 2 is componentized by definition, you can reuse a framework to provide a lot of the glue that holds your application together. A couple of examples of Model 2 frameworks are Apache Struts and OpenSymphony's WebWork.
Scalability	Because you have separated out the components, it is easy to add more components where necessary. Plus, you can cache your data components more easily because of the separation of concerns — your view doesn't care if it is handling a cached version of an object or a real version.
Security	By handling all actions through a central controller, you can easily configure and manage access control to your data and actions.

However, there is no perfect solution. There are disadvantages to using the Model 2 Architecture, which are illustrated in the following table.

Disadvantage	Description
Learning curve	You cannot use the Model 2 Architecture if you do not understand it. Furthermore, if you want to reuse a framework, then you must learn the particulars of that application. Of course, you are reading this chapter, so this should be fairly well mitigated after you read all about WebWork.
Complexity	There are many things to learn about Model 2 Architecture in order to use it effectively. Learning curves are different, but compared to JSP, it can be quite intimidating to the average Web developer who has been building page-centric database-driven Web applications for quite a while.
Programming vs. scripting	Many Web developers are used to developing their applications interactively — as if they were scripting their Web site. The concept of compiling and dependencies is simply something foreign to them, particularly if they came to Web development out of graphical design rather than programming. Now, you can still separate responsibilities among the team and allow these scripters to handle the views of the application, which are still conventional JSP.

The critical concept in deciding whether to go with Model 2 is to decide whether it is overkill or not. A rule of thumb could be that if you have more than five or six pages in your Web application, you really should use Model 2 Architecture. Note that this assumes that you will *never* have more than five or six pages, or that you are building a throwaway application.

The example application in this chapter deals directly with this issue of Model 1 versus Model 2. Too many explanations of Model 2 find it necessary to describe a system sufficiently complex to demonstrate the utility of Model 2, while ignoring the fact that the bigger the scope, the harder it is to wrap your mind around it. This application, a contact manager, would probably be a good candidate for Model 1, if it were not going to change or grow.

That is the fundamental distinction in Model 1 versus Model 2 — "Pay me now or pay me later." Either way you are not really saving any effort with Model 1 unless you intend not to be around later — because the project is not expected to undergo further development (as opposed to some untimely demise).

Now that you understand the concepts, advantages, and disadvantages of the Model 2 Architecture, you will want to look at an implementation of a Model 2 Architecture. For this chapter, you will see a simple example of building a Model 2 application using the popular Web application framework called WebWork.

Developing an Application with WebWork

Building applications with the Model 2 Architecture is not very helpful if you have to build all of this additional glue code that provides the framework that implements the architecture. It is far better if you use a framework like Struts to implement Model 2. In this chapter, you will see one of the more popular emerging frameworks known as WebWork, or more specifically, WebWork2. WebWork is a Web application framework built upon a generic command framework that provides for modularizing code through a concept known as *Inversion of Control* (IoC). While WebWork could be used to build a Model 1 Web application, it is really geared towards being a great Model 2 framework.

What Is Inversion of Control and Why Is It Useful?

To explain Inversion of Control, you should be familiar with a couple of concepts that are widely used by software/system architects to categorize components and services of a bigger system. These categories are

- ❑ **Vertical.** When a component or service is referred to as being vertical, it is focused on a business process. For example, a billing application would be a vertical application.

- ❑ **Horizontal.** Conversely, a component or service that is horizontal provides something that is relevant to all of the vertical services and components. A security manager and database connection pool are examples of horizontal components.

What has become increasingly painful in developing enterprise applications, that is, vertical components, is interfacing to horizontal services and components. Outside of the obvious performance benefit, how much better is it to have to do a custom, configurable lookup of a database connection pool than just creating the connection yourself? Furthermore, you don't want to have to account for all of the horizontal services in all of your application components, so you end up creating another layer of indirection on top of the horizontal service in order to provide the role for that service in your application.

Here is what that would look like in code:

```
package org.advancedjava.ch08;
import javax.naming.Context;
import javax.naming.InitialContext;
import javax.naming.NamingException;
import javax.sql.DataSource;
public class LookupMethod {
  private DataSource ds;
  public LookupMethod() {
    try {
      Context initCtxt = new InitialContext();
      ds = (DataSource) initCtxt.lookup("/jdbc/DS");
    } catch (NamingException e) {
      e.printStackTrace();
    }
  }
  /**
   * @return
   */
  public DataSource getDs() {
    return ds;
  }
  /**
   * @param source
   */
  public void setDs(DataSource source) {
    ds = source;
  }
}
```

Note in the constructor how you must go to the trouble to look up a component using the Java Naming and Directory Interface — and you tie yourself to that name. Now, this wouldn't be such a big problem in such a limited circumstance, but consider that this class is not the start point for your application, rather it is just a component of the application. You may have many of these components, all looking things up for themselves.

What if you inverted the whole equation and you simply declared your need for a given horizontal service? This is what Inversion of Control does; it allows you to develop your application components independent of how they will actually be provided. You simply declare the need for a given component, and allow the framework to inject the dependency — that is, provide the needed component at run time for you.

Instead, you could write it as what they call a Plain Old Java Object (POJO), which simply declares a member variable for the needed dependency and leaves the how and where of satisfying that dependency to the framework that runs it. So, your class would look something like this:

```
package org.advancedjava.ch08;
import javax.sql.DataSource;
public class InjectorMethod implements Injector {
  private DataSource ds;
  public InjectorMethod() {
  }
  /**
   * @return
   */
  public DataSource getDs() {
    return ds;
  }
  /**
   * @param source
   */
  public void setDs(DataSource source) {
    ds = source;
  }
}
```

Note how you have implemented an interface known as Injector, to declare the method through which you expose your dependency. Here is what that interface looks like:

```
package org.advancedjava.ch08;

import javax.sql.DataSource;
public interface Injector {
  public void setDs(DataSource ds);
}
```

By doing this, you are keeping your objects based more purely on solving the domain problems of your application, and deferring the context (setting up resources and finding them, and so on) to another part of the application. You have inverted the control, that is let the infrastructure call your code to do its specific part, rather than having your code and every other piece of code call the infrastructure to suit their needs.

Before you stop reading under the pressure of having to understand every nuance of all these complex pieces and abstract concepts, realize that you are learning these things as the background to understanding how things work under the hood. The nice thing about frameworks is that they handle a lot of the heavy lifting for you.

Now that you have learned the foundation concepts of WebWork—Inversion of Control and Model 2 Architecture—you will get some background in the WebWork framework in particular.

Architecture

You don't need to know every intricacy of WebWork in order to use it, but this text will provide you with some of the fundamental concepts so that you understand how it all fits together. Figure 8-2 demonstrates how the framework fits together.

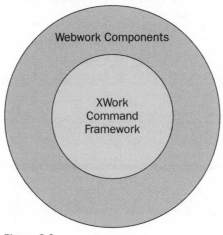

Figure 8-2

Note how the WebWork components (JSP tags, servlets, listeners, and servlet filters) are really just Web extensions to the generic command pattern framework known as XWork. In fact, you could easily wrap your exact same XWork Actions with RMI or Web service interfaces, or even embed them within a Swing application. That is the key concept; you are only applying the Web context to your core POJOs that represent your domain.

The essence of WebWork (and XWork) is that you write basic Java objects called Actions, and then allow the framework to inject the dependencies that you need. By configuring interceptors, you can inject the dependencies that your Java object requires. Figure 8-3 shows how the request-response flow works in WebWork.

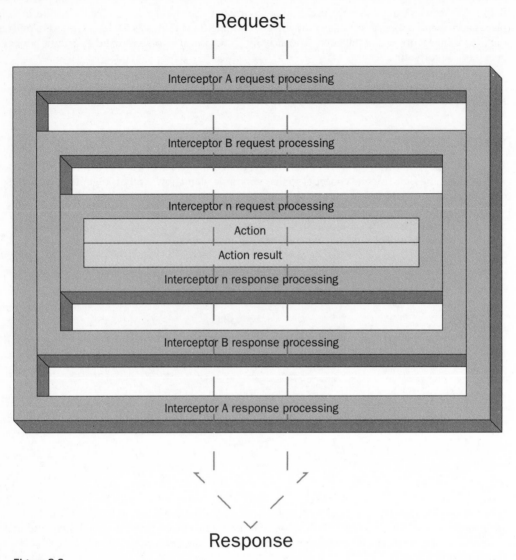

Figure 8-3

The request comes into the interceptor stack and is processed in the order of the interceptors until it gets to your developed Action class. Then, in reverse sequence, it makes its way back out through the response processing. This allows you to configure interceptors to provide facilities that are independent of the domain action, you can thus inject those dependencies, without burdening your Action with unneeded code.

Interceptors

Several Interceptors come with the WebWork framework; here is what each of them provides.

Interceptor	Description
LoggingInterceptor	Provides a logging statement before and after the execution of an action. Helpful for tracing through the application.
TimerInterceptor	Tracks the time taken to execute a given action. Useful for isolating bottlenecks, particularly in multiple action chains.
StaticParametersInterceptor	Maps the configuration parameters provided in your xwork.xml to the Action.
ParametersInterceptor	Populates the Action with the parameters passed in with the request.
ModelDrivenInterceptor	Unlike the other parameter interceptors, which only apply parameters directly to the member variables in the Action, this interceptor will allow you to map them into more complex domain objects in your action.
ChainingInterceptor	Applies the result of the previous action to the next action, useful for tying together multiple actions to form a useful composite. For example, you may have an action for calculating the sales tax which is chained to an action that handles the totaling of the whole bill.
DefaultWorkflowInterceptor	If the `Action` implements `Validateable`, it will call `validate()`. If the `Action` implements `Validation-Aware`, it will call `hasErrors()` to see if there are any registered error messages; if there are, it will return the `INPUT` status. If neither of these occur, it will invoke the `Action` execute method.

Of course, you can implement your own interceptors, and later in the chapter, you will see this in action, as it is used to provide support for Hibernate.

ValueStack

Remember how you learned earlier in the chapter about how your domain specific objects are "along for the ride?" The `ValueStack` is where they ride. Much like Java uses a stack to hold the relevant objects it uses within a given method or code block, XWork uses the `ValueStack` to accumulate the results of what has happened through your request's life cycle. This is useful because the View components can simply build themselves using JSP (or Velocity) tags that interact with the `ValueStack`.

The way that your views interact with the `ValueStack` is through something called the Object Graph Navigation Language (OGNL).

OGNL

OGNL, pronounced like it would sound if you tried to say it, provides you with a useful and easy way to express how you retrieve objects from an object graph. It also does things like automatic type conversion. (You think to yourself, "*Sure, the request sends all of its parameters as String objects and yes, the domain object takes an int, so why do I have to always tell it to execute Integer.parseInt()?")* In effect, it is very useful for providing simple expressions for manipulations of objects that otherwise take several lines of code.

Not only does the WebWork tag library make great use of OGNL for traversing the `ValueStack`, but WebWork also uses it to populate Action objects from request parameters.

Components

As you learned earlier, WebWork is built upon IoC. The first way that IoC is used is in injecting dependencies into Actions. However, WebWork also provides the ability to use a Component to inject resources into various scopes. You can configure your WebWork application to inject components into three different scopes:

1. **Request.** The Component will be attached to every user request, making it accessible to each Action.
2. **Session.** The Component will be attached when each new user session is created.
3. **Application.** The Component will exist throughout the life cycle of the application.

However, a practical example would probably make it easier to understand how components are used. Next, you will see how Hibernate is configured as a set of WebWork components to provide a complementary solution for persisting your objects.

Extending the Framework to Support Hibernate

The nice thing about Model 2 Architecture frameworks in general and WebWork in particular is that they are easily componentized and extended. One of the more exciting open source tools available online is the Hibernate tool, which provides object/relational persistence. Put more simply, it allows you to persist your objects more easily to a relational database than conventional SQL. For more discussion of the problem that Hibernate seeks to address, see Chapter 6: "Persisting Your Application Using Databases.

The genius behind Hibernate is a guy named Gavin King. King wanted to demonstrate how easily Hibernate pulled into a Model 2 Framework, so he created a sample application to provide user and role administration for Tomcat by linking Hibernate to WebWork.

In order to make it more focused, King's example has been stripped down to the point that it would probably not be recognizable to him, but he still deserves credit for the concepts. Plus, you can refer to his application if you want to see a more sophisticated use of these techniques. It can be downloaded at `hibernate.org`.

The fundamental component in building your Hibernate applications is the `HibernateFactory` object. This object performs the setup and configuration of Hibernate, and then provides Session objects for users to interact with the framework. As you might imagine, you only need one of these for your application, any more would be excessive and inefficient.

So what if you could create one at startup time and share it among all of your applications? That is where WebWork components come into play. As demonstrated in Figure 8-4, WebWork will initialize a `HibernateFactory` at startup and inject that dependency into your application's context.

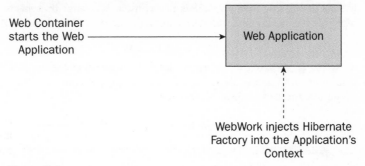

Figure 8-4

But WebWork doesn't stop with just injecting a `HibernateFactory` into your application; it also provides the ability to inject a Hibernate Session object into every user request. Figure 8-5 demonstrates how a Session object is injected into the request object that is created to service a given request.

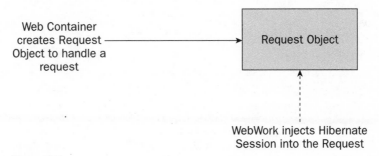

Figure 8-5

Now that you have learned how WebWork components inject Hibernate into your Model 2 Architecture application, you will see how that comes in very useful.

Preventing the Hanging Session

A tough problem in matching up Model 2 Architecture applications with object/relational mapping tools is that they tend to have two common operating models that can work against each other:

❑ A Model 2 application wants to conduct an action to retrieve a given graph of objects in the domain model and then forward it along to the view. In effect, it wants to disconnect from the database to prevent unnecessary binding. Also, it allows for clear packaging and handling of unanticipated actions in processing, namely exceptions and errors. Model 2 wants to consider the View part of the model to be about rendering data, independent of where it comes from.

❑ An ORM tool (like Hibernate) tends to prefer deferring initializing all of the objects on a given graph until they are needed, to avoid performance problems, data latency issues, and so on. Basically, the more data you pull, the slower and less efficient your application can become. Furthermore, the longer it is disconnected, the less likely it is to be current.

Now, before you start dismissing the two models as inconsistent, realize that this is a hiccup in two otherwise very compatible techniques. So, there is clearly a motivation to try to make the two work together more cleanly.

This is where the `HibernateInterceptor` comes into play. The short answer to what it does is allow you to maintain an open Hibernate session during the rendering of your view, because it intercepts the request model going out and closes the session cleanly.

Here is what the `HibernateInterceptor` looks like:

```
package org.advancedjava.ch08.interceptor;
import net.sf.hibernate.HibernateException;
import org.apache.commons.logging.Log;
import org.apache.commons.logging.LogFactory;
import org.advancedjava.ch08.HibernateAction;
import org.advancedjava.ch08.component.HibernateSession;
import com.opensymphony.xwork.Action;
import com.opensymphony.xwork.ActionInvocation;
import com.opensymphony.xwork.interceptor.Interceptor;
public class HibernateInterceptor implements Interceptor {
  private static final Log LOG =
    LogFactory.getLog(HibernateInterceptor.class);
  public void destroy() {
  }
  public void init() {
  }
  public String intercept(ActionInvocation invocation)
    throws Exception {
    Action action = invocation.getAction();
    if (!(action instanceof HibernateAction))
      return invocation.invoke();
    HibernateSession hs =
      ((HibernateAction) action).getHibernateSession();
    try {
      return invocation.invoke();
    }
    // Note that all the cleanup is done
    // after the view is rendered, so we
    // have an open session in the view
    catch (Exception e) {
      hs.setRollBackOnly(true);
      if (e instanceof HibernateException) {
        LOG.error("HibernateException in execute()", e);
        return Action.ERROR;
      } else {
        LOG.error("Exception in execute()", e);
        throw e;
      }
    } finally {
      try {
        hs.disposeSession();
      } catch (HibernateException e) {
        LOG.error("HibernateException in dispose()", e);
        return Action.ERROR;
      }
```

```
        }
    }
}
```

This brings the discussion back to the aforementioned `HibernateAction` class. Simply extending this class will allow your other actions to use these advantages rather transparently:

```java
package org.advancedjava.ch08;
import net.sf.hibernate.HibernateException;
import net.sf.hibernate.Session;

import org.advancedjava.ch08.component.HibernateSession;
import org.advancedjava.ch08.component.HibernateSessionAware;
import org.apache.commons.logging.Log;
import org.apache.commons.logging.LogFactory;

import com.opensymphony.xwork.ActionSupport;

public abstract class HibernateAction
  extends ActionSupport
  implements HibernateSessionAware {
  private static final Log LOG =
    LogFactory.getLog(HibernateAction.class);
  private HibernateSession session;
  public String execute() throws Exception {
    if (hasErrors()) {
      LOG.debug("action not executed, field or action errors");
      LOG.debug("Field errors: " + getFieldErrors());
      LOG.debug("Action errors: " + getActionErrors());
      return INPUT;
    }
    LOG.debug("executing action");
    return go();
  }
  protected abstract String go() throws HibernateException;
  public void setHibernateSession(HibernateSession session) {
    this.session = session;
  }
  public HibernateSession getHibernateSession() {
    return session;
  }
  /**
   * Get the Hibernate Session instance
   */
  protected Session getSession() throws HibernateException {
    return session.getSession();
  }
  protected void setRollbackOnly() {
    session.setRollBackOnly(true);
  }
}
```

Now that you have seen all that the WebWork2 and Hibernate frameworks have to offer, it is time to move on to a more concrete example of using them — your contact manager.

Defining Your Domain Model

One of the first things you will do in your project is get your hands around what things your system will manage. Whether you call them entities or objects, and no matter where you store them (in a database or file system), there are still a set of conceptual classes that hold your system (and your business) together.

When it comes to defining your domain model, you have three things to consider:

❑   What domain objects already exist in the form of databases, documents, and so on?

❑   If I don't have them, what is available to help me make them up?

❑   What if my domain already exists, but is unsatisfactory for the users?

In essence, you generally fall into one of these two scenarios: Either you already are managing this data, in which case you are probably already in possession of a database, or you are starting from something new. The third way, having something already and needing something new, is the most painful.

Since data modeling and data migration are beyond the scope of this chapter (and book), focus instead on the domain on a basic model. Figure 8-6 demonstrates the conceptual classes for our small contact management system.

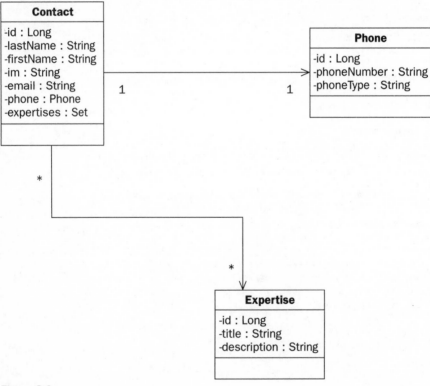

Figure 8-6

This model provides you with a basic capability to track a person and their relevant phone number and expertise. A person can be related to many expertise objects, but only one phone number, as well as the inverse being true. There are many experts in Java, and someone can be an expert in many things.

There are no methods represented in this diagram, although you could assign behaviors to domain objects if they were to make sense. An example of where you may want to capture a behavior would be something like a calculator object where you would have obvious domain behaviors. The diagram in Figure 8-6 demonstrates what is the primary domain of this application—storing information on contacts and their expertise.

Models really embody the core concept behind Object Oriented Programming, creating software objects that represent the system-relevant attributes and behaviors of a real-world object.

Now, the model is turned into a set of JavaBeans, with accessor and mutator methods (the "getters and setters"). For the sake of brevity, you will not have to look through all of them here, but instead they are provided with the source on the companion Web site.

Hibernate is going to handle our object persistence to a database, so you should take a look at the Hibernate mapping file to see how the object and the database model are resolved. In this first section, you declare your mapping package, and the first part of your first class, Contact. In there you define your basic properties and to which columns they bind. An interesting thing to note here: You are letting the database handle creating unique Ids for your contact objects, so you should leave the id property alone in your code. It will be null until the database assigns it an identifier:

```xml
<?xml version="1.0"?>
<!DOCTYPE hibernate-mapping PUBLIC
    "-//Hibernate/Hibernate Mapping DTD 2.0//EN"
    "http://hibernate.sourceforge.net/hibernate-mapping-2.0.dtd">
<hibernate-mapping package="org.advancedjava.ch08.model">
    <class name="Contact" table="contacts">
        <id name="id" column="ID"
            unsaved-value="null">
            <generator class="increment"/>
        </id>
        <property name="firstName" column="FIRST_NAME" />
        <property name="lastName" column="LAST_NAME"/>
        <property name="email" column="EMAIL"/>
        <property name="im" column="IM"/>
```

In this next section of code, you are mapping the set of Expertise objects for a given Contact. Note how it specifies your conventional many-to-many join table, with the key column referring to the key of the containing object and the many-to-many column referring to the key of the related class:

```xml
        <set name="expertises"
            table="contact_expertise"
            cascade="save-update">
            <!-- the foreign key of the Contact -->
            <key column="CONTACT_ID"/>
            <many-to-many column="EXPERTISE_ID"
                class="Expertise"/>
        </set>
```

The last section shows an example of mapping a complex type with a one-to-one relationship (`phone`), and then gives the mapping definitions for the other classes in our domain model. Note that generally mappings are defined each in its own file, but for brevity, they are defined together here. It is important to recognize that you must not define the same class twice:

```xml
            <one-to-one name="phone" cascade="all"/>
    </class>

    <class name="Expertise" table="expertise">
        <id name="id" column="ID"
            unsaved-value="null">
            <generator class="increment"/>
        </id>
        <property name="title" column="TITLE" />
        <property name="description" column="DESCRIPTION"/>
    </class>

    <class name="Phone" table="phone">
        <id name="id" column="ID"
            unsaved-value="null">
            <generator class="increment"/>
        </id>
        <property name="phoneNumber" column="PHONENUMBER" />
        <property name="phoneType" column="PHONETYPE"/>
    </class>
</hibernate-mapping>
```

Wait a second! You may be thinking that now you have to go and create the database, being careful to set everything up to match this mapping file. You may also be thinking: "There is no way I am going to do this myself for this little sample application, where is the SQL script to load this database?"

Not so fast. Now that you have defined the semantics of how the database should look, you can just use Hibernate's `SchemaExport` tool to create the database for you!

Along with the Hibernate distribution, there is a Windows batch file called `SchemaExport.bat` that looks a little like this (the actual paths are changed in this one from the one that ships with Hibernate):

```
@echo off
rem ------------------------------------------------------------------
rem Execute SchemaExport tool
rem ------------------------------------------------------------------

set JDBC_DRIVER=C:\jakarta-tomcat-4.1.24-LE-jdk14\webapps\contact\WEB-
INF\lib\mysql-connector-java-3.0.9-stable-bin.jar
set HIBERNATE_HOME=..
set LIB=%HIBERNATE_HOME%\lib
set PROPS=C:\jakarta-tomcat-4.1.24-LE-jdk14\webapps\contact\WEB-INF\classes
set CP=%JDBC_DRIVER%;%PROPS%;%HIBERNATE_HOME%\hibernate2.jar;%LIB%\commons-logging-
1.0.3.jar;%LIB%\commons-collections-2.1.jar;%LIB%\commons-lang-1.0.1.jar;%LIB%\cgli
b-2.0-rc2.jar;%LIB%\dom4j-1.4.jar;%LIB%\odmg-3.0.jar;%LIB%\xml-
apis.jar;%LIB%\xerces-2.4.0.jar;%LIB%\xalan-2.4.0.jar

java -cp %CP% net.sf.hibernate.tool.hbm2ddl.SchemaExport C:\jakarta-tomcat-4.1.24-
LE-jdk14\webapps\contact\WEB-INF\classes\org\advancedjava\ch08\model\Model.hbm.xml
```

If you are using Linux or Unix, it probably goes without saying that you would have to change this script for the shell that you use. It is incredibly unlikely that you would choose to use Linux or Unix without understanding any of the shells. In essence, you are just building a big Java command for the tool, so conceivably you could type all of this by hand (and probably still save time over writing the DDL by hand!)

Note that somewhere in the classpath it will look for a properties file to tell it how to configure Hibernate for your purposes. The one that comes with the Hibernate distribution has a tremendous number of options and examples, so this one is simplified for our purposes. Here is what that properties file will look like for your MySQL implementation:

```
hibernate.query.substitutions true 1, false 0, yes 'Y', no 'N'
hibernate.dialect net.sf.hibernate.dialect.MySQLDialect
hibernate.connection.driver_class com.mysql.jdbc.Driver
hibernate.connection.url jdbc:mysql:///contact
hibernate.connection.username root
hibernate.connection.password
hibernate.connection.pool_size 5

#Comment this out as soon as you have seen the SQL
hibernate.show_sql true

#Left these in here to set properties for hbm2ddl
#hibernate.hbm2ddl.auto create-drop
#hibernate.hbm2ddl.auto create
#hibernate.hbm2ddl.auto update

hibernate.jdbc.batch_size 0
hibernate.jdbc.use_streams_for_binary true
hibernate.max_fetch_depth 1

#If you are having Hibernate problems, set this to true
#very helpful for debug.
#hibernate.cglib.use_reflection_optimizer false
hibernate.cache.use_query_cache true
hibernate.cache.provider_class net.sf.ehcache.hibernate.Provider
```

Of course, most of the examples for other databases have been taken out for the sake of brevity, but you could easily substitute another database for this one. You will reuse this properties file later to configure your Web application:

```
<!DOCTYPE hibernate-configuration PUBLIC
    "-//Hibernate/Hibernate Configuration DTD//EN"
    "http://hibernate.sourceforge.net/hibernate-configuration-2.0.dtd">

<hibernate-configuration>
    <session-factory>
        <mapping resource="org/advancedjava/ch08/model/Model.hbm.xml"/>
    </session-factory>
</hibernate-configuration>
```

It is very interesting to see what happens when you run the `SchemaExport` utility, as it offers much insight into how Hibernate operates. In this first section, Hibernate does its setup and configuration:

```
C:\hibernate-2.1.4\bin>SchemaExport
Jun 12, 2004 3:15:46 PM net.sf.hibernate.cfg.Environment <clinit>
INFO: Hibernate 2.1.4
Jun 12, 2004 3:15:46 PM net.sf.hibernate.cfg.Environment <clinit>
INFO: loaded properties from resource hibernate.properties: {hibernate.connectio
n.driver_class=com.mysql.jdbc.Driver, hibernate.cglib.use_reflection_optimizer=t
rue, hibernate.cache.provider_class=net.sf.ehcache.hibernate.Provider, hibernate
.cache.use_query_cache=true, hibernate.max_fetch_depth=1, hibernate.dialect=net.
sf.hibernate.dialect.MySQLDialect, hibernate.jdbc.use_streams_for_binary=true, h
ibernate.jdbc.batch_size=0, hibernate.query.substitutions=true 1, false 0, yes '
Y', no 'N', hibernate.connection.username=root, hibernate.connection.url=jdbc:my
sql:///contact, hibernate.connection.password=, hibernate.connection.pool_size=5
}
Jun 12, 2004 3:15:46 PM net.sf.hibernate.cfg.Environment <clinit>
INFO: using java.io streams to persist binary types
Jun 12, 2004 3:15:46 PM net.sf.hibernate.cfg.Environment <clinit>
INFO: using CGLIB reflection optimizer
Jun 12, 2004 3:15:46 PM net.sf.hibernate.cfg.Configuration addFile
```

Now that it has configured the environment, it starts picking up the mapping files or, in this case, the only mapping file. On the first pass, it maps all of the entities, and then it does a second pass to map the relationships and constraints:

```
INFO: Mapping file: C:\jakarta-tomcat-4.1.24-LE-jdk14\webapps\contact\WEB-INF\cl
asses\org\advancedjava\ch08\model\Model.hbm.xml
Jun 12, 2004 3:15:46 PM net.sf.hibernate.cfg.Binder bindRootClass
INFO: Mapping class: org.advancedjava.ch08.model.Contact -> contacts
Jun 12, 2004 3:15:46 PM net.sf.hibernate.cfg.Binder bindCollection
INFO: Mapping collection: org.advancedjava.ch08.model.Contact.expertises -> cont
act_expertise
Jun 12, 2004 3:15:46 PM net.sf.hibernate.cfg.Binder bindRootClass
INFO: Mapping class: org.advancedjava.ch08.model.Expertise -> expertise
Jun 12, 2004 3:15:46 PM net.sf.hibernate.cfg.Binder bindRootClass
INFO: Mapping class: org.advancedjava.ch08.model.Phone -> phone
Jun 12, 2004 3:15:46 PM net.sf.hibernate.dialect.Dialect <init>
INFO: Using dialect: net.sf.hibernate.dialect.MySQLDialect
Jun 12, 2004 3:15:46 PM net.sf.hibernate.cfg.Configuration secondPassCompile
INFO: processing one-to-many association mappings
Jun 12, 2004 3:15:46 PM net.sf.hibernate.cfg.Configuration secondPassCompile
INFO: processing one-to-one association property references
Jun 12, 2004 3:15:46 PM net.sf.hibernate.cfg.Configuration secondPassCompile
INFO: processing foreign key constraints
Jun 12, 2004 3:15:46 PM net.sf.hibernate.cfg.Configuration secondPassCompile
INFO: processing one-to-many association mappings
Jun 12, 2004 3:15:46 PM net.sf.hibernate.cfg.Configuration secondPassCompile
INFO: processing one-to-one association property references
Jun 12, 2004 3:15:47 PM net.sf.hibernate.cfg.Configuration secondPassCompile
INFO: processing foreign key constraints
```

Here it sets up its database connection, using the specified parameters (This is a good place to check if your database isn't where you expect it.):

```
Jun 12, 2004 3:15:47 PM net.sf.hibernate.tool.hbm2ddl.SchemaExport execute
INFO: Running hbm2ddl schema export
Jun 12, 2004 3:15:47 PM net.sf.hibernate.tool.hbm2ddl.SchemaExport execute
INFO: exporting generated schema to database
Jun 12, 2004 3:15:47 PM net.sf.hibernate.connection.DriverManagerConnectionProvi
der configure
INFO: Using Hibernate built-in connection pool (not for production use!)
Jun 12, 2004 3:15:47 PM net.sf.hibernate.connection.DriverManagerConnectionProvi
der configure
INFO: Hibernate connection pool size: 5
Jun 12, 2004 3:15:47 PM net.sf.hibernate.connection.DriverManagerConnectionProvi
der configure
INFO: using driver: com.mysql.jdbc.Driver at URL: jdbc:mysql:///contact
Jun 12, 2004 3:15:47 PM net.sf.hibernate.connection.DriverManagerConnectionProvi
der configure
INFO: connection properties: {user=root, password=}
```

Finally, it spits out the SQL that it will execute and reports on its success with the export. It then reports that it is cleaning up after itself:

```
drop table if exists phone
drop table if exists contacts
drop table if exists contact_expertise
drop table if exists expertise
create table phone (ID BIGINT not null, PHONENUMBER VARCHAR(255), PHONETYPE VARC
HAR(255), primary key (ID))
create table contacts (ID BIGINT not null, FIRST_NAME VARCHAR(255), LAST_NAME VA
RCHAR(255), EMAIL VARCHAR(255), IM VARCHAR(255), primary key (ID))
create table contact_expertise (CONTACT_ID BIGINT not null, EXPERTISE_ID BIGINT
not null, primary key (CONTACT_ID, EXPERTISE_ID))
create table expertise (ID BIGINT not null, TITLE VARCHAR(255), DESCRIPTION VARC
HAR(255), primary key (ID))
alter table contact_expertise add index FK750E78B22540BDBA (CONTACT_ID), add con
straint FK750E78B22540BDBA foreign key (CONTACT_ID) references contacts (ID)
alter table contact_expertise add index FK750E78B2B1D44A29 (EXPERTISE_ID), add c
onstraint FK750E78B2B1D44A29 foreign key (EXPERTISE_ID) references expertise (ID
)
Jun 12, 2004 3:15:47 PM net.sf.hibernate.tool.hbm2ddl.SchemaExport execute
INFO: schema export complete
Jun 12, 2004 3:15:47 PM net.sf.hibernate.connection.DriverManagerConnectionProvi
der close
INFO: cleaning up connection pool: jdbc:mysql:///contact
```

In this case, you are using the MySQL database, so you can execute the Show Tables command and view that they were actually created:

```
mysql> show tables;
+-------------------+
| Tables_in_contact |
+-------------------+
| contact_expertise |
```

(continued)

```
| contacts           |
| expertise          |
| phone              |
+--------------------+
5 rows in set (0.01 sec)
```

Now that you have handled the domain model for this application, it is time to bring this application to life and actually do something by implementing your Action classes.

Implementing Your Use Cases with Actions

So now what is it that your system does? Your use cases describe what a user hopes to achieve through interacting with your system. They describe the behavior of your system, or the actions that your system can provide. Now, the chicken and egg argument is only slightly older than the old software argument concerning whether you should describe your system's behavior or structure first. In this case, you have described the structure first for two reasons:

1. This sample is an overwhelmingly data-centric application.

2. Because it is a data-centric application, the easiest way to restrict the scope is to define the data first.

Now, you develop the use cases that comprise this application. Here is a set of use cases for the system.

Use Case	Description
Browse Contacts	If you specify a given expertise, it will display the contacts that have that expertise.
Add Contact	Gather the relevant information to add a contact to the contact manager.
Remove Contact	Remove a contact from the contact manager.

Each of these use cases maps into an XWork Action. Here is the XWork Action used to handle the Browse Contacts use case. The interesting points about it are

❑ It is just one plain old Java object; its simplicity is that it has methods for accessing and mutating its member variables and a go method to handle executing its intended function.

❑ It extends HibernateAction providing easy access to the Hibernate framework.

❑ It only takes a handful of lines of code to implement the use case. Even novice developers could start doing the basics very quickly. In this case, you execute a query based on the Id of the expertise for which you seek to find Contacts, and assign it to your List of contacts. Simply return SUCCESS; if anything should fail in terms of the database, query, and so on, it will be handled by the HibernateInterceptor:

```
package org.advancedjava.ch08;
import java.util.List;
import net.sf.hibernate.HibernateException;
import net.sf.hibernate.Query;
public class BrowseContactAction extends HibernateAction {
```

```
    private Integer expertiseId;
    private List contacts;
    public String go() throws HibernateException {
      Query q =
        getSession().createQuery(
          "select con from Contact con  join con.expertises as exp where exp.id =
:ids");
      q.setParameter("ids", expertiseId);
      contacts = q.list();
      return SUCCESS;
    }
    /**
     * @return
     */
    public List getContacts() {
      return contacts;
    }
    /**
     * @return
     */
    public Integer getExpertiseId() {
      return expertiseId;
    }
    /**
     * @param list
     */
    public void setContacts(List list) {
      contacts = list;
    }
    /**
     * @param integer
     */
    public void setExpertiseId(Integer integer) {
      expertiseId = integer;
    }
}
```

Of course, there is nothing to browse if you do not add contacts to the database. Here is the Action that adds a Contact into the database. Note a couple of interesting things here:

❑ You are not handling the individual form elements or parameters and mapping them into the domain objects. WebWork is doing that for you, along with the tedious type conversion code.

❑ Since you only got the Ids for the types of expertise, you need to pull the actual objects from the database and assign them as a set to your Contact object.

```
package org.advancedjava.ch08;
import java.util.HashSet;
import net.sf.hibernate.HibernateException;
import net.sf.hibernate.Query;
import org.advancedjava.ch08.model.Contact;
import org.advancedjava.ch08.model.Phone;
public class AddContactAction extends HibernateAction {
  private Integer[] selectedExpertises;
  private Contact contact;
```

```
    private Phone phone;
    public AddContactAction() {
      contact = new Contact();
      phone = new Phone();
    }
    public String go() throws HibernateException {
      Query q =
        getSession().createQuery(
          "from Expertise exp where exp.id in (:ids)");
      q.setParameterList("ids", selectedExpertises);
      contact.setExpertises(new HashSet(q.list()));
      contact.setPhone(phone);
      getSession().save(contact);
      return SUCCESS;
    }
```

The remainder of this code demonstrates just the conventional accessor and mutator methods of the object. Though frequently overlooked, and rarely considered very seriously, you must not forget them when they are necessary, and with two frameworks like Hibernate and WebWork that make such extensive use of reflection, they are very often necessary:

```
/**
 * @return
 */
public Contact getContact() {
  return contact;
}
/**
 * @return
 */
public Phone getPhone() {
  return phone;
}
/**
 * @return
 */
public Integer[] getSelectedExpertises() {
  return selectedExpertises;
}
/**
 * @param contact
 */
public void setContact(Contact contact) {
  this.contact = contact;
}
/**
 * @param phone
 */
public void setPhone(Phone phone) {
  this.phone = phone;
}
/**
```

```
    * @param integers
    */
   public void setSelectedExpertises(Integer[] integers) {
     selectedExpertises = integers;
   }
}
```

Of course, note that you could have written validation rules in your code, but instead it is easier to leverage XWork's validation framework. Here is the validation XML file for this Action. It is pretty straightforward; you specify the types of validators that you wish to apply to each field, as well as a message if it fails. You can consult XWork's documentation for all of its validation features:

```xml
<!DOCTYPE validators
    PUBLIC "-//OpenSymphony Group//XWork Validator 1.0//EN"
    "http://www.opensymphony.com/xwork/xwork-validator-1.0.dtd">

<validators>
    <field name="contact.firstName">
        <field-validator type="requiredstring">
            <message>You must enter a first name.</message>
        </field-validator>
    </field>
    <field name="contact.lastName">
        <field-validator type="requiredstring">
            <message>You must enter a last name.</message>
        </field-validator>
    </field>
    <field name="contact.email">
        <field-validator type="email">
            <message>Please correct the e-mail address.</message>
        </field-validator>
        <field-validator type="required">
            <message>Please enter an e-mail address.</message>
        </field-validator>
    </field>
</validators>
```

These `Action` classes provide the core business logic of your application, but no application would be complete without considering the user interface.

Developing Your Views

Now, it is time to specify what the user will see as they traverse through the Web application. You will now describe your system's user interface. Given different actions, what will the user see? In Figure 8-7, you have a drawing of how this Web application flows.

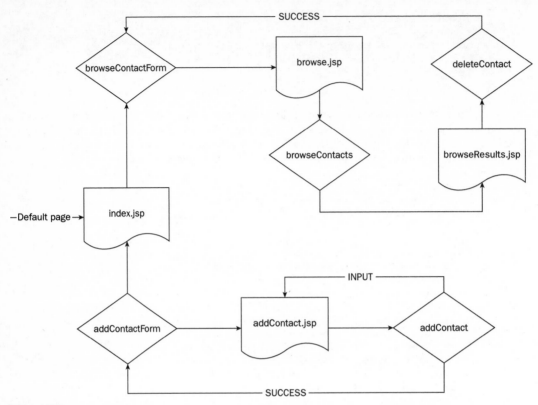

Figure 8-7

The flow starts with the default page of the Web application (specified just like any other J2EE Web application, in the web.xml file) — index.jsp. This page just serves as the front page for the application, which gives you links to your two major branches of the application: browsing contacts and adding contacts. Figure 8-8 shows you the simplicity of this page.

As you start to mock up your view elements, it becomes obvious that you will need to pull expertise data in order to populate the lists of expertise available in order to assign to a given contact, or by which to browse your contacts. Thus, based on these views, you have now derived two use cases in support of them.

Derived Use Case	Description
Browse Contact Form	This action will retrieve the relevant domain information required to build the browse contact view. In this case, it will just be a list of types of expertise.
Add Contact Form	In the same way, you will need to gather that expertise list in order to provide the user with the ability to assign which types of expertise a contact brings.

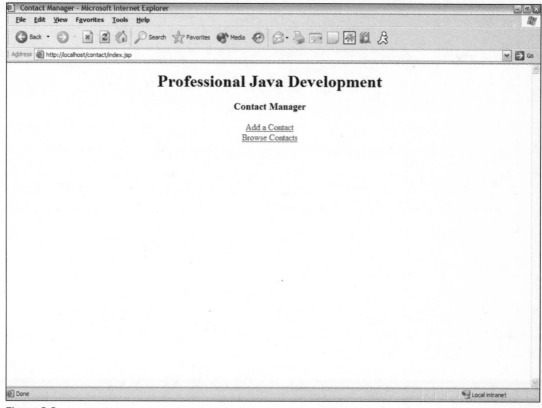

Figure 8-8

Often in situations like this one, where you have use cases specified simply to build the view, you will make a small departure from Model 2 purity and allow these pages to call their own application code specific to just building the view. WebWork provides the ability to reference its Actions and framework from within its WebWork JSP custom tags. However, for the sake of this chapter, since you used JSP custom tags extensively in the last chapter, you will use the pure approach.

Adding Contacts to the System

In order to browse the contacts in the system, first you must add some contacts to the system. Following the Add a Contact link on the Web application's homepage leads you to this screen, displayed in Figure 8-9.

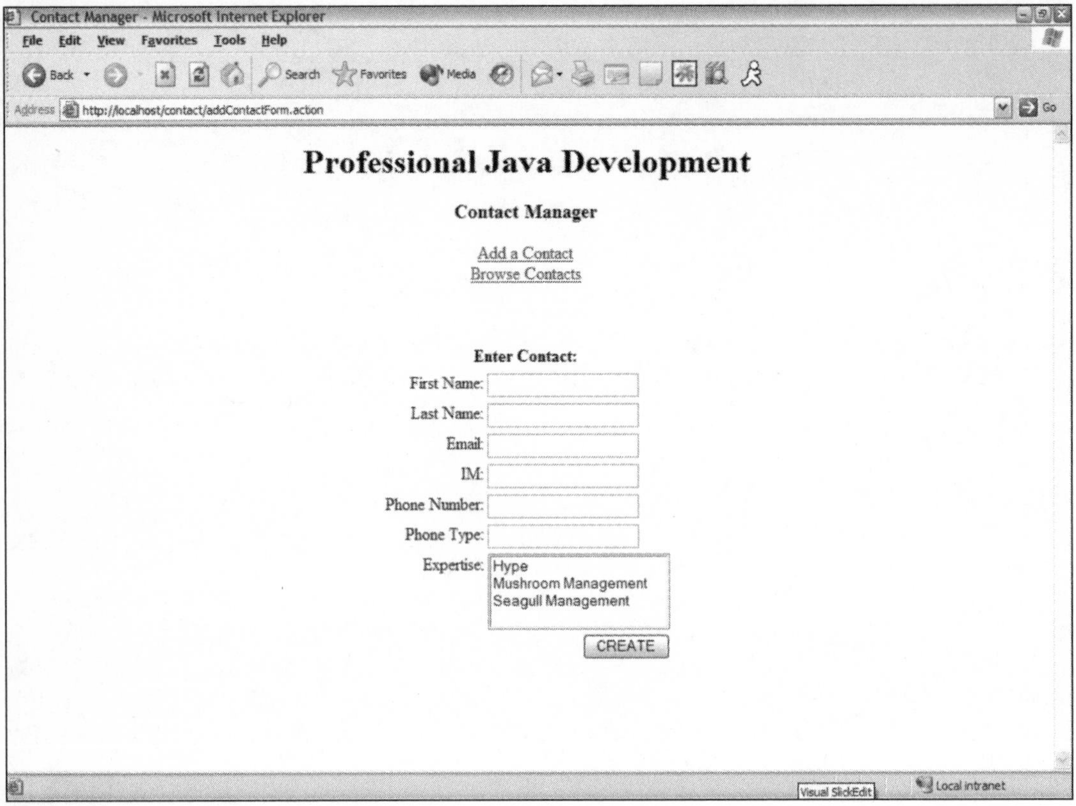

Figure 8-9

Here is addContact.jsp, which renders the input form. The important point to take away from this important form is how it maps onto your Action class, right down to the internal attributes of its domain objects (like Contact and Phone).

```
<%@ taglib prefix="ww" uri="webwork" %>
<jsp:include page="index.jsp"/>
<table cellspacing="0" cellpadding="0" border="0">
    <tr>
        <th>Enter Contact:</th>
    </tr>
    <tr>
        <td class="mask">
  <ww:form name="'createContactForm'"
               action="'addContact.action'" method="'POST'">
      <ww:textfield label="'First Name'" name="'contact.firstName'"/>
      <ww:textfield label="'Last Name'" name="'contact.lastName'"/>
      <ww:textfield label="'Email'" name="'contact.email'"/>
      <ww:textfield label="'IM'" name="'contact.im'"/>
      <ww:textfield label="'Phone Number'" name="'phone.phoneNumber'"/>
      <ww:textfield label="'Phone Type'" name="'phone.phoneType'"/>
```

```
            <ww:select label="'Expertise'" name="'selectedExpertises'"
                        listKey="id"
                        listValue="title"
                        list="expertises"
                        multiple="true"
            />
    <ww:submit value="'CREATE'" />
    </ww:form>
        </td>
    </tr>
</table>
```

Of course, after you submit your new Contact, it brings you right back to the same page, with the form already filled in. This would be an ill-advised thing in production, but for a personal use system, it would probably save some data entry. Either way, in this case, you are just doing this to reduce the scope of the application so it can focus on the critical concepts of Model 2.

Browsing Contacts

Now that you have contacts, you can browse through them based on their expertise. Clicking on "Browse Contacts" leads you to the screen displayed in Figure 8-10.

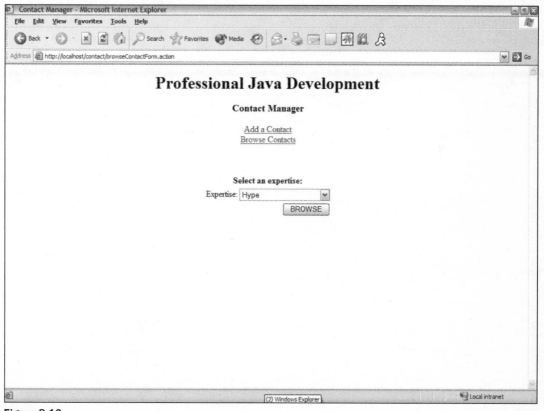

Figure 8-10

This page was built by using the Browse Contact Form use case, which provides an opportunity to demonstrate how to map the domain object into a Select box. Here is the code for browse.jsp. Note how the WebWork select tag maps to the List of Expertise objects that this page renders. The listKey attribute provides the value for each of the options within the HTML select, while the listValue provides the display value:

```
<%@ taglib prefix="ww" uri="webwork" %>
<jsp:include page="index.jsp"/>
<table cellspacing="0" cellpadding="0" border="0">
    <tr>
        <th>Select an expertise:</th>
    </tr>
    <tr>
        <td class="mask">
    <ww:form name="'browseContactForm'"
                    action="'browseContacts.action'" method="'POST'">
    <ww:select label="'Expertise'" name="'expertiseId'"
                    listKey="id"
                    listValue="title"
                    list="expertises"
            />
    <ww:submit value="'BROWSE'" />
    </ww:form>
        </td>
    </tr>
</table>
```

When you submit this page, you get a table of contacts with their relevant information. This table is shown in Figure 8-11.

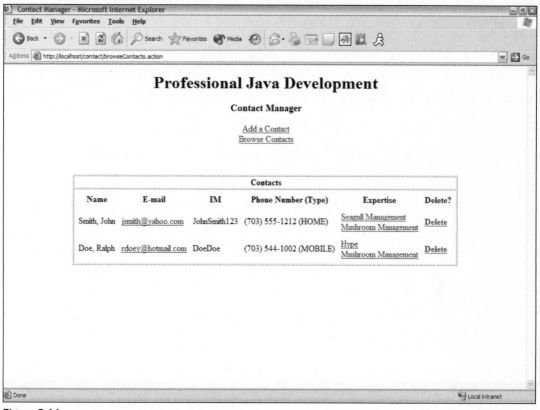

Figure 8-11

This screen is rendered by `browseContacts.jsp`. In it you see the use of the WebWork `iterator` tags to traverse the list of contacts and print out the relevant details about each contact:

```
<%@ taglib prefix="ww" uri="webwork" %>
<jsp:include page="index.jsp"/>
<table cellspacing="1" cellpadding="1" border="">
  <tr>
    <th>Contacts</th>
  </tr>
  <tr>
    <td class="mask">
      <table cellspacing="4" cellpadding="4">
        <tr>
          <th>Name</th>
          <th>E-mail</th>
          <th>IM</th>
          <th>Phone Number (Type)</th>
          <th>Expertise</th>
          <th>Delete?</th>
        </tr>
        <ww:iterator id="curContact" value="contacts">
```

```
        <tr>
          <td>
            <ww:property value="firstName"/>, <ww:property value="lastName"/>
          </td>
          <td><a href="mailto:<ww:property value="email"/>"/>
            <ww:property value="email"/>
            </a></td>
          <td>
            <ww:property value="im"/>
          </td>
          <td>
            <ww:property value="phone.phoneNumber"/>
            (
            <ww:property value="phone.phoneType"/>
            )</td>
          <td>
            <ww:iterator id="expertiseCur" value="expertises">
            <a href="browseContacts.action?expertiseId=<ww:property value="id"/>">
            <ww:property value="title"/>
            <br>
            </a>
            </ww:iterator>
          </td>
          <td><a href="deleteContact.action?selectedContact=<ww:property
value="id"/>">
            <b>Delete</b></a></td>
        </tr>
        </ww:iterator>
      </table>
    </td>
  </tr>
</table>
```

Of course, the link to Delete will remove a given Contact from the database, but it returns the user back to the Browse Contacts screen, so it is unnecessary to review again.

Now that you have put together all of the components of a WebWork application, you need to review how to configure all of them to work together.

Configuring Your Application

In putting together all of these components that you have built using the WebWork framework, the first thing to remember is that WebWork is a J2EE Web application first and foremost. Therefore, it is useful to start with the Web application deployment descriptor, commonly called the web.xml:

```
<?xml version="1.0" encoding="ISO-8859-1"?>

<!DOCTYPE web-app
    PUBLIC "-//Sun Microsystems, Inc.//DTD Web Application 2.3//EN"
    "http://java.sun.com/dtd/web-app_2_3.dtd">

<web-app>
```

```
        <display-name>Contact manager</display-name>
        <description>Example of Model 2 using Hibernate</description>
        <filter>
            <filter-name>container</filter-name>
            <filter-
class>com.opensymphony.webwork.lifecycle.RequestLifecycleFilter</filter-class>
        </filter>
        <filter-mapping>
            <filter-name>container</filter-name>
            <url-pattern>/*</url-pattern>
        </filter-mapping>
        <listener>
            <listener-
class>com.opensymphony.webwork.lifecycle.ApplicationLifecycleListener</listener-cla
ss>
        </listener>
        <listener>
            <listener-
class>com.opensymphony.webwork.lifecycle.SessionLifecycleListener</listener-class>
        </listener>
        <servlet>
            <servlet-name>velocity</servlet-name>
            <servlet-
class>com.opensymphony.webwork.views.velocity.WebWorkVelocityServlet</servlet-class
>
            <load-on-startup>1</load-on-startup>
        </servlet>
        <servlet>
            <servlet-name>webwork</servlet-name>
            <servlet-
class>com.opensymphony.webwork.dispatcher.ServletDispatcher</servlet-class>
        </servlet>
        <servlet-mapping>
            <servlet-name>webwork</servlet-name>
            <url-pattern>*.action</url-pattern>
        </servlet-mapping>
        <servlet-mapping>
            <servlet-name>velocity</servlet-name>
            <url-pattern>*.vm</url-pattern>
        </servlet-mapping>
        <welcome-file-list>
            <welcome-file>index.jsp</welcome-file>
        </welcome-file-list>
        <taglib>
            <taglib-uri>webwork</taglib-uri>
            <taglib-location>/WEB-INF/webwork.tld</taglib-location>
        </taglib>
</web-app>
```

Note that the WebWork wrapper to XWork is composed of a servlet filter, a listener, two servlets, and a tag library. You could always modify the mappings as you see fit, for example, if you prefer to make your actions more like those of Struts and end in .do, rather than .action.

The XWork framework, of course, defines the flow of the application, and that is defined within the xwork.xml file:

```
<!DOCTYPE xwork
    PUBLIC "-//OpenSymphony Group//XWork 1.0//EN"
    "http://www.opensymphony.com/xwork/xwork-1.0.dtd">
<xwork>
    <include file="webwork-default.xml"/>
    <package name="default" extends="webwork-default">
        <default-interceptor-ref name="defaultStack"/>
        <action name="browseContactForm"
class="org.advancedjava.ch08.BrowseContactFormAction">
            <result name="success" type="dispatcher">
                <param name="location">/browse.jsp</param>
            </result>
            <interceptor-ref name="defaultStack"/>
        </action>
        <action name="addContactForm"
class="org.advancedjava.ch08.AddContactFormAction">
            <result name="success" type="dispatcher">
                <param name="location">/addContact.jsp</param>
            </result>
            <interceptor-ref name="defaultStack"/>
        </action>
        <action name="addContact" class="org.advancedjava.ch08.AddContactAction">
            <result name="input" type="dispatcher">
                <param name="location">/addContact.jsp</param>
            </result>
            <result name="success" type="chain">
                <param name="actionName">addContactForm</param>
            </result>
            <interceptor-ref name="defaultStack"/>
            <interceptor-ref name="validation"/>
        </action>
        <action name="browseContacts"
class="org.advancedjava.ch08.BrowseContactAction">
            <result name="success" type="dispatcher">
                <param name="location">/browseResults.jsp</param>
            </result>
            <interceptor-ref name="defaultStack"/>
        </action>
        <action name="deleteContact"
class="org.advancedjava.ch08.DeleteContactAction">
            <result name="success" type="chain">
                <param name="actionName">browseContactForm</param>
            </result>
            <interceptor-ref name="defaultStack"/>
        </action>
    </package>
</xwork>
```

As you learned earlier in the chapter, WebWork provides the ability to inject dependencies into a Web application, which was used to strap Hibernate into the application. In the components.xml, you specify the components and the enabler interfaces:

```
<components>
    <component>
        <scope>request</scope>
        <class>org.advancedjava.ch08.component.HibernateSession</class>
        <enabler>org.advancedjava.ch08.component.HibernateSessionAware</enabler>
    </component>
    <component>
        <scope>application</scope>
        <class>org.advancedjava.ch08.component.HibernateSessionFactory</class>
        <enabler>org.advancedjava.ch08.component.HibernateSessionFactoryAware
</enabler>
    </component>
</components>
```

Now, that you have built the components and configured the application, you are ready to deploy and use your application.

Adapting to Changes

Now that the contact manager is up and running, what if you wanted to add an attribute to your `Contact` object? Since your application has become so wildly successful, you have forgotten who all of these contacts are and need to add a description to your contact. To accomplish this, change the UML diagram in Figure 8-6 to look like Figure 8-12.

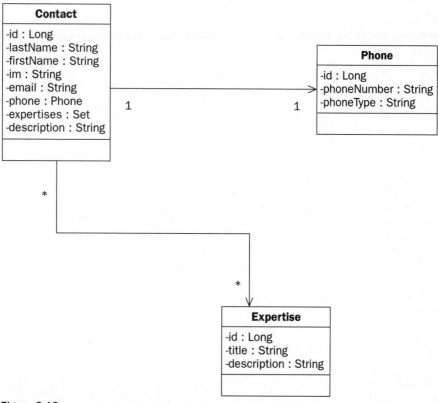

Figure 8-12

397

Of course, you would have to modify the Hibernate mapping file to accommodate the change to the domain model. Here is the change to `Model.hbm.xml`:

```xml
<?xml version="1.0"?>
<!DOCTYPE hibernate-mapping PUBLIC
    "-//Hibernate/Hibernate Mapping DTD 2.0//EN"
    "http://hibernate.sourceforge.net/hibernate-mapping-2.0.dtd">
<hibernate-mapping package="org.advancedjava.ch08.model">
    <class name="Contact" table="contacts">
        <id name="id" column="ID"
            unsaved-value="null">
            <generator class="increment"/>
        </id>
        <property name="firstName" column="FIRST_NAME" />
        <property name="lastName" column="LAST_NAME"/>
        <property name="email" column="EMAIL"/>
        <property name="description" column="DESCRIPTION"/>
        <property name="im" column="IM"/>
```

Now, that you have added your addition column, you could do one of two things: You can modify the database schema by hand, or you can run Hibernate's `SchemaUpdate` tool to resynchronize your database with your Hibernate mappings.

Once you have gotten your database and mappings back up to date, you will need a place to enter the data. This is the change to your `addContact.jsp` file:

```jsp
<%@ taglib prefix="ww" uri="webwork" %>
<jsp:include page="index.jsp"/>
<table cellspacing="0" cellpadding="0" border="0">
    <tr>
        <th>Enter Contact:</th>
    </tr>
    <tr>
        <td class="mask">
    <ww:form name="'createContactForm'"
            action="'addContact.action'" method="'POST'">
    <ww:textfield label="'First Name'" name="'contact.firstName'"/>
    <ww:textfield label="'Last Name'" name="'contact.lastName'"/>
    <ww:textfield label="'Email'" name="'contact.email'"/>
    <ww:textfield label="'IM'" name="'contact.im'"/>
    <ww:textfield label="'Description'" name="'contact.description'"/>
    <ww:textfield label="'Phone Number'" name="'phone.phoneNumber'"/>
    <ww:textfield label="'Phone Type'" name="'phone.phoneType'"/>
    <ww:select label="'Expertise'" name="'selectedExpertises'"
                    listKey="id"
                    listValue="title"
                    list="expertises"
                    multiple="true"
        />
    <ww:submit value="'CREATE'" />
    </ww:form>
        </td>
    </tr>
</table>
```

Other than the obvious change to your `Contact.java`, that is all you need to do in order to add an attribute to your model. This is the key point in using the Model 2 Architecture: Modularity allows flexibility.

Summary

You have built a contact manager using the Model 2 Architecture leveraging WebWork framework (and Inversion of Control) to add support for the Hibernate Object persistance framework. While the application is simplified in order to keep the examples easy to understand, it clearly demonstrates how you can easily adapt your application to new requirements.

In this chapter, you learned the following things:

❑   Web applications do not have to be developed using a page-centric approach, but rather there is an approach towards building modular Web applications known as the Model 2 Architecture.

❑   In a popular Web application framework called WebWork, the Model 2 Architecture is combined with a concept known as Inversion of Control, to allow Plain Old Java Objects (POJOs) to implement your functionality independent of the burdens of configuring external components.

❑   The modularity of WebWork allows you to plug in useful tools like Hibernate to build very streamlined applications that focus directly on your business domain.

The next chapter will discuss how to leverage code developed in other languages through the Java Native Interface.

Interacting with C/C++ Using Java Native Interface

This chapter discusses connecting Java programs to programs written in C/C++. Java Native Interface (JNI) provides a sophisticated mechanism for invoking routines written in native code, and also provides a mechanism for native code to call routines that are written in Java.

A First Look at Java Native Interface

Creating a Java program that uses native code is fundamentally simple. First, you write the Java code and mark certain methods as *native* and leave the method un-implemented (as if you were writing an abstract method). Next, you run a utility that comes with the JDK to create a C/C++ header file. The native methods are then implemented in C/C++, with signatures matching the version in the generated header file. The Java code must then load this library in order to obtain access to the native routines. This process is illustrated in Figure 9-1.

To get a basic idea of how to write a program using JNI, create a small library of math routines implemented in C++ and invoke this from Java.

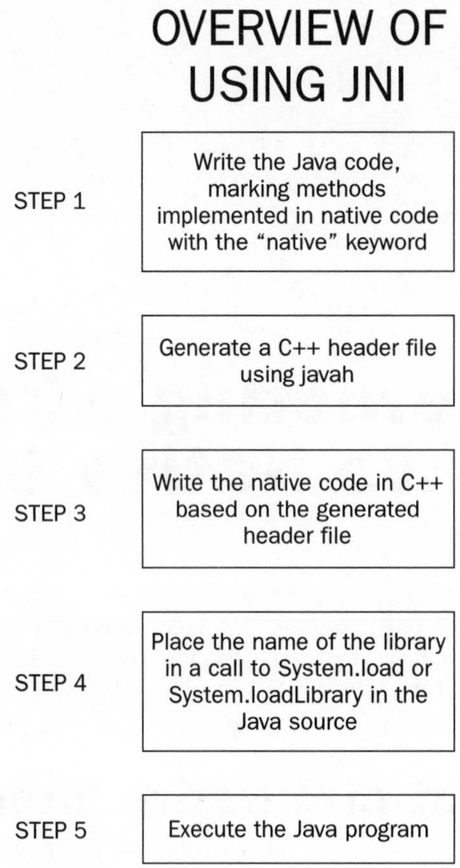

OVERVIEW OF USING JNI

STEP 1

> Write the Java code, marking methods implemented in native code with the "native" keyword

STEP 2

> Generate a C++ header file using javah

STEP 3

> Write the native code in C++ based on the generated header file

STEP 4

> Place the name of the library in a call to System.load or System.loadLibrary in the Java source

STEP 5

> Execute the Java program

Figure 9-1

Creating the Java Code

The Java code is straightforward. Two methods are created, `addTwoNumbers` and `multiplyTwoNumbers`. These methods have no method bodies and are marked with the native keyword:

```java
public class JNIMathClient {
    public native int addTwoNumbers(int one, int two);
    public native int multiplyTwoNumbers(int one, int two);

    static {
        System.loadLibrary("MathLibrary");
    }

    public static void main(String args[])
    {
        JNIMathClient client = new JNIMathClient();
```

```
        int num1, num2;

        num1 = 5;
        num2 = 100;
        System.out.println(num1 + " + " + num2 + " = " +
                           client.addTwoNumbers(num1, num2));
        System.out.println(num1 + " * " + num2 + " = " +
                           client.multiplyTwoNumbers(num1, num2));
    }
}
```

The rest of the Java program is written as expected. The native methods are called as if they were normally implemented routines in Java. The static initializer is used to ensure the native library is loaded before it can be used inside the program. The discussion of the loadLibrary call is saved for the next section since it requires details of the native library.

Creating the Native Code and Library

In order to write the code in C++, javah—a tool that comes with the JDK—must be used to generate a header file. This header file contains the prototypes for the functions that must be implemented in C++. The Java code is first compiled and then this tool is executed on the class file. You execute javah by specifying the name of the class (not a filename) as the first parameter. The output of javah is a header file that has the same name as the class, and h as the file extension.

The resulting header file after executing javah JNIMathClient is JNIMathClient.h:

```
/* DO NOT EDIT THIS FILE - it is machine generated */
#include <jni.h>
/* Header for class JNIMathClient */

#ifndef _Included_JNIMathClient
#define _Included_JNIMathClient
#ifdef __cplusplus
extern "C" {
#endif
/*
 * Class:     JNIMathClient
 * Method:    addTwoNumbers
 * Signature: (II)I
 */
JNIEXPORT jint JNICALL Java_JNIMathClient_addTwoNumbers
  (JNIEnv *, jobject, jint, jint);

/*
 * Class:     JNIMathClient
 * Method:    multiplyTwoNumbers
 * Signature: (II)I
 */
JNIEXPORT jint JNICALL Java_JNIMathClient_multiplyTwoNumbers
  (JNIEnv *, jobject, jint, jint);

#ifdef __cplusplus
}
#endif
#endif
```

Each native method declaration is translated into a counterpart in C++. Each function always takes as its first two parameters a handle to the Java VM environment and a handle to the object that called the native method. Each parameter after those are the parameters specified in the original declaration of the function in the Java code.

After creating the header file, it can then be used in a C++ project. Using Visual Studio 6.0, create a simple DLL project and include this header file. Implementing the functions is a simple matter of copying the function signatures and filling in the bodies.

Select File ⇨ New and navigate to the Projects tab. Choose Win32 Dynamic-Link Library and give it a name. Figure 9-2 shows an example. On the first step of the wizard, choose A Simple DLL Project in order to already have the boilerplate code for a DLL. Click on Finish and then OK. Look at Figure 9-2 to see these options chosen in the Visual C++ wizard.

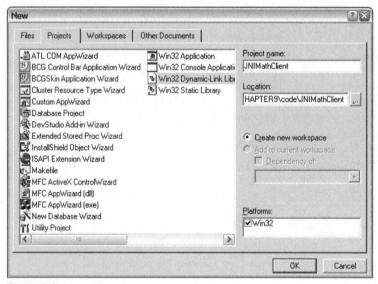

Figure 9-2

Continuing this example, the routines in the source file MathLibrary.cpp will be filled in. Don't forget to include the generated header file at the top of the source file:

```
// MathLibrary.cpp : Defines the entry point for the DLL application.
//

#include "stdafx.h"
#include "..\JNIMathClient.h"

JNIEXPORT jint JNICALL Java_JNIMathClient_addTwoNumbers
  (JNIEnv *, jobject, jint one, jint two)
{
    return(one + two);
```

```
}

JNIEXPORT jint JNICALL Java_JNIMathClient_multiplyTwoNumbers
  (JNIEnv *, jobject, jint one, jint two)
{
    return(one * two);
}

BOOL APIENTRY DllMain( HANDLE hModule,
                       DWORD  ul_reason_for_call,
                       LPVOID lpReserved
                     )
{
   return TRUE;
}
```

After the native methods are implemented in C++, build the project. If there are no errors, you end up with a DLL file. This is the native library that then must be referenced in a call to System.load or System.loadLibrary. The library must be in the same directory as the Java program, or found somewhere in the paths specified in the system property java.library.path. If you use System.loadLibrary, specify only the base name of the native library — don't include the extension or a path. If you use System.load, you can specify a full path and must specify the extension of the library. The name of the library has nothing to do with the routines inside it, so feel free to name this file anything you want, but preserve the extension.

Executing the Code

If all is configured correctly, executing the Java code loads the native library, calls the routines, and uses the returned results. Executing the above Java code provides the following output:

```
5 + 100 = 105
5 * 100 = 500
```

If the library (MathLibrary.dll) is not found, you will end up with the following error:

```
java.lang.UnsatisfiedLinkError: no MathLibrary in java.library.path
    at java.lang.ClassLoader.loadLibrary(ClassLoader.java:1644)
    at java.lang.Runtime.loadLibrary0(Runtime.java:817)
    at java.lang.System.loadLibrary(System.java:986)
    at JNIMathClient.<clinit>(JNIMathClient.java:7)
Exception in thread "main"
```

You will also get this error if you try to use the native routines before you've called System.load or System.loadLibrary. By placing this call in the static initializer, you ensure the native library will be loaded well before it is needed.

> Prototypes, also known as function signatures, follow a specific naming convention. The full package name comes first (following the prefix _Java) with each dot replaced with an underscore, then the name of the class, another underscore, then the name of the method. A native method named addNumbers defined in a package com.mathlib and inside a class named Math becomes _Java_com_mathlib_Math_addNumbers in the header file.

Java Native Interface

JNI provides many functions, such as string and array handling, and a complete set of functions to create and use Java objects. These functions all take a pointer to the Java environment as the first parameter. However, in order to simplify programming, these functions all have an alias that is defined in the JNIEnv structure. This means you can invoke any JNI function by calling it through the pointer to the JNI environment. The rest of this chapter describes functions that are defined in this structure instead of the full version that includes this first parameter. Each function's full declaration will precede its explanation throughout the rest of this chapter.

Data Types

The most important aspect of interfacing with other languages is the treatment of various data types such as strings. Different languages store strings in different ways. For example, character array strings in C and C++ are null-terminated. Strings in Java store the length separately, but are also 0-indexed. JNI provides a number of functions to manipulate strings, described in detail later. The primitive data types are provided with natural analogs on the native side. Consult the following table to see how data types in Java translate to types in C++.

Primitive Type	Native Type	Size (Bits)
boolean	jboolean	8, unsigned
byte	jbyte	8
char	jchar	16, unsigned
short	jshort	16
int	jint	32
long	jlong	64
float	jfloat	32
double	jdouble	64
void	void	n/a

Strings in JNI

The jstring data type is used to handle Java strings in C/C++. This type should not be used directly. If you try to use it in a call to printf (a C function to output text to the screen), for example, you run the risk of crashing the Java virtual machine. The jstring must first be converted to a C-string using one of several string conversion functions that JNI provides.

Java passes strings to the native environment in a slightly modified UTF-8 format. Take a look at Figure 9-3 to see how UTF-8 characters are organized in memory. If the high bit is set for a particular byte, the byte is part of a multibyte character. This means that ASCII characters from value 1 to 127 stay the same, and though you can't count on it, if all the characters in the jstring are in this range, you can use the jstring directly in C/C++ code. Java does not use UTF-8 characters longer than three bytes, and the null character (ASCII 0) is represented by two bytes, not one. This means you will never have a character that has all its bits set to 0.

UTF-8 Character Encoding

A single byte accounts for
characters in the range \u0001
to \u007F. The high bit is
always 0.

0 (Bit 7)	Bits 0-6

Two bytes account for
characters in the range \u0080
to \u07FF, and the null
character, \u0000

1	1	0	Bits 6-10		1	0	Bits 0-5

High Byte   Low Byte

Three bytes account for
characters in the range \u0800
to \uFFFF

1	1	1	0	Bits 12-15		1	0	Bits 6-11		1	0	Bits 0-5

High Byte   Low Byte

Figure 9-3

There are also routines that work with Unicode strings. Unicode characters always take up two bytes. If you're writing a program that uses localized strings, always handle your strings in Unicode since UTF-8 does not support internationalization. There are five functions that work with UTF-8 strings, and each has a counterpart for Unicode strings. Two additional functions round out the set of string functions. These last two functions obtain a lock or release a lock on the string for purposes of synchronizing strings when in a threaded environment. Each string function takes as its first parameter a pointer to the Java environment. This is already passed in when a native function is called, so this is easily available:

```
jstring NewString(const jchar *unicodeChars, jsize len);
jstring NewStringUTF(const char *bytes);
```

The Unicode version of NewString takes a sequence of characters (jchar, which is two bytes) and the length in number of characters (not number of bytes). The UTF version simply takes a sequence of bytes.

Each byte may form part of a one-, two- or three-byte character, and the end of the string is marked by a two-byte NULL character:

```
jsize GetStringLength(jstring string);
jsize GetStringUTFLength(jstring string);
```

Both the Unicode and UTF versions of GetStringLength take a jstring and return its size in number of characters:

```
const jchar *GetStringChars(jstring string, jboolean *isCopy);
const char *GetStringUTFChars(jstring string, jboolean *isCopy);
```

These two GetStringChars functions return a pointer to the sequence of characters in a specified jstring. These are the main functions used to take a jstring and turn it into a string that can be easily used in native code. The pointer is valid until the accompanying version of `ReleaseStringChars` is invoked. The Unicode version returns a pointer to jchar, and the UTF returns a pointer to jbyte. The `isCopy` parameter is set to JNI_TRUE if a copy of the string is made, or set to NULL or JNI_FALSE if no copy is made:

```
void ReleaseStringChars(jstring string, const jchar *chars);
void ReleaseStringUTFChars(jstring string, const char *utf);
```

Invoking one of the ReleaseStringChars functions tells the VM that the native code no longer needs to use the character sequence obtained in the call to the accompanying version GetStringChars. The pointer to the characters is no longer valid after this function is called. The original string must be passed in along with the pointer obtained from the GetStringChars call:

```
void GetStringRegion(jstring str, jsize start, jsize len, jchar *buf);
void GetStringUTFRegion(jstring str, jsize start, jsize len, char *buf);
```

The GetStringRegion functions transfer a substring of the string `str` to a character buffer. The substring starts at position `start` and stops at len-1 (therefore transferring len number of characters). This may throw a StringIndexOutOfBoundsException:

```
const jchar *GetStringCritical(jstring string, jboolean *isCopy);
```

The GetStringCritical function returns a pointer to the characters in the specified string. If necessary, the characters are copied and the function returns with isCopy set to JNI_TRUE. Otherwise, isCopy is NULL or set to JNI_FALSE. After this function is invoked, and up to the point ReleaseStringCritical is invoked, the functions used cannot cause the current thread to block:

```
void ReleaseStringCritical(jstring string, const jchar *carray);
```

The ReleaseStringCritical function releases the pointer obtained from the call to GetStringCritical.

String Example

Here's an example of implementing a string-replace function in native code. The function replaceString takes a source string and replaces a string inside of the source string with another, then returns the new string. The Java code sets up what is needed on the native side:

```java
public class StringExamples {
    public native String replaceString(String sourceString, String strToReplace,
                                        String replaceString);

    static {
        System.loadLibrary("StringLibrary");
    }

    public static void main(String args[])
    {
        StringExamples ex = new StringExamples();
        String str1 = "";
        String str2 = "";

        str1 = "Sky Black";
        str2 = ex.replaceString(str1, "Black", "Blue");
        System.out.println("The string before: " + str1);
        System.out.println("The string after: " + str2);
    }
}
```

The C++ implementation of the replaceString method, shown next, makes use of the string functions that you just learned:

```cpp
JNIEXPORT jstring JNICALL Java_StringExamples_replaceString
  (JNIEnv *env, jobject obj,
   jstring _srcString, jstring _strToReplace, jstring _replString)
{
    const char *searchStr, *findStr, *replStr, *found;
    jstring newString = NULL;
    int index;

    searchStr = env->GetStringUTFChars(_srcString, NULL);
    findStr = env->GetStringUTFChars(_strToReplace, NULL);
    replStr = env->GetStringUTFChars(_replString, NULL);

    found = strstr(searchStr, findStr);

    if(found != NULL) {
        char *newStringTemp;

        index = found - searchStr;
        newStringTemp =
            new char[strlen(searchStr) + strlen(replStr) + 1];

        strcpy(newStringTemp, searchStr);
        newStringTemp[index] = 0;
        strcat(newStringTemp, replStr);
        strcat(newStringTemp, &searchStr[index+strlen(findStr)]);

        newString = env->NewStringUTF((const char*)newStringTemp);
```

```
    }

    env->ReleaseStringUTFChars(_srcString, searchStr);
    env->ReleaseStringUTFChars(_strToReplace, findStr);
    env->ReleaseStringUTFChars(_replString, replStr);

    return(newString);
}
```

The GetStringUTFChars function is used to convert the string to a string guaranteed useable in native code. The code within the `if` clause performs the search and replace, and finally allocates a new UTF string with the affected string. This reference is returned, so it is the only reference not released using ReleaseStringUTFChars.

Arrays in JNI

JNI supports the use of both arrays of primitive types and arrays of objects. Each primitive type has an array type counterpart. These array types are listed in the following table.

Name of Primitive Data Type	Array Type (For Use in C/C++ Code)
boolean	jbooleanArray
byte	jbyteArray
char	jcharArray
short	jshortArray
int	jintArray
long	jlongArray
float	jfloatArray
double	jdoubleArray

Much like strings in JNI, arrays cannot be used directly. JNI provides a complete set of functions to access, get information about, create, and synchronize both arrays of objects and arrays of primitive data types. The following is an example of how Java arrays should NOT be used in C/C++:

```
JNIEXPORT jint JNICALL
int findNumber(JNIEnv *env, jobject obj, jintArray intArray,
               jint arraySize, jint numberToFind)
{
    int i;

    for(i=0; i<arraySize; i++) {
        if(intArray[i] == numberToFind) {
            return(i);
        }
    }

    return(-1);
}
```

This piece of code does not take into account any of the functions provided by JNI for processing arrays. JNI has a function to get the length of an array, and functions to access the array elements since the elements cannot be accessed directly. If you attempt to compile and execute the above code, it will crash the VM.

Array Functions

This section separates the array functions into those that work with arrays of objects and those that work with arrays of primitive data types. The function GetArrayLength works with any array. This is what the function looks like:

```
jsize GetArrayLength(jarray array);
```

The GetArrayLength function returns the length of the array. This is the same value you get when accessing the `length` property of the array in Java code.

Functions for Arrays of Objects

There are three functions that are provided for working with arrays of Java objects in native code. These are NewObjectArray, GetObjectArrayElement, and SetObjectArrayElement:

```
jobjectArray NewObjectArray(jsize length, jclass elementClass,
                            jobject initialElement);
```

The NewObjectArray function creates a new object array of size `length` that holds objects of type `elementClass`. All elements in the array are set to initialElement, thus providing an easy way to initialize the entire array to null (or to another value):

```
jobject GetObjectArrayElement(jobjectArray array, jsize index);
```

The GetObjectArrayElement function retrieves an object inside the `array` at the index specified by index. If the index is out of bounds, an IndexOutOfBoundsException is thrown:

```
void SetObjectArrayElement(jobjectArray array, jsize index, jobject value);
```

The SetObjectArrayElement function sets the array element inside `array` at position `index` to `value`. If the index is out of bounds, an IndexOutOfBoundsException is thrown.

Functions for Arrays of Primitive Types

There are five core functions for use with each primitive data type. There is one version of each function for each primitive data type. Because there are so many functions, this section uses an abbreviation for each function. Certain information must be replaced with correct data types. In the following list of functions, the [Type] is replaced with the exact name of a primitive type from the first column in the following table. The [ArrayType] is replaced with the exact name of the array data type from the second column in the table. The [NativeType] is replaced with the exact name of the native data type from column three in the table. For example, to create a new integer array, you use the function NewIntArray that returns jintArray.

Name of Primitive Data Type	Array Type (For Use in C/C++ Code)	Primitive Type (For Use in C/C++ Code)
boolean	jbooleanArray	jboolean
byte	jbyteArray	jbyte
char	jcharArray	jchar
short	jshortArray	jshort
int	jintArray	jint
long	jlongArray	jlong
float	jfloatArray	jfloat
double	jdoubleArray	jdouble

```
[ArrayType] New[Type]Array(jsize length);
```

The NewArray function returns a newly created Java array that is `length` elements in size.

```
[NativeType] *Get[Type]ArrayElements([ArrayType] array, jboolean *isCopy);
```

The GetArrayElements function returns a pointer to an array of the native type that corresponds to the Java data type. The parameter isCopy is set to JNI_TRUE if the memory returned is a copy of the array from the Java code, or JNI_FALSE if the memory is not a copy.

```
void Release[Type]ArrayElements([ArrayType] array, [NativeType] *elems, jint mode);
```

The ReleaseArrayElements function releases the memory obtained from the call to Get**[Type]**ArrayElements. If the native array is not a copy, then the mode parameter can be used to optionally copy memory from the native array back to the Java array. The values of mode and their effects are listed in the following table.

Value of Mode	Description
0	Copies the memory from the native array to the Java array and deallocates the memory used by the native array
JNI_COMMIT	Copies the memory from the native array to the Java array, but does NOT deallocate the memory used by the native array
JNI_ABORT	Does not copy memory from the native array to the Java array. The memory used by the native array is still deallocated.

```
void Get[Type]ArrayRegion([ArrayType] array, jsize start, jsize len,
                          [NativeType] *buf);
```

The GetArrayRegion function operates much like Get[Type]ArrayElements. However, this is used to copy only a subset of the array. The parameter start specifies the starting index to copy from, and len specifies how many positions in the array to copy into the native array:

```
void Set[Type]ArrayRegion([ArrayType] array, jsize start, jsize len,
                          [NativeType] *buf);
```

The SetArrayRegion is the counterpart to Get[Type]ArrayRegion. This function is used to copy a segment of a native array back to the Java array. Elements are copied directly from the beginning of the native array (index 0) but are copied into the Java array starting at position start and len elements are copied over:

```
void *GetPrimitiveArrayCritical(jarray array, jboolean *isCopy);
```

The GetPrimitiveArrayCritical function returns a handle to an array after obtaining a lock on the array. If no lock could be established, the isCopy parameter comes back with a value JNI_TRUE. Otherwise, isCopy comes back NULL or as JNI_FALSE:

```
void ReleasePrimitiveArrayCritical(jarray array, void *carray, jint mode);
```

The ReleasePrimitiveArrayCritical releases the array previously returned from a call to GetPrimitiveArrayCritical. Look at the next table to see how the mode parameter affects the array and carray parameters.

Value for Mode	Meaning
0	Copies the values from carray into array and frees the memory associated with carray
JNI_COMMIT	Copies the values from carray into array but does not free the memory associated with carray
JNI_ABORT	Does not copy the values from carray to array, but does free the memory associated with carray

Array Examples

Here's an example of implementing a sort routine in native code. In order to keep things simple, the insertion sort is used. The Java code, as usual, is fairly simple. The native method is declared, then the library is statically loaded, and the native method is invoked in the main method:

```
public class PrimitiveArrayExample {
    public native boolean sortIntArray(int[] numbers);

    static {
        System.loadLibrary("PrimitiveArrayLibrary");
    }

    public static void main(String args[])
    {
        PrimitiveArrayExample pae = new PrimitiveArrayExample();
```

```
        int numberList[] = {4, 1, 2, 20, 11, 7, 2};

        if(pae.sortIntArray(numberList)) {
            System.out.print("The sorted numbers are: ");
            for(int i=0; i<numberList.length; i++) {
                System.out.print(numberList[i] + " ");
            }
            System.out.println();
        } else {
            System.out.println("The sort operation failed because " +
                               "the array memory could not be allocated.");
        }
    }
}
```

The native code uses the array functions to work with an array of integers:

```
JNIEXPORT jboolean JNICALL Java_PrimitiveArrayExample_sortIntArray
            (JNIEnv *env, jobject obj, jintArray intArrayToSort)
{
    jint *intArray;
    jboolean isCopy;
    int i, j, num;

    intArray = env->GetIntArrayElements(intArrayToSort, &isCopy);

    if(intArray == NULL) {
        return(false);
    }

    for(i=1; i<env->GetArrayLength(intArrayToSort); i++) {
        num = intArray[i];

        for(j=i-1; j >= 0 && (intArray[j] > num); j--) {
            intArray[j+1] = intArray[j];
        }

        intArray[j+1] = num;
    }

    env->ReleaseIntArrayElements(intArrayToSort, intArray, 0);
    return(true);
}
```

This sortIntArray function uses the GetIntArrayElements in order to work with the array in a native form. The GetArrayLength function is used to know how many elements are in the array, and finally, ReleaseIntArrayElements is used to both save the changed memory to the Java array and deallocate the memory.

As one final example of arrays, create an array of strings and then implement a find function that returns the index to the string:

```
public class ObjectArrayExample {
    public native int findString(String[] stringList, String stringToFind);

    static {
        System.loadLibrary("ObjectArrayLibrary");
    }

    public static void main(String args[])
    {
        ObjectArrayExample oae = new ObjectArrayExample();
        String[] colors = {"red","blue","black","green","grey"};
        int foundIndex;

        System.out.println("Searching for 'black'...");
        foundIndex = oae.findString(colors, "black");

        if(foundIndex != -1) {
            System.out.println("The color 'black' was found at index "
                                + foundIndex);
        } else {
            System.out.println("The color 'black' was not found");
        }
    }
}
```

An array of strings is created and passed to the native method findString. If the string is not found, the method returns -1 and otherwise returns the index to the string from the array:

```
JNIEXPORT jint JNICALL Java_ObjectArrayExample_findString
  (JNIEnv *env, jobject obj, jobjectArray strList, jstring strToFind)
{
    const char *findStr;
    jint i;
    int arrayLen;

    arrayLen = env->GetArrayLength(strList);
    findStr = env->GetStringUTFChars(strToFind, NULL);

    if(findStr == NULL) {
        return(-1);
    }

    for(i=0; i<arrayLen; i++) {
        jstring strElem = (jstring)env->GetObjectArrayElement(strList, i);

        if(strElem != NULL) {
            const char *strTemp = env->GetStringUTFChars(strElem, NULL);

            if(strcmp(strTemp, findStr) == 0) {
                env->ReleaseStringUTFChars(strElem, strTemp);
                env->ReleaseStringUTFChars(strToFind, findStr);
                env->DeleteLocalRef(strElem);
```

```
            break;
        }

        env->ReleaseStringUTFChars(strElem, strTemp);
        env->DeleteLocalRef(strElem);
    }

    env->ReleaseStringUTFChars(strToFind, findStr);
}

if(i == arrayLen) {
    return(-1);
} else {
    return(i);
}
}
```

The GetArrayLength function is used to retrieve the length of the object array. The object array is then accessed using the GetObjectArrayElement function to retrieve a specific element. Note that the object is then cast to a jstring in order to get a handle to the array element's specific type. Also note that since the GetObjectArrayElement function returns a local reference, the reference is freed using DeleteLocalRef. As explained in the local reference section, this call to DeleteLocalRef isn't necessary here, but it helps to remind you that many native functions return a local reference.

Working with Java Objects in C/C++

Java Native Interface also provides a set of functions to manipulate Java objects (using methods/fields), handle exceptions, and synchronize data for threads. These functions provide greater access to Java objects on the native side, allowing for more sophisticated applications. One way that these functions can be used is to make callbacks to Java methods, perhaps to communicate information. You will see this in action in the mail client example at the end of this chapter.

Accessing Fields in JNI

There are two types of member variables in Java classes — static fields, that belong to classes, and non-static fields, that belong to individual objects. In order to gain access to a field, you must pass a field descriptor and the name of the field to GetFieldID or GetStaticFieldID. A field descriptor is one or more characters that fully describe a field's type. For example, the field int number has as its field descriptor I. Consult the next table for a full list of descriptors for primitive types. The descriptor for an array type is prefixed with the character [for each dimension of the array. Therefore, the type int[] numbers is described by [I, and int[][] numbers is [[I. For reference types, the fully qualified name of the class is used but the dots are replaced with a forward slash and the descriptor is surrounded by an L at the beginning and a semicolon at the end. For example, the type java.lang.Integer is described by Ljava/lang/Integer.

Primitive Type	Field Descriptor
boolean	Z
byte	B
char	C
short	S
int	I
long	J
float	F
double	D

Much like the variety of functions for use with arrays of primitive types, each primitive type has its own Get and Set function for fields. This section also uses the abbreviated version for compactness. The [NativeType] is replaced by a string from the first column of the next table, and [Type] is replaced by the corresponding string from the second column in the table.

Name of Primitive Data Type	Primitive Type (For Use in C/C++ Code)
boolean	jboolean
byte	jbyte
char	jchar
short	jshort
int	jint
long	jlong
float	jfloat
double	jdouble

Here are the functions that are provided to access fields inside Java classes:

```
jfieldID GetFieldID(jclass clazz, const char *name, const char *sig);
```

The GetFieldID function returns a handle to the specified field for use in the Get and Set functions. The GetObjectClass function (described later) can be used to get a jclass suitable for the first parameter to this function. The name is the name of the field, and the sig parameter is the field descriptor. If this function fails, it returns NULL:

```
[NativeType] Get[Type]Field(jobject obj, jfieldID fieldID);
```

The GetField function returns the value of a particular field specified by fieldID that belongs to the Java object obj:

```
void Set[Type]Field(jobject obj, jfieldID fieldID, [NativeType] val);
```

The SetField function sets the value of a particular field specified by fieldID that belongs to the Java object obj to the value val:

```
jfieldID GetStaticFieldID(jclass clazz, const char *name, const char *sig);
```

The GetStaticFieldID function works the same as GetFieldID but is used for getting a handle to a static field:

```
[NativeType] GetStatic[Type]Field(jclass clazz, jfieldID fieldID);
```

The GetStaticField function returns the value of a static field specified by the fieldID handle and belonging to the class described by clazz:

```
void SetStatic[Type]Field(jclass clazz, jfieldID fieldID, [NativeType] value);
```

The SetStaticField function sets the value of a static field specified by the fieldID that belongs to the class described by clazz:

Here's an example of accessing fields on an object. The Java code defines a Point class and the native code performs some transformation on that point:

```
class Point {
    public int x, y, z;

    public String toString()
    {
        return("(" + x + ", " + y + ", " + z + ")");
    }
}

public class FieldAccessExample {
    public native void transformPoint(Point p);

    static {
        System.loadLibrary("FieldAccessLibrary");
    }

    public static void main(String args[])
    {
        FieldAccessExample fae = new FieldAccessExample();
        Point p1 = new Point();

        p1.x = 17;
        p1.y = 20;
        p1.z = 10;
        System.out.println("The point before transformation: " + p1);
```

```
        fae.transformPoint(p1);
        System.out.println("The point after transformation: " + p1);
    }
}
```

The native library is loaded as usual. An instance of the Point class is created and set up, then the native function is called. The native code accesses the fields in the Point object and modifies these fields. Note that the object passed in isn't a copy—any changes done to it in native code take effect in the Java code when the native function returns:

```
JNIEXPORT void JNICALL Java_FieldAccessExample_transformPoint
  (JNIEnv *env, jobject obj, jobject thePoint)
{
    jfieldID x_id, y_id, z_id;
    jint x_value, y_value, z_value;
    jclass cls;

    cls = env->GetObjectClass(thePoint);

    x_id = env->GetFieldID(cls, "x", "I");
    y_id = env->GetFieldID(cls, "y", "I");
    z_id = env->GetFieldID(cls, "z", "I");

    x_value = env->GetIntField(thePoint, x_id);
    y_value = env->GetIntField(thePoint, y_id);
    z_value = env->GetIntField(thePoint, z_id);

    x_value = x_value;
    y_value = 10*y_value + 5;
    z_value = 30*z_value + 2;

    env->SetIntField(thePoint, x_id, x_value);
    env->SetIntField(thePoint, y_id, y_value);
    env->SetIntField(thePoint, z_id, z_value);
}
```

The GetObjectClass function is used to get a handle to the class behind a specified object. In this case, GetObjectClass returns a handle to the Point class. Each field is an integer, so the field descriptor used is simply I. After the field ID's are retrieved, accessing the value of the field happens through GetIntField and the field values are written back using SetIntField.

Invoking Java Methods Using JNI

Just like fields, there are static and nonstatic methods in Java. JNI provides functions to execute methods on Java objects and also static methods on Java classes. Much like accessing fields, the name and a descriptor for the method are used in order to get a handle to a specific Java method. Once you have this handle, you pass it to one of the CallMethod functions along with the actual parameters for the method. There are actually a number of CallMethod functions—one for each possible return type from a method. Consult the previous table for a listing of the various return types.

419

The method descriptor is formed by placing all the method's parameter types inside a single set of parentheses, and then specifying the return type after the closing parenthesis. Types for parameters and return type use the field descriptor described in the previous section. If the method returns void, the descriptor is simply V. If the method does not take any parameters, the parentheses are left empty. The method descriptor for the main method that you are familiar with is ([Ljava/lang/String;)V. The parameters to main are placed inside the parentheses. The square bracket followed by the String object type corresponds to the data type String []args. Outside the parentheses is a single V since main has void as its return type. If you wish to invoke the constructor, use the method name <init>, and for static constructors, use the name <clinit>.

> A shortcut to deriving field and method descriptors can be found in the javap utility that comes with the JDK. By passing the command-line option -s to javap, you get a listing of the descriptors for the methods and fields of a class. For example, running javap on the Point class generates the following output:
>
> ```
> H:\CHAPTER9\code>javap -s Point
> Compiled from FieldAccessExample.java
> class Point extends java.lang.Object {
>     public int x;
>         /*   I   */
>     public int y;
>         /*   I   */
>     public int z;
>         /*   I   */
>     Point();
>         /*   ()V   */
>     public java.lang.String toString();
>         /*   ()Ljava/lang/String;   */
> }
> ```
>
> Both field descriptors and method descriptors are output. You can copy these descriptors directly into the calls to the GetFieldID or GetMethodID functions instead of figuring the descriptors out manually.

Following is a list of functions for use when invoking methods on Java objects. The various CallMethod functions have versions for each data type, much like the functions for accessing fields, so the abbreviation is also used here. Replace the [NativeType] with a native data type, and replace the [Type] with the type name to finish the name of the function:

```
jclass GetObjectClass(jobject obj);
```

The GetObjectClass function returns a jclass that represents the class of the Java object obj that is passed in:

```
jmethodID GetMethodID(jclass clazz, const char *name, const char *sig);
jmethodID GetStaticMethodID(jclass clazz, const char *name, const char *sig);
```

The GetMethodID and GetStaticMethodID functions return a handle to the specified method for use in the various CallMethod functions. The GetObjectClass function can be used to get a jclass suitable for the first parameter to this function. The name is the name of the method, and the sig parameter is the method descriptor. If this function fails it returns NULL:

```
[NativeType] Call[Type]Method(jobject obj, jmethodID methodID, ...);
[NativeType] Call[Type]MethodV(jobject obj, jmethodID methodID, va_list args);
[NativeType] Call[Type]MethodA(jobject obj, jmethodID methodID,
                               const jvalue *args);
```

The CallMethod functions (and variants) are used to invoke an instance method on a Java object. The first two parameters to all these functions are a handle to the object that has the method, and the handle to the specific method to invoke. The other parameters are the actual parameters to the Java method about to be invoked. The first function accepts a variable number of arguments and passes these arguments directly to the Java method. The second function accepts the list of arguments as a va_list structure that is prepackaged with the list of arguments. The third function accepts the method arguments as an array of jvalue, which is a union able to take the form of any of the native data type versions of the Java data types, including jobject. If you wish to invoke a constructor or a private method, the method ID has to be obtained based on the actual class of the object, not one of the object's super-classes:

```
[NativeType] CallNonvirtual[Type]Method(jobject obj, jclass clazz,
                                        jmethodID methodID, ...);
[NativeType] CallNonvirtual[Type]MethodV(jobject obj, jclass clazz,
                                         jmethodID methodID, va_list args);
[NativeType] CallNonvirtual[Type]MethodA(jobject obj, jclass clazz,
                                         jmethodID methodID,
                                         const jvalue *args);
```

The CallNonvirtual functions also invoke an instance method of an object, but which Java method to invoke is based on the clazz parameter. These enable you to invoke a specific method somewhere in the hierarchy of the object's class instead of invoking a method based on just the object's class. Just like the normal CallMethod functions, these allow you to pass in arguments to the Java method in the same three different ways:

```
[NativeType] CallStatic[Type]Method(jclass clazz, jmethodID methodID, ...);
[NativeType] CallStatic[Type]MethodV(jclass clazz, jmethodID methodID,
                                     va_list args);
[NativeType] CallStatic[Type]MethodA(jclass clazz, jmethodID methodID,
                                     const jvalue *args);
```

The CallStaticMethod functions (and variants) invoke a static method belonging to the class clazz that is passed in. Use GetStaticMethodID to obtain a handle to the specific method to invoke. Arguments to the method can be passed in to this function in the same three ways as described above.

Along with showing how to invoke Java methods, the following example shows the relationship of the Call and CallNonvirtual functions to combinations of an object and a handle to a class and a handle to a method:

```
class InvokeMethodParentClass {
    public void printMessage()
    {
        System.out.println("Inside InvokeMethodParentClass");
    }
}

public class InvokeMethodExample extends InvokeMethodParentClass {
    public native void execMethods();

    static {
        System.loadLibrary("InvokeMethodLibrary");
    }

    public void printMessage()
    {
        System.out.println("Inside InvokeMethodExample");
    }

    public static void main(String args[])
    {
        InvokeMethodExample ime = new InvokeMethodExample();

        ime.execMethods();
    }
}
```

The Java source defines a parent and a child class and both classes define the same method. The execMethods native method invokes the Call and CallNonvirtual functions in a variety of ways:

```
JNIEXPORT void JNICALL Java_InvokeMethodExample_execMethods
  (JNIEnv *env, jobject obj)
{
    jclass childClass, parentClass;
    jmethodID parent_methodID, child_methodID;

    childClass = env->GetObjectClass(obj);
    parentClass = env->FindClass("InvokeMethodParentClass");

    if(childClass == NULL || parentClass == NULL) {
        printf("Couldn't obtain handle to parent or child class");
        return;
    }

    parent_methodID = env->GetMethodID(childClass, "printMessage", "()V");
    child_methodID = env->GetMethodID(parentClass, "printMessage", "()V");

    if(parent_methodID == NULL || child_methodID == NULL) {
        printf("Couldn't obtain handle to parent or child method");
        return;
    }

    // These two calls invoke the method on the child class
    env->CallVoidMethod(obj, parent_methodID);
```

```
        env->CallVoidMethod(obj, child_methodID);

        // These two calls invoke the method on the parent class
        env->CallNonvirtualVoidMethod(obj, childClass, parent_methodID);
        env->CallNonvirtualVoidMethod(obj, parentClass, parent_methodID);

        // These two calls invoke the method on the child class
        env->CallNonvirtualVoidMethod(obj, childClass, child_methodID);
        env->CallNonvirtualVoidMethod(obj, parentClass, child_methodID);
    }
```

Here's the output from this example:

```
Inside InvokeMethodExample
Inside InvokeMethodExample
Inside InvokeMethodParentClass
Inside InvokeMethodParentClass
Inside InvokeMethodExample
Inside InvokeMethodExample
```

Using the regular version, CallVoidMethod, the child's method is always invoked, regardless of which method ID is used (the one for the parent class or the one for the child). The CallNonvirtualVoidMethod must be used to cause the method of the parent class to execute. Note that regardless of which class type is passed in, the determining factor for which method to execute is the method ID that is passed in.

Handling Java Exceptions in Native Code

JNI provides hooks to the Java exception mechanism in order to handle exceptions that are thrown in the course of executing methods that are implemented in Java code, or native methods written to throw Java exceptions. This mechanism has no bearing on standard error handling for regular functions implemented in C/C++. JNI provides a set of functions for checking, analyzing, and otherwise handling Java exceptions in native code. This section explores these functions and shows how to go about handling Java exceptions in native code in order to maintain Java's approach to exception handling:

```
jboolean ExceptionCheck();
```

The ExceptionCheck function returns JNI_TRUE if an exception has been thrown, or JNI_FALSE if one hasn't:

```
jthrowable ExceptionOccurred();
```

The ExceptionOccurred function retrieves a local reference to an exception that is being thrown. The native code or the Java code must handle this exception:

```
void ExceptionDescribe();
```

The ExceptionDescribe function prints information about the exception that was just thrown to the standard error output. This information includes a stack trace:

```
void ExceptionClear();
```

The ExceptionClear function clears an exception if one was just thrown:

```
jint Throw(jthrowable obj);
```

The Throw function throws an exception that has already been created. If the exception was successfully thrown, 0 is returned; otherwise, a negative value is returned:

```
jint ThrowNew(jclass clazz, const char *msg);
```

The ThrowNew function creates an exception based on clazz, which should inherit from Throwable, with the exception text specified by msg (in UTF-8 format). If the construction and throwing of the exception is successful, this function returns 0; otherwise, a negative value is returned:

```
void FatalError(const char *msg);
```

The FatalError function causes the signaling of a fatal error. A fatal error is only for situations where recovery is not possible. The VM is shut down upon calling this function.

You should always check for exceptions that might occur in the course of executing native code. If an exception is left unhandled, it will cause future calls to most JNI functions to fail. Here's a simple scenario using the FindClass function to try to find a class that isn't there and then handle the exception:

```
JNIEXPORT void JNICALL Java_ExceptionExample_testExceptions
  (JNIEnv *env, jobject obj)
{
    // Try to find a class that isn't there to trigger an exception
    env->FindClass("NoSuchClass");

    // If an exception happened, print it out and then clear it
    if(env->ExceptionCheck()) {
        env->ExceptionDescribe();
        env->ExceptionClear();
    }
}
```

The first statement in the function triggers a NoClassDefFoundError exception. When running this native function, the following output is generated:

```
java.lang.NoClassDefFoundError: NoSuchClass
        at ExceptionExample.testExceptions(Native Method)
        at ExceptionExample.main(ExceptionExample.java:13)
Exception in thread "main"
```

The exception details are printed, specifying which exception was thrown, extra information (in this case, the name of the class passed to FindClass), and the stack trace showing the method calls up to the native method, where the exception was thrown. The stack trace doesn't include line numbers in the native code since Java does not have native code line number information immediately available to it.

Working with Object References in Native Code

JNI provides sets of functions to utilize Java objects in native code, as you've seen with strings, arrays, and general objects. This raises an important question that you may have already considered — how are references to objects handled? More specifically, how does the garbage collector handle object references and know when to collect garbage? JNI provides three different types of references:

❑ **Local References.** For use only in a single native method.

❑ **Global References.** For use across multiple invocations of native methods.

❑ **Weak Global References.** Just like global references, but these do not prevent the object from being garbage collected.

Local References

Local references are explicitly created using the NewLocalRef function, though a number of JNI functions return a local reference. These references are intended only for use while a native function executes and disappear when that function returns. Local references should not be cached on the native side (such as in a local static variable) since they are not valid across multiple calls to the native method. As soon as the native function returns, any local references that existed are now eligible for garbage collection. If you want to deallocate the local reference before the function returns, you can explicitly deallocate the local reference using the DeleteLocalRef function. Local references are also only valid in the thread that created them, so don't try to store a local reference and use it in a different thread.

The following functions are available to explicitly create and destroy local references:

```
jobject NewLocalRef(jobject ref);
```

The NewLocalRef function returns a new local reference to the object reference passed in. If NULL is passed in, the function returns NULL:

```
void DeleteLocalRef(jobject obj);
```

The DeleteLocalRef function deallocates the local reference that is passed in.

All local references are available for garbage collection when a native function returns. Local references are created by many JNI functions, such as GetStringUTFChars. Most local references are created and cleaned up automatically. Since local references are so common, look at the example in the next section to see an example of explicitly accounting for local references.

Managing Local References

You must be conscious of how many local references are currently in use since many functions return local references. JNI only allows for a set maximum number of local references. Also, if you create references to large objects, you run the risk of exhausting the available memory. The following functions are provided for management of local references:

```
jint EnsureLocalCapacity(jint capacity);
```

This function ensures that at least capacity number of local references can be created. The VM ensures that at least 16 local references can be created when a native method is called. If you try to create more local references than are available, FatalError is invoked. This function returns 0 on success and a negative number on failure along with throwing an OutOfMemoryException:

```
jint PushLocalFrame(jint capacity);
```

The PushLocalFrame is a useful function to create a new scope of local references. This makes it simple to release all local references allocated in this frame by using the PopLocalFrame function. When this is called, at least capacity number of local references can be created in this frame. This function returns 0 on success and a negative number on failure along with throwing an OutOfMemoryException:

```
jobject PopLocalFrame(jobject result);
```

The PopLocalFrame function releases all local references in the current frame (pops up a level). Since storing the result of this function (the return value) might cause a local reference creation in the about-to-be-popped frame, this function accepts a parameter that causes the reference creation to happen in the topmost frame after the current one is popped. This ensures you maintain a reference that stores the result of this function.

Here's an example showing the usage of the local reference management functions:

```
JNIEXPORT void JNICALL Java_LocalRefExample_testLocalRefs
  (JNIEnv *env, jobject obj)
{
    jint count;

    // Let's figure out just how many local references
    // we can create...
    for(count=16; count<10000; count++) {
        if(env->EnsureLocalCapacity(count+1)) {
            break;
        }
    }

    printf("I can create up to %d local references\n", count);

    // Now let's create a few...
    jcharArray charArray;
    jintArray intArray;
    jstring str;

    str = env->NewStringUTF("This is a test");

    if(env->PushLocalFrame(10)) {
        charArray = env->NewCharArray(13);

        if(charArray == NULL) {
            printf("Failed to create character array\n");
```

```
            return;
        }

        if(env->PushLocalFrame(10)) {
            intArray = env->NewIntArray(14);

            if(intArray == NULL) {
                printf("Failed to create integer array\n");
                return;
            }

            // intArray created. Use PopLocalFrame to free all allocated
            // references in this scope level, in this case just intArray
            env->PopLocalFrame(NULL);
        }

        // charArray created. Use PopLocalFrame to free all allocated
        // references in this scope level, in this case just charArray
        env->PopLocalFrame(NULL);
    }

    // 'str' is freed after this function exits
}
```

When I ran this function, it printed that it can allocate 4,096 local references. The Java VM only guarantees 16 local references, so always call the EnsureLocalCapacity function if you need a large number of local references. Each call to PushLocalFrame allocates a new scope level for allocating local references. All local references that are allocated are automatically freed when PopLocalFrame is called. Only intArray is freed when the first PopLocalFrame is called, and only charArray is freed when the second call to PopLocalFrame happens.

Global and Weak Global References

Global references are meant for use across different invocations of a native method. They are created only by using the NewGlobalRef function. Global references can also be used across separate threads. Since global references give you these added benefits, there is a small trade-off: Java cannot control the lifetime of a global reference. You must determine when the global reference is no longer needed and deallocate it manually using the DeleteGlobalRef function. Weak global references are much like global references, but the underlying object might be garbage collected at any time. JNI provides a special invocation of IsSameObject for finding out if the underlying object is still valid.

The following functions are used for creating and destroying global references:

```
jobject NewGlobalRef(jobject lobj);
jweak NewWeakGlobalRef(jobject obj);
```

NewGlobalRef creates a new global reference and returns it, and NewWeakGlobalRef creates and returns a new weak global reference. The parameter to these functions is the class of the object to create. If you don't have a handle to a class, you can obtain one by invoking the FindClass function. If you try to create a reference to the null object, or the object cannot be created, these functions return NULL. If the reference cannot be created due to no more available memory, an OutOfMemoryException is thrown:

```
void DeleteGlobalRef(jobject gref);
void DeleteWeakGlobalRef(jweak ref);
```

The DeleteGlobalRef/DeleteWeakGlobalRef functions deallocate the global (or weak global) reference that was previously allocated in a call to NewGlobalRef or NewWeakGlobalRef.

Here's an example of how to cache a class for use across multiple calls to this native function:

```
JNIEXPORT void JNICALL Java_GlobalRefExample_testGlobalRef
  (JNIEnv *env, jobject obj)
{
    static jstring globalString = NULL;
    const char *gStr;

    if(globalString == NULL) {
        // First time through, create global reference
        jstring localStr;

        localStr = env->NewStringUTF("This is a string");

        if(localStr == NULL) {
            return;
        }

        printf("Global reference does not exist, creating...\n");
        globalString = (jstring)env->NewGlobalRef(localStr);
    }

    gStr = env->GetStringUTFChars(globalString, NULL);

    printf("The contents of globalString: %s\n", gStr);
    fflush(stdout);

    env->ReleaseStringUTFChars(globalString, gStr);
}
```

The globalString is marked static so it is preserved across multiple calls to the function. The globalString reference must be created using NewGlobalRef so that the underlying object is also preserved across multiple calls to this function. The first time this is invoked, a local reference to a string is created. This local reference is then used to create a global reference, which is then stored in globalString. The output from the above function, invoked twice, shows how the globalString is created only the first time through:

```
--- FIRST TIME CALLING ---
Global reference does not exist, creating...
The contents of globalString: This is a string
--- SECOND TIME CALLING ---
The contents of globalString: This is a string
```

Don't forget to build in code to deallocate the global reference. This example shows only how to create a global reference. When to call DeleteGlobalRef depends on your application design.

Comparing References

JNI provides a special function, IsSameObject, in order to test whether the object behind two references is the same. In C++, the keyword NULL corresponds to a null object in Java. Thus, you can pass NULL as a parameter to IsSameObject or compare an object reference directly to NULL. The IsSameObject function has the following prototype:

```
jboolean IsSameObject(jobject obj1, jobject obj2);
```

The IsSameObject function returns JNI_TRUE if the objects are the same, and JNI_FALSE otherwise. If you attempt to compare a weak global reference to NULL using IsSameObject, it returns JNI_TRUE if the underlying object hasn't been garbage collected, and JNI_FALSE if the object has.

Advanced Programming Using JNI

JNI provides several other capabilities to the programmer of native routines. Since Java is a multithreaded environment, routines related to threading are available on the native side. JNI also supports a way of exposing native routines to Java code singly, rather than making all native functions immediately available through a call to System.load or System.loadLibrary. In addition to these features, Java exposes the reflection library natively.

Java Threading

Since Java is a multithreaded environment, it is possible that one or more threads in a system will invoke native methods. This makes it important to know how native methods and things like global references in native libraries relate to threading in Java. The pointer to the Java environment is thread specific, so don't use one thread's environment pointer in another thread. If you plan to pass a local reference from one thread to another, convert it to a global reference first. Local references are also thread specific.

Thread Synchronization

JNI provides two native functions for synchronizing objects, MonitorEnter and MonitorExit. These are the only threading functions that are exposed directly at the native level since these are time-critical functions. Other functions such as wait and notify should be invoked using the method invocation functions described in an earlier section:

```
jint MonitorEnter(jobject obj);
```

Invoking the MonitorEnter function is equivalent to using synchronized(obj) in Java. The current thread enters the specified object's monitor, unless another thread has a lock on the object, in which case the current thread pauses until the other thread releases the object's monitor. If the current thread already has a lock on the object's monitor, a counter is incremented for each call to this function for the object. Returns a 0 on success, or a negative value if the function failed:

```
jint MonitorExit(jobject obj);
```

The MonitorExit function decrements the object's monitor counter by 1, or releases the current thread's lock on the object if the counter reaches 0. Returns a 0 on success, or a negative value if the function failed.

Native NIO Support

Introduced to JNI in the 1.4 version of Java are three functions that work with NIO direct buffers. A direct byte buffer is a container for byte data that Java will do its best to perform native I/O operations on. JNI defines three functions for use with NIO:

```
jobject NewDirectByteBuffer(void* address, jlong capacity);
```

Based on a pointer to a memory address and the length of the memory (capacity), this function allocates and returns a new java.nio.ByteBuffer. Returns NULL if this function is not implemented for the current Java virtual machine, or if an exception is thrown. If no memory is available, an OutOfMemoryException is thrown:

```
void *GetDirectBufferAddress(jobject buf);
```

The GetDirectBufferAddress function returns a pointer to the address referred to by the java.nio.ByteBuffer object that is passed in. Returns NULL if the function is not implemented, if the buf is not an object of the java.nio.ByteBuffer type, or if the memory region is not defined:

```
jlong GetDirectBufferCapacity(jobject buf);
```

The GetDirectBufferCapacity function returns the capacity (in number of bytes) of a java.nio.ByteBuffer object that is passed in. Returns -1 if the function is not implemented or if the buf is not an object of the java.nio.ByteBuffer type.

Manually Registering Native Methods

JNI provides a way to register native methods at run time. This dynamic registration is especially useful when a native application initiates an instance of the virtual machine at run time. Native methods in this application cannot be loaded by the VM (since they aren't in a native library), but can still be used by the Java code after the functions have been manually registered. It is also possible to register a native function multiple times, changing its implementation at run time. The only requirement for native functions is that they follow the JNICALL calling convention. In this section you will see how to utilize these functions to perform more sophisticated coding tasks using JNI:

```
jint RegisterNatives(jclass clazz, const JNINativeMethod *methods,
                     jint nMethods);
```

The RegisterNatives function is used to register one or more native methods. It returns 0 if successful, or a negative value otherwise. The parameter clazz is a handle to the Java class that contains the native methods about to be registered. The nMethods parameter specifies how many native methods are in the list to register. The methods parameter is a pointer to a list of native methods (can be one or more methods). Each element of the methods array is an instance of the JNINativeMethod structure. The JNINativeMethod structure is as follows:

```
typedef struct {
    char *name;
    char *signature;
    void *fnPtr;
} JNINativeMethod;
```

The strings are UTF-8 encoded strings. The name member contains the name of the native method to register (from the Java class) and signature is the method descriptor that fully describes the method's type. The fnPtr member is a function pointer that points to the C function to register. The function behind this pointer must adhere to the following prototype:

```
[ReturnType] (*fnPtr)(JNIEnv *env, jobject objectOrClass, ...);
```

The [ReturnType] must be one of the native equivalents of the Java data types. The first two parameters to all native method implementations are a pointer to the Java environment and a reference to the class/object invoking the native method. The variable argument list is for the regular parameters passed to the method:

```
jint UnregisterNatives(jclass clazz);
```

The UnregisterNatives function should not be used except in highly specialized situations. This function unregisters all native methods registered with the class passed in. This function returns 0 on success and a negative value otherwise.

Here's an example of manually registering a native method. The Java code defines two native functions, one that is used to select which sort routine to use, and the other to perform the sort. The sortNumbers method has no implementation when the library is loaded. The setSort function uses an input parameter to know which sort routine to manually register:

```
import java.io.*;

public class RegisterNativeExample {
    public native boolean sortNumbers(int strList[]);
    public native void setSort(int whichSort);

    static {
        System.loadLibrary("RegisterNativeLibrary");
    }

    public static void main(String args[])
    {
        RegisterNativeExample rne = new RegisterNativeExample();
        int sortType = 1;
        int nums[] = {23, 1, 6, 1, 2, 7, 3, 4};

        try {
            BufferedReader br = new BufferedReader(
                                        new InputStreamReader(System.in));

            System.out.println("Choose a sort routine");
            System.out.println("  1. Bubble");
            System.out.println("  2. Insertion");
```

```
            System.out.print("% ");
            sortType = Integer.parseInt(br.readLine());
            rne.setSort(sortType);
            rne.sortNumbers(nums);
            System.out.print("Sorted numbers are: ");
            for(int i=0; i<nums.length; i++) {
                System.out.print(nums[i] + " ");
            }
            System.out.println("");
        } catch(IOException ioe) {
            System.out.println("IOException occurred");
            ioe.printStackTrace();
        }
    }
}
```

Much like the example of using primitive arrays, the list of numbers is hard-coded. The user is asked to choose which sort to use, and the setSort function manually registers the chosen sort routine.

Here's the native code. The sort routines are what you would expect, so just their signatures are listed here, along with the setSort function. The full code is available online:

```
jboolean JNICALL bubbleSort(JNIEnv *env, jobject obj, jintArray intArrayToSort)
{ /* ... */ }

jboolean JNICALL insertionSort(JNIEnv *env, jobject obj, jintArray intArrayToSort)
{ /* ... */ }

JNIEXPORT void JNICALL Java_RegisterNativeExample_setSort
  (JNIEnv *env, jobject obj, jint which)
{
    JNINativeMethod sortMethod;

    sortMethod.name = "sortNumbers";
    sortMethod.signature = "([I)Z";

    if(which == 1) {
        sortMethod.fnPtr = bubbleSort;
    } else {
        sortMethod.fnPtr = insertionSort;
    }

    env->RegisterNatives(env->GetObjectClass(obj), &sortMethod, 1);
}
```

The name of the sort method in the Java code is sortNumbers and its signature is ([I)Z; that is, it takes an array of integers and returns a boolean. The final member of the JNINativeMethod structure is the function pointer and is set to either bubbleSort or insertionSort. Finally the RegisterNatives function is called to register the single method that was just configured. After this call, the sortNumbers method can be invoked in the Java code.

Reflection

JNI provides a set of reflection functions that mirror those in the Java API. Using these functions makes it possible to discover information about classes such as a class's super-class or whether one type can be cast to another. Functions are also provided to convert jmethodID and jfieldID types to and from their corresponding method or field:

```
jclass FindClass(const char *name);
```

The FindClass function searches all classes/jar files found in the CLASSPATH for the class name passed in. If the class is found, a handle to that class is returned. The name is a UTF-8 string that includes the full package name and class name, but the dots are replaced with forward slashes. If the class is not found, NULL is returned and one of the following exceptions are thrown:

❑ **ClassFormatError.** The class requested is not a valid class.

❑ **ClassCircularityError.** Tthe class/interface is its own super-class/superinterface.

❑ **OutOfMemoryError.** There is no memory for the handle to the class.

```
jclass GetObjectClass(jobject obj);
```

The GetObjectClass function returns a handle to the class of the object passed in:

```
jclass GetSuperclass(jclass sub);
```

The GetSuperclass function returns a handle to the super-class of the class passed in. If java.lang.Object is passed in, or an interface is passed in, this function returns NULL:

```
jboolean IsAssignableFrom(jclass sub, jclass sup);
```

The IsAssignableFrom function is used to determine if an object of the class described by sub can be successfully cast to the class described by sup. Returns JNI_TRUE if sub and sup are the same classes, sub is a subclass of sup, or sub implements the interface sup. Returns JNI_FALSE otherwise:

```
jboolean IsInstanceOf(jobject obj, jclass clazz);
```

The IsInstanceOf function returns JNI_TRUE if obj is an instance of clazz, and JNI_FALSE otherwise. Passing in NULL for obj causes the function to always return JNI_TRUE since null objects can be cast to any class:

```
jmethodID FromReflectedMethod(jobject method);
```

The FromReflectedMethod function accepts a handle to an object of the java.lang.reflect.Method and returns a jmethodID suitable for use in the functions that require a jmethodID:

```
jobject ToReflectedMethod(jclass cls, jmethodID methodID, jboolean isStatic);
```

The ToReflectedMethod function accepts a handle to a Java class and a handle to a specific method (which might be a constructor) and returns a java.lang.reflect.Method object corresponding to that method. Set isStatic to JNI_TRUE if the method is a static method, and JNI_FALSE (or 0) otherwise. If the function fails, it returns NULL and throws an OutOfMemoryException:

```
jfieldID FromReflectedField(jobject field);
```

The FromReflectedField function accepts a handle to an object of the java.lang.reflect.Field and returns a jfieldID suitable for use in the functions that require a jfieldID:

```
jobject ToReflectedField(jclass cls, jfieldID fieldID, jboolean isStatic);
```

The ToReflectedField function accepts a handle to a Java class and a handle to a specific field and returns a java.lang.reflect.Field object corresponding to that field. Set isStatic to JNI_TRUE if the field is a static field, and JNI_FALSE (or 0) otherwise. If the function fails, it returns NULL and throws an OutOfMemoryException.

Developing an E-Mail Client

To wrap up this chapter, look at a larger program that will retrieve information stored in MS Outlook. This example is based on a project I worked on in the past and provides a way to bring different aspects of JNI together to show what a real-world application of JNI might look like. The e-mail client will provide a user interface to check mail and send mail. This is displayed in a Swing user interface. The mail and mail folder information is accessed using the MAPI routines through COM. The JNI portion is the most important, so the complete user interface is not included here (but is available in the code online for this chapter). In order to retrieve e-mail on the client side, CDO (Collaborative Data Objects) is used, so this example assumes you are running Outlook and it is configured to send mail. Note that due to security updates in Outlook, you might be presented with a dialog cautioning you that an external program is attempting to access information from Outlook or attempting to send mail.

System Design

Take a look at Figure 9-4 to see how the Java code relates to the native code. The MailClient contains the user interface (using Swing). The MailClient class communicates with the JNIMailBridge, which has the native functions to invoke the send and check e-mail native functions. The native library then uses COM to access the information stored in Outlook.

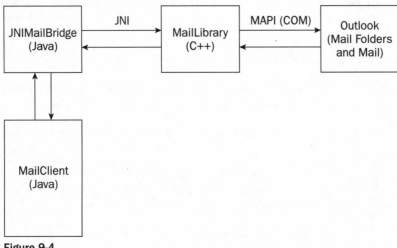

Figure 9-4

User Interface

The following two figures, Figures 9-5 and 9-6, are screen shots of the actual mail client. In the first screen shot, the Mail Folders tree contains all the folders beneath the top folder from Outlook. The table in the top right shows all the messages in the Example folder (shown after double-clicking on Example). The bottom right contains the body of the message (shown after double-clicking on a specific message in the table).

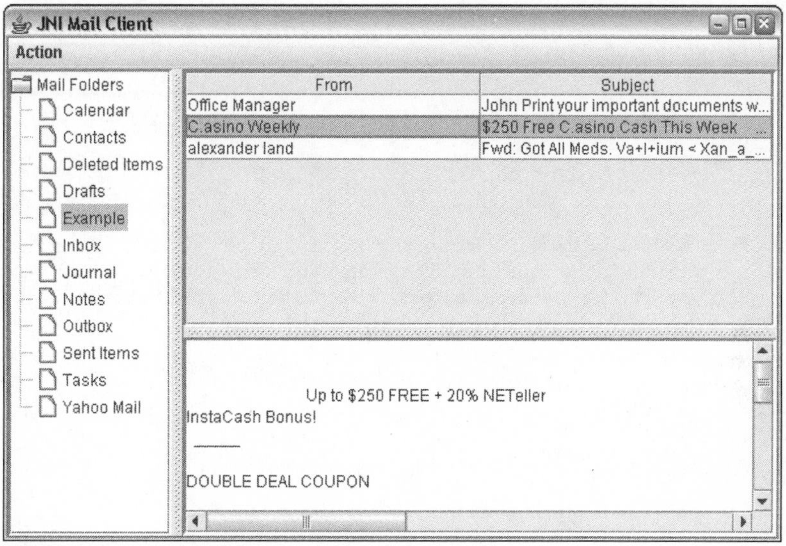

Figure 9-5

This second screen shot contains a basic set of fields to address an e-mail, write the e-mail, and send it (after hitting the Send Mail button).

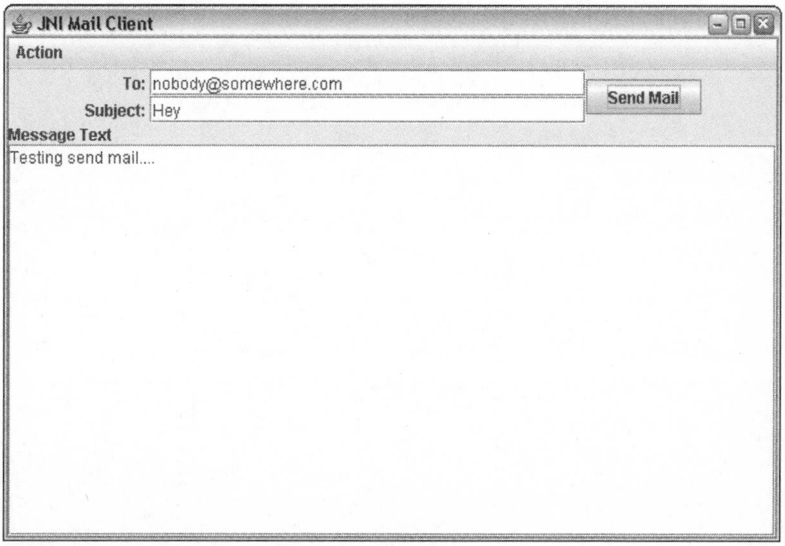

Figure 9-6

The JNIMailBridge class contains all the code related to the retrieval and storage of messages from Outlook. The native code uses the method-calling functions in order to pass data back to the Java application. Two helper classes are defined as follows in order to store the folder/e-mail information:

```java
class MailMessage {
    public String fromAddress;
    public String subject;
    public String body;

    public MailMessage(String from, String subj, String b)
    {
        fromAddress = from;
        subject = subj;
        body = b;
    }

    public String toString()
    {
        return("FROM: " + fromAddress + "  SUBJECT: " + subject);
    }
}

class MailFolder {
    String folderName="";
    ArrayList<MailMessage> messageList;

    public MailFolder(String name)
    {
        setFolderName(name);
        messageList = new ArrayList<MailMessage>();
    }

    public String getFolderName()
    {
        return(folderName);
    }

    public void setFolderName(String name)
    {
        folderName = name;
    }

    public int getMessageCount()
    {
        return(messageList.size());
    }

    public MailMessage getMessage(int index)
    {
        if(index < 0 || index >= messageList.size()) {
            return(null);
        }

        return((MailMessage)messageList.get(index));
```

```
    }

    public void addMessage(MailMessage msg)
    {
        messageList.add(msg);
    }

    public void clearMessages()
    {
        messageList = new ArrayList<MailMessage>();
    }

    public String toString()
    {
        return(folderName);
    }
}
```

The MailMessage class stores basic information about a single e-mail message. The MailFolder class stores a collection of these MailMessage objects in an ArrayList and allows for ease of saving and retrieving e-mail messages. The real work on the Java side happens in the JNIMailBridge class:

```
public class JNIMailBridge {
    ArrayList<MailFolder> mailFolders;

    public native void sendMail(String profile, String to,
                                String subject, String body);
    public native void getFolderContents(String profile,
                                String topFolderName, String folderName);
    public native void getFolderList(String profile, String topFolderName);

    static {
        System.loadLibrary("MailLibrary");
    }
```

These methods establish the functions that will be implemented on the native side. The sendMail method sends an e-mail from the user associated with the profile. The getFolderContents returns a list of all pieces of mail inside a specified folder. The getFolderList returns a list of all folders within a top-level folder. The following methods are used to store and retrieve lists of folders and mail messages:

```
    public void clearFolderList()
    {
        mailFolders = new ArrayList<MailFolder>();
    }

    public void addFolder(String folderName)
    {
        mailFolders.add(new MailFolder(folderName));
    }

    public int getFolderCount()
    {
```

```
            return(mailFolders.size());
    }

    public MailFolder getFolder(int index)
    {
        if(index < 0 || index >= mailFolders.size()) {
            return(null);
        }

        return(mailFolders.get(index));
    }

    public MailFolder findFolder(String folderName)
    {
        int index;
        MailFolder folder;

        for(index=0; index<mailFolders.size(); index++) {
            folder = mailFolders.get(index);

            if(folder.getFolderName().equals(folderName)) {
                return(folder);
            }
        }

        return(null);
    }

    public void clearMessageList(String folderName)
    {
        MailFolder folder;

        folder = findFolder(folderName);

        if(folder != null) {
            folder.clearMessages();
        }
    }

    public void addMessage(String folderName, String from,
                           String subj, String body)
    {
        MailFolder folder;
        MailMessage msg;

        folder = findFolder(folderName);

        if(folder != null) {
            msg = new MailMessage(from, subj, body);
            folder.addMessage(msg);
        }
    }
}
```

The JNIMailBridge class defines three native functions. The profile parameter is used to select a specific profile in Outlook. Each user generally has one profile for storing mail and other data in Outlook. The other parameters to sendMail are the address to send the mail message to, and the subject and text of the mail message. The getFolderContents method transfers messages from a specified folder in Outlook (using the two parameters top folder; that is, the folder that contains other folders, and the individual folder that has the messages) to the JNIMailBridge class using the clearMessageList and addMessage methods. The getFolderList method transfers all folders that are located beneath the top folder. For purposes of this example, Outlook has the set of standard folders beneath the folder named *Top of Personal Folders* and the profile name is *Outlook*.

The code on the native side performs the necessary communication with Outlook. The three native functions are implemented using COM to utilize the MAPI routines. MAPI provides an interface to access mail data and send mail through Outlook:

```
JNIEXPORT void JNICALL Java_JNIMailBridge_getFolderList
    (JNIEnv *env, jobject obj, jstring _profile, jstring _topFolder)
{
    const char *folderName = env->GetStringUTFChars(_topFolder, 0);
    const char *profile = env->GetStringUTFChars(_profile, 0);

    _SessionPtr pSession("MAPI.Session");

    // Log on with a specific profile.
    // If this isn't specified a logon box would pop up.
    pSession->Logon(profile);

    InfoStoresPtr pInfoStores;
    InfoStorePtr pInfoStore;
    FolderPtr pTopFolder;
    FoldersPtr pPSTFolders;
    long l;

    pInfoStores = pSession->GetInfoStores();

    if(pInfoStores == NULL) {
        env->ThrowNew(env->FindClass("java/lang/Exception"),
            "Can't obtain handle to InfoStores");
        return;
    }

    // Search for the specific folder name
    for(l=1; l <= (long)(pInfoStores->GetCount()); l++) {
        pInfoStore = pInfoStores->GetItem(l);
        pTopFolder = pInfoStore->GetRootFolder();

        _bstr_t fName = folderName;
        _bstr_t compName = (_bstr_t)pTopFolder->GetName();

        if(fName == compName) {
            // We've found it, exit the loop
            break;
        }
```

```
        }

        if(pTopFolder == NULL) {
            env->ThrowNew(env->FindClass("java/lang/Exception"),
                "Can't obtain handle to top folder");
            return;
        }

        pPSTFolders = pTopFolder->GetFolders();

        if(pPSTFolders == NULL) {
            env->ThrowNew(env->FindClass("java/lang/Exception"),
                "Can't obtain handle to PST folders");
            return;
        }
```

This block of code will look familiar to you shortly. This code establishes a connection to the data stored in Outlook via the MAPI object. The InfoStores contains all top-level folders. This collection is searched for the top-level folder that contains the various mail folders:

```
        jclass cls = env->GetObjectClass(obj);
        jmethodID clearFolderID =
            env->GetMethodID(cls, "clearFolderList", "()V");
        jmethodID addFolderID =
            env->GetMethodID(cls, "addFolder", "(Ljava/lang/String;)V");
```

This code establishes handles to the clearFolderList and addFolder methods defined in the Java code. These handles are then used to invoke the methods on the Java side in order to communicate data back to the Java object:

```
        // First reset the list of folders
        env->CallVoidMethod(obj, clearFolderID);

        // Loop over all available folders
        for(l=1; l <= (long)(pPSTFolders->GetCount()); l++) {
            FolderPtr tempFolder = pPSTFolders->GetItem(l);

            _bstr_t pstName = tempFolder->GetName();

            // Add folder. Remember that the string must be transformed
            // into a Java string using NewStringUTF.
            env->CallVoidMethod(obj, addFolderID,
                            env->NewStringUTF((char *)pstName));
        }

        env->ReleaseStringUTFChars(_topFolder, folderName);
        env->ReleaseStringUTFChars(_profile, profile);
    }
```

The getFolderList function retrieves the list of folders beneath a specified top folder. Note how the strings are allocated and released at the end. The method invocation functions are used to make callbacks to the Java code in order to first reinitialize the list of folders (invoking clearFolderList) and then adding each folder to the collection in Java by invoking addFolder. The getFolderContents function, listed next, performs a retrieval of e-mail messages in a specified folder using similar callback semantics to getFolderList. Take a look at this function piece by piece:

```
JNIEXPORT void JNICALL Java_JNIMailBridge_getFolderContents
    (JNIEnv *env, jobject obj,
    jstring _profile, jstring _folderName, jstring _searchName)
{
    jclass mapiSupportClass;
    jmethodID mAddMessage, mClearMessages;

    const char *folderName = env->GetStringUTFChars(_folderName, 0);
    const char *searchName = env->GetStringUTFChars(_searchName, 0);
    const char *profile = env->GetStringUTFChars(_profile, 0);

    mapiSupportClass = env->GetObjectClass(obj);

    if(mapiSupportClass == NULL) {
        env->ThrowNew(env->FindClass("java/lang/Exception"),
                    "Can't obtain class handle from object passed in");
        return;
    }

    _SessionPtr pSession("MAPI.Session");

    // Log on with a specific profile.
    // If not specified a logon box would pop up.
    pSession->Logon(profile);
```

The three jstrings that are passed in must first get converted to strings suitable for use in the native code. Next, since methods will be invoked on a Java object, a handle to the Java object must be obtained. This happens via the call to GetObjectClass. Next, a pointer to the MAPI.Session object is obtained and then Logon is called in order to work with the MAPI object since it requires authentication:

```
    InfoStoresPtr pInfoStores;
    InfoStorePtr pInfoStore;
    FolderPtr pTopFolder;
    FoldersPtr pPSTFolders;
    long l;

    pInfoStores = pSession->GetInfoStores();

    if(pInfoStores == NULL) {
        env->ThrowNew(env->FindClass("java/lang/Exception"),
                    "Handle to info stores is invalid");
        return;
    }

    // First we search for the correct collection of folders.
    for(l=1; l <= (long)(pInfoStores->GetCount()); l++) {
        pInfoStore = pInfoStores->GetItem(l);
```

```
            pTopFolder = pInfoStore->GetRootFolder();

            _bstr_t fName = folderName;
            _bstr_t compName = (_bstr_t)pTopFolder->GetName();

            if(fName == compName) {
                break;
            }
        }

    pPSTFolders = pTopFolder->GetFolders();

    if(pPSTFolders == NULL) {
        env->ThrowNew(env->FindClass("java/lang/Exception"),
                        "Can't create global reference to Java class");
        return;
    }
```

The InfoStores collection contains all the top-level folders. This loop executes in order to find the root folder of the mail folders. If at any point an object is NULL, an exception is thrown:

```
    // Second we need a handle to the correct folder,
    // so search for folderName.
    for(l=1; l <= (long)(pPSTFolders->GetCount()); l++) {
        FolderPtr tempFolder = pPSTFolders->GetItem(l);
        _bstr_t pstName = tempFolder->GetName();

        _bstr_t compSearchName = searchName;

        if(pstName == compSearchName) {
            break;
        }
    }

    // Get a handle to the first message (after getting
    // a handle to the folder, then the folder's
    // message collection)
    FolderPtr pFoundFolder = pPSTFolders->GetItem(l);

    if(pFoundFolder == NULL) {
        env->ThrowNew(env->FindClass("java/lang/Exception"),
                        "Folder requested was not found");
        return;
    }

    MessagesPtr pMessages = pFoundFolder->Messages;

    if(pMessages == NULL) {
        env->ThrowNew(env->FindClass("java/lang/Exception"),
                        "Can't obtain handle to message collection");
        return;
```

```
    }

    MessagePtr pMessage = pMessages->GetFirst();

    if(pMessage == NULL) {
        env->ThrowNew(env->FindClass("java/lang/Exception"),
                    "Can't obtain handle to first message in collection");
        return;
    }
```

After obtaining a handle to the correct top-level folder, its contents are searched to obtain a handle to the mail folder. A MessagePtr is then configured to point to the first message in this folder:

```
    mAddMessage = env->GetMethodID(mapiSupportClass,
        "addMessage",
        "(Ljava/lang/String;Ljava/lang/String;"
        "Ljava/lang/String;Ljava/lang/String;)V");

    mClearMessages = env->GetMethodID(mapiSupportClass,
        "clearMessageList",
        "(Ljava/lang/String;)V");

    if(mAddMessage == NULL || mClearMessages == NULL) {
        printf("Can't obtain handle to class\n");
        env->ThrowNew(env->FindClass("java/lang/Exception"),
                    "Can't obtain handle to addMessage"
                    " or clearMessageList Java method");
        return;
    }
```

These two calls to GetMethodID return handles to the Java methods that will soon get called in order to pass information back to the Java object. If either of these handles are NULL, an exception is thrown:

```
    // Call the clearMessageList method to reset the
    // message collection
    env->CallVoidMethod(obj, mClearMessages, _searchName);

    // Loop through all messages in the folder, using the
    // addMessage method to store each message
    while(pMessage != NULL) {
        _bstr_t subject, sender, text, sent;
        subject = pMessage->GetSubject();

        sender = pMessage->GetSender();
        text = pMessage->GetText();

        jstring jsSubject, jsSender, jsText;

        jsSubject = env->NewStringUTF((char *)subject);
        jsSender = env->NewStringUTF((char *)sender);
```

```
        jsText = env->NewStringUTF((char *)text);

        env->CallVoidMethod(obj, mAddMessage, _searchName,
                            jsSender, jsSubject, jsText);

        pMessage = NULL;
        pMessage = pMessages->GetNext();
    }
```

The first CallVoidMethod is invoked to cause the clearMessageList method to execute. This resets the collection of messages inside the Java object, allowing multiple calls to this function, each returning a different set of messages. For each message in the folder, the appropriate information (subject, sender, and recipient information) is converted to a jstring via NewStringUTF and then passed to addMessage via the CallVoidMethod invocation. This sends basic information about each message, one message at a time, to the Java code for storage and later processing:

```
    pFoundFolder = NULL;
    pMessages = NULL;
    pMessage = NULL;

    // Release the strings
    env->ReleaseStringUTFChars(_searchName, searchName);
    env->ReleaseStringUTFChars(_folderName, folderName);
}
```

The Java code and C++ code work together to create a miniature e-mail client. The Java code is responsible for the user interface and storing the message and folder information. The C++ code is responsible for using COM to access the folders and e-mail in MS Outlook. Java Native Interface is the technology that allows Java code to work with C++ code with a minimum of hassle to you, the developer. This application demonstrates many elements of JNI that were discussed in this chapter and should serve as an instructive example of using JNI to solve real problems.

Summary

Java Native Interface is a powerful mechanism for writing advanced systems in Java. Linking Java to native code enables a developer to leverage functionality provided by the operating system, such as utilizing COM in Windows or perhaps using a native user interface library (presenting vast speed improvements over Swing). This chapter has given you a lot of information about how to utilize JNI, presenting you with plenty of examples that demonstrate common constructs on both the native and Java side. You should now be able to judge if, when, and where to use JNI in your projects.

10

Communicating between Java Components with RMI and EJB

This chapter explains how to communicate between two Java components using Remote Method Invocation (RMI) and how to also use Enterprise JavaBeans (EJB) for more enterprise-oriented architectures. It will explore the different intricacies of each Java technology and explain why one technology may not always be the right fit for all of your architecture needs. Client/server development is becoming extremely hot in the marketplace today. Applications that just exist on a desktop and are tied to a particular operating system are few and far between on the list of development tasks that are going on. With the rise of the Internet, homeland security, online banking, and online shopping, there is a significant need for applications to share information in a quick and secure manner. Therefore, new technologies continue to be developed every day to try and meet those needs.

Web services using SOAP seem to be the latest rage, but if you have ever tried to build a large-scale system and imposed stringent security requirements on Web services, you can quickly see major degradation in performance. The concept of Web services that use SOAP for their protocol is grand, but the tools are not yet there from a performance and interoperability standpoint. While these tools are maturing, developers have other alternatives that perform better and are already highly scalable. RMI and EJBs have been the mature favorites and continue to prove why they are some of the best technologies to use if performance and scalability is your concern. So get started and explore these two technologies.

Remote Method Invocation

Java's claim to fame is the "Write once, run anywhere" model. What about the need for a "Write once, communicate anywhere" model? Java's Remote Method Invocation (RMI) is Java's answer to writing distributed objects, and coupled with Java's Native Interface (JNI), the need to "communicate anywhere" with different languages can be met.

In the past, the use of sockets was the primary way for applications to communicate with each other. This of course was not an object-oriented approach to communication and, if you have ever worked with socket code, you realized real fast just how tedious it was to create a client/server architecture that had some complexity to it and performed all the necessary operations you may have needed.

Remote Procedure Call (RPC) services were the next attempt at eliminating the complicated communication layer of using sockets and to also make it easier for programmers to call remote procedures, but the parameters that could be passed to these procedures usually weren't very complex. If the need to pass more complex parameters arose, the burden would lie on the programmer to process the types and perform monotonous conversions. Plus, the parameters were usually not very portable between languages.

RMI picks up where RPC services left off by being designed in an object-oriented fashion which allows programmers to communicate using objects and not just predefined data types that are language-centric. These objects can be as complex as you need them to be and values that are returned can be of any type. The communication layer is completely hidden from the programmer, which allows you to concentrate on more important aspects of programming, like the business logic.

RMI makes applet coding a dream since you can now have your applets easily communicate with back-end distributed systems. RMI is also very secure and uses security managers to prevent malicious code from attacking your network. If your applications require multithreading, RMI also supports threads flawlessly.

Exploring RMI's Architecture

RMI's basic architectural components usually consist of a client, a server, and an RMI registry, which exists on the server side. The client is able to look up and retrieve the remote objects from the server. The server receives client requests for objects and looks for them in the RMI registry. The server also has the task of registering any remote objects with the RMI registry when it is started. Figure 10-1 shows the basic RMI architecture that was just described.

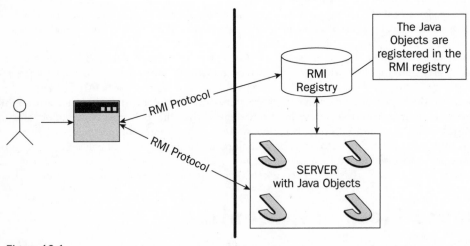

Figure 10-1

The communication transport protocol is completely handled by RMI and is invisible to the programmer. There is no need for you to have to worry about writing any socket code or other transport methods to establish communication with the server. However, you do need to process remote exceptions because at various points, communication breakdowns can occur.

The beauty of RMI is that it lets you call methods on remote objects in the same way you would call methods of a normal Java object. It appears to be almost completely transparent to the programmer. Now, there are certain things you do need to know that affect only RMI applications:

❏ Clients only interact with remote objects that are tied to a remote interface. They can never actually interface with the implementation classes of those interfaces.

❏ Networks can fail, and because at any given time the network connection to the server can drop, you must capture java.rmi.RemoteExceptions. Also, servers must have the method signatures they expose to clients throw java.rmi.RemoteExceptions in the event of a communication failure.

❏ Arguments are passed by value (copy) instead of by reference. When you are programming in Java, objects are passed by reference; with RMI applications, you are dealing with separate Java Virtual Machines, so you can only pass object arguments by value. However, keep in mind that remote objects are passed by reference. A simple rule to remember when dealing with passing objects is that if it is not a remote object, it is passed by value instead of reference.

❏ It is important that you also consider your security architecture when you are dealing with RMI applications. All of your object calls are being transmitted over the network and therefore can be intercepted by someone who could then alter the contents of your calls or simply monitor what you are transmitting. Therefore, for applications that need to be security aware, it is imperative that you do your upfront security design work before developing your applications. Security should never be an afterthought. It will cost you valuable development time if you ignore security requirements in the beginning.

❏ Another design consideration when dealing with RMI is performance. Make sure that you try to design your RMI applications to be as lightweight as possible and avoid any unnecessary overhead. You should definitely plan out your scalability requirements ahead of time during the design phase of your project.

❏ The other aspect of RMI that is transparent to you is remote garbage collecting. Java RMI has incorporated a remote garbage collector for you so you do not need to worry about cleaning up any unused objects.

Although it may seem like there are lots of differences between normal Java applications and RMI Java applications, the differences are relatively simple to grasp and use. The more you develop with RMI, the more the differences will make sense, and you will also discover that all the differences are extremely valuable to you when developing RMI applications. For instance, without remote exceptions, you would never be able to tell when a network error occurred. Having this capability allows you to not only make correct programming decisions when remote exceptions occur, but to also display useful error messages to the users of your applications.

Developing RMI Applications

When developing RMI applications, there is a component called *stubs* that you need to know about in order to develop and communicate successfully with an RMI application. Stubs basically act as remote object proxies that are local to a client. Stubs are generated after you have defined your remote interface containing all the methods you wish to expose to clients. To generate the stubs, you will need to use the *rmic tool* that comes with your installation of Java. The rmic tool will take a specified class and generate the stub file for that class, which exposes all the methods to be used by the client. Stub classes are named with the name of the class that is used followed by a _Stub tag. So if you had a class called RMIChatImpl.class and ran the rmic tool against it, the resulting file would be called RMIChatImpl_Stub.class.

> *Note:* **The new Java 5 SDK supports dynamic generation of stub classes at run time, which eliminates the need to use the rmic tool to pregenerate your stub classes for your remote objects. However, you will still need to use the rmic tool if you plan to support clients that use earlier versions of the Java SDK.**

Stubs are then used transparently by the client. Clients will call methods that reside in the local stub and then the local stub will execute the necessary protocol to call the method on the remote object. The protocol the stub uses involves the following steps:

❑ Establish a connection with the remote JVM that contains the remote object to be used.

❑ Take the parameters for the remote method and marshall them to the remote JVM.

> *Note: Marshalling* **is the act of taking an object and converting it into a byte stream that is compatible with the connection protocol you are using for communication and sending it through the connection pipe. Java accomplishes this by using its serialization specification. Unmarshalling is the act of taking the byte stream and converting it back to its original object form.**

❑ Wait for the results that may be returned from the process of invoking the remote object.

❑ Unmarshall the results back to their original object forms.

All the communication layers, including marshalling, are hidden from the clients calling the remote object methods and the developer. Figure 10-2 depicts the usage of stubs and the basic RMI architecture.

Using Threads in RMI

Threading is usually great for performance issues but can be a bit cumbersome when dealing with remote objects. The RMI specification has no set way of mapping remote objects to threads that the clients use. Therefore you must make sure that your application is thread-safe when it needs to deal with remote object calls. This simply means that if you plan to use threads, then you need to take the necessary time to architect your application in a manner that will be thread-friendly and also to make sure that you have considered any potential thread pitfalls in your architectural design.

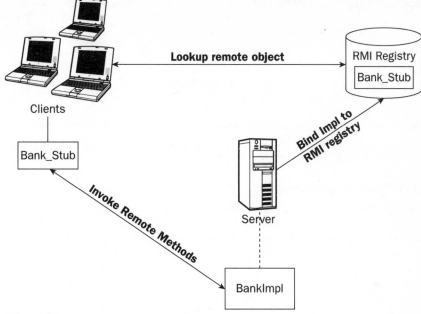

Figure 10-2

Using Dynamic Class Loading

One of the greatest features of RMI is its ability to download classes from another virtual machine that may not exist in the receiving virtual machine. The ability to download almost any object type as long as it is serializable makes RMI extremely simple to use from a development standpoint and eliminates the need for the developer to be concerned with doing any type of custom marshalling and unmarshalling of Java objects. The large benefit is that you can use the downloaded class objects just like you would use any other Java object and call its methods. The only real requirement is to make sure that you capture RemoteExceptions.

Distributed Garbage Collection

A mess that can occur with distributed systems is the need to keep track of all the remote objects you are creating and make sure that you destroy them so that you are not creating memory leaks anywhere. Luckily for you, RMI has a distributed garbage collector that keeps track of all the remote objects and deletes them when they are no longer in use. Without this feature, you would have to do your own garbage collecting, which could be quite burdensome and error-prone.

Examining Remote Object Activations

Systems that would use an RMI type of architecture could potentially be systems that need to support thousands of object creations, and at any given time there could be a need to have access to all those objects if the situation arose. For instance, say you developed a super IM chat system that covered the entire east coast and a certain event happened that caused users to get on and chat with each other all at the same time. Even though all the users are logged on, would you want to continuously keep their

449

objects in memory? RMI has a mechanism, called *Remote Object Activations*, that allows on-demand access to remote objects. These are called *activatable remote objects*. To make activatable remote objects work, two things were developed:

❑ A class called *java.rmi.activation.Activatable*, which makes remote objects activatable.

❑ An activation daemon called *rmid*. The rmid manages the creation of activatable objects and it also manages how the objects are executed.

So just how do you make your remote interfaces activatable, you might ask? Well, first you must include the java.rmi.activation package, and then you must extend the class Activatable for your class while implementing your remote interface. Here is a quick example demonstrating how to use basic activations.

TestRemoteInterface Interface

This TestRemoteInterface looks like a standard remote interface class for RMI. Basically, there is no difference between creating a remote interface with activations and a remote interface without activations. The changes start to come into play when you create the implementation and client classes. The following code demonstrates how to create the TestRemoteInterface:

```
import java.rmi.*;

public interface TestRemoteInterface extends Remote {

    public String rmiWelcome() throws RemoteException;

}
```

TestActivationImpl Class

The implementation class is the first exposure to the activation world in this text. In this class, you need to extend the java.rmi.activation.Activatable class and set up a constructor that takes two new parameters. In the constructor, you must call the parent construct to register the new object with the parent class and have it assign an anonymous port to the class:

```
import java.rmi.*;
import java.rmi.activation.*;

public class TestActivationImpl extends Activatable implements TestRemoteInterface
{

    public TestActivationImpl(ActivationID activationID, MarshalledObject mObject)
                                        throws RemoteException {
        // Register the object
        super(activationID, 0);
    }

    // Now you will need to implement your remote interface methods here
    public String rmiWelcome() throws RemoteException {
        return (String) "Welcome to activatable RMI!";
    }
}
```

At this point, you have achieved the creation of a remote interface and an implementation of the remote interface. You now need to turn your attention to the client class and how it uses activations.

TestClient Class

In order to test out the activation capability, a client must be created to look up the remote objects and execute the methods associated with them. The following code will demonstrate to you all the intricacies involved in creating the client code:

```
import java.rmi.*;

public class TestClient {

    public static void main(String args[]) {

        String sURI = "rmi://127.0.0.1/TestActivationImpl";

        // Get a security manager
        RMISecurityManager rmSM = new RMISecurityManager();
        System.setSecurityManager(rmSM);
```

The preceding code creates a variable to hold the URL to the TestActivationImpl. This variable is currently pointing to localhost but could easily point to any server available on the network. The security manager must be set up so that the client can download and access the remote objects stub. That is accomplished with the method call System.setSecurityManager(rmSM):

```
        try {

            TestRemoteInterface testRI = (TestRemoteInterface)Naming.lookup(sURI);

            String sResponse = (String)testRI.rmiWelcome();

            System.out.println("Received the following response from " +
                    "activatable remote object: " + sResponse);

        } catch (Exception e) {
          e.printStackTrace();
        }
    }
}
```

The URL is looked up using the call Naming.lookup(sURI), and if everything is successful, a TestRemoteInterface object should be received. After obtaining the remote object, the remote method TestRemoteInterface.rmiWelcome can now be executed to create the welcome message. That is all there is to the basics of activations. It gets a little more hairy when you introduce the Register class. This text explores that class next.

Register Class

The main purpose of this class is to handle the registration of the implementation class with the *RMI registry* and the *rmid daemon*. Once the implementation class has been registered, the class can then be looked up remotely:

```
import java.rmi.*;
import java.rmi.activation.*;
import java.util.Properties;

public class Register {

        public static void main(String[] args) throws Exception {

        RMISecurityManager rmiMGR = new RMISecurityManager();

        System.setSecurityManager(rmiMGR);
```

The first thing you need to do is get and set a security manager to use so that you have access to the necessary files to perform your registration options:

```
        Properties pProperties = new Properties();
        pProperties.put("java.security.policy", "C:/rmitest/policy");

        ActivationGroupDesc.CommandEnvironment actCommandEnv = null;

        ActivationGroupDesc actGroup = new ActivationGroupDesc(
                                       pProperties, actCommandEnv);


        ActivationGroupID actGroupID =
                       ActivationGroup.getSystem().registerGroup(actGroup);
```

The activation groups above will provide the rmid with the required information it needs to contact the VM of the activatable object. Here you are simply setting up a policy that will allow the VM to be contacted:

```
        String sFileLocations = "file:///C:/rmitest/";

        // Create the rest of the parameters that will be passed to
        // the ActivationDesc constructor
        //
        MarshalledObject mObject = null;

        ActivationDesc actDesc = new ActivationDesc(actGroupID,
                     "TestActivationImpl", sFileLocations, mObject);
```

The activation description shown above will provide the rmid with the necessary info it needs to create a new instance of the implementation class. Here you are telling the rmid the name of the implementation class and the file location and are also providing it with a MarshalledObject:

```
            // Register with rmid
            TestRemoteInterface trInterface =
                        (TestRemoteInterface)Activatable.register(actDesc);

            // Bind the stub that we received with the RMI registry
            Naming.rebind("TestActivationImpl", trInterface);


    }


}
```

Finally, you need to register with the rmid and the RMI registry. This now allows you to test the sample code fully. Remember, you must also have a policy file created and located in `C:\rmitest\policy`. Here is an example of the contents of a policy file that grants the program all permissions:

```
grant {
  permission java.security.AllPermission;
};
```

You have not yet started the RMI registry or the rmid daemon server. These must be started for the code to function properly and for the registration to occur.

Starting the Activation Tools

There are two main tools that you need to start before running the above code. You must start the RMI registry and you must start the rmid daemon.

To start the RMI registry, type the following from a command prompt:

`start rmiregistry`

To start the rmid daemon, you will need to type following from a command prompt:

`start rmid -J-Djava.security.policy=rmid.policy`

After both tools are running, you should then be able to run your remote-activatable object code and register with the RMI registry and rmid daemon tools.

In the next section of this chapter I will show you an example of a nonactivatable application called RMIChat. The RMIChat example is much more complex than the previous activatable example and it will dive into the more intricate details of RMI.

RMIChat Example

The RMIChat example that I will discuss here shows you how to create a chat server, a chat applet, and how to register the objects with the RMI registry. The RMIChat example allows multiple users to communicate with each other via an applet that is embedded in a Web browser. A single server will be used for communication. The following illustration, Figure 10-3, shows the graphical user interface (GUI) of the RMIChat application.

Figure 10-3

Figure 10-4 shows the chat application being used by multiple users at the same time from different browsers. There are two users, Bob and Jenna, who are currently using the chat application. This is Jenna's view of the application.

Figure 10-4

This type of design would normally require an enormous amount of upfront socket work just to establish the communication layer that RMI provides you with. It is pretty amazing how fast you can build your own chat application with little effort. So, with that said, dive into the example and explore the different classes and methods that it uses to achieve its communication and presentation goals.

RMIChat Interface

This RMIChat interface is the interface that exposes the methods that can be accessed remotely by RMI clients. For this interface to function properly, it must extend the java.rmi.Remote interface. This interface will be used by the RMIChatImpl as a guideline for implementation.

You should also take note that all the methods that will be exposed remotely to RMI clients must throw RemoteExceptions. RemoteExceptions are what the RMI clients will receive when an error occurs during communication with the RMI server:

```java
import java.rmi.Remote;
import java.rmi.RemoteException;
import java.util.ArrayList;

/**
 * RMIChat is the main remote interface for the RMIChat application.
 */
public interface RMIChat extends Remote {

    public ChatUser logIn(String sNickName) throws RemoteException;
    public boolean logOut(ChatUser cu) throws RemoteException;

    void sendMessage(String sMessage, ChatUser cu) throws RemoteException;
    String getMessage() throws RemoteException;

    ChatUser findUser(String sNickName)throws RemoteException;
    ArrayList getUsers() throws RemoteException;

    int getUserCount() throws RemoteException;

}
```

RMIChatImpl Class

The RMIChatImpl class is the class that is the implementation of the RMIChat interface. It defines each of the methods that exist in the RMIChat interface and its primary purpose is to act as a server for connecting RMIClients. So when new chat sessions are created via the chat applet, they will communicate with the RMIChatImpl class. This class is also registered with the RMI registry so that clients can look it up in the registry and obtain a remote object to the class:

```java
import java.rmi.RemoteException;
import java.rmi.server.UnicastRemoteObject;
import java.rmi.Naming;
import java.rmi.RMISecurityManager;

import java.util.ArrayList;

/*
 * The RMIChatImpl class is the implementation of the RMIChat interface class.
 */
public class RMIChatImpl extends UnicastRemoteObject implements RMIChat {

  private String m_sServerName;
    private String m_sLastMsg;
    private int nGUID;
    public ArrayList m_alUsers;
```

The RMIChatImpl class implements the RMIChat interface and begins to define its methods. In case you haven't noticed, the class also extends the UnicastRemoteObject. The reason for this is that RMI requires

you to export the object and bind it to a port. In order to do this you can use the method
UnicastRemoteObject.exportObject(this, 3432) in your default constructor or you can simply extend
UnicastRemoteObject as demonstrated in this example and allow it to do the export for you.

In the preceding code, there are also four variables that are explicitly used by this class for tracking user,
server, and message information. They are described in the following table.

Variable	Description
String m_sServerName	Allows you to associate a name with the server. Not a critical variable, but it can be useful if you were to set up multiple servers.
String m_sLastMsg	This variable holds the last chat message that was submitted by a client to the server.
int nGUID	This variable is called the Global Unique Identifier. It is used to assign a unique ID to each client that is using the chat server.
ArrayList m_alUsers	This array list holds ChatUser objects, each which represents an individual chat user or client of the server.

The main variables that are constantly changing throughout the life of the server are the m_alUsers,
nGUID, and the m_sLastMsg:

```
// Default Constructor
public RMIChatImpl() throws RemoteException {
    super();

    nGUID = 0;

    m_sLastMsg = "";
    m_alUsers = new ArrayList();
}

// Constructor which excepts a server name
public RMIChatImpl(String sServerName) throws RemoteException {

    super();
    nGUID = 0;

    m_sLastMsg = "";
    m_sServerName = sServerName;
    m_alUsers = new ArrayList();

}
```

The contructors for the RMIChatImpl class reset all the variables and call their respective super constructors. One thing to note is that the nGUID and the array list of users are always reinitialized when the
RMIChatImpl server is created:

```
public ChatUser logIn(String sNickName) throws RemoteException {

    ChatUser cu = this.findUser(sNickName);

    if (cu != null) {
        return cu;
    }

    cu = new ChatUser(sNickName, nGUID);

    m_alUsers.add(cu);

    nGUID++;

    return cu;
}
```

The first real remote method is shown above and it is called the logIn method. Its main purpose is to allow chat users to log in to the server. When users log in, they must supply the nickname that they wish to use. When the server receives a login request, it will first check to see if the user already exists on the server. If the user doesn't exist, a new ChatUser object is associated with the user and the new user is added to the array list of users:

```
public boolean logOut(ChatUser cuUser) throws RemoteException {

    if (cuUser == null) {
        return false;
    }

    return m_alUsers.remove(cuUser);
}
```

The logOut remote method is just the opposite of the logIn remote method. It allows users to disconnect from the chat server. When users invoke the logOut method, they must supply their credentials in the form of a ChatUser object. Once this is received, the server will then attempt to log the user out and perform any necessary cleanup operations:

```
public void sendMessage(String sMessage, ChatUser cuUser) throws
RemoteException {

    if (cuUser != null) {
        m_sLastMsg = "<" + cuUser.getUserName() + "> " + sMessage;
    }
}
```

The sendMessage remote method is a bit deceiving. It requires a user to submit their credentials and a message to be displayed to all the other chat clients. However, if you look closely, the code doesn't physically send the message anywhere; it simply stores the message in the m_sLastMsg variable. The reason for this is that the chat clients (users) are constantly pinging the server for the last message that was sent. If the last message has changed, they will display the new message. This was an easy approach to take to make this sample code smaller in size and more understandable:

457

```
public String getMessage() throws RemoteException {
    return m_sLastMsg;
}
```

The getMessage remote method is the method that the clients continuously poll for new messages:

```
public ChatUser findUser(String sNickName) throws RemoteException {
    if (m_alUsers != null && this.getUserCount() > 0) {
        int alSize = m_alUsers.size();
        ChatUser cuTemp;

        for (int i = 0; i < alSize; i++) {
            cuTemp = (ChatUser) m_alUsers.get(i);

            if (cuTemp != null) {
                String sTmp = cuTemp.getUserName();

                if (sTmp.equalsIgnoreCase(sNickName)) {
                    return cuTemp;
                }
            }
        }
    }

    return null;
}
```

The findUser remote method allows clients or servers to retrieve a user's credentials or ChatUser object based on the user's nickname. You may have noticed that this is the first RMI remote method that returns a custom object. RMI is so powerful that it allows you to utilize your own custom objects with one main constraint—the custom object you are returning must be serializable. ChatUser is the object being returned and it is serializable, so it is perfectly valid:

```
public ArrayList getUsers() throws RemoteException {
    return m_alUsers;
}

public int getUserCount() throws RemoteException {
    if (m_alUsers == null) {
        return 0;
    }

    return m_alUsers.size();
}

public String getServerName() throws RemoteException {
    return m_sServerName;
}
```

The above code is used to retrieve the values of different variables. You can retrieve a list of users on the server that could possibly be used by the clients to show a list of users in a listbox. I did not add this to the present example. However, it would be a good exercise for you to try:

```
    public static void main(String[] args) {
        // Setup a security manager
        if (System.getSecurityManager() == null) {
            System.setSecurityManager(new RMISecurityManager());
        }

        try {
            RMIChatImpl rmiObj = new RMIChatImpl();

            // Bind this object to "RMIChatServer"
            Naming.rebind("RMIChatServer", rmiObj);

            System.out.println("RMIChatServer registered with the RMI registry");
        } catch (Exception ex) {
            System.out.println("RMIChatImpl error: " + ex.getMessage());
            ex.printStackTrace();
        }
    }
}
```

The main method of the class is important because it is used when the RMIChatImpl class is registered with the RMI registry. Following is a list of necessary steps that it performs:

1. First it sets up a security manager for the server. You can tailor the security manager to fit your individual architectural needs. This simple example just uses the default system security manager.

2. It then constructs an RMIChatImpl object that will be registered with the RMI registry.

3. Finally it uses the Naming.bind method to bind the RMIChatImpl object with the name "RMIChatServer" in the RMI registry. Clients can search for "RMIChatServer" to obtain a remote RMIChatImpl object.

The RMI registry must be started before the steps above are executed to ensure proper registration with the RMI registry.

ChatUser Class

The ChatUser class is used to store specific information about users of the RMIChatImpl server. The server uses this class extensively to track, search, and accept messages, and authenticate users. While there isn't much to this class, there is something important that must be noted. Since this class is being returned through a remote object via one of the RMIChatImpl server's methods, it must be serializable. If it were not serializable, exceptions would be thrown and the server would not work:

```
public class ChatUser implements java.io.Serializable {
    private String m_sUserName;
    private int m_nUserID;

    protected Object clone() throws CloneNotSupportedException {
        return super.clone();
    }

    protected void finalize() throws Throwable {
```

```
            super.finalize();
    }

    public boolean equals(Object arg0) {
        return super.equals(arg0);
    }

    public int hashCode() {
        return super.hashCode();
    }
```

The preceding code is mainly used for serialization purposes to make sure that the class is utilizing serialization as specified by the interface java.io.Serializable. The code shown below is simply used to track user information such as the user's name (or nickname) and the user's unique ID:

```
    public ChatUser(String sUserName, int nUserID) {
        m_sUserName = sUserName;
        m_nUserID = nUserID;
    }

    public int getUserID() {
        return m_nUserID;
    }

    public void setUserID(int userID) {
        m_nUserID = userID;
    }

    public String getUserName() {
        return m_sUserName;
    }

    public void setUserName(String userName) {
        m_sUserName = userName;
    }
}
```

ChatApplet Class

The ChatApplet class is the main class for the client. It contains the Swing code for the GUI and it also contains the client code for sending and receiving messages. Since the Swing code can be very large, I will eliminate most of it from the chapter discussion. However you can find all of the working code on http://www.wrox.com:

```
import javax.swing.*;
import java.rmi.Naming;

public class ChatApplet extends JApplet implements Runnable {
    private JPanel jContentPane = null;

    private JButton jButton = null;
    private JTextField jTextField = null;
    private JButton jButton1 = null;
```

```
            private JScrollPane jScrollPane = null;
            private JList jList = null;
            private JLabel jLabel = null;
            private DefaultListModel listModel = null;

            private RMIChat m_rmiChat = null;
            private ChatUser m_ChatUser = null;

            private boolean m_bIsConnected = false;
```

The ChatApplet class does not extend or implement any specific RMI interfaces or classes, nor is it required to. The code for accessing the remote objects of the RMIChatImpl object will be shown shortly. Throughout the explanation of this class there are three variables that are considered global. They are described in the following table.

Variable	Description
RMIChat m_rmiChat	This represents an RMIChat object that will be used later to communicate with the remote objects on the server.
ChatUser m_ChatUser	This variable contains specific user information that pertains to the client.
Boolean m_bIsConnected	This is a boolean flag that lets you constantly know what your status is with the server. So if the value is set to true, you are connected to the server, otherwise you are not.

```
            public void start() {
              super.start();

              Thread t = new Thread(this);
              t.start();
            }

            public void stop() {
              super.stop();
            }
```

The start and stop methods can be used to determine when an applet has been started or when it has been stopped. In the start method, you are spawning off a thread which will be used to poll the server for new chat messages:

```
            public void run() {
                String sOldMsg = "";
                String sNewMsg = "";

              while (true) {
                if (this.m_bIsConnected) {
                    try {
                        if (this.m_rmiChat != null) {
```

```
                    sNewMsg = this.m_rmiChat.getMessage();
                    if (!sNewMsg.equalsIgnoreCase(sOldMsg)) {
                        listModel.addElement(sNewMsg);
                        sOldMsg = sNewMsg;
                    }
                }
            } catch (Exception e) {
                System.out.println(e.getMessage());
                e.printStackTrace();
            }
        }

    try {
            Thread.currentThread().sleep(500);
        } catch (Exception e) {
          System.out.println(e.getMessage());
          e.printStackTrace();
        }
      }
    }
```

The run method is the body of the thread that was spawned in the start method. This method checks to see if you are connected and that you have a valid remote RMIChat object. If you do, it polls the chat server every 500 milliseconds using the RMIChat object, m_rmiChat, for new messages with the rmiChat.getMessage method:

```
public ChatApplet() {
    super();
    init();
}


public void init() {
    listModel = new DefaultListModel();
    listModel.addElement("Chat Client loaded successfully.");
    listModel.addElement("Chat messages will appear below.");

    jList.setModel(listModel);

    try {
        m_rmiChat = (RMIChat) Naming.lookup("RMIChatServer");

    } catch (Exception ex) {
        System.out.println("ChatApplet error: " + ex.getMessage());
        ex.printStackTrace();
    }

}
```

The init method contains your core RMI code. It looks up the RMIChatServer remote object using the Naming.lookup method and returns an RMIChat object upon success. If the operation was successful, you can immediately begin using the RMIChat object to call remote methods on the server. It is that easy!

```
                private javax.swing.JButton getJButton() {
            if (jButton == null) {
                jButton = new javax.swing.JButton();
                jButton.setText("Send");
                jButton.setName("btSend");
                jButton.addActionListener(new java.awt.event.ActionListener() {
                    public void actionPerformed(java.awt.event.ActionEvent e) {
                        if (m_bIsConnected) {
                            if (m_rmiChat != null && m_ChatUser != null) {
                                try {
                                    m_rmiChat.sendMessage(jTextField.getText(), m_ChatUser);
                                } catch (Exception ex) {
                                    System.out.println(ex.getMessage());
                                    ex.printStackTrace();
                                }
                            }
                        }

                    }
                });
            }
            return jButton;
        }
```

The getJButton method is where you will perform your send message code. When the send button is pressed, you should grab the text from the jTextField control and then send a message to the server using the m_rmiChat.sendMessage method. This method simply takes as parameters the message you want to send in String form and your credentials in the form of a ChatUser object:

```
        private javax.swing.JButton getJButton1() {
            if (jButton1 == null) {
                jButton1 = new javax.swing.JButton();
                jButton1.setText("Connect");
                jButton1.setName("btConnect");
                jButton1.addActionListener(new java.awt.event.ActionListener() {
                    public void actionPerformed(java.awt.event.ActionEvent e) {
                      if (jButton1.getText().equalsIgnoreCase("Connect")) {
                    // Create user here
                    m_bIsConnected = true;

                        if (m_rmiChat != null) {
                            String sUserName = jTextField.getText();

                            if (sUserName.equalsIgnoreCase("")) {
                        sUserName = "noname";
                            }
                            try {
                                m_ChatUser = m_rmiChat.logIn(sUserName);
                            } catch (Exception ex) {
                              System.out.println(ex.getMessage());
                              ex.printStackTrace();
                            }
                        }
```

When the user clicks the Connect or Disconnect button, the above ActionEvent is fired. What occurs is the applet will send a message to the server requesting to log in with a particular username using the m_rmiChat.logIn method. If the network layer is present and the method succeeds, an m_ChatUser object is returned. If a connection already exists, then the logOut code below will be executed. The applet will attempt to disconnect the client from the server once the m_rmiChat.logOut method is called:

```
                    jButton1.setText("Disconnect");
                } else {
                m_bIsConnected = false;
                    jButton1.setText("Connect");

                if (m_rmiChat != null && m_ChatUser != null) {
                    try {
                        m_rmiChat.logOut(m_ChatUser);
                    } catch (Exception ex) {
                        System.out.println(ex.getMessage());
                        ex.printStackTrace();
                    }
                }
            }
        }
    });

    }
    return jButton1;
    }

}
```

The final piece of code in this example is the HTML code for loading the applet. This code will embed the applet in your Web browser of choice:

```
<html>
  <body>
    <applet code=ChatApplet.class width="300" height="200" >
    </applet>
  </body>
</html>
```

Compiling the RMIChat Application

So far, this chapter has briefly touched on the subject of compiling RMI applications and using the rmic tool to generate stubs, but it has not yet shown you an example of how to do so. Below are the necessary steps to compile an RMI application:

1. The first step is to compile all the source files as you normally would do with any Java application.

2. You will need to then run the rmic tool on the RMIChatImpl class to generate the appropriate stub. From a command prompt in the directory where your compiled source files are located, type the following:

   rmic RMIChatImpl

3. Once you have compiled the source files and generated the appropriate stubs, you will then need to start the RMI registry using the command stated below:

```
start rmiregistry
```

4. The final step is to start the RMIChatImpl server. This will register the server with the RMI register and cause it to await client connections.

```
java   -Djava.rmi.server.codebase=http://host/username/dir/
         -Djava.security.policy=policy RMIChatImpl
```

And that is all there is to creating a very significant RMI application. This example has covered the most important functionalities of RMI, and this knowledge hopefully will provide you with a solid foundation for building future RMI applications. Now turn your attention to Enterprise JavaBeans.

Enterprise JavaBeans

Enterprise JavaBeans, or EJBs, are a server-side component-based architecture that is used to build applications that are scalable, transactional, distributable, portable, and secure. If you think in terms of reusable code, then you will see why EJBs are so vital. EJBs are only concerned with the business logic of the application; the system logic is the requirement of the EJB container. EJB containers are basically application servers that provide you with a server platform to deploy your EJBs on. They handle all the scalability, transactional, security, connection pools, and other system logic components, thus making your job as a developer much easier. Because EJBs are a standard, and application servers must implement the EJB specification, EJBs can be deployed on different application servers with very little configuration changes and almost no code changes. Therefore EJBs are very portable.

RMI, on the other hand, is great if you never really plan to have a very robust enterprise application. In order to make a robust RMI enterprise application, it would require much more work to write all the transaction, security, and connection pools that EJB containers provide. So, depending on your needs, you can decide which technology is best for your architectural requirements.

RMI is also involved in EJB development. EJBs are accessed via RMI, so all that you learned about RMI will apply nicely to EJB development. Several of the components you used in RMI you will also use in EJBs, like remote interfaces and remote exceptions, but you won't have to deal with complex system logic components like transaction support.

EJB Basics

Just like RMI, EJB clients interact with interfaces that expose methods that they can use to communicate with the server. Therefore, clients never need access to the implementation code on the server in order to communicate and use its methods. EJBs also do not need to manage resources; they simply interact with their container in order to obtain connections to external resources like databases. Developers can leverage these resources quickly and easily and do not need to worry about setting up connection pools, transaction support, or security restrictions. Those tasks fall on the administrator of the container and keep the EJB code itself portable.

Types of EJBs

There are four basic types of EJBs that compose the following discussion: Stateless-Session, Stateful-Session, Entity, and Message-Driven beans. Each type has a specific purpose and it is important that you understand each type before deciding on the EJB architectural design for your system.

Session Beans

Session beans contain session information about the clients they are interacting with. Session beans operate on a single client and their life spans are usually very short-lived. They can be transaction aware and interface with shared data sources. The container class can handle a large number of session beans concurrently. If the container was to crash, session beans would lose all the information that they contain. This means the clients would have to reconnect to the session beans and start over.

Stateless-Session

The name stateless simply means that an instance of the bean contains no state information for a particular client. Therefore, many instances of this bean can be created and used by any client that requires its uses. The container can manage different instances of these beans as needed. Only one thread can be associated with a bean at any time, so it is sometimes necessary to have multiple instances of stateless-session beans available for use. Otherwise, clients would have to wait for the instance of the stateless-session bean to be released before they could use it.

Stateful-Session

The opposite of stateless-session beans, stateful-session beans are dedicated to a particular client. The container manages this dedication. In the event that the container has an enormous amount of client stateful-session beans to manage, it can remove the bean from RAM and store it on disk in a state called passivate. When the bean is needed again by the container, it can read it into memory from disk. This prevents the container from filling up the machine's RAM with stateful-session beans.

A good example of a stateful-session bean is an online Web site that possesses a shopping cart mechanism. An online shopping cart keeps track of items that a user wishes to purchase as the user continues to navigate the site. Stateful-session beans can be used to keep track of this user information.

Entity

Entity beans can be thought of as beans that are used to persist data to a database. They basically represent a single row within a given database. It is important to put emphasis on the word single since entity beans access one row of data at a time. A session bean can have more than one representation of data by simply having multiple instances of itself. Entity beans cannot do that; in fact, an entity bean's life span is directly tied to its relationship with the data, whereas session beans care about clients and not data.

Message Driven

Message-driven beans are message consumers that clients use transparently when they send messages to specific destinations or endpoints that the message-driven beans are aware of. Message-driven beans are asynchronous and in the past only used JMS for communication. With the arrival of the EJB 2.1 specification, message-driven beans are no longer tied completely to JMS.

Message-driven beans are generally invoked and managed by containers. They are completely transparent to the clients that use them to reach a specific destination. When a client makes a request to send a message to a particular destination, the container can then execute the message-driven bean to handle the communication needs.

Examining EJB Containers

As the name suggests, EJB containers are complete systems that house EJBs and allow clients to access the EJBs through the Java Naming and Directory Interface (JNDI) by exposing the EJBs home interface. Here is an example of how clients can look up EJBs locally using JNDI calls:

```
Context initialContext = new InitialContext();

TestHome testHome = (TestHome) initialContext.lookup("java:comp/env/ejb/test");
```

The home interfaces of the EJBs can actually reside on multiple machines on multiple networks. The location of the EJBs would be totally transparent to the user. It is the container's job to find the EJB's home interfaces and provide them to the clients. Figure 10-5 shows the client asking for the EJBRocket home interface, and container 1 gets the interface from container 2 and returns it to the client without the client having any knowledge of where the EJB was located.

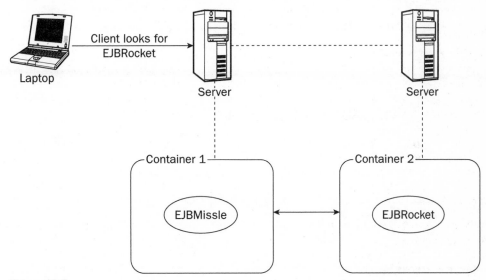

Figure 10-5

Some of the more popular application servers that are EJB containers provide a great amount of functionality — including caching, security, connection pools, thread pools, and transaction support — that the EJBs can leverage. This allows EJB developers to separate the business logic of the application from the system logic and also prevents the developer from having to reinvent the wheel every time the developer needs to create an EJB that requires transaction or database support. This adds to interoperability and is exactly what the architects of J2EE had in mind.

All of the system logic can now be controlled by an administrator of the EJB container, and therefore it gives corporations and government agencies more control over security, scalability, and performance.

If you are looking for a good application server/EJB container to develop EJBs in, try the open-source solution, JBoss.

EJB Loan Calculator Example

The EJB Loan Calculator example will demonstrate how to use a stateless-session bean for the purpose of calculating the monthly payment of a loan given the loan amount, loan term (in months), and interest rate. The beauty of the EJB is that it can be used by any client that requires its loan calculating services. This really shows the benefit of creating EJBs versus individual applications to do all the work. Now, multiple clients can simply call this EJB to perform loan calculations by looking up the loan calculator bean with JNDI.

LoanObject Interface

The first thing you need to do in the example is design the remote interface that clients will be interfacing with. This remote interface must extend the javax.ejb.EJBObject class in order to become a valid remote interface. Any methods associated with this interface must throw a RemoteException in the event of an error. The LoanObject interface is your remote interface that will be used by clients to gain access to its only method that is used for calculating a loan payment. The method calculateLoanPayment takes three doubles and returns the result in double form:

```
package sample.loanejb;

import java.rmi.RemoteException;

/**
 *    The LoanObject class is the remote interface of the EJB
 *    and it contains a method which can be invoked remotely by
 *    clients.
 */
public interface LoanObject extends javax.ejb.EJBObject {

    // The method to calculate monthly payments on a given loan.
    public double calculateLoanPayment(double dLoanAmount, double dLoanTerm,
                                       double dLoanRate) throws RemoteException;
}
```

LoanHome Interface

The LoanHome interface is the EJB home interface that is used to create the LoanObjects and distribute them to clients as needed. The LoanHome interface contains only one method called create to accomplish its task. You may have noticed that the create method not only throws a RemoteException but also a CreateException, which is a requirement for the create method:

```
package sample.loanejb;

import java.rmi.RemoteException;
import javax.ejb.CreateException;

/**
```

```
 *    LoanHome is the home interface of the EJB. We have one method create
 *    which is used to create a LoanObject.
 *
 */
public interface LoanHome extends javax.ejb.EJBHome {

    // Creates a LoanObject
    public LoanObject create() throws CreateException, RemoteException;

}
```

LoanBean Class

The LoanBean class is the implementation of the LoanObject interface. It contains the remote methods
that clients will use when connecting to the EJB. The calculateLoanPayment method is implemented
fully along with the ejbCreate method below:

```
package sample.loanejb;

import javax.ejb.*;
import javax.naming.*;

/**
 *    The LoanBean class is the implementation of the
 *    remote interface. It contains the implementations of the
 *    LoanObject class.
 */
public class LoanBean implements SessionBean
{
    // Used to store the name of the EJB
    String m_ObjectName;

    /**
     *    This method is used to obtain the monthly payment of a given loan
     */
    public double calculateLoanPayment(double dLoanAmount, double dLoanTerm,
                                                       double dLoanRate) {

        double dLoanPayment = 0.0d;
        double dRate        = 0.0d;


        dRate = dLoanRate / 1200;


        // Algorithm =  dLoanAmount * dRate /
        //                  (1 - (Math.pow(1/(1 + dRate), dLoanTerm)))

        dLoanPayment = dLoanAmount * dRate /
                          (1.0d - (Math.pow(1.0d/(1.0d + dRate), dLoanTerm)));

        return dLoanPayment;
    }
```

The ejbCreate method is used to give the developer a chance to execute commands when the EJB is created. In this case, the name of the EJB is being retrieved in the form of a string and then it is saved for later use:

```
public void ejbCreate() throws CreateException
{
    try {

        // Get and save our name
        m_ObjectName = (String) new
InitialContext().lookup("java:comp/env/loanEJB");

    } catch (NamingException ne) {
        throw new CreateException("Could not obtain the name for this EJB");
    }
}
```

The methods below are required but not used for stateless-session beans. This example does not need to use them, but they must be implemented because they are required methods of the SessionBean interface that must be implemented for the LoanBean class:

```
public void setSessionContext(SessionContext ctx)
{
    // Not required
}

public void ejbActivate()
{
    // used only for stateful session beans
}

public void ejbPassivate()
{
    // used only for stateful session beans
}

public void ejbRemove()
{
    // Any clean up code you need to do should go here for the
    // EJB.
}
}
```

LoanClient Class

The LoanClient class is the class that communicates with the EJB and performs the necessary operations to calculate the loan payments due each month. The class expects three command-line arguments to be passed to it:

❑ **The loan amount.** This amount will be converted to a double internally so decimal points in the amount are excepted. An example of a loan amount, if you were financing a car, would be 20000.00.

❑ **The loan term.** The program expects the loan term to be in months. An example of loan term would be 60 months (which is the equivalent of five years).

❑ **The loan rate.** This is the percentage rate you expect for the loan. In order to enter a percentage rate of 7 ½ percent, simply send in the number 7.5.

Take a look at the code. The significant aspects of the class will be explained as the code is presented:

```
package sample.loanejb;

import java.rmi.RemoteException;
import javax.ejb.CreateException;

import javax.naming.*;
import sample.loanejb.LoanHome;
import sample.loanejb.LoanObject;
```

In order to use the LoanHome and LoanObject classes, they must be imported since they are a significant part of the design of this class:

```
/**
 *   This is the LoanClient that will communicate with the EJB.
 */
public class LoanClient {

    private LoanHome m_LoanHome;


    public LoanClient() throws Exception {

      try {
        Context ctx = new InitialContext();
        m_LoanHome = (LoanHome) javax.rmi.PortableRemoteObject.narrow(
                    ctx.lookup("LoanEJB"), LoanHome.class);

        ctx.close();

      } catch (NamingException e) {
        System.out.println("Could not lookup LoanEJB home");
        throw e;
      }
    }
```

The default constructor performs a crucial operation of looking up the remote object LoanEJB that is required in order to use its remote methods. Once the object is found, it is then stored in a LoanHome variable for later use:

```
    public LoanHome getHome() {
        return m_LoanHome;
    }

    public static void main(String[] args) throws Exception {

        if (args.length != 3) {
```

```
            System.out.println("Usage: java -jar client.jar " +
                    "loanAmount (5000.00, loanTerm (in months, 60), " +
                    "loanRate (7.5)");
        System.exit(0);
    }
```

The main method expects three arguments to be sent to it as was discussed earlier in this section. If they do not exist, the program will print out a usage statement to the user and exit without further execution:

```
    // Obtain a client object
    LoanClient lcClient = new LoanClient();

    // Collect arg info into appropriate variables
    double dLoanAmount = Double.parseDouble(args[0]);
    double dLoanTerm   = Double.parseDouble(args[1]);
    double dLoanRate   = Double.parseDouble(args[2]);

    // Create LoanEJB
    LoanObject loanObj;

    try {
        // Create the EJB object
        loanObj = lcClient.getHome().create();

    } catch (CreateException ex) {
        System.out.println("Error creating EJB!");
        throw ex;
    }
```

There are many neat things happening in this segment of the client class. First a LoanClient object is created, which is an object of this class. This triggers the default constructor, which looks up the LoanEJB and stores it in the m_LoanHome variable of the class. Once the home object is obtained, an EJB object is created by calling `lcClient.getHome().create()` and then it is stored in the loanObj variable which is of type LoanObject. Now you are ready to continue and make remote calls as needed:

```
    double dResult;

    try {

      dResult = loanObj.calculateLoanPayment(dLoanAmount,dLoanTerm,dLoanRate);

    } catch (RemoteException ex)      {

      System.out.println("Error calling loanObj.calculateLoanPayment()");
      throw ex;
    } finally {
        // perform clean up
        loanObj.remove();
    }
```

Using the loanObj, a call to calculateLoanPayment is made to get the monthly payment for the loan specified. Since the object is no longer needed, loanObj.remove is called to perform any cleanup routines that may be needed prior to the EJB being garbage collected:

```
        // Print out result
        System.out.println("The amount it will cost you each month for a" +
            " period of " + dLoanTerm +
            " month(s)\non a $"+ dLoanAmount +" loan with an interest rate of " +
            dLoanRate + " percent is: $" + dResult);

    }
}
```

Finally, the result of the loan is printed out. Here is the printout of a sample result for a loan that has a loan amount of $20,352.07 with a term of 60 months at an interest rate of 7.5 percent.

> **The amount it will cost you each month for a period of 60.0 month(s) on a $20352.07 loan with an interest rate of 7.5 percent is: $407.81373247452996.**

Examining the EJB-JAR.XML File

The ejb-jar.xml file is the basic EJB deployment descriptor that is used by containers to locate classes and interfaces, impose security restrictions, and set up transaction support. Depending on the application server you are using for your EJBs, you may be required to fill out another XML file that is specific to your application server. The ejb-jar.xml file generally coexists with the application server's deployment descriptor file. For example, JBoss uses both ejb-jar.xml and jboss.xml. The file jboss.xml is obviously jboss-specific and is not compatible with other application servers:

```xml
<?xml version="1.0" encoding="UTF-8"?>

<ejb-jar>
  <description>
        LoanEJB example takes a loan amount, term in months and interest
        rate then computes and returns the monthly payment for the loan
  </description>

  <display-name>LoanEJB example</display-name>
```

These are the basic description and name tags for the EJB that may show up in the container's administrator page or elsewhere. They are not critical configurations, but are worth noting:

```xml
    <enterprise-beans>
      <session>
        <display-name>Loan EJB</display-name>
        <ejb-name>LoanEJB</ejb-name>

        <home>sample.loanejb.LoanHome</home>
        <remote>sample.loanejb.LoanObject</remote>
        <ejb-class>sample.loanejb.LoanBean</ejb-class>

        <session-type>Stateless</session-type>
        <transaction-type>Container</transaction-type>
```

Explore the elements shown above a little closer. The `<ejb-name>` element specifies the name for the EJB. The `<home>` element must point to the EJB home interface. The `<remote>` element must point to the remote interface. For this example, that is the LoanObject interface. The `<ejb-class>` element must point to the fully qualified name of the enterprise bean's class. The `<session-type>` has only two possible values, Stateful or Stateless. Stateless is what was required for this example. Finally, the `<transaction-type>` element must specify the type of management that will occur, either Bean or Container:

```
        <env-entry>
            <env-entry-name>loanEJB</env-entry-name>
            <env-entry-type>java.lang.String</env-entry-type>
             <env-entry-value>LoanEJB</env-entry-value>
        </env-entry>
      </session>

  </enterprise-beans>
```

The `<env-entry>` section contains environment entries that are optionally set for the EJB's environment. These entries can be looked up by JNDI as shown in this example. The `<env-entry-name>` element contains the name of the EJB's environment entry. The `<env-entry-type>` describes the Java type of the value of the environment entry. The `<env-entry-value>` contains the value of the environment entry:

```
  <assembly-descriptor>

    <security-role>
      <role-name>guest</role-name>
    </security-role>

    <method-permission>
      <description>This is the guest account to access the EJB</description>
      <role-name>guest</role-name>

      <method>
            <ejb-name>LoanEJB</ejb-name>
        <method-name>*</method-name>
      </method>

    </method-permission>

    <container-transaction>
      <description>LoanEJB transaction</description>

      <method>
        <ejb-name>LoanEJB</ejb-name>
        <method-name>*</method-name>
      </method>

      <trans-attribute>Supports</trans-attribute>
    </container-transaction>

  </assembly-descriptor>

</ejb-jar>
```

The final code segment above is contained in the element `<assembly-descriptor>`. This element can contain information on security roles, method permissions, and transaction attributes. There are so many here to examine that the best way to describe them is in a table. Here are the descriptions of each child element of the `<assembly-descriptor>` element.

Element	Description
<security-role>	This element contains info about a security role such as a description and role name
<role-name>	This element contains a security role name that must conform to the NMTOKEN lexical rules.
<method-permission>	This element sets permissions for individual methods of an EJB and it ensures that one or more security roles can be allowed to access the methods.
<method>	This element allows you to associate all methods or specific methods of an EJB with a specific security role of the method-permission element.
<container-transaction>	This element has child elements that manage how transactions apply to EJB methods.
<trans-attribute>	When dealing with EJB methods, this element tells the container how it should manage transaction boundaries. Valid values are as follows: NotSupported, Supports, Required, RequiresNew, Mandatory, Never.

Summary

This chapter explored RMI and EJB Java technologies that allow Java components to communicate with each other on different levels using different protocols. It also demonstrated how EJBs are the better approach of the two technologies for communication between Java components and for interoperability needs when dealing with enterprise applications. RMI is still very useful, and depending on your architecture needs, you should choose the technology that works best for you.

The next chapter will focus in on how to perform communication between Java components using other technologies, such as Web services, CORBA, and sockets.

11

Communicating between Java Components and Components of Other Platforms

Java is an ideal platform for server-side development. Many of the ongoing professional and open source Java development projects are for various server-side applications. J2EE dominates this Java server space, providing a strong open platform for many different types of server applications. One of the core principles and architectural themes in J2EE is the ability to segregate and distribute various *components* of the same software system to different machines. Remote communication between Java objects and components to other Java objects and components is at the heart of J2EE. Since J2EE is an open platform, it also defines how external objects and components in other applications (and even other programming languages) communicate with J2EE components. In today's heterogeneous Internet-centric computing world, this communication is absolutely essential.

> *Components*–Component is an ambiguous term that can mean many different things to many different developers. In the context of this chapter, component refers to any software object or collection of objects that are network-aware, either sending information to other components or receiving it from the latter. For example, a Web server could be considered a component. Web browsers and other client applications need to communicate with this component. Enterprise JavaBeans (EJBs; see Chapter 10, "Communicating between Java Components with RMI and EJB") could also be thought of as components.

In this chapter, you will investigate the general high-level design of component-to-component communication as well as some concrete examples for coding the actual communication. The `java.net` package will be looked at first for its socket's API, since sockets are the basic building block for all other communication technologies. A brief discussion of Remote Method Invocation (RMI) and the Common Object Request Broker Architecture (CORBA) will follow. Concluding the chapter will be information on how best to utilize the latest and greatest craze in distributed software development, Web services.

Component Communication Scenarios

A few examples of where component-to-component communication takes place will aid the understanding of where sockets, CORBA, RMI, and Web services fit into a given application's architecture. In each of the scenarios shown, almost any of these technologies *could* be used. Being equipped with more in-depth knowledge of these technologies later on in the chapter will allow the software developer to weigh the pros and cons of each in their particular situation and pick the right technology for the job.

News Reader: Automated Web Browsing

Little software utilities can often eliminate tedious tasks such as constantly watching and monitoring particular Web sites. Software can be developed to automate these tasks as much as possible. Developing an application for monitoring Web sites would involve communicating with the remote Web server to check various news sites for new stories and information on topics of interest every ten minutes. Whenever a new story popped up, fitting your criteria, the user would be notified, eliminating the need to constantly check and refresh certain Web sites. Writing client components that monitor data sources for new information is a common task in distributed computing.

A Bank Application: An EJB/J2EE Client

Because of J2EE's component-based nature, existing systems can often be extended by simply adding new software components, without destroying their existing infrastructure. Suppose a bank wants to modernize their client software that their tellers use to access the banking infrastructure. The terminals the bank tellers use daily are all running Microsoft Windows 2000 and the application must run on this existing infrastructure. The bank already has a J2EE-based back end to keep track of all banking data, and the application merely needs to interface with it. This J2EE system exposes a Web front end, which is good for personal use over the Internet by various members of the bank, but not for the heavy daily use necessary for tellers. A thick client is needed. The EJB components on the server will need to be accessed by the client. Writing client applications that access EJBs (or other J2EE components) is typical in professional Java development.

A Portal: Integrating Heterogeneous Data Sources and Services

Many Web portals, such as *Yahoo!*, integrate various pieces of data such as stock tickers, sports scores, and news headlines. The software design of such a portal must be flexible enough to integrate many of these different pieces of data, oftentimes from many different locations. Many larger corporations have their own internal intranet portal. These portals need to access information from a variety of sources. Component-to-component communication is crucial to access the databases, files, and information from other software applications necessary for the functionality of the portal.

Overview of Interprocess Communication and Basic Network Architecture

In the development of these distributed software applications, it is often necessary for components running in one process to communicate with components running in another process. For instance, a database runs in one process on a server, and the client application that reads and writes information from and to this database runs in a separate process (and possibly on a different machine). There must be some mechanism through which these two processes communicate. Often, these other processes that your Java application must communicate with are not written in Java and are not running inside a virtual machine. Whether or not another process is running in a Java Virtual Machine, any communication between two processes must follow some sort of *protocol*. Protocols are the language two disparate components use to speak to one another. Your Web browser speaks the HyperText Transfer Protocol (HTTP) to Web servers to retrieve Web content to your local machine. Your instant messaging client speaks a certain protocol back to its server and potentially to other users of an instant messaging service. Peer-to-peer file-sharing services speak protocols to allow the searching and sharing of files (Gnutella is one popular example of a common protocol allowing many different file-sharing clients to communicate with each other.).

All of the applications and protocols mentioned can communicate over a network. They can also communicate to another process on the same machine. This is because these protocols have been abstracted from their transport. They could run locally, or over a TCP/IP network. In communicating between Java components and components of other platforms, you must always consider possible network transports. The Open Systems Interconnection (OSI) network architecture gives a high-level abstraction of some of the layers in any form of interprocess network communication. For the discussion in this chapter, you can think of an even higher-level architecture (derived from the OSI architecture) for understanding component-to-component communication. Figure 11-1 shows the derived architecture with three main layers: the application layer, the protocol layer, and the transport layer.

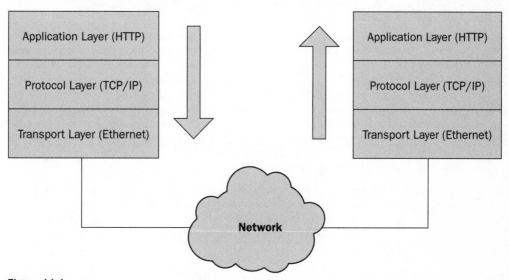

Figure 11-1

Two disparate components communicate by sending data through each of the layers as shown. The application layer represents high-level protocols such as HTTP or FTP. The protocol layer represents lower-level transport protocols such as TCP or UDP running over IP. The transport layer represents the actual physical transport, such as Ethernet, as its corresponding mechanisms for sending and retrieving data. For distributed components to communicate, they must speak the same protocol at the application level.

This chapter focuses on the application level; the lower-level hardware transport is out of the scope of this book. For most distributed application development, the application layer is most important to software developers. In Web applications, for example, HTTP is the application level protocol that dictates many of the application's design decisions. HTTP does not support stateful connections, and therefore the state of any user's session must be simulated by the use of session cookies or session identification parameters. Designing *any* network-aware application, or in other words, any application that must communicate between separate components, Java or non-Java, locally or remote, requires the knowledge of the limitations and features of the various application level and transport level protocols available to facilitate such communication.

> **Note:** *Threads are a critical aspect of designing any good I/O-intensive application, especially I/O over a network and between two disparate processes.*

Sockets

Sockets are the basic mechanism for interprocess communication provided by the operating system. In most development projects, they will probably not have to be used explicitly, since they are fairly low-level. However, *any* type of interprocess communication is built on top of sockets, and in any type of network communication, sockets are used implicitly. Therefore, it would be prudent to understand just some simple background as to how they work. This section of the chapter will provide a broad overview of sockets for the purposes of better understanding RMI, CORBA, and Web services.

A *socket* is essentially a defined endpoint for communication between two processes. It provides a full duplex channel to two different parties (potentially more if it is multicasting) involved in communication — there are two separate data streams, one going in and one going out. There are two types of sockets:

❑   **User Datagram Protocol (UDP).** Sockets using UDP provide a *datagram* service. They receive and send discrete packets of data. UDP is a connectionless protocol, meaning that there is no connection setup time as there is in TCP. However, UDP is unreliable — packets are not guaranteed to be sent or received in the right order. UDP is mainly used for applications such as multimedia streaming and online gaming, where not all data is necessary, for which the UDP's best-effort service model is well suited.

❑   **Transmission Control Protocol (TCP).** Sockets using TCP provide a reliable byte-stream service. TCP guarantees delivery of all packets sent and the reception of them in the correct order. TCP is a connection-oriented protocol, which allows it to provide the byte-stream service. TCP is best suited for applications that cannot allow data transmitted to be lost, such as for file transfer, Web browsing, or Telnet.

This section will only consider using TCP sockets, since UDP is more for advanced network applications that require the development of their own low-level protocols or multimedia streaming algorithms, which are out of the scope of this book. For the purposes of this text, sockets simply allow you an input and output stream to another process, either running locally or remotely.

The Java Socket API

The Java Socket API is the core Java interface to network programming. As such, all of the core socket classes are found in the java.net package. Java implements the two types of sockets: TCP sockets, which communicate using the Transmission Control Protocol, and UDP sockets, which communicate via the Universal Datagram Protocol. In addition to the normal UDP socket implementation, Java also provides a UDP multicast socket implementation, which is a socket that sends data to multiple clients simultaneously. Since Java was built from the ground up as an object-oriented language, you will find that the socket library interacts heavily with the Java I/O libraries (both java.io and java.nio). If you need a refresher on some of the aspects of Java I/O and serialization, see Chapter 5, "Persisting Your Application Using Files." This section concentrates on TCP sockets throughout, because they are far more prevalent than UDP sockets in most client/server or distributed systems.

Key Classes

The following table shows the four major classes used for socket communication in Java. The Socket and DatagramSocket classes implement TCP and UDP, respectively. Both TCP and UDP use an IP address and port number as the demultiplexing key, or address, to another process. InetSocketAddress represents this address. Both Socket and DatagramSocket use an InetSocketAddress to locate the machine and process that should be the recipient of any data sent.

Class (From java.net)	Function
Socket	Class used to represent a client socket endpoint for sending and receiving data over TCP connections.
DatagramSocket	Both client and server class for sending and receiving data sent via UDP.
ServerSocket	Class used for TCP servers. Once a client connects, this class returns a Socket class to actually send and receive data.
InetSocketAddress	Represents an IP address (or hostname) along with a port number. For example, InetSocketAddress could represent www.*example*.com:8080.

Client Programming

The Socket and InetSocketAddress classes are used by a client to connect to a server running in another process (whether remote or local). Once a connection is set up, all communication takes place utilizing normal Java I/O classes. There is a stream of data coming in, and a stream of data going out. To set up a connection, first create the address object that defines which server and port to connect:

```
InetSocketAddress address = new InetSocketAddress("www.example.com", 80);
```

InetSocketAddress objects can also be created with an IP address:

```
InetSocketAddress address = new InetSocketAddress("127.0.0.1", 80);
```

Once the address of the remote endpoint has been defined, a connection can be attempted. Be sure to catch java.io.IOException, as this exception will be thrown if there are any problems connecting (such as the network is down, the server is busy, the server cannot be located, and so on). In network programming, it is important to pay extra attention to error-handling details, as communication problems aren't just a possibility—they are pretty much guaranteed to happen at some point. Now that you have defined an address, you can create a new `Socket` class to attempt a connection:

```
Socket socket = new Socket();
socket.connect(address);
```

If the connection succeeds, either Java I/O classes or NIO (`java.nio`) classes can be used to send and receive data. In these examples, you will use normal Java I/O because it is often easier to understand and provides better code readability. Once the socket is connected, both `InputStream` and `OutputStream` objects from the `java.io` package can be retrieved and communication can begin:

```
InputStream in = socket.getInputStream();
OutputStream out = socket.getOutputStream();
```

These objects are often wrapped around other higher-level and easier to use I/O classes just as they are in normal Java I/O programming. Suppose, for example, that all the communication you are going to send and receive over the socket is textual data. Java provides the `BufferedReader` and `PrintWriter` objects that can be wrapped around the input and output stream objects:

```
PrintWriter out = new PrintWriter(out);
BufferedReader br  = new BufferedReader(new InputStreamReader(in));
out.println("Hello, remote computer");
out.flush();
String serverResponse = br.readLine();
```

> *Note: The call to **flush()** in the preceding code segment is important. **PrintWriter** and other I/O classes buffer data before writing them to their underlying output stream. To have the send take place immediately, you flush the underlying output stream so the data you have written to the **PrintWriter** is immediately written to the underlying output stream, in this case, the **OutputStream** from the **Socket**, which then sends the data over the network. **PrintWriter** can also be created to automatically flush any output written straight to the underlying output stream, at the disadvantage of losing the ability to buffer data before it is sent to optimize network performance.*

That's really all there is to sockets. The difficult aspect of sockets comes when determining and implementing the *protocol* by which two different processes agree to communicate. In the "Implementing a Protocol" section, the difficulties will be explored, and a small portion of HTTP will be implemented.

Server Programming

Programming server-side sockets with Java is just as easy as on the client-side. The `ServerSocket` class is used to initiate a passive TCP connection. A passive TCP connection monitors a particular port on the host machine and waits for a remote client to connect. Once a connection is initiated by a client, the `ServerSocket` class dispatches a `Socket` class, which in turn can be used to get the input and output streams associated with the connection (as well as the hostname and address of the client machine). Certain ports on computers are generally associated with certain protocols, port 80 is HTTP, 23 is Telnet, 25 is SMTP, and so on. When picking a port to use for your application, the general rule of thumb is to keep it above 1000, as most common server applications do not use ports in this range. If a `ServerSocket` is created on a port that is already in use, an exception will be thrown, and the server socket will not be created. Only *one* application on a machine can use any given port at one time. The code below creates a `ServerSocket` and prepares it to accept incoming connections on port 1500:

```
ServerSocket serverSocket = new ServerSocket(1500);
Socket incomingClient = serverSocket.accept();
```

The `accept()` method blocks until a client connects. Once a client connects, a `Socket` instance is returned that represents the connection to the remote process. Input and output streams can be obtained to facilitate communication using the same mechanisms described in the preceding section. You do not have to call `connect()` on the incoming `Socket` though, since the connection setup has already occurred.

The previous code segment listed will accept one connection, and one connection only. Server-side applications generally need to service more than one client simultaneously however. Imagine if eBay or other popular Web sites could only serve one client at a time! The `accept()` method on the `ServerSocket` negotiates another port on the server for the client's connection to move to, freeing up the original port the `ServerSocket` was created on for another incoming connection. You could call `accept()` again to wait for another connection. However convenient the behavior of `accept()` is though, it does not solve the problem of allowing multiple *simultaneous* connections. This is solved through the use of threads. The code below is a simple example of how a server could allow for multiple simultaneous connections:

```
boolean conditionToKeepRunning = true;

while (conditionToKeepRunning) {
    Socket client = serverSocket.accept();

Thread clientServiceThread = new Thread(new ClassThatImplementsRunnable(client));
    clientServiceThread.start();
}
```

Notice how every time your server receives a connection, it spawns off a worker thread to handle the incoming request. This allows the incoming request to be serviced *while* the server waits for another connection. Since each request receives its own thread, more than one request can also be processed at the same time.

> *Note: This model of one thread per request is not the most efficient solution; it is used here for simplicity. Creation and destruction of threads is an expensive operation, and a thread pool would be a better solution. Keeping a fixed number of active threads and using them as they become available can keep the server from being overloaded, as well as virtually eliminating the cost of thread creation and destruction.*

Putting It All Together: An Echo Server

Writing a simple server application will demonstrate a full application using sockets. This cleverly-named echo server will echo any text sent to it back to the client. Whenever a client connects, they will receive a welcome message, and after the message is sent, your server will simply begin its loop of echoing back to the client any text the client sends.

Our server class, `SocketEcho`, will implement `java.lang.Runnable` since every instance you create of `SocketEcho` will be running in a separate thread, allowing you to process multiple simultaneous connections. All of the server logic will reside in the `SocketEcho.run()` method (for the threading). In its constructor, `SocketEcho` is passed a `Socket` with which it conducts all communications with its client in the run() method. The run() method is shown below, and as you can see after the welcome message is printed, the application simply loops on receiving textual input from its client. Every time a new character is received, the server checks to see if it was the exit character (the ? in this case). If the exit character was received, the application breaks out of its loop and the socket is closed in the finally block. Any other character besides the exit character is sent back to the client:

```java
public void run() {
    try {
        BufferedReader br = new BufferedReader(new
                             InputStreamReader(socket.getInputStream()));
        PrintWriter out = new PrintWriter(socket.getOutputStream());

        // print a welcome message
        out.println("Hello, you've contacted the Echo Server.");
        out.println("\tWhatever you type, I will type back to you...");
        out.println("\tPress '?' to close the connection.");
        out.println();
        out.println();
        out.flush();

        int currChar = 0;
        while ((currChar = br.read()) != -1) {
            char c = (char) currChar;

            // if '?' is typed, close the connection
            if (c == '?')
                break;

            out.print(c);
            out.flush();
        }
    } catch (IOException ioe) {
        ioe.printStackTrace();
    } finally {
        try {
            if (socket != null) {
                socket.close();
            }
        } catch (IOException ex) {
            ex.printStackTrace();
        }
    }
}
```

The main() function simply launches the server, using a ServerSocket. In here, the code for accepting client connections and spawning new threads is found. Every time a client connects, a new instance of SocketEcho is created with the client's corresponding Socket instance, and a thread to run it is produced. Once this new thread is started, the control flow for the client that connected goes to the run() method in SocketEcho (which is in a different thread). While one or many clients are connected, the server can still wait for new connections, because the server handles each client in a separate thread:

```java
try {
    ServerSocket serverSocket = new ServerSocket(port);

    System.out.println("Echo Server Running...");
```

```
      int counter = 0;
      while (true) {
        Socket client = serverSocket.accept();

        System.out.println("Accepted a connection from " +
                             client.getInetAddress().getHostName());

        // use multiple threads to handle simultaneous connections
        Thread t = new Thread(new SocketEcho(client));
        t.setName(client.getInetAddress().getHostName() + ":" + counter++);
        t.start(); // starts up the new thread and SocketEcho.run() is called
      }
    } catch (IOException ioe) {
      ioe.printStackTrace();
    }
```

The full listing of the code for SocketEcho is found below:

```
package book;

import java.io.BufferedReader;
import java.io.IOException;
import java.io.InputStreamReader;
import java.io.PrintWriter;
import java.net.ServerSocket;
import java.net.Socket;

public class SocketEcho implements Runnable {

  private Socket socket;

  public SocketEcho(Socket socket) {
    this.socket = socket;
  }

  public void run() {
    try {
      BufferedReader br = new BufferedReader(new
                           InputStreamReader(socket.getInputStream()));
      PrintWriter out = new PrintWriter(socket.getOutputStream());

      // print a welcome message
      out.println("Hello, you've contacted the Echo Server.");
      out.println("\tWhatever you type, I will type back to you...");
      out.println("\tPress '?' to close the connection.");
      out.println();
      out.println();
      out.flush();

      int currChar = 0;
      while ((currChar = br.read()) != -1) {
        char c = (char) currChar;

        // if '?' is typed, close the connection
        if (c == '?')
```

```
            break;

        out.print(c);
        out.flush();
      }
    } catch (IOException ioe) {
      ioe.printStackTrace();
    } finally {
      try {
        if (socket != null) {
          socket.close();
        }
      } catch (IOException ex) {
        ex.printStackTrace();
      }
    }
  }

  public static void main(String[] args) {
    // our default port
    int port = 1500;

    // use port passed in by the command line, if one was
    if (args.length >= 1) {
      try {
        port = Integer.parseInt(args[0]);
      } catch (NumberFormatException nfe) {
        System.out.println("Error: port must be a number -- using 1500 instead.");
      }
    }

    try {
      ServerSocket serverSocket = new ServerSocket(port);

      System.out.println("Echo Server Running...");
      int counter = 0;
      while (true) {
        Socket client = serverSocket.accept();

        System.out.println("Accepted a connection from " +
                            client.getInetAddress().getHostName());

        // use multiple threads to handle simultaneous connections
        Thread t = new Thread(new SocketEcho(client));
        t.setName(client.getInetAddress().getHostName() + ":" + counter++);
        t.start(); // starts up the new thread and SocketEcho.run() is called
      }
    } catch (IOException ioe) {
      ioe.printStackTrace();
    }
  }
}
```

Running the Echo Server

To start up the echo server, simply run it like any other Java application from the command prompt:

```
java book.SocketEcho
```

Once the server is started, it will begin accepting connections on port 1500 (or what was specified as a parameter in the command line). Whenever a connection is accepted, information about who connected is outputted to the screen as seen in Figure 11-2.

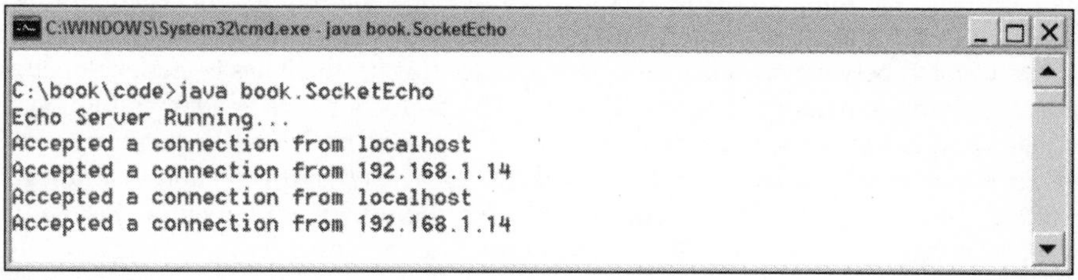

```
C:\WINDOWS\System32\cmd.exe - java book.SocketEcho                    _ □ ×

C:\book\code>java book.SocketEcho
Echo Server Running...
Accepted a connection from localhost
Accepted a connection from 192.168.1.14
Accepted a connection from localhost
Accepted a connection from 192.168.1.14
```

Figure 11-2

To connect to your client, run Telnet. Because you are running your server on a different port than Telnet's default, you have to specify the port to which you want Telnet to connect:

```
telnet localhost 1500
```

Notice the welcome message displays. Now anything you type will be sent to the server and then echoed back to your screen. If you press the *?* character, the server closes the connection. Figure 11-3 shows an example conversion between the client and server.

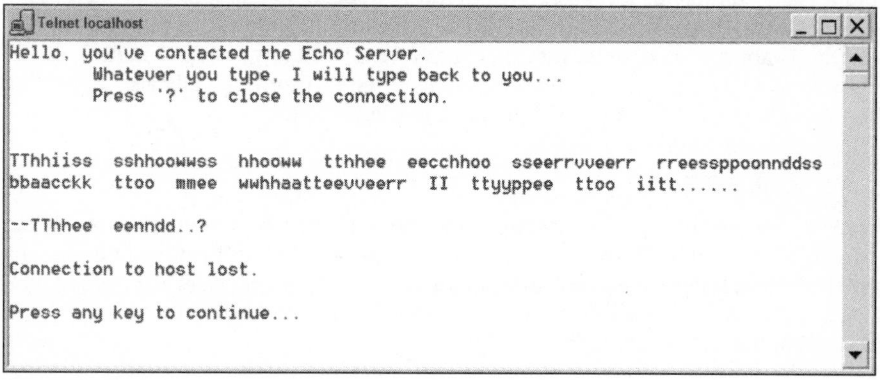

```
Telnet localhost                                                      _ □ ×

Hello, you've contacted the Echo Server.
        Whatever you type, I will type back to you...
        Press '?' to close the connection.


TThhiiss  sshhhhoowwss  hhooww  tthhee  eecchhoo  sseerrvveerr  rreessppoonnddss
bbaacckk  ttoo  mmee  wwhhaatteevveerr  II  ttyyppee  ttoo  iitt......

--TThhee  eennddd..?

Connection to host lost.

Press any key to continue...
```

Figure 11-3

Implementing a Protocol

Sockets provide the building blocks for developing communication languages, or protocols, between two separate applications. TCP sockets provide input and output streams, but any data sent on one end is simply bytes to the other end unless the other end understands its meaning. In the previous echo server example, the server did not *understand* any of the data sent to it. It only read the data, and passed it back to the client. In practice, applications such as these are really only good to test network connectivity. They can serve no other purpose. To have any sort of meaningful communication, both a client and server must talk the same language, or protocol. Implementing protocols is a difficult task. As you have seen previously, sockets in Java are not difficult to program — they are simply another way of reading from an input stream and writing to an output stream. Many of the hard tasks associated with socket programming are the same hard problems associated with reading certain types of files. Files are structured in some sort of meaningful way — for instance, bitmaps are basically a two-dimensional array of color values. Programs that can read and display bitmaps must understand how to *parse* the file format. Writing parsers for anything more involved than simple text commands can be a daunting task, and is out of the scope of this chapter. Implementing a protocol requires agreeing on some form of a contract (or file/data *format*) between the client and server. Once this protocol has been developed, clients and servers can then implement it to talk to each other. The protocol needs to be unambiguous for two separate implementations to work correctly with each other. *It is no trivial task to specify an unambiguous protocol, and then have two separate implementations work with each other*. In this section, a simple implementation of one of the commands in the HTTP protocol will be explored. By implementing just a minute fraction of a simple textual protocol like HTTP, you will appreciate the difficulty in writing and implementing more detailed protocols. Other options will then follow that spare application programmers the need to recreate the wheel by writing new protocols for every application they develop.

Protocol Specification

During the development of an application that employs the use of sockets, there will be some point where either a custom protocol is defined, or the definition of an existing protocol is used as the foundation for the logic in all socket programming in the application. Only for the development of specialized applications is there ever a need to develop a custom protocol. For example, the communications modules of the Mars Landers from NASA probably have to use sockets to issue commands to the robot and receive its status (or if not sockets, some other software abstraction of communication for which you would develop your own protocol). A custom protocol would need to be specified and implemented for this unique set of commands for the Lander. In most applications though, there is probably a protocol out there that suits the application's needs. There are many different ways to write a protocol specification, and this chapter will not delve into such matters, as it is a large subject on its own. In this section, HTTP is used as a test case for implementing someone else's protocol. Only a small portion of the HTTP specification will be looked at and a simple piece implemented.

Basic Elements of HTTP

HTTP follows the simple request/response paradigm. A client sends a request to an HTTP server, issuing a particular command. The server then returns a response to the client based upon what command was sent. HTTP is a stateless protocol, meaning that the HTTP server does not need to retain information about a particular client *across* different requests. Every request is treated the same, no matter what requests a client has previously made.

> **Note:** *There are ways to simulate state over HTTP, and this is what all Web applications do. They use session identifiers and cookies to retain information about a particular client across multiple requests. This is how sites like amazon.com can identify particular users and provide one of the building blocks necessary for e-commerce.*

HTTP was developed purposely to be a simple protocol and easy to implement. This is why things such as stateful-session support had to be built on top of HTTP later — HTTP was originally designed just to be a mechanism for transferring HTML pages across a network. In HTTP, a client merely connects to a port (usually 80) on a remote machine and issues an HTTP command. The main HTTP commands are

- ❑ **GET.** Retrieves the content found at the URL specified.

- ❑ **POST.** Sends data to the HTTP server and retrieves the content found at the URL specified. Oftentimes the content the HTTP server passes back is based on the data sent in by the POST command (that is, form data passed to a server).

- ❑ **PUT.** Asks the HTTP server to store the data sent with the request to the URL specified.

- ❑ **HEAD.** Retrieves only the HTTP headers of a request, and not the actual content.

- ❑ **DELETE.** Asks the HTTP server to delete the content found at the URL specified.

After receiving an HTTP command, an HTTP server returns a response. It returns a response code to indicate something about the response. I'm sure you have seen some of these response codes while simply browsing the Web. Depending on which response code is returned, content may be returned along with the response code. The client can then parse through the content and display it as necessary. Some of the more common HTTP response codes are

- ❑ **200.** Response OK, the request was fulfilled.

- ❑ **404.** The requested URL could not be found.

- ❑ **403.** The request for the URL was forbidden.

- ❑ **500.** The server encountered an internal error that prevented it from fulfilling the request.

See the actual HTTP specification online at the following URL:

```
http://www.w3.org/Protocols/HTTP/
```

It is detailed and precise, and gives a good idea of what a specification for even a protocol as simple as HTTP looks like. For this example, you are going to look at a simple implementation of GET, and how it is be implemented.

A Simple Implementation of HTTP GET

By implementing a small portion of a protocol, the inherent complexity and difficulty of implementing a full protocol specification will be revealed. Writing custom protocols is no picnic, and often leads to hard-to-maintain systems. Open protocols such as HTTP, which are published, are among the easiest to implement. The source code to reference and sample implementations can often be found. Freely available test suites to test the validity of an implementation often exist for open protocols. In the next example, first some of the details of HTTP GET (though not all by any means) must be examined. Your implementation of a simple stripped-down version of GET can then commence, concluding with a look at some methods for testing the validity of the implementation.

Background on HTTP GET

HTTP GET is probably the most commonly used HTTP request operation. Anytime a user types a URL into the address bar of his or her browser and navigates to that URL, GET is used. GET simply asks the server to retrieve a particular file. The server returns a response code indicating whether or not it was successful and, if successful, returns the file. A sample HTTP GET request looks like this:

```
GET / HTTP/1.1
Accept: */*
Accept-Language: en-nz
Accept-Encoding: gzip, deflate
User-Agent: Mozilla/4.0 (compatible; MSIE 6.0; Windows NT 5.0; .NET CLR 1.1.4322)
Host: www.cnn.com
Connection: Keep-Alive
```

Notice the format of the request. First the HTTP command line is given:

```
GET / HTTP/1.1
```

GET signifies the HTTP GET command. The / signifies the file on the server (in this case the root file) —
for example it could be /index.html, which would correspond to the URL http://www.cnn.com/
index.html. The HTTP/1.1 signifies which version of HTTP is being used by this request — this request
is using the 1.1 version of the protocol. HTTP/1.0 is the other valid entry in this field.

After the HTTP command line, HTTP headers follow. An HTTP header follows the format:

```
Key: Value
```

Headers are optional in HTTP 1.0, but in 1.1 certain headers are defined to be required, though most
HTTP servers are lenient and do not enforce these requirements. Many of the optional features of HTTP
are built on top of headers. Features, such as compressing responses or setting cookies, are all based on
HTTP headers. This part of the book will not delve further into the meaning of individual HTTP headers
as this simple implementation of HTTP GET will not make use of them. At the end of the headers, the
request is ended by two line-feeds, or new line characters. This notifies the server that no more HTTP
headers will be sent, and the server can begin sending the response.

An HTTP response is similar in structure to an HTTP request. The first line of a response contains the
HTTP response status code. Headers follow, and then the content of the file requested (in the case of a successful HTTP GET). The response you receive from your request in the previous example looks like this:

```
HTTP/1.1 200 OK
Server: Netscape-Enterprise/6.1 AOL
Date: Tue, 08 Jun 2004 10:33:25 GMT
Last-modified: Tue, 08 Jun 2004 10:33:23 GMT
Expires: Tue, 08 Jun 2004 10:34:23 GMT
Cache-control: private,max-age=60
Content-type: text/html
Transfer-Encoding: chunked

<!DOCTYPE HTML PUBLIC "-//W3C//DTD HTML 4.01 Transitional//EN"><html
lang="en"><head><title>CNN.com</title>
... (more html follows)
```

The first line of the response contains the HTTP protocol version, the status code of the response, and a
brief textual message indicating the nature of the response code. Following are headers, and then the
actual content of the page requested. An implementation of HTTP GET must be able to read the status
code to determine and report back to the user the success or failure to retrieve a page.

HttpGetter: The Implementation

Our implementation of HTTP GET will be a simple command-line Java application. It will save a remote HTML file specified by the user to a local file. Your application will do four main tasks in a simple sequential order:

1. Parse URL and file location to save the remote file from the command-line parameters.

2. Set up the `Socket` and `InetSocketAddress` corresponding to the URL parsed from the command line, and connect to the remote host.

3. Write the HTTP GET request to the Socket's `OutputStream`.

4. Read the HTTP GET response from the server from the Socket's `InputStream`, and write the remote file to disk in the file location specified in the command line.

To parse the URL from the command line, you will use the `java.net.URL` class. This class breaks up a URL into its components, such as host, port, and file. The code to parse the URL and local filename to save the URL to disk from the command-line parameters is straightforward:

```
URL url = new URL(args[0]);
File outFile = new File(args[1]);
```

*Note: Persons experienced with the URL class will note that it already has HTTP protocol capabilities —
we will not be using them, as the exercise is to show the HTTP protocol via sockets.*

Now that the URL has been successfully parsed, the connection to the remote server can be set up. Using socket programming techniques learned from the previous section, the connection is set up as follows:

```
Socket socket = new Socket();

int port = url.getPort();
if (port == -1)
  port = url.getDefaultPort();

InetSocketAddress remoteAddress = new InetSocketAddress(url.getHost(), port);
socket.connect(remoteAddress);
```

One of the idiosyncrasies of the URL class is that if no port is explicitly set in the URL (like `http://www.example.com:1234`), `getPort()` returns `-1`, meaning you have to check for it. Once you have the port, you can create the `InetSocketAddress`, representing the endpoint on the remote server to connect, and then connect to it.

Now connected to the remote server, you simply write the request to the socket's output stream, and then read the HTTP server's response from the input stream. Since HTTP is a text-based protocol, `PrintWriter` is the perfect class to wrap your `Socket`'s `OutputStream` and use to send character data over the socket. Notice in the code below how the two HTTP headers, User-Agent and Host, are sent. User-Agent tells the HTTP server what client software is making the request. Since your client software is called HttpGetter, that is the value put in the header. This header is mainly a courtesy to the server, since many Web servers return different content based on the value of User-Agent (that is, Netscape compatible pages or Internet Explorer compatible pages). The Host value is simply the hostname of the remote server to which you are connecting:

```
PrintWriter out = new PrintWriter(socket.getOutputStream());

// write our client's request
out.println("GET " + url.getFile() + " HTTP/1.0");
out.println("User-Agent: HttpGetter");
out.println("Host: " + url.getHost());
out.println();
out.flush();
```

After you send the request, you must now read the response. The first line of any HTTP response contains the status code for the request. That is the first thing you must check—if the response code is anything other than 200 (OK), you do not want to save the contents of the input to a file, since the only content that could be sent back would be some sort of error message. In the first line of the response, the status code is the second of the three groups of information:

```
HTTP/1.1 200 OK
```

We want to parse out the 200 in the case above and then continue on in this case, since the 200 is HTTP OK, meaning your request was successfully processed and the content of the page you request will follow. In the following code, first use a `BufferedReader` to begin reading character data from the remote server. To parse the status code out of the first line, use a `StringTokenizer` to separate the three groups of values and then choose the second one to convert to an integer:

*Note: Since you are using a **BufferedReader**, you can only read character data from the remote server. This means that your implementation will not be able to request any file in your HTTP GET command that contains binary data (such as an image file, a zip file, and so on).*

```
InputStream in = socket.getInputStream();
boolean responseOK = true;

BufferedReader br = new BufferedReader(new InputStreamReader(in));
String currLine = null;


// get http response code from first line of result
currLine = br.readLine();
if (currLine != null) {
   System.out.println(currLine);
   StringTokenizer st = new StringTokenizer(currLine, " \t");
   st.nextToken();
   String responseCode = st.nextToken();

   int httpResponseCode = Integer.parseInt(responseCode.trim());

   if (httpResponseCode != 200) {
      // response not OK
      responseOK = false;
   }
} else {
   System.err.println("Server returned no response!");
   System.exit(1);
}
```

The last step is to print out the headers, and then save the content of the request to the file specified at the command line by the user. The headers follow the status-code line of the response until a blank line is encountered. In the first loop in the code below, simply print the headers out on the standard output stream for the user to see until you encounter a blank line when you break out of your loop, knowing the content will immediately follow. If the status code previously parsed was 200, save the remaining content found in the `Socket`'s `InputStream` (which is wrapped in a `BufferedReader`) to the file specified by the user:

```java
// read headers
  while ((currLine = br.readLine()) != null) {
    System.out.println(currLine);

    // done reading headers, so break out of loop
    if (currLine.trim().equals(""))
      break;
  }

if (responseOK) {
  FileOutputStream fout = new FileOutputStream(outFile);

  int currByte;
  while ((currByte = br.read()) != -1)
    fout.write(currByte);

  fout.close();
  System.out.println("** Wrote result to " + args[1]);
} else {
  System.out.println("HTTP response code not OK -- file not written");
}
```

The following is the full listing for the code for `HttpGetter`:

```java
package book;

import java.io.BufferedReader;
import java.io.File;
import java.io.FileOutputStream;
import java.io.IOException;
import java.io.InputStream;
import java.io.InputStreamReader;
import java.io.PrintWriter;
import java.net.InetSocketAddress;
import java.net.MalformedURLException;
import java.net.Socket;
import java.net.URL;
import java.util.StringTokenizer;

public class HttpGetter {
  public static void main(String[] args) {
    try {
      if (args.length < 2) {
        System.out.println("Usage");
        System.out.println("\tHttpGetter <Http URL> <file to save>");
        System.out.println
                ("\tExample: HttpGetter http://www.google.com/ google.html");
```

```
    System.exit(1);
}

URL url = new URL(args[0]);
File outFile = new File(args[1]);

Socket socket = new Socket();

int port = url.getPort();
if (port == -1)
  port = url.getDefaultPort();

InetSocketAddress remoteAddress = new
                          InetSocketAddress(url.getHost(), port);
socket.connect(remoteAddress);
PrintWriter out = new PrintWriter(socket.getOutputStream());

// write our client's request
out.println("GET " + url.getFile() + " HTTP/1.0");
out.println("User-Agent: HttpGetter");
out.println("Host: " + url.getHost());
out.println();
out.flush();

// read remote server's response
InputStream in = socket.getInputStream();
boolean responseOK = true;

BufferedReader br = new BufferedReader(new
                          InputStreamReader(in));
String currLine = null;


// get http response code from first line of result
currLine = br.readLine();
if (currLine != null) {
  System.out.println(currLine);
  StringTokenizer st = new StringTokenizer(currLine, " \t");
  st.nextToken();
  String responseCode = st.nextToken();

  int httpResponseCode =
                Integer.parseInt(responseCode.trim());

  if (httpResponseCode != 200) {
    // response not OK
    responseOK = false;
  }
} else {
  System.err.println("Server returned no response!");
  System.exit(1);
}

// read headers
while ((currLine = br.readLine()) != null) {
```

```
      System.out.println(currLine);

      // done reading headers, so break out of loop
      if (currLine.trim().equals(""))
        break;
    }

    if (responseOK) {
      FileOutputStream fout = new FileOutputStream(outFile);

      int currByte;
      while ((currByte = br.read()) != -1)
        fout.write(currByte);

      fout.close();
      System.out.println("** Wrote result to " + args[1]);
    } else {
      System.out.println("HTTP response code not OK -- file not written");
    }

    socket.close();
  } catch (MalformedURLException me) {
    me.printStackTrace();
  } catch (IOException ioe) {
    ioe.printStackTrace();
  }
 }
}
```

Congratulations, you have implemented part of a real protocol. There a couple of things to note about this simple implementation. First, as noted before, your implementation can only read text, not binary, which makes it not too robust, since images and other binary files are frequently served from HTTP servers. Secondly, it does not handle errors gracefully, and in reality would require more of a full-fledged parser than your handyman `java.io` usage. This implementation is a minimal amount of code and logic to implement HTTP GET.

The command-line screen shot in Figure 11-4 shows a user downloading the root Web page of `http://www.google.com/` to `google.html`.

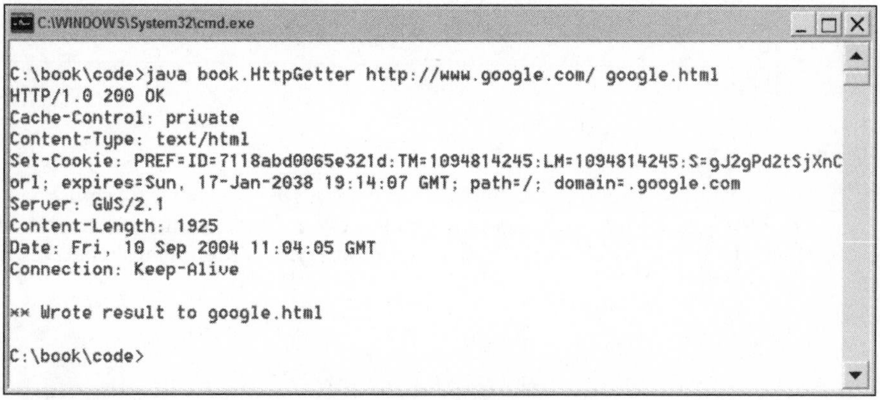

```
C:\WINDOWS\System32\cmd.exe                                              _ □ X

C:\book\code>java book.HttpGetter http://www.google.com/ google.html
HTTP/1.0 200 OK
Cache-Control: private
Content-Type: text/html
Set-Cookie: PREF=ID=7118abd0065e321d:TM=1094814245:LM=1094814245:S=gJ2gPd2tSjXnC
orl; expires=Sun, 17-Jan-2038 19:14:07 GMT; path=/; domain=.google.com
Server: GWS/2.1
Content-Length: 1925
Date: Fri, 10 Sep 2004 11:04:05 GMT
Connection: Keep-Alive

** Wrote result to google.html

C:\book\code>
```

Figure 11-4

TCP Monitoring: Testing with Apache TCPMon

Testing and debugging protocol implementations is far more difficult and tedious than testing and debugging a standalone application. To make sure the protocol implementation you are developing is correct, it is extremely helpful to see what is being sent and received over the wire with the remote server. There are utilities available to do just that — view what is being sent and received over a TCP/IP socket connection. For `HttpGetter`, I used the Apache utility, TCPMon, to monitor my TCP/IP connection with remote Web servers. Being able to read my request from the utility let me know that my request was following the HTTP specification. If there was any trouble parsing the response, I could look at exactly what was sent back from the server using the monitoring utility. Parsing the input from a socket is very similar to parsing a file — the data is in a certain format, and the code must read in that format. With sockets though, there is no file to view and test against. If there is a bug, it is difficult to see what in the protocol could be causing it. This is why the TCPMon utility is invaluable; it lets the developer look at the server's response as if it were a file on the local machine. It is useful for the implementation of any protocol based on TCP/IP, or during development with Web services. This chapter will also discuss using TCPMon in the "Web Services" section.

Getting, Building, and Running TCPMon

TCPMon is included as part of Apache AXIS. Apache AXIS is an implementation of SOAP that will be discussed in more detail in the "Web Services" section. However, the TCPMon utility, which is also useful in Web services development (hence it is included with AXIS), can also be useful for socket development as well, especially when implementing a protocol. The AXIS distribution can be downloaded from the following URL:

```
http://ws.apache.org/axis/index.html
```

Make sure to download a source distribution of AXIS. You will also need the Apache Ant build tool to build and run TCPMon (as well as the AXIS distribution). See Chapter 2, "Tools and Techniques for Developing Java Solutions," for more information regarding Ant. In the AXIS source distribution /docs folder, there is documentation on building AXIS (`building-axis.html` at the time of this writing). You will have to download a few libraries before you can actually build AXIS. Look at the "Building without Any Optional Components" and the "Building with Servlets" sections (in `building-axis.html`) for the links to these libraries. After all the required jars are in /lib of the AXIS source distribution, build AXIS by running the following in the directory with `build.xml` (the root directory of the distribution):

```
ant compile
```

After AXIS has been successfully built, run TCPMon by again using ANT:

```
ant -buildfile tcpmon.xml
```

Using TCPMon

To have TCPMon be able to print out your requests and the server's responses, it must be set up as a middleman between your local machine and the remote server. To test your program, it will have to connect to TCPMon, which in turn connects it to the remote server. TCPMon relays whatever is sent to it to

the remote server, and whatever the remote server sends it, it relays back to your application. To configure TCPMon in this manner, it must be set up as a `Listener`, and given a port number on the local
machine. The screen in Figure 11-5 is the first screen and main configuration screen of TCPMon. The figure shows the configuration necessary for TCPMon to act as a `Listener` on port 8079. TCPMon will
relay any connection made to port 8079 on the local machine to www.google.com, port 80 (the default
HTTP port). Once the Add button is clicked, TCPMon will set up the relay.

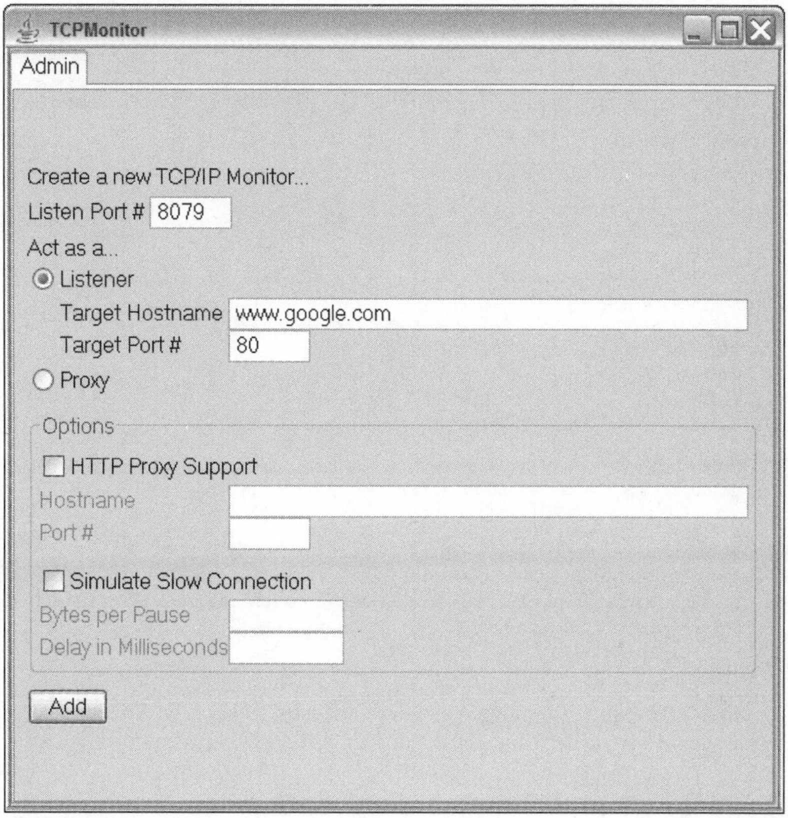

Figure 11-5

Now that the relay is running, `HttpGetter` can be tested by running:

```
java book.HttpGetter http://localhost:8079/ tester.html
```

`HttpGetter` connects to TCPMon, which in turn, connects it to www.google.com. Going to the Port
8079 tab on TCPMon yields a list of all connection attempts made to www.google.com in this session.
Figure 11-6 shows each request and response in detail.

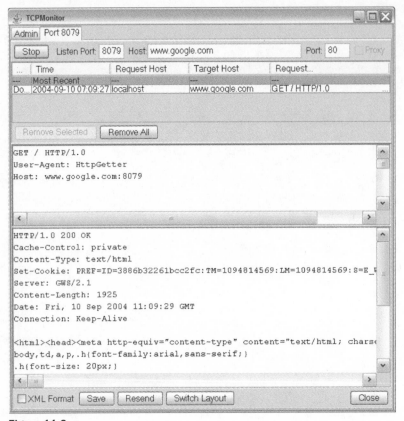

Figure 11-6

Debugging a protocol implementation is far easier with a utility such as Apache TCPMon, which allows the developer to view the data sent and received over a TCP/IP connection.

Proprietary Protocols and Reverse Engineering

Some protocols are not open. The instant messaging protocols for AOL's Instant Messenger and Microsoft's Messenger clients are proprietary information that currently is not shared (although the FCC is trying to force an open instant messaging standard to allow various clients to interoperate). If your software must communicate with servers such as these, whose protocol is either unknown or proprietary, there are not a whole lot of options. Some groups such as Gaim (http://gaim.sourceforge.net), an open-source, instant messaging client, have attempted to reverse-engineer the instant messaging protocols. This is done by monitoring the TCP connections and data sent between proprietary clients and servers. Sometimes portions of a protocol can be identified. When designing a proprietary protocol, taking into account how easy it would be to reverse-engineer is important (especially if security is a high priority). For extra security, some sort of encryption may be necessary for the protocol to avoid being reverse-engineered. Most of the time, protocols should be open. The specifications are generally easier for everyone to implement, since they have the advantage of being reviewed by many different sets of eyes. HTTP, for example, has undergone a number of performance-improving amendments from version 1.0 to 1.1. The most robust and stable implementations of protocols generally result from free and open protocols that have been in use for a while. High-quality reference implementations have been developed for protocols such as HTTP, TCP/IP, and X-Windows precisely because those protocols are open.

Utilizing Existing Protocols and Implementations

Developers will want to avoid designing and writing their own protocol if at all possible. Some existing protocol somewhere usually will fulfill the requirements of almost any application. There is no point in reinventing the wheel, and oftentimes using open protocols is a good avenue to ease the difficulty of interoperating with the outside world. If your app needs to interface to other applications, writing and designing a custom protocol has even more costs. Any other application that wishes to interface with your application must now implement a custom protocol. Getting two disparate implementations of a protocol to work robustly together is no easy task in itself, let alone in addition to normal application development. There are many protocols out there that already have high-quality implementations freely available to Java developers. The Jakarta Project from Apache hosts many open source projects. The Jakarta Commons Net package, for example, provides an API that implements FTP, NNTP, SMTP, POP3, Telnet, TFTP, and more. You can find more information about it at the following URL:

```
http://jakarta.apache.org/commons/net/
```

Even though in your HttpGetter example, you found that implementing one small section of HTTP was fairly simple, implementing the entire protocol with all of its optional components would be far more difficult. There are already optimized implementations of HTTP out there, and using one would be a far better design choice in *any application* that requires HTTP client support. The JDK provides limited support for HTTP via the `java.net.URL` class. It is good for simple HTTP operations, but sometimes more control over *how* HTTP is used is necessary. For example, to view and set HTTP headers, an HTTP client library that exposes more HTTP details than the `java.net.URL` class found in the JDK would be required. The HTTP Client project in the Jakarta Project provides a high-quality HTTP implementation. More information on HTTP Client can be found here:

```
http://jakarta.apache.org/commons/httpclient/
```

You have just looked at some freely available client libraries. There are also freely available libraries for servers. The Jakarta Project provides an HTTP server implementation with its servlet container, Tomcat. There are implementations of POP3 mail servers available. It should, almost 100 percent of the time, make sense to use an existing protocol in your application for communicating between your Java components and components on other platforms. You also should not have to implement the protocol yourself as there are high-quality robust open source implementations available for almost all of the major open protocols in use today.

Some great resources for finding and aggregating open source Java projects into your application are listed in the following table.

Resource	URL
The Jakarta Project	`http://jakarta.apache.org`
OpenSymphony Quality Components	`http://www.opensymphony.com`
JBoss: Professional Open Source	`http://www.jboss.org`
The Apache XML Project	`http://xml.apache.org`
The Eclipse Project	`http://www.eclipse.org`

Remote Method Invocation

Remote Method Invocation is the Java platform's standard for remote procedure calls (RPC). Remote procedure calls are abstractly the same concept as a normal procedure call within a program, except that the calls can happen over a network, and are between two separate processes. Different forms of RPC have been around for a while, but the concepts are similar. There is a client program and a server program, each running on separate machines (or at the very least, on two separate processes on the same machine). The client program calls a procedure (or in Java terminology, a method) on the server, and waits till the server returns the method result before continuing its normal execution (just like a normal local method call). Figure 11-7 illustrates a high-level view of object-to-object communication over a network in different JVMs.

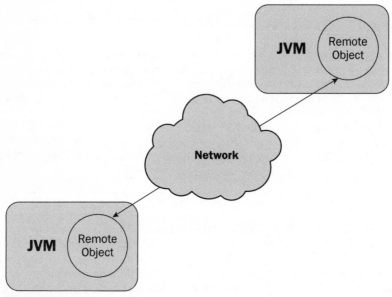

Figure 11-7

Remote Method Invocation (RMI) is such a large topic that it has its own chapter. See Chapter 10, "Communicating between Java Components with RMI and EJB," for detailed information on how to use RMI in your applications. This chapter will take a more abstract view of RMI and see how it fits as a technology into distributed systems.

Core RPC/RMI Principles

The Java platform makes writing client/server programs fairly simple. In Java, you can call methods on an object, and not even necessarily *know* that the object resides on a remote machine. The code for the method call is no different than a normal local method call. In J2EE, you generally have to look object instances up from a naming service before using them. When you look the object up and receive a reference to it, it may be a local reference *or a remote reference*. The code does not change though, and it is one of the reasons Java is such a powerful server language — a lot of the complex details of technologies such as RMI have been abstracted away. Now, this does not mean developers can be completely oblivious to whether an object instance is remote or local. Remote objects have certain design trade-offs that must be taken into account. Method calls happen across a network, and thus are limited to the reliability and speed of the network. RMI is a powerful mechanism for writing distributed systems. The following sections look into the basic core principles common to almost all RPC mechanisms, and show how they relate to RMI.

In RPC, all method calls must be transformed into a format that can be sent over the network and understood by a remote process. In order to call methods on a remote object, three main steps occur:

1. **A *reference* to the remote object must be obtained.** The remote object must be looked up on the remote server

2. **Marshalling and unmarshalling of parameters.** When a method is invoked on the remote reference, the parameters must be *marshalled* into a byte stream that can be sent over the network. On the server side, these parameters must be *unmarshalled* from the byte stream into their original values and then passed to the appropriate method.

3. **Transmission of data through a common protocol.** There must be a protocol defined for the transport and delivery of these method calls and returns. A standard format for parameters is necessary, along with standards to tell the server which method on which object is to be invoked.

To make the remote call appear like a local call, a local implementation exists with the same interface (*all RMI objects must be defined as Java interfaces*). This local implementation is called a *stub* and is essentially a proxy to the real implementation. Whenever a method is called on this local implementation or stub, the local implementation performs the operations necessary to send the method call to a remote implementation of the same interface on another server. The stub marshalls the parameters and sends them over the network using a common RMI protocol. In turn, a stub on the server side implementing the same interface unmarshalls the parameters and then passes them on to the actual remote object in a normal method call. This process is reversed for the return value; the stub on the server side marshalls and sends it, and the stub on the client unmarshalls and returns it to the original caller. Figure 11-8 displays this entire process graphically.

Marshalling and Unmarshalling

The parameters and method call must be flattened into a byte stream before they can be sent over the network. This process is called marshalling. The reverse is called unmarshalling, when the byte stream is decoded into the original parameters and method call information. After unmarshalling the parameters and method call, the server dispatches the method call to the appropriate object that actually implements the remote method and then marshalls the return value back to the client. By serializing the parameters and method into a byte stream, RMI protocols can work on top of network protocols which provide a reliable byte stream, such as TCP/IP.

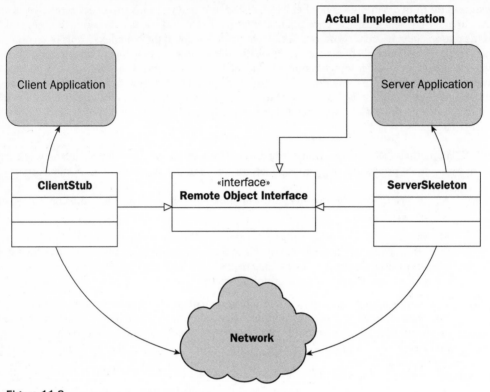

Figure 11-8

In RMI, there are two types of objects besides primitives that can be passed as parameters. Objects that implement the `java.rmi.Remote` interface or objects that implement the `java.io.Serializable` interface. These two interfaces do not contain any methods, instead they mark objects with a particular property. Java's RMI mechanism knows that `Remote` objects could be on another virtual machine, and will have stubs. Objects that implement `Serializable`, on the other hand, can be transformed into a byte stream (to save to disk, or in RMI's case, to send over a network). In RMI, objects that implement `Remote` are passed by reference while objects that implement `Serializable` (and not `Remote`) are passed by value. When parameters are marshalled over the network and transformed into a byte stream, any object that must be passed via an RMI call must be `Serializable`. So now for the first time, objects in Java can be passed by value. This is not as confusing as it sounds — `Remote` objects are passed by reference and `Serializable` objects are passed by value. This helps reduce the number of network calls that must occur. If an object being passed contains a large number of properties that must be accessed through `getXXX` methods, there would be a large number of network calls taking place. By serializing the object, all these calls become local calls on the remote server and use up far less network bandwidth. Method calls on `Remote` objects passed in, on the other hand, will go over the network and must be taken into consideration.

Suppose this is an implementation of a method on a server that is being invoked remotely by a client:

```
public void myTestMethod(A a, B b) {
    a.remoteMethod();
    Data d = b.getData();
...
}
```

In this example, A implements java.rmi.Remote, and thus a call to remoteMethod() is a remote callback to your client. B implements Serializable and hence getData() is a local call to b which was unmarshalled from its serialized state back into an object now running on the server.

> *Note:* **Any objects passed by value in RMI must be in the classpath of the JVM running on the remote server.**

See Chapter 5, "Persisting Your Application Using Files," for more information on **java.io.Serializable** *and serializing objects to disk.*

Protocols

In RPC, all method calls must be transformed into a standard format that can be sent over a network. In other words, two programs running on two separate processes must be able to read and write this same format. RPC mechanisms have their own protocols. Sometimes these protocols are built on top of TCP/IP, or at other times they define their own transport protocol in addition to the RPC protocol, combining the transport layer and the application layer protocols for optimal performance. Operating systems sometimes provide system-level services in this manner.

RMI is implemented such that it can support more than one underlying transport protocol (though obviously only one protocol can be used between any two objects). There are two main choices as the transport protocol for RMI:

❑   Java Remote Method Protocol (JRMP)

❑   Internet InterORB Protocol (IIOP)

Either one of these protocols could be used in a given system, and both have their trade-offs. IIOP offers compatibility with CORBA, which will be discussed later in this chapter. IIOP, since it was not designed specifically for Java remote procedure calls, does not support some of the features JRMP supports, such as security and distributed garbage collection. Using IIOP as the underlying protocol for RMI makes it easy to integrate legacy objects written in other languages however (discussed more in the "Common Object Request Broker Architecture" section of this chapter). JRMP is the default protocol for RMI. IIOP stubs differ from JRMP stubs and must be generated separately. See rmic tool documentation for more details.

RMI Registry

Object instances must be made available in a registry on the server before they can be used by remote clients. Clients obtain an instance by looking up a particular name—for example, the string EmployeeData might refer to a class containing the data for the employees of a particular company.

When a server is starting up, it creates instances of the objects it wishes to be available, and registers them in a registry. Since these objects are globally available, they must be thread safe (since their methods can be called at the same time by different threads). The code to look up a particular instance of a class is not very difficult, and uses the Java Naming and Directory Interface (JNDI) API (found in `javax.naming`). A small snippet of code to look up an object on a remote server follows:

```
import javax.naming.InitialContext;
...

InitialContext ctx = new InitialContext();

EmployeeData data = (EmployeeData) ctx.lookup("CompanyX\\MyEmployeeDataInstance");
...
```

JNDI is configured by setting certain Java system properties to tell it the location and protocol of the registry. This is how objects can be transparently remote or local. If the registry is configured locally, in the same JVM, then all calls to `data` will be local. If `data` is an instance on a remote server, all calls will go through RMI, using whatever protocol was specified.

See Chapter 10, "Communicating between Java Components with RMI and EJB," for more detailed information on the mechanics and details of RMI.

Distributed Objects

RMI allows a developer to abstract away where objects physically reside from his application. Object-oriented applications can be transparently spread across multiple machines. Objects that do heavy processing or provide server-side functionality, such as mail services, transactional database services, or file serving services, can be located on server-class machines. Typical desktop client applications can then access these objects as if they were local and part of the same object-oriented application. Location-independent objects are powerful since they can be dynamically moved around from machine to machine. If mail services' objects on a server become too bogged down, they can be spread across multiple machines, all transparently to the client applications using them. Java's platform independence adds even more value to its location-independent objects. Server objects could reside on a Unix-based operating system for example, and client objects on a Microsoft Windows platform. Figure 11-9 shows many objects communicating from different JVMs on different machines.

Middleware and J2EE

Most of time, the main reasons for distributing objects onto various machines is to give access to various services provided by these machines. Mail services, transactional-database services, and file-server services all can be encapsulated by various software components, or in this case, Java objects. By allowing all these objects to communicate in a standard, distributed way, server-side applications can be developed with ease. Location-independent objects allow for server applications to scale, since when one server no longer provides enough horsepower for a server application, you just add a couple more machines and spread the objects around.

Middleware is a software layer between various data sources and their client applications. RMI distributed objects is one way to implement middleware for different applications. Middleware abstracts away the details of the one-or-many data sources. RMI is the perfect building block for middleware because of its location and platform independence. Java is most prevalent in server-side applications and middleware because of the foundation it provides for building stable and reliable software systems.

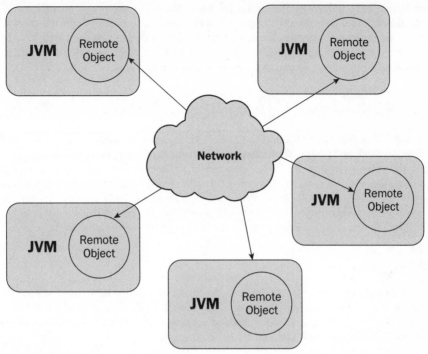

Figure 11-9

The Java 2 Enterprise Edition (J2EE) platform uses RMI as one of its core technologies. J2EE provides reliable messaging, rock-solid transactional storage capabilities, remote management and deployment, and frameworks for producing Web-enabled server-side applications. J2EE is a standard platform for developing middleware and other server-side services. RMI enables J2EE to be location-independent and distributed. Rather than developing one's own middleware solely with RMI, it is far better to build on the J2EE standard for writing server-side applications.

Common Object Request Broker Architecture

The Common Object Request Broker Architecture, or CORBA for short, is a set of specifications by the Object Management Group (OMG) for language-independent distributed objects. It allows for objects written in a number of different programming languages to interoperate and communicate with one another. C++ classes can talk to Java classes. C# can talk to C++ or Java. Programs written in C are supported by some CORBA implementations, as well as even scripting languages such as Python. CORBA is similar to RMI conceptually, but supports more languages than simply Java. CORBA itself is a set of specifications, not an actual implementation. For it to be possible for a language to support CORBA and other CORBA objects, it must have an implementation in its native language (or somehow be bound to an implementation). For instance, the Java Development Kit (JDK) includes an implementation of the CORBA 2.3.1 specification. That means that, out of the box, Java supports CORBA implementations up to and including the 2.3.1 specification (the latest CORBA specification at the time of this writing is 3.02).

Though there has been industry criticism for the age of the JDK's support for CORBA, 2.3.1 includes many of CORBA's modern features, and is certainly enough to implement and use most CORBA distributed objects. There are many implementations of CORBA that can be used with Java besides the implementation that comes with the JDK. A list of free CORBA downloads (either trials of commercial implementations or free open-source implementations) can be found on OMG's Web site at the following URL:

```
http://www.omg.org/technology/corba/corbadownloads.htm
```

CORBA is a massive set of specifications and has been an immense undertaking. CORBA has a history of having slow, bloated, and buggy implementations — on top of being extremely complex and difficult to develop with. Today though, as CORBA is a stable and mature technology, its implementations are much faster and reliable, and it is used in many mission-critical environments. CORBA is still complex and not as developer friendly as technologies such as RMI though, and usually for newer systems, J2EE-based servers are the best design choice if the Java platform is the primary development environment. This chapter will briefly examine CORBA, though not in any depth worthy of its complexity.

CORBA Basics

There are four main concepts of the CORBA specification that define how distributed objects written in different languages communicate with one another. Like RMI, there is a naming service, where remote object references can be registered, to be retrieved at some point in time by one or more clients. The Internet InterORB Protocol (IIOP) is used for the communication between clients and servers. This is the protocol that is responsible for defining the format of the marshalling and unmarshalling of remote method invocations and parameter passing. Object Request Brokers (ORBs) are responsible for processing all remote method calls and dispatching them to the appropriate object, both on the client and server. Figure 11-10 demonstrates these CORBA concepts.

The paradigm for object-to-object communication is similar to RMI:

1. Remote object references are obtained using the COS Naming Service.

2. Method call information and parameters are marshalled into a byte stream to send over the network via the Internet InterORB Protocol (IIOP).

3. An Object Request Broker (ORB) receives incoming requests on the remote server, and dispatches them to the object implementing the CORBA interface called.

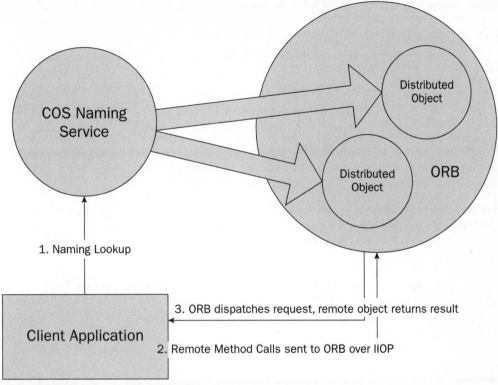

1. Naming Lookup

3. ORB dispatches request, remote object returns result

2. Remote Method Calls sent to ORB over IIOP

Figure 11-10

IDL: Interface Definition Language

The Interface Definition Language (IDL) is a CORBA specification for writing an interface. In CORBA, all distributed objects must implement a CORBA interface. These interfaces are similar to Java's concept of an interface — an interface allows for multiple implementations. CORBA interfaces though, can be implemented by any language that supports CORBA. Figure 11-11 shows a class diagram of a CORBA being implemented both in Java and C#.

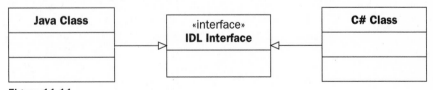

Figure 11-11

Three things can be declared in CORBA interfaces:

- ❑ Operations (like Java methods)
- ❑ Attributes (like JavaBean properties, implemented by getXXX and setXXX methods)
- ❑ Exceptions

A CORBA interface for each distributed object allows IDL compilers to compile IDL to stub classes in an existing language. For instance, the JDK provides tools that map CORBA IDL types to Java types, and generate stub classes for any given IDL file. These stub classes allow Java programmers to see the CORBA object as a Java class, and call its methods with Java syntax just like any other Java class. IDL is the link between different languages — it provides the description of an interface that can be transformed into the corresponding class in a concrete programming language.

When using remote CORBA objects, the client programmer is using the *interface*, not the specific object implementing it. The ORB running on the remote machine resolves the request, and dispatches it to the correct implementation. The client never knows which language the remote object was written in, it is all transparent.

In the "Distributed Filesystem Notifications: An Example CORBA System" section that follows at the end of this CORBA section, a CORBA interface called FileNotification will be defined. Seeing the Java representation will help you understand the CORBA representation. Here is the Java representation of that interface:

```
package book;

public interface FileNotification
{
   public void fileModified (String fileName);
   public void fileDeleted (String fileName);
   public void fileCreated (String fileName);
}
```

The equivalent definition of this Java interface in IDL looks like this:

```
#include "orb.idl"

#ifndef __book_FileNotification__
#define __book_FileNotification__


module book {

    interface FileNotification {

        void fileModified(
            in ::CORBA::WStringValue fileName );
        void fileDeleted(
            in ::CORBA::WStringValue fileName );
        void fileCreated(
            in ::CORBA::WStringValue fileName );
```

```
    };

#pragma ID FileNotification "RMI:book.FileNotification:0000000000000000"

};

#endif
```

If you have developed with C++ before, you will notice that the IDL syntax is similar to the C++ syntax, since C++ was the dominant language at the time of CORBA's inception. This chapter will not go heavily into the IDL syntax, as that is better left to books dedicated solely to CORBA. The main concept of IDL is simple: Separate the interface from the implementation. This principle applies to good software design in general, but is absolutely essential when an implementation could be written in more than one language. There would be no other way to have two disparate languages communicate with one another if not for a common interface.

ORB: Object Request Broker

The Object Request Broker is responsible for mediating incoming CORBA method invocations. ORBs are the core infrastructure of any CORBA implementation. They provide a common entry point for all CORBA requests to any given server. Many different method invocations on a number of CORBA objects go through the same entry point, the ORB. The ORB then dispatches the request to the correct CORBA object instance corresponding to the client's reference.

Common Object Service (COS) Naming

The Common Object Service (COS) Naming provides a registry to hold references to CORBA objects. It is similar in concept to the RMI registry. When a server wants to expose CORBA object instances to remote clients, it registers each instance with the naming service. Each instance gets a unique name on the server. Clients use the name to retrieve the reference and call its methods.

JNDI provides an InitialContext that can interact with COS Naming and look up various CORBA objects in the same fashion as one would look up an RMI object. As long as the correct stubs for IIOP are in place, setting the following system properties (which is the URL containing the correct hostname and port for the remote COS Naming service), client Java programs can access CORBA objects transparently:

```
java.naming.factory.initial=com.sun.jndi.cosnaming.CNCtxFactory
java.naming.provider.url=iiop://hostname:1049
```

Once these properties are set (using the -D option at the command line is one way to set them), the JNDI lookup occurs normally.

> Note: Client programs can also use the **org.omg.CORBA** package to manually access CORBA references, and have all of the many intricacies of CORBA at their disposal.

IIOP: Internet InterORB Protocol

The Internet InterORB Protocol is the protocol that CORBA ORBs use to communicate with one another over a network. All method calls and parameters are marshalled and unmarshalled over this protocol. It is an efficient binary protocol. JDK 1.5 supports version 2.3.1 of the IIOP specification.

RMI-IIOP: Making RMI Compatible with CORBA

RMI-IIOP combines some of the best aspects of RMI with the language independence of CORBA. RMI is far simpler for developers to use than CORBA. The main limitation of RMI is that it only supports the Java language. Though Java is platform independent, sometimes there are legacy components or systems written in other languages that must be interacted with. CORBA provides that channel of communication but can be a painful experience for developers. RMI-IIOP is Java RMI, but uses the IIOP protocol for communication, meaning normal RMI objects can be exposed as CORBA objects to external systems. By the same token, external CORBA objects can be accessed through the RMI APIs, again because of the use of IIOP as the underlying communication protocol.

It would be a perfect world if RMI-IIOP had exactly the same feature set as RMI over JRMP. IIOP was not designed for Java though. Objects passed by value over IIOP (ones that implement `java.io.Serializable` instead of `java.rmi.Remote`—see "Marshalling and Unmarshalling" in the RMI section of this chapter) get passed in the byte stream as Java objects. *This means that any parameters passed by value over RMI-IIOP can only be read by Java clients!* Fortunately, CORBA has a mechanism to deal with value types. It does, however, mean that the same interface of the value type must be implemented by the client. For example, suppose a Java RMI object returns a value type of `java.util.ArrayList`. A CORBA client cannot read this value type. The CORBA client application then must implement the interface for `ArrayList` (and make it compatible with the binary representation passed in!). Because of this large extra burden placed by objects passed by value on CORBA systems being communicated with using RMI-IIOP, it generally makes sense to try to make the interfaces pass only primitive types or objects by reference.

CORBA IDL unfortunately does not support method overloading. This, combined with the non-use of value types in passing parameters, can be a burden to designing a distributed system using RMI-IIOP. One design approach is to start thinking from the limiting IDL perspective when you are creating your Java interface for your remote object (if the system must communicate with CORBA clients). Your code may not be as clean using only primitive types, but the ease of interoperability makes it by far worth the price. The client-side development is tremendously simplified when value types do not have to be implemented also. Doing so is essentially implementing an object twice, once in Java and once in the CORBA client's language, and is asking for buggy and incompatible implementations, not to mention the synchronization nightmare of keeping their functionality and IDL up to date.

In most situations though, RMI-IIOP makes CORBA programming far simpler, and is the preferred method of integrating with CORBA in Java if the advanced features of CORBA are not necessary. The programming model is the same as RMI, and allows the Java developer to easily integrate with other platforms.

How to Turn an RMI Object into an RMI-IIOP Object

To take an existing RMI object and expose it via RMI-IIOP requires a minimal amount of work. Suppose you have a simple RMI HelloWorld interface:

```
package simple.rmi;

import java.rmi.Remote;
import java.rmi.RemoteException;

public interface HelloWorld extends Remote {
    public void hello() throws RemoteException;
}
```

Normal RMI object implementations extend `java.rmi.UnicastRemoteObject`. Your simple `HelloWorldImpl` as a normal RMI object looks like this:

```
package simple.rmi;

import java.rmi.RemoteException;
import java.rmi.server.UnicastRemoteObject;

public class HelloWorldImpl extends UnicastRemoteObject implements HelloWorld {

  public HelloWorldImpl() throws RemoteException {
    super();
  }

  public void hello() throws RemoteException {
    System.out.println("Hello");
  }
}
```

> **Note that** `UnicastRemoteObject` **above is in context.**

To allow this object to be used over RMI-IIOP, the first step is to make the class extend `javax.rmi.PortableRemoteObject` instead of `java.rmi.UnicastRemoteObject`:

```
package simple.rmi;

import java.rmi.RemoteException;

import javax.rmi.PortableRemoteObject;

public class HelloWorldImpl extends PortableRemoteObject implements HelloWorld {

  public HelloWorldImpl() throws RemoteException {
    super();
  }

  public void hello() throws RemoteException {
    System.out.println("Hello");
  }
}
```

Now HelloWorldImpl is ready to be used over RMI-IIOP. The last step is to generate the IDL and IIOP stubs from your class. The IIOP stubs allow the object to be sent over the wire using IIOP. The IDL allows CORBA clients to generate the stubs necessary to use the class. To generate both the stubs and the IDL, use the `rmic` tool from the JDK (in the `bin` directory under the JDK home). Running `rmic` from the command line, make sure that `simple.rmi.HelloWorldImpl` is on the classpath:

```
rmic -iiop -idl simple.rmi.HelloWorldImpl
```

The last step is to write the main program that actually starts up the RMI-IIOP server. This book will talk more about communicating with the Java ORB daemon included with the JDK, `orbd`, in the "Distributed Filesystem Notifications: An Example CORBA System" section, including registering objects and communicating with remote CORBA ORBs.

When to Use CORBA

CORBA is a difficult platform to develop software. It is robust and successful in mission-critical software systems, but the learning curve is high and development costs can rise. CORBA is best used in distributed systems that must have components written in more than one language, or have the potential to be written in more than one language. J2EE is a more ubiquitous standard for server-side applications today. It also provides CORBA support for some of its components. If you are creating a new server-side application in Java, sticking with J2EE is most certainly your best choice. CORBA support can always be added on later should you need to support clients written in other languages. Here are a couple of good instances of where to add CORBA to your distributed system:

❑ When you have to integrate with legacy systems that support CORBA in your middleware

❑ When there are components written in other languages just not available in Java that are essential to your server-side application (and would require less effort to build a CORBA link than to rewrite the component in Java)

CORBA as a distributed technology is simply not used as much in industry practice as J2EE-based component technologies (or COM/COM+/DCOM). It is a solid platform since it has been around for about ten years. Most of the complaints CORBA developers had originally have been rectified. CORBA implementations are fast and efficient now, and more than robust enough to use in mission-critical applications. CORBA has a steep learning curve, and the only value it adds over J2EE component technology is the ability to write components in different languages than Java. If your system is all Java, it just does not make sense to use CORBA — especially since J2EE can expose Java components to CORBA systems already through RMI-IIOP. It is best to use CORBA when you must integrate with a system that supports it.

CORBA may be a good technology to use when integrating with the Microsoft .NET platform. There has recently been an open source project, IIOP.NET, that integrates .NET Remoting (.NET's equivalent to RMI) with IIOP. This product is becoming mature, and allows for easy integration between RMI-IIOP and .NET Remoting. This is a big step towards an easier integration between .NET and Java components. The IIOP.NET project can be found at the following URL:

```
http://iiop-net.sourceforge.net/
```

IIOP.NET provides an exciting new way to use CORBA. By integrating with .NET Remoting, it allows programmers in the .NET environment and the Java environment to use their remote objects seamlessly (with normal IIOP limitations, of course, with value types, and so on). You have already seen how you can expose a Java component to CORBA using RMI-IIOP; the process is quick and easy, and better yet, can be *automated*. The process on the .NET side is the same way. CORBA can be used in this manner to allow .NET and Java components to interact transparently. The following example will examine such a system. A .NET component is wrapped with a CORBA interface and components in Java can access it like a normal Java component via RMI-IIOP.

Distributed File System Notifications: An Example CORBA System

Java does not contain any classes in the JDK to monitor for file system events. File system events occur when a file is deleted, modified, created, or renamed. These operations are platform specific and work different depending not only on the file system type, but on the host operating system. The only pure Java way to achieve this effect is to run a program that polls the file system and looks for updates — hardly an efficient mechanism of monitoring the file system. It would be far better if you could hook into the operating system and whenever a file system event occurred, be notified. Try to find a component that meets these needs and then provide a CORBA wrapper to access the component from your Java application.

Fortunately, one of the components of the .NET framework fits your needs. The `FileSystemWatcher` class from the `System.IO` namespace hooks into the Windows operating system, and notifies the user of file system events. Since your application is written in Java, you need somehow to integrate this non-Java component into your application. CORBA is a fine choice in this case, especially because of the advent of IIOP.NET, which was discussed in the proceeding section. IIOP.NET allows .NET Remoting to run over IIOP, which basically means you can access .NET remote objects from Java's RMI-IIOP. For this example, you will wrap the `FileSystemWatcher` class in a .NET remote object, expose this object through CORBA, and then implement the Java client. This text will not go into any code details for the .NET side, since this is a Java book and not a C# book. However, the code for the .NET side can be downloaded from this book's Web site at www.wrox.com. Figure 11-12 is a high-level diagram of the architecture for the communication between .NET and Java.

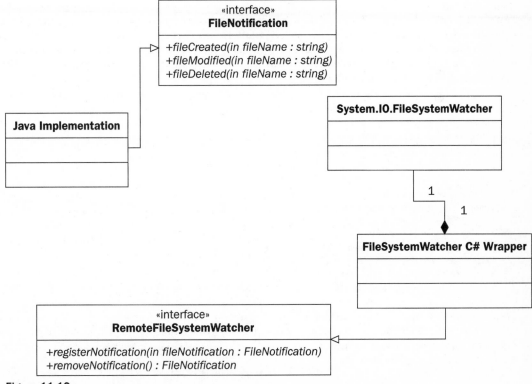

Figure 11-12

You have the IDL for the remote .NET components. The CORBA object that wraps the .NET component, `FileSystemWatcher`, has the following IDL:

```
#include "orb.idl"
#include "Predef.idl"

#include "FileNotification.idl"
#ifndef __ConsoleCorbaServer_RemoteFileSystemWatcher__
#define __ConsoleCorbaServer_RemoteFileSystemWatcher__
module ConsoleCorbaServer {

interface RemoteFileSystemWatcher {

void registerNotfication(in ::book::FileNotification notification) raises
(::Ch::Elca::Iiop::GenericUserException);
void removeNotification(in ::book::FileNotification notification) raises
(::Ch::Elca::Iiop::GenericUserException);
void setDirectory(in ::CORBA::WStringValue path) raises
(::Ch::Elca::Iiop::GenericUserException);
};

#pragma ID RemoteFileSystemWatcher
"IDL:ConsoleCorbaServer/RemoteFileSystemWatcher:1.0"

};

#endif
```

You can run `idlj`, the Java IDL compiler, to generate stub classes that will proxy your requests to these methods to the CORBA ORB running on the .NET platform's host machine. Notice how the IDL generated includes other IDL files, namely, `orb.idl`, `predef.idl`, and `FileNotification.idl`. These other files must be in the same directory when you run `idlj` for the compilation to work properly. The file `orb.idl` is the Java mapping definitions from IDL to Java specific types. The IIOP.NET provides `predef.idl` for some types specific to its .NET to CORBA mappings. The Java IDL compiler is included in JDK 5.0. Running the `idlj` compiler is simple:

```
idlj RemoteFileSystemWatcher.idl
```

By running `idlj` on the IDL, the following files were generated:

```
RemoteFileSystemWatcherStub.java
RemoteFileSystemWatcher.java
RemoteFileSystemWatcherHelper.java
RemoteFileSystemWatcherHolder.java
RemoteFileSystemWatcherOperations.java
GenericUserException.java
GenericUserExceptionHolder.java
GenericUserExceptionHelper.java
```

These are the stub and interfaces necessary to use the remote CORBA object, `RemoteFileSystemWatcher` (which wraps the .NET component, `FileSystemWatcher`). Note that since the IDL contained exceptions, exception classes were also generated. The `RemoteFileSystemWatcherOperations.java` defines the interface methods available to you:

```
package ConsoleCorbaServer;


/**
* ConsoleCorbaServer/RemoteFileSystemWatcherOperations.java .
* Generated by the IDL-to-Java compiler (portable), version "3.1"
* from RemoteFileSystemWatcher.idl
* Friday, June 11, 2004 5:56:29 PM EDT
*/

public interface RemoteFileSystemWatcherOperations
{
  void registerNotfication (book.FileNotification notification) throws
Ch.Elca.Iiop.GenericUserException;
  void removeNotification (book.FileNotification notification) throws
Ch.Elca.Iiop.GenericUserException;
  void setDirectory (String path) throws Ch.Elca.Iiop.GenericUserException;
} // interface RemoteFileSystemWatcherOperations
```

Notice how `registerNotification()` and `removeNotification()` have a
`book.FileNotification` object as their parameter. `FileNotification` is the callback interface
defined by `RemoteFileSystemWatcher`. `FileNotification` is defined in `FileNotification.idl`.
You will have to generate Java stubs for this CORBA object as well. The difference, though, is that you
will have to provide an implementation of `FileNotification` if you want to receive these filesystem
events. By providing an implementation of `FileNotification`, you will be able to pass to the remote
CORBA ORB a local instance which can receive events from the remote server. To implement
`FileNotification`, you must run `idlj` with a different parameter, one to generate both the client stubs
and the server stubs necessary for you to provide your own implementation. Here is the IDL for
FileNotification:

```
#include "orb.idl"

#ifndef __book_FileNotification__
#define __book_FileNotification__


module book {

    interface FileNotification {

        void fileModified(
            in ::CORBA::WStringValue fileName );
        void fileDeleted(
            in ::CORBA::WStringValue fileName );
        void fileCreated(
            in ::CORBA::WStringValue fileName );

    };

#pragma ID FileNotification "RMI:book.FileNotification:0000000000000000"

};

#endif
```

Now run `idlj` to produce client and server stubs (to produce both client and server stubs, the `-fall` option is used):

```
idlj -fall FileNotification.idl
```

The following files were then generated:

```
FileNotificationStub.java
FileNotification.java
FileNotificationHelper.java
FileNotificationHolder.java
FileNotificationOperations.java
FileNotificationPOA.java
```

Notice how the only additional file generated with the `-fall` option was `FileNotificationPOA.java`. This is an abstract class that gives you the means to provide an implementation of `FileNotification`. By extending it and providing the implementation of the methods defined in the interface, you will have a CORBA Portable Object Adapter (POA) that can be connected to a running ORB. By connecting the POA to the ORB, the ORB will be able to route incoming requests for `FileNotification` to the correct instance.

The Implementation

Our implementation of `FileNotification` will extend `FileNotificationPOA`. Here you will have to provide simple implementations for the methods found in the file `FileNotificationOperations.java`, since `FileNotificationPOA` implements `FileNotificationOperations`. This chapter will then go through the code necessary to do the following:

1. Implement the `FileNotificationOperations` interface.
2. Connect to the local ORB.
3. Create a Portable Object Adapter for your implementation of `FileNotification`.
4. Connect the POA to the ORB's root POA.
5. Register your instance of `FileNotification` with the local COS Naming Service.
6. Connect to the remote COS Naming Service.
7. Obtain an instance of `RemoteFileSystemWatcher`.
8. Register your instance of `FileNotification` with `RemoteFileSystemWatcher` to receive the filesystem notification events.
9. Wait for filesystem events.

The key CORBA classes used in the example code are summarized in the following table. They are the minimal set of classes necessary to use a local ORB and COS Naming service to publish an instance of a CORBA object for use by remote clients.

Class	Function
org.omg.CORBA.Object	Class used to represent any CORBA remote object reference.
org.omg.CORBA.ORB	Class used to represent a CORBA ORB. This class provides the core CORBA infrastructure services, and brokers incoming and outgoing CORBA object method invocations.
org.omg.CosNaming.NamingComponent	Class used for representing a CORBA Name. Names refer to instances of a particular object running on a COS Naming service. With a name, a client can look up a particular object and receive a reference to it, and then begin to use the object.
org.omg.CosNaming.NamingContext	Class used to represent the actual COS Naming service. This class is used to perform the actual object lookups to receive references to remote CORBA objects.
org.omg.PortableServer.POA	Represents a Portable Object Adapter. Since JDK 1.4, the POA feature of the CORBA specification was added to the Java implementation. POAs allow for CORBA objects to be easily deployed on different implementations of CORBA ORBs. They connect a CORBA object reference to the ORB, allowing for incoming requests for that reference to be processed.

Your first task is to implement `FileNotificationOperations` in your class that extends the abstract class `FileNotificationPOA` that was generated by the `idlj` tool. Your implementation will simply print out what file system notifications were received to standard output:

```java
public class FileNotificationImpl extends FileNotificationPOA {

    public FileNotificationImpl() {
    }

    // next three methods are the implementation of FileNotification.idl
    public void fileModified(String fileName) {
        System.out.println(fileName + ": Modified");
    }

    public void fileDeleted(String fileName) {
        System.out.println(fileName + ": Deleted");
    }

    public void fileCreated(String fileName) {
        System.out.println(fileName + ": Created");
    }

...
```

These methods implement the CORBA interface found in the `FileNotification.idl` file. Now that you have the interface implemented, you must create the `main()` method that starts up your server, registers an instance of your `FileNotification` implementation with a local ORB, retrieves an instance of `RemoteFileWatcher`, and registers your instance of `FileNotification` with this remote instance to receive file system events.

Our main method begins by setting the properties necessary for the local ORB to find the COS Naming service daemon running in a separate process on your local machine. This is the naming service you will be using to register your instance of `FileNotification`. The `java.util.Properties` object in the code below stores where your ORB is running with its initial port. These parameters allow your ORB to connect to the COS Naming service running on port 1049:

```
public static void main(String[] args) throws Exception {

    Properties props = new Properties();
    props.put("org.omg.CORBA.ORBInitialHost", "localhost");
    props.put("orb.omg.CORBA.ORBInitialPort", "1049");

    ORB orb = ORB.init(args, props);

    ...
```

Once you have your ORB instance, you must get the root Portable Object Adapter (POA). Every ORB has a root POA. From this POA, all additional POAs are attached in a treelike structure with the root POA being the root of the tree:

```
POA rootPOA = POAHelper.narrow(orb.resolve_initial_references("RootPOA"));
```

You must activate the root POA so that the ORB will accept incoming requests:

```
rootPOA.the_POAManager().activate();
```

Now that the root POA is active, you need to create the POA that contains your implementation of `FileNotification`. Once created, you connect your POA to the root POA so it can actively accept requests. To retrieve the actual CORBA reference of your implementation, you use the `FileNotificationHelper` object. The `FileNotificationHelper` object was also generated by the `idlj` tool and the `narrow()` method was used to take an `org.omg.CORBA.Object reference` and cast it to a `FileNotification` object (with CORBA, a standard Java cast would not do the trick):

```
    FileNotificationPOA nPOA = new FileNotificationImpl();

    // attach File Notification POA to the root and register a reference
    org.omg.CORBA.Object ref = rootPOA.servant_to_reference(nPOA);
    FileNotification fileNotification = FileNotificationHelper.narrow(ref);
```

The next step is to bind your reference to the COS Naming service. You will name your reference FileNotification. You then bind your CORBA object reference `ref` to the naming service. Your `FileNotification` instance is now ready to receive incoming requests:

```
    // bind the reference to the local cos naming server
    NamingContext ctx =
NamingContextHelper.narrow(orb.resolve_initial_references("NameService"));
```

```
NameComponent comp = new NameComponent("FileNotification", " ");

ctx.rebind(new NameComponent[] {comp}, ref);
```

Now you must look up the remote CORBA object reference of the type `RemoteFileSystemWatcher`. This object allows you to register your local instance of `FileNotification` with it to receive file system events. The first step is to find the remote COS Naming service and lookup the object. To do this you must inform JNDI that you want to use a COS Naming context. The Java system property `java.naming.factory.initial` is set to reflect this. The `java.naming.provider.url` tells JNDI where to look for the remote COS Naming service (though in this example, the so-called remote COS Naming service is running on the local machine, and hence the hostname `localhost`). You then perform a normal JNDI lookup. However, since you are using IIOP for the underlying protocol with RMI, you cannot simply cast the object returned to the appropriate type. You must use the static `javax.rmi.PortableRemoteObject.narrow()` instead:

```
Hashtable env = new Hashtable();
env.put("java.naming.factory.initial", "com.sun.jndi.cosnaming.CNCtxFactory");
env.put("java.naming.provider.url", "iiop://localhost:1500");

// connect to the remote cos naming service and lookup the RemoteFileSystemWatcher
InitialContext remoteCtx = new InitialContext(env);
java.lang.Object fswRef = remoteCtx.lookup("FileSystemWatcher");

// register our File Notification reference to receive events from the watcher
RemoteFileSystemWatcher watcher = (RemoteFileSystemWatcher)
PortableRemoteObject.narrow(fswRef, RemoteFileSystemWatcher.class);
```

Now that you have a reference to `RemoteFileSystemWatcher`, you can register your local reference of `FileNotification` and start receiving file system events: You tell the ORB to `run()` and your program blocks so you can receive file system events:

```
//remote call to register our local FileNotification instance on the remote server
watcher.registerNotfication(fileNotification);

System.out.println("File Notification registered on remote server.");
System.out.println("Waiting for file notification events...");
System.out.println();

// let our server run and wait for events
orb.run();
```

That is all there is to it. Your implementation is finished. You implemented a CORBA interface, `FileNotification`, in Java. You produced stubs for another CORBA interface, `RemoteFileSystemWatcher`, to proxy requests to a remote implementation. You then set up a local ORB with your implementation of `FileNotification`, looked up the remote instance of `RemoteFileSystemWatcher`, and then registered your reference of `FileNotification` with the remote CORBA object. The remote CORBA object now calls your local `FileNotification` reference whenever a file system event occurs.

The following is the full code listing for `FileNotificationImpl.java`:

```java
package book;

import java.util.Hashtable;
import java.util.Properties;

import javax.naming.InitialContext;
import javax.rmi.PortableRemoteObject;

import org.omg.CORBA.ORB;
import org.omg.CosNaming.NameComponent;
import org.omg.CosNaming.NamingContext;
import org.omg.CosNaming.NamingContextHelper;
import org.omg.PortableServer.POA;
import org.omg.PortableServer.POAHelper;

import ConsoleCorbaServer.RemoteFileSystemWatcher;


public class FileNotificationImpl extends FileNotificationPOA {

  public FileNotificationImpl() {
  }

  // next three methods are the implementation of FileNotification.idl
  public void fileModified(String fileName) {
    System.out.println(fileName + ": Modified");
  }

  public void fileDeleted(String fileName) {
    System.out.println(fileName + ": Deleted");
  }

  public void fileCreated(String fileName) {
    System.out.println(fileName + ": Created");
  }

  public static void main(String[] args) throws Exception {

    Properties props = new Properties();
    props.put("org.omg.CORBA.ORBInitialHost", "localhost");
    props.put("orb.omg.CORBA.ORBInitialPort", "1049");

    // connect to the local cos naming server, get and activate
    // the RootPOA
    ORB orb = ORB.init(args, props);
    POA rootPOA =
                  POAHelper.narrow(orb.resolve_initial_references("RootPOA"));

    rootPOA.the_POAManager().activate();
    FileNotificationPOA nPOA = new FileNotificationImpl();

    // attach File Notification POA to the root and register a reference
    org.omg.CORBA.Object ref = rootPOA.servant_to_reference(nPOA);
```

```java
    FileNotification fileNotification = FileNotificationHelper.narrow(ref);

    // bind the reference to the local cos naming server
    NamingContext ctx =
        NamingContextHelper.narrow(orb.resolve_initial_references("NameService"));
    NameComponent comp = new NameComponent("FileNotification", " ");

    ctx.rebind(new NameComponent[] {comp}, ref);

    System.out.println("File Notification bound to local ORB");


    Hashtable env = new Hashtable();
    env.put("java.naming.factory.initial",
                    "com.sun.jndi.cosnaming.CNCtxFactory");
    env.put("java.naming.provider.url", "iiop://localhost:1500");

    // connect to the remote naming service and lookup the RemoteFileSystemWatcher
    InitialContext remoteCtx = new InitialContext(env);
    java.lang.Object fswRef = remoteCtx.lookup("FileSystemWatcher");

    // register our FileNotification reference to receive events from the watcher
    RemoteFileSystemWatcher watcher = (RemoteFileSystemWatcher)
                PortableRemoteObject.narrow(fswRef, RemoteFileSystemWatcher.class);
    watcher.registerNotfication(fileNotification);

    System.out.println("File Notification registered on remote server.");
    System.out.println("Waiting for file notification events...");
    System.out.println();

    // let our server run and wait for events
    orb.run();
  }
}
```

Running the Example

To run your example, you first need to start up the remote CORBA server. You do this by running `ConsoleCorbaServer.exe` (a compiled .NET binary):

```
ConsoleCorbaServer
```

This `ConsoleCorbaServer` creates a C# instance of `RemoteFileSystemWatcher`, and registers it for use over IIOP via a COS Naming service. `ConsoleCorbaServer.exe` has the instance of `RemoteFileSystemWatcher` set up by default to monitor the directory `d:\book`. This can be changed by calling its `setDirectory()` method (which is exposed via CORBA), but for the purposes of running the example, the default is fine.

Next you must start up your local COS Naming service with which you will register your instance of FileNotification. The JDK provides a CORBA COS Naming service with its `orbd` tool. To start up the naming service, simply run `orbd` from the command line:

```
orbd
```

With no parameters specified, `orbd` runs on port 1049 (where your code will be looking for it). After `orbd` is running, you can now start your client program:

```
java book.FileNotificationImpl
```

The output screen shot in Figure 11-13 shows your program receiving some file system events after I created, modified, and deleted a text file in the `d:\book` directory.

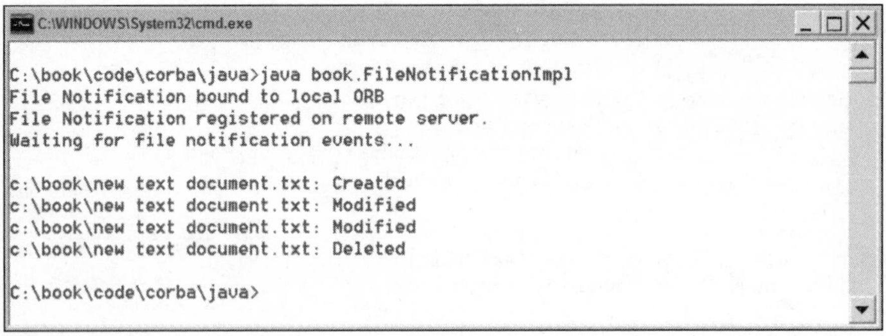

```
C:\WINDOWS\System32\cmd.exe                                       _ □ X

C:\book\code\corba\java>java book.FileNotificationImpl
File Notification bound to local ORB
File Notification registered on remote server.
Waiting for file notification events...

c:\book\new text document.txt: Created
c:\book\new text document.txt: Modified
c:\book\new text document.txt: Modified
c:\book\new text document.txt: Deleted

C:\book\code\corba\java>
```

Figure 11-13

Web Services

Sometimes it is difficult to pin down any sort of definition to the term Web services. Web services are drowned in hype. Some proclaim them as the enabling technology for the next generation World Wide Web, the Semantic Web. Others say they will revolutionize business-to-business communication. Still others insist that every new server-side application *must* support them — in fact, any legacy systems that do not support Web services should be retrofitted or rewritten. Web services are more than just the latest craze in distributed programming, but only an understanding of the technology itself will help you design your software system — don't do Web services for the sake of doing Web services.

So what are Web services exactly? Web services, from a technical vantage point, are actually pretty simple. They enable remote procedure calls. The protocol they are generally run over is not revolutionary, it is HTTP. XML defines the actual data being transported. In fact, Web services do not even support sessions out of the box. They do not support distributed objects out of the box. They do not come close to either RMI or CORBA in terms of features or reliability. They are not scalable, robust, or good for mission-critical applications. So why the hype? Web services quite frankly are so simple to understand and implement, that they become a very powerful tool. Web services value interoperability above anything else. Interoperability is a goal in CORBA, but with Web services, it is *the* number one priority. Web services are not fast. They simply make it easy to interoperate from a large range of platforms. Even Microsoft is fully on board, and officially supports Web services as the recommended method for communicating between their new .NET platform and the Java platform. You know it's big when Microsoft commits itself to interoperability with *any* other platform, especially Java.

Web services allow the exchange of structured data over the simple HTTP protocol. Yes, they can be used over other protocols. Yes, they can be forced to simulate the more advanced features of RMI and CORBA. But they shouldn't. Web services must stay simple to be effective. They make no sense otherwise. (Otherwise the wheel has just again been reinvented.) CORBA or RMI are stable and quality implementations for distributed objects and components. Web services are *simply intended to facilitate the sending and receiving of structured data over HTTP*. Your Web browser displays HTML pages. Since you can read, all the computer must do is display the Web page. It does not understand the content. All it knows is that a table goes here, an image goes there, and the title of the document is News. This is a fine model, and the World Wide Web has thrived. However, what if these Web pages were machine-readable? If the data served on HTTP servers was structured in formats that computer programs could be easily written to make use of the data, a whole new slew of applications could be written. This is why Web services are drowned in hype. It's not because the technology is revolutionary, because it's not; it's beautifully simple, and some would say a regression from either RMI or CORBA. Web services are revolutionary because they will enable a whole generation of new computer applications that maximize the knowledge and information stored in the World Wide Web.

Evolution of the World Wide Web

Tim Berners-Lee, the visionary who created the foundation for what you now know as the World Wide Web, envisions a greater evolution of that Web for tomorrow. Slowly over time the Web has been transitioning. The first Web sites were simple and only served up static content. Later on, database-backed Web sites allowed for the dynamic query and creation of content served over HTTP. Today, you can manage bank accounts, pay credit card bills, purchase merchandise, and compete in online auctions. The major limitation of today's Web, though, is the fact that almost all of the content currently in place, the vast wealth of information, is only good for human consumption. The best technology behind search engines still is limited by keywords, simple site usage statistics, and primitive categorization. Advances in artificial intelligence haven't been all that advancing for a field where the same principles that applied 30 years ago still apply today and aren't changed a whole lot by the more powerful machines of today.

Web services are one technology to bridge the gap from a human-readable Web to a machine-consumable one. Imagine if the popular retailers, search engines, online auction sites, stock tickers, and news services all had simple APIs to programmatically access their content. Entirely new information-centric applications could be written that simply cannot exist now — portals like my.yahoo are the best we've got. I've created a hypothetical weather Web site. I say hypothetical because it doesn't exist online, and it produces completely random weather forecasts. It does, however, give a good view of what the Web looks like today. Figure 11-14 shows a screen shot from this hypothetical site, random-weather.org.

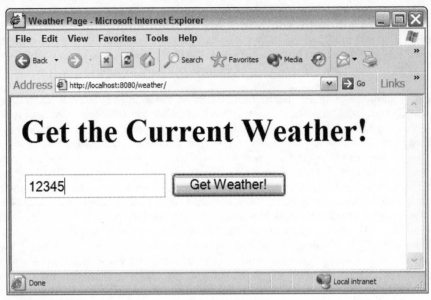

Figure 11-14

It is a simple site; users enter their zip code into the form and then receive their weather forecast — not all that different from real weather sites, except of course, that this one is hideous. This page is encoded in HTML, and works with the browser to send the Web server whatever zip code was typed in (as with any Web application). Here is the simple HTML of this page:

```html
<html>
<head>
  <title>Weather Page</title>
</head>
<body>
<h1>Get the Current Weather!</h1>

<form method="get" action="weather.jsp">

<table border="0" cellspacing="2" cellpadding="2">
  <tr>
    <td><input name="zipcode" type="textbox"/></td>
    <td><input type="submit" value="Get Weather!"/></td>
  </tr>
</table>

</form>

</form>
</body>
</html>
```

Note that there are only a couple of input tags, and this is where the information is exchanged. Figure 11-15 shows what the resulting Web page from this dynamic site looks like.

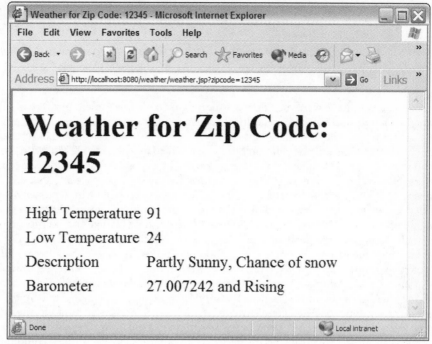

Figure 11-15

A nice, simple little page displays the random weather forecast. The HTML looks like this:

```
<html>
<head>
  <title>Weather for Zip Code: 12345</title>
</head>

<body>

  <h1>Weather for Zip Code: 12345</h1>

<table border="0" cellspacing="2" cellpadding="2">
  <tr>
    <td>High Temperature</td>
    <td>93</td>
  </tr>
  <tr>
    <td>Low Temperature</td>
    <td>73</td>
  </tr>
  <tr>
    <td>Description</td>
    <td>Partly Cloudy</td>
  </tr>
  <tr>
    <td>Barometer</td>
```

```
        <td>26.11519 and Rising</td>
    </tr>
</table>

</body>
</html>
```

Now, what if you wanted to write a computer program to access this same repository of information. It's easy enough as a user to enter the Web address, type in your zip code, and view the weather forecast. Writing a program to do the same thing, though, is a tedious task and easy to break. These types of dynamic sites intermingle the presentation format of the data (encoded in HTML) with the data itself. If a program were to attempt to access this information (and it is possible), it would have to know what parameters the server needed (in this case, the name of the zip code variable and that it is an HTTP GET request), and then know exactly what format the HTML generated will be in. A parser would have to be written that knows exactly where the high temperature and the low temperature reside in the Web page, parse them out, and then do something with the data. This is not only tedious, painful, and difficult, but it is extremely prone to breakage. If random-weather.org decided to change how it presented the data, your parser would have to be rewritten. If they modified almost any aspect of either HTML page, some part of your program would have to be rewritten. This just does not make sense. Separating data from its presentation is a key principle in any software design, and in the continuing evolution of the Web, may someday become a ubiquitous reality. Web services were mainly designed to help this process. Web services allow these types of Web queries for information to occur in a structured format, using XML, that can be easily parsed and read by computer programs. Google is offering a sample Web services API so developers can programmatically access the Google search engine. Developers could then write applications that integrate the Google search engine easily into their applications. Other sites are playing around with various Web services APIs. Amazon.com offers an API to allow developers to search their product catalog. Any site that offers dynamic content could expose useful Web services to developers (should they so desire).

Platform Independent RPC

Web services are an implementation of platform independent remote procedure calls. Think of each individual Web service as a remote method. An XML-encoded request is sent to a server, and an XML-encoded response is returned. Normally, Web services are sent over the HTTP protocol via the HTTP POST operation. XML is posted to the Web server, and XML is returned from the HTTP POST operation. Since XML was built to be a data description language, any form of data can be encoded. Though some would call XML a bloated data format, since it stores information in plaintext, no one argues with the robustness of the XML parsers available to developers. Since XML is plaintext and the rules are not overly complicated (XML specification designers originally wanted the spec to be simple enough that any graduate-level computer science student could implement a parser in about two weeks), it is easy to write parsers. The XML specification is simple and clear enough that different parsers do not have a problem interoperating. A sample XML request/response posted via HTTP is diagrammed in the following Figure 11-16.

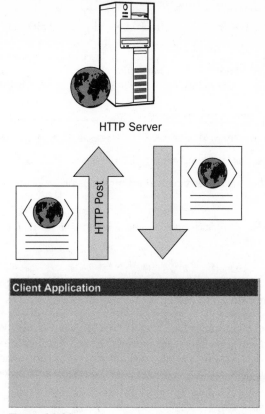

HTTP Server

Client Application

Figure 11-16

There are other advantages to implementing RPC via XML over HTTP. HTTP is another rock-solid protocol, again because of its simplicity. Earlier in this chapter, you easily implemented part of the specification. Technologies such as RMI or CORBA have specifications that are orders of magnitude more complex than either HTTP or XML. These protocols are also binary protocols, which makes them more efficient over the wire as more information can be encoded in less space. Debugging these protocols, though, is no simple task. Some would argue that distributed objects themselves are just too complex of a technology and not worth the considerable amount of design and development time required to truly implement a server-side application consisting entirely of distributed objects. By taking the simple route, Web services have ensured their ease of implementation. Ease of implementation is one of the single most critical elements to a cross-platform technology.

XML Web services do not have certain features built into them out of the box. They do not support sessions (since HTTP does not truly support sessions). They do not support procedure callbacks. They have no understanding of a distributed object. They are not at all object oriented, in fact. Security, transactions, and scalability — no, no, and no again. They are not meant to be a pillar supporting a mission-critical application. They merely enable current Web technologies to support a new generation of applications.

Chapter 11

Web Services Description Language (WSDL)

The Web Services Description Language is the Web services equivalent of CORBA IDL — in the sense that it is an interface document. It describes how to communicate with a particular Web service. Some would say you can be more descriptive with data you are passing; since all data is defined in XML, you are not limited to primitive data types and particular classes like you are in CORBA IDL. Web services described in WSDL can have the following pieces of information attached to them:

❑ **Types.** The XML data types are defined here.

❑ **Messages.** The content of Web services messages is described here.

❑ **Port Types.** Specifies input and/or output messages for a particular operation or method.

❑ **Binding.** Specifies the underlying communications protocol and transport protocol the Web services run over.

WSDL itself is described in XML and the complete specification for its format can be found at the following URL:

```
http://www.w3.org/TR/wsdl
```

Apache AXIS is an open-source Java project for Web service development and hosting. It ships with a couple of sample Web services. One simply returns the current version of the AXIS server. This section will later discuss in more detail about how to use AXIS. Here is a sample WSDL document from the Apache Version service. Note how messages, port types, and bindings are defined. There are no custom types; this WSDL document simply describes one service (WSDL documents can describe one or more Web services). The one service returns a string, just the version string of the AXIS server:

```
<?xml version="1.0" encoding="UTF-8"?>
<wsdl:definitions targetNamespace="http://localhost:8080/axis/services/Version"
xmlns:apachesoap="http://xml.apache.org/xml-soap"
xmlns:impl="http://localhost:8080/axis/services/Version"
xmlns:intf="http://localhost:8080/axis/services/Version"
xmlns:soapenc="http://schemas.xmlsoap.org/soap/encoding/"
xmlns:wsdl="http://schemas.xmlsoap.org/wsdl/"
xmlns:wsdlsoap="http://schemas.xmlsoap.org/wsdl/soap/"
xmlns:xsd="http://www.w3.org/2001/XMLSchema">
<!--WSDL created by Apache Axis version: 1.2beta
Built on Mar 31, 2004 (12:47:03 EST)-->

    <wsdl:message name="getVersionResponse">
        <wsdl:part name="getVersionReturn" type="soapenc:string"/>
    </wsdl:message>
    <wsdl:message name="getVersionRequest">
    </wsdl:message>
    <wsdl:portType name="Version">
        <wsdl:operation name="getVersion">
            <wsdl:input message="impl:getVersionRequest" name="getVersionRequest"/>
            <wsdl:output message="impl:getVersionResponse" name="getVersionResponse"/>
        </wsdl:operation>
    </wsdl:portType>
    <wsdl:binding name="VersionSoapBinding" type="impl:Version">
        <wsdlsoap:binding style="rpc"
transport="http://schemas.xmlsoap.org/soap/http"/>
```

```
        <wsdl:operation name="getVersion">
          <wsdlsoap:operation soapAction=""/>
          <wsdl:input name="getVersionRequest">
            <wsdlsoap:body
encodingStyle="http://schemas.xmlsoap.org/soap/encoding/"
namespace="http://axis.apache.org" use="encoded"/>
          </wsdl:input>
          <wsdl:output name="getVersionResponse">
            <wsdlsoap:body
encodingStyle="http://schemas.xmlsoap.org/soap/encoding/"
namespace="http://localhost:8080/axis/services/Version" use="encoded"/>
          </wsdl:output>
        </wsdl:operation>
      </wsdl:binding>
      <wsdl:service name="VersionService">
        <wsdl:port binding="impl:VersionSoapBinding" name="Version">
          <wsdlsoap:address location="http://localhost:8080/axis/services/Version"/>
        </wsdl:port>
      </wsdl:service>
    </wsdl:definitions>
```

We will not be going into too much depth for the actual details of WSDL — that is better left to books or chapters dedicated solely to WSDL. In CORBA or RMI, you generate stub classes to use distributed objects transparently in code. WSDL allows the same sort of functionality for Web services. There are toolkits and compilers for WSDL in a number of languages. This chapter will later examine how to generate Java classes from WSDL and then use them in code. You never even need to know what goes on under the hood, but it certainly helps in understanding. Since Web services, boiled down to their core, are really just XML posted via HTTP, you could use an XML API and an HTTP API and write Web services. This is almost always not the best way to go about using Web services though. Bindings generated from WSDL provide far more accurate implementations (and are much more likely to be bug free). Because of the simplicity of Web services, there is no real speed or efficiency advantage to reinventing the wheel either. This chapter will look more at code generation from WSDL and generating WSDL from Java methods that you wish to expose as Web services.

Simple Object Access Protocol (SOAP)

Every RPC system needs a communications protocol. RMI uses either JRMP or IIOP. CORBA uses IIOP. Web services use the Simple Object Access Protocol, or SOAP. SOAP is a message format defined in XML. SOAP is inherently platform independent because it is based entirely on XML. Like WSDL, SOAP is also a W3C standard, and its specification can be found at the following URL:

```
http://www.w3.org/TR/soap/
```

Every SOAP message has the following structural attributes:

❑ **Envelope.** The entire XML message has as its root element the SOAP Envelope — all content of the message is contained here.

❑ **Headers.** XML Data can be placed in the header of a SOAP message away from the actual content — keeping things like usernames and passwords (if required) separate from the actual content of the message.

❑ **Body.** The XML content delivered in a SOAP message is contained in the body.

SOAP is a fairly straightforward protocol, assuming you understand XML and XML namespaces. An example SOAP message for the AXIS version service is listed below:

```
<?xml version="1.0" encoding="UTF-8"?>
<soapenv:Envelope xmlns:soapenv="http://schemas.xmlsoap.org/soap/envelope/"
xmlns:xsd="http://www.w3.org/2001/XMLSchema"
xmlns:xsi="http://www.w3.org/2001/XMLSchema-instance">
<soapenv:Body>
  <ns1:getVersion soapenv:encodingStyle="http://schemas.xmlsoap.org/soap/encoding/"
xmlns:ns1="http://axis.apache.org"/>
</soapenv:Body>
</soapenv:Envelope>
```

The SOAP message returned from this version request looks like:

```
<?xml version="1.0" encoding="utf-8"?>
<soapenv:Envelope xmlns:soapenv="http://schemas.xmlsoap.org/soap/envelope/"
xmlns:xsd="http://www.w3.org/2001/XMLSchema"
xmlns:xsi="http://www.w3.org/2001/XMLSchema-instance">
<soapenv:Body>
  <ns1:getVersionResponse
soapenv:encodingStyle="http://schemas.xmlsoap.org/soap/encoding/"
xmlns:ns1="http://axis.apache.org">
    <getVersionReturn xsi:type="soapenc:string"
xmlns:soapenc="http://schemas.xmlsoap.org/soap/encoding/">Apache Axis version:
1.2beta
Built on Mar 31, 2004 (12:47:03 EST)</getVersionReturn>
  </ns1:getVersionResponse>
 </soapenv:Body>
</soapenv:Envelope>
```

Notice how both messages are rooted with the XML element envelope. There are no headers for these messages, and the Body for each is straightforward. This text will not go into any further depth describing SOAP. Most of its details are not as important. Learning the ins and outs of WSDL is probably more worth your while; the exact syntax of SOAP is not as big of an issue, since most Web service toolkits will handle it all for you (much the same way as you wouldn't think of knowing how JRMP or IIOP work).

Sadly, perhaps one of the most exciting elements of SOAP is that Microsoft has made it a key part of its new .NET platform. SOAP is here to stay, and will hopefully continue to provide the cornerstone protocol for enabling Web service communication.

Underlying Transport Protocols

SOAP can be transported over a variety of protocols. The normal course of action is over HTTP, which is over TCP/IP. However, SOAP messages can also be sent over:

❑   Straight TCP/IP (no HTTP)

❑   Simple Mail Transport Protocol (SMTP)

❑   Java Messaging Service Protocols

The real power of SOAP lies with HTTP over TCP/IP though. Web services become normal Web requests, can be sent through firewalls, and are just structured data requests from Web servers.

Weather Web Site Example

Going back to the `random-weather.org` site from before, this section will take a look under the hood of how it is currently implemented. After looking at its current implementation, you will enable it for Web services. In addition to finding out your local random weather forecast from your Web browser, developers can programmatically access this same information. Your weather Web site has a particular class that does most of the work, `WeatherGetter`. `WeatherGetter` randomly generates a weather forecast for a certain zip code. This forecast changes daily and randomly. If you ran a real Web site, you could think of `WeatherGetter` as providing accurate weather information, maybe from a database, probably conglomerated from local weather stations. Your weather forecasts will consist of four items:

- ❑ High Temperature
- ❑ Low Temperature
- ❑ Weather Description
- ❑ Barometer and Description

You develop a JavaBean, `Weather`, to hold these properties:

```java
package book;

public class Weather {
  private String description;

  private int lowTemp;
  private int highTemp;

  private float barometer;
  private String barometerDescription;

  public float getBarometer() {
    return barometer;
  }

  public void setBarometer(float barometer) {
    this.barometer = barometer;
  }

  public String getBarometerDescription() {
    return barometerDescription;
  }

  public void setBarometerDescription(String barometerDescription) {
    this.barometerDescription = barometerDescription;
  }

  public String getDescription() {
    return description;
  }

  public void setDescription(String description) {
    this.description = description;
  }
```

```
  public int getHighTemp() {
    return highTemp;
  }

  public void setHighTemp(int highTemp) {
    this.highTemp = highTemp;
  }

  public int getLowTemp() {
    return lowTemp;
  }

  public void setLowTemp(int lowTemp) {
    this.lowTemp = lowTemp;
  }
}
```

The `WeatherGetter` class is also straightforward. This section will not go into detail explaining exactly how the forecasts are generated; if you are curious, though, look at the `java.util.Random` class in the JDK. The code listing is important later on so you can see how to expose it as a Web service. Here is the code listing:

```
package book;

import java.util.Calendar;
import java.util.GregorianCalendar;
import java.util.Random;

public class WeatherGetter {

  private Random random;

  public WeatherGetter() {
    this.random = new Random();
  }

  public Weather getWeather(int zipCode) {
    Calendar cal = new GregorianCalendar();
    // changes the weather value daily
    random.setSeed(zipCode + cal.get(Calendar.DAY_OF_YEAR) +
cal.get(Calendar.YEAR));

    Weather w = new Weather();

    int x = random.nextInt(100);
    int y = random.nextInt(100);

    if (x >= y) {
      w.setHighTemp(x);
      w.setLowTemp(y);
    } else {
      w.setHighTemp(y);
      w.setLowTemp(x);
```

```
      }

      w.setBarometer(25 + random.nextFloat() * 8);
      if (random.nextBoolean()) {
        if (random.nextBoolean()) {
          w.setBarometerDescription("Rising");
        } else w.setBarometerDescription("Falling");
      } else w.setBarometerDescription("Holding Steady");

      String adjective;
      String noun;

      if (random.nextBoolean()) {
        adjective = "Partly";
      } else adjective = "";

      if (random.nextBoolean()) {
        noun = "Sunny";
      } else noun = "Cloudy";

      if (("Partly".equals(adjective) || "Cloudy".equals(noun))
          && random.nextBoolean()) {
        noun += ", Chance of ";
        if (w.getLowTemp() < 32)
          noun += "snow";
        else noun += "rain";
      }

      w.setDescription((adjective + " " + noun).trim());

      return w;
    }
  }
```

The weather Web application is fairly straightforward. There is one Java Server Page (JSP) that handles incoming weather requests and outputs the current random forecast for that zip code (like the screen shots and HTML code from earlier). The JSP uses `WeatherGetter` to generate the weather requests. This is a standard way to build dynamic sites — JSPs backed by Java classes that access data (or in this simple case, generate data). See Chapter 7, "Developing Web Applications Using the Model 1 Architecture," and Chapter 8, "Developing Web Applications Using the Model 2 Architecture," for more information on building Web applications with Java. You will now look at how to have this same functionality exposed as a Web service, using Apache AXIS.

Apache AXIS

Apache AXIS is an implementation of SOAP and is a rewrite of the original Apache SOAP project. It is also the most used Java toolkit for developing Web services. One of the primary goals of the AXIS project is to work well with other SOAP implementations. It works seamlessly with Microsoft's .NET platform. AXIS provides a strong toolkit for any developer wishing to implement Web services. It includes:

❑ Web application archive (WAR file) to deploy and manage Web services in standard Java Web containers

❑ WSDL2Java and Java2WSDL toolsets — converts WSDL to Java classes and generates WSDL from existing Java classes

❑ TCPMon — the TCP Monitoring utility you looked at earlier in this chapter

❑ Rich set of sample Web services

Since AXIS includes a Web application, it is complemented perfectly by Apache Tomcat, a servlet container and HTTP server. Combing these two open-source projects yields a production quality environment for deploying Web services and Web applications.

The main alternative in the Java world to using AXIS is Sun's Java Web Services Developer Package (JWSDP). The current version at the time of this writing is 1.3, though 1.4 is due out soon, and will probably be the current version when you are reading this. Either AXIS or JWSDP can be used, although I have personally found AXIS to be simpler to use, and used more widely in production. The remainder of the "Web Services" section will discuss AXIS.

Setting up the Environment

There are four main steps to making your environment Web services ready:

1. Download and install Apache Tomcat.

   There is a windows installer distribution of Apache Tomcat that makes installation a breeze (there are also `zip` files and `tar.gz` files — for those, simply unpack them, they are ready as is). This file can be downloaded from the following URL:

   ```
   http://jakarta.apache.org/site/binindex.cgi
   ```

   This site lists all of the products the Jakarta Project offers, so you'll have to scroll down to find the `.exe` file for Tomcat.

2. Download the Apache AXIS source distribution, build it (as per its instructions), and place the AXIS Web application in the Tomcat's directory for deploying Web applications.

   AXIS can be downloaded from the following URL:

   ```
   http://ws.apache.org/axis/index.html
   ```

   After downloading and unzipping AXIS, go under the `<AXIS_HOME>/webapps` directory to find the AXIS Web app. Copy this directory and all of its contents to the `<TOMCAT_HOME>/webapps` directory. The next time you start up Tomcat, you will be able to go to the local URL:

   ```
   http://localhost:8080/axis/
   ```

   From here you can view the status of the AXIS installation and see what Web services have been deployed.

3. Download the Java Activation Framework and install `activation.jar` to the lib directory of the AXIS Web application.

   You'll need to download the Java Activation Framework from the following URL:

   ```
   http://java.sun.com/products/javabeans/glasgow/jaf.html
   ```

   After downloading and unpacking the file, you'll find `activation.jar`. Copy this file to the `<TOMCAT_HOME>/webapps/axis/WEB-INF/lib` directory.

4. Modify the `web.xml` configuration file of the AXIS Web application to enable the administration servlet.

To be able to deploy Web services, you have to enable the AXIS administration servlet. Modify the `<TOMCAT_HOME>/webapps/axis/WEB-INF/web.xml` file to uncomment the administration servlet (note the comments around the servlet-mapping element below). The next time you start Tomcat, your Web services environment will be ready:

```
...
<!-- uncomment this if you want the admin servlet -->
    <!--
  <servlet-mapping>
    <servlet-name>AdminServlet</servlet-name>
    <url-pattern>/servlet/AdminServlet</url-pattern>
  </servlet-mapping>
  -->
...
```

Deploying a Service

Getting back to your `random-weather.org` Web site, suppose you want to expose the following method of `WeatherGetter` as a Web service:

```
public Weather getWeather(int zipcode) {...}
```

Doing so would enable client programmers, as well as normal Web-browsing end users, to access the functionality of your `random-weather.org` Web site.

AXIS makes it easy to expose the method as a Web service — all you need is a Web Services Deployment Descriptor, which is an AXIS-specific file type used for deploying a Web service. This text will not go into too much detail regarding the actual format for this file; see the AXIS documentation for more information. Here is what your deployment descriptor, `desploy.wsdd`, looks like:

```
<?xml version="1.0" encoding="UTF-8"?>
<deployment xmlns="http://xml.apache.org/axis/wsdd/"
xmlns:java="http://xml.apache.org/axis/wsdd/providers/java">

  <service name="Weather" provider="java:RPC">
    <parameter name="allowedMethods" value="getWeather"/>
    <parameter name="className" value="book.WeatherGetter"/>
    <beanMapping qname="ns:weather" xmlns:ns="http://randomweather.org"
languageSpecificType="java:book.Weather"/>
  </service>

</deployment>
```

Notice how the `service` definition in the deployment descriptor defines the Java class and methods exposed as the Web service. Any class used as a service in this manner by AXIS must have a default, no-argument constructor, so the AXIS engine can create instances of it. Since the type `Weather` is not a primitive type, there is some extra configuration necessary for AXIS to be able to properly serialize and deserialize the class to and from XML. There are powerful predefined mechanisms in AXIS for defining exactly how to serialize and deserialize data. If a predefined serializer cannot be found to properly serialize a nonprimitive Java type, custom serializers can be written for the utmost control over the serialization process. Since the `Weather` type follows JavaBean conventions, the easiest mechanism in your case is to use the AXIS bean serializer. The AXIS bean serializer takes a JavaBean and defines an XML mapping for it. This mapping is included when AXIS generates WSDL for the service, making third-party developers writing client programs to use the Web service not have to write any custom code—the WSDL generated allows them to auto-generate stubs, which then allow them to use the service transparently in their code. The `<beanMapping>` tag in the deployment descriptor identifies your JavaBean, and tells AXIS what XML namespace to use when serializing the type.

Note how, in the `<service>` tag, the provider is defined as `java:RPC`. There are essentially three main types of Web services. Each of these three services is encoded differently and possesses different attributes:

❑ **Remote Procedure Call Services.** The weather example seen so far in this chapter is an example of an RPC-based Web service. Though other styles of Web services can be similar to RPC-based services in the sense that all normally follow a request-response paradigm, services designated as RPC use the SOAP encoding of types rather than XML schema. A huge emphasis on interoperability has made RPC-based services generally the most interoperable out of the box of the three.

❑ **Document-Based Services.** Document-based Web services use XML schema to define the data types passed in SOAP messages. This support is useful when you want to pass XML data itself (and not simply encode in XML data that is not normally stored in XML). When you have existing XML schemas for certain XML file types, this format makes the most sense. This format has been gaining ground in terms of support and is almost as interoperable as RPC. In-depth knowledge of WSDL and XML schema is required to create and deploy document-based Web services.

❑ **Message-Style Services.** Message services are the most generic of the three types. They give the developers complete control over the incoming XML. Message style services are less of a type of Web service as they are a method for implementing them. Message-style services are AXIS specific, but since the developer is given complete control over the XML, they can be used to implement document-based services. Implementing services in AXIS using the message-style is the most complex, but the most control possible is given to the developer. Message-style services are necessary when implementing advanced features such as session management, transactions, security, and other functionality on top of normal Web services.

RPC makes the most sense for your weather Web service for interoperability and simplicity's sake. This method `getWeather()` is simple, and is not transporting a predefined XML data type, so there is no need for using document-based Web services (or its more complex sibling, message-style).

To actually deploy your Web service, the Java classes, `book.Weather` and `book.WeatherGetter`, must be in the classpath of the AXIS Web application. To do so, put the class files under the `<TOMCAT_HOME>/webapps/axis/WEB-INF/classes` directory.

The last step to deploying your service is running the AXIS admin tool. This can be done as an ANT task. Here is the `build.xml` file to use to deploy the service:

```
<project name="weatherService" default="deploy" basedir=".">
  <path id="axis.classpath">
    <fileset dir="${axis.home}/build/lib">
      <include name="**/*.jar" />
    </fileset>
  </path>
```

```
<taskdef resource="axis-tasks.properties"
    classpathref="axis.classpath" />

<target name="deploy">
  <axis-admin
      port="8080"
      hostname="localhost"
      failonerror="true"
      servletpath="/axis/services/AdminService"
      debug="true"
      xmlfile="deploy.wsdd"
      />
  </target>
</project>
```

Deploy.wsdd and build.xml need to be in the same directory, and then ant can be run normally to deploy the service.

The service is now deployed to the URL:

```
http://localhost:8080/axis/services/Weather
```

WSDL for this service is found simply by appending ?wsdl to the URL:

```
http://localhost:8080/axis/services/Weather?wsdl
```

Now Web service clients can programmatically access the weather forecasts from random-weather.org.

Writing a Web Service Client

Writing a Web services client when you have the WSDL handy for the Web service is quick and simple. Since WSDL defines the interface and data types in a particular Web service (or multiple Web services), classes to use the Web service can be auto-generated. AXIS provides a tool, WSDL2Java, that does just that. This tool can be run as an ant task as well, and the build.xml file to create the client classes necessary to communicate with your weather Web service looks like this:

```
<project name="weatherServiceClient" default="wsdl" basedir=".">
  <path id="axis.classpath">
    <fileset dir="${axis.home}/build/lib">
      <include name="**/*.jar" />
    </fileset>
  </path>

  <taskdef resource="axis-tasks.properties"
      classpathref="axis.classpath" />

  <target name="wsdl">
    <axis-wsdl2java
      output="output"
      testcase="true"
      verbose="true"
```

```
         url="http://localhost:8080/axis/services/Weather?wsdl" >

      </axis-wsdl2java>

   </target>
</project>
```

After creating the output directory (that is specified in the `<axis-wsdl2java>` tag), in this case, called `output`, running ant generates the following classes:

```
localhost.axis.services.Weather.WeatherGetter
localhost.axis.services.Weather.WeatherGetterService
localhost.axis.services.Weather.WeatherGetterServiceLocator
localhost.axis.services.Weather.WeatherGetterSoapBindingStub
org.randomweather.Weather
```

These generated classes depend on the jar files in the `<AXIS_HOME>/build/lib` directory to build a simple client application that accesses the Web service. Only three lines of code are required to access the Web service. It really is too easy:

```
int zipcode;
URL endpoint = new URL("http://localhost:8080/axis/services/Weather");

WeatherGetterService serviceLocator = new WeatherGetterServiceLocator();
WeatherGetter wg = serviceLocator.getWeather(endpoint);

Weather weather = wg.getWeather(zipcode);
```

The `WeatherGetterServiceLocator` class is used to bind a URL endpoint to the service. After that, the service can be accessed. The strength of Web services is in their simplicity, and as you can see, there really is not a whole lot to using a Web service. The complete code listing for the simple client application looks like the following code:

```
package book;

import java.net.URL;

import org.randomweather.Weather;

import localhost.axis.services.Weather.WeatherGetter;
import localhost.axis.services.Weather.WeatherGetterService;
import localhost.axis.services.Weather.WeatherGetterServiceLocator;

public class WeatherClient {
  public static void main(String[] args) throws Exception {
    int zipcode = 12345;
    URL endpoint = null;

    if (args.length >= 1) {
      zipcode = Integer.parseInt(args[0]);
      if (args.length >= 2) {
        endpoint = new URL(args[1]);
```

```
        }
    }

    if (endpoint == null)
        endpoint = new URL("http://localhost:8080/axis/services/Weather");

    WeatherGetterService serviceLocator = new WeatherGetterServiceLocator();
    WeatherGetter wg = serviceLocator.getWeather(endpoint);

    Weather weather = wg.getWeather(zipcode);

    System.out.println("Weather for " + zipcode);
    System.out.println("\tDescription:\t\t" + weather.getDescription());
    System.out.println("\tHigh Temperature:\t" + weather.getHighTemp());
    System.out.println("\tLow Temperature:\t" + weather.getLowTemp());
    System.out.println("\tBarmometer:\t\t" + weather.getBarometer() + " and "
                            + weather.getBarometerDescription());
    }
}
```

To see what gets sent and received over the HTTP connection, the Apache TCPMon application can again be used. You will set it to listen on port 8079 (and forward to port 8080), and run your client application as follows (assuming your CLASSPATH environment variable includes all the jars in the <AXIS_HOME>/build/lib directory):

```
java book.WeatherClient 12345 http://localhost:8079/axis/services/Weather
```

The output follows:

```
Weather for 12345
    Description:        Partly Sunny, Chance of snow
    High Temperature:  91
    Low Temperature:   24
    Barmoter:          27.007242 and Rising
```

Looking at the TCPMon screenshot in Figure 11-17, you can see the SOAP message sent and the reply received. TCPMon is useful for debugging document-based and message-style Web services (since you have more control over the XML passed).

Client-Side Possibilities

There are more things you could do with your random-weather.org Web service than simply write a program that prints the information out. In Windows, you could write an application using the .NET framework that runs in the system tray. It would check the weather every hour or so, and update the information for the zip code of your choice. If someone ever wanted to write a larger client-side application that included the current random weather forecast, it could be easily integrated, no matter what language the application was being developed with, or what platform on which it ran. Other Web sites that wanted to include the weather could connect to your Web service and then display the results on their page. Because the data for your weather Web site is structured, it can now be used in a variety of places *besides the Web browser.*

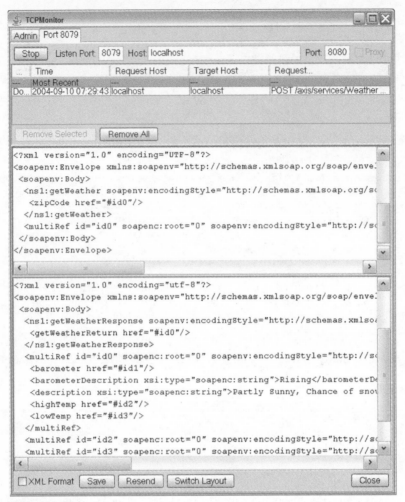

Figure 11-17

The Future

The future of Web services is unknown. There are many standards floating around, some by the W3C, some by OASIS. Standards for implementing secure Web services, transactional Web services, and reliable Web services are all being written and implemented. Once the major vendor implementations of Web services, such as Sun's Java Web Services Developer Pack and Microsoft's .NET framework, support these features out of the box, they may be practical to implement. Right now, there is minimal support for transactions and reliable messaging, and if your application needs those features today, Web services probably are not the best choice. Web services are moving away from simply enabling existing Web sites' dynamic data to be accessed by a new generation of rich client-side applications, to enabling the same securely and transactionally.

Summary

In this chapter, you have learned some possible ways to enable Java components in your application to communicate with external components in other applications or systems that could have been written in a variety of languages. Sockets provide the building blocks for all other technologies discussed in this chapter. With TCP/IP, they provide a reliable byte stream over a network that any language with a socket API can use. This is the lowest level of interprocess communication. Sockets are, however, not in themselves a guarantee of communication between two different components, a common protocol must also be spoken. In this chapter you implemented a small portion of the HTTP specification to gain an understanding of the immense undertaking it can be. RMI, CORBA, and Web services are all built on top of sockets and TCP/IP. RMI and CORBA implement complex protocols allowing them to provide such features as reliability, sessions, and transactions. They are cornerstone technologies for many enterprise systems. J2EE makes extensive use of RMI, as RMI combined with JNDI allows for the objects of a system to be transparently spread across multiple machines without any changes in the application's code. RMI and CORBA have become intertwined to some degree since support for CORBA's IIOP protocol was added to RMI. Now RMI and CORBA have basic interoperability, and this makes it easier for developers to integrate legacy CORBA systems into their modern J2EE equivalents.

Web services are the latest craze in distributed computing, and enable the evolution of the current World Wide Web of unstructured information to one of structured information. Web services are not as advanced technologically as RMI or CORBA, but there is power in their simplicity. Web services require minimal development effort to implement and, because all of their underlying protocols are human readable, are easy to debug. Web services have been prophesized to enable the next generation of applications that can better make use of the vast wealth of information found on the Internet.

None of the technologies used in this chapter is inherently better than any other. The right tool is needed for the right job. Sockets provide a low-level API that allows for the optimization and creation of new protocols. Some projects may require this — the remote control of external hardware, such as robotic devices, can usually be done best starting with sockets, and then building a more developer-friendly API layered on top. RMI and CORBA provide great foundations for distributed systems, and an understanding of them is necessary to utilize the full power of J2EE. The network latency implications of remote method calls must also be considered in any distributed system. Web services complement existing Web portals. They will be the simple mechanism by which information on the World Wide Web is shared for use by machines, not just by human eyes. Distributed applications and systems will probably make use of more than one component-to-component technology. As the integration of systems and information becomes easier with more platform-agnostic APIs and technologies, a whole new breed of information-centric applications can arise.

12

Distributed Processing with JMS and JMX

This chapter shows you how to build distributed processing applications using two standard Java APIs. You can use this application as a starting point for CPU intensive processing tasks that require scaling beyond a single computer. In addition to scaling, the application discussed in this chapter can be managed very easily. It can be configured, deployed, even changed completely at run time using a standard Web browser.

Tough software problems often require large amounts of processing power. In some cases it is necessary to distribute this processing across several servers to meet the required demand. These systems are susceptible to bottlenecks and are difficult to manage. The two technologies discussed in this chapter — JMS and JMX — reduce the inherent complexities of this problem.

Java Message System (JMS) is the Java standard API for developing Message Oriented Middleware (MOM). JMS is one of the APIs that make up the J2EE architecture. JMS provides a robust message capability allowing you to send and process messages across several servers within a network.

Java Management Extensions (JMX) is also a Java standard API. JMX defines a way to provide manageable resources to other applications, provided they comply with the same architectural standard. This allows you to configure and manage applications at run time through standard management tools.

The first section, "Basic Concepts," will explore the fundamentals of both JMS and JMX. It will not be an extensive laundry list of every method in the APIs; instead, it will be about the basics that you need to understand to be able to build a usable application. The focus of this chapter will be to expose you to a high value percentage of capabilities of these technologies that you can put to use in similar processing architecture problems. The second section, "Building a Distributed Application," will show you how to build a usable example application. This application example will show how to model a generic business process. The third section, "Deploying the

Application," will show you how to leverage JMX technology to deploy and manage an application remotely at run time.

The code in this chapter can then be extended to support any business process that might meet your needs. You will also be able to download the complete example from the publishers Web site. The Web site will give you the specific details on configuring and running the application.

Again, this chapter will not cover every detail regarding JMS and JMX. The intent is to understand enough of the two APIs to guide the design decision-making process, and then allow you to test out and extend the example application. The example will also help you navigate the standard API documentation with confidence after becoming familiar with the core capabilities of these two technologies.

Basic Concepts

This first section of the chapter discusses the fundamental concepts of both JMS and JMX API. With JMS, you will look at the object model required to send and receive messages using the JMS architecture. The second section introduces the JMX architecture for deploying standard manageable application components.

JMS Fundamentals

Messaging systems are made up of application components that do not communicate directly with each other. All communication goes through an intermediary, called a *destination*. In JMS terms, a *destination* is either a *queue* or a *topic*. The first thing to understand when building a message system is the difference between these two concepts.

The difference between a queue and a topic involves how messages are delivered. It is critical to understand the two delivery models when selecting the correct destination type for the problem at hand. The best way to illustrate the difference between the two is to use two analogies.

Everything you want to learn about a queue you can observe with a visit to a bank on a Friday at 5:00 p.m. The line, or queue, is long. There are too many customers and not enough tellers. Each customer represents a Message or work the system needs to perform, while each teller represents a Message Receiver or a processing node of the system. As you add tellers, each teller processes fewer customers effectively distributing the processing load of the system. The key takeaway from this is that a queue allows you to scale processing.

A topic solves a completely different problem. An analogy that describes a topic well would be a newspaper delivery route. A Subscription List defines who gets a copy of the newspaper. The newspaper represents the message of the system. Unlike the queue delivery model, the adding of subscribers does not distribute the processing; it is for notification. It increases the total work the system must perform.

A rough guideline used to determine the destination type is to look at the purpose of the message being sent. If the purpose is to *do something* with the message, then use a queue. If the purpose is to *inform or notify* the component, then use a topic. Now you ought to understand the conceptual difference between a queue and a topic. The next section will provide an overview of the classes used in sending and receiving a message from a JMS destination.

Distributed Processing with JMS and JMX

Sending and Receiving a JMS Message

In this section, you will learn how to send and receive messages from a message destination in Java. A JMS application is a contract between a messaging system and a client API that processes messages. The message system is a server that manages the destinations, listens for client connections, and manages transactions. A JMS messaging system is provided commercially or through the open source vendor. The first part of this section is an overview of the client API that interacts with a messaging system. The second section will show how to send and receive messages using the client API.

The following table contains the classes used to communicate with a JMS messaging system. These are interfaces defined in the *javax.jms.** package. As of JMS 1.1, the object model for handling both the queue and topic destination type is identical.

Class	Purpose
ConnectionFactory	Defines the behavior for creating a Connection to a JMS server. ConnectionFactory is an administered object bound to the JNDI context. The messaging system will exhibit different behavior depending on what type of ConnectionFactory is bound to the context. This behavior is related to message delivery, message persistence, and transaction support.
Destination	An object representing the queue or topic. Logically, it is where messages are stored between processing steps.
Connection	The Connection provides a unique link between the JMS server and your client-messaging component. It is also responsible for addressing security and permission issues.
Session	The Session object coordinates the Message Traffic between the JMS server and the client and is associated to a specific Connection object. It also makes sure the communication between the server and client are thread-safe.
MessagePublisher	Message publisher is able to send messages to a destination object.
MessageConsumer	A Message consumer has the ability to take messages from a destination, either synchronously or asynchronously.
MessageListener	Implementing the Message listener interface allows a client component to register to receive messages asynchronously when they are available.
Message	Last, but not least, the Message object represents the information moving through the system.

Now that you understand the purpose of the JMS interfaces that you will be working with, the next step is to look at the code required to send and receive messages. There are four important steps to sending a message:

1. Create a connection to the Message system.

2. Establish a JMS session.

545

3. Create a message publisher.

4. Explicitly send the message.

The code that follows will walk you through each step in the process of sending a message.

To be able to send or receive messages, you need to create a Session with the JMS server. The Session object allows you to create the Message, MessageConsumer, and MessagePublisher objects for the specific send and receive tasks. The session object is created with the sequence of method calls found in Figure 12-1.

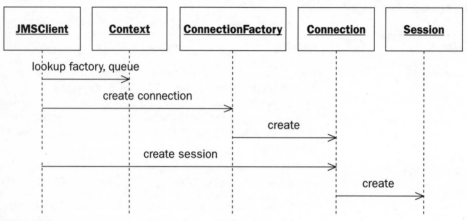

Figure 12-1

The following is the code for creating a session as described in Figure 12-1:

```
connection.createSession(boolean transaction, int acknowledgement);
```

The previous code for creating a session is very important because it defines transaction support and message acknowledgment. The first parameter defines transaction support. If the session supports transactional messages and the second specifies how the client will acknowledge receipt of the messages sent. Message acknowledgment can either be done automatically per message or by client request (in a large batch). Once you have a reference to a *Session* object, you can use it to create a *Message* and a *Message Publisher*. Figure 12-2 shows the UML for sending a message once a session object has been created.

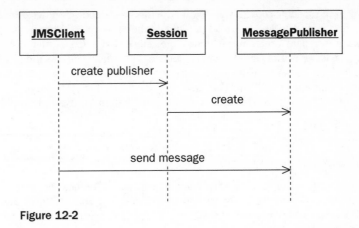

Figure 12-2

The code for creating a publisher that was described in UML by Figure 12-2 is listed here for clarification:

```
MessagePublisher publisher = session.createPublisher();
publisher.send( session.createTextMessage("message body"));
```

It is important to note from the code above that the publisher sent the message, not the session. This allows you to send and receive messages from the same session. By using the same session, the message can exist in the same transaction, which is important for fault-tolerant applications.

A JMS client can be notified when a message arrives at a JMS queue. The client must implement the *MessageListener* interface from the *javax.jms* package.

The next section walks through this process, starting with Figure 12-3, which shows the conceptual process for registering to receive messages from a JMS system.

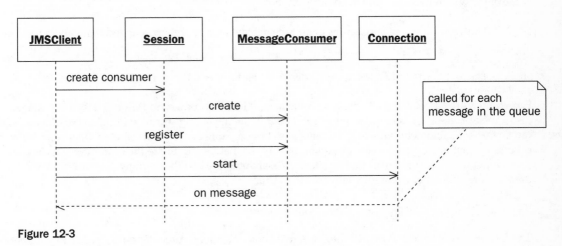

Figure 12-3

Now, take a look at the specific code that is involved with the collaboration described in Figure 12-3. The class that registers with the JMS server must implement the *MessageListener* interface found in the *javax.jms.** package. You pass a reference to a message listener to the Consumer and the consumer will call back the messageListener as messages become available. The callback is specified by the Messagelistener interface by the method `onMessage(Message m)`. The code for registering as a message consumer follows. Please note the `start()` method. This method is used to tell the JMS server to start sending messages to the registered client class. This will be covered in detail in the example application:

```
MessageConsumer consumer = session.createConsumer(queue);
consumer.addListener( this );
consumer.start();
```

From this section, you have learned the important conceptual differences between a queue and a topic, as well as how to send and receive messages using a JMS system. That is a large percentage of the JMS object model. The next section looks at the overview of JMX architecture and the capabilities it provides to the application developer.

JMX Fundamentals

In this section of the chapter, the fundamentals of the JMX architecture will be looked at. After reading this section, you will understand the capabilities that JMX provides the application developer, an overview of the architecture, and how to create your own JMX components that can leverage these management capabilities.

Java Management Extensions (JMX) is a framework that allows you to expose the methods of a Java object to other application. The Java objects that you expose are called MBeans. MBeans are the building blocks of JMX. An MBean is deployed to a JMX Agent where it is managed. The Agent provides a common set of services to interact with the MBean. These common services provide the application developer with a large number of capabilities.

Some of the capabilities available to an MBean follow:

❑ The agent allows the properties of an MBean to be read as well as changed remotely at run time.

❑ The agent allows the methods of an MBean to be invoked at run time.

❑ The agent allows the MBeans to be deployed and undeployed at run time.

Hopefully, these capabilities will give you some insight into how powerful JMX can be for building a distributed processing system. The application built in the upcoming section will consist of MBeans that can be managed remotely. By taking advantage of these capabilities you can remotely deploy additional processing components across several servers at runtime. Before moving to the example in this chapter, there ought to be a further investigation of the JMX architecture and the naming convention an MBean must adhere to in order to comply with the architecture.

Figure 12-4 is a logical depiction of the JMX architecture.

The architecture is logically divided into an Agent layer and an Instrumentation layer. The instrumentation layer is a collection of MBeans that provide the functionality that your application requires. This is supported by the Agent layer providing a common set of services for each component. These services handle component registration, event notification, and monitoring.

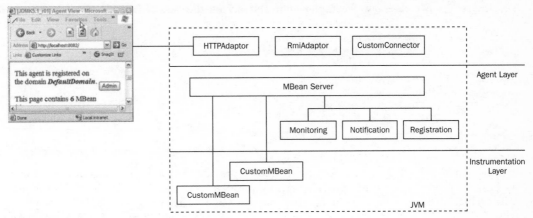

Figure 12-4

In order to use an MBean, it must be deployed to an *MBeanServer*. All communication with an MBean is done indirectly through the server. This server has a standard interface for manipulating MBeans. This standard communication is extended one step further with the use of MBean Adaptors and Connectors. An Adaptor communicates with an MBeanServer using a standard protocol. In the example later in this chapter, an HTTPAdaptor will be used to communicate with deployed MBeans using a standard Web browser.

The next three sections will describe the specifics of the JMX architecture, including using standard MBeans, deploying an MBean for management, and using Adaptors and Connectors.

Using Standard MBeans

An MBean is made up of an interface and an implementing class. The interface and class must subscribe to a specific standard so that it can be managed by an MBeanServer. The following are the standard rules to which an MBean must subscribe:

❑   The Interface must have the same name as the implementing class plus an MBean Suffix.

❑   The Interface must reside in the same package as the implementing class.

The following code is an example of a standard MBean interface. In this example, the MBean interface exposes one read-only property, isRunning, and two operations, stop() and start(), to the MBeanServer:

```
package wrox.processing.jmx;
public interface ExampleMBean {
  public boolean isRunning();
  public void stop();
  public void start();
}
```

The next section of code shows the implementing class. Note the class names and package declarations:

```
package wrox.processing.jmx;
public class Example implements ExampleMBean {
private Boolean running;

public Boolean isRunning() {
   return running;
}


}
```

In the example that will be created, four more MBeans provide various applications logic in support of the business process. This section provided an example of a standard MBean; there are other types of MBeans that are beyond the scope of this chapter, however, the same principles apply by complying with the standard common services and management that are available through the JMX architecture. The next section will describe the process of deploying an MBean to an MBeanServer.

Deploying MBean for Management

The MBeanServer is the heart of the Agent layer of the JMX Architecture. It provides the ability to register an MBean. This makes them available to other components that can connect to the MBeanServer.

The interaction with the server takes place through the *MBeanServer* interface. The next code listing shows an abbreviated version of the methods available in the MBeanServer. This interface allows you to invoke methods on an MBean that has been deployed through the server. Methods of an MBean are invoked indirectly via the MBeanServer:

```
public Object getAttribute(ObjectName on, String name);
public void setAttribute(ObjectName on, Attribute att);
public Object invoke(ObjectName on, String method, Object[] param, String[] sig);
public ObjectInstance registerMBean(Object obj, ObjectName on);
public Set queryMBeans(ObjectName on, QueryExp qe);
```

The server identifies each MBean through a unique name assigned when it is registered with the server. This is called the objectName. It is made up of two parts: the domain and the keys separated by a colon (:). In the example that follows, the domain is processing and the key is name=message-processor. An object name can have any number of keys separated by a comma (,):

```
BeanServer server= MBeanServerFactory.createMBeanServer();
ObjectName objectname = new ObjectName( "processing:name=message-processor");
server.register( new MessageProcessor(), objectName );
```

Once an MBean has been registered with the MBeanServer, it is possible to get and set attributes, invoke methods, and query for an MBean using the ObjectName. For example, to invoke the method public void read(String file) on an MBean registered with the name processing:name=message-processor, you would execute the following line of code:

```
ObjectName on = new ObjectName("processing:name=message-processor");
Object[] args = { "file.txt"};
String [] sig = { "java.lang.String"};
server.invoke( on, "read", args,sig);
```

The previous code is fairly long-winded for the invocation of a single method. Fortunately, there are several adaptors available that make interacting with an MBean easier. This is discussed in the next section on adaptors and connectors.

Using Adaptors and Connectors

An adaptor exposes the MBeanServer to other applications external to the JMX Agent. The adaptor communicates via a defined protocol. The MBeanServer is exposing MBean to external applications using the adaptor. Every JMX agent needs to deploy at least one adaptor.

There are several Adaptors available that support various protocols. These include HTTP for Web-based management, RMI for remote method invocation, and SNMP for communicating with network devices such as routers and switches. This chapter will work with an HttpAdaptor allowing the management of the example through a Web browser. The HttpAdaptor is used extensively in the "Deploying the Application" section of this chapter.

This concludes the "Basic Concepts" section of this chapter. The next section will show how to design and build an application using these two technologies and implement an order-processing system.

Building a Distributed Application

The objective of this chapter, and specifically this section, is to build a flexible distributed processing application. By now it should be clear why you are using JMS and JMX to accomplish this task. JMS allows you to partition work requests into messages and distribute these messages to numerous processing nodes seamlessly across a network of computers. Furthermore, your processing components will be built as MBeans. This allows you to monitor and communicate with them remotely at run time.

The example application will show how to perform the business process described in Figure 12-5.

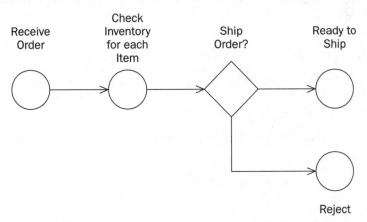

Figure 12-5

The goal of the example is to build three components that implement the messaging behavior. The result will be an abstraction that separates the JMS messaging logic from the actual business logic specific to the business process. These fundamental message components can then be tied together in various ways to support different, more complex, business processes.

The three components in the JMS processing architecture example define the system responsibilities required to process messages, route messages, and split and aggregate messages. Each processing step is mapped to a messaging component. The following diagram in Figure 12-6 shows how the example messaging components are mapped to the example business process.

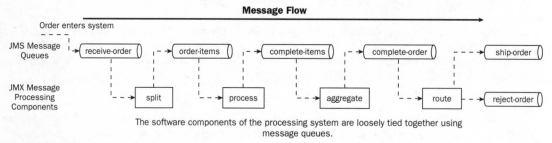

Figure 12-6

There are several benefits to this design. The primary benefit of this design is scalability. Any number of components running on several different physical machines can process a message from a queue. This creates a location-independent processing architecture. In addition, components have no direct dependencies. All dependencies are established by receiving and sending messages between queues. This is an example of a loose coupling of system components. There is also a significant amount of design flexibility. Changing the flow of messages between components can be done without modifying the components themselves, but by simply changing the queue.

The next section will discuss the various types of messages that are available through JMS. Once a type is selected that matches the criteria, the sections that follow will describe in the detail how to build the three types of messaging components used in the example.

Deciding on the Message Type

Before beginning the component design, it is important to select a message type appropriate to your processing requirement. Choosing a message type is important because it affects the persistence, performance, and interoperability of the application.

The three types of JMS messages are described by the contents they can transport. They include the following:

❑ *ObjectMessage* allows any serialized object to be passed as the payload of a JMS message.

❑ *MapMessage* provides a hashmap of properties, useful when sending flat data that can be represented as name value pairs.

❑ *Text Message* can store a Java string, which lends itself to sending messages represented as XML.

ObjectMessage allows you to wrap any serializable Java object within a message and pass it between destinations.

Of the three message types provided by JMS, the ObjectMessage type is the easiest to implement in a pure Java environment. However, there can be issues persisting Java objects. For example, a message history needs to be saved; it will be persisted as a binary object in the underlying relational storage system. If the class definition of the object message changes over time, the older message stored would no longer be retrievable.

It's for that reason that the text Message approach will be used in this example. Plus, by using XML text messages you gain XML's structure and flexibility. In addition, XML text messages lend themselves well to integration with a Web service interface.

Since the focus of the application is to distribute computer processing work across several computers on a network, this application will use queue as its JMS destination. Remember, a queue is a point-to-point communication model. Once a message is taken from a queue, no other queue consumers will receive the message. This allows you to divide and conquer requests across several message consumers.

Understanding the Three-Component Architecture

The component architecture will support any business process. The application will implement an order processing example. The application itself will model the behavior of a business process. A business process is really just a collection of steps. In this example, those steps fall into one of three categories. The categories are processing, routing, and splitting and aggregating. Each category will be abstracted and modeled as a JMX component.

The design goal of this application is to create an abstract business process — for example, if you needed to process documents into a search index. It's possible to extend the processing component described in this application to suit your specific needs. By doing that you will be able to leverage the processing scalability gained from working with queues, as well as the manageability of working with the JMX framework with very little infrastructure code.

The next three sections will describe how to build the three MBeans required to implement your application. The message components deployed as MBeans are the following:

❑   The MessageProcessor

❑   The MessageRouter

❑   The MessageSplitter and Aggregator

These three components represent the abstract behavior of most any business process. The concepts expressed are based on design patterns from *Enterprise Integration Patterns* by Gregor Hohpe. The following sections will show what is required to build on each of these three components. Each component section will examine the classes and interfaces required to implement the component. For each class, the code will be divided into logical units and discussed. The complete code listing can be downloaded from the publisher's Web site.

Creating a Component to Process JMS Messages

The first component to tackle will be the message processing component. A message processing component performs three functions: It takes a message from a source queue, performs work on that message, and then puts the resulting message on a destination queue. Figure 12-7 shows the UML design of the message processor component.

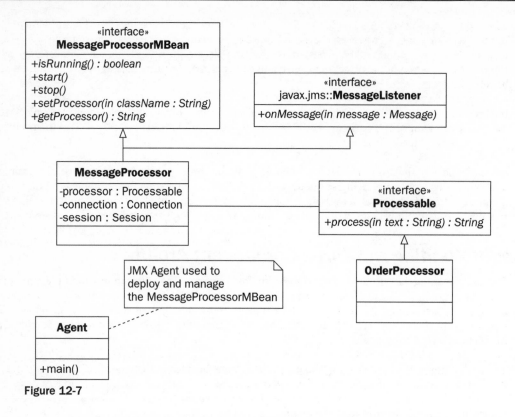

Figure 12-7

The following are a few things to take away from the design:

❑ By leveraging the JMX architecture, you expose class methods so that they can be discovered and invoked at run time.

❑ By leveraging a simple processable interface, you are able to create a separation of concern between the JMS message logic of the MessageProcessor and the business logic of the Order Processor class. Reducing the dependences between the JMS class and the business logic class increases the reuse of the message code.

> **Make sure the JMX naming conventions are followed when creating standard MBeans. The MessageProcessor and the interface MessageProcessorMBean need to be named identically, except for the MBean suffix on the interface. The MBean suffix needs to have the M and the B capitalized; otherwise it will not be recognized by the MBeanServer.**

The following table shows the classes and interfaces that are involved in the message processing component.

Component	Responsibility
MessageProcessorMBean	The MBean interface defines the operations and properties that will be exposed for management using the JMX standard architecture.
MessageProcessor	The MessageProcessor is the implementing class of the MBean interface. This class is responsible for sending and receiving messages by connecting and registering with the JMS server.
Processable	The Processable interface removes the JMS dependencies from the specific processing task, allowing the reuse of the MessageProcessingMBean.
OrderProcessor	OrderProcessor is a specific example of a class implementing the processable interface. By implementing Processable interface, the OrderProcessor class can focus on the business logic of the problem domain.
MessageListener	Message listener declares the onMessage method to be called when a message arrives at a queue.

MessageListener

The message listener interface is part of the JMS specification. Having the MessageProcessor implement MessageListener allows the MessageProcessor to be registered with the JMS server when the connection to the JMS server is established. When a message arrives at a queue, the message is sent to one of the MessageListeners registered with that queue:

```
package javax.jms.MessageListener;

public interface MessageListener {
 public void onMessage( Message message) ;
}
```

MessageProcessorMBean

The MessageProcessorMBean interface complies with the standard MBean naming conventions. It defines the methods that will be exposed to the JMX Agent. In the case of the Message processing component, it will publish the isRunning(), stop(), and start() methods. These methods can then be invoked at run time via any application that has access to the management agent. You will not write any code to interact with the JMX agent, instead, you will use the standard HTTPAdapter and interact with the agent with a common Web browser. The following section shows the code for the MessageProcessorMBean interface.

First, the code that follows is the package declaration:

```
package wrox.processing.jmx;
```

The interface declaration for the MBean must match the <class name>MBean pattern of its implementing class and be in the same package. Because you are creating the MessageProcessor class from scratch, this is an easy requirement to satisfy; however, if you are deploying a legacy application, this may not be possible. The Dynamic MBean interface and meta data classes of the JMX API allow you to deal with that requirement:

```
public interface MessageProcessorMBean {
```

The isRunning method will provide the status of the MBeans connection to the JMS server. The status is read-only, but the value is controlled by the start and stop methods below. The start and stop methods allow you to control the message processing:

```
public boolean isRunning();
public void stop();
public void start();
```

The remaining methods of the interface define the properties exposed through the JMX Agent. These will allow you to parameterize your component and change the source and destination queues at run time:

```
public void setSource(String source);
public String getSource();
public void setDestination(String destination);
public String getDestination();
public void setProcessor(String name);
public String getProcessor();
}
```

JndiHelper

Since you are using JMS, you need to connect to the JMS server using JNDI context lookup. The following code is a utility class that establishes a connection with a JMS server as well as looks up the Queues in the JNDI context:

```
package wrox.processing.util;
import java.util.Properties;
import javax.jms.ConnectionFactory;
import javax.jms.Destination;
import javax.naming.Context;
import javax.naming.InitialContext;
import javax.naming.NamingException;

public class JndiHelper {
  private JndiHelper() {
  }
```

The getContext() method returns a reference to the JNDI tree associated with the JMS server:

```
public static synchronized Context getContext() {
    Context context= null;
    Properties props= new Properties();
```

Context properties are specific to the different JMS vendors' implementations. In this example, you are using JBOSS 4.0, so their JNDI lookup client properties must be provided. They are shown in the code for clarity. It's also important to include the vendor-specific jar containing the NamingContextFactory class. In this case, it is fr.dyade.aaa.jndi2.client.NamingContextFactory:

```
    properties.put(Context.INITIAL_CONTEXT_FACTORY,"org.jnp.interfaces.NamingContextFac
tory");
    properties.put(Context.URL_PKG_PREFIXES, "org.jnp.interfaces");
properties.put(Context.PROVIDER_URL,"localhost");

    try {
      context= new InitialContext(props);
    } catch (NamingException e) {
      throw new RuntimeException("could not create context", e);
    }
    return context;
  }
```

This is a convenience method for looking up a destination from the JNDI context.

```
  public static synchronized Destination getDestination(String name) {
    Context context= getContext();
    Destination destination= null;
    try {
      destination= (Destination)context.lookup(name);
    } catch (NamingException e) {
      e.printStackTrace();
    }
    if (destination == null) {
      throw new RuntimeException("could not find destination" + name);
    }
    return destination;
  }
```

This method is for looking up connection factory objects. It includes an option to specify whether transaction support is needed:

```
  public static synchronized ConnectionFactory getConnectionFactory(boolean
txSupport) {
    Context context= getContext();
    ConnectionFactory factory= null;
    try {
      if (txSupport) {
        factory= (ConnectionFactory)context.lookup("XAConnectionFactory");
      } else {
        factory= (ConnectionFactory)context.lookup("ConnectionFactory");
      }
    } catch (NamingException e) {
      e.printStackTrace();
    }
    if (factory == null) {
      throw new RuntimeException("Could not find connection factory. " );
    }
    return factory;
  }
  public static synchronized ConnectionFactory getConnectionFactory( ){
    return getConnectionFactory(false);
  }
}
```

Chapter 12

MessageProcessor

The following shows the code for the heart of the message processing component — the message processor implementing class. The messageProcessor class implements both the MessageListener interface and
the MessageProcessorMBean. The interface and implementing class must be declared in the same package. In this case, both the interface and implementing classes are declared in the wrox.processing.jmx
package:

```
package wrox.processing.jmx;

import java.lang.reflect.Constructor;
```

There are several classes to import from the javax.jms package. Fortunately, these interfaces represent the
unified domain of the JMS 1.1 specification. They are a vast improvement over the previous 1.0 specification. Previously, to send a message to a queue required a specific QueueConnectionFactory,
QueueConnection, QueueSession, et cetera.

> **Other than the hassle of the programming overhead associated with queues and top-
> ics, the real problem was that you couldn't receive from a queue and send to a topic
> with the same session. Since the session performs transaction management, this
> implies that you cannot send and receive between destination types in a transaction-
> safe way. JMS 1.1 corrected that problem.**

It's important to note that the JMS-specific classes are imported and used in the MessageProcessor class.
This is because it is the only class that has a dependency to JMS. A good practice in application design is
to localize dependency on external APIs. This minimizes the impact to an application if a change needs
to be made:

```
import javax.jms.Connection;
import javax.jms.ConnectionFactory;
import javax.jms.Destination;
import javax.jms.JMSException;
import javax.jms.Message;
import javax.jms.MessageConsumer;
import javax.jms.MessageListener;
import javax.jms.MessageProducer;
import javax.jms.Session;
import javax.jms.TextMessage;
```

The *processable* interface defines the link between the JMS coding and the business logic of the application:

```
import wrox.processing.Processable;
import wrox.processing.util.JndiHelper;
```

The class declaration for the MBean needs to follow the naming conversion. The Message processor can
also implement or extend classes; however, only the methods specified in the *MessageProcessorMBean*
interface will be exposed for management. In this example, the onMessage() method in the
MessageListener interface will not be accessible via the MBeanServer:

```
public class MessageProcessor implements MessageListener, MessageProcessorMBean {

  private boolean running= false;
  private String sourceName, destinationName;
  private String processorName;
  private Processable processable;

  private ConnectionFactory factory;
  private Connection connection;
  private Session session;
  private MessageConsumer consumer;
  private MessageProducer producer;
  private Destination source, destination;
```

Setting the destination and source queue as managed attributes allows you to configure the message processor component at run time. This will be reviewed when the component is deployed:

```
public String getDestination() {
  return destinationName;
}
public void setDestination(String name) {
  this.destinationName= name;
}
public String getSource() {
  return sourceName;
}
public void setSource(String name) {
  this.sourceName= name;
}
```

Continuing with the description of the MessageProcessor code, this is the start method that will be exposed to the JMX Agent. The start method is responsible for creating the connection with the JMS server and registering the client to receive messages as they arrive to the queue:

```
public void start() {
  ConnectionFactory factory= null;
```

Before establishing a connection to the JMS server, you need to look up the connectionFactory object in the JNDI object registry. An example of using the JndiHelper class to simplify this lookup of the destination objects is listed in the following code:

> JNDI plays a key role in abstracting out the vendor-specific classes from the standard interfaces defined in the javax.jms.* package. The object bound to the context is the concrete implementation. The lookup casts the object to standard interface, removing vend specifics from application developers' code. This is a common practice in a number of J2EE APIs.

```
factory= JndiHelper.getConnectionFactory();
source= JndiHelper.getDestination(sourceName);
destination= JndiHelper.getDestination(destinationName);
try {
```

Establish a unique connection for this client:

```
connection= factory.createConnection( );
```

Create the session object. The first parameter determines transaction support. The second parameter specifies acknowledgment of messages delivered to the client. AUTO_ACKNOWLEDGE tells the JMS server to mark the message as received when the method call to onMessage returns. Another option is to explicitly call message.acknowledge() to confirm message delivery. If the connection is lost or the session is rolled back before the acknowledge method is called, the message will be resent:

```
session= connection.createSession(false, Session.AUTO_ACKNOWLEDGE);
consumer= session.createConsumer(source);
```

Pass a reference to this object to receive a message from the server:

```
consumer.setMessageListener(this);
```

Create a producer object for sending to the next destination:

```
producer= session.createProducer(destination);
```

Starting the connection is a very important step. It tells the JMS server to begin sending messages as they are available. Without that one line of code, you will spend a great deal of time wondering why there aren't any messages being sent from the queue:

```
        connection.start();
        running= true;

    } catch (JMSException e) {
        throw new RuntimeException("could not start message processor", e);
    }
}

public boolean isRunning() {
    return running;
}
```

Stop is the operation to return resources to the JMS server and close out all connections:

```
public void stop() {
    try {
        connection.stop();
        producer.close();
        consumer.close();
        session.close();
        connection.close();
    } catch (JMSException e) {
        e.printStackTrace();
    } finally {
        running= false;
    }
}
```

The goal here is to be able to pass in the name of the class implementing the processable interface:

```
public void setProcessor(String name) {
   processorName= name;
   try {
```

The code then uses reflection to take the class name and turn it into an object instance of that class. Note that the class described by the processorName parameter must be available in the classpath:

```
Class clazz=Class.forName(processorName);
Constructor ct= clazz.getConstructor(null);
Object obj = ct.newInstance(null);
 If ( obj instanceof Processable){
     processable= (Processable)obj;
 } else {
     throw new RuntimeException("processor"+name+"is not an instance of
Processable", e);
   }
 } catch (Exception e) {
     throw new RuntimeException("could not create processor class", e);
 }
}
```

This is part of the MBean interface and will return the fully qualified name of the class implementing the processable interface:

```
public String getProcessor() {
  return processorName;
}
/* (non-Javadoc)
 * @see javax.jms.MessageListener#onMessage(javax.jms.Message)
 */
```

The algorithm for the message processor component is really expressed in the onMessage method:

```
public void onMessage(Message message) {
   TextMessage inMessage = null, outMessage = null;
   try {
     try {
```

The MessageProcessor is only designed to handle text messages. ObjectMessage and MapMessage types will be ignored:

```
if (message instanceof TextMessage) {
   inMessage= (TextMessage)message;
```

Get the body of the input message and pass it to the processable interface. Create the output message from the session and send the new message to the next destination queue moving the message down the processing chain:

```
String body= inMessage.getText();
if (processable != null) {
String result = processable.process(body);
```

```
                    outMessage = session.createTextMessage();
                    outMessage.setText(result);
                    producer.send(outMessage);
    }
```

The process method on the Processable interface throws a ProcessingException. If this is thrown, send the input message to the error queue. This would take place if there was something functionally wrong with the current message:

```
        } catch (ProcessingException pe) {
            inMessage.setObjectProperty("exception", pe);
            producer.send(JndiHelper.getDestination(JndiHelper.ERROR_QUEUE),
    inMessage);
        }
     } catch (JMSException e) {
        e.printStackTrace();
     }
   }
  }
```

This concludes the code for the MessageProcessor MBean implementing class. Note that the processable interface is responsible for the specific business logic. The next section shows the processable interface and an example implementing class.

Processable

The processing interface defines a single method. The method takes a string parameter. This parameter is the body of the text message to be processed. In implementing this design approach, this message body will be a string message:

```
package wrox.processing;

public interface Processable {

   public String process( String text ) throws ProcessingException;
}
```

OrderProcessor

The OrderProcessor class is an example implementation of the processable interface. This would be replaced with any application-specific behavior you need to implement. OrderProcessor is the concrete implementation of the Processable interface. The goal of this component is to implement this one interface for each of the business processing steps that need to be accomplished. The implementation of the process method has been stubbed out for testing purposes:

```
public class OrderProcessor implements Processable {

   public OrderProcessor( ){

   }
   /* (non-Javadoc)
    * @see wrox.jmx.Processable#process(java.lang.String)
    */
   public String process(String xml) throws ProcessingException {
```

```
//TODO replace dummy response
  return "<order><id>100</id><item><status>instock</status></item></order>"
  }
```

JMXAgent

The final class needed is for the JMX Agent, and the code you need to write is for the JMX Agent. The Agent is a simple application containing a main method. The Agent will create the MbeanServer and create the HttpAdaptor. The results of running the JMXAgent class as a standalone executable will be the deployment of the MessageProcessor MBean, HttpAdaptor, and the starting of the JMX Agent:

```
package wrox.processing.jmx;
```

Here are the imports required for the JMX Agent:

```
package wrox.processing.jmx;
import javax.management.MBeanServer;
import javax.management.MBeanServerFactory;
import javax.management.ObjectName;
```

The next import is for the HTTP adaptor. This will allow management of the application via a Web browser over HTTP protocol. As you can see, it is not part of the standard javax.management package. At this time, adaptors are not part of the specification. This example is using an httpAdaptor, but there are numerous protocols available. Some of the protocols include RMI for remote method invocation, and SNMP for communicating with network devices such as a routers and switches.

The following code shows the main method for starting the deployment process for deploying a JMX application:

```
import com.sun.jdmk.comm.HtmlAdaptorServer;
/**
 * @author Scot
 */
public class Agent {
  public static void main(String[] args) {
```

The first step is to create the MBean server:

```
MBeanServer server= MBeanServerFactory.createMBeanServer();

ObjectName adaptorName= null;
    try {
```

Next, create the adaptor and create an object name to uniquely identify the adaptor once it is registered with the MBean server:

```
HtmlAdaptorServer htmlAdaptor= new HtmlAdaptorServer();
    adaptorName= new ObjectName("Adaptor:name=html,port=8082");
```

Then, register the adaptor with the MBean server. As you can see, the method to register the adaptor reads registerMBean. That is because, just like the MessageProcessor MBean created in the previous section, the httpadaptor also follow the JMX standard:

```
        server.registerMBean(htmlAdaptor, adaptorName);

        System.out.println("adaptor starting..");
```

The final step is to start the HTML adaptor. This will tell the htmlAdaptor object to open a Socket connection and listening port 8082 for HTTP requests:

```
        htmlAdaptor.start();

        } catch (Exception e) {
        System.out.println("Errors starting jmx agent");
        e.printStackTrace();
        return;
      }
    }
  }
```

That is all the code that needs to be written for the message-processing component. The next section is the second of three message components: the routing component.

Creating a Component that Directs Messages through the Business Process

The second component that you will be implementing in this solution is a message routing component. Think of this component as the decision diamond of a business process. The message routing component takes a message from a source queue and — based on the message content — determines the next appropriate message *Destination*.

This component acts as a message control gate or traffic intersection. This is an explicit design decision to segregate the processing logic from the message routing logic. It's just a good practice; by separating responsibility of components, you increase the level of reuse the component exhibits.

Just to clarify the motivation, the goal of building a process application in this manner is to be able to support a complex business process built with simple components loosely tied together with message queues and/or topics. For example, if you wanted to build a system that manages files on a network, you could create a component that copies a file from one directory to another and then reuse that component, without modification, whenever you needed to copy files.

This component helps simplify the overall system design by doing the following things:

1. Separating flow and processing logic, reducing the dependencies between each component.
2. Providing reuse of business logic.
3. Limiting the number of components that can modify each message. By design, the routing components will not be given access to the messages.

Figure 12-8 shows the UML design for the message routing component.

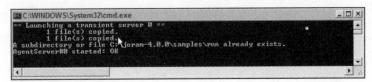

Figure 12-8

The message router design uses the same concepts as the MessageProcessor. There, collaboration is the same as the message processor. The only difference is the behavior specified by the Routable interface. The algorithm in the onMessage method does not modify the message, but instead determines the next queue in the processing chain. The responsibility of determining the next queue in the processing chain is left to the Routable Implementer, in this case the OrderRouter class.

The MessageRouter class also implements a standard MBean interface to expose the configuration and life-cycle methods of the component to the JMX agent. That way, the component methods will be accessible to other JMX compliant applications through any JMX-compliant adaptor.

The message routing component is similar to the message processing component in that it contains an MBean interface, an Implementing class, as well as an interface to extend the specific application behavior.

Routeable

The *Routeable* interface defines the behavior of the routable component. Unlike the *Processable* interface, the Routeable interface does not modify the incoming message. The Routeable interface consists of a single method: accepting the body of the JMS message as text and returning a string that represents the name of a queue:

```
package wrox.processing;

public interface Routeable {

  public String route( String message);
}
```

MessageRouter

The MessageRouter class will implement the *MessageRouterMBean* and *MessageListener*. By implementing the MessageRouterMBean interface, its methods will be exposed for management via the JMX server. By implementing the MessageListener interface, the MessageRouter class can register with the JMS server and receive messages as they arrive at the JMS destination:

```
package wrox.processing.jmx;
import java.lang.reflect.Constructor;

//JMS imports omitted

import wrox.processing.Routeable;
import wrox.processing.util.JndiHelper;

public class MessageRouter implements MessageRouterMBean, MessageListener {
private boolean running= false;
private Routeable routeable;
```

Life-cycle methods are the same as the Message Processor, as shown following:

```
public void start(){
//method bodies omitted
}
public void stop() {
//method bodies omitted
}
```

The setRouter method uses reflection to take the string parameter and create an instance of a Routeable object:

```
public void setRouter(String className) {
    try {
        Class clazz= Class.forName(className);
        Constructor ct= clazz.getConstructor(null);
        routeable= (Routeable)ct.newInstance(null);
    } catch (Exception e) {
        e.printStackTrace();
    }
}
```

The onMessage method passes the message body to the routable interface and the interface returns the name of the queue to look up in the JNDI context:

```
public void onMessage(Message message) {
    TextMessage textMessage= (TextMessage)message;
    try {
        String text= textMessage.getText();
        String name= routeable.route(text);
        Destination queue = JndiHelper.getDestination(name);
        producer.send(queue, message );

    } catch (JMSException e) {
        e.printStackTrace();
    }
}
```

So far, you have built the components to process messages and route messages between queues based on the message content. The next component takes distributed processing a step further by dividing large processing tasks into smaller pieces that can be executed in parallel.

Creating a Component to Divide Large Tasks for Parallel Processing

Often, large tasks need to be divided up into small tasks that can be processed in parallel. This next component allows large messages to be broken up into smaller messages such that each submessage can be processed separately; however, a common scenario is that the workflow cannot continue until all submessages are processed. This component uses JMS correlating messages that were created from the same initial request.

This component uses two MBeans: one to split a message into submessages, and another to join the submessages together after they have been processed individually. Think of these two components as bookends of a smaller subprocess.

The two MBeans follow the same pattern as the previous components in that they contain a behavior interface, an MBean interface, and an implementing class. The first class discussed is the behavior interface for splitting a JMS message.

Splitable

The splitable interface takes the message text as an argument and returns a list of strings for creating submessages:

```
package wrox.processing;
import java.util.List;

public interface Splitable {

  public List getSubMessage( String text);

}
```

MessageSplitter

The message splitter is similar in design to the other components already built, except that this component creates several messages from a single input message:

```
package wrox.processing.jmx;
import java.lang.reflect.Constructor;
import java.util.Iterator;
import java.util.List;
// jms import statements omitted.
import wrox.processing.Splitable;
import wrox.processing.util.JndiHelper;

public class MessageSplitter implements MessageListener, MessageSplitterMBean {
  private boolean running;
  private Splitable splitable;
  private String splitterName;
```

The JMX exposed properties are as follows:

```
  public String getDestination() {
    return destinationName;
  }

  public void setDestination(String name) {
    destinationName= name;
  }

  public String getSource() {
    return sourceName;
  }
```

```
public void setSource(String name) {
   sourceName= name;
}
```

Again, the onMessage method is where the algorithm for the component is implemented:

```
public void onMessage(Message m) {
  try {
    TextMessage textMessage= (TextMessage)m;
```

Get the Unique message ID assigned by the JMS server when the message was created:

```
        String correlationId= m.getJMSMessageID();
        String text= textMessage.getText();
```

The onMessage method takes an input text message and splits it into submessages:

```
    List messages= splitable.getSubMessage(text);

    int count= messages.size();
```

The getJMSCorrelationID is a header parameter used to show that several message are related to one another. In this example, you will split one message into several submessages. Using the messageID of the source message as the correlationID of all the submessage, you will be able to identify which message produced a given submessage. This creates a relationship between all the new submessages that can be looked up in the MessageAggregator component. You have also set a property count on the message header. This will tell the MessageAggregator how many messages exist with this correlationId:

```
        for (Iterator iter= messages.iterator(); iter.hasNext();) {
          TextMessage subMessage= session.createTextMessage();
          subMessage.setJMSCorrelationID(correlationId);
          subMessage.setStringProperty("count", count);
          String subText= (String)iter.next();

          subMessage.setText(subText);
          producer.send(subMessage);
        }
    } catch (JMSException e) {
      e.printStackTrace();
    }
  }
```

Given the example message described in the following code, the OrderSplitter would transform the input message into submessages by applying an XML transformation that extracts each of the items in order, as in the following example message:

```
<order>
 <id>400</id>
 <customer>
         <name>Heather</name>
 </customer>
 <items>
         <item>
            <id>4034</id>
             <description>VW Jetta,Blue</description>
             <quantity>1</quantity>
         </item>
         <item>
             <id>4500</id>
             <description>...</description>
             <quantity>2</quantity>
         </item>
   </items>
 </order>
```

An example result of splitting the above message is shown by the following:

```
<!-- Message 1 of 2 ->
<item>
 <order-reference>400</order-reference>
 <id>4034</id>
 <quantity>1</quantity>
</item>

<!-- Message 2 of 2 ->
<item>
 <order-reference>400</order-reference>
 <id>450</id>
 <quantity>1</quantity>
</item>
```

That concludes the portion of this component that is responsible for splitting the initial message into submessages. The next sections look at the process of taking submessages and correlating them back together. Figure 12-9 shows an overview of the classes and interfaces that make up the design of the AggregatorMBean.

It's important to understand from the design that there is no guarantee that submessages will be processed in any particular order. For that reason, the aggregator acts as a stateful message filter. It collects and stores submessages until all the submessages for a particular correlationId have been processed.

It's possible to see one of the benefits of the loose coupling design strategy. For example, the specific sub-processing step is not tied to the split or aggregate component. So therefore, numerous subprocessing steps can be configured without modifying the application code of this component.

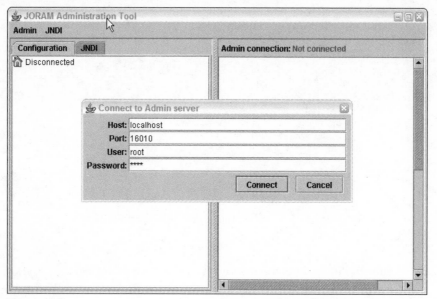

Figure 12-9

Aggregateable

The aggregateable interface defines the aggregator life cycle. This defines the aggregateable strategy. The strategy can be changed by providing a different implementation of the isComplete() and getResultMessage():

```
package wrox.processing;

public interface Aggregateable {

  public void setCorrelationId(String correlationId);
  public void addMessage(String messageId, int count, String message);
  public boolean isComplete();
  public String getResultMessage( );
}
```

MessageAggregator

This class is responsible for implementing the logic of receiving the submessages and tracking them via the correlationId:

```
package wrox.processing.jmx;
import java.lang.reflect.Constructor;
import java.util.HashMap;
import java.util.Map;
//omitted jms imports
import wrox.processing.Aggregateable;
import wrox.processing.util.JndiHelper;

public class MessageAggregator implements MessageListener, MessageAggregatorMBean {
```

The Map defines the collection of aggregators, one for each correlationId as shown here:

```
private Map aggregators= new HashMap();
 // jmx properties omitted.

public void onMessage(Message m) {
  TextMessage textMessage= (TextMessage)m;
   try {

     String correlationId= textMessage.getJMSCorrelationID();

     if (correlationId != null) {
       String messageId= textMessage.getJMSMessageID();
       int count= textMessage.getIntProperty("count");
```

The basic steps of the algorithm are to look up an aggregator in the aggregator map. If it doesn't exist, create an aggregator for that correlationId:

```
        String text= textMessage.getText();
        Aggregateable aggregateable= (Aggregateable)aggregators.get(correlationId);
        if (aggregateable == null) {

          aggregateable= createAggregateable();
          aggregateable.setCorrelationId(correlationId);
          aggregators.put(correlationId, aggregateable);
        }
```

Next, add the message text, count property, and message ID to the aggregateable interface. Check to see if the aggregator isComplete(), meaning the last message has been received. If it has, get the resulting message from the aggregator and send it to the next destination queue:

```
        aggregateable.addMessage(messageId, count, text);
        if (aggregateable.isComplete()) {
          String result= aggregateable.getResultMessage();
          TextMessage resultMessage= session.createTextMessage(result);
          producer.send(destination, resultMessage );
          aggregators.remove(correlationId);
        }
      }
    } catch (JMSException e) {
      e.printStackTrace();
    }
}
```

The next section of code shows the method of using reflection to create an instance of the agreeable interface. You need to have an aggregateable class for each correlationID. This method is a variation on the previous setProcessor, setRouter method. It will be called by the onMessage when a new correlation Id is discovered:

```
protected Aggregateable createAggregateable() {
  try {
    Class clazz= Class.forName(aggregatorClassName);
    Constructor ct= clazz.getConstructor(null);
    return (Aggregateable)ct.newInstance(null);
  } catch (Exception e) {
```

```
        throw new RuntimeException("couldn't create aggregateable object.", e);
    }
  }
  // JMX properties getSource, getDestination omitted

  public void start() {
  //omitted
  }

  public void stop() {
  //omitted
  }
}
```

The only thing left to implement is the concrete aggregator used in this example. The next section shows the OrderAggregator class. This handles the logic for your order processing example.

OrderAggregator

This section describes the orderAggregator class. This is an example aggregator used in this chapter's business process. It receives submessages from the queue it is registered with and saves each with a correlationId until all the messages for that correlationId have been processed. Once all message have been received, it sends the dummy message stating that the order has been processed:

```
package wrox.processing.order;
import wrox.processing.Aggregateable;

public class OrderAggregator implements Aggregateable {

  int received= 0;
  boolean done= false;
  String correlationId;
  List savedMessages = new ArrayList();
  public OrderAggregator( ) {

  }
  public void setCorrelationId(String correlationId ){
    this.correlationId = correlationId;
  }
```

The specific behavior of the OrderAggregator is to save each submessage and check the number of messages received against the number specified in the count:

```
public void addMessage(String messageId, int count, String message) {

  savedMessages.add(message);
  if (count == received) {
    done= true;
  }
}

public String getResultMessage() {
  // transform savedmessageList into an xml result message
  //TODO transform resulting xml.
  return "<order><id>300</id><status>complete</status></order>";
}
public boolean isComplete() {
  return done;
}
}
```

This concludes the components required to implement the example business process. In review, this section covered the development of three messaging components used in realizing an order processing system. Each component was designed as a standard MBean. Now that these MBeans have been developed, they can be deployed across several servers. The next section goes into the deployment process in great detail.

Deploying the Application

Deploy the application using one of the two methods described hereafter. The "Basic Deployment" section walks through all the pieces of the application step-by-step. Once you understand how each piece plays together, the next section, "Advanced Deployment," shows how to configure the application to deploy dynamically using a built-in service that reads a text descriptor file that describes the MBean to be deployed.

Basic Deployment

1. Start the JMS server. For the chapter examples, use JORAM JMS Server. JORAM implements the JMS 1.1 specification and it is available free to the open source community. The server starts up using the bat file common (see Figure 12-10):

```
C:\joram-4.0.0\samples\bin\windows\single_server.bat
```

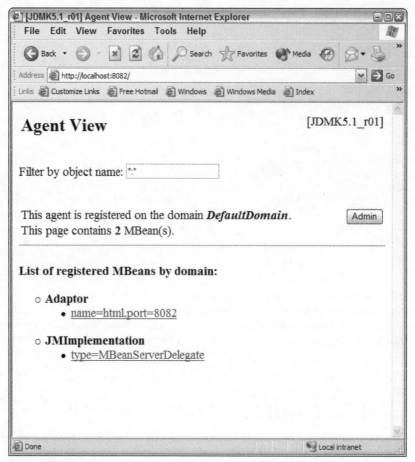

Figure 12-10

2. Create the administered objects using the JMS admin tool (this is vendor specific). Once the
    server is started, connect to it by running the JORAM administration console (see Figure 12-11):

```
C:\joram-4.0.0\samples\bin\windows\admin.bat
```

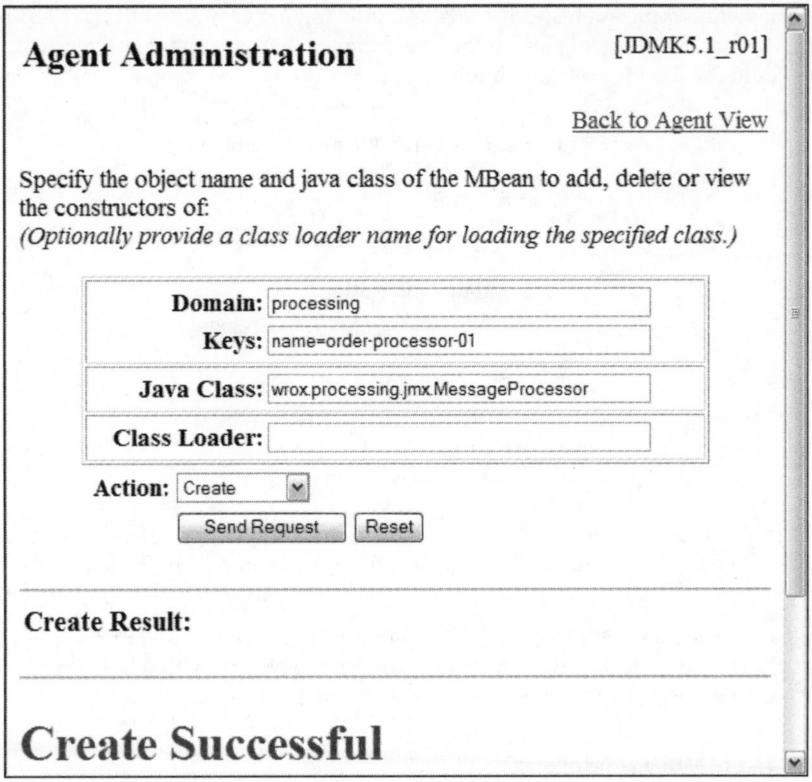

Figure 12-11

The admin console allows you to create the applications ConnectionFactory and Destinations objects. They are bound to the JNDI context, to be accessed through the *lookup(<name>)* method of the javax.naming.Context object from your application code.

Note: In this chapter, all the queues and topics will reside on the same server, but it is possible to connect to and manage multiple JMS servers through a single console.

3. Start the JMX Agent containing the MBeanServer. The agent is just a standalone Java application. The classpath environment variable must include the classes from the example as well as the jmxri.jar from Sun's JMX reference implementation:

```
java wrox.processing.jmx.Agent
```

4. Deploy your application-specific MBeans. Point a Web browser at `http://localhost:8082`. This brings up the agent view of the htmlAdaptor that was just registered with the MBean server in the Agent class (see Figure 12-12).

List of registered MBeans by domain:

○ **Adaptor**
- name=html.port=8082

○ **JMImplementation**
- type=MBeanServerDelegate

○ **processing**
- name=order-processor-01

Figure 12-12

As you can see from Figure 12-12, the html adaptor shows two MBeans registered with the MBeanServer. The htmlAdaptor is getting this information from the MBean Server's query capability.

5. Let's add the message processing MBean to the MBeanServer. The first step is to select the admin button in the top-right corner of the agent view as pictured in Figure 12-12. This will bring up the Agent Administration screen pictured in Figure 12-13.

List of MBeans attributes:

Name	Type	Access	Value
Destination	java.lang.String	RW	destination-queue
Processor	java.lang.String	RW	wrox.processing.order.OrderProcessor
Running	boolean	RO	**false**
Source	java.lang.String	RW	source-queue

Figure 12-13

6. Specify the domain field; this can be anything you would like. The one used here is *processing*. Then enter a unique key in the format key=value1,key=value..n. Then specify the fully qualified name of the messageProcessor class and select send request. Once that is done, you should see the Create Successful message below the registration form. Now, select Back to Agent View in the upper-right corner and you should see what's shown in Figure 12-14. The MBeans register should include the name=order-processor-01 in domain processing.

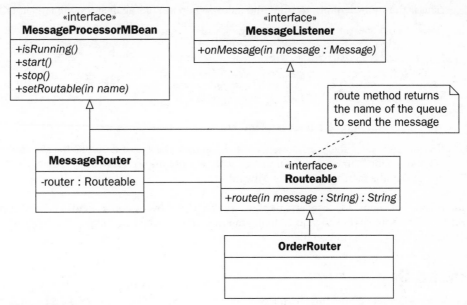

Figure 12-14

The htmlAdaptor took the values posted by the form submission and used them to register processor MBean with the MBean Server. That is how to create an MBean using the HtmlAdaptor, but you can do the same programmatically as shown here:

```
MessageProcessor processor= new MessageProcessor();
processorName= new ObjectName("processing:name=order-processor-01");
server.registerMBean(processor, processorName);
```

7. Go back to the agent page and select the name=order-processing-01 link. This will bring up the MBean view for the order processing MBean. This page renders as HTML the attributes and methods specified in the MessageProcessorMBean interface.

8. In the attributes section, specify the names of the source and destination queues as well as the name of the class implementing the processing interface. Once this is done, select Apply (see Figure 12-15).

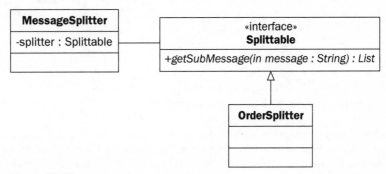

Figure 12-15

This is the equivalent of executing the following operations against the MBeanServer:

```
processorName= new ObjectName("wrox.processing:name=order-processor");
server.setAttribute(processorName, new Attribute("Source", "source-queue"));
server.setAttribute(processorName, new Attribute("Destination", "destination-
    queue"));
server.setAttribute(processorName, new Attribute("Processor",
    "wrox.processing.order.OrderProcessor"));
```

9. Configure and start each message component.

10. Finally, go back to the MBean view of the MessageProcessor and invoke the start message. You should see the Start Successful message at the start of the screen. This will invoke the start method of the message processor MBean.

Start to finish, that is how to create and deploy a message processing component. The next section will show how to use some of the advanced deployment options available through JMX to deploy MBeans dynamically from a configuration file.

Advanced Deployment

So far, the example has shown how to deploy MBeans directly to the MBean Server as well as indirectly using an htmlAdaptor MBean. This provides a great deal of flexibility to deploy and configure MBeans at run time. This section will demonstration how to deploy MBeans automatically using the M-Let Service.

M-Let is an abbreviation for managed applet. It is an agent service that works with the MBean server to allow remote deployment of MBeans. The logical view of how this works is pictured in Figure 12-16.

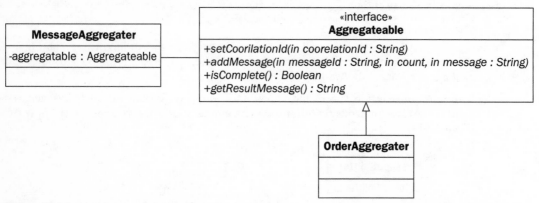

Figure 12-16

There are two benefits to using the M-Let service:

❑ The M-Let service supports Remote deployment. In a distributed processing architecture; one server can prove the MBean configuration for all the other servers in the processing architecture. At startup, all the severs would look to the M-Let server for their configuration settings.

❑ The agent does not need to be restarted to add classes to the JVM classpath providing true hot deployment. This allows a production environment to maintain continuity of operations, which in turn prevents service interruptions and downtime for maintenance and software upgrades.

There are three steps to using the M-Let service: Deploy the M-Let service to the JMX Agent, configure the M-Let deployment descriptor, and add the descriptor URL to the M-Let service.

Deploy the M-Let Service

Working with the same Agent class for creating the earlier examples, all that needs to be done is to deploy the M-Let services as a standard MBean:

```
package wrox.processing.jmx;
import javax.management.loading.MLet;
public class Agent {
public static void main(String[] args) {
    MBeanServer server= MBeanServerFactory.createMBeanServer();
    try {
      // htmlAdaptor omitted for brevity

      MLet mlet= new MLet();
      mletName= new ObjectName("Services:type=MLet");
      server.registerMBean(mlet, mletName);


}
```

Once this is complete, it is possible to configure and manage this MBean via the HTML adaptor just like the other MBeans in this chapter. Point a Web browser at `http://localhost:8082/` to inspect the method and properties exposed by the M-Let service.

Configure the Deployment Descriptor

The M-Let deployment descriptor is a text file that contains the definitions of MBeans to be deployed as well as the required supporting Java classes needed to run the application. An M-Let deployment description is shown following this paragraph. The file is called wrox.mlet and it is located in a Web server directory so it can be viewed by selecting `http://localhost/mbeans/wrox.mlet`. Only the CODE, NAME, and ARCHIVE parameters are required:

```
<MLET
```

The code attribute is the fully qualified class name of the MBean:

```
CODE="wrox.processing.jmx.MessageProcessor"
```

The name attribute is equivalent to the string in the ObjectName constructor uniquely identifying the MBean:

```
NAME = MLetDeployed:name=processor-03
```

The archive attribute specifies the jar file that contains the class name from the code attribute as well as any other support classes needed to run the application. The archive attribute can also be a comma-separated list of jar files:

```
ARCHIVE="wrox.jar"
```

The code base attribute is a file path to the jar file. In this example, absolute path is used, but the path can also be relative to the directory where the JVM was started:

```
CODEBASE="file:c:\mlet">
```

It is also possible to specify constructor parameters for nonzero parameter constructors. You can only specify primitive types using this method:

```
<arglist>
 <arg type="java.lang.String value="source-queue />
 <arg type="java.lang.String value="destination-queue />
</arglist>
</MLET>
```

The M-Let file can have several <MLET> tag declarations. In most cases, it is recommended that you use one M-Let config file for each type of server being deployed.

> The M-Let descriptor file is part of the standard JMX specification. But there are a few complaints about some of its limitations.
>
> The first is, "Why is it not an XML file?" The descriptor is in an XML-like text file, but it is not XML. This makes it a bit harder to validate and parse.
>
> The second is that there is no built-in way of supporting deployment dependencies. If MBean A needs to deploy before MBean B, there is no way of expressing that in the M-Let descriptor file.
>
> Some JMX vendors have provided extensions to the M-Let service in order to make up for these limitations. One of the JMX implementations available under open source license, JBoss, has a nonstandard approach to address both of these limitations.
>
> The JBoss Group (www.jboss.org) has a custom MBean descriptor file. The Jboss JMX Agent assumes that all files using the <serviceName>-service.xml naming convention contain Mbeans. Each Mbean description can have a <depends> tag. This tells the server to make sure the MBean described in the depends tag is deployed prior to this one.
>
> JBoss also recognizes custom MBean lifecycle methods, calling create() and then start() on each MBean as the server loads, followed by stop() and destroy() as the server is shut down.

Add the M-Let Configuration File to the M-Let Service

The M-Let file describes the MBeans that need to be deployed. All that is left to do is to point the M-Let service to the M-Let descriptor file. This can be done through the HttpAdaptor by adding the URL `http://localhost/mbeans/wrox.mlet`, to the M-Let service. The easiest way to do this is through the htmlAdaptor. This is pictured in Figure 12-17.

The steps to load the M-Let descriptor file are as follows:

1. Load the httpAdaptor by pointing the Web browser to `http://localhost:8082`.

2. Select the Services:type=MLet from the list of MBeans.

3. Enter in the URL of the M-Let descriptor file.

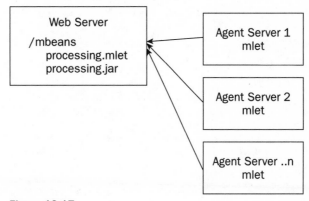

Figure 12-17

Click the Submit button. Once you see the Success message, return to the Agent view and the MBeans described by the wrox.mlet file will be visible and the jar file containing the depend classes deployed remotely through the Web browser. MBeans deployed through the M-Let service can be managed as any other MBean.

Summary

In this chapter, you have learned about building scalable and manageable distributed processing systems through JMS and JMX. The first section illustrated using some of the concepts of asynchronous message systems to scale processing ability. Following that, you built a series of basic messaging components. These components handled the message responsibility of processing, routing, and splitting and aggregating. Then, the example showed how to link theses basic components to implement a business process. The final section discussed how to deploy and manage these components remotely in a distributed computing environment.

There are other JMS design patterns to handle integration scenarios, and third-party tools built on top of JMS for workflow management problems. JMX has applications in managing network devices and includes methods and classes for event notification and component relationships not covered in this chapter.

13

Java Security

Security becomes ever more important as people flock to the Web and a large number of sites (such as amazon.com and online banks) store personal information about their customers, not to mention a wide variety of uses in custom enterprise solutions with multiple users. Java provides for security in two major ways. Java Cryptography provides for user identification/authentication and signing of digital messages. Java Authentication and Authorization Services provides programmatic access control and user authentication, granting a set of the program's features based on permissions and security policies. This chapter will give you a solid foundation in these APIs and show you how to utilize them effectively.

The Java implementation of security addresses many standard facets of security such as access control, public/private key generation and management, signing of digital content, and management of digital certificates. Just what are all these components of a security package? Let's look at what Java provides in its various security packages and delve into the concepts of security.

Java Cryptography Architecture and Java Cryptography Extension (JCA/JCE)

The *Java Cryptography Architecture (JCA)* was first introduced in JDK 1.1. Since its initial release, the JCA went from providing APIs for digital signatures and message digests to including certificate management and fine-grained configurable access control. The other important features of a security implementation are encryption of data for communication, key management and exchange, and Message Authentication Code (MAC) support. These features are all found in the *Java Cryptography Extension (JCE)*, which was integrated into the standard Java API in version 1.4 of the Java 2 SDK release. Combining the functionality provided by JCA with JCE presents you with a rich set of security and cryptography-related routines for your security needs.

JCA Design and Architecture

The Java Cryptography Architecture (JCA) forms the core of the security API. It was designed with two important principles in mind. First, the JCA is implementation-independent and interoperable. Implementation independence is achieved through the use of *cryptographic service providers* (or, more simply, *providers*). A provider implements a cryptographic service such as generating random numbers or creating digital signatures. Interoperability ensures that different providers will still work with each other. For example, different providers implementing routines using the same algorithm should work such that a message encrypted by one provider can be decrypted by another provider. The second principle is that of algorithm independence and extensibility. Algorithm independence is achieved through the specification of *engine classes* that provide a specific cryptographic service, such as a key generator or a message digest service. Algorithm extensibility ensures that these engine classes can be updated with new algorithms easily.

The JDK comes with a default implementation of the cryptographic service providers. This provider package is named SUN and has the providers listed below:

- Implementation of DSA (Digital Signature Algorithm)
- Implementation of MD5 and SHA-1 message digest algorithms
- Key pair generator to generate public and private key pairs for the DSA algorithm
- DSA algorithm parameter generator
- DSA algorithm parameter manager
- DSA key factory that supports converting public keys to and from private keys
- SHA1PRNG pseudo-random number generator
- X.509 Certificate path builder and validator for PKIX
- A certificate store using the PKIX LDAP V2 Schema
- Certificate factory for X.509 certificates and *Certificate Revocation Lists (CRLs)*
- A keystore

All of these providers will be discussed in more detail in this chapter. All examples in this chapter will use the default implementation of providers in the SUN package. Consult the third-party documentation if you are using another provider package.

Engine Classes

An engine class provides the interface to a specific cryptographic service. This interface dictates how programmers use a particular service. There can be a number of different implementations for a particular engine class, such as Signature implementations that use SHA-1 or MD5 algorithms. Each engine class has a corresponding *Service Provider Interface (SPI)*, which is an abstract class that is encapsulated by the engine class. The SPI class must be subclassed in order to create a concrete implementation. Each engine class also has a factory class that is used to create a specific instance of the engine class (and its enclosed SPI class) using the getInstance factory method.

The Java SDK defines 12 engine classes. Three of which (the certificate path classes and the certificate store) were introduced in the 1.4 version of the Java 2 SDK. These engine classes and their descriptions are shown in the following table.

Engine Class	Description
MessageDigest	Calculates the message digest (or hash) of data
Signature	Digitally signs data and verifies signatures
KeyPairGenerator	Generates a public and private key pair
KeyFactory	Converts opaque cryptographic keys into transparent representations of the underlying key material
CertificateFactory	Creates public key certificates and CRLs
KeyStore	Creates and manages a keystore, which stores and managers public/private keys and certificates
AlgorithmParameters	Manages parameters for a particular algorithm, including encoding/decoding of parameters
AlgorithmParameterGenerator	Generates a set of parameters for a specified algorithm
SecureRandom	Generates random (or pseudo-random) numbers
CertPathBuilder	Builds certificate chains (or certification paths)
CertPathValidator	Validates certificate chains
CertStore	Retrieves certificates and CRLs from a repository

The naming convention of SPI classes is the text Spi appended to the engine class name. For example, the SPI for the SecureRandom engine class is SecureRandomSpi. Each engine class has a `getInstance` method that is used to request a particular algorithm and also a particular provider if needed.

Installing a different provider package is done by either placing the JAR file in your classpath or deploying the JAR file as an extension in your JRE. The provider must then be placed in the list of approved providers in the java.security file. This file is found in the lib/security directory of your JDK or JRE installation. The property in this file takes the following form:

```
security.provider.n=masterClassName
```

The n is replaced with a number, such as 1 or 2. Using numbers provides a way to rank providers, and this list of providers is searched top down when no specific provider is specified in a call to one of the engine classes' `getInstance` methods. The masterClassName is replaced with the fully qualified class name of the master class for the provider package. This file contains the following lines for specifying providers in the JRE that comes with the current Java 5.0 SDK:

```
security.provider.1=sun.security.provider.Sun
security.provider.2=sun.security.rsa.SunRsaSign
security.provider.3=com.sun.net.ssl.internal.ssl.Provider
security.provider.4=com.sun.crypto.provider.SunJCE
security.provider.5=sun.security.jgss.SunProvider
security.provider.6=com.sun.security.sasl.Provider
```

Next, let's take a closer look at using each of the engine classes. Examples utilize the default implementations provided by the SUN package.

Calculating and Verifying Message Digests

The MessageDigest engine class takes an arbitrary length byte array as input and calculates a fixed-length hash value, known as a message digest. This is a one-way operation. It is impossible to take a message digest and derive the original input. If this was possible, then the world would have the best compression algorithm in existence, which a guy I know actually tried to implement in high school. This is a vital aspect of a message digest because it keeps the original input out of the picture. Additionally, with the complexity of the message digest algorithms, it is computationally infeasible to find two sets of input that hash to the exact same value. Therefore, you can view a message digest as a fingerprint of data because each input set hashes to an (almost) unique value.

Let's take a look at using the factory creation method in action. This is the same across all engine classes, so it will be described in detail here but glossed over for the other engine classes. Each engine class has three static methods that conform to the following signatures:

```
static [engine class name] getInstance(String algorithm)
static [engine class name] getInstance(String algorithm,
                                        String provider)
static [engine class name] getInstance(String algorithm,
                                        Provider provider)
```

The second two forms of the getInstance method allow you to specify a particular provider. The last form allows you to pass in an instance of a provider, and the second form lets you just use the name of a provider. All strings, including algorithm, are case-insensitive. The [engine class name] is replaced with the actual class name of the engine class.

The SUN package comes with two message digest algorithms: MD5 and SHA-1. The MD5 algorithm accepts input and generates a 128-bit message digest for the given input. For those familiar with MD4, the MD5 algorithm is slightly slower than MD4 but has greater assurance of security. One key benefit to the MD5 algorithm is that it can be coded in a fairly straightforward manner, not needing any complicated or large lookup tables. Although secure, it has actually been discovered that it is computationally feasible to find two sets of input that hash to the same value. This violates one of the principles of message digests. Due in part to this fact, SHA-1 is also available. SHA-1, short for Secure Hash Algorithm, was developed by the NSA and first published in 1995. It is based on some of the same principles as MD5, but produces a message digest that is 160 bits long. The maximum input size SHA-1 can take is in the neighborhood of 2 quintillion bytes (2^{64} bits).

After invoking the getInstance factory method, an initialized MessageDigest is available. The next step is to provide the MessageDigest object with the input and then ask it to calculate the message digest. There are three methods available to pass input data to the MessageDigest:

```
void update(byte input)
void update(byte[] input)
void update(byte[] input, int offset, int len)
```

The first form accepts a single byte of input. The second takes an array of bytes, and the length of the array is used as the length of the input. The last form takes an array of bytes, but it allows for the calculation of a message digest based on a subset of the array starting at position offset. The input size is described by len.

There are three methods that calculate the message digest, which is then returned as an array of bytes:

```
byte[] digest()
byte[] digest(byte[] input)
int digest(byte[] buf, int offset, int len)
```

The first `digest` method calculates the message digest based on the input already passed in via one of the update methods. The second form is a convenience method that returns a message digest based on input passed in to the method. The third form is not a convenience method. It calculates the message digest based on the input set via one of the update methods and then stores the message digest in the buf byte array that is passed in to the method. The len parameter dictates the maximum length available for the message digest, and offset dictates where in the array the message digest should start getting written. The return value is how many bytes were stored in buf.

You can use the MessageDigest engine class to ensure the integrity of data. Say you're writing the security and data integrity component of a system that is used globally. You want to ensure that data is not altered. One way to accomplish this is to store a collection of message digests that correspond to sensitive data that is communicated across the globe. These message digest values are stored in a base system and then the message digest can be recalculated when each piece of data arrives at its destination. A component can be developed to look up the message digests from the base system (because they are small and shouldn't be communicated with the data) and compare them to a newly calculated message digest. Here's an example implementation of a class that instantiates and computes the message digest and then compares it to an already looked up message digest value:

```java
import java.security.MessageDigest;
import java.security.NoSuchAlgorithmException;

public class MessageDigestExample {
    public static void main(String args[])
    {
        try {
            MessageDigest sha = MessageDigest.getInstance("SHA-1");
            byte[] data1 = {65,66,67,68,69};
            byte[] data2 = {70,71,72,73,74};

            sha.update(data1);
            sha.update(data2);
            byte[] msgDigest = sha.digest();

            // Can also combine the final update with digest like this:
            // byte[] msgDigest = sha.digest(data2);

            System.out.println("--- Message Digest ---");
            for(int i=0; i<msgDigest.length; i++) {
                System.out.print(msgDigest[i] + " ");
            }

            System.out.println("");
        } catch(NoSuchAlgorithmException nsae) {
            System.out.println("Exception: " + nsae);
            nsae.printStackTrace();
        }
    }
}
```

The SHA-1 algorithm is specified in the call to getInstance, returning an initialized MessageDigest object that computes the message digest according to the SHA-1 algorithm. The update method is invoked twice, simulating a multipart operation. The message digest that is calculated is a series of numbers shown in the following output:

```
--- Message Digest ---
-97 103 -17 -58 -81 -87 95 26 -17 -101 51 81 -42 -80 29 126 5 -111 -73 72
```

This array of numbers can be recomputed and compared on the recipient's side to ensure the data is the same that was originally communicated.

Digital Signing and Verification of Data

Digitally signing data is accomplished using a private key, and the verification of that signature is done with the public key. This ensures that the data originated from the specific person that signed it with their private key, much like signing a credit card receipt. The private key is used to sign a collection of bytes, and a short, fixed-length signature is generated (much like a message digest). This signature can then be verified using the public key. This process is illustrated in Figure 13-1. This is a primarily programmatic view of using the DSA algorithm. In actuality, the DSA algorithm is used with a message digest algorithm such as MD5 or SHA-1 (to which you already have access through the MessageDigest engine class). The actual message digest becomes input to the DSA algorithm along with the private key. On the other side, the data is then encoded into a message digest again and serves as input to DSA along with the public key in order to verify the integrity of the data.

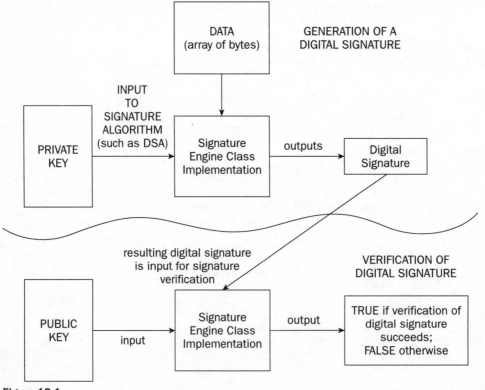

Figure 13-1

588

Much like message digests, there are two vital principles for a Digital Signature Algorithm. The first principle is that the public key that corresponds to the private key can be used to verify the integrity of the data. The second is that the digital signature and the public key do not reveal anything about the private key. The actual Signature object can be in one of three states. Consult the following table for the list of states that an object of the Signature class can assume.

Signature State	Description
UNINITIALIZED	The state assumed immediately after creation.
SIGN	Signifies the object is initialized for signing. Set after a call to initSign.
VERIFY	Signifies the object is initialized for verifying a signature. Set after a call to initVerify.

The SUN package comes with an implementation of the Digital Signature Algorithm (DSA). DSA is part of the Digital Signature Standard (DSS) that was developed by the NSA in 1991. Either SHA-1 or MD5 can be used with the DSA algorithm. Hopefully, the value of engine classes is making itself apparent. It becomes easy to combine a message digest function with a digital signature function. Just like the MessageDigest engine class, the Signature engine class has the same three getInstance methods. An instance of a Signature class must be initialized after creation using the following method in order to prepare it to digitally sign data:

```
final void initSign(PrivateKey privateKey)
```

After this method is called, the Signature class assumes the SIGN state. The next step is to send data to the Signature object and actually sign it. This is accomplished by the update and sign methods:

```
final void update(byte b)
final void update(byte[] data)
final void update(byte[] data, int offset, int len)
```

The first form accepts a single byte of data. The second takes an array of bytes, and the length of the array is used as the length of the data. The last form takes an array of bytes, but it allows for the calculation of a signature based on a subset of the array starting at position offset. The data size is described by `len`:

```
final byte[] sign()
final int sign(byte[] outbuf, int offset, int len)
```

The first form of the sign method returns the signature in an array of bytes. The second form places the signature in the outbuf array starting at offset and going for a maximum length of len. The value returned is how many bytes were stored in the outbuf array. After a sign method returns, the Signature object is left in the SIGN state and is still configured with the programmed private key. Call initSign again to utilize a different private key.

The other operation that the Signature engine class supports is verifying data. The Signature object must first be set to verify data by invoking an initVerify method:

```
final void initVerify(PublicKey publicKey)
final void initVerify(Certificate certificate)
```

Either a public key object or a certificate can be used to verify a digital signature. After initVerify is invoked, the Signature object assumes the VERIFY state. The update methods are used to send data into the Signature object to verify. Their usage does not differ from passing in data for signing. A verify method is then invoked to determine if the signature generated from the data and public key match the private key:

```
final boolean verify(byte[] signature)
final boolean verify(byte[] signature, int offset, int length)
```

The digital signature takes the form of a byte array. The second form of verify is used to specify the location (at offset) and the length (specified by length) of the signature in the byte array. If it all matches up, verify returns true. However, if the public key does not match the signature or the signature is invalid, false is returned. After verify returns, the Signature object is left in the VERIFY state still programmed with the public key that was passed in to initVerify. Call initVerify again to use a different public key.

One common use of public and private keys is signing and then verifying the source of communication. For example, assume you work for a government contractor and are tasked with constructing a secure communication system that is essentially secure e-mail. The secure e-mail client must have the capability to digitally sign messages going out and also verify messages that are delivered. The details of generating and managing keys are saved for subsequent discussion. Assume the keys are available. You might develop a utility class listed in the following example to assist with the signing and verifying of secure communication:

```
import java.security.Signature;
import java.security.KeyPair;
import java.security.PublicKey;
import java.security.PrivateKey;
import java.security.NoSuchAlgorithmException;
import java.security.InvalidKeyException;
import java.security.SignatureException;

public class SignatureExample {
    public byte[] signData(byte[] data, PrivateKey key)
    {
        try {
            Signature signer = Signature.getInstance("SHA1withDSA");

            signer.initSign(key);

            signer.update(data);

            return(signer.sign());
        } catch(NoSuchAlgorithmException nsae) {
            System.out.println("Exception: " + nsae);
            nsae.printStackTrace();
        } catch(InvalidKeyException ike) {
            System.out.println("Exception: " + ike);
            ike.printStackTrace();
        } catch(SignatureException se) {
            System.out.println("Exception: " + se);
            se.printStackTrace();
        }

        return(null);
```

```
    }

    public boolean verifySig(byte[] data, PublicKey key, byte[] sig)
    {
        try {
            Signature signer = Signature.getInstance("SHA1withDSA");

            signer.initVerify(key);

            signer.update(data);

            return(signer.verify(sig));
        } catch(NoSuchAlgorithmException nsae) {
            System.out.println("Exception: " + nsae);
            nsae.printStackTrace();
        } catch(InvalidKeyException ike) {
            System.out.println("Exception: " + ike);
            ike.printStackTrace();
        } catch(SignatureException se) {
            System.out.println("Exception: " + se);
            se.printStackTrace();
        }

        return(false);
    }

    public static void main(String args[])
    {
        SignatureExample sigEx = new SignatureExample();
        KeyPairGeneratorExample kpge = new KeyPairGeneratorExample();
        KeyPair keyPair = kpge.generateKeyPair(717);

        byte[] data = {65,66,67,68,69,70,71,72,73,74};
        byte[] digitalSignature = sigEx.signData(data,
                                        keyPair.getPrivate());
        boolean verified;

        // This verification will succeed
        verified = sigEx.verifySig(data, keyPair.getPublic(),
                                    digitalSignature);
        if(verified) {
            System.out.println("** The digital signature " +
                            "has been verified");
        } else {
            System.out.println("** The digital signature is " +
                            "invalid, the wrong " +
                            "key was used, or the data has" +
                            " been compromised");
        }

        System.out.println("");

        // Generate a new key pair. Guaranteed to be different
        // and incompatible with first set.
        keyPair = kpge.generateKeyPair(517);
        // This verification will fail
```

```
            verified = sigEx.verifySig(data, keyPair.getPublic(),
                                    digitalSignature);
            if(verified) {
                System.out.println("** The digital signature has" +
                                " been verified");
            } else {
                System.out.println("** The digital signature is " +
                                    "invalid, the wrong " +
                                    "key was used, or the data " +
                                    "has been compromised");
            }
        }
    }
```

The KeyPairGeneratorExample, explained subsequently, is used to obtain a public and private key. The data is signed with the private key and verified with the public key.

Digital Key Creation and Management

There are two representations of keys made available by the security API. *Transparent representations* of keys allow you to retrieve specific information about the key, such as the algorithm parameter values used to calculate the key. *Opaque representations* of keys keep these values hidden and only allow you access to the algorithm used to create the key, the encoding used, and the encoded form of the key itself. Transparent representations of keys inherit from a tagging interface called KeySpec. Since this is a tagging interface, no methods are defined inside the interface. Key interfaces provided in the java.security.spec package are listed in the following table.

Key Interface	Description
DSAPrivateKeySpec	A DSA private key specification
DSAPublicKeySpec	A DSA public key specification
RSAPrivateKeySpec	An RSA private key specification
RSAPrivateCrtKeySpec	An RSA private key specification using Chinese remainder theorem
RSAMultiplePrimePrivateCrtKeySpec	An RSA multiple prime private key specification using the Chinese remainder theorem
RSAPublicKeySpec	An RSA public key specification
EncodedKeySpec	An encoded key specification PKCS8Encoded-KeySpec and X509EncodedKeySpec are two provided implementers.

As opposed to transparent representations of keys, opaque representations inherit from the Key interface. Unlike the KeySpec interface, the Key interface defines three methods that all concrete implementations must implement. These three methods are described next:

```
String algorithm()
```

The `algorithm` method returns a string representation of the algorithm used to create the key:

```
byte[] getEncoded()
```

The `getEncoded` method returns the encoded version of the key (which can then be packaged and transmitted) according to a standard encoding format such as X.509 or PKCS #8.

```
String getFormat()
```

The `getFormat` method returns the name of the particular encoding format used to encode the key. The java.security.interfaces package contains 12 interfaces that inherit directly from the Key interface. These are the various types of keys that are standard in the Java API. These are listed in the following table.

Key Interface	Description
DHPrivateKey	A Diffie-Hellman private key
DHPublicKey	A Diffie-Hellman public key
DSAPrivateKey	A DSA private key
DSAPublicKey	A DSA public key
PBEKey	A PBE (password-based encryption) key, supporting a SALT value
RSAMultiPrimePrivateCrtKey	An RSA multiprime private key using the Chinese remainder theorem. Consult PKCS#1 for more information.
RSAPrivateCrtKey	An RSA private key using the Chinese remainder theorem. Consult PKCS#1 for more information.
RSAPrivateKey	An RSA private key
RSAPublicKey	An RSA public key
PublicKey	Used as a tagging interface for all public key interfaces/classes
PrivateKey	Used as a tagging interface for all private key interfaces/classes
SecretKey	Used as a tagging interface for all secret key interfaces/classes

The KeyFactory engine class is used to convert transparent representations of keys to opaque representations and vice versa. The standard getInstance methods are available to create a KeyFactory. There are two methods to convert a transparent representation to an opaque representation: one for public keys and one for private keys. There is one method defined for the reverse operation. These methods are described subsequently:

```
PublicKey generatePublic(KeySpec keySpec)
PrivateKey generatePrivate(KeySpec keySpec)
```

The generatePublic and generatePrivate methods take a transparent representation of a key (a class that inherits from KeySpec—directly or indirectly) and return either the opaque representation of the public key or the opaque representation of the private key:

```
KeySpec getKeySpec(Key key, Class keySpec)
```

The getKeySpec method accepts the opaque representation of the key through the key parameter and a class that specifies which key specification class to convert the key to and return.

From more of a client perspective, the KeyPair class and KeyPairGenerator and KeyStore engine classes are used to create, store, and manage public/private keys and certificates. The KeyPair class defines the following two methods:

```
PrivateKey getPrivate()
PublicKey getPublic()
```

The first method returns the private key currently stored, and the second returns the public key. The KeyPairGenerator engine class is used to generate these pairs of private and public keys and uses the KeyPair class to store them.

The KeyPairGenerator engine class generates a pair of keys in either an algorithm-independent manner or an algorithm-specific manner. Which of these is used depends on how the KeyPairGenerator is initialized. The following two methods are for algorithm-independent initialization. Because all algorithms use the basic concepts of size and randomness, this initialization is available when initialization based on a specific algorithm isn't necessary:

```
void initialize(int keysize, SecureRandom random)
void initialize(int keysize)
```

The meaning of the keysize parameter varies for each algorithm. Other algorithm parameters are given preconfigured parameters. For example, a DSA algorithm might assign its parameters different values based on the specified keysize. If a random number generator is not passed in, randomness is generated via a default system generator:

```
void initialize(AlgorithmParameterSpec params, SecureRandom random)
void initialize(AlgorithmParameterSpec params)
```

These forms of initialize perform the initialization based on specific parameters that are passed through the params parameter. If a random number generator is not passed in, randomness is generated from the system:

```
KeyPair generateKeyPair()
```

This method creates and returns a KeyPair object. Each call to this method returns a separate and distinct pair of keys.

Here's an example implementation of a method that utilizes the KeyGenerator class to generate a private key and public key and store them in a KeyPair object (this is used in other examples in this chapter):

```
import java.security.KeyPairGenerator;
import java.security.KeyPair;
import java.security.SecureRandom;
```

```
import java.security.NoSuchAlgorithmException;
import java.security.NoSuchProviderException;
import java.security.PublicKey;
import java.security.PrivateKey;

public class KeyPairGeneratorExample {
    public KeyPair generateKeyPair(long seed)
    {
        try {
            // Get a DSA key generator from first
            // provider that provides it

            KeyPairGenerator keyGenerator =
                            KeyPairGenerator.getInstance("DSA");

            // Get a random number generator using
            // algorithm SHA1PRNG from the SUN provider package.
            SecureRandom rng =
                    SecureRandom.getInstance("SHA1PRNG", "SUN");

            // Configure RNG and initialize key pair generator
            rng.setSeed(seed);
            keyGenerator.initialize(1024, rng);

            return(keyGenerator.generateKeyPair());
        } catch(NoSuchProviderException nspe) {
            System.out.println("Exception: " + nspe);
            nspe.printStackTrace();
        } catch(NoSuchAlgorithmException nsae) {
            System.out.println("Exception: " + nsae);
            nsae.printStackTrace();
        }

        return(null);
    }

    public static void main(String args[])
    {
        KeyPairGeneratorExample kpge = new KeyPairGeneratorExample();

        KeyPair kp = kpge.generateKeyPair(717);
        System.out.println("-- Public Key ----");
        PublicKey pubKey = kp.getPublic();
        System.out.println("  Algorithm=" + pubKey.getAlgorithm());
        System.out.println("  Encoded=" + pubKey.getEncoded());
        System.out.println("  Format=" + pubKey.getFormat());

        System.out.println("\n-- Private Key ----");
        PrivateKey priKey = kp.getPrivate();
        System.out.println("  Algorithm=" + priKey.getAlgorithm());
        System.out.println("  Encoded=" + priKey.getEncoded());
        System.out.println("  Format=" + priKey.getFormat());
    }
}
```

This class utilizes a specific random number generator, SHA1PRNG, from the SUN provider package. It is then seeded with the value specified in the call to generateKeyPair. If you take a look at the output, you will see a difference between the private and public key:

```
-- Public Key ----
    Algorithm=DSA
    Encoded=[B@1a46e30
    Format=X.509

-- Private Key ----
    Algorithm=DSA
    Encoded=[B@3e25a5
    Format=PKCS#8
```

The public key is encoded in the X.509 format, and the private key is encoded in the PKCS#8 format. PKCS stands for Public Key Cryptography Standards, and the eighth standard defines the format for private keys. The usage of X.509 for the public key means that a public key certificate was generated. A certificate allows the connecting of a trusted source with a public key, ensuring the public key is coming from the person that it claims it is.

Storing and Managing Keys

A *keystore* is a database of public keys, private keys, and certificates. By default, this database is stored in a file named keystore in the user's home directory. The SUN provider package provides this behavior through a proprietary format named JKS. Each private key in this file is protected by a password, and the file itself is also protected by a password. The KeyStore engine class provides a robust interface for implementing a keystore provider. There are two types of entries that a KeyStore stores. The first, a *key entry*, contains sensitive key information such as private keys and the authenticating certificate chain, or a secret key. The second, a *trusted certificate entry*, contains a certificate authenticating the owner of a specific public key. The manner in which the keystore is persisted depends upon the implementation; thus, it is not specified by this engine class. The KeyStore engine class provides methods to load and save a keystore, access aliases of entries, determine entry types, manage the entries themselves, and retrieve information about the keystore. The standard getInstance methods are available to create a keystore:

```
final void load(InputStream stream, char[] password)
```

The load method loads a keystore from the specified input stream. The optional password is used as a way to verify the integrity of the keystore. If no password is specified, this integrity check is not performed. Pass in null in place of an input to create an empty keystore:

```
final void store(OutputStream stream, char[] password)
```

The store method saves the current keystore to the specified output stream. If a password is specified, it is used to calculate a checksum of the keystore data and is appended to the end of the output stream. This checksum is used by load to perform an integrity check:

```
final Enumeration aliases()
```

Each keystore entry has an associated alias that takes the form of a string. The aliases method returns an enumeration of the entry aliases in the keystore:

```
final boolean isKeyEntry(String alias)
final boolean isCertificateEntry(String alias)
```

The isKeyEntry and isCertificateEntry methods provide a way to check the type of a keystore entry. The first, isKeyEntry, returns true if the entry specified by alias is a key entry, and returns false otherwise. The second, isCertificateEntry, returns true if the entry specified by alias is a certificate entry, and returns false otherwise:

```
final void setKeyEntry(String alias, Key key,
                       char[] password, Certificate[] chain)
final void setKeyEntry(String alias, byte[] key,
                       Certificate[] chain)
```

The setKeyEntry method adds a new key entry to the keystore (if alias does not correspond to an existing entry) or changes the key at the preexisting alias in the keystore. If the key is passed in as an array of bytes, the key should be in protected format, such as an EncryptedPrivateKeyInfo in the PKCS #8 standard. The alternate form of setKeyEntry uses a password to protect the key. The chain parameter is used to pass in a certificate chain as a trust source for the key:

```
final void setCertificateEntry(String alias, Certificate cert)
```

The setCertificateEntry method adds a new certificate entry to the keystore (if alias does not correspond to an existing entry) or changes the certificate at the entry named by alias (if a certificate entry already exists):

```
final void deleteEntry(String alias)
```

The deleteEntry method removes the entry associated with alias from the keystore:

```
final Key getKey(String alias, char[] password)
```

The getKey method returns the key entry from the keystore that is associated with alias. The password is used to retrieve the key:

```
final Certificate getCertificate(String alias)
final Certificate[] getCertificateChain(String alias)
```

The getCertificate and getCertificateChain methods return the certificate or certificate chain (array of Certificate) specified by alias in the keystore:

```
final String getCertificateAlias(Certificate cert)
```

The getCertificateAlias method returns the alias associated with a specified certificate from the keystore.

Algorithm Management

Algorithms have parameters associated with them, such as values of constants for the DSA algorithm. The actual values of these parameters are revealed in transparent representations through classes that implement the AlgorithmParameterSpec interface. This interface defines no methods, which thus makes it a tagging interface. Opaque representations of algorithm parameters are addressed by the AlgorithmParameters engine class. No direct access to the values of the algorithm parameters is available. The following methods, along with the expected getInstance methods, are defined in the AlgorithmParameters engine class. After object creation using getInstance, one of the init methods must be invoked to initialize the object:

```
void init(AlgorithmParameterSpec paramSpec)
void init(byte[] params)
void init(byte[] params, String format)
```

The byte array params contains the parameters in an encoded format. The form of init that only takes a byte array uses the default decoding format ASN.1 to decode the parameters. The last form of init accepts the byte array of parameters and format, the string representation of a decoding scheme. The first form accepts a reference to a transparent representation of the algorithm parameters. Note that initialization can only occur once. You cannot reuse an AlgorithmParameter object like you can a SecureSignature object:

```
byte[] getEncoded()
byte[] getEncoded(String format)
```

These methods return a byte array containing the encoded parameters. The default decoding used is ASN.1. You can specify a specific decoding format by passing its name in format. The default implementation of this engine class as provided in the SUN provider package disregards the format parameter:

```
AlgorithmParameterSpec getParameterSpec(Class paramSpec)
```

This returns a reference to a transparent representation of the encoded parameters. The paramSpec parameter is used to specify a particular AlgorithmParameterSpec class, such as passing in DSAParameterSpec.class to get a DSAParameterSpec object returned.

The AlgorithmParameterGenerator is an engine class to generate parameters for a particular algorithm. Creating an object of this class is the same as any other engine class. A particular algorithm and possibly a provider are passed to a getInstance method. After object creation, the object must be initialized using one of the init methods. After initialization, you can invoke generateParameters to actually generate the parameters for the specified algorithm:

```
void init(int size, SecureRandom random)
void init(int size)
void init(AlgorithmParameterSpec genParamSpec, SecureRandom random)
void init(AlgorithmParameterSpec genParamSpec)
```

Each algorithm uses two core pieces of information to generate parameters: a size and a way to create random numbers. This size could be a number of bits or a number of bytes, all depending on the specific algorithm. The use of SecureRandom shows the interoperability of the engine classes. Any provider's random number generator can be used with any other provider's AlgorithmParameterGenerator to generate parameters. If no random number generator is specified, a system-provided source of random numbers is used. The first two forms only allow the specification of a single size, so default values are used for other algorithm parameters. The last two forms provide for the specification of each algorithm's parameter. Because there are no requirements made based on the AlgorithmParameterSpec, each algorithm has its own AlgorithmParameterGenerator that works with the algorithm's AlgorithmParameterSpec to generate the parameters:

```
AlgorithmParameters generateParameters()
```

This generates and returns a set of algorithm parameters encoded in an AlgorithmParameters object.

Random Number Generation

A *random number generator (RNG)* is a vital part of encryption algorithms. Because most random number generators start with a *seed value*, a value that causes a predictable string of numbers to get generated, random number generators are often termed *pseudo-random* because they are not truly random. The engine class for random number generators is SecureRandom and, as expected, has the standard set of `getInstance` methods.

The operations available on the random number generator are seeding the generator, obtaining a random number (or sequence of random numbers), and obtaining a random seed that can be used to seed a random number generator. These operations are accomplished via the following methods:

```
synchronized public void setSeed(byte[] seed)
public void setSeed(long seed)
```

Invoking a `setSeed` method isn't strictly necessary. When the `getInstance` method is invoked, the random number generator should set itself to a random state. However, it is possible to increase the randomness by which the generator works by passing in a long value or a sequence of bytes as a seed. Each subsequent call to setSeed increases the randomness. A seed passed in later does not replace an earlier seed; it extends it into a more random organization:

```
synchronized public void nextBytes(byte[] bytes)
```

The byte array bytes is filled with a sequence of randomly generated bytes up to the array's allocated length:

```
byte[] generateSeed(int numBytes)
```

This method returns a byte array of size numBytes. This byte array can then be used as a seed to the random number generator.

Here's a brief example using the SecureRandom class to generate random numbers:

```
import java.security.SecureRandom;
import java.security.NoSuchAlgorithmException;

public class SecureRandomExample {
    public static void main(String args[])
    {
        try {
            SecureRandom rng = SecureRandom.getInstance("SHA1PRNG");
            rng.setSeed(711);

            int numberToGenerate = new Integer(args[0]).intValue();
            byte randNumbers[] = new byte[numberToGenerate];

            rng.nextBytes(randNumbers);
            for(int j=0; j<numberToGenerate; j++) {
                System.out.print(randNumbers[j] + " ");
            }

            System.out.println("");
```

```
        } catch(NoSuchAlgorithmException nsae) {
            System.out.println("Exception: " + nsae);
            nsae.printStackTrace();
        }
    }
}
```

In this example, the user passes in how many numbers to generate on the command line as the first (and only) parameter. The same seed is used every time this program is executed, so the same sequence of numbers will always get generated. If you execute this program and ask for five numbers, you will get the same output as listed in the following example:

```
111 100 -92 -59 -49
```

Certificate Management

Certificates are a vital part of the security picture. Because public keys are, by definition, public, how can you verify that the public key truly belongs to the person that claims to own it? This is accomplished using a certificate. A trusted third party, such as Verisign or Entrust, issues a certificate to an entity (a person, an organization, and so forth) verifying that this entity is trusted. A public key associated with a certificate is then trusted to come from the owner of the associated certificate. A *certification path* is a sequence of trust from one authority to another. For example, one certificate authority (CA) can issue a certificate for one public key, and the subject of this certificate is then used as a CA for another public key. This establishes a path of trust, and each step must be validated for the entire trust relationship to stand up.

The Java Security Architecture provides classes in the java.secuity.cert package to manage and utilize certificates. The CertificateFactory creates certificates, certification paths, and certification revocation lists (CRLs) from their corresponding encodings. The CertPathBuilder builds certification paths (or chains). The CertPathValidator provides the functionality to validate the certification path stored in a CertPath object. The CertStore class provides a repository for storing both trusted and untrusted certifications and CRLs. All of these classes are engine classes and thus have the standard getInstance methods for creating an instance of one of these classes.

CertificateFactory

The CertificateFactory engine class is a factory class that can generate certificates, certificate paths, and CRLs. The standard getInstance methods are available for object creation.

To generate a certificate, one of the following methods is used:

```
final Certificate generateCertificate(InputStream inStream)
final Collection generateCertificates(InputStream inStream)
```

The first form creates a single certificate from a provided input stream, and the second creates a collection of zero or more certificates from a provided input stream.

Creating a CRL is similar to creating certificates:

```
final CRL generateCRL(InputStream inStream)
final Collection generateCRLs(InputStream inStream)
```

The first form creates a single CRL from a provided input stream, and the second creates a collection of zero or more CRLs from a provided input stream. The CertificateFactory can also create a certification path from a provided input stream:

```
final CertPath generateCertPath(InputStream inStream)
final CertPath generateCertPath(InputStream inStream, String encoding)
```

These methods provide a way to create a certification path from the input stream. The second form allows you to specify the encoding used for the certification path:

```
final CertPath generateCertPath(List certificates)
```

This method creates a CertPath object and initializes it with the list of certificates passed in:

```
final Iterator getCertPathEncodings()
```

A list of certificate encodings supported by this factory is returned. The default encoding is listed first.

CertPathBuilder

The CertPathBuilder engine class is used to create a CertPath from a set of CertPathParameters. The nature of these parameters is algorithm-specific. The standard `getInstance` methods are provided for object creation. A single method is provided to build the CertPath:

```
public final CertPathBuilderResult build(CertPathParameters params)
        throws CertPathBuilderException, InvalidAlgorithmParameterException
```

The CertPathBuilderResult contains a getCertPath method that returns the CertPath that is built using this method. Using this interface allows for ease of grouping and copying (via clone) of the path that is built.

CertPathValidator

The CertPathValidator is an engine class that validates a certiticate path. The standard `getInstance` methods are provided. A single method is provided to validate the certificate path:

```
public final CertPathValidatorResult validate(CertPath certPath,
                                        CertPathParameters params)
        throws CertPathValidatorException,
               InvalidAlgorithmParameterException
```

If the validation succeeds, an instance of a class implementing the CertPathValidatorResult interface is returned. Otherwise, a CertPathValidatorException is thrown, signaling an invalid certificate path. The CertPath and CertPathParameters that are passed in must be compatible with the algorithm, or an InvalidAlgorithmParameterException is thrown.

CertStore

The CertStore is an engine class designed to store certificates and CRLs. The `getInstance` methods are augmented with a CertStoreParameters parameter. The revised `getInstance` methods are listed next:

```
public static CertStore getInstance(String type,
                                    CertStoreParameters params)
public static CertStore getInstance(String type,
                                    CertStoreParameters params,
                                    String provider)
public static CertStore getInstance(String type,
                                    CertStoreParameters params,
                                    Provider provider)
```

The type parameter represents the name of a repository type, such as LDAP or Collection for Java collections. The specific CertStoreParameters are specific to each repository type.

The parameters used to initialize the CertStore can be retrieved using the following method:

```
public final CertStoreParameters getCertStoreParameters()
```

To retrieve certificates and CRLs from a CertStore, the concept of a *selector* is introduced. This selector defines the criteria used to select a set of certificates or CRLs to return. The following methods are provided to select and return a set of certificates or CRLs:

```
public final Collection getCertificates(CertSelector selector)
       throws CertStoreException
public final Collection getCRLs(CRLSelector selector)
                       throws CertStoreException
```

Each method returns a collection of their corresponding objects. The selector interfaces both define a single method named match that accepts a certificate or a CRL and returns true if the specified object matches some criteria, or false otherwise. There are concrete implementations of these interfaces that are available as part of the security library, such as X509CertSelector and X509CRLSelector, which verify whether a certificate or CRL matches the format of X509 certificates/CRLs.

Java Cryptography Extension

The Java Cryptography Extension (JCE) specifies other cryptographic services that are important for a more complete security package. The JCE is based on the same architecture as the JCA and is thus provider-based. The default provider package that comes with J2SDK 1.5 is named SunJCE. The services provided by the JCE are as follows:

❑ Encryption/Decryption: Converts a nonencrypted *plaintext* (or *cleartext)* message into an encrypted form using a key or performing the opposite operation.

❑ Password-Based Encryption (PBE): Derives an encryption key from a given password, sometimes based on a salt (a random number) to extend the time needed for a brute force attack, which thus makes a brute force attack more infeasible.

❑ Cipher: An object that carries out the encryption and decryption of information based on a particular algorithm.

❑ Key Agreement: A protocol that enables two or more parties to establish the same cryptographic keys without needing to share secret information.

❑ Message Authentication Code (MAC): A short code that is used to verify the integrity/origination of information, similar to using a digital signature to verify data integrity/origination.

The engine classes provided by the JCE are Cipher, KeyGenerator, KeyAgreement, and Mac. These engine classes and classes related to each are discussed in detail in this section.

The Cipher Engine Class

The Cipher engine class is the largest engine class in the JCE. It provides both encryption and decryption support. The JCE also introduces CipherInputStream and CipherOutputStream, which provide secure input and output streams when combined with a Cipher object. The getInstance methods available on the Cipher object differ from the getInstance methods of engine classes from the JCA:

```
public static Cipher getInstance(String transformation);
public static Cipher getInstance(String transformation,
                                 String provider);
```

The parameter transformation is used to specify a particular transforming and takes the form of algorithm/mode/padding or just algorithm. Specifying DES or DES/ECB/PKCS5Padding (the default algorithm/mode/padding provided by the SunJCE) are both valid. The provider parameter lets you specify which provider should be used. If no provider is specified, a provider is located that provides the requested transformation.

After object creation, the Cipher object must be initialized with an operating mode and other information. There are eight forms of the init method:

```
public void init(int opmode, Key key)
public void init(int opmode, Certificate certificate)
public void init(int opmode, Key key, SecureRandom random)
public void init(int opmode, Certificate certificate,
                 SecureRandom random)
public void init(int opmode, Key key,
                 AlgorithmParameterSpec params)
public void init(int opmode, Key key,
                 AlgorithmParameterSpec params, SecureRandom random)
public void init(int opmode, Key key,
                 AlgorithmParameters params)
public void init(int opmode, Key key,
                 AlgorithmParameters params, SecureRandom random)
```

The opmode parameter can take one of four integer values that are defined as final integers in the Cipher class. These operating modes are listed in the following table.

Operating Mode Constant's Name	Description
ENCRYPT_MODE	Configures Cipher to encrypt data
DECRYPT_MODE	Configures Cipher to decrypt data
WRAP_MODE	Configures Cipher in key wrapping mode to convert a key to bytes that can be securely transported
UNWRAP_MODE	Configures Cipher to unwrap a previously wrapped key

You can pass in a key through the key or certificate parameters (for a certificate that contains a key). The params parameter contains parameters for the particular algorithm requested, and random is used to utilize a different random number generator than the system source of randomness.

If the mode is DECRYPT_MODE, the Cipher requires a key and appropriate parameters. If these are not specified, an InvalidKeyException or InvalidAlgorithmParameterException is thrown. If the Cipher is configured for ENCRYPT_MODE, these parameters are configured with already defined values unless explicitly passed in to the init method.

Encrypting/Decrypting Data

Data can be passed to a Cipher object in parts or all at once. The update method is used to pass in a chunk of data at a time, and the doFinal method is used to either pass in all of the data at a single time or signal the end of a sequence of data that was passed in through the update method:

```
public byte[] update(byte[] input)
public byte[] update(byte[] input, int inputOffset,
                     int inputLen)
public int update(byte[] input, int inputOffset,
                  int inputLen, byte[] output)
public int update(byte[] input, int inputOffset,
                  int inputLen, byte[] output, int outputOffset)
```

These methods allow you to pass a piece of data to the Cipher. Using these methods lets you process more data than you have at a single time. The last two forms store the encrypted/decrypted data in a buffer passed in, as opposed to returning the data in the first two forms:

```
public byte[] doFinal(byte[] input)
public byte[] doFinal(byte[] input, int inputOffset,
                      int inputLen)
public int doFinal(byte[] input, int inputOffset,
                   int inputLen, byte[] output)
public int doFinal(byte[] input, int inputOffset,
                   int inputLen, byte[] output,
                   int outputOffset)
public byte[] doFinal();
public int doFinal(byte[] output, int outputOffset)
```

These methods are used to either process all the input at once or signal the end of input after repeated calls to update. The first four forms let you combine the operation of passing in the rest of the data and retrieving the result. The last two forms signal the end and then obtain the result. The last form returns the length of the output.

Wrapping and Unwrapping Keys

```
public final byte[] wrap(Key key)
```

This method is used to take a key and convert it to a sequence of bytes that can be safely and easily transported. The key is encrypted using the Cipher so that secure transmission is possible. In order for the recipient to unwrap the key, you need to also transmit the name of the key algorithm and the type of the key (either SECRET_KEY, PRIVATE_KEY, or PUBLIC_KEY):

```
public final Key unwrap(byte[] wrappedKey, String wrappedKeyAlgorithm,
                        int wrappedKeyType)
```

This method takes a wrapped key and unwraps it using the specified algorithm and key type. The wrappedKeyType is either SECRET_KEY, PRIVATE_KEY, or PUBLIC_KEY:

```
public int getOutputSize(int inputLen)
```

This method is useful to determine the size of the output in order for the client code to allocate enough space in its buffer for the encrypted/decrypted data.

Two classes are provided for chaining a cipher in file input/output operations. The CipherInputStream inherits from the FilterInputStream class. The CipherOutputStream inherits from FilterOutputStream. Data passing through the each of these is encrypted or decrypted using an associated Cipher object. Usage of CipherInputStream and CipherOutputStream are straightforward. Take a look at the example to see them in action.

Here is a class that provides an interface to using the Cipher class by itself and also utilizing the CipherInputStream and CipherOutputStream classes. This example could be modified rather easily to work as a utility class using the Cipher engine class:

```
import java.security.*;
import java.security.spec.*;
import javax.crypto.*;
import javax.crypto.spec.*;
import java.io.*;

public class CipherExample {
    private Cipher m_encrypter;
    private Cipher m_decrypter;

    public void init(SecretKey key)
    {
        // for CBC; must be 8 bytes
        byte[] initVector = new byte[]{0x10, 0x10, 0x01, 0x04,
                                       0x01, 0x01, 0x01, 0x02};

        AlgorithmParameterSpec algParamSpec =
                                new IvParameterSpec(initVector);

        try {
            m_encrypter = Cipher.getInstance("DES/CBC/PKCS5Padding");
            m_decrypter = Cipher.getInstance("DES/CBC/PKCS5Padding");

            m_encrypter.init(Cipher.ENCRYPT_MODE, key, algParamSpec);
            m_decrypter.init(Cipher.DECRYPT_MODE, key, algParamSpec);
        } catch (InvalidAlgorithmParameterException e) {
            System.out.println("Exception: " + e);
        } catch (NoSuchPaddingException e) {
            System.out.println("Exception: " + e);
        } catch (NoSuchAlgorithmException e) {
            System.out.println("Exception: " + e);
        } catch (InvalidKeyException e) {
```

```
                System.out.println("Exception: " + e);
        }
    }

    public void write(byte[] bytes, OutputStream out)
    {
        try {
            CipherOutputStream cos =
                        new CipherOutputStream(out, m_encrypter);

            cos.write(bytes, 0, bytes.length);

            cos.close();
        } catch(IOException ioe) {
            System.out.println("Exception: " + ioe);
        }
    }

    public void read(byte[] bytes, InputStream in)
    {
        try {
            CipherInputStream cis =
                        new CipherInputStream(in, m_decrypter);

            int pos=0, intValue;

            while( (intValue = cis.read()) != -1) {
                bytes[pos] = (byte)intValue;
                pos++;
            }
        } catch(IOException ioe) {
            System.out.println("Exception: " + ioe);
        }
    }

    public byte[] encrypt(byte[] input)
    {
        try {
            return(m_encrypter.doFinal(input));
        } catch(IllegalBlockSizeException ibse) {
            System.out.println("Exception: " + ibse);
        } catch(BadPaddingException bpe) {
            System.out.println("Exception: " + bpe);
        }

        return(null);
    }

    public byte[] decrypt(byte[] input)
    {
        try {
            return(m_decrypter.doFinal(input));
        } catch(IllegalBlockSizeException ibse) {
            System.out.println("Exception: " + ibse);
        } catch(BadPaddingException bpe) {
```

```
        System.out.println("Exception: " + bpe);
    }

    return(null);
}

public static void main(String args[])
{
    try {
        CipherExample ce = new CipherExample();

        SecretKey key =
                KeyGenerator.getInstance("DES").generateKey();

        ce.init(key);

        System.out.println("Testing encrypt/decrypt of bytes");
        byte[] clearText = new byte[]{65,73,82,68,65,78,67,69};
        byte[] encryptedText = ce.encrypt(clearText);
        byte[] decryptedText = ce.decrypt(encryptedText);

        String clearTextAsString = new String(clearText);
        String encTextAsString = new String(encryptedText);
        String decTextAsString = new String(decryptedText);

        System.out.println("   CLEARTEXT: " + clearTextAsString);
        System.out.println("   ENCRYPTED: " + encTextAsString);
        System.out.println("   DECRYPTED: " + decTextAsString);

        System.out.println("\nTesting encrypting of a file\n");

        FileInputStream fis = new FileInputStream("cipherTest.in");
        FileOutputStream fos =
                        new FileOutputStream("cipherTest.out");

        int dataInputSize = fis.available();

        byte[] inputBytes = new byte[dataInputSize];
        fis.read(inputBytes);
        ce.write(inputBytes, fos);
        fos.flush();
        fis.close();
        fos.close();

        String inputFileAsString = new String(inputBytes);
        System.out.println("INPUT FILE CONTENTS\n" +
                            inputFileAsString + "\n");

        System.out.println("File encrypted and saved to disk\n");

        fis = new FileInputStream("cipherTest.out");

        byte[] decrypted = new byte[dataInputSize];
        ce.read(decrypted, fis);
```

```
                     fis.close();
                     String decryptedAsString = new String(decrypted);

                     System.out.println("DECRYPTED FILE:\n" +
                                         decryptedAsString + "\n");
            } catch(IOException ioe) {
                     System.out.println("Exception: " + ioe);
            } catch(NoSuchAlgorithmException e) {
                     System.out.println("Exception: " + e);
            }
        }
    }
```

The KeyGenerator engine class is used to generate a SecretKey. This class accepts a SecretKey as an initialization parameter, which is then used by the various instances of the Cipher class.

KeyGenerator

This engine class is used to generate secret keys for symmetric algorithms. The standard getInstance methods are available. After object creation, one of the following methods is used to initialize the KeyGenerator.

The following are the algorithm-independent initialization methods:

```
public void init(SecureRandom random)
public void init(int keysize)
public void init(int keysize, SecureRandom random)
```

The following are the algorithm-specific initialization methods:

```
public void init(AlgorithmParameterSpec params)
public void init(AlgorithmParameterSpec params, SecureRandom random)
```

The algorithm-independent initialization allows you to specify a RNG or a keysize — or both — as parameters used to initialize the key generator. The algorithm-specific initialization methods accept a set of parameters (and possibly a RNG also) that are used with the chosen algorithm. What these parameters are depend on the algorithm used:

```
public SecretKey generateKey()
```

After the KeyGenerator is created and initialized, the generateKey method is called to generate a secret key. Consult the previous Cipher example for a use of the KeyGenerator in action.

SecretKeyFactory

This is very much like the KeyFactory in the java.security package; however, this engine class only works on secret (symmetric) keys. This class is used to convert keys back and forth between their transparent and opaque representations. The standard getInstance methods are used to create a SecretKeyFactory object. Three main methods are used to manipulate keys: generateSecret, getKeySpec, and translateKey:

```
SecretKey generateSecret(KeySpec keySpec)
```

This converts a key specification into a SecretKey object. If the factory cannot convert the key using the current algorithm, an InvalidKeySpecException is thrown:

```
KeySpec getKeySpec(SecretKey key, Class keySpec)
```

This converts a key into a key specification in the format specified by the keySpec parameter. If the factory cannot perform the conversion due to the algorithm or some other mismatch (such as incompatible formats), an InvalidKeySpecException is thrown:

```
SecretKey translateKey(SecretKey key)
```

This translates a key object from an unknown or untrusted provider to a key object from this factory.

Protecting Objects through Sealing

The SealedObject class is used to encrypt any class that is serializable. It is used with an instance of the Cipher class. The constructor of SealedObject is used to specify an object to seal an initialized Cipher object. One of three getObject methods is later used to decrypt the object. The name of the algorithm used to encrypt the object can be retrieved using the getAlgorithm method:

```
Object getObject(Cipher c)
Object getObject(Key key)
Object getObject(Key key, String provider)
```

The first form decrypts the object using a provided Cipher. The second decrypts the object using the algorithm that encrypted the object and requires a key for decryption. The final form allows you to specify a specific provider along with the key needed to decrypt the object.

Here's an example of creating a custom class, sealing it, and then unsealing it:

```java
import java.security.*;
import java.security.spec.*;
import javax.crypto.*;
import javax.crypto.spec.*;
import java.io.*;

class CustomerData implements Serializable {
    public String name;
    public String password;
}

public class SealedObjectExample {
    private SecretKey secretKey;
    private Cipher encrypter, decrypter;

    public SealedObjectExample()
    {
        try {
            secretKey = KeyGenerator.getInstance("DES").generateKey();

            encrypter = Cipher.getInstance("DES");
            encrypter.init(Cipher.ENCRYPT_MODE, secretKey);

            decrypter = Cipher.getInstance("DES");
```

```
            decrypter.init(Cipher.DECRYPT_MODE, secretKey);
        } catch(NoSuchAlgorithmException e) {
        } catch(InvalidKeyException e) {
        } catch(NoSuchPaddingException e) {
        }
    }

    public SealedObject seal(Serializable obj)
    {
        try {
            return(new SealedObject(obj, encrypter));
        } catch(IOException e) {
        } catch(IllegalBlockSizeException e) {
        }

        return(null);
    }

    public Object unseal(SealedObject so)
    {
        try {
            String algorithmName = so.getAlgorithm();

            // can use algorithmName to construct a decrypter

            return(so.getObject(decrypter));
        } catch(IOException e) {
        } catch(IllegalBlockSizeException e) {
        } catch(BadPaddingException e) {
        } catch(ClassNotFoundException e) {
        }

        return(null);
    }

    public static void main(String args[])
    {
        CustomerData cust, unsealed;
        SealedObject sealed;
        SealedObjectExample soe = new SealedObjectExample();

        // configure a CustomerData object
        cust = new CustomerData();
        cust.name = "Paul";
        cust.password = "password";

        // Seal it, storing it in a SealedObject
        sealed = soe.seal(cust);

        // Try unsealing it
        unsealed = (CustomerData)soe.unseal(sealed);

        System.out.println("NAME: " + unsealed.name);
        System.out.println("PASSWORD: " + unsealed.password);
    }
}
```

The only requirement on the class that will be sealed is that it inherits from serializable. The SealedObject class contains the sealed object, and to unseal the object, all that is necessary is the SealedObject object. It is possible to retrieve the name of the algorithm used to seal it using the getAlgorithm method on the SealedObject class. A Cipher object is also needed to perform the unsealing operation.

Computing Message Authentication Codes

The Mac engine class computes a hash, similar to a message digest, for input data given a secret key. The Mac class has the standard getInstance methods for object creation. After creation, the object must be initialized using one of the following methods:

```
public void init(Key key)
public void init(Key key, AlgorithmParameterSpec params)
```

The key must be a key class that inherits from the javax.crypto.SecretKey interface, such as KeyGenerator.generateKey() or KeyAgreement.generateSecret(). Certain algorithms require that the algorithm used to generate the key be compatible with the algorithm specified in the getInstance call. If this is the case and the two algorithms are not compatible, an InvalidKeyException is thrown.

The Mac class follows similar semantics for sending data to the computation engine. Data can be passed in all at once using the doFinal method or passed in piece by piece using the update method (and then invoking doFinal to signal the end of the input):

```
public byte[] doFinal(byte[] input)
public byte[] doFinal()
public void doFinal(byte[] output, int outOffset)
```

The first doFinal method accepts a byte array containing the input data, computes the message authentication code, and returns that in a byte array. The second form is used to signal the end of input after several invocations of the update method. The last form can be used after a sequence of update methods to both accept the last chunk of data and signal the end of input. The outOffset parameter specifies where in the output array to start reading data, and the data ends at the end of the array:

```
public void update(byte input)
public void update(byte[] input)
public void update(byte[] input, int inputOffset, int inputLen)
```

These methods are useful for sending data to the Mac class a piece at a time. The first method accepts a single byte of input. The second method takes an array of bytes. The third allows you to pass in an array and specify where in the array (starting at inputOffset) to read the data, and the length of the data (inputLen). After you are done calling update, don't forget to call a version of doFinal to signal the end of input and calculate the message authentication code.

Here's an example of creating an instance of the Mac class and computing the message authentication code for data. This example leverages the previous KeyGeneratorExample:

```
import java.security.*;
import javax.crypto.*;
import java.io.*;

public class MacExample {
```

```
        public static void main(String args[])
        {
            try {
                String inputString = "Test input string";

                KeyGenerator keyGen = KeyGenerator.getInstance("HmacMD5");
                SecretKey secretKey = keyGen.generateKey();

                Mac mac = Mac.getInstance(secretKey.getAlgorithm());
                mac.init(secretKey);

                // the Mac class needs data in byte format
                byte[] byteData = inputString.getBytes("UTF8");

                // Compute the MAC for the data all in one operation
                byte[] macBytes = mac.doFinal(byteData);

                String macAsString =
                        new sun.misc.BASE64Encoder().encode(macBytes);

                System.out.println(
                    "The computed message authentication code is: "
                    + macAsString);
            } catch (InvalidKeyException e) {
            } catch (NoSuchAlgorithmException e) {
            } catch (UnsupportedEncodingException e) {
            }
        }
    }
```

Computing the message authentication code is very similar to computing the message digest using the MessageDigest engine class. The main difference is that a key is required. Here, the key is generated via the KeyGenerator. Normally, this key would be saved or transmitted for verifying that the MAC matches the data. The Mac class is created with the same algorithm used for the key and then initialized with the key.

Program Security Using JAAS

JAAS stands for Java Authentication and Authorization Service. This package used to be an extension, but it was made part of the J2SDK in the 1.4 release of the JDK. Authentication is the process by which the user of the application (any type of Java program, including applets, servlets, and so forth) is verified. Authorization is the process by which an authenticated user is granted permission for executing actions, such as modifying specific files that are access-controlled. Authentication and authorization work together to provide access control for your program, but these are separate concepts.

User Identification

In order for access control to work, there must be a way of storing the user's identity. This is accomplished using a *Subject*, a grouping of information that identifies the source of all requests, such as a particular user that is logged in to the system. A Subject has associated principals, which are other identifying characteristics of a subject, such as a user's social security number or name. A Subject also has public and private credentials, such as a public and private key, but it can be any object.

You won't usually need to instantiate a Subject; however, there are two constructors provided:

```
public Subject();
public Subject(boolean readOnly, Set principals,
               Set pubCredentials, Set privCredentials);
```

The first constructor creates a Subject that isn't read-only and has empty (not null) sets of principals, and public and private credentials. The second constructor gives you an idea of the information the Subject possesses:

```
public void setReadOnly();
public boolean isReadOnly();
```

These two methods allow you to change and retrieve the read-only state of the subject. If the Subject is marked read-only and an attempt is made to change the principals or credentials, an IllegalStateException is thrown:

```
public Set getPrincipals();
public Set getPrincipals(Class c);
public Set getPublicCredentials();
public Set getPublicCredentials(Class c);
public Set getPrivateCredentials();
public Set getPrivateCredentials(Class c);
```

These methods allow you to retrieve a handle to the set of principals, or public or private credentials. Once you have this handle, you can use the methods on the Set class to manipulate the contents of the set. Modifying this set modifies the set in the Subject.

Each version of this access method has a Class parameter that allows you to retrieve only those principals/credentials that are of a specific type. However, these methods return a new set that does not correspond to the internal set of the Subject.

A Subject can be associated with an AccessControlContext. This is a snapshot of context from an AccessController that governs how security checks are performed. You can access this through the following method:

```
public static Subject getSubject(final AccessControlContext acc);
```

Note that this is a static method. This method returns the Subject currently associated with the specified AccessControlContext or null if there is no association.

Executing Code with Security Checks

The Subject class provides doAs and doAsPrivileged methods to execute code that contains security restrictions. The java.security.PrivilegedAction interface must be implemented by another class in order to package code for use with the doAs or doAsPrivleged methods. Only one method is defined in this interface:

```
public Object run();
```

Any code in the run method executes with the Subject passed to the doAs or doAsPrivileged method. If permission for all the operations in the code is not granted to the Subject/principals, then a SecurityException is thrown. The value returned can have any meaning you wish to associate with it or simply return null if you don't need to pass any information back.

The doAs method executes a specified block of code as a particular Subject:

```
public static Object doAs(final Subject subject,
                          final java.security.PrivilegedAction action);

public static Object doAs(final Subject subject,
                    final java.security.PrivilegedExceptionAction action)
        throws java.security.PrivilegedActionException;
```

These methods first associate the Subject with the current thread's AccessControlContext and then execute the action. The first form expects the method to return, and the second allows checked exceptions to be thrown from the executing code.

The doAsPrivileged method operates the same as the doAs method, but it allows you to specify which AccessControlContext to use instead of the one attached to the current thread:

```
public static Object doAsPrivileged(final Subject subject,
                          final java.security.PrivilegedAction action,
                          final java.security.AccessControlContext acc);

public static Object doAsPrivileged(final Subject subject,
                    final java.security.PrivilegedExceptionAction action,
                    final java.security.AccessControlContext acc)
          throws java.security.PrivilegedActionException;
```

These provide a third parameter to both methods for using a different AccessControlContext.

Principals

A principal can be of any class type as long as the class inherits from java.security.Principal and java.io.Serializable. The Principal interface defines the following methods:

```
boolean equals(Object another)
```

The equals method returns true if the principal passed in matches the current principal and returns false otherwise:

```
String toString()
```

The toString method returns a string representation of this principal:

```
int hashCode()
```

The hashCode method returns a hash code for this principal:

```
String getName()
```

The getName method returns the name of this principal.

Credentials

Credentials can be of any type, and no requirements are placed on what interfaces a credential class must implement. However, JAAS provides two interfaces that bestow behavior on a credential class that might prove useful. These interfaces are Refreshable and Destroyable.

The javax.security.auth.Refreshable is useful for a credential that requires a refresh of its state (perhaps the credential is valid only for a specific length of time). Three methods are defined on this interface:

```
boolean isCurrent()
```

The isCurrent method should return true if the credential is current or return false if it has expired or needs a refresh of its state:

```
void refresh() throws RefreshFailedException
```

The refresh method refreshes the current state of the credential, making it valid again. The javax .security.auth.Destroyable interface gives a credential semantics for destroying its contents:

```
boolean isDestroyed()
```

The isDestroyed method returns true if the credential's contents have been destroyed and returns false otherwise:

```
void destroy() throws DestroyFailedException
```

The destroy method destroys the contents of the credential. Methods that require contents to be valid should throw the IllegalStateException after destroy is called.

Authenticating a Subject

The basic manner in which a subject is authenticated is through a LoginContext object. A LoginContext then consults another class for the specific authentication services. The sequence of steps that occurs when a LoginContext is used for authentication is as follows:

1. A LoginContext object is instantiated.
2. The LoginContext consults a Configuration to load all LoginModules for the current application.
3. The login method of the LoginContext is called.
4. Each LoginModule then attempts to authenticate the subject. The LoginModule should associate principals/credentials with a successfully authenticated user.
5. The success or failure of the authentication is communicated back to the application.

Configuration

The configuration file contains a number of configurations per application for authentication. Each configuration has a name (usually the application name) and then a list of login modules to use for authentication. The configuration can have one set of login modules under the name other to specify an authentication scheme to use when no others match the name specified. Each set of login modules adheres to the following syntax:

```
NAME {
     LoginModuleClass   FLAG   ModuleOptions;
     LoginModuleClass   FLAG   ModuleOptions;
}
```

The LoginModuleClass is the fully qualified name of a LoginModule. The FLAG can be one of the values in the following table.

Flag Name	Description
Required	The LoginModule is required to succeed; however, if it fails, LoginModules specified after the current one still execute.
Requisite	The LoginModule is required to succeed. If it fails, control returns to the application. No further LoginModules are executed.
Sufficient	The LoginModule is not required to succeed. If the LoginModule succeeds, control is immediately returned to the application. Control passes down the list of LoginModules even if this one fails.
Optional	The LoginModule is not required to succeed, and control passes down the list if this one succeeds or fails.

The ModuleOptions is a space-separated list of login module-specific name=value pairs.

LoginContext

The LoginContext class provides a clean approach to authenticating subjects while leaving the authentication details to LoginModules. This makes it easy to change the configuration for an application by adding or removing a LoginModule. The LoginContext class provides the following constructors:

```
public LoginContext(String name) throws LoginException
public LoginContext(String name, Subject subject) throws LoginException
public LoginContext(String name, CallbackHandler callbackHandler)
       throws LoginException
public LoginContext(String name, Subject subject,
                    CallbackHandler callbackHandler)
       throws LoginException
```

The name parameter corresponds to an entry in the configuration used for the application. The first and third forms of the constructor create an empty subject because one isn't passed in. If a LoginModule has to communicate with the user, it can do so through a CallbackHandler. For example, if a username and password are required, a class can inherit from javax.security.auth.callback.CallbackHandler and retrieve the information from the user. The CallbackHandler interface defines a single method:

```
void handle(Callback[] callbacks)
     throws java.io.IOException, UnsupportedCallbackException
```

One or more callbacks can be specified, allowing you to separate username and password entries into two separate callbacks all managed by a single CallbackHandler.

The LoginContext also provides `login` and `logout` methods:

```
public void login() throws LoginException
```

This method causes all configured LoginModules to authenticate the subject. If authentication succeeds, you can retrieve the subject via `getSubject()`. The subject may have revised credentials and principals after all authentication is performed:

```
public void logout() throws LoginException
```

The `logout` method removes credentials/principals from the authenticated subject.

Essentially, the code used for an application to log in, obtain an authenticated subject, and then log out looks like the following snippet of code:

```
LoginContext loginContext = new LoginContext("BasicConsoleLogin");

try {
    loginContext.login(); // utilizes callbacks
    Subject subject = loginContext.getSubject();

    // ... execute specific application code here ...

    loginContext.logout();
} catch(LoginException le) {
    // authentication failed
}
```

The LoginContext retrieves the set of LoginModules to execute from the configuration under the name BasicConsoleLogin.

Authorization

Authentication provides for more of a black-and-white approach to security. The user (or other entity) is either authenticated or not. JAAS provides authorization for granting degrees of access to an entity. Each application can use a policy file that contains a list of permissions for various targets. The policy file provides a way to grant permissions to both code and principals.

The javax.security.auth.AuthPermission class exists to guard access to the Policy, Subject, LoginContext, and Configuration objects, providing a layer of security on these classes as well. Consult the documentation for this class for a full list of permissions that it provides.

The policy file contains a list of grant sections that grant permissions to code or principals. The grant keyword is used to start a grant section, followed by zero or more optional elements: signedBy, codeBase, and principal. The basic format looks like the following:

```
grant signedBy "signer_names",
      codeBase "URL",
      principal principal_class_name "principal_name",
      principal principal_class_name "principal_name",
```

```
        ... {

    permission permission_class_name "target_name", "action",
                    signedBy "signer_names";
    permission permission_class_name "target_name", "action",
                    signedBy "signer_names";
    ...
    };
```

You can only specify signedBy and codeBase a maximum of one time, but the principal element can be specified more than once. All of these are optional elements. By not specifying any at all, the permissions specified apply to all executing code, regardless of its source.

As one example of a policy file, the java.policy that is located in the jre/lib/security directory that comes with JDK 5 has a policy that opens permissions wide to Java extensions:

```
    grant codeBase "file:${{java.ext.dirs}}/*" {
        permission java.security.AllPermission;
    };
```

The codeBase element is used to specify all code that is located in the java.ext.dirs (a system property) directory, which hence grants AllPermission to all code in the Java extensions directory.

The signedBy element is used to grant permissions only when the code is signed by the specified entity.

There are many available permissions in the Java API, such as java.io.FilePermission, java.net .NetPermission, and java.security.AllPermission. Each permission has its own set of actions, such as FilePermission, needing to know which operations are valid on a particular file (read, write, and so forth). Consult the online documentation for specific details on each permission.

Summary

In this chapter, you learned about Java Cryptography and Security. Security is very important in online systems and systems that have multiple users. You now know some of the basics of security, such as generating and using keys, including digital signing and key management. You have seen how Java supports a variety of security mechanisms from data encryption to access control, and you have an overview of how to go about securing your application.

14

Packaging and Deploying Your Java Applications

This chapter describes how to package and deploy your Java applications including client-side and server-side applications. It discusses technologies like Java Web Start, JAR packaging, JAR signing, building WAR files, and CLASSPATH manipulation. You'll walk through the different types of Java applications and get a brief introduction to each as well as information on a few useful utilities that you can use when creating, configuring, and deploying your own applications.

Examining Java CLASSPATHs

One of the most potentially frustrating aspects of Java is the classpath. If you have coded in Java even for a short length of time, you're already familiar with the classpath. It is a system environment variable that directs the Java Virtual Machine (VM) to a set of classes and/or JAR files. This is how the VM knows where code used by the program resides.

At times, you wind up needing a class and have no idea which JAR file has this class. You might add a bunch of JAR files to your classpath, hoping you'll accidentally add the right one in, never truly knowing which JAR files are not needed. Many people complain about DLL Hell on Windows, but a similar mismanagement of the classpath and the many files it points to can create the same situation with Java. If you use a development environment such as Eclipse, you are somewhat insulated from this problem because it is easy to manage your classpath through the GUI. However, in a deployment scenario, you may not have the luxury of a graphical tool to help manage the classpath. A seemingly small problem (one JAR left off the classpath, for example) may take seconds to fix if you know where the class is, or — if you don't know — much longer.

Another problem with classpaths is length limits on the classpath environment variable imposed by the environment. I've seen more than one project with an insane number of JAR files (each with a long path) specified within the classpath. Sometimes, there is no great solution to this problem.

If the classpath works and nobody needs to tweak it after deployment, you should be fine. However, long classpaths are troublesome during development and might even grow too long for the environment space after deployment.

Here are a few suggestions to attempt to manage long classpaths. First, know where your application is executing from and utilize relative paths instead of absolute paths. Second, attempt to group your application and its libraries into as few JAR files as possible. A more complicated but useful solution is grouping the common utility JAR files (perhaps third-party JAR files used by your application) and placing these in the extensions directory within the installed JRE. By default, this extensions directory is lib/ext beneath the JRE directory. By installing a JAR file as an extension, it no longer needs to appear on the classpath. You must ensure that the JAR file is placed within the correct JRE though. This might entail you installing your own JRE with your application, but this too cannot be done lightly. Utilizing the extensions directory is not a great idea because you are technically not extending the Java environment, but it is one solution to consider in managing a classpath that is too long.

In hoping to alleviate your burden a little, here are a couple of utility programs that may help you in managing your classpath. The first class is a straightforward utility that accepts a list of classes stored inside a file and verifies that each class is present somewhere within the classpath (or in one of the JAR files in the classpath). The file containing the class list is passed in on the command line. Each line in the file contains a single fully qualified class name:

```
import java.io.*;

public class ClassPathVerifier {
    public static void main(String args[])
    {
        try {
            BufferedReader br = new BufferedReader(
                              new InputStreamReader(
                                new FileInputStream(args[0])));
            String clsName="";

            while( (clsName = br.readLine()) != null) {
                try {
                    Class.forName(clsName);
                    System.out.print(".");
                } catch(Exception e) {
                    System.out.println("\nNOT FOUND: " + clsName);
                }
            }

            br.close();
        } catch(IOException ioe) {
            System.out.println("IOException: " + ioe);
            ioe.printStackTrace();
        }
    }
}
```

This class uses the simple technique of passing a class name into the Class.forName method. If no exception is thrown, the class is found. In order to show progress, a single period is printed for each class that is successfully loaded. If you manage multiple classpaths, this utility can be used to ensure that a set of classes is always available.

A utility that packs more of a punch is listed next. The purpose of this next utility is to find which JAR file(s) a class is inside. You need not specify a fully qualified class name — any portion of the class name and package will do. This means that you can even search for a package instead of a particular class:

```
import java.io.*;
import java.util.zip.*;
import java.util.StringTokenizer;

public class ClassSearch {
    private String m_baseDirectory;
    private String m_classToFind;
    private int m_resultsCount=0;
```

A very interesting method that uses a bit more complex code is the searchJarFile. This method, shown in the following example, actually opens a JAR file and searches inside it for a given class name:

```
public void searchJarFile(String filePath)
{
    try {
        FileInputStream fis = new FileInputStream(filePath);
        BufferedInputStream bis = new BufferedInputStream(fis);
        ZipInputStream zis = new ZipInputStream(bis);
        ZipEntry ze = null;

        while((ze=zis.getNextEntry()) != null) {
            if(ze.isDirectory()) {
                continue;
            }

            if(ze.getName().indexOf(m_classToFind) != -1) {
                System.out.println("  " + ze.getName() +
                                        "\n    (inside " + filePath + ")");
                m_resultsCount++;
            }
        }
    } catch(Exception e) {
        System.out.println("Exception: " + e);
        e.printStackTrace();
    }
}
```

The findHelper method searches directories and subdirectories for JAR files:

```
public void findHelper(File dir, int level)
{
    int i;
    File[] subFiles;

    subFiles = dir.listFiles();

    for(i=0; i<subFiles.length; i++) {
        if(subFiles[i].isFile()) {
            if(subFiles[i].getName().toLowerCase().indexOf(".jar") != -1) {
                // found a jar file, process it
```

```
                    searchJarFile(subFiles[i].getAbsolutePath());
            }
        } else {
            // directory, so recur
            findHelper(subFiles[i], level+1);
        }
    }
}
```

The method `searchClassPath` is used to find a class in the JAR files specified in the given classpath:

```
public void searchClassPath(String classToFind)
{
    String classPath = System.getProperty("java.class.path");
    System.out.println("Searching classpath: " + classPath);
    StringTokenizer st = new StringTokenizer(classPath, ";");

    m_classToFind = classToFind;

    while(st.hasMoreTokens()) {
        String jarFileName = st.nextToken();
        if(jarFileName != null &&
            jarFileName.toLowerCase().indexOf(".jar") != -1) {
            searchJarFile(jarFileName);
        }
    }
}
```

The `findClass` method is kicked off from the main method and takes two parameters. One parameter is the base directory that will be used as a starting point to begin the class search. The second parameter is the class name that you are looking for. If the class name is found in any JAR files that exist in the base directory or its subdirectories, the JAR filename and location are printed out to the console:

```
public void findClass(String baseDir, String classToFind)
{
    System.out.println("SEARCHING IN: " + baseDir);
    m_baseDirectory = baseDir;
    m_classToFind = classToFind;
    m_classToFind = m_classToFind.replaceAll("\\.", "/");

    File start = new File(m_baseDirectory);

    System.out.println("SEARCHING FOR: " + m_classToFind);
    System.out.println("\nSEARCH RESULTS:");

    findHelper(start, 1);

    if(m_resultsCount == 0) {
        System.out.println("No results.");
    }
}
```

The main method shown in the following example is the driver method of the utility class and takes a base directory and class name for which to search:

```java
public static void main(String args[])
{
    if(args.length < 1 || args.length > 2) {
        System.out.println("Incorrect program usage");
        System.out.println("  java ClassSearch <base directory>" +
                            " <class to find>\n");
        System.out.println("    searches all jar files beneath base" +
                            " directory for class\n");
        System.out.println("");
        System.out.println("  java ClassSearch <class to find>\n");
        System.out.println("    searches all jar files in classpath" +
                            " for class\n");
        System.exit(1);
    }

    ClassSearch cs = new ClassSearch();

    if(args.length == 1) {
        cs.searchClassPath(args[0]);
    } else if(args.length == 2) {
        cs.findClass(args[0], args[1]);
    }
}
}
```

This class uses the zip library in Java along with the directory search facilities of the File class to search for a class/package specified on the command line. An alternate usage allows you to search for a class within the JAR files listed in the classpath. This allows you to find every JAR file that has a class, which thus resolves a mess in the classpath. Here's an example usage of the program. This assumes that the JDK is installed in D:\j2sdk1.5.0:

```
D:\writing\code>java ClassSearch d:\j2sdk1.5.0 ArrayList
SEARCHING IN: d:\j2sdk1.5.0
SEARCHING FOR: ArrayList

SEARCH RESULTS:
  java/util/Arrays$ArrayList.class
    (inside d:\j2sdk1.5.0\jre\lib\rt.jar)
  java/util/concurrent/CopyOnWriteArrayList$1.class
    (inside d:\j2sdk1.5.0\jre\lib\rt.jar)
  java/util/concurrent/CopyOnWriteArrayList$COWIterator.class
    (inside d:\j2sdk1.5.0\jre\lib\rt.jar)
  java/util/concurrent/CopyOnWriteArrayList$COWSubList.class
    (inside d:\j2sdk1.5.0\jre\lib\rt.jar)
  java/util/concurrent/CopyOnWriteArrayList$COWSubListIterator.class
    (inside d:\j2sdk1.5.0\jre\lib\rt.jar)
  java/util/concurrent/CopyOnWriteArrayList.class
    (inside d:\j2sdk1.5.0\jre\lib\rt.jar)
  sun/swing/BakedArrayList.class
    (inside d:\j2sdk1.5.0\jre\lib\rt.jar)
  java/util/ArrayList.class
    (inside d:\j2sdk1.5.0\jre\lib\rt.jar)
```

This execution of the utility shows the various ArrayList classes in the various packages inside the core runtime JAR that comes with every JRE. If you search for a more obscure class, such as ByteToCharDBCS_EBCDIC, you'll find the charsets.jar file in your search results. This utility can be used to find which JAR file a class is in but also every JAR file that contains this class. You can find a class you need or resolve classpath confusion if the same class is in a number of JAR files and an older version of a class you developed is being used although you've specified the newer version on the command line.

Investigating the Endorsed Directory

In an installation of a Java Runtime Environment, there are packages that are not part of the standard Java API. These packages are common third-party libraries and are considered *endorsed*, which means they are distributed as an extension to the Java API. One example of an endorsed package is the org.omg.CORBA package providing CORBA functionality. Because these packages are available to Java programs, it is possible that there is a conflict when you distribute third-party libraries that already exist in the endorsed directory. Java provides a mechanism called the *Endorsed Standard Override Mechanism*, which gives you a way to install newer versions of libraries in the endorsed directory.

In order to override the endorsed standards, place JAR files in the endorsed directory within the JRE. This directory is named endorsed and is located in the JRE installation beneath the lib directory, both on Windows and on Unix. If you have multiple JREs or JDKs installed, make sure you place the JAR files in the correct endorsed directory such that the VM that executes will recognize these JAR files. If you want to use a different directory for overriding the endorsed standards, specify it in the java.endorsed.dirs system property. In this property, you can list one or more directories that have JAR files you wish to use. These directories are delimited by the value of the File.pathSeparatorChar, which is system-specific.

There is a fixed list of standard API's that you can override, shown in the following table. Note that you cannot arbitrarily override a package in the standard Java API.

Packages that Can Be Overridden	Packages that Can Be Overridden
javax.rmi.CORBA	org.omg.DynamicAny
org.omg.CORBA	org.omg.DynamicAny.DynAnyFactoryPackage
org.omg.CORBA.DynAnyPackage	org.omg.DynamicAny.DynAnyPackage
org.omg.CORBA.ORBPackage	org.omg.IOP
org.omg.CORBA.portable	org.omg.IOP.CodecFactoryPackage
org.omg.CORBA.TypeCodePackage	org.omg.IOP.CodecPackage
org.omg.CORBA_2_3	org.omg.Messaging
org.omg.CORBA_2_3.portable	org.omg.PortableInterceptor
org.omg.CosNaming	org.omg.PortableInterceptor.ORBInitInfoPackage
org.omg.CosNaming.NamingContextExtPackage	org.omg.PortableServer
org.omg.CosNaming.NamingContextPackage	org.omg.PortableServer.CurrentPackage
org.omg.Dynamic	

Exploring Java Archives

Java wouldn't be where it is today without the creation of its archive file format. The JAVA archive, which programmers generally refer to as a JAR file, is a way to bundle multiple files, including other JARs, into a single file that is suffixed with the .jar extension. JAR files use the same format to compress their files as those of the zip format. So, you can open a JAR file in a program that understands the normal zip compression and edit away. This makes the format of JAR files very portable across different operating systems because most operating systems understand the zip format or have utilities that were created for them to manipulate zip files. JAR files can greatly reduce the download time of classes, images, audio, and other large files by compressing them. Applets and their resources can be compressed into a JAR file, significantly reducing the amount of time it takes to download the applet.

JAR files can also be digitally signed for architectures that require a substantial amount of security requirements to be imposed on the applications being constructed. By digitally signing a JAR file, you can always tell who the author of the JAR file was and if it has been tampered with. In Java 5, there have been two new enhancements of the JAR format:

❏ Faster access to the contents of JAR files has been accomplished with a new parameter addition, -i, to the command-line JAR tool that allows you to create a JAR file index.

❏ A new API has been added for the *delete-on-close* mode that is used when opening JAR files.

The major feature that separates the JAR file from a normal zip file is that of its *manifest* file that is contained in the JAR files META-INF directory. The manifest file allows you to invoke special features like package sealing and the ability to specify the JAR as an executable JAR file. The manifest file is similar to the format of a properties file in that it accepts NAME-VALUE pair entries that are used for changing specific settings about the JAR file. Along with the manifest file, there are also other files that can be created in the META-INF directory of a JAR file. More about this subject will be discussed subsequently. The new Java 5 allows you to include an INDEX.LIST in the META-INF directory, which is automatically generated when you invoke the JAR tool and specify the -i option. This allows for quicker class loading times.

Manipulating JAR files

The Java Development Kit (JDK) contains a command-line tool called the *Java Archive Tool* that is used to create JAR files via the command line. You execute the JAR tool by simply typing **jar** at a console window. If you can't get the tool to run, it's most likely that you don't have Java set up correctly for your environment. Reread the install instructions for your environment that comes with your JDK. You can always run the tool from the JDK/BIN directory, but it is highly recommended that you adjust your environment so that you can run the tool from almost anywhere. The correct syntax for executing the JAR tool is shown in the following example:

```
jar {ctxu}[vfm0Mi] [jar-file] [manifest-file] [-C dir] files ...
```

Before you create your first JAR file, it is important to understand the options that can be used to create a JAR file. Otherwise, it will seem like a big mystery as to why certain options were chosen to create the JAR file. The following table lists the options and a description of the options for the JAR tool.

Option	Description
c	This option is simply used to create a new archive.
t	This option will list the table of contents for the archive file. This is a great way to inspect the contents of the JAR file right after you have created it to make sure it was created successfully and the way you anticipated. **Note:** The f option is usually combined with the t option to reduce the amount of typing you have to do.
x	This option is used to extract the specified files or all the files from the JAR file.
u	This option allows you to update a JAR file with specified new or changed files. It is more likely that you will use a tool that knows how to update a zip file format or an IDE that can update JAR files for you because this task can be quite cumbersome if you have a lot of files to update.
v	The verbose option allows you to get more feedback from the JAR tool as it creates the JAR. It is very helpful when debugging issues.
f	This option specifies that the JAR file to update is on the command line.
m	This option signifies that you are supplying the JAR tool with a manifest file that is to be included in the JAR.
0	The zero option tells the JAR tool to not compress the files and just package them into the archive.
M	This option prevents the default manifest file from being created. Manifest files are optional in JAR files.
i	One of the new features in Java 5, this option is used to generate index information for the JAR file into its META-INF directory under the file named INDEX.LIST.
C [DIR]	This option instructs the JAR tool to change the directory to the one specified and to JAR the files that are being referenced.

Now it is time to show you just how easy it is to create a JAR file. This example will contain two Java files and an images directory. Normally, the Java files would be compiled into classes, and the source code would be removed, but this example simply demonstrates how almost any type of file can be contained in a JAR file. Figure 14-1 shows the directory structure prior to issuing a JAR command.

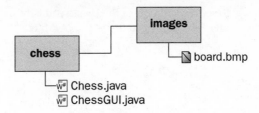

Figure 14-1

Once you know the files and directories you want to archive, you can issue a JAR tool command with the options cvf from the root directory and literally compress the entire chess directory as well as any subdirectories under it. The c option is used to create the archive, the v option specifies verbose, and the f option signifies that you will be supplying the name of the JAR file to create on the command line. Here is an example of the JAR tool in action:

```
C:\>jar -cvf chess.jar chess
added manifest
adding: chess/(in = 0) (out= 0)(stored 0%)
adding: chess/Chess.java(in = 0) (out= 0)(stored 0%)
adding: chess/ChessGUI.java(in = 0) (out= 0)(stored 0%)
adding: chess/images/(in = 0) (out= 0)(stored 0%)
adding: chess/images/board.bmp(in = 0) (out= 0)(stored 0%)
```

The chess.jar file is now created and contains all the files under the C:\chess directory. There is a default manifest file that was automatically generated by the JAR tool in the META-INF directory of the JAR file. It contains nothing more than a version string. Figure 14-2 shows the new JAR structure.

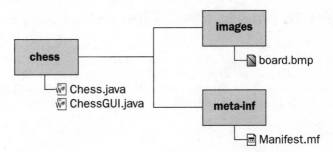

Figure 14-2

You can also use the JAR tool to see the contents of the chess.jar file by specifying the t option on the file. Here is an example of how to view the table of contents of a JAR file:

```
C:\>jar -tf chess.jar
META-INF/
META-INF/MANIFEST.MF
chess/
chess/Chess.java
chess/ChessGUI.java
chess/images/
chess/images/board.bmp
```

Besides viewing the contents of a JAR file, you can also extract the contents of the JAR file. This may be necessary if you ever get into a situation when you need to unpack the JAR to patch or edit files in the JAR file. To extract a JAR file, you will need to specify the x option. In this example, the xvf options are used. Refer to the option table in this section for more information on options and their uses:

```
C:\>jar -xvf chess.jar
   created: META-INF/
  inflated: META-INF/MANIFEST.MF
   created: chess/
 extracted: chess/Chess.java
 extracted: chess/ChessGUI.java
   created: chess/images/
 extracted: chess/images/board.bmp
```

The command simply extracts the JAR file to the current working directory. Now you can edit the files and repackage them if need be.

Examining the Basic Manifest File

The manifest file can be thought of as a file that contains meta data information about the JAR file it belongs to. By using the manifest file, you can version control, digitally sign, and seal the JAR files, packages, and extensions. When you first create your JAR file, if you didn't specify the -M option, a default manifest will be created for you. The M option prevents the default manifest file from being created. The default manifest file looks something like this, depending on the version of Java you are using:

```
Manifest-Version: 1.0
Created-By: 1.5.0 (Sun Microsystems Inc.)
```

The manifest file is broken up into two general parts: a main section and an individuals section where information about different files or packages can be listed. You don't have to list every file you have in the JAR file in the manifest file. In fact, you don't have to list any unless you plan to sign particular files in the JAR file. If you do, then those files must be listed.

Information in the manifest is broken up by name-value pair entries. The colon (:) character is used to separate the name from the value. This is similar to property files except for, in property files, the delimiter is an equals (=) sign. Any attributes that Java can't understand are ignored, but the attributes can still be used by the application. Therefore, these attributes are sometimes referred to as application-specific attributes. The following table describes several of the most common main attributes you will run across and gives a brief description of each.

Attribute	Description
Manifest-Version	The value of this attribute is the manifest file version.
Created-By	Generated by the JAR tool, this is the version of Java that was used to create the JAR. It also includes the name of the vendor who created the Java implementation.
Signature-Version	The value of this attribute contains the signature version of the JAR file and must contain a valid version number string with this specific format: digit+{.digit+}*
Class-Path	The class loader uses this value to create an internal search path that will look for extensions or libraries that this application needs. URLs are separated by spaces.
Main-Class	This attribute is needed if you are creating a self-executing JAR file. You need to specify the name of the class file that contains the main method. When you specify the name, do not include the .class extension, or your JAR will not execute.
Sealed	This attribute has only two possible values: true or false. If true, all the packages in the JAR file are sealed unless they are defined individually to be different.

Though the manifest is not a very exciting file to read about, it definitely is worth exploring so that you have a general understanding of the power and flexibility it provides JAR files with.

Examining Applets and JARs

One of the most common uses for JAR files is to bundle applet code inside of JAR files and make them accessible, like any other applet via a Web browser. Because of this feature, a special attribute called an extension in the manifest can be used to incorporate other packages in your applets. For more information on applets, see the "Analyzing Applets" section within this chapter.

Here is a list of the extension attributes that can be used to optimize your applets.

Attribute	Description
Extension-List	This attribute is where you list the optional packages that you would like to include in your applets. The package names should be separated by a single space.
(extension)-Extension-Name	The unique name of the package that the Java plug-in will use to determine if the package is installed is stored in this attribute.
(extension)-Specification-Version	This attribute lets the Java plug-in know which is the minimum version required of the package to use.
(extension)-Implementation-Version	This attribute lets the Java plug-in know which is the minimal version of the package that is required. If the version is too old, the plug-in will attempt to download a newer version of the package.
(extension)-Implementation-Vendor-Id	This attribute is used to assign a vendor ID to the optional package. Again, the Java plug-in will compare the vendor IDs to make sure it is getting the correct optional package.
(extension)-Implementation-URL	In order for the Java plug-in to know where to get the latest version of the package, this attribute would have to be set with the URL that tells the Java plug-in where to download the latest optional package.

Signing JAR Files

Signing JAR files is important for security-aware applications. It ensures that the JAR file has not been tampered with and the file is from the original author. JAR files are signed using a special utility tool called jarsigner, which can be found in your JAVA_HOME/BIN directory. JAR files can also be signed by using the java.security API via code. The jarsigner tool signs the JAR files by accessing a keystore that has been created by the keytool utility that is used to create public and private keys, issue certificate requests, import certificate replies, and determine if public keys belonging to third parties are trusted. The private key is used to sign the JAR file by the jarsigner tool, and only people who know the private key's password can sign the JAR file with it.

When a JAR file is signed by the jarsigner tool, all of the entries in the META-INF directory are signed. Even nonsignature-related files will be signed. Generally speaking, signature-related files end in the following extensions: *.RSA, *.SF, *.DSA, and SIG-*.

You can sign the JAR file using the Java.security API; however, compared to using the jarsigner tool, there will be a lot more work for you to do. When a JAR file is successfully signed, it must contain an updated manifest file, signature file, and signature block file. Entries for each file signed are created in the manifest file and look like the following example:

```
Name: com/wrox/SampleSigned.class
SHA1-Digest: fcavHwerE23Ff4355fdsMdS=
```

Now that you know the theory about JAR signing, it is time to show you a concrete example of how to sign a JAR and use all the wonderful tools that the Java SDK provides you with. Note that all these tests will not be with valid certificates or keystores; rather, it will be example keystores that you will create for testing purposes. This is great when you need to develop applications that require you to sign JAR files but don't have access to a certificate or keystore. The following example will show you how to use the keytool to generate a keystore and create a self-signed test certificate that you can use with the jartool to sign the chess.jar file that you created earlier in this chapter.

The first thing you want to do is create a keystore that you can use for creating a self-signed certificate. The following are the steps involved in generating the key:

1. Execute the keytool as shown. This will create a myKeystore file that will contain your key:

```
C:\>keytool -genkey -keystore myKeystore -alias myself
```

2. It will prompt you to enter a password for the keystore. Simply enter **password**:

```
Enter keystore password:  password
```

3. Next, you will be asked to fill in several lines of data about yourself. Here is what you enter to generate the key:

```
What is your first and last name?
  [Unknown]:  John Doe
What is the name of your organizational unit?
  [Unknown]:  IT
What is the name of your organization?
  [Unknown]:  Wrox
What is the name of your City or Locality?
  [Unknown]:  Springfield
What is the name of your State or Province?
  [Unknown]:  Ohio
What is the two-letter country code for this unit?
  [Unknown]:  US
Is CN=John Doe, OU=IT, O=Wrox, L=Springfield, ST=Ohio, C=US correct?
  [no]:  Yes
```

4. The last step is to enter a password for the private key. Here, you'll see the word *password* entered again:

```
Enter key password for <myself>
        (RETURN if same as keystore password):  password
```

Your new myKeystore file should be generated. You can open it up and view it in a text editor if you want, but the majority of the contents are encrypted. Even though you have a keystore, you still cannot sign a JAR file until you have a certificate that you can use for signing. Fortunately, the keytool is able to generate a self-signed certificate for you. This is simply done by issuing the following command:

```
C:\>keytool -selfcert -alias myself -keystore myKeystore
```

This command will prompt you for your keystore password. When you created the keystore, you made it using the word *password* as your password so that is what you should enter. This command can sometimes take a minute or two to complete, depending on your system:

```
Enter keystore password:  password
```

You now have a certificate and are ready to sign the JAR file. However, how do you know for sure that the certificate and the keystore are okay? The easiest way is to issue a keytool command with the option -list on the command line. This will display the contents of the keystore. Here is the output of the command:

```
C:\>keytool -list -keystore myKeystore
Enter keystore password:  password
```

Again, you have to enter your password to access the information in the keystore. The output after entering your password is shown in the following example:

```
Keystore type: jks
Keystore provider: SUN

Your keystore contains 1 entry

myself, Jul 21, 2004, keyEntry,
Certificate fingerprint (MD5): 96:0B:2C:20:EA:DB:87:7A:64:DA:9F:68:21:85:B6:9A
```

The output shows the type of keystore you are using, the provider, and the certificate fingerprint. If you get the above printout, you are ready to sign the JAR file. In order to sign the JAR file, you must now use the jarsigner tool. Taking the keystore you generated earlier, issue the following command at a command prompt:

```
C:\>jarsigner -keystore myKeystore chess.jar myself
Enter Passphrase for keystore: password

Warning: The signer certificate will expire within six months.
```

You have now successfully signed your first JAR file! To verify that the jarsigning tool successfully signed the JAR file that you specified, extract the JAR file and review its contents. You should now see two new files in the JAR file: one called Myself.dsa and the other called Myself.sf. The .dsa (digital signature) file is unreadable, but the .sf file can be read. The contents of it are shown in the following example:

```
Signature-Version: 1.0
Created-By: 1.5.0 (Sun Microsystems Inc.)
SHA1-Digest-Manifest-Main-Attributes: XpKykodQ7e3bKKW8wqLFO8VocOU=
SHA1-Digest-Manifest: eL4xJ2eU5oyO7h4VVYW0hs1pEj0=

Name: chess/images/board.bmp
SHA1-Digest: wvxwx9Dqd+jbKoe8e7raVxSfNzI=

Name: chess/ChessGUI.java
SHA1-Digest: JlWKkQ915/82bHxMdf4nzrmphH0=

Name: chess/Chess.java
SHA1-Digest: Y4jUlkFH64RojRERTRBEIZRC+uc=
```

These three new entries show the signature for each of the files that were signed by the jarsigner. These entries are now also shown in the manifest.mf file:

```
Manifest-Version: 1.0
Created-By: 1.5.0(Sun Microsystems Inc.)

Name: chess/images/board.bmp
SHA1-Digest: 2jmj7l5rSw0yVb/vlWAYkK/YBwk=

Name: chess/ChessGUI.java
SHA1-Digest: 2jmj7l5rSw0yVb/vlWAYkK/YBwk=

Name: chess/Chess.java
SHA1-Digest: 2jmj7l5rSw0yVb/vlWAYkK/YBwk=
```

Another way to verify that the jarsigner signed the JAR file correctly is to run the jarsigner tool with the -verify option on the JAR file you want to verify. So, go ahead and issue the following command on the JAR file you just signed:

```
C:\>jarsigner -verbose -verify chess.jar
```

You should see the following output if it was successful:

```
           289 Wed July 21 21:28:58 EDT 2004 META-INF/MANIFEST.MF
           410 Wed July 21 21:28:58 EDT 2004 META-INF/MYSELF.SF
          1008 Wed July 21 21:28:58 EDT 2004 META-INF/MYSELF.DSA
             0 Wed July 21 13:36:18 EDT 2004 META-INF/
             0 Wed July 21  13:27:02 EDT 2004 chess/
sm           0 Wed July 21  13:26:32 EDT 2004 chess/Chess.java
sm           0 Wed July 21  13:26:42 EDT 2004 chess/ChessGUI.java
             0 Wed July 21 13:27:14 EDT 2004 chess/images/
sm           0 Wed July 21 13:27:08 EDT 2004 chess/images/board.bmp

  s = signature was verified
  m = entry is listed in manifest
  k = at least one certificate was found in keystore
  i = at least one certificate was found in identity scope

jar verified.
```

If the validation failed, the jarsigner tool would either throw a security exception, or, if the JAR file was not signed at all, it would send a message back stating that the JAR file is unsigned (signature missing or not parsable).

If you have made it through all of these steps, congratulations! You now know how to sign your own JAR files. This is critical when you need to ensure security on a JAR file. JAR files are generally signed when using Java Web Start applications and especially applets, but signing can definitely be done for all the JAR files you create.

JAR files can also be signed by multiple people. What will happen is the signatures for each of the people who ran the jarsigner tool will be stored in the META-INF directory just as is the case when one person signs it. You can even sign the JAR file with different versions of the JDK so that there are a lot of security options you can do using the tools that have been mentioned for signing JAR files and creating keystores. Before moving on, take a closer look at the options that can be used with the jarsigner tool.

Option	Description
keystore <url>	This option is required when signing a JAR file and will default to the .keystore file in your user.home directory if you do not specify the keystore file to use. You can specify a full path and filename of the keystore file for the URL parameter.
storepass <password>	This is used to supply the password that is required to access the keystore you plan to use when signing your JAR file.
storetype <storetype>	This is used to specify the keystore type to be used. The security .properties file has an entry called keystore.type, and the jarsigner tool will default to that value if no storetype is provided.
keypass <password>	This is your password for your private key if it is different from the store password. If you don't supply this option, you will be prompted for the password, if necessary.
sigfile <filename>	This specifies the base of the filename to use for generating the .sf and .dsa files. This option allows you to override the default values generated by the jarsigner tool.
signedjar <filename>	You can specify another name for the JAR file that will be signed. If you don't specify a name, the JAR file you are issuing the command on is overwritten. For example, you could use chess_secure.jar for the name if you want to have signed and unsigned copies of chess.jar.
verify <jarfile>	This is an option for verifying that the JAR file is signed properly.
verbose	Verbose tells the jarsigner tool to output more information during the signing process to help with debugging issues.
certs	This option should be used with verbose and verify together. It will display certificate information for each signer of the JAR file.
tsa <url>	This allows you to specify the location of the Time-Stamping Authority.

Examining the JAR Index Option

Downloading JAR files that are required by applets can be slow and painful, and searching them for the appropriate classes they contain used to be very linear. Linear searching of a JAR file for its class can result in slow performance, wasted bandwidth, and waiting too long to initiate a download of a JAR file the applet may be missing. With the JARIndex algorithm, all the JAR files in an applet can be stored into an index file, which thus makes class loading times much faster — especially in determining what needs to be downloaded.

The jar tool has a new option, -i, which means index. This option will generate index information about the classes, packages, and resources that exist inside the JAR file. This makes access times much quicker. The information is stored in a small text file under the META-INF directory called INDEX.LIST. When the JAR is accessed by the class loader, it reads the INDEX.LIST file into a hash map that will contain all the files and package names in the hash map. Instead of searching linearly in the JAR file for the class file or resource that the class loader needs, it can now query the hash map, resulting in quicker access times. The INDEX.LIST file is always trusted by the class loader, so manipulating it manually is not wise. If you make a mistake and the class loader can't locate a resource or file, it will throw an InvalidJarIndexException so that you can capture the error and correct it. You can generate an index of the JAR file chess.jar that you created in previous examples by issuing the following command:

```
C:\>jar -iv chess.jar
```

The contents of the JAR file now contain an INDEX.LIST file in the META-INF directory:

```
C:\>jar -tf chess.jar
META-INF/INDEX.LIST
META-INF/
META-INF/MANIFEST.MF
chess/
chess/Chess.java
chess/ChessGUI.java
chess/images/
chess/images/board.bmp
```

The INDEX.LIST file contains the following information:

```
JarIndex-Version: 1.0

chess.jar
chess
chess/images
```

The INDEX.LIST file is simply text and is compressed inside the JAR file, so the memory footprint of the INDEX.LIST file is very light, to say the least.

Creating an Executable JAR

Java supports the ability to make JAR files executable. If a JAR file is executable, it can be run from a console or command prompt by typing:

```
java -jar jar-file-name
```

Also, if you are in Windows and your application is GUI-driven, simply double-click an executable JAR, and it will automatically run.

Making your JAR file executable is extremely simple. Just follow these procedures when creating your JAR file, and you will instantly be able to make it executable:

1. Compile all of your Java source code.

2. Create a manifest file, and enter in (at a bare minimum) the Manifest-Version and Main-Class properties. The Main-Class should point to the name of the class that contains the main method in the JAR file:

```
Manifest-Version: 1.0
Main-Class: Test
```

3. Create the JAR file using the following syntax:

```
Jar -cmf myManifest.mf test.jar *
```

4. Execute the JAR using the -jar option:

```
java -jar test.jar
```

The test.jar that was created should now execute without any problem if you specified the appropriate class in the manifest file that contains the main method for the application. It is extremely useful to make JAR files self-executing when the JAR files are GUI-driven applications and not based upon initial user input that would normally be supplied to the program via its ARG list in the main method of the application.

Analyzing Applets

Java applets are one of the very elite features of the Java programming language. Applets are programs that are designed to run within Web browsers that are compatible with and support Java. Applets can be embedded directly in HTML and can be used on Web pages to process user input or display information such as the current weather forecast. Applets can also exist outside of the Web browser and can have a much more robust feature set built into them like a standalone application would. The downside of making an applet that contains the same amount of features as say a standalone Swing application is that, the larger the applet, the more time it would take to download the applet for the user to use. The reason for this is that applets are downloaded every time a user accesses the Web page containing the applet. However, this is becoming less of an issue as the caching abilities of the Java plug-in improve with each new release of Java.

Basic Anatomy of an Applet

The basic anatomy of an applet is shown in the following class. You'll notice that there is no main method as is required by a standard Java application. Applets do not require such a method and only require you to extend the class that will be run from the Applet class. Instead of having a starting point method, applets have methods that are event-driven. There are five basic event-driven methods that are very useful when developing a basic applet: init, start, stop, destroy, and paint. These methods are demonstrated in the following code:

```
import javax.swing.*;
import java.awt.*;

public class Welcome extends JApplet {

    public void init() {
        System.out.prinln("Initializing Applet");
        repaint();
    }

    public void start() {
        System.out.println("Starting Applet");
        repaint();
    }

    public void paint(Graphics g) {
        g.drawString("Welcome to Java Applets!", 100, 50);
    }

    public void stop() {
        System.out.println("Stopping Applet");
        repaint();

    }

    public void destroy() {
        System.out.println("Destroying Applet");
        repaint();
    }

}
```

The five methods shown in the code above are described in the following table.

Method	Description
init	This method is used to initialize the applet when it is either loaded for the first time or reloaded thereafter.
start	After the applet has been initialized, the start method will be called. Here, you can fire off threads or begin execution of code.
stop	If the user leaves the Web page that the applet is on or exits the Web browser, this method is called. This allows you a chance to clean up code such as threads or code that is in the middle of being executed.
destroy	This method is your last chance to perform any final cleanup that is necessary before the applet is unloaded.
paint	The paint method is called any time the GUI needs to be updated based on users' interaction with the applet.

You do not have to override all of the above events to get a basic applet to work. For example, you could just override the `paint` method that displays a string containing the words, "Hello World!" and the applet would function just fine. There are also many other event methods that you can override that will allow you to react to user actions. For example, if you need to capture the mouse-down event, you could do this by overriding the method `mouseDown`. These are standard AWT events. In more advanced applet implementations, you would most likely use Swing to build your applet.

Packaging an Applet for Execution

Applets are not executed the same way as normal Java applications. They are generally embedded in an HTML page and executed by a Java-compatible browser such as Internet Explorer. Internet Explorer uses the Java plug-in to execute applet code. For development purposes, you can also execute applets that are embedded in HTML files by using the appletviewer command. For example:

```
appletviewer com/wrox/Welcome.html
```

The example above executes the applet that is embedded in the Welcome.html file. The HTML code is shown in the following example:

```
<HTML>
  <HEAD>
      <TITLE> Welcome to Java Applet </TITLE>
  </HEAD>
  <BODY>
    <APPLET CODE="Welcome.class" CODEBASE="com/wrox/" WIDTH=200 HEIGHT=50>
        <PARAM NAME="exampleParam" VALUE="whatever">
    </APPLET>
  </BODY>
</HTML>
```

The `<APPLET>` and `</APPLET>` tags designate the specific tags belonging to the applet that will be executing. The CODE attribute is used to reference the class name that contains the compiled applet class. The CODEBASE attribute is optional and specifies the base directory of where the applet's class is stored. If you do not use this attribute, then the directory where the HTML file resides is used as the base directory.

The `<PARAM>`and `</PARAM>` tags allow you to specify specific parameters that you may want to pass to the applet when it is loaded. These tags have two attributes: a NAME and a VALUE. The VALUE can then be retrieved in code via the `init` method of the applet as depicted in the following example:

```
public void init() {
    String sValue = getParameter("exampleParam");

    if (sValue != null) {
        // This will print out the value "whatever"
        System.out.println(sValue);
    }
}
```

The `getParameter` method is used to retrieve the value of a specified parameter. In this case, you are retrieving the exampleParam value and displaying it to the user.

Examining Applet Security

When creating an applet and deploying it, there are certain security restrictions that are enforced upon applets by the Java Environment. Applets usually cannot make network connections to any other machines except to that of the host they were downloaded from. Applets are generally restricted from writing or reading files from the client's machine. Also, applets cannot start applications that reside on the client's machine. These are not all the restrictions that are enforced on applets, but rather the most obvious. You can relax security restrictions by using SecurityObjects and Access Control Lists.

Applets cannot read or write files if they are considered untrusted. All applets that are downloaded are considered untrusted unless specified otherwise. In order to make an applet trusted, applets must be signed by an identity marked as trusted in your database of identities. Generally, your Web browser can also ask you if you trust the server that the applet is coming from. This aids in giving the applets more rights to your computer. When developing applets on your machine, they are generally trusted because they are being accessed from your local machine. So, you may not see the security restrictions that a remote user would see when downloading your applet. It is important that you understand what your applet users can and cannot do before deploying your applet. Refer to your Java documentation for more information on Applet Security specifics.

Exploring Web Applications

Web applications are applications that can be deployed on application servers as Web Archive files or, as the Java community calls them, WAR files. WAR files are the same format as JAR files, and, in fact, developers use the JAR tool to create WAR files. The difference is the directory structure and files that comprise the WAR file are different than a standard JAR. WAR files generally contain JSPs, servlets, HTML, images, audio files, XML files, and numerous other files that you may find while surfing a normal Web site.

So, static and dynamic content make up WAR files, but WAR files themselves are used for two basic reasons. One is to be front-end presentation oriented, concentrating heavily on user experience. The second is a service-oriented approach, which means that the WAR file is used to provide a service to other applications that are calling it. The most common term used for this type of Web application is *Web Service*. You can have an enormous architecture that is comprised of Web Services that may use the *Simple Object Access Protocol* (otherwise known as SOAP) to communicate. If you add security on top of the SOAP layer, you will have a very complicated system to package and deploy because you will need to manage certificates, keystores, signed JARs, SSL, and other security-related components and protocols. Therefore, WAR files can become much more difficult to deploy in enterprise-level usages.

However, in its simplest form, WAR files are very easy to use and are a dream for packaging and compressing Web site resources that are comprised of static and dynamic data like form processing or shopping carts. The WAR file format allows the whole Web site to be portable and makes it very easy to deploy on other vendor application servers that are J2EE compliant.

Examining the WAR Directory Structure

As stated previously, there are differences between a JAR file and a WAR file. WAR files have additional file and directory structures that are used for deploying the WAR file on to the application server of choice. Figure 14-3 is an example of a Web application that is deployed on Tomcat.

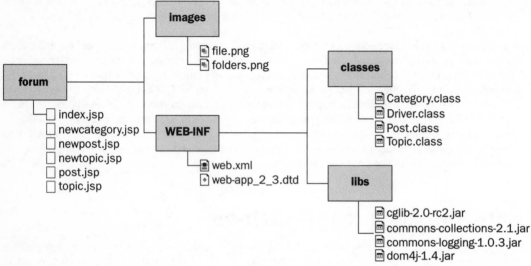

Figure 14-3

The above is the forum example Web application directory structure that was used in Chapter 6. This file is named forum.war, and, at the root level, it contains all the JSPs needed for the user interface components. The images directory simply stores images that are used by the JSPs. The WEB-INF is the important directory and is the directory that distinguishes a WAR file from a JAR file. The web.xml in the directory is a required file and is officially called the Web application deployment descriptor. The classes directory is where you would store your compiled classes that can be used by JSPs or servlets. The libs directory contains all the necessary JAR files to make your Web application work.

Understanding the WAR Deployment Descriptor

The Web application deployment descriptor is used to configure your Web application. In this example, this deployment descriptor is called web.xml. The deployment descriptor contains the following basic XML elements that are configurable and must appear in this order.

Element	Description
icon	The icon element has two child elements that represent the small icon and the large icon for a GUI tool.
display-name	This element contains a short name this is intended for tools to use. It doesn't have to be unique.
description	This element is used to describe information to the parent element and is used in a number of different elements.

Element	Description
distributable	By having the distributable element present, you are signifying that the Web application is programmed to be distributed in a servlet container.
context-param	This element is used to initialize a Web application's servlet context.
filter	Filter elements are specifically used to map servlets or URL patterns for Web applications.
filter-mapping	The filter-mapping element is used by the container to decide which filters to map a request to.
listener	This element and its subelements are used to declare Web application listener beans. You simply specify the class that is the listener bean.
servlet	The servlet element and its subelements are used to designate a specific class or JSP as a servlet and to provide specific configurations for that servlet.
servlet-mapping	This element simply defines a mapping between a servlet and a specific URL pattern.
session-config	This is a useful element for configuring the session information for a Web application.
mime-mapping	The mime-mapping element allows you to map between a file extension and a mime type.
welcome-file-list	This is the element that is used to determine the first page to be displayed when users hit your Web application.
error-page	When errors occur, the mapping in this element allows you to map and error code to an error page. Very handy.
taglib	You should use this element to describe the JSP tag library.
resource-ref	This element allows you to specify external resources to use in your Web application.
security-constraint	With this element you can associate security restraints with a particular resource.
login-config	This element is used to specify the authentication method to be used for the Web application as well as any authentication constraints.
security-role	This element allows you to define security roles for your Web application.
env-entry	This element is used to specify environment entries that can be picked up by classes, JSPs, and so forth that exist in your Web application.

Though the table explains the different elements and attributes used when creating a deployment descriptor, it can be confusing to try and understand how to use them. The following is a sample web.xml file for Tomcat that will hopefully shed some light on how to appropriately use some of the elements discussed in the previous table:

```
<?xml version="1.0" encoding="ISO-8859-1"?>

<!DOCTYPE web-app
    PUBLIC "-//Sun Microsystems, Inc.//DTD Web Application 2.3//EN"
    " http://java.sun.com/dtd/web-app_2_3.dtd">
<web-app>
```

Deployment descriptors are XML files; therefore, they require a standard prolog that is displayed in the previous example:

```
    <display-name>HelloWAR</display-name>
    <description> HelloWAR </description>


<servlet>
    <servlet-name>HelloServlet</servlet-name>
    <servlet-class>HelloServlet</servlet-class>
    <load-on-startup>1</load-on-startup>
</servlet>
```

The `<servlet>` element allows you to specify information about a servlet that exists in the Web application. In this case, I am referring to the servlet, HelloServlet. The `<load-on-startup>` attribute signifies that the application server should load the servlet upon startup:

```
<!--Creating mime type mappings -->
<mime-mapping>
    <extension>txt</extension>
    <mime-type>text/plain</mime-type>
</mime-mapping>
<mime-mapping>
    <extension>html</extension>
    <mime-type>text/html</mime-type>
</mime-mapping>
<mime-mapping>
    <extension>htm</extension>
    <mime-type>text/html</mime-type>
</mime-mapping>
<mime-mapping>
    <extension>gif</extension>
    <mime-type>image/gif</mime-type>
</mime-mapping>
<mime-mapping>
    <extension>jpg</extension>
    <mime-type>image/jpeg</mime-type>
</mime-mapping>
```

The `<mime-mapping>` element contains two attributes called `<mime-type>` and `<extension>`. These are used specifically for mapping mime types to file extensions:

```
<welcome-file-list>
    <welcome-file>index.html</welcome-file>
</welcome-file-list>
```

One of the most common elements, `<welcome-file-list>`, is shown in the previous example. This element has an attribute called `<welcome-file>` that lets you specify the file to be loaded when a user first accesses your Web application:

```
<security-constraint>
      <web-resource-collection>
            <web-resource-name>Hello View</web-resource-name>
            <url-pattern>/hello.jsp</url-pattern>
      </web-resource-collection>
      <auth-constraint>
            <role-name>tomcat</role-name>
      </auth-constraint>
</security-constraint>

  <login-config>
      <auth-method>BASIC</auth-method>
      <realm-name>Hello View</realm-name>
  </login-config>

  <security-role>
      <description>
        An example role defined in "conf/tomcat-users.xml"
      </description>
      <role-name>tomcat</role-name>
  </security-role>

</web-app>
```

The `<security-constraint>` element contains attributes that allow you to assign roles to specific Web resources. In this example, the role of Tomcat is being assigned to hello.jsp. This means that only users with the specified role of Tomcat can view the JSP. The `<security-role>` element shows you how to define a role in the Web application deployment descriptor.

Packaging Enterprise Java Beans

Chapter 10 discusses the various classes that are needed to develop different types of EJBs and also has a very good loan calculator example that will help you get your feet wet with EJBs. The inherent problem with deploying EJBs is that the EJB specification isn't specific enough about the deployment process and allows the vendors of application servers to interpret the art of deploying EJBs the way they see fit. Now, the vendors have an opportunity to interject their own proprietary deployment requirements. This makes it a painful experience if you want to move your EJBs from one vendor to another. So, the best advice is to simply read the specific documentation on the vendor of choice that you want to house your EJBs.

All is not lost though in terms of deployment standardization. There is one common file that must exist in all EJBs, and that is the *ejb-jar.xml* that resides in the META-INF directory of your EJBs' JAR file. The ejb-jar.xml file is the basic EJB deployment descriptor that must be used by the EJB container to locate the necessary classes, interfaces, security restrictions, and transaction management support. The ejb-jar.xml file will usually coexist with the vendor's application server deployment descriptor. For example, if you were to use JBoss as your application server, you would have to also configure a jboss.xml file with your EJBs. Chapter 10 has a very good demonstration and explanation of what type of information is contained in the ejb-jar.xml file. It is recommended that you review the examples that are in Chapter 10 for specific information on how to deploy and package an EJB application.

Inspecting Enterprise Archives

Once you have developed your EJBs and WARs, you should have all the components of a full application — from the business logic (and maybe database logic) to the user interface for the Web. You may have just a couple files or perhaps a large number of files. Either way, you might be looking at your application and wondering if there is a way to tidy up that directory. If you have multiple applications that use distinct EJBs and WARs, then you're almost definitely thinking "there must be some way to easily group and distinguish these two applications." You would be correct in thinking this, and this is where Enterprise Archives (EARs) come into the picture. Even though mistakenly called Enterprise Applications at times, this name might be more meaningful, because inside an EAR file resides all your EJBs and WARs.

An EAR file has its own descriptor file, much like EJBs and WARs. Other than that the directory structure of an EAR is arbitrary, you can develop any scheme that best suits your application. An EAR file may look like Figure 14-4. Note that there is one WAR file but multiple EJB JAR files packaged inside the EAR. This grouping is useful to make your application a single logical unit.

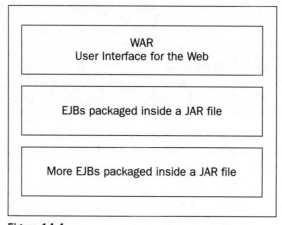

Figure 14-4

The EAR Descriptor File

The descriptor file is named application.xml and is located in the META-INF directory in the EAR file. The main component of this file is the module element. The following is an example of this file:

```
<?xml version="1.0" encoding="UTF-8"?>

<application xmlns="http://java.sun.com/xml/ns/j2ee"
             xmlns:xsi="http://www.w3.org/2001/XMLSchema-instance"
             xsi:schemaLocation="http://java.sun.com/xml/ns/j2ee
             http://java.sun.com/xml/ns/j2ee/application_1_4.xsd"
             version="1.4">

   <display-name>Example EAR file</display-name>
   <description>Simple example</description>
```

```
    <module>
      <ejb>ejb1.jar</ejb>
    </module>

    <module>
      <ejb>ejb2.jar</ejb>
    </module>

    <module>
      <web>
        <web-uri>mainUI.war</web-uri>
        <context-root>web</context-root>
      </web>
    </module>
  </application>
```

Each instance of the module element specifies a particular module to load. This module can be an EJB (using the ejb element), a Web application (using the Web element), a connector (using the connector element), or a Java client module (using the Java element). The context-root element for Web applications specifies the root directory to use for the execution of the Web application.

Deployment Scenario

The previous section described a straightforward approach to packaging and using EAR files. What happens, though, if you have multiple applications that all depend upon some central component? Take a look at Figure 14-5. In this scenario, a second EAR file depends upon a component packaged in the first.

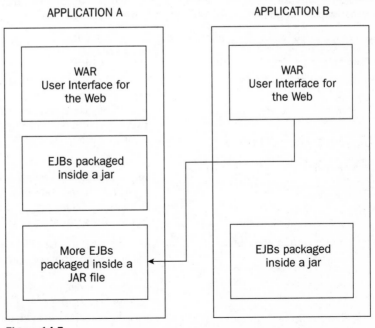

Figure 14-5

Though this scenario may seem like it solves the problem, it just ends up creating new deployment problems. First, application A has no dependency on application B, but the opposite is not true. If application A were to fail or be brought down for maintenance, then application B would also be down. Second, you have to create some way of adding the stub code to application B that is necessary to utilize the EJBs in application A. This is not addressed by the J2EE specification.

Another option is to package all these components into the same EAR file, effectively combining multiple applications into a single file. Of course, this approach has problems, too. In the real world, two different applications will have different deployment and uptime requirements. One application might have to always be available to its users, but the other one might have different memory requirements or only need to be up during the night. This makes packaging both applications within the same EAR file a poor choice due to the disparate requirements.

Another significant problem whenever there is a shared component between two or more applications is version incompatibility. Because the shared component usually has a single owning entity, classes inside the shared component might change method signatures, and this may break other applications that weren't expecting the method to change.

So, any route you choose seems to have its own set of problems. There is one other deployment scenario. You can take the shared component and place it inside each application's EAR file. This makes one EAR file totally separate from another. This still presents a deployment problem though. What happens when the API changes but the component used by all EARs is only updated in one EAR? This scenario makes it easy for different EAR files to all have different versions of this common component.

The basic approach you should take when deciding how to package your various enterprise applications and shared components is to consider each deployment scenario and pick the one that will (hopefully) cause the fewest nightmares for you in the future. Consult the following table for a summary of these deployment scenarios and rough guidelines as to when to use each one.

Scenario	When to Use
Shared component external to EARs	— Applications have different runtime requirements. — API of shared component is not expected to change, or it is easy to update all applications that use the shared API.
Shared component packaged in a single EAR	— Applications have compatible uptime requirements and system requirements. — API of shared component is not expected to change, or it is easy to update all applications that use the shared API.
Placing shared component in each EAR	— Each EAR is on a different system, and the systems cannot communicate with each other. — The shared component is expected to stay relatively the same over time, or updating each EAR with a new version is easy.

Jumping into Java Web Start

Web-based solutions have become the standard for delivering client/server applications even though Web browsers were never intended to be used to deliver anything other than static content. Developers continue to stretch the bounds of Web technologies in search of the best solution. Applets appeared to be the answer because they delivered such a strong feature set and were able to be embedded in a Java-supporting Web browser. Applets still require a significant amount of download time and are still not as rich as a thick client is. Sun is again proving to be very innovative and removing the limitations of browser-based technology by introducing a solid, rich client technology called *Java Web Start*. Java Web Start is based on the Java Network Launch Protocol (JNLP) and the Java 2 platform. Java Web Start was introduced as a standard component in Java 1.4. Because of Java Web Start's unique architecture, it only takes one click to download the application you wish to launch from a Web browser. The link that you click is the JNLP file that tells Java to launch Web Start and download the application.

This section will teach you how to package and deploy a Java Web Start application through an example of an all-time favorite game, tic-tac-toe.

Examining the TicTacToe Example

This example goes into detail on how to create, package, deploy, and launch a Java Web Start application. The game is not exceptionally smart and could be enhanced by adding an artificial intelligence (AI) capability. An AI would have been overkill for the purpose of this demonstration. The following table is a list of files that make up the TicTacToe example.

File	Description
tictactoe.jnlp	This is the Java Network Launch Protocol file that contains all the specific attributes to tell Java Web Start how to launch the application. It is also the file that the user clicks on to execute the application.
ttt.htm	This HTML file contains a link to the tictactoe.jnlp file used to launch the application.
TTTMain.java	This is the source file with the main method in it that drives the application.
TTTGui.java	This file contains all the Swing code necessary to handle the user interaction with the game.
TTTLogic.java	This file contains all the game logic and is used to determine who wins, whose move it is, and what positions are open on the board. This is the perfect spot to add an artificial intelligence capability.
tictactoe.jar	This is the signed JAR file that contains the compiled code and will be launched by Java Web Start.

The tictactoe.jar file, the ttt.htm file, and the tictactoe.jnlp must all be deployed to a Web server so that the user can download the application. When the user clicks the link that is in the ttt.htm file, the following window is displayed to the user (see Figure 14-6).

Figure 14-6

This window is displayed until the application is downloaded. Once it is downloaded, the application is launched, and the user can begin using it. If there is no specific code to tie the application to network use, the user can also use the application offline! Try that with an applet! The TicTacToe application shown in Figure 14-7 appears as any normal thick client would.

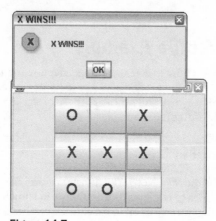

Figure 14-7

This is what makes Java Web Start so powerful and the technology of the future. It is just now starting to catch on in the world of distributed computing and is proving to have all the security features required to be a strong enterprise solution to complicated applications that require heavy client-side processing. Also, by moving the processing to the client, you eliminate the load on the server.

Examing the TicTacToe.JNLP

Before you actually create and deploy the JNLP file, you do have to make sure that whatever Web server you are using is configured to properly handle the JNLP mime type. To do this, simply add an entry in your deployment descriptor for the JNLP extension. In Tomcat, you can do this in the WEB-INF/web.xml file with the following XML entry:

```
<mime-mapping>
    <extension>jnlp</extension>
    <mime-type>application/x-java-jnlp-file</mime-type>
</mime-mapping>
```

Now that you are sure the Web server can handle the JNLP extension, you can create the JNLP file:

```
<?xml version="1.0" encoding="utf-8"?>
<jnlp
  spec="1.0+"
  codebase="http://localhost/ttt"
  href="tictactoe.jnlp">
```

The `<spec>` attribute is used to denote the JNLP specification version. The next attribute, `<codebase>`, is used as a base directory to locate resources on the Web server. The final attribute, `href`, is used to point to the JNLP file:

```
<information>
   <title>TIC TAC TOE</title>
   <vendor>TTT Team</vendor>
   <homepage href="http://localhost/ttt/ttt.htm"/>

   <description>TICTACTOE GAME</description>

   <description kind="short">
      A demo of the capabilities of JAVA WebStart.
   </description>

   <offline-allowed/>
</information>
```

The `<information>` element supplies Java Web Start with general information about the application. It has a `<title>` attribute to signify the title of the application. It also has a `<vendor>` attribute to denote the company, organization, or supplier of the application. There is also a `<homepage>` attribute that is used to tell the person where to go to get more information on the application. The `<description>` attribute is used to give the application a description. There is also a short `<description>` attribute if you need to supply one; finally, there is the `<offline-allowed>` attribute that signifies the application can be used offline. If this attribute is not supplied, the application cannot be launched without being first connected to the network:

```
<security>
   <all-permissions/>
</security>
<resources>
  <j2se version="1.5"/>
  <jar href="tictactoe.jar"/>
</resources>
<application-desc main-class="com.wrox.TTTMain"/>
</jnlp>
```

The security of a Java Web Start application is the same as that of an applet. It is very restrictive unless instructed otherwise. You are specifying an `<all-permissions/>` attribute that gives the application full access to the client's machine. The `<resources>` element defines attributes that are needed in order to run properly. The `<j2se>` attribute signifies which Java platform to run the application on. The `<jar>` attribute tells Java Web Start which classes are required to run the application. Keep in mind that there can be multiple `<jar>` tags depending on your needs. The final element is the `<application-desc>` element that is instructing Java Web Start to run the com.wrox.TTTMain class. The importance of the `<application-desc>` tag is to let Java Web Start know that it is to run an application and not an applet:

```
<html>
<head>
<meta http-equiv="Content-Language" content="en-us">
<meta http-equiv="Content-Type" content="text/html; charset=windows-1252">

<title>TIC TAC TOE GAME!</title>
</head>

<body topmargin="0" leftmargin="0" link="#000080" vlink="#000080">

<center><A HREF="tictactoe.jnlp">Click Here to Launch TICTACTOE Game</A></center>

</body>
</html>
```

The ttt.htm file is shown in the previous example and is illustrated to teach you how to set up an HTML file to launch a Java Web Start application. As you can see, all that is required is to have the HREF tag point to the JNLP file.

TTTMain.java

The TTTMain class is the simple driver class for the application. Java Web Start calls this class to launch the application:

```
public class TTTMain {
 public static void main(String[] args) {
    TTTLogic tLogic = new TTTLogic();
    TTTGui tg = new TTTGui(tLogic);

    // Set the GUI visible
    tg.setVisible(true);
 }
}
```

This class creates the TTTLogic object that is to be used by the GUI. So, when users interact with the application, the GUI can track their interactions using this object.

TTTLogic.java

This class contains the most complicated code for the example. It keeps track of player moves, player turns, player positions, and if there is a winner or not. There is a member variable called m_nBoard, which is a two-dimensional array that always keeps track of which squares are occupied on the board:

```
public class TTTLogic {
 int [][]m_nBoard;
 int m_nX, m_nO;

 boolean m_bXTurn;
```

The TTTLogic constructor sets the values for X and O in the m_nX and m_nO variables and sets the default to turn to X. Finally, it clears the board array by setting it with all zeros:

```
public TTTLogic() {

  m_nX = 1;
  m_nO = 2;

  m_bXTurn = true;

  // Initialize array
  m_nBoard = new int[3][3];

  // Clear the board
  for (int x = 0; x < 3; x++){
    for (int y = 0; y < 3; y++) {
      m_nBoard[x][y] = 0;
    }
  }
}
```

The getMarker method takes an x and y parameter. The x parameter represents a row, and the y parameter represents a column. The method will return the value for the particular square on the board that is requested. For example, an x value of 0 and a y value of 2 would result in the value of the upper-right corner square being returned:

```
public int getMarker(int x, int y) {
  return m_nBoard[x][y];
}
```

The setMarker is the opposite of getMarker and actually sets the marker value of a specified square. It knows which mark to put in by determining whose turn it is using the this.getXTurn method. Once the marker has been set, the method advances the turn to the next player:

```
public boolean setMarker(int x, int y) {
  int nIsFree = 0;

  nIsFree = getMarker(x, y);

  if (nIsFree == 0) {
    if (this.getXTurn() == true) {
      m_nBoard[x][y] = m_nX;
      this.setXTurn(false);
    } else {
      m_nBoard[x][y] = m_nO;
      this.setXTurn(true);
    }
```

```
    return true;
  }
  return false;
}
```

The getWinner method is a very large method that determines who the winner is by executing different checks on the board. The checking for the O winner was purposely removed to save space in the chapter:

```
public int getWinner() {
  // 1 = X
  // 2 = O
  int nWinner = 0;
  int nCount = 0;

  // -------- CHECK FOR an X winner
  // check the across boxes first for X
  for (int x = 0; x < 3; x++){
    nCount = 0;
    for (int y = 0; y < 3; y++) {
      if (m_nBoard[x][y] == m_nX) {
        nCount++;
      } else {
        break;
      }
    }
    if (nCount == 3) {
      nWinner = m_nX; // X Wins!
      return nWinner;
    }
  }
```

So far, you have checked the across squares to see if there is a winner. If the winner is X, the value of m_nX is returned. Next, you will check the down squares and see if X has won:

```
  // check the down boxes first for X
  for (int y = 0; y < 3; y++){
    nCount = 0;
    for (int x = 0; x < 3; x++) {
      if (m_nBoard[x][y] == m_nX) {
        nCount++;
      } else {
        break;
      }
    }
    if (nCount == 3) {
      nWinner = m_nX; // X Wins!
      return nWinner;
    }
  }
```

Finally, you need to check diagonally to see if X has won. If not, then you will need to search to see if O has won:

```
           // Check Diagonals
           if (m_nBoard[0][0] == m_nX && m_nBoard[1][1] == m_nX &&
               m_nBoard[2][2] == m_nX) {

               nWinner = m_nX; // X Wins!
               return nWinner;
           } else if (m_nBoard[2][0] == m_nX && m_nBoard[1][1] == m_nX &&
                      m_nBoard[0][2] == m_nX) {
               nWinner = m_nX; // X Wins!
               return nWinner;
           }

           return nWinner;
       }
```

The method getXTurn is used to determine if it is player X's turn or not. The setXTurn allows you to set whether it is player X's turn or not:

```
public boolean getXTurn() {
    return m_bXTurn;
}
public void setXTurn(boolean bTurn) {
    m_bXTurn = bTurn;
}

}
```

TTTGui.java

The TTTGui is too big to display here, so what you are seeing is an example of what occurs when the button representing square 0,0 is pressed by the user. The same code exists for almost all other buttons with a few coordinate changes:

```
private javax.swing.JButton getJbtOne() {
    if (jbtOne == null) {
        jbtOne = new javax.swing.JButton();
        jbtOne.setName("jbtOne");
        jbtOne.setPreferredSize(new java.awt.Dimension(55,55));
        jbtOne.setText("");
        jbtOne.setFont(new java.awt.Font("Dialog", java.awt.Font.BOLD, 24));

        jbtOne.addActionListener(new java.awt.event.ActionListener() {
            public void actionPerformed(java.awt.event.ActionEvent e) {
                boolean bXTurn = m_TLogic.getXTurn();
                if (m_TLogic.setMarker(0,0)) {
                    if (bXTurn) {
                        jbtOne.setText("X");
                    } else {
                        jbtOne.setText("O");
                    }
                }
            }
```

When the button is pressed, the first thing that happens is the code saves the player's turn in the bXTurn variable and then tries to set the marker on the space. If setMarker is successful, the appropriate symbol is used to mark the square the user chose:

```
            int nWinner = m_TLogic.getWinner();

            if (nWinner != 0) {
                if (nWinner == 1) {
                    JOptionPane.showMessageDialog(null, "X WINS!!!",
                                "X WINS!!!", JOptionPane.OK_OPTION);
                } else {
                    JOptionPane.showMessageDialog(null, "O WINS!!!",
                                "O WINS!!!", JOptionPane.OK_OPTION);
                }
            }
        }
        });
    }
    return jbtOne;
}
```

Before the method is complete, it checks to see if it has a winner. If the user who clicked the square has won, the method will pop up a message box declaring the winner! The application must now be reset in order to play another game.

Summarizing Java Web Start

From the examples of code that you have seen, there is one step that wasn't mentioned — signing the JAR file. The necessary steps to sign JAR files are discussed under the JAR section of this chapter. To summarize, you should configure your Web server to understand requests for JNLP files. You'll then need to create the JNLP file that describes the application to be launched with Java Web Start. You should package your application in a JAR file and sign the JAR file using the jarsigner tool. Finally, you should create the HTML page that will be used to access your JNLP file. That's all that is needed to turn your application into a Java Web Start application!

Using ANT with Web Archives

ANT is an open source application used for generally building Java applications. It has a vast array of built-in configuration management functions that are configured through XML tags. Ant essentially is a tool to do away with the dreaded makefiles of the past that required programmers to write an enormous amount of fragile, shell-based commands that had to be flexible enough for the user's environment and demands. ANT uses Java to do its necessary work, and, instead of shell-based commands, ANT has a concept called *ANT tasks* that performs almost every configuration/build task a programmer could want. You can download the latest binary distribution of ANT from http://ant.apache.org.

Installing ANT

Once you have downloaded your ANT distribution of choice, you simply extract the file to a directory of choice. When ANT is exploded, it creates the following main directory structure that is illustrated and explained in the following diagram, Figure 14-8.

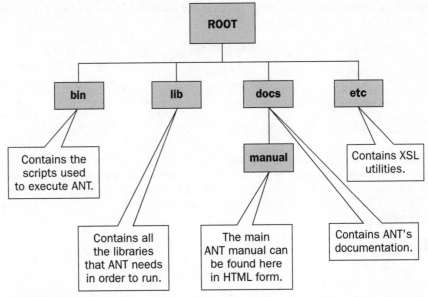

Figure 14-8

The main directory of interest should be the bin directory because this directory contains the scripts that execute ANT. You will need to configure your environment to be able to execute the ANT scripts from a console or command prompt. In order to do so, simply follow these three steps:

1. Set JAVA_HOME to point to the directory where your JDK is installed.

2. Create an environment variable called ANT_HOME, and set it to the directory that you have installed Ant to. Example: ANT_HOME= C:\apache-ant-1.6.2

3. Finally, add the ANT_HOME\bin directory to your PATH environment variable so that Ant can be accessible from any directory in any console window.

If you did not download a binary distribution of ANT, then you will have to consult the instructions that come with ANT on how to build the source code for the particular platform you are on.

Building Projects with ANT

ANT is extremely easy to build with once you understand the basics of what is involved with creating Ant build files. ANT requires you to create an XML file called a build file that contains a project element and at least one target element. Each target can have multiple task elements that can perform a variety of operations from deleting files to compiling source code. With ANT, you can incorporate property files that you can read in, and you can also access system properties at any time during the execution of the build file.

A basic ANT system for building a project generally consists of a simple build.xml file and sometimes a properties file for loading in specific settings like a location of a third-party JAR. The build.xml file will need to contain a project and a target element. Here is a quick example of the syntax of a very basic build.xml file that just displays a "Hello World!" message:

```
<project name="antTest" default="Hello" basedir=".">
  <description>A very simple build.xml file</description>

  <target name="Hello">
    <echo message="Hello World!"/>
  </target>
</project>
```

In order to run this example, you would change directory to the directory that contains the build.xml file from a console window and simply type **ant**. ANT will automatically look for the file named build.xml as a default. Once ANT finds the file, it executes it based on the default target supplied in the project element of the build file. In this case, the default target and only target is Hello. The output is shown in the following example:

```
C:\btest>ant
Buildfile: build.xml

Hello:
     [echo] Hello World!

BUILD SUCCESSFUL
Total time: 0 seconds
```

The ANT manual does a terrific job of explaining the different XML elements such as project, target, classpath, filesets, and so forth, so there isn't a need to explain them in-depth here. What is needed is to show you how to glue them all together. This next example will show you how to create a complete Web Archive (WAR) file using ANT. This example contains two files: a mybuild.properties file to contain the properties you will read in for Ant to use, and the staple build.xml file that is the main build file that Ant will execute. The following is the content of the mybuild.properties file:

```
# Xerces home directory
xerces.home  = C:\\xerces-2_6_2

# The name of the .jar file to create
jar.name     = myantwebapp.jar

# The name of the .war file to create
war.name     = myantwebapp.war
```

The first property shows a third-party tool location that you will need for compiling and packaging the source code. The next two properties list the name that you want the JAR and the final WAR file to be called. It's time now to dissect the complex build.xml file. This file is made up of four targets, three of which are dependent upon another target. When a dependency occurs in an ANT target, ANT must execute the dependency first. So, if target D is dependent on target C, and target C is dependent on target B, and target B is dependent on target A, ANT would execute the targets in the following order: A, B, C, then D:

```
<project name="MYANTWEBAPP" default="createWAR" basedir=".">
    <description>This a real world example of using ANT.</description>
```

The `<project>` tag defines a name for the project and requires you to supply a default target to execute. In this case, you want ANT to run the createWAR target first. The createWAR target has a dependency chain, as I explained in the A, B, C, and D target example. The basedir attribute is asking which directory it should use as a base for execution. The . signifies the current directory:

```
<property file="mybuild.properties"/>

<!-- set global properties for this build -->
<property name="src"        location="src"/>
<property name="jsps"       location="jsp"/>
<property name="build"      location="build"/>
<property name="dist"       location="dist"/>
```

Now, you are telling ANT to read in the properties from mybuild.properties and to also create four additional properties: src, jsps, build, and dist. These can now all be accessed by their property name with the following syntax — ${propertyname} — in the ANT build file:

```
<path id="everything">
    <fileset dir="${xerces.home}">
        <include name="xercesImpl.jar"/>
        <include name="xml-apis.jar"/>
    </fileset>
    <pathelement location="${build}"/>
</path>
```

The `<path>` tag will be used by the build file to incorporate the files in the path into a classpath that will be used to compile source code. Here, two Xerces jar files are being built into a path element named everything:

```
<target name="clean" description="Deletes the build and dist directories" >
    <delete dir="${build}"/>
    <delete dir="${dist}"/>
</target>
```

The first target, clean, gets executed first and simply deletes the build and distribution directories. The `<delete>` tag is an ANT task. ANT has a multitude of tasks that can perform many operations. Refer to the Ant manual for more information:

```
<target name="init" depends="clean">
    <mkdir dir="${build}"/>
    <mkdir dir="${dist}"/>
</target>
```

The second target, init, depends on clean. Once clean deletes the build and dist directories, the init target recreates them. These two targets ensure that the build and dist directories will be empty before you start compiling your source code:

```
<target name="createJAR" depends="init"
        description="Compiles source and creates new JAR" >

    <javac classpathref="everything" classpath="${src}" srcdir="${src}"
```

```
                                destdir="${build}"/>

        <mkdir dir="${dist}/lib"/>

        <echo message="Creating jar: ${dist}\lib\${jar.name}"/>
        <jar destfile="${dist}/lib/${jar.name}" includes="**/*.class"
             basedir="${build}" compress="true" index="true" update="true"/>
    </target>
```

The third target, createJAR, depends on init and uses the ANT task <javac> to compile any source code that is in the SRC directory. You should also take note that the classpathref references the path that was built earlier called everything. The <javac> task will use the *everything* path in its classpath for compiling the source files. After the files are compiled, a very handy Ant task called <jar> is used to create a JAR file into the lib directory that was created:

```
    <target name="createWAR" depends="createJAR">

        <copy preservelastmodified="true" overwrite="true"
                                         todir="${jsps}/WEB-INF/lib">
            <fileset dir="${dist}/lib">
                <include name="${jar.name}"/>
            </fileset>
        </copy>

        <mkdir dir="${dist}/war"/>

        <war destfile="${dist}/war/${war.name}" webxml="${jsps}/WEB-INF/web.xml"
                        update="true">

            <fileset dir="${jsps}" includes="*.html,*.jsp,*.doc"
                        excludes="*.jar,*.war"/>

            <webinf dir="${jsps}/WEB-INF" includes="*.wsdd,*.lst"/>
            <lib dir="${jsps}/WEB-INF/lib" includes="*.jar,*.war,*.zip"/>
            <zipfileset dir="${jsps}/images" prefix="images" excludes="*.psd"/>

        </war>
    </target>

</project>
```

The final target, createWAR, depends on createJAR and is used to create a WAR file. The JAR file was created and moved to the WAR files WEB-INF/lib directory because it has utilities that the WAR file needs. The other files, which you can see in the fileset, are then moved into position to create the WAR file. The WAR file is created using another handy ANT task called <WAR>.

This ANT build file example can now be run over and over every time you need to recompile and package your program. This example shows just how useful and easy it is to use ANT. If you need to replace Xerces with a new version, all that is required is a property change to mybuild.properties. However, this example barely touches on all the different ANT tasks that are available to you. The ANT manual that comes with the Ant distribution should explain all the tasks in great detail.

Summary

Packaging and deploying Java applications vary depending on the program you are currently working on. This chapter touched on the most popular types of Java applications that you will come across. It took you through the intricacies of the different Java archive files — JAR, WAR, and EAR — and kept going right into applet land. It also supplied you with a few helpful tools for managing your classpath and an explanation of already existing Java tools that can aid you in your packaging efforts such as the jarsigner and keytool tools.

This chapter discussed the great innovations of Java Web Start and how it can be the technology of the future for deploying thick, rich clients to users over browser-based technologies. Finally, this chapter examined the usefulness of ANT and how it can make a developer's building and configuration management woes a thing of the past.

References

[AMBLER] Ambler, Scott M. *Agile Modeling: Effective Practices for Extreme Programming and the Unified Process*. Indianapolis, IN: John Wiley & Sons, 2002.

[BECK] Beck, Kent. *Extreme Programming Explained*. Boston, MA: Addison Wesley, 1999.

[FOWLER] Fowler, Martin. *Refactoring*. Boston, MA: Addison Wesley, 1999.

[LARMAN] Larman, Craig. *Applying UML and Patterns: An Introduction to Object-Oriented Analysis and Design and the Unified Process*, second edition, Upper Saddle River, NJ: Prentice Hall PTR, 2002.

Index

D

W

WAR (Web ARchive File)
in AXIS, for Web services, 533
creating, 104, 658
definition of, 639–640
deploying, 640–643
in EAR (Enterprise Archive), 644–646
`warning()` **method,** `Logger` **class, 33**
Waterfall methodology, 82–83, 86–87
weak global references to objects, 425, 427–429
weather example
JavaBean for, 531–532
WeatherGetter class, 532–533
without Web services, 523–526
Web services for, 533–540
Web application archive. *See* **WAR**
Web applications. *See also* **Model 1 Architecture;**
    Model 2 Architecture
applets
definition of, 636
in JAR files, 629–630
packaging for execution, 638
RMI for, 446
security of, 639
structure of, 636–638
deploying, 639–643
Java Web Start, 647–654
visualizations
developing with JSP, 350–363
developing with JSTL, 344–350
Web ARchive File (WAR)
in AXIS, for Web services, 533
creating, 104, 658
definition of, 639–640
deploying, 640–643
in EAR (Enterprise Archive), 644–646
Web services
client for, writing with AXIS, 537–539
definition of, 522–523, 639
deploying with AXIS, 535–537
example using, 523–526, 531–540
future of, 540
limitations of, 445, 522, 527
remote procedure calls with, 526–527
SOAP and, 529–530
types of, 536
when to use, 522–523, 540
WSDL and, 528–529

Web Services Description Language (WSDL),
    528–529, 537
Web sites
The Apache XML Project, 499
The Eclipse Project, 499
Gaim, 498
IIOP.NET project, 512
The Jakarta Project, 499
JBoss: Professional Open Source, 499
JDBC drivers, 282
JMeter tool, 107–108
JNDI (Java Naming and Directory Interface), 287
King's Hibernate example application, 374
OMG (Object Management Group), 506
OpenSymphony Quality Components, 499
SourceForge, XDoclet tool, 101
WSDL (Web Services Description Language), 528
Web Start
definition of, 647, 654
TicTacToe example of
definition of, 647–648
JNLP file for, 648–650
TTTGui class, 653–654
TTTLogic class, 650–653
TTTMain class, 650
Web tier, J2EE, 87
WebRowSetImpl RowSet implementation, 309
WebWork framework
architecture of, 371–374
definition of, 368–369
extending with Hibernate, 374–377
Interceptors in, 372–373
IoC (Inversion of Control), 369–371
OGNL (Object Graph Navigation Language) for,
    373–374
scopes of components, 374
`ValueStack` in, 373
`weightx` **variable,** `GridLayout` **manager, 178**
`weighty` **variable,** `GridLayout` **manager, 178**
`<welcome-file-list>` **element, WAR deployment**
    descriptor, 641, 642
World Wide Web, evolution of
description of, 523
example illustrating, 524–526
Web services and, 523, 526
`wrap()` **method,** `Cipher` **class, 604–608**
`writeObject()` **method, Java Serialization API,**
    243–245

Licenses

Apache License

Version 2.0, January 2004

`http://www.apache.org/licenses/`

Terms and Conditions for Use, Reproduction, and Distribution

1. Definitions.

    "License" shall mean the terms and conditions for use, reproduction, and distribution as defined by Sections 1 through 9 of this document.

    "Licensor" shall mean the copyright owner or entity authorized by the copyright owner that is granting the License.

    "Legal Entity" shall mean the union of the acting entity and all other entities that control, are controlled by, or are under common control with that entity. For the purposes of this definition, "control" means (i) the power, direct or indirect, to cause the direction or management of such entity, whether by contract or otherwise, or (ii) ownership of fifty percent (50%) or more of the outstanding shares, or (iii) beneficial ownership of such entity.

    "You" (or "Your") shall mean an individual or Legal Entity exercising permissions granted by this License.

    "Source" form shall mean the preferred form for making modifications, including but not limited to software source code, documentation source, and configuration files.

    "Object" form shall mean any form resulting from mechanical transformation or translation of a Source form, including but not limited to compiled object code, generated documentation, and conversions to other media types.

    "Work" shall mean the work of authorship, whether in Source or Object form, made available under the License, as indicated by a copyright notice that is included in or attached to the work (an example is provided in the Appendix below).

    "Derivative Works" shall mean any work, whether in Source or Object form, that is based on (or derived from) the Work and for which the editorial revisions, annotations, elaborations, or other modifications represent, as a whole, an original work of authorship. For the purposes of this License, Derivative Works shall not include works that remain separable from, or merely link (or bind by name) to the interfaces of, the Work and Derivative Works thereof.

    "Contribution" shall mean any work of authorship, including the original version of the Work and any modifications or additions to that Work or Derivative Works thereof, that is intentionally submitted to Licensor for inclusion in the Work by the copyright owner or by an individual or Legal Entity authorized to submit on behalf of the copyright owner. For the purposes of this definition, "submitted" means any form of electronic, verbal, or written communication sent to the Licensor or its representatives, including but not limited to communication on electronic mailing lists, source code control systems, and issue tracking systems that are managed by, or on behalf of, the Licensor for the purpose of discussing and improving the Work, but excluding communication that is conspicuously marked or otherwise designated in writing by the copyright owner as "Not a Contribution."

"Contributor" shall mean Licensor and any individual or Legal Entity on behalf of whom a Contribution has been received by Licensor and subsequently incorporated within the Work.

2. Grant of Copyright License. Subject to the terms and conditions of this License, each Contributor hereby grants to You a perpetual, worldwide, non-exclusive, no-charge, royalty-free, irrevocable copyright license to reproduce, prepare Derivative Works of, publicly display, publicly perform, sublicense, and distribute the Work and such Derivative Works in Source or Object form.

3. Grant of Patent License. Subject to the terms and conditions of this License, each Contributor hereby grants to You a perpetual, worldwide, non-exclusive, no-charge, royalty-free, irrevocable (except as stated in this section) patent license to make, have made, use, offer to sell, sell, import, and otherwise transfer the Work, where such license applies only to those patent claims licensable by such Contributor that are necessarily infringed by their Contribution(s) alone or by combination of their Contribution(s) with the Work to which such Contribution(s) was submitted. If You institute patent litigation against any entity (including a cross-claim or counterclaim in a lawsuit) alleging that the Work or a Contribution incorporated within the Work constitutes direct or contributory patent infringement, then any patent licenses granted to You under this License for that Work shall terminate as of the date such litigation is filed.

4. Redistribution. You may reproduce and distribute copies of the Work or Derivative Works thereof in any medium, with or without modifications, and in Source or Object form, provided that You meet the following conditions:

    (a) You must give any other recipients of the Work or Derivative Works a copy of this License; and

    (b) You must cause any modified files to carry prominent notices stating that You changed the files; and

    (c) You must retain, in the Source form of any Derivative Works that You distribute, all copyright, patent, trademark, and attribution notices from the Source form of the Work, excluding those notices that do not pertain to any part of the Derivative Works; and

    (d) If the Work includes a "NOTICE" text file as part of its distribution, then any Derivative Works that You distribute must include a readable copy of the attribution notices contained within such NOTICE file, excluding those notices that do not pertain to any part of the Derivative Works, in at least one of the following places: within a NOTICE text file distributed as part of the Derivative Works; within the Source form or documentation, if provided along with the Derivative Works; or, within a display generated by the Derivative Works, if and wherever such third-party notices normally appear. The contents of the NOTICE file are for informational purposes only and do not modify the License. You may add Your own attribution notices within Derivative Works that You distribute, alongside or as an addendum to the NOTICE text from the Work, provided that such additional attribution notices cannot be construed as modifying the License.

    You may add Your own copyright statement to Your modifications and may provide additional or different license terms and conditions for use, reproduction, or distribution of Your modifications, or for any such Derivative Works as a whole, provided Your use, reproduction, and distribution of the Work otherwise complies with the conditions stated in this License.

5. Submission of Contributions. Unless You explicitly state otherwise, any Contribution intentionally submitted for inclusion in the Work by You to the Licensor shall be under the terms and conditions of this License, without any additional terms or conditions. Notwithstanding the above, nothing herein shall supersede or modify the terms of any separate license agreement you may have executed with Licensor regarding such Contributions.

6. Trademarks. This License does not grant permission to use the tradenames, trademarks, service marks, or product names of the Licensor, except as required for reasonable and customary use in describing the origin of the Work and reproducing the content of the NOTICE file.

7. Disclaimer of Warranty. Unless required by applicable law or agreed to in writing, Licensor provides the Work (and each Contributor provides its Contributions) on an "AS IS" BASIS, WITHOUT WARRANTIES OR CONDITIONS OF ANY KIND, either express or implied, including, without limitation, any warranties or conditions of TITLE, NON-INFRINGEMENT, MERCHANTABILITY, or FITNESS FOR A PARTICULAR PURPOSE. You are solely responsible for determining the appropriateness of using or redistributing the Work and assume any risks associated with Your exercise of permissions under this License.

8. Limitation of Liability. In no event and under no legal theory, whether in tort (including negligence), contract, or otherwise, unless required by applicable law (such as deliberate and grossly negligent acts) or agreed to in writing, shall any Contributor be liable to You for damages, including any direct, indirect, special, incidental, or consequential damages of any character arising as a result of this License or out of the use or inability to use the Work (including but not limited to damages for loss of goodwill, work stoppage, computer failure or malfunction, or any and all other commercial damages or losses), even if such Contributor has been advised of the possibility of such damages.

9. Accepting Warranty or Additional Liability. While redistributing the Work or Derivative Works thereof, You may choose to offer, and charge a fee for, acceptance of support, warranty, indemnity, or other liability obligations and/or rights consistent with this License. However, in accepting such obligations, You may act only on Your own behalf and on Your sole responsibility, not on behalf of any other Contributor, and only if You agree to indemnify, defend, and hold each Contributor harmless for any liability incurred by, or claims asserted against, such Contributor by reason of your accepting any such warranty or additional liability.

GNU LESSER GENERAL PUBLIC LICENSE

Version 2.1, February 1999

Copyright © 1991, 1999 Free Software Foundation, Inc.

59 Temple Place, Suite 330, Boston, MA 02111-1307 USA

Preamble

The licenses for most software are designed to take away your freedom to share and change it. By contrast, the GNU General Public Licenses are intended to guarantee your freedom to share and change free software — to make sure the software is free for all its users.

This license, the Lesser General Public License, applies to some specially designated software packages — typically libraries — of the Free Software Foundation and other authors who decide to use it. You can use it too, but we suggest you first think carefully about whether this license or the ordinary General Public License is the better strategy to use in any particular case, based on the explanations below.

When we speak of free software, we are referring to freedom of use, not price. Our General Public Licenses are designed to make sure that you have the freedom to distribute copies of free software (and charge for this service if you wish); that you receive source code or can get it if you want it; that you can change the software and use pieces of it in new free programs; and that you are informed that you can do these things.

To protect your rights, we need to make restrictions that forbid distributors to deny you these rights or to ask you to surrender these rights. These restrictions translate to certain responsibilities for you if you distribute copies of the library or if you modify it.

For example, if you distribute copies of the library, whether gratis or for a fee, you must give the recipients all the rights that we gave you. You must make sure that they, too, receive or can get the source code. If you link other code with the library, you must provide complete object files to the recipients, so that they can relink them with the library after making changes to the library and recompiling it. And you must show them these terms so they know their rights.

We protect your rights with a two-step method: (1) we copyright the library, and (2) we offer you this license, which gives you legal permission to copy, distribute and/or modify the library.

To protect each distributor, we want to make it very clear that there is no warranty for the free library. Also, if the library is modified by someone else and passed on, the recipients should know that what they have is not the original version, so that the original author's reputation will not be affected by problems that might be introduced by others.

Finally, software patents pose a constant threat to the existence of any free program. We wish to make sure that a company cannot effectively restrict the users of a free program by obtaining a restrictive license from a patent holder. Therefore, we insist that any patent license obtained for a version of the library must be consistent with the full freedom of use specified in this license.

Most GNU software, including some libraries, is covered by the ordinary GNU General Public License. This license, the GNU Lesser General Public License, applies to certain designated libraries, and is quite different from the ordinary General Public License. We use this license for certain libraries in order to permit linking those libraries into non-free programs.

When a program is linked with a library, whether statically or using a shared library, the combination of the two is legally speaking a combined work, a derivative of the original library. The ordinary General Public License therefore permits such linking only if the entire combination fits its criteria of freedom. The Lesser General Public License permits more lax criteria for linking other code with the library.

We call this license the "Lesser" General Public License because it does Less to protect the user's freedom than the ordinary General Public License. It also provides other free software developers Less of an advantage over competing non-free programs. These disadvantages are the reason we use the ordinary General Public License for many libraries. However, the Lesser license provides advantages in certain special circumstances.

For example, on rare occasions, there may be a special need to encourage the widest possible use of a certain library, so that it becomes a de facto standard. To achieve this, non-free programs must be allowed to use the library. A more frequent case is that a free library does the same job as widely used non-free libraries. In this case, there is little to gain by limiting the free library to free software only, so we use the Lesser General Public License.

In other cases, permission to use a particular library in non-free programs enables a greater number of people to use a large body of free software. For example, permission to use the GNU C Library in non-free programs enables many more people to use the whole GNU operating system, as well as its variant, the GNU/Linux operating system.

Although the Lesser General Public License is Less protective of the users' freedom, it does ensure that the user of a program that is linked with the Library has the freedom and the wherewithal to run that program using a modified version of the Library.

The precise terms and conditions for copying, distribution and modification follow. Pay close attention to the difference between a "work based on the library" and a "work that uses the library". The former contains code derived from the library, whereas the latter must be combined with the library in order to run.

GNU LESSER GENERAL PUBLIC LICENSE

Terms and Conditions for Copying, Distribution and Modification

0.   This License Agreement applies to any software library or other program which contains a notice placed by the copyright holder or other authorized party saying it may be distributed under the terms of this Lesser General Public License (also called "this License").

     Each licensee is addressed as "you".

A "library" means a collection of software functions and/or data prepared so as to be conveniently linked with application programs (which use some of those functions and data) to form executables.

The "Library", below, refers to any such software library or work that has been distributed under these terms. A "work based on the Library" means either the Library or any derivative work under copyright law: that is to say, a work containing the Library or a portion of it, either verbatim or with modifications and/or translated straightforwardly into another language. (Hereinafter, translation is included without limitation in the term "modification".)

"Source code" for a work means the preferred form of the work for making modifications to it. For a library, complete source code means all the source code for all modules it contains, plus any associated interface definition files, plus the scripts used to control compilation and installation of the library. Activities other than copying, distribution and modification are not covered by this License; they are outside its scope. The act of running a program using the Library is not restricted, and output from such a program is covered only if its contents constitute a work based on the Library (independent of the use of the Library in a tool for writing it). Whether that is true depends on what the Library does and what the program that uses the Library does.

1. You may copy and distribute verbatim copies of the Library's complete source code as you receive it, in any medium, provided that you conspicuously and appropriately publish on each copy an appropriate copyright notice and disclaimer of warranty; keep intact all the notices that refer to this License and to the absence of any warranty; and distribute a copy of this License along with the Library.

   You may charge a fee for the physical act of transferring a copy, and you may at your option offer warranty protection in exchange for a fee.

2. You may modify your copy or copies of the Library or any portion of it, thus forming a work based on the Library, and copy and distribute such modifications or work under the terms of Section 1 above, provided that you also meet all of these conditions:

   a) The modified work must itself be a software library.

   b) You must cause the files modified to carry prominent notices stating that you changed the files and the date of any change.

   c) You must cause the whole of the work to be licensed at no charge to all third parties under the terms of this License.

   d) If a facility in the modified Library refers to a function or a table of data to be supplied by an application program that uses the facility, other than as an argument passed when the facility is invoked, then you must make a good faith effort to ensure that, in the event an application does not supply such function or table, the facility still operates, and performs whatever part of its purpose remains meaningful.

   (For example, a function in a library to compute square roots has a purpose that is entirely well defined independent of the application. Therefore, Subsection 2d requires that any application-supplied function or table used by this function must be optional: if the application does not supply it, the square root function must still compute square roots.)

   These requirements apply to the modified work as a whole. If identifiable sections of that work are not derived from the Library, and can be reasonably considered independent and separate works in themselves, then this License, and its terms, do not apply to those sections when you distribute them as separate works. But when you distribute the same sections as part of a whole that is a work based on the Library, the distribution of the whole must be on the terms of this License, whose permissions for other licensees extend to the entire whole, and thus to each and every part regardless of who wrote it.

Thus, it is not the intent of this section to claim rights or contest your rights to work written entirely by you; rather, the intent is to exercise the right to control the distribution of derivative or collective works based on the Library.

In addition, mere aggregation of another work not based on the Library with the Library (or with a work based on the Library) on a volume of a storage or distribution medium does not bring the other work under the scope of this License.

3. You may opt to apply the terms of the ordinary GNU General Public License instead of this License to a given copy of the Library. To do this, you must alter all the notices that refer to this License, so that they refer to the ordinary GNU General Public License, version 2,instead of to this License. (If a newer version than version 2 of the ordinary GNU General Public License has appeared, then you can specify that version instead if you wish.) Do not make any other change in these notices.

Once this change is made in a given copy, it is irreversible for that copy, so the ordinary GNU General Public License applies to all subsequent copies and derivative works made from that copy.

This option is useful when you wish to copy part of the code of the Library into a program that is not a library.

4. You may copy and distribute the Library (or a portion or derivative of it, under Section 2) in object code or executable form under the terms of Sections 1 and 2 above provided that you accompany it with the complete corresponding machine-readable source code, which must be distributed under the terms of Sections 1 and 2 above on a medium customarily used for software interchange.

If distribution of object code is made by offering access to copy from a designated place, then offering equivalent access to copy the source code from the same place satisfies the requirement to distribute the source code, even though third parties are not compelled to copy the source along with the object code.

5. A program that contains no derivative of any portion of the Library, but is designed to work with the Library by being compiled or linked with it, is called a "work that uses the Library". Such a work, in isolation, is not a derivative work of the Library, and therefore falls outside the scope of this License.

However, linking a "work that uses the Library" with the Library creates an executable that is a derivative of the Library (because it contains portions of the Library), rather than a "work that uses the library". The executable is therefore covered by this License. Section 6 states terms for distribution of such executables. When a "work that uses the Library" uses material from a header file that is part of the Library, the object code for the work may be a derivative work of the Library even though the source code is not. Whether this is true is especially significant if the work can be linked without the Library, or if the work is itself a library. The threshold for this to be true is not precisely defined by law. If such an object file uses only numerical parameters, data structure layouts and accessors, and small macros and small inline functions (ten lines or less in length), then the use of the object file is unrestricted, regardless of whether it is legally a derivative work. (Executables containing this object code plus portions of the Library will still fall under Section 6.) Otherwise, if the work is a derivative of the Library, you may distribute the object code for the work under the terms of Section 6. Any executables containing that work also fall under Section 6,whether or not they are linked directly with the Library itself.

6. As an exception to the Sections above, you may also combine or link a "work that uses the Library" with the Library to produce a work containing portions of the Library, and distribute that work under terms of your choice, provided that the terms permit modification of the work for the customer's own use and reverse engineering for debugging such modifications. You must give prominent notice with each copy of the work that the Library is used in it and that the Library and its use are covered by this License. You must supply a copy of this License. If the work during execution displays copyright notices, you must include the copyright notice for the Library among them, as well as a reference directing the user to the copy of this License. Also, you must do one of these things:

a) Accompany the work with the complete corresponding machine-readable source code for the Library including whatever changes were used in the work (which must be distributed under Sections 1 and 2 above); and, if the work is an executable linked with the Library, with the complete machine-readable "work that uses the Library", as object code and/or source code, so that the user can modify the Library and then relink to produce a modified executable containing the modified Library. (It is understood that the user who changes the contents of definitions files in the Library will not necessarily be able to recompile the application to use the modified definitions.)

b) Use a suitable shared library mechanism for linking with the Library. A suitable mechanism is one that (1) uses at run time a copy of the library already present on the user's computer system, rather than copying library functions into the executable, and (2) will operate properly with a modified version of the library, if the user installs one, as long as the modified version is interface-compatible with the version that the work was made with.

c) Accompany the work with a written offer, valid for at least three years, to give the same user the materials specified in Subsection 6a, above, for a charge no more than the cost of performing this distribution.

d) If distribution of the work is made by offering access to copy from a designated place, offer equivalent access to copy the above-specified materials from the same place.

e) Verify that the user has already received a copy of these materials or that you have already sent this user a copy.

For an executable, the required form of the "work that uses the Library" must include any data and utility programs needed for reproducing the executable from it. However, as a special exception, the materials to be distributed need not include anything that is normally distributed (in either source or binary form) with the major components (compiler, kernel, and so on) of the operating system on which the executable runs, unless that component itself accompanies the executable.

It may happen that this requirement contradicts the license restrictions of other proprietary libraries that do not normally accompany the operating system. Such a contradiction means you cannot use both them and the Library together in an executable that you distribute.

7. You may place library facilities that are a work based on the Library side-by-side in a single library together with other library facilities not covered by this License, and distribute such a combined library, provided that the separate distribution of the work based on the Library and of the other library facilities is otherwise permitted, and provided that you do these two things:

a) Accompany the combined library with a copy of the same work based on the Library, uncombined with any other library facilities. This must be distributed under the terms of the Sections above.

b) Give prominent notice with the combined library of the fact that part of it is a work based on the Library, and explaining where to find the accompanying uncombined form of the same work.

8.   You may not copy, modify, sublicense, link with, or distribute the Library except as expressly provided under this License. Any attempt otherwise to copy, modify, sublicense, link with, or distribute the Library is void, and will automatically terminate your rights under this License. However, parties who have received copies, or rights, from you under this License will not have their licenses terminated so long as such parties remain in full compliance.

9.   You are not required to accept this License, since you have not signed it. However, nothing else grants you permission to modify or distribute the Library or its derivative works. These actions are prohibited by law if you do not accept this License. Therefore, by modifying or distributing the Library (or any work based on the Library), you indicate your acceptance of this License to do so, and all its terms and conditions for copying, distributing or modifying the Library or works based on it.

10. Each time you redistribute the Library (or any work based on the Library), the recipient automatically receives a license from the original licensor to copy, distribute, link with or modify the Library subject to these terms and conditions. You may not impose any further restrictions on the recipients' exercise of the rights granted herein. You are not responsible for enforcing compliance by third parties with this License.

11. If, as a consequence of a court judgment or allegation of patent infringement or for any other reason (not limited to patent issues), conditions are imposed on you (whether by court order, agreement or otherwise) that contradict the conditions of this License, they do not excuse you from the conditions of this License. If you cannot distribute so as to satisfy simultaneously your obligations under this License and any other pertinent obligations, then as a consequence you may not distribute the Library at all. For example, if a patent license would not permit royalty-free redistribution of the Library by all those who receive copies directly or indirectly through you, then the only way you could satisfy both it and this License would be to refrain entirely from distribution of the Library.

If any portion of this section is held invalid or unenforceable under any particular circumstance, the balance of the section is intended to apply, and the section as a whole is intended to apply in other circumstances.

It is not the purpose of this section to induce you to infringe any patents or other property right claims or to contest validity of any such claims; this section has the sole purpose of protecting the integrity of the free software distribution system which is implemented by public license practices. Many people have made generous contributions to the wide range of software distributed through that system in reliance on consistent application of that system; it is up to the author/donor to decide if he or she is willing to distribute software through any other system and a licensee cannot impose that choice.

This section is intended to make thoroughly clear what is believed to be a consequence of the rest of this License.

12. If the distribution and/or use of the Library is restricted in certain countries either by patents or by copyrighted interfaces, the original copyright holder who places the Library under this License may add an explicit geographical distribution limitation excluding those countries, so

that distribution is permitted only in or among countries not thus excluded. In such case, this License incorporates the limitation as if written in the body of this License.

13. The Free Software Foundation may publish revised and/or new versions of the Lesser General Public License from time to time. Such new versions will be similar in spirit to the present version, but may differ in detail to address new problems or concerns. Each version is given a distinguishing version number. If the Library specifies a version number of this License which applies to it and "any later version," you have the option of following the terms and conditions either of that version or of any later version published by the Free Software Foundation. If the Library does not specify a license version number, you may choose any version ever published by the Free Software Foundation.

14. If you wish to incorporate parts of the Library into other free programs whose distribution conditions are incompatible with these, write to the author to ask for permission. For software that is copyrighted by the Free Software Foundation, write to the Free Software Foundation; we sometimes make exceptions for this. Our decision will be guided by the two goals of preserving the free status of all derivatives of our free software and of promoting the sharing and reuse of software generally.

NO WARRANTY

15. BECAUSE THE LIBRARY IS LICENSED FREE OF CHARGE, THERE IS NO WARRANTY FOR THE LIBRARY, TO THE EXTENT PERMITTED BY APPLICABLE LAW. EXCEPT WHEN OTHERWISE STATED IN WRITING THE COPYRIGHT HOLDERS AND/OR OTHER PARTIES PROVIDE THE LIBRARY "AS IS" WITHOUT WARRANTY OF ANY KIND, EITHER EXPRESSED OR IMPLIED, INCLUDING, BUT NOT LIMITED TO, THE IMPLIED WARRANTIES OF MERCHANTABILITY AND FITNESS FOR A PARTICULAR PURPOSE. THE ENTIRE RISK AS TO THE QUALITY AND PERFORMANCE OF THE LIBRARY IS WITH YOU. SHOULD THE LIBRARY PROVE DEFECTIVE, YOU ASSUME THE COST OF ALL NECESSARY SERVICING, REPAIR OR CORRECTION.

16. IN NO EVENT UNLESS REQUIRED BY APPLICABLE LAW OR AGREED TO IN WRITING WILL ANY COPYRIGHT HOLDER, OR ANY OTHER PARTY WHO MAY MODIFY AND/OR REDISTRIBUTE THE LIBRARY AS PERMITTED ABOVE, BE LIABLE TO YOU FOR DAMAGES, INCLUDING ANY GENERAL, SPECIAL, INCIDENTAL OR CONSEQUENTIAL DAMAGES ARISING OUT OF THE USE OR INABILITY TO USE THE LIBRARY (INCLUDING BUT NOT LIMITED TO LOSS OF DATA OR DATA BEING RENDERED INACCURATE OR LOSSES SUSTAINED BY YOU OR THIRD PARTIES OR A FAILURE OF THE LIBRARY TO OPERATE WITH ANY OTHER SOFTWARE), EVEN IF SUCH HOLDER OR OTHER PARTY HAS BEEN ADVISED OF THE POSSIBILITY OF SUCH DAMAGES.

END OF TERMS AND CONDITIONS

How to Apply These Terms to Your New Libraries

If you develop a new library, and you want it to be of the greatest possible use to the public, we recommend making it free software that everyone can redistribute and change. You can do so by permitting redistribution under these terms (or, alternatively, under the terms of the ordinary General Public License).

To apply these terms, attach the following notices to the library. It is safest to attach them to the start of each source file to most effectively convey the exclusion of warranty; and each file should have at least the "copyright" line and a pointer to where the full notice is found.

<one line to give the library's name and a brief idea of what it does.>

Copyright © *<year> <name of author>*

This library is free software; you can redistribute it and/or modify it under the terms of the GNU Lesser General Public License as published by the Free Software Foundation; either version 2.1 of the License, or (at your option) any later version.

This library is distributed in the hope that it will be useful, but WITHOUT ANY WARRANTY; without even the implied warranty of MERCHANTABILITY or FITNESS FOR A PARTICULAR PURPOSE. See the GNU Lesser General Public License for more details.

You should have received a copy of the GNU Lesser General Public License along with this library; if not, write to the Free Software Foundation, Inc., 59 Temple Place, Suite 330, Boston, MA 02111-1307 USA

Also add information on how to contact you by electronic and paper mail.

You should also get your employer (if you work as a programmer) or your school, if any, to sign a "copyright disclaimer" for the library, if necessary. Here is a sample; alter the names:

Yoyodyne, Inc., hereby disclaims all copyright interest in the

library `Frob' (a library for tweaking knobs) written by James Random Hacker.

<signature of Ty Coon>, 1 April 1990

Ty Coon, President of Vice

That's all there is to it!

The OpenSymphony Software License, Version 1.1